Management Research
Custom Publication

Management Research
Custom Publication

PRIFYSGOL
BANGOR
UNIVERSITY

palgrave
macmillan

© Jill Collis, Roger Hussey, Harvey Maylor, Kate Blackmon and Les Oakshott 2011

All rights reserved. No reproduction, copy or transmission of this publication may be made without written permission.

No portion of this publication may be reproduced, copied or transmitted save with written permission or in accordance with the provisions of the Copyright, Designs and Patents Act 1988, or under the terms of any licence permitting limited copying issued by the Copyright Licensing Agency, Saffron House, 6–10 Kirby Street, London EC1N 8TS.

Any person who does any unauthorized act in relation to this publication may be liable to criminal prosecution and civil claims for damages.

The authors have asserted their rights to be identified as the authors of this work in accordance with the Copyright, Designs and Patents Act 1988.

First published 2011 by
PALGRAVE MACMILLAN

Business Research © Jill Collis and Roger Hussey 1997, 2003, 2009 Researching Business and Management © Harvey Maylor and Kate Blackmon 2005 Essential Quantitative Methods
© Les Oakshott 1998, 2001, 2006, 2009

Palgrave Macmillan in the UK is an imprint of Macmillan Publishers Limited, registered in England, company number 785998, of Houndmills, Basingstoke, Hampshire RG21 6XS.

Palgrave Macmillan in the US is a division of St Martin's Press LLC,
175 Fifth Avenue, New York, NY 10010.

Palgrave Macmillan is the global academic imprint of the above companies and has companies and representatives throughout the world.

Palgrave® and Macmillan® are registered trademarks in the United States, the United Kingdom, Europe and other countries.

ISBN 978–0–230–29104–1   paperback

This book is printed on paper suitable for recycling and made from fully managed and sustained forest sources. Logging, pulping and manufacturing processes are expected to conform to the environmental regulations of the country of origin.

A catalogue record for this book is available from the British Library.

A catalog record for this book is available from the Library of Congress.

10 9 8 7 6 5 4 3 2 1
20 19 18 17 16 15 14 13 12 11

Printed and bound in Great Britain by
CPI Antony Rowe, Chippenham and Eastbourne

Contents

Acknowledgements vii

Part 1   Defining the research

1. Understanding research 3
   Collis and Hussey: Business Research

2. What is business and management research? 23
   Maylor and Blackmon: Researching Business and Management

Part 2   Understanding research philosophies and designs

3. Identifying your research paradigm 47
   Collis and Hussey: Business Research

4. Scientist or ethnographer? 67
   Maylor and Blackmon: Researching Business and Management

5. Quantitative research designs 97
   Maylor and Blackmon: Researching Business and Management

6. Designing qualitative research 147
   Maylor and Blackmon: Researching Business and Management

7. Case studies and multi-method design 169
   Maylor and Blackmon: Researching Business and Management

Part 3   Literature review and writing your research proposal

8. Searching and reviewing the literature 195
   Collis and Hussey: Business Research

9. What should I study? 217
   Maylor and Blackmon: Researching Business and Management

10. Writing your research proposal 253
    Collis and Hussey: Business Research

Part 4 Sampling and data collection

11. Collecting data — 293
    Oakshott: Essential Quantitative Methods

12. Collecting qualitative data — 313
    Collis and Hussey: Business Research

13. Collecting data for statistical analysis — 337
    Collis and Hussey: Business Research

Part 5 Data analysis

14. Analysing qualitative data — 377
    Maylor and Blackmon: Researching Business and Management

15. Analysing data using descriptive statistics — 401
    Collis and Hussey: Business Research

16. Analysing data using inferential statistics — 441
    Collis and Hussey: Business Research

Part 6 Describing your research

17. Answering your research questions — 479
    Maylor and Blackmon: Researching Business and Management

18. Describing your research — 501
    Maylor and Blackmon: Researching Business and Management

Name index — 535

Subject index — 539

Acknowledgements

This custom publication for Bangor University draws on chapters from the following books:

Collis and Hussey, (2009) *Business Research: A Practical Guide for Undergraduate and Postgraduate Students 3rd Edition*, Basingstoke: Palgrave Macmillan

Maylor and Blackmon, (2005) *Researching Business and Management*, Basingstoke: Palgrave Macmillan

Oakshott, (2009) *Essential Quantitative Methods for Business, Management and Finance 4th Edition*, Basingstoke: Palgrave Macmillan

Every effort has been made to trace all copyright holders, but if any have been inadvertently overlooked the publishers will be pleased to make the necessary arrangements at the first opportunity.

PART 1
Defining the research

CHAPTER 1
Understanding research

LEARNING OBJECTIVES

When you have studied this chapter, you should be able to:
- explain the nature and purpose of research
- classify different types of research
- identify the main stages in the research process
- identify the characteristics of a good research project.

1.1 Introduction

Whether you are merely at the stage where you are contemplating carrying out business research or you have already begun planning your study, you will find this chapter useful for clarifying your initial thoughts. We start by examining the nature and purpose of academic research that focuses on business issues and the different ways in which studies can be categorized. We also look at the general differences between undergraduate, postgraduate and doctoral research projects before going on to discuss what makes a good project.

1.2 Nature and purpose of business research

Although *research* is central to both business and academic activities, there is no consensus in the literature on how it should be defined. One reason for this is that research means different things to different people. However, from the many definitions offered, there is general agreement that research is:

- a process of enquiry and investigation
- systematic and methodical, and
- increases knowledge.

Looking at the *nature* of research, this tells us that researchers need to use appropriate methods for collecting and analysing research data, and to apply them rigorously. It tells us that the *purpose* of research is to investigate a research question with a view to generating knowledge. The research question you investigate will relate to a particular problem or issue that you identify from studying a particular topic. Research is much more than mere speculation or assumptions about business events, transactions and activities. You will need to study your chosen topic and the choice of research methods. Students need to meet the criteria that relate to their degree programme, and all researchers will need to meet the standards expected by their institutions and/or funding body.

Key definitions

Research is a systematic and methodical process of enquiry and investigation with a view to increasing knowledge.

A research project offers both undergraduate and postgraduate students an opportunity to identify and select a research problem and investigate it independently under the guidance of a supervisor. It allows you to apply theory to or otherwise analyse a real problem, or to explore and analyse more general issues. It also enables you to apply techniques and procedures to illuminate the problem and contribute to our greater understanding of it or to generate solutions. Thus, the typical objectives of research can be summarized as follows:

- to review and synthesize existing knowledge
- to investigate some existing situation or problem
- to provide solutions to a problem
- to explore and analyse more general issues
- to construct or create a new procedure or system
- to explain a new phenomenon
- to generate new knowledge
- a combination of any of the above.

Our summary illustrates that research is purposeful, as it is conducted with a view to achieving an outcome. The nature of that outcome will depend on the type of research you are conducting and the level at which you are operating. The outcome may be presented in the form of a *dissertation* for an undergraduate or taught Master's degree or for a Master of Philosophy (MPhil). Alternatively, it is likely to take the form of a *thesis* for a doctoral degree such as Doctor of Business Administration (DBA) or Doctor of Philosophy (PhD). Academic research can also be conducted for the purpose of publishing the study as a book or an article in an academic journal or for consultancy purposes. This book focuses primarily on the needs of students carrying out some form of business research for a qualification and those pursuing academic careers.

Key definitions

A **discourse** is 'a lengthy treatment of a theme'.
A **dissertation** is a 'detailed discourse, esp. as submitted for academic degree'.
A **thesis** is a 'dissertation, esp. by candidate for a higher degree'.
(*Oxford Compact Dictionary & Thesaurus*, 1997, pp. 211, 216 and 801 respectively)

Types of enterprise to research include small and medium-sized enterprises (SMEs), businesses with limited liability (such as companies), and organizations in the not-for-profit or public sectors. The focus in the media is mainly on big business, yet 99% of businesses are small or medium-sized enterprises (SMEs) and you may find yourself employed by one or even starting one. Whatever type of entity you choose as the focus of your research, you will find a wide range of issues to investigate.

The typical users of business research are:

- The government – for developing/monitoring policies, regulations and so on
- Owners, managers and business advisers – for keeping up to date with new ideas and specific developments in business
- Management – for developing internal policies and strategies (for example comparing research results relating to their own business with those with previous periods, their competitors and/or industry benchmarks)
- Academics – for further research and educational purposes.

1.3 Classifying research

As there are many ways of *classifying research*, it can be bewildering at first. However, studying the various characteristics of the different types of research helps us to identify and examine the similarities and differences. Research can be classified according to the:

- *purpose* of the research – the reason why it was conducted
- *process* of the research – the way in which the data were collected and analysed
- *logic* of the research – whether the research logic moves from the general to the specific or vice versa
- *outcome* of the research – whether the expected outcome is the solution to a particular problem or a more general contribution to knowledge.

For example, the aim of your research project might be to describe a particular business activity (purpose) by collecting qualitative data that are quantified and analysed statistically (process), which will be used to solve a business problem (outcome). Table 1.1 shows the classification of the main types of research according to the above criteria.

1.3.1 Exploratory, descriptive, analytical and predictive research

If we are classifying research according to its *purpose*, we can describe it as being exploratory, descriptive, analytical or predictive. At the undergraduate level,

Table 1.1 Classification of main types of research

Type of research	Basis of classification
Exploratory, descriptive, analytical or predictive research	Purpose of the research
Quantitative or qualitative research	Process of the research
Applied or basic research	Outcome of the research
Deductive or inductive research	Logic of the research

Table 1.2 Examples of research classified by purpose

Type of research	Example
Exploratory	An interview survey among clerical staff in a particular office, department, company, group of companies, industry, region and so on, to find out what motivates them to increase their productivity (that is, to see if a research problem can be formulated).
Descriptive	A description of how the selected clerical staff are rewarded and what measures are used to record their productivity levels.
Analytical	An analysis of any relationships between the rewards given to the clerical staff and their productivity levels.
Predictive	A forecast of which variable(s) should be changed in order to bring about a change in the productivity levels of clerical staff.

research is usually exploratory and/or descriptive. At postgraduate or doctoral level it is always analytical or predictive. Table 1.2 shows this classification in increasing order of sophistication and gives examples. One drawback of increasing the level of sophistication in research is that the level of complexity and detail also increases.

Exploratory research is conducted into a research problem or issue when there are very few or no earlier studies to which we can refer for information about the issue or problem. The aim of this type of study is to look for patterns, ideas or hypotheses, rather than testing or confirming a hypothesis. A *hypothesis* is a proposition that can be tested for association or causality against empirical evidence. *Empirical evidence* is data based on observation or experience, and *data** are known facts or things used as a basis for inference or reckoning. In exploratory research, the focus is on gaining insights and familiarity with the subject area for more rigorous investigation at a later stage.

Typical techniques used in exploratory research include case studies, observation and historical analysis, which can provide both quantitative and qualitative data. Such techniques are very flexible as there are few constraints on the nature of activities employed or on the type of data collected. The research will assess which existing theories and concepts can be applied to the problem or whether new ones should be developed. The approach to the research is usually very open and concentrates on gathering a wide range of data and impressions. As such, exploratory research rarely provides conclusive answers to problems or issues, but gives guidance on what future research, if any, should be conducted.

Descriptive research is conducted to describe phenomena as they exist. It is used to identify and obtain information on the characteristics of a particular problem or issue. Descriptive research goes further in examining a problem than exploratory research, as it is undertaken to ascertain and describe the characteristics of the pertinent issues. The following are examples of research questions in a descriptive research study:

- What is the absentee rate in particular offices?
- What are the feelings of workers faced with redundancy?

*This term is a Latin plural noun, the singular of which is 'datum'.

- What are the qualifications of different groups of employees?
- What type of packaging for a box of chocolates do consumers prefer?
- What information do consumers want shown on food labels?
- Which car advertisements on television do men and women of different ages prefer?
- How many students study accounting in China compared with students in Australia?
- How do commuters travel to work in capital cities?

You will notice that many of these questions start with 'what' or 'how' because the aim is to describe something. However, further clarification would be required before the study could begin. For example, we cannot ask everyone in the world about which car advertisements or chocolate box packaging they prefer. Even a study that compared the number of students studying accounting in China and Australia requires clarification of the type of students (for example age, sex and nationality) and what is studied (for example level/stage in the course, main subjects covered and qualification). Therefore, even in a descriptive study, you must spend time refining your research questions and being specific about the phenomena you are studying. We will explain how this can be achieved in later chapters.

Key definitions

Data are known facts or things used as a basis for inference or reckoning.
Empirical evidence is data based on observation or experience.
A **hypothesis** is a proposition that can be tested for association or causality against empirical evidence.
A **variable** is a characteristic of a phenomenon that can be observed or measured.

Analytical or *explanatory research* is a continuation of descriptive research. The researcher goes beyond merely describing the characteristics, to analysing and explaining why or how the phenomenon being studied is happening. Thus, analytical research aims to understand phenomena by discovering and measuring causal relations among them. For example, information may be collected on the size of companies and the levels of labour turnover. A statistical analysis of the data may show that the larger the company the higher the level of turnover, although as we will see later, research is rarely that simple. An important element of explanatory research is identifying and, possibly, controlling the *variables* in the research activities, as this permits the critical variables or the causal links between the characteristics to be better explained. A variable is a characteristic of a phenomenon that can be observed or measured.

Predictive research goes even further than explanatory research. The latter establishes an explanation for what is happening in a particular situation, whereas the former forecasts the likelihood of a similar situation occurring elsewhere. Predictive research aims to generalize from the analysis by predicting certain phenomena on the basis of hypothesized, general relationships. Thus, the solution to a problem in a particular study will be applicable to similar problems elsewhere, if the predictive research can provide a valid, robust solution based on a clear understanding of the relevant causes. Predictive research provides 'how', 'why' and 'where' answers to current events and also to similar events in the future. It is also helpful in situations where 'what if' questions are being asked. The following are examples of research questions in a predictive research study:

- In which city would it be most profitable to open a new retail outlet?.
- Will the introduction of an employee bonus scheme lead to higher levels of productivity?.
- What type of packaging will improve the sales of our products?.
- How would an increase in interest rates affect our profit margins?.
- Which stock market investments will be the most profitable over the next three months?.
- What will happen to sales of our products if there is an economic downturn?.

1.3.2 Quantitative and qualitative research

Looking at the approach adopted by the researcher can also differentiate research. Some people prefer to take a *quantitative* approach to addressing their research question(s) and design a study that involves collecting quantitative data (and/or qualitative data that can be quantified) and analysing them using statistical methods. Others prefer to take a *qualitative* approach to addressing their research question(s) and design a study that involves collecting qualitative data and analysing them using interpretative methods. As you will see in later chapters, a large study might incorporate elements of both as their merits are often considered to be complementary in gaining an understanding in the social sciences.

Referring to a research approach as quantitative or qualitative can be misleading, as a researcher can design a study with a view to collecting qualitative data (for example published text or transcripts of interviews) and then quantifying them by counting the frequency of occurrence of particular key words or themes. This allows researchers to analyse their data using statistical methods. On the other hand, a researcher can collect qualitative data with the intention of analysing them using non-numerical methods, or collect data that are already in numerical form and use statistical methods to analyse them. In this chapter, we will continue to refer to quantitative and qualitative approaches, but we will discuss alternative terms you may wish to use later in the book.

Some students avoid taking a quantitative approach because they are not confident with statistics and think a qualitative approach will be easier. Many students find that it is harder to start and decide on an overall design for a quantitative study, but it is easier to conduct the analysis and write up the research because it is highly structured. Qualitative research is normally easier to start, but students often find it more difficult to analyse the data and write up their final report. For example, if you were conducting a study into stress caused by working night shifts, you might want to collect quantitative data such as absenteeism rates or productivity levels, and analyse these data statistically. Alternatively, you might want to investigate the same question by collecting qualitative data about how stress is experienced by night workers in terms of their perceptions, health, social problems and so on.

There are many arguments in the literature regarding the merits of qualitative versus quantitative approaches, which we will examine later on in the book. At this stage, you simply need to be aware that your choice will be influenced by the nature of your research project as well as your own philosophical preferences. Moreover, you may find that the access you have been able to negotiate, the type of data available and the research problem persuade you to put your philosophical preferences to one side.

1.3.3 Applied and basic research

A standard classification of research divides projects into *applied research* and *basic research*. Applied research is a study that has been designed to apply its findings to solving a specific, existing problem. It is the application of existing knowledge to improve management practices and policies. The research project is likely to be short term (often less than 6 months) and the immediacy of the problem will be more important than academic theorizing. For example, you might be investigating the reorganization of an office layout, the improvement of safety in the workplace or the reduction of wastage of raw materials or energy in a factory process. The output from this type of research is likely to be a consultant's report, articles in professional or trade magazines and presentations to practitioners.

Key definitions

Applied research describes a study that is designed to apply its findings to solving a specific, existing problem.

Basic (or pure) research describes a study that is designed to make a contribution to general knowledge and theoretical understanding, rather than solve a specific problem.

When the research problem is of a less specific nature and the research is being conducted primarily to improve our understanding of general issues without emphasis on its immediate application, it is classified as basic or pure research. For example, you might be interested in whether personal characteristics influence people's career choices. Basic research is regarded as the most academic form of research, as the principal aim is to make a contribution to knowledge, usually for the general good, rather than to solve a specific problem for one organization.

Another example of applied research that is conducted in academic institutions often goes under the general title of *educational scholarship* (or *instructional research* or *pedagogic research*). This type of study is concerned with improving the educational activities within the institution and the output is likely to be case studies, instructional software or textbooks.

Basic research may focus on problem solving, but the problem is likely to be theoretical rather than practical. The typical outcome of this type of research is knowledge. Basic research may not resolve an immediate problem, but will contribute to our knowledge in a way that may assist in the solution of future problems. The emphasis, therefore, is on academic rigour and the strength of the research design. The output from basic research is likely to be papers presented at academic conferences and the articles published in academic journals.

1.3.4 Deductive and inductive research

Deductive research is a study in which a conceptual and theoretical structure is developed and then tested by empirical observation; thus, particular instances are deduced from general inferences. For this reason, the deductive method is referred to as moving from the general to the particular. For example, you may have read about theories of motivation and wish to test them in your own workplace. This will involve collecting specific data of the variables that the theories have identified as being important.

Key definitions

Deductive research describes a study in which a conceptual and theoretical structure is developed which is then tested by empirical observation; thus particular instances are deducted from general inferences.

Inductive research describes a study in which theory is developed from the observation of empirical reality; thus general inferences are induced from particular instances.

Inductive research is a study in which theory is developed from the observation of empirical reality; thus, general inferences are induced from particular instances, which is the reverse of the deductive method. Since it involves moving from individual observation to statements of general patterns or laws, it is referred to as moving from the specific to the general. For example, you may have observed from factory records in your company that production levels go down after two hours of the shift and you conclude that production levels vary with length of time worked.

All the different types of research we have discussed can be helpful in allowing you to understand your research and the best way to conduct it, but do not feel too constrained. It is important to recognize that one particular project may be described in a number of ways, as it will have purpose, process, logic and outcome. For example, you may conduct an applied, analytical study using a quantitative approach. In a long-term project, you may wish to use qualitative and quantitative approaches, deductive and inductive methods, and you will move from exploratory and descriptive research to analytical and predictive research. The key classifications we have examined can be applied to previous studies that you will review as part of your research and you can use these typologies to describe your own study in your proposal and later on in your dissertation or thesis.

1.4 Academic levels of research

The *academic level* of your research in terms of the sophistication of the research design and duration of the project will depend on your reasons for undertaking it. The requirements for undergraduates are very different from those for postgraduate students and doctoral students. However, the basic principles, issues and practicalities are the same.

1.4.1 Undergraduate level

If you are an undergraduate student, you may be required to undertake a research project as part of a course or it may even be a complete course. You are normally expected to be familiar with the main concepts and terms as explained in this book and undertake one or more of the following activities:

- Design a research project – On some courses you will be expected to design a research project and then write a report that explains the rationale for your chosen design and describes its strengths and weaknesses.
- Write a research proposal – A research proposal requires you to design a project as above, but also to include a preliminary review of the literature.
- Conduct a research project – In many cases you will be required not only to design a project and write a proposal, but also to do some actual research. This would entail writing a review of the literature and also collecting and analysing existing data or new data (for example from interviews or a questionnaire survey). In some cases, you may be allowed to base your entire project on a critical literature review, where you will analyse the literature on a chosen topic and draw conclusions. In all cases, you will be required to write a research report, which may be called a dissertation or thesis.

1.4.2 Postgraduate and doctoral students

If you are on an MBA programme or a specialized Master's programme, you will normally be expected to design a research project, write a proposal, conduct the study and write a report (which may be called a dissertation or thesis). In some cases, you may find that you are allowed to conduct a critical literature review only, where you will be expected to analyse and synthesize the literature on a chosen topic and draw conclusions. The processes are very similar to undergraduate research, but a more comprehensive approach is needed and higher quality of work will be required.

If you are doing a Master's degree by research or a doctorate, the intensity of the research will be much greater and you will need to read this book thoroughly and the recommended reading that is relevant to your subject. It is important to remember that, at this level, the country in which you are studying and the expectations of your institution will have a significant influence on the process and outcome of your research.

1.4.3 Academic researchers

If you are seeking an academic post, looking for promotion or engaged in research as part of your job, this book will reinforce your knowledge or give you a new perspective on a particular issue you have not considered previously, and help you to write conference papers and journal articles.

1.5 Overview of the research process

Whatever type of research or approach is adopted, there are several fundamental stages in the *research process* that are common to all scientifically based investigations. The simplified diagram shown in Figure 1.1 illustrates a traditional and highly structured view of the research process.

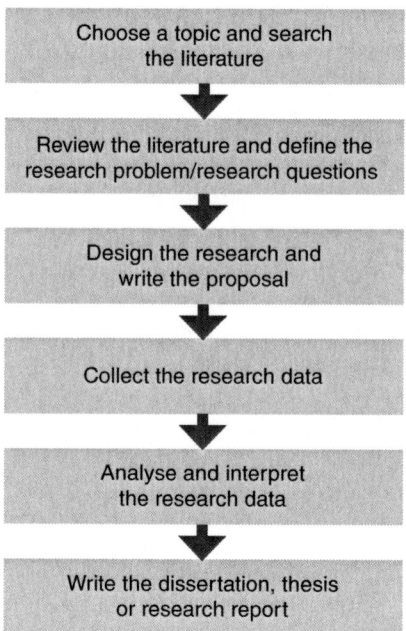

Figure 1.1 Overview of the research process

This model presents research as a neat, orderly process, with one stage leading logically on to the next stage. However, in practice, research is rarely like that. For example, failure at one stage means returning to an earlier stage and many stages overlap. Thus, if you were unable to collect the research data, it may be necessary to revise your definition of the research problem or amend the way you conduct the research. This is often a good reason for conducting some exploratory research before commencing a full project.

We will look briefly at each stage in the research process now to give you an overview of the nature of research, but greater detail is provided in the subsequent chapters.

1.5.1 The research topic

The starting point is to choose a *research topic,* which is a general subject area that is related to your degree if you are a student or your discipline if you are an academic. You may find a research topic suggests itself as a result of your coursework, job, interests or general experience. For example, you may be interested in the employment problems of minority groups in society, the difficulties of funding small businesses, what makes managers successful, or the commercial sponsorship of sport.

1.5.2 The literature

Once you have chosen a general topic, you need to search the literature for previous studies and other relevant information on that subject and read it. By exploring the existing body of knowledge, you should be able to see how your topic is divided into a number of different areas that will help you focus your ideas on a particular research problem.

Key definitions

The **literature** is all sources of published data on a particular topic.

1.5.3 The research problem

All students experience some difficulty in narrowing down their general interest in a research topic to focus on a particular *research problem* or issue that is small enough to be investigated. This is often referred to as defining the research problem and leads on to setting the *research question(s)*. The classic way in academic research to identify a research problem is to consider the literature and identify any gaps, as these indicate original areas to research. You will also find that many academic articles incorporate suggestions for further research in their conclusions. If you have conducted an undergraduate dissertation already, that subject area may lead you to your Master's or doctoral research questions. If you are an academic, you may also have conducted previous academic or consultancy research that suggests research questions for your present study. You will need to focus your ideas, decide the scope of your research and set parameters. For example, perhaps your study will investigate a broad financial issue, but focus on a particular group of stakeholders, size of business, industry, geographical area, or period of time.

1.5.4 The research design

The starting point in *research design* is to determine your research *paradigm*. A research paradigm is a framework that guides how research should be conducted, based on people's philosophies and assumptions about the world and the nature of knowledge. Your overall approach to the entire process of the research study is known as your *methodology*. Although, in part, this is determined by the research problem, the assumptions you use in your research and the way you define your research problem will influence the way you conduct the study.

Key definitions

A **methodology** is an approach to the process of the research encompassing a body of methods.

A **paradigm** is a framework that guides how research should be conducted, based on people's philosophies and their assumptions about the world and the nature of knowledge.

1.5.5 Collecting research data

There are a variety of ways in which you can collect research data and we look at the main *methods of data collection* later in Chapters 8 and 10. Because of the many differences between quantitative and qualitative methods, these are explained in separate chapters. If you have a quantitative methodology, you will be attempting to measure variables or count occurrences of a phenomenon. On the other hand, if you have a qualitative methodology, you will emphasize the themes and patterns of meanings and experiences related to the phenomena.

1.5.6 Analysing and interpreting research data

A major part of your research project will be spent analysing and interpreting research data. The main *methods of data analysis* used will depend on your research paradigm and whether you have collected quantitative or qualitative data. We will be looking at this in more detail in Chapters 9, 11 and 12. It is important to realize, however, that although data collection and data analysis are discussed separately in this book, the stages are sometimes simultaneous. You should not make decisions about your data collection methods without also deciding which analytical methods you will use.

1.5.7 Writing the dissertation or thesis

It is at the writing-up stage that many students experience problems, usually because they have left it until the very last minute! It is important to start writing up your research in draft as soon as you start the early stages of the project, and continue to do so until it is completed. To a large extent, the stages outlined above will be captured in the structure of your dissertation or thesis. It is valuable at the outset to consider a possible structure, as it will give you an idea of what you are aiming for and Table 1.3 shows a typical structure. The title should be descriptive but not lengthy. Remember that any planned structure will have the disadvantage of

Table 1.3 Indicative structure of a dissertation or thesis

	% of report

1. Introduction
  – The research problem or issue and the purpose of the study
  – Background to the study and why it is important or of interest
  – Structure of the remainder of the report
	10

2. Review of the literature
  – Evaluation of the existing body of knowledge on the topic
  – Theoretical framework (if applicable)
  – Where your research fits in and the research question(s) and propositions or hypotheses, if applicable)
	30

3. Methodology
  – Identification of paradigm (*doctoral students will need to discuss*)
  – Justification for choice of methodology and methods
  – Limitations of the research design
	20

4. Findings/Results (*more than one chapter if appropriate*) – Presentation and discussion of the analysis of your research data/statistical tests and their results	30

5. Conclusions
  – Summary of what you found out in relation to each research question you investigated
  – Your contribution to knowledge
  – Limitations of your research and suggestions for future research
  – Implications of your research for practice or policy (if appropriate)
	10
	100

References (*do not number this section*) – A detailed, alphabetical (numerical, if appropriate) list of all the sources cited in the text	
Appendices – Detailed data referred to in the text, but not shown elsewhere	

making the research process look much more orderly than it really is. Although all research reports differ in structure according to the problem being investigated and the methodology employed, there are some common features.

1.6 Developing a research strategy

Research is a time-consuming and expensive activity and therefore you will need to develop a *research strategy* to ensure you meet your objectives. A humorous view of the challenges facing researchers is shown in Figure 1.2. However, this map was drawn in 1969 and in the intervening years many techniques and methods have been developed that help researchers overcome the difficulties depicted in this cartoon.

Although a few lucky individuals are in a position to conduct studies purely out of interest, most require some definite outcomes. This may be a dissertation or thesis that gets you a good grade as a student, transferable skills that improve your employability or a journal publication that will help you further your academic career. The main steps are:

- Getting organized
- Identifying your desired outcome(s)
- Choosing a research topic

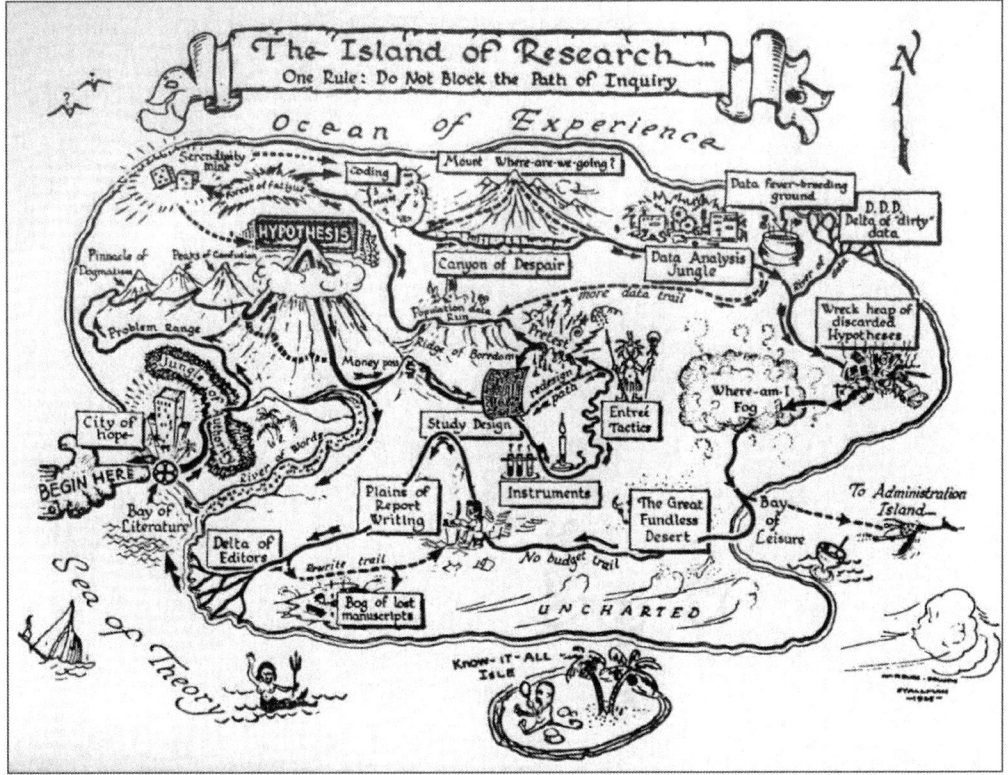

Figure 1.2 Island of research

Source: Agnew and Pyke (1969, frontispiece)

- Determining the research problem/question(s)
- Drawing up a detailed table of contents
- Establishing a timetable or schedule
- Being serious about writing.

These aspects will be discussed in depth throughout this book, but so that you can start developing your research strategy straightaway, we give some helpful pointers now.

1.6.1 Getting organized

You will not be successful in doing research if you are not organized. We can all think of exceptions of brilliant researchers who ignore this rule but, for most of us, success depends on being administratively competent. This entails having a good filing system, dating and recording all your research activities and committing everything to paper or computer. At this stage, you need to work out how much time you have, what financial resources you need and what physical resources you have in terms of computer hardware and software and any other technology. You will also need to draw up a list of contacts, groups and institutions that may be helpful. They may be able to help by offering advice and guidance, allowing you access to facilities such as a library or to collect data, or by assisting you in some way to achieve your desired outcomes.

1.6.2 Identifying the outcome(s)

You need to be specific when identifying the outcome(s) of your research. It is not sufficient to say that you want a high grade for your research project or to publish in one of the top academic journals. If you want to get the top grades for your dissertation or thesis, you need to understand the requirements you have to satisfy, and these are discussed in Chapter 2. If you want your work to be published, you need to read articles in the journal you have chosen and understand the editorial policy. We offer advice on this in Chapter 13.

1.6.3 Choosing a research topic

There is often a conflict between what you would like to do and what is feasible. The level of research and the outcome you desire will frequently determine the research you will conduct. You may be very interested in the history of sea bathing, but this may not be suitable if the particular aspect of sea bathing you choose is not relevant to your degree programme. If you are pursuing an academic career, you will need to think whether the topic you choose will provide you with a research niche upon which to build an impressive reputation. At the other end of the scale, the time constraints you face on a Bachelor's or Master's programme make it unlikely that you will be able to conduct a large survey of the opinions of directors of the world's top companies. Even a seasoned researcher with an enviable reputation would find such a project a challenge. Your research must be feasible and lead to your expected outcome(s).

1.6.4 Determining the research problem/question(s)

Do not focus solely on the immediate outcome(s) of your research only, but think about how you might be able to develop your work. For example, if you are a student, you might want to examine an issue in a particular industry where you hope to find employment when you graduate. For those pursuing research to further their careers, there is a good argument for choosing an issue that will help you to build a reputation and become one of the experts in a particular field.

1.6.5 Being serious about writing

You will be judged by your ability to communicate, particularly your written output; a poorly crafted dissertation, thesis, conference paper or article can destroy what may have been a well-designed and carefully executed study. We give considerable guidance on writing in the later chapters but the immediate advice is to start writing notes and drafts now and to continue to write, review and revise your work so that your final draft will represent the highest quality in terms of substance, structure, grammar and spelling.

Key definitions

Methodological rigour refers to the appropriateness and intellectual soundness of the research design and the systematic application of the research methods.

1.7 Characteristics of good research

Many of the characteristics of good research can be developed by adopting a methodical approach. *Methodological rigour* is very important and this term refers to the appropriateness and intellectual soundness of the research design and the systematic application of the methods used. Therefore, it requires a careful, detailed, exacting approach to conducting the research.

The characteristics of a good research project vary according to the philosophical assumptions that underpin your research. These assumptions are discussed later in Chapter 4 and are very important at all academic levels. A soundly based research design should allow a degree of flexibility to enable you to pursue new developments in the topic if they are relevant to the study and you have sufficient time. In subsequent chapters, we will explain how this can be achieved At this stage, it is useful to have an overview of what makes a good research project. Therefore, Table 1.4 compares the main characteristics of good and poor projects.

1.8 Conclusions

This chapter has examined the purpose and nature of research, and the ways in which it can be classified. We have given an overview of the different types of research and the factors that need o be considered at various levels. A research project offers an opportunity to identify and select a research problem to investigate independently under the guidance of a supervisor. It gives you the opportunity to apply theory or otherwise analyse a real business problem or issue. Your research needs to be systematic and methodical and your study will illuminate the problem

Table 1.4 Characteristics of good and poor research projects

Criteria	Poor project	Good project
Research problem and scope	Unclear and unfocused	Sharply focused Related to academic debate
Literature review	A list of items Relevance unclear Little or no evaluation Research questions missing, impractical or unfocused	Critical evaluation of relevant, up-to-date literature Linked to focused, feasible research questions
Methodology	Little appreciation of research design No justification of choice Not linked to the literature	Cohesive design Excellent review of research design options Linked to the literature
Analysis and discussion	Unclear findings, unrelated to research questions Little or no attempt to discuss in relation to literature review	Clear findings discussed in an analytical manner that generates new knowledge and insight Linked to the literature
Conclusions	Some conclusions but not linked to research questions Implications and limitations of results not addressed	Conclusions clearly linked to research questions Attention given to implications and limitations
Referencing	Plagiarism through omission or inadequate referencing	All sources cited in the text and full bibliographic details listed at the end
Communication	Difficult to follow Many spelling and grammar mistakes	Clear flow of ideas Appropriate spelling and grammar

or issue and contribute towards our greater understanding of it. To ensure you are satisfied with your research and achieve the outcomes you desire, you must develop a research strategy. The most important part of that strategy from the onset is to start writing. You should make sure that you keep careful records to ensure that other people's contribution to knowledge is not confused with yours.

Activities

1. Select two academic journals from your discipline in the library and construct a table that classifies articles according to whether the research is exploratory, descriptive, analytical or predictive.
2. Construct a second table that classifies the same articles according to whether the research is quantitative or qualitative.
3. Now construct a third table that classifies the same articles according to whether the research is applied or basic.
4. Finally, construct a table that classifies the same articles according to whether the research is deductive and inductive.
5. Reflect on the results shown in your four tables and write notes on similarities and differences in these classifications. Summarize your notes in the form of a diagram.

UNDERSTANDING RESEARCH

PROGRESS TEST

Complete the following sentences:

1. Research is a process of enquiry and investigation that is conducted in a systematic and methodical way with a view to increasing _____.
2. A study in which theory is developed from the empirical evidence is known as _____ research.
3. A study in which theory is tested against empirical evidence is known as _____ research.
4. An idea or proposition that can be tested against empirical evidence is called a _____.
5. Empirical evidence is data based on experience or _____.

Are the following statements true or false?

6. A research paradigm is a lengthy treatment of a theme that is submitted for an academic degree.
7. Descriptive research can take a quantitative or qualitative approach.
8. A qualitative approach to research does not require IT skills.
9. An exploratory study is always used to test or confirm a hypothesis.
10. Research that has been designed to resolve a specific problem is known as applied research.

Multiple choice questions:

11. The result of building up information from other information is known as:
    a) an analysis
    b) a dialysis
    c) a synopsis
    d) a synthesis
12. The result of setting out a reasoned argument in steps is known as:
    a) a comparison
    b) a debate
    c) an evaluation
    d) an evasion
13. The classification of studies into exploratory, descriptive, analytical or predictive research is based on:
    a) the logic of the research
    b) the outcome of the research
    c) the process of the research
    d) the purpose of the research
14. The classification of studies into applied or basic research is based on:
    a) the logic of the research
    b) the outcome of the research

c) the process of the research
d) the purpose of the research

15. Inductive research seeks to:
    a) classify theory
    b) confirm theory
    c) develop theory
    d) test theory

References

Agnew, N. M. and Pyke, S. W. (1969) *The Science Game: An Introduction to Research in Behavioral Sciences*, Englewood Cliffs, NJ: Prentice-Hall.
Oxford Compact Dictionary & Thesaurus (1997) Oxford: Oxford University Press.

Glossary

Analytical research	A study where the aim is to understand phenomena by discovering and measuring causal relations among them.
Applied research	Describes a study that is designed to apply its findings to solving a specific, existing problem.
Basic (or pure) research	Describes a study that is designed to make a contribution to general knowledge and theoretical understanding, rather than solve a specific problem.
Data (singular is datum)	Known facts or things used as a basis for inference or reckoning.
Deductive research	A study in which a conceptual and theoretical structure is developed which is then tested by empirical observation; thus particular instances are deducted from general inferences.
Descriptive research	A study where the aim is to describe the characteristics of phenomena.
Dissertation	'A detailed discourse, esp. as submitted for [an] academic degree'. A discourse is 'a lengthy treatment of a theme' (*Oxford Dictionary & Thesaurus*, 1997, pp. 216 and 211).
Exploratory research	A study where the aim is to investigate phenomena where there is little or no information, with a view to finding patterns or developing propositions, rather than testing them. The focus is on gaining insights prior to a more rigorous investigation.
Hypothesis (plural is hypotheses)	A proposition that can be tested for association or causality against empirical evidence.
Inductive research	A study in which theory is developed from the observation of empirical reality; thus general inferences are induced from particular instances.
Methodological rigour	The appropriateness and intellectual soundness of the research design and the systematic application of the research methods.
Paradigm	A framework that guides how research should be conducted based on people's philosophies and their assumptions about the world and the nature of knowledge.
Predictive research	A study where the aim is to generalize from an analysis of phenomena by making predictions based on hypothesized general relationships.

UNDERSTANDING RESEARCH

Research	A systematic and methodical process of enquiry and investigation with a view to increasing knowledge.
Research design	The detailed plan for conducting a research study.
Research topic	The general area of research interest.
Secondary data	Data collected from an existing source, such as publications, databases and internal records.
Thesis	'A dissertation, esp. by [a] candidate for a higher degree' (*Oxford Dictionary & Thesaurus*, 1997, p. 801).
Variable	A characteristic of a phenomenon that can be observed or measured.

CHAPTER 2
What is business and management research?
An introduction to the research process

KEY QUESTIONS

- What is business and management research?
- Why do we do business and management research?
- What are the benefits of taking a systematic approach to a research project?
- What critical issues should you consider as you get started?
- Who are the key project stakeholders?

LEARNING OUTCOMES

At the end of this chapter, you should be able to:

- Explain what business and management research is, and why we do it
- Describe a systematic research process for doing research
- Identify the issues you should address before starting your project

CONTENTS

Introduction
2.1 What is business and management research?
2.2 Business and management research in wider context
2.3 Before you get started
Summary
Answers to key questions
References
Additional resources
Key terms
Discussion questions
Workshop and discussion questions

Introduction

Business and management research plays a familiar part in our everyday lives, even if we don't always recognise it as research. For instance, you often do research without explicitly thinking about it as such, using the library, internet, newspapers and other publications to find out more about organisations and their products and activities. You are doing business and management research when you collect and use information to solve a practical problem, such as visiting a supplier's website to find out more about a new bicycle, using a phone directory to locate a taxi firm or purchasing an air travel ticket over the web.

Businesses and other organisations constantly conduct research. People who work in organisations do research to meet organisational needs, for example to find out about competitors and their products. Sometimes this research is obvious – someone approaches you in the street or contacts you via telephone or email asking you to answer a market survey. Less obviously, organisations unobtrusively collect information on you as a customer using 'cookies' and other software when you visit a website or customer loyalty cards when you visit a shop.

You are also constantly bombarded with new information about business and management. Newspapers report stories about organisations and people, management consultants present their analyses of clients' problems and make recommendations to solve them and organisations themselves churn out a steady flow of information for shareholders, analysts, regulators and the general public.

If you are already doing research, why should you study or learn more about research methods by reading this book? The fact that you are reading this paragraph may mean that you are studying research methods or doing a research project as part of your studies. Or, you may be working in an organisation and need to do some research to solve an organisational problem. Either way, you can benefit from a better understanding of the research process. You can apply the research skills you develop through studying a research problem in depth, as well as the learning and self-reflection that come from the process, in your studies and career. Furthermore, what you learn about research can help you to become a more critical consumer of what you learn in your studies, which are in turn based on business and management research done by professional researchers.

This chapter provides a general introduction to business and management research. **Section 2.1** provides an overview of business and management research. **Section 2.2** explains the wider context of business and management research. **Section 2.3** discusses some critical issues that you should think about as you begin learning about research. Examples of real-life student and scholarly research are a continuing theme in this chapter and throughout this book.

2.1 What is business and management research?

Our goal in writing this book is not only to present a range of information so that you can pass a research methods course or carry out a particular research project, but also to help you develop skills and understanding that let you manage research through taking a **systematic approach**. You should think of research as a **process** that consists of a specific set and sequence of activities, with tangible and intangible inputs and outputs, such as information, time, resources and knowledge. Something (such as knowledge about the world and actions that are taken based on that knowledge) is transformed as a result of the research process. With this understanding, you can manage research rather than being managed by it or simply hoping that it will all happen for you.

This systematic approach is based on our 4-D model of the **research process** outlined in the **Introduction**. Positioning your research project within this more general framework allows you to identify the choices you will make as a researcher about what to research and how to research it, and the logic that guides these choices. In the research process, even if some aspects of research are always uncertain and unpredictable, a systematic approach will help you manage this uncertainty.

To get you started on thinking about research as a systematic process, this chapter will:

- Describe business and management research
- Introduce our framework for managing the research process
- Show how research fits in the context of business and management.

2.1.1 What is research?

Research is a process of finding out information and investigating the unknown to solve a problem. For many people, 'researcher' conjures up an image of a white-coated scientist beavering away in a laboratory, whilst 'investigator' suggests a hard-boiled private eye snooping around to try to uncover some piece of evidence and thereby solve a crime. However, business and management research generally involves neither 'ivory tower' research in a laboratory nor undercover investigation.

Even before you started reading this book, you probably had some ideas about what business and management research is. You probably know that research involves identifying and gathering information. True, in some small projects, you may only need to find and report information, requiring nothing more than a simple internet search or a quick visit to your library. Although gathering information is an integral research skill, doing business and management research involves much more than searching for information using the library, internet or other resources. Research also requires using this information to solve a problem that is relevant to business and management. This problem can be a practical one faced by a real organisation, or a theoretical one posed by a gap in management knowledge. Research involves identifying a problem, understanding what information is relevant to addressing that problem, getting the information and interpreting that information and its context.

To reflect this larger role of research, we define research as:

> A systematic process that includes defining, designing, doing and describing an investigation into a research problem.

What business and management researchers study

Saunders et al. (2003: 3) define business and management research as 'undertaking systematic research to find things out about business and management'. So what exactly does this entail? The scope of business and management research is not as neatly bounded as, for example, inorganic chemistry or nuclear physics. Business and management research covers diverse areas: accounting, finance and economics; human resources and organisational behaviour; strategy and international business; marketing; operations, management science and information systems. Business and management research covers a diverse set of research activities because of its range of topics, links to other areas and study of different social units. Even a single area such as accounting includes a broad range of topics, starting with the distinction between managerial accounting and financial accounting.

This diversity is increased because business and management research draws on other academic areas, including mathematics, statistics, economics, psychology, computing, sociology, anthropology and law. Finance, for example, draws heavily on both economics and mathematics, so if you wanted to study financial markets you would probably need some knowledge of these two areas as well.

Business and management researchers study a diverse set of social units ranging from individuals to nations and even regions. Researchers may study *individuals* such as employees, managers or executives in organisations, and other individuals such as customers and suppliers who interact with them. These shareholders, directors, managers, workers, customers and clients are sometimes described as 'organisational actors'. Researchers also study *groups* of individuals such as work groups, who act together to achieve common goals, or who interact, such as frontline employees and customers. Researchers also study *organisations*, formal or informal groupings of people, including firms and other businesses, and not-for-profit entities such as charities, government agencies or non-government organisations (NGOs). They may also study levels higher than the organisation, such as the supply chain, industry, nation, region of the world or even global organisation. This higher level may be defined around patterns of interaction, such as markets, or location, such as the European Union (EU).

Given these three dimensions of business and management research, you can see the huge range of possible subjects facing the business and management researcher. As we shall see in **Chapter 3**, this can leave you rather spoilt for choice! When you think about what you are interested in studying, you might think about how these individuals and organisations relate to each other. The hierarchy presented in **Figure 2.1** is one way of making sense of the interrelationships and where business and management disciplines fit with these levels.

If business and management research spans nearly every type of human activity, is there anything that makes business and management research unique? How does it differ from other areas such as economics, psychology or sociology that study many of the same issues?

Because business and management is a professional, rather than an academic discipline, research needs to be relevant as well as academically rigorous. Academic researchers are often primarily concerned with increasing knowledge, which may be applied in the future, not just to aid understanding, but also to improve individual and organisational performance. On the other hand, many people, academics and managers alike, believe that the ultimate goal of research should be to help organisations to improve their performance. A major focus of business and management research is on the link between practices and organisational performance. Practices

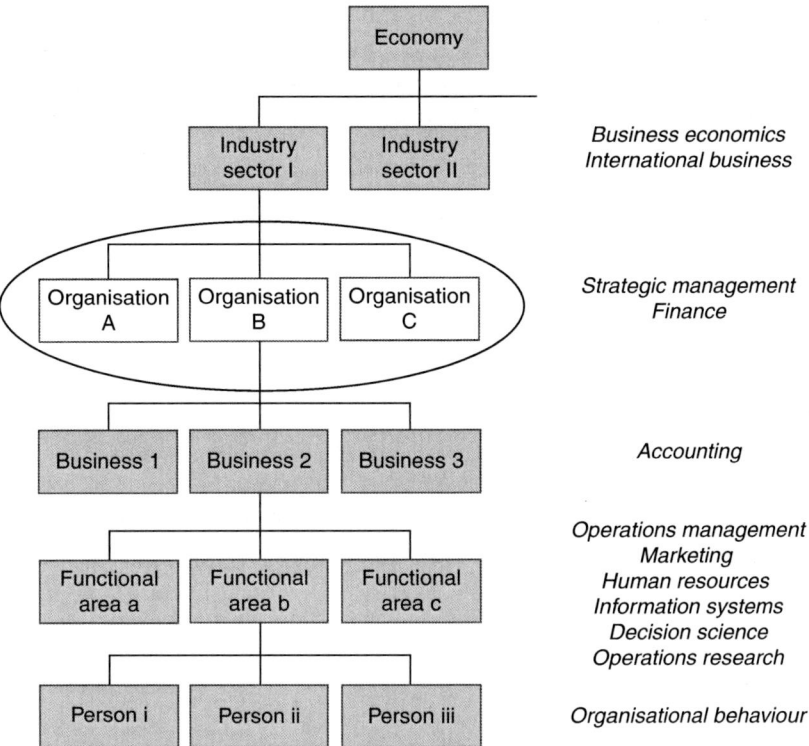

Figure 2.1 A hierarchy of business and management research objects

that affect individual and organisational performance may be external – for example the role of national regulation – or internal – for example specific accounting, operations or human resources (HR) practices.

2.1.2 What research is not!

Even if business and management research is diverse, it is not so broad that any problem you could investigate qualifies as research. There are significant differences between a systematic research process – the journey you are embarking on – and activities such as journalism or consulting.

It can sometimes be hard to tell research, journalism and consulting apart – all three share many characteristics. However, business and management research isn't just a process of collecting and reporting information; it involves creating new knowledge by analysing, interpreting and reporting that information, and by integrating this new knowledge with what we already know. A major goal of business and management research is to create better and more widely applicable theories (we will discuss more precisely what we mean by 'theory' in **Chapter 3**) that will help other people to solve a similar practical problem or understand a research problem better. Further, professional business and management research (what gets published in management journals) must be rigorously checked by other academic researchers (peer review, which we discuss in **Chapter 4**), and is constantly revised or even replaced over time.

Research is not journalism

Many students find it difficult to distinguish between journalism and research. In **journalism**, journalists report information about business and management organisations, people and trends in newspapers such as the *Financial Times* and the *Wall Street Journal* and magazines such as *The Economist* and *Fortune*. A common purpose of both journalism and research is to gather information and present it in an appropriate format. However, a journalist's job is to report the news – what is new or novel – to sell newspapers or magazines or attract television or radio viewers. 'Man bites dog' makes the news headlines because it is new or unusual, not because it adds to our knowledge, or helps us to understand deeper truths about the world or solve particular problems.

An important difference between journalism and research is that other researchers must verify the research findings before they are published. Checking and challenging is an essential, not optional, element of the systematic research process discussed in this book. Newspapers and magazines, however, seldom do much factual checking of the information they report, apart from spell-checking and so fall well short of the standards of peer review. This means that information provided by journalists is not always reliable, even if it is eye-catching and timely.

Of course, journalism and academic research are not always mutually exclusive. Journalists report on noteworthy research findings and the presentations and ideas of leading academic researchers. Some journalists contribute to knowledge as well as just providing information. Some investigative journalism even comes close to or surpasses academic research; however, it is unlikely to have been peer reviewed.

In addition, many academic researchers cross over into journalism, appearing on news programmes and chat shows; providing 'sound bites' on the topic of the day; writing books, magazine articles and newspaper columns for popular audiences; and even presenting television and radio programmes. However, even if someone has immense credibility as a researcher, if what they are saying has not been arrived at through a systematic research process and been checked and challenged by other academics, it is still opinion and/or journalism and not research.

Research is not consulting

The difference between journalism and research is obvious when they are done by different people and reported in different places. (We will discuss the credibility of different sources in **Chapter 4**.) It can be more difficult to tell the difference between **consulting** and research, because they are often done by the same people and reported in the same places (for example *Harvard Business Review*). Professional consultants report their work in books and in-house journals that resemble academic publications, in order to publicise their ideas and promote their services. Some academics wear both hats, carrying out consulting projects and reporting their work as research findings. Famous business 'gurus' such as Michael Porter and Gary Hamel run consulting companies, teach business and management, and publish in academic and non-academic forums.

To understand the difference between consulting and research, let's take a closer look at what consultants do. A consultant is typically engaged by an organisation to solve an organisational problem. The consultant must gather, analyse and interpret information to solve that problem. The output of the consulting engagement will be a set of recommendations, developed by the consultant based on this information, describing how the company should solve the problem. For example, a consultant might be hired by an organisation to provide advice on how to restructure the organisation, and so will need to gather information about the organisation, including finding out the organisation's current structure and defining its objectives. The consultant's report would describe how to restructure the company and address any potential problems in how it might be implemented.

In deciding whether a project is more consulting or research, you should consider both the means and the ends. Whether a project is research or consulting depends on what the consultant then does with that information. Most consulting engagements begin with and end with the specific organisational problem, although a consultant will build up a stock of expertise over time and consulting companies often specialise in particular areas of expertise.

Consultants value the information they gain in a consultancy engagement primarily as an input to future consulting engagements. In fact, consulting firms typically want to keep that knowledge proprietary. When consultants do report their work, it is typically to advertise this expertise in order to attract clients rather than increase the sum of business and management knowledge. As a result, consultants rarely have to justify how and what they investigate except to their client and employer, because the quality of their work is judged by how well it lets the organisation solve a particular problem, not whether it would help other organisations solve similar problems.

Researchers, on the other hand, have a primary responsibility to create and share original knowledge. This means that they must link their research to previous research on the subject, and show that they are adding something new to that knowledge as a result of their investigation. Research by its nature is meant to be shared, not hidden. Finally, as we noted for journalism, it isn't 'research' until it has been validated by other researchers, or peer reviewed.

2.2 Business and management research in wider context

If we can define business and management research by what it is not, neither journalism nor consulting, we can also define it by what it is, a form of social research and of research in general. This makes it possible for us to identify some characteristics of research projects that both make them unique and create challenges in trying to manage them.

2.2.1 Originality in research

First of all, as we noted above, a business and management research project makes a unique contribution to knowledge. This doesn't necessarily have to be a 'great discovery' or 'grand new theory'. Your project will typically aim to apply existing business and management knowledge in a new context or add a small bit of new knowledge to what we already know. Your unique contribution to existing knowledge may come through:

- new or improved evidence
- new or improved methodology

- new or improved analysis
- new or improved concepts or theories.

Second, business and management research focuses on asking questions and solving problems, rather than just finding out information, as we note above. As we will see in **Chapter 3**, the first step in the research process is to identify a research problem that you want to find out more about. A **research problem** can come from either a practical problem (real-life situation) or a theoretical problem (general principles or observations). You might identify a practical problem based on an issue that you have observed in a real-life setting, for example receiving poor service in a store might lead you to study how stores handle customer complaints. A practical problem could also come from issues that have been identified in your courses, or problems that face your organisation or other setting you are interested in investigating.

You could also start with a theoretical problem posed by a business or management topic about which you would like to know more but for which there is incomplete information, for example the best way to motivate workers. Such problems often emerge as you think about how to apply the theories and models learnt in your course-work to real-life settings, or try to understand which of several competing theories best explains how people or organisations actually behave. For example which is better for understanding corporate strategy, Porter's five forces or the resource-based view? It is not always possible to answer either type of problem completely by what you find out in a single research project.

You need to ask one or more **research questions** about your research problem in order to understand more about it. **Chapter 3** will identify a systematic process for identifying research problems and questions that you can transform into research projects, and how these problems and questions can be used to structure your research project.

For example, if you were interested in researching whether agricultural subsidies affect farmers in developing countries, you might investigate the practical problem presented by agricultural subsidies to farmers in developed regions such as the EU, which could potentially put farmers in developing countries out of business. Another way you might approach this problem is from an international business perspective, focusing on the implications of trade barriers. You could start with the theoretical problem of trade barriers, then narrow it down to agricultural subsidies and even further to developing countries.

Either way, you might come up with some questions that you want to answer, such as:

- Do agricultural subsidies to farmers in developed countries make imported products less competitive?
- Should governments in developed countries change their policies to aid farmers in developing countries?

Your research problem and questions *define* your research project and become key inputs to the next stage of the process, *designing* your research, which we cover in **Part 2**. The research design, in turn, drives the *doing* stage of the research process, which is detailed in **Part 3**. Finally, the inputs from these first three stages allow you to *describe* your research, which is the subject of **Part 4**. We described these stages in detail in the **Introduction**.

WHAT IS BUSINESS AND MANAGEMENT RESEARCH?

Table 2.1 Three types of research activity

Stage in research	Role of this type of research
Basic research	Research that is conducted to increase knowledge, with little consideration of future applications. Many social science researchers consider their work to be of this type. For instance, research on the behaviour of people under certain conditions may be undertaken (as in Milgram's experiment at the end of this chapter).
Development	This involves taking an original idea, possibly a basic research project, and looking for applications. This may include combining it with other ideas, or changing the original intention. For instance, knowing that people behave in a certain way, considering how this might be applied in practice, for example as part of a training package for in-company use.
Commercial	This involves taking an idea from the possibility of application through to commercial usage. This is a particular skill set of consultants. For instance, they may take the behavioural work developed above and sell it into a firm as part of a training package. There could be further research to evaluate its usefulness in practice.

2.2.2 Types of research activities

We might classify research projects depending on how much they are targeted towards a specific practical problem versus how much they are targeted towards a general theoretical problem. This leads to three general types of project, which are basic research, development and commercial projects and are described in more detail in **Table 2.1**.

Some research projects may fit into more than one classification. You might start by investigating a practical problem and then use your findings to add to the knowledge about a theoretical problem, or you might investigate a theoretical problem in a specific practical context and then identify how to solve similar problems in other practical contexts. A series of research projects that starts with basic research and carries the same kind of investigation through to development, or vice versa, is known as a 'stream' of research.

2.2.3 General issues for research projects

Because many researchers are interested in how ideas are developed and how they are turned into new products or other concrete outcomes, they have conducted much academic study on research projects. **Table 2.2** summarises some other key dimensions or characteristics of research.

2.3 Before you get started

> I keep six honest serving-men, they taught me all I knew. Their names are what and why and when, and how and where and who.
>
> (**Kipling** [1902]1987: *69*)

You can use Kipling's six question words to start thinking about your research project:

1. Why am I doing this research project, and what do I want to get out of it?
2. What do I want to find out?

Table 2.2 Key dimensions of business and management research

Type	Comments
Scholarly versus commercial research	The main motivation for conducting scholarly research is usually to increase our knowledge about business and management. The knowledge that is created may not be immediately – if ever – applicable to a practical problem faced by businesses or managers.
	Commercial research is research that is sponsored (and paid for) by the organisation or individual that intends to apply the knowledge, usually to a practical problem facing the organisation. Commercial research usually has a purpose connected with the central objective of the organisation, be it making money or carrying out a governmental or charitable mission.
	The customers of the output of the project are different in nature. In the first, the acquisition of knowledge is the driver. Commercial research is usually intended for immediate use by the business sponsor, whilst academic research has no clear customer in mind. In the second, the application of the knowledge is the driver.
Scholarly versus student research	Scholarly research is expected to contribute to our knowledge about business and management, whilst student research may only need to apply such knowledge to a practical or theoretical problem.
	To ensure that scholarly research is both original and correct, it usually undergoes peer review – other academics who are knowledgeable about the research topic and/or methods review it to ensure it meets an acceptable level of quality before it is published or presented.
	Student research is usually assessed by a small set of examiners, who must assess it against the project requirements and standards of the institution.
Assigned versus interest-driven topics	The more choice you are given by your project guidelines, the more time you will need to spend defining and designing your research, but you will have a greater opportunity to reflect your own interests and skills.
	The challenges for each are different. Choosing a project is the subject of **Chapter 3** and can be an extensive activity. The assigned project would appear to have an easier start, but defining precisely what the project is about (scoping) can be as extensive an activity as choosing your own project.
Indirect versus direct contact with organizations to gather data	Research projects can involve considerable contact with external organisations or other parties or none at all. Some research, generally known as 'desk' or 'library' research, involves only indirect contact with the organisations or individuals you are studying. In desk research, you will have no direct contact with the source of the data you are analysing, but instead may use the library, internet, archives, computer databases or other sources of data. This is often used when you are studying organisations that are distant in time and/or space.
	Alternately, you may have direct contact with the organisation and/or individuals you are studying, either face to face, as in interviews or case study research, or by other means, such as postal surveys.
Individual versus research	Research projects may be conducted alone or as part of a group group. Group projects require managing group processes (interactions between group members) as well as the content and the process of the research project. This group process creates the potential for group conflict, although a group can often create synergies.
Single discipline versus interdisciplinary research	Business and management research draws on many base disciplines, including economics, psychology, sociology and mathematics. Your research can be based in one of these disciplines or consider inputs from a number of areas. This will be discussed below and in **Chapters 2** and **3**.

3. Where is the information that I want to find out?
4. Who will want to know what I find out?
5. How will I be assessed?
6. When can I start, and when must I finish, my work?

We suggest that, before you start your project, you consider what you are trying to do and why, so that you *begin with the end in mind* (see Stephen Covey's book *The Seven Habits of Highly Effective People* (2005) for a discussion of why this is important). Some of the most successful research projects we have supervised began with students visualising the final project report and then deciding how they would make it happen. Think of your research project not as an arrow that you shoot into the air, which may hit a target only by luck, but as a target pulling the arrow towards it. You might also think about the different people who will be involved in your project and the impact your work might actually make on the world.

2.3.1 Why are you doing a research project?

As you reach the end of this first chapter, you should also consider why you are reading this book, and/or why you are doing a research project. If you are doing research as part of a coursework assignment or degree requirement, one immediate benefit will be to pass the course or get your degree. If you are doing research as part of a work assignment, the immediate benefit will be to satisfy your manager and help your organisation. In both cases, you will be assessed, either formally or informally, on the quality and the outcomes of your research project. Therefore, you may answer the question 'why are you doing research?' with 'to complete an assigned task!'.

However, we argue that learning to do research and becoming a competent researcher are themselves worthwhile. You may find that doing research has long-term benefits, such as improving:

- Your understanding of the research problem you study
- Your competence in doing a research project
- Your ability to manage research as a systematic process
- Your ability to build on other people's research, increasing the credibility of your own work.

Additionally, you can apply your research skills beyond business and management, to:

- Test accepted or new ideas to see if they are true
- Discover new things about the world
- Make sense of the world around you.

To manage research as a systematic process you will need to develop not only practical and analytic skills, but also critical skills. This point is key – if you are not an informed consumer of research, you can't tell what is true and what is merely opinion. Doing research helps you to understand and critically assess research carried out by other researchers, including the research presented in textbooks, academic journals and the popular press. Without this ability to critically assess other people's arguments, as Carl Sagan (1997: 42) commented: 'We become a nation of suckers, up for grabs by every charlatan that comes along' (more of this in **Chapter 5**).

Our experience supports the need for everyone – students, journalists, consultants and managers – to develop a questioning approach to journalists' reports, consultants' recommendations and researchers' findings, as shown in **Research in action 1.1**.

Research in action 2.1
CHECK THE ASSUMPTIONS

One company continually worked hard to reduce new product lead times, that is, how long from start to finish it took them to develop new products. Reducing lead times became a real obsession in the firm, but whenever anyone was asked why it was so important, they usually answered: 'Oh, you know that study …'. However, not one person could identify the original source of 'that study'.

From detailed questioning of the managers, it became clear to the researcher that this study was actually a one-line statement quoted in *Fortune* magazine based on some simplistic calculations carried out by a consultancy. Perhaps not coincidentally, the consultancy trained companies to reduce new product lead times. If the managers had approached the study from a more critical perspective, they might have raised questions such as: How reliable is this study? Do these recommendations apply to us?

The point is that we must be able to evaluate the foundations on which we are basing our work or decisions.

2.3.2 Key players in the project

Whether you undertake a research project alone or as part of a team, you need to know what you should be doing at any point in the research process. In the following chapters, we will consider the activities that should be undertaken in each of the project stages. If you are part of a research team, you will also need to know what role each person will be playing. **Chapter 2** will consider the role of the project team in more detail.

Some questions that you might want to ask are:

- Who will be carrying out this research project?
- What will I be doing or be responsible for?
- How should I work with my supervisor?
- How should I work with any external stakeholders for my work?
- What are the requirements of any assessment body?

Your supervisor's role

An important **project stakeholder** will be your main advisor, typically your academic supervisor, but potentially your project sponsor if you have one. The role your main supervisor plays may vary according to the kind of project, for example supervisor implies much more 'hands-on' involvement than coordinator. In coursework projects or job-related research projects, your supervisor will set the project assignment, and may even be the person who marks or assesses it.

If you have a chance to choose your own supervisor or project coordinator, you should try to find out:

- What do other students that he or she has supervised think about him or her for this specific type of project?
- Is he or she interested in the research you will be doing?
- Does his or her personality complement or conflict with your personality?
- How quickly can he or she provide feedback on your work?
- What are his or her plans for the period of research?

Finding out what other students think about a potential supervisor can help you to decide whether he or she might be a good match for your project. Project supervisors who can provide quick, accurate feedback on your research are worth their weight in gold. A good sign is whether your proposed supervisor takes an interest in this kind of project, especially if he or she is interested in the topic and/or research approach you will be taking. However, interest alone is no guarantee of success: every student–supervisor relationship is unique. Personal habits, administrative and other teaching duties, and the number of students he or she supervises can detract from your academic supervisor's time and attention. Furthermore, whether your supervisor is available to provide feedback and other guidance can be affected by sabbaticals, leave of absence, taking a job at another university, retirement or plans to spend the summer in a house in France.

Whether or not you are able to choose your supervisor, you should think carefully about the relationship you are about to embark on. Students sometimes make unrealistic assumptions about their advisors, which can only lead to disappointment. You can use the issues listed in **Figure 2.2** to manage your expectations of what your supervisor will and will not do.

Because this relationship can have such a large impact on a research project's process and outcomes, many institutions now explicitly state what each party is responsible for. The guidelines given in **Student research in action 2.1** are just an example, but you can see how they set out the ground rules right from the start of the project.

Other people who play a role
You will also need to manage other project stakeholders besides yourself and your supervisor. Try to identify those people who have the information you need. Also try to identify those to whom you will report your findings or make your recommendations. They may or may not be the same people. You should identify these people and start to work proactively with them from the start of your project, since they can help but can also hinder your work. How well you manage them can affect how smoothly the process goes and how successful your project is. This is discussed in more detail in **Chapter 2**.

Always have two plans; leave something to chance.

(**Napoleon**)

A key research skill is managing everyone involved in the research project. This includes not only you and any other project team members, but all the project's **stakeholders**. These stakeholders will provide information and/or other inputs that you need. They are also the people who will be the customers for your project's output.

My advisor:

Is interested in me as a person	⇔	Is not interested in me as a person
Is interested in my topic	⇔	Is not interested in my topic
Is experienced and competent to advise on my topic	⇔	Is inexperienced and not competent to advise on my topic
Has reasonable expectations as to what I can do and how long it will take me	⇔	Has unreasonable expectations about the amount of work I can do and how long it will take me
Provides comments and feedback on my work in a reasonable time period	⇔	Takes a long time or never provides comments or feedback on my work
Is consistent in words and actions	⇔	Is inconsistent
Has integrity and is responsible	⇔	Cannot be relied on
Looks out for my best interests and takes pride in my work	⇔	Makes unfair demands on me or doesn't protect me from others
Respects me as a person	⇔	Doesn't respect me as a person

Figure 2.2 Issues to consider in working with a project supervisor

Source: Based on Davis and Parker (1997: 44)

Student research in action 2.1

EXAMPLE GUIDELINES

The student's responsibilities

The student will be expected to:

- Submit a research proposal to the format and timetable as set down in the guidelines
- Draw up a timetable of activities
- Submit an outline of the project report showing what each chapter will cover
- Submit an agreed chapter to generate supervisor feedback
- Keep his/her supervisor informed of any holidays or trips that may affect his/her performance
- Keep the project coordinator and supervisor informed of any circumstances that may affect the submission of his/her project
- Work with an allocated supervisor who may not be his/her first choice
- Be aware of the supervisor's availability during the period of the project, particularly in July, August and September.

The supervisor's responsibilities

The supervisor will provide general guidance in the conduct of a research programme and will act as a 'sounding board' to test various ideas and help in deciding appropriate courses of action (this can include referral to appropriate specialists within the school). This is to help to ensure that the progress made throughout the project and the writing-up of these activities will fulfil the academic requirements of the school.

It is expected that a supervisor will:

- Discuss and assist in the development of the submitted proposal
- Agree a timetable of activities
- Discuss the structure of the written project, that is, chapter coverage and purposes
- Comment on one chapter to advise on how well it matches the set purpose for that chapter and the style of writing
- Advise on issues relating to the theory and/or methodology used in the project
- Examine and mark the completed project.

A supervisor will not:

- Keep track of a student's progress and chase him/her when deadlines are not adhered to
- Read an entire draft copy of the finished project
- Arrange access to organisations used as part of any field work
- Visit any organisations as part of any field work
- Necessarily be an expert in the theoretical or methodological area of a project he/she is supervising.

Summary

In this chapter, we have addressed three main issues about business and management research. First, we have given you an overview of business and management research, and tried to draw a boundary between what research is and is not. Second, we have explained the benefits of understanding business and management research, doing a business and management research project and why you should approach it as a systematic and structured process. Finally, we have explained some issues that you need to consider as you are getting started on your research project, including why you are doing it, what you want to get out of it and who else will be involved in it.

Answers to key questions

What is business and management research?

- It is a process that starts with the determination of a research problem or question, based on an issue of interest
- Research is not journalism or consulting, although there are parallels in the processes with both these activities
- Business and management research considers the roles of organisations, organisational actors and their actions and interactions

Why do we do business and management research?
- Research is conducted for a wide range of intrinsic and extrinsic reasons, including the possibility of discovering new things about something of interest, testing ideas and making sense of complex situations
- Basic research is carried out to establish ideas or principles
- Developmental research is carried out to take these ideas or principles on and bring them one step closer to commercialisation

What are the benefits of taking a systematic approach to a research project?
- A systematic approach allows you to identify the choices you will make as a researcher and the logic that guides these choices
- A systematic approach will remove some of the uncertainty from the process, and allow you to manage the remainder
- The research life cycle is defined by the 4-Ds, from definition, to designing to doing the research and then describing your work
- The process is not linear, but iterative

What critical issues should you consider as you get started?
- Begin with the end in mind
- Look for previous work in this or similar areas, key themes and hot topics, consider methods and look at your timescales and available resources

Who are the key project stakeholders?
- Yourself
- Other members of the project team (if applicable)
- Supervisors
- Examiners
- Project sponsors (if applicable)

References

Covey, Stephen R. 2005. *The Seven Habits of Highly Effective People*, rev. edn. London: Simon & Schuster.
Davis, Gordon B. and Parker, Clyde A. 1997. *Writing the Doctoral Dissertation: A Systematic Approach.* Hauppage, NY: Barron's Educational Series.
Kipling, Rudyard. [1902]1998. 'The Elephant's Child' in *Just So Stories*. London: Puffin.
Milgram, S. 1974. *Obedience to Authority.* New York: Harper Perennial.
Roethlisberger, F.J. and Dickson, W.J. 1939. *Management and the Worker.* Cambridge, MA: Harvard University Press.
Sagan, Carl. 1997. *The Demon-Haunted World: Science as a Candle in the Dark.* New York: Ballantine Books.
Saunders, Mark N.K., Lewis, Philip and Thornhill, Adrian. 2003. *Research Methods for Business Students*, 3rd edn. Harlow: Financial Times/Prentice Hall.
Taylor, F.W. [1911]1998. *The Principles of Scientific Management.* London: Dover Publications.
Whyte, William F. 1955. *Street Corner Society.* Chicago: University of Chicago Press.

Additional resources

Collis, Jill and Hussey Roger. 2003. *Business Research,* 2nd edn. Basingstoke: Palgrave Macmillan.
Easterby-Smith, Mark, Thorpe, Richard and Lowe, Andy. 2002. *Management Research: An Introduction,* 2nd edn. London: Sage.
Gill, John and Johnson, Phil. 2002. *Research Methods for Managers,* 3rd edn. London: Sage.
Jankowicz, A.D. 2000. *Business Research Projects,* 3rd edn. London: Business Press/Thomson Learning.
Partington, David. 2002. *Essential Skills for Management Research.* London: Sage.
Robson, Colin. 2002. *Real World Research,* 2nd edn. Oxford: Blackwell.
Saunders, Mark, Lewis, Phillip and Thornhill, Adrian. 2003. *Research Methods for Business Students,* 3rd edn. Harlow: Financial Times/Prentice Hall.
Sekaran, U. 2000. *Research Methods for Business,* 3rd edn. Chichester: Wiley.
Zikmund, W.G. 2000. *Business Research Methods,* 6th edn. Orlando, FL: Dryden Press/Harcourt College.

Key terms

consulting, 28
journalism, 28
project stakeholder, 34
research problem, 30
research process, 25

research questions, 30
stakeholders, 35
systematic approach, 24

Discussion questions

1. Identify five ways in which organisations gather information about you for business and management purposes.
2. Can a single research project satisfy the needs of both academic research and consulting? Academic research and journalism?
3. Why do we argue that research reports published in newspapers or business magazines are less credible than those published in journals where they must be reviewed by other researchers before they are published?
4. Review **Table 2.2**. Can you identify a category of research that has been missed out of this table?
5. What do business and management researchers study? Identify at least one study from your classes or textbooks for each level of the hierarchy presented in **Figure 2.1**.
6. What research projects have you carried out so far in your course of study? Why did you do them? What did you find out?
7. Which of the projects would we classify as academic research projects, and which as practical research projects, and what are the differences between the two?
8. Which is more important in business and management research – solving practical problems or increasing knowledge?
9. What are the four stages of business and management research?

10. How can project stakeholders influence the definition, design, doing and description of a research project?

11. Identify the stakeholders in a recent research project or other project you have carried out. What were the needs of each stakeholder and how were they expressed, if at all? If you have carried out projects previously, what have you learnt about the management of stakeholders from this experience?

Workshop

Read the seven mini-cases below, each describing a particular research project carried out by either students or professional researchers, and then answer the questions at the end.

1: The good student project

A student was asked by a regional development agency (RDA) to investigate how effective the RDA was in promoting good business practice in the region. Early on, the student identified two key customers for this report, the university and the RDA, so she worked with both to make sure that she understood their requirements. The university's requirements were laid out in the project guidelines, which she clarified with her academic supervisor. Her main contact at the RDA put his requirements in writing at an early stage, giving her a definable end objective.

Based on these two sets of requirements, the student decided that the best way to approach the project was from an economic perspective, in which she identified and narrowed down the relevant research done by other people in similar areas, and organised these findings into a framework for evaluating the RDA's practices based on work done elsewhere. The findings reported by other researchers also provided a point of comparison when she evaluated what the agency was doing. Her further investigation of the roles that other agencies were reported to be playing allowed some small-scale benchmarking of the RDA's activities against other agencies.

The project was a phenomenal success. The university awarded it a prize and the agency came away with a much better understanding of how it was supporting businesses in order to innovate. This success reflected an understanding of the needs of both the university and the sponsoring organisation – not always an easy task – and the fact that these needs could be converted into products.

2: The bad student project

The project started with the student demonstrating to the supervisor a piece of software he had been involved in writing. 'This is what managers today need to help them to manage', he confidently stated. 'I want to use my project to validate that this is the case.' Despite objections from his supervisor, he proceeded with his work and tried to construct tests to prove this. As he saw this as 'a practical project', he dismissed any prior academic research as irrelevant to his work. He also rejected using established methods for collecting and analysing data in his testing, preferring to invent these methods himself.

The project failed. It lacked key facets that must be present in all academic projects. These include a basis in prior research – this shows that you have covered what is known already before you start reinventing anything. Furthermore, the use of any method is not self-validating. Justifying your methods is vital to demonstrate that you are able to conceptualise, design, carry out, analyse and report research. This is valued in most academic qualifications.

3: A professional laboratory study: Milgram's experiment

Stanley Milgram (1974) conducted one of the most well-known experiments in the study of human behaviour. His objective was to study obedience to authority. He constructed a laboratory-style experiment using human subjects – in this case male adults residing in New Haven aged 20–50, and selected from a wide variety of occupations. He carried out the experiment twice, using 40 new participants for each experiment.

Each test was carried out on a pair of test subjects. The initial briefing given to the subjects told them that the test was designed to test memory and learning. Unknown to one of the pair was the fact that the other was actually a paid confederate of the researcher. Each was paid and told that their performance in no way affected their pay.

Following a short introduction to memory and learning, a rigged draw took place in which the (naive) subject was assigned the role of teacher, and the confederate the role of learner. A white-coated experimenter stayed in the room with the 'teacher'. The 'learner' was taken to an adjacent room and strapped into an electric chair. The experimenter told the subject that he had to teach the learner a list of paired words. Subsequently he was to test the learner on his recall of the list and to administer an increasing level of electric shocks to punish him for each mistake in the test. The 'teacher' was instructed to increase the intensity of shock by one level for each mistake. The dial was marked with 30 shock levels (15–450 volts), labelled from 'slight shock' to 'danger: severe shock'. The learner, according to the plan, provided many wrong answers, so that before long the subject would have to administer the strongest level of shock. Increases in shock level were met by increasingly insistent demands from the learner that the experiment be stopped. However, the experimenter kept instructing the teacher to continue. (The confederate was not really being shocked, but behaved as though he was increasingly being shocked, up to the level of no response, implying that he was unconscious or even dead.)

Milgram recorded that only 14 out of 40 people withdrew from the test before they thought they had administered the maximum shock. All participants administered at least slight shocks. The remaining majority, despite stating that they would rather not hurt the presumed victim, felt obligated to follow the orders of the experimenter. Although admitting that they had ultimate control over the switch, the experimenter exerted sufficient pressure by simply urging that the experiment must continue to create behaviour antithetical to personal and social ideals. (All the subjects were carefully debriefed following the experiment and reconciled with their 'victim'.)

4: In-house study of text message banking

A high-street bank wanted to know whether it should invest time and significant resources into developing text message banking. With such a service, customers would be able to have balance and transaction information sent directly to their mobile phones, as well as access to other services, including making payments. The overall question was relatively straightforward – should the company invest in this service?

A student research team was assembled to consider this further. They broke the main question down into a number of sub-questions, including:

- What is the main market for text message banking?
- Do people in this group want such a service?
- Would they like it enough to pay for the service?
- How many people would want to sign up for the service if it were free and how many would sign up for it if it were a pay-as-you-go service?

The initial study involved the students finding out who were the greatest users of mobile phones and text messaging services in particular. Their findings were that by far most users of these services were aged 18–30, especially students. Given that the bank was trying to compete in the student market, this presented an intriguing opportunity, which might ultimately be useful outside the single issue of text message services.

The students used various databases such as Mintel to find out more about the usage of mobile phones in this age group. Having established the potential market size, they designed and carried out two further studies. The first was a survey to determine whether this service would be of interest to the market. They chose their respondents carefully and carried out a pilot study of their questionnaire. In addition, they used focus groups to get more information about what kind of service people would be willing to pay for. They obtained many insights from the focus groups, and gained agreement from the bank to launch a small-scale trial of a text message service. From the trial, they were able to answer the third and fourth of their key questions, including estimating the potential market for the service. By rigorously applying well-established marketing research methods, they were able to obtain highly credible results, and produce a report of significance for both their sponsors and their academic institution.

5: The professional ethnographic study – *Street Corner Society*

Whyte (1955) studied groups of young men who socialised together in a thinly disguised Boston in the 1940s. Whyte lived and socialised with these 'disadvantaged' youths, even going bowling and generally living as they did for the period of the study. This gave him a unique insight into the complex social dynamics of the groups – he was able to get 'inside their heads' to understand their thinking processes, in a way that an external observer would never be able to. In this study he 'went native' – completely immersing himself in the environment for the purposes of the research.

6: The professional in-company study: F.W. Taylor's studies of work

F.W. Taylor has been credited with inventing the whole science of 'time-and-motion studies'. In these, a work task is analysed in scientific terms to determine the optimal way for it to be carried out. The time that it takes and the way that it is carried out are the subject of analysis. Taylor developed his techniques in the early years of the last century in a foundry. He studied many manual tasks that were carried out, including the shovelling of ore and ashes into and from furnaces. He would analyse the elements of each task – in the case of ore shovelling, push shovel into ore stack, turn and throw ore in a particular direction at a particular height. By carrying out extensive experimentation and measurement (watching and recording the times and movements on hundreds of occasions), he was able to conclude that the optimum load for a shovel was 21 pounds for the people that he was studying. This meant that they would need different sized shovels – for instance one for ore (small) and a different one for ash (much larger). Redesigning the shovels also increased the productivity of the people doing the shovelling. Other aspects of the job, including the placement of piles of work were likewise optimised. He also paid the workers a bonus for this increased productivity in return for using his scientifically derived methods (see Taylor [1911]1998).

7: The professional in-company study: Roethlisberger and Dickson's Hawthorne studies

The study started as an experiment with a small group of workers in 1927 to determine the conditions that led to fatigue in workers. By doing so, the researchers hoped to be able to determine the optimum conditions under which people could work to increase their productivity. The researchers were very confident about their method and that they would be able to isolate the key variables that would enhance productivity. As is so often the case in research, what they found was not what they expected.

One small part of the study concerned the impact of lighting levels on the productivity of a group of workers. By isolating the group from the rest of the factory, other factors could be eliminated, providing near-laboratory conditions. Initially the lighting level was raised and it was noted that the productivity increased. At the end of the experiment, the levels were lowered again, and the productivity increased again. This was not expected. The researchers changed their approach to try to uncover why this was happening. They discovered that what was underlying these changes in output were not any of the influences of management (for example through incentives). They found that it was the social processes in the group and their accepted norms (particularly relating to output) that determined their productivity (see Roethlisberger and Dickson 1939).

Discussion questions for Chapter 2 Workshop

1. What question or problem do you think the researcher was addressing in each case?
2. How did each researcher go about his/her task? Briefly summarise the method for his/her research.
3. What were the resource requirements in each case in terms of time, level of expertise, and so on for the researchers and how applicable would each approach be for a student project?
4. What were the key findings of each project?
5. How generalisable are the findings in each case, that is, could the finding apply to environments other than the one in which they were carried out?

PART 2
Understanding research philosophies and designs

CHAPTER 3
Identifying your research paradigm

LEARNING OBJECTIVES

When you have studied this chapter, you should be able to:
- describe the main features of positivism
- describe the main features of interpretivism
- compare the assumptions of the two main paradigms
- discuss the strengths and weaknesses of pragmatism
- identify your research paradigm.

3.1 Introduction

Now you have begun to understand the nature of research and we have dealt with some of the practical issues, it is time to look at the philosophical issues that underpin research. This chapter introduces a number of new terms that will help you to extend your knowledge of how research is conducted. We introduce the ideas in a way that allows you to develop your knowledge incrementally and you will soon be using your extended vocabulary with confidence. Your new understanding will provide a valuable framework for expressing your ideas about your proposed research when you talk to your supervisor and other researchers, and will also help you absorb information from any preliminary reading you are doing.

If you are an undergraduate or on a taught Master's degree, you will probably face two major constraints when doing your research. The first is the relatively short period of time you will have to conduct your research, and the second is the relatively short length of your dissertation. Therefore, you may not find it possible or necessary to explore the philosophical issues in this chapter in any great depth. However, other Master's students and all doctoral students need greater understanding of research philosophies and should use the references in this chapter as a guide to further reading.

3.2 The two main paradigms

A *research paradigm* is a philosophical framework that guides how scientific research should be conducted. Philosophy is 'the use of reason and argument in seeking truth and knowledge, especially of ultimate reality or of general causes and principles' (*Oxford Compact Dictionary and Thesaurus*, 1997, p. 557). People's ideas about reality and the nature of knowledge have changed over time and, therefore, new research paradigms emerge in response to the perceived inadequacies of earlier paradigms. This is captured in Kuhn's definition: 'Paradigms are universally recognized scientific achievements that for a time provide model problems and solutions to a community of practitioners' (Kuhn, 1962, p. viii).

For many hundreds of years there was only one research paradigm because the 'scientific achievements' referred to by Kuhn (1962) stemmed from one source. Today we refer to that source as the *natural sciences* to distinguish them from the *social sciences*. The emergence of the social sciences led to the development of a second research paradigm.

Key definitions

A **research paradigm** is a framework that guides how research should be conducted, based on people's philosophies and their assumptions about the world and the nature of knowledge.

According to Smith (1983), until the late nineteenth century, research had focused on inanimate objects in the physical world, such as physics, which focuses on the properties matter and energy and the interaction between them. The systematic methods used by these scientists, involved observation and experiment, and they applied inductive logic to discover explanatory theories that could be used for prediction. Their beliefs about the world and the nature of knowledge were based on *positivism,* which has its roots in the philosophy known as realism. Positivism was developed by theorists such as Comte (1798–1857), Mill (1806–1873) and Durkheim (1859–1917).

With the advent of industrialization and capitalism, researchers began to turn their attention to social phenomena. A phenomenon (plural phenomena) is 'an observed or apparent object, fact or occurrence, especially one where the cause is uncertain' (*Oxford Compact Dictionary & Thesaurus*, 1997). Initially, the new social scientists used the methods established by the natural scientists, but the suitability of the traditional scientific methods was challenged by a number of theorists, which led to a debate that lasted many decades (Smith, 1983). The alternative to positivism can be loosely labelled as *interpretivism*,* which is based on the principles of idealism, a philosophy associated with Kant (1724–1804) and subsequently developed by Dilthey (1833–1911), Rickert (1863–1936) and Weber (1864–1920).

3.2.1 Positivism

As you can see from the historical developments outlined above, *positivism* provided the framework for the way research was conducted in the natural sciences and the scientific methods are still widely used in social science research today. Positivism

---

* Some authors refer to phenomenology (as we did in previous editions of this book), but we have now decided to use interpretivism as it suggests a broader philosophical perspective.

is underpinned by the belief that reality is independent of us and the goal is the discovery of theories, based on empirical research (observation and experiment). Knowledge is derived from 'positive information' because 'every rationally justifiable assertion can be scientifically verified or is capable of logical or mathematical proof' (Walliman, 2001, p. 15). Today, researchers conducting business research under a paradigm that stems from positivism still focus on theories to explain and/or predict social phenomena. They still apply logical reasoning so that precision, objectivity and rigour underpin their approach, rather than subjectivity and intuitive interpretation. Because positivists believe reality is independent of us, they assume the act of investigating social reality has no effect on that reality (Creswell, 1994).

Under positivism, theories provide the basis of explanation, permit the anticipation of phenomena, predict their occurrence and therefore allow them to be controlled. Explanation consists of establishing causal relationships between the variables by establishing causal laws and linking them to a deductive or integrated theory. Thus, social and natural worlds are both regarded as being bound by certain fixed laws in a sequence of cause and effect. You will remember from Chapter 1 that a variable is an attribute of a phenomenon that can change and take different values, which are capable of being observed and/or measured; and a theory is a set of interrelated variables, definitions and propositions that specifies relationships among the variables. Since it is assumed that social phenomena can be measured, positivism is associated with quantitative methods of analysis.

Key definitions

Positivism is a paradigm that originated in the natural sciences. It rests on the assumption that social reality is singular and objective, and is not affected by the act of investigating it. The research involves a deductive process with a view to providing explanatory theories to understand social phenomena.

3.2.2 Interpretivism

Since *interpretivism* developed as a result of the perceived inadequacy of positivism to meet the needs of social scientists, it is important to understand the main criticisms of positivism. Box 3.1 sets out the main arguments.

Box 3.1 Main criticisms of positivism

- It is impossible to separate people from the social contexts in which they exist.
- People cannot be understood without examining the perceptions they have of their own activities.
- A highly structured research design imposes constraints on the results and may ignore other relevant findings.
- Researchers are not objective, but part of what they observe. They bring their own interests and values to the research.
- Capturing complex phenomena in a single measure is misleading (for example it is not possible to capture a person's intelligence by assigning numerical values).

Key definitions

Interpretivism is a paradigm that emerged in response to criticisms of positivism. It rests on the assumption that social reality is in our minds, and is subjective and multiple. Therefore, social reality is affected by the act of investigating it. The research involves an inductive process with a view to providing interpretive understanding of social phenomena within a particular context.

Interpretivism is underpinned by the belief that social reality is not objective but highly subjective because it is shaped by our perceptions. The researcher interacts with that being researched because it is impossible to separate what exists in the social world from what is in the researcher's mind (Smith, 1983; Creswell, 1994). Therefore, the act of investigating social reality has an effect on it. Whereas positivism focuses on measuring social phenomena, interpretivism focuses on exploring the complexity of social phenomena with a view to gaining interpretive understanding. Therefore, rather than adopt the quantitative methods used by positivists, interpretivists adopt a range of methods that 'seek to describe, translate and otherwise come to terms with the meaning, not the frequency of certain more or less naturally occurring phenomena in the social world' (Van Maanen, 1983, p. 9). These important differences lead to a very broad conclusion that interpretive research is any type of research where the findings are not derived from the statistical analysis of quantitative data (Strauss and Corbin, 1990).

3.2.3 Approaches within the two main paradigms

Just as realism gave way to positivism and idealism gave way to what we are loosely referring to as interpretivism, many new paradigms have emerged over the years and few researchers now adopt the pure forms of the main paradigms. New paradigms are distinguished by differences in the philosophical assumptions on which they rest. You may find it helpful to think of positivism and interpretivism as the extremities of a continuous line of paradigms that can exist simultaneously, as illustrated in Figure 3.1. As you move along the continuum, the features and assumptions of one paradigm are gradually relaxed and replaced by those of the next (Morgan and Smircich, 1980).

In addition to reading about different paradigms that were developed towards the end of the nineteenth century and beyond (for example hermeneutics, phenomenology, existentialism, critical rationalism, linguistics, conventionalism), you may also come across a number of terms that describe different approaches with the main paradigms. You will find the term 'paradigm' is used somewhat inconsistently in the literature because it has different meanings for different people in different disciplines, in different parts of the world and over different periods of time. For example, Mingers (2001) points out that the version of paradigms described by Kuhn (1970) is less restrictive than that described by Burrell and Morgan (1979). To

Figure 3.1 A continuum of paradigms

Table 3.1 Approaches within the two main paradigms

Positivism	Interpretivism
Quantitative	Qualitative
Objective	Subjective
Scientific	Humanist
Traditionalist	Phenomenological

help clarify the uncertainties, Morgan (1979) suggests paradigm can be used at three different levels:

- at the philosophical level, where the term is used to reflect basic beliefs about the world
- at the social level, where the term is used to provide guidelines about how the researcher should conduct his or her endeavours
- at the technical level, where the term is used to specify the methods and techniques, which ideally should be adopted when conducting research.

Table 3.1 shows some of the more common terms used to describe approaches within the two main paradigms. You should be aware that the terms under a particular category are not necessarily interchangeable, as they were coined by researchers wishing to distinguish their approach from others. In some cases, the term is being used at the social level (for example a subjectivist approach) or at the technical level where it refers to a particular method for collecting and/or analysing data (for example a qualitative approach). At the undergraduate level, these nuances may not be important, but a postgraduate researcher may be required to argue the appropriateness of the paradigm and the terms he or she is using.

3.3 Assumptions of the main paradigms

Drawing on a number of other authors, Creswell (1994 and 1998) provides a summary of the philosophical assumptions that underpin the two main paradigms, which he refers to as the quantitative and the qualitative paradigms. Table 3.2 is adapted from his work.

Before you can design your research project, you must consider the above questions. If you are still developing your understanding of research, you will probably find some of the questions difficult. Your answers will give you some indication of your orientation at this stage by indicating whether your paradigm is broadly positivist (most answers in the quantitative column) or interpretivist (most answers in the qualitative column). However, this may change as you progress with your studies. To help you with your analysis, we will provide some explanations of the terms used in the table. Remember that we are describing the assumptions that underpin the pure forms of the main paradigms. The first three assumptions are interrelated and if you accept one of them within a particular paradigm, you will find the other two assumptions for that paradigm are complementary.

Table 3.2 Assumptions of the main paradigms

Philosophical assumption	Positivism	Interpretivism
Ontological assumption (the nature of reality)	Reality is objective and singular, separate from the researcher	Reality is subjective and multiple, as seen by the participants
Epistemological assumption (what constitutes valid knowledge)	Researcher is independent of that being researched	Researcher interacts with that being researched
Axiological assumption (the role of values)	Research is value-free and unbiased	Researcher acknowledges that research is value-laden and biases are present
Rhetorical assumption (the language of research)	Researcher writes in a formal style and uses the passive voice, accepted quantitative words and set definitions	Researcher writes in an informal style and uses the personal voice, accepted qualitative terms and limited definitions
Methodological assumption (the process of research)	Process is deductive Study of cause and effect with a static design (categories are isolated beforehand)	Process is inductive Study of mutual simultaneous shaping of factors with an emerging design (categories are identified during the process)
	Research is context free Generalizations lead to prediction, explanation and understanding Results are accurate and reliable through validity and reliability	Research is context bound Patterns and/or theories are developed for understanding Findings are accurate and reliable through verification

Source: Adapted from Creswell (1994, p. 5 and 1998, p. 75)

3.3.1 Ontological assumption

The *ontological assumption* is concerned with the nature of reality:

- Positivists believe social reality is objective and external to the researcher. Therefore, there is only one reality.
- Interpretivists believe that social reality is subjective because it is socially constructed. Therefore, each person has his or her own sense of reality and there are multiple realities.

3.3.2 Epistemological assumption

The *epistemological assumption* is concerned with what we accept as valid knowledge. This involves an examination of the relationship between the researcher and that which is researched:

- Positivists believe that only phenomena that are observable and measurable can be validly regarded as knowledge. They try to maintain an independent and objective stance.
- On the other hand, interpretivists attempt to minimize the distance between the researcher and that which is researched. They may be involved in different forms of participative enquiry. This polarity between the two approaches has been captured by Smith (1983, pp. 10–11) who argues, 'In quantitative research facts act to

constrain our beliefs; while in interpretive research beliefs determine what should count as facts.'

3.3.3 Axiological assumption

The *axiological assumption* is concerned with the role of values:

- Positivists believe that the process of research is value-free. Therefore, positivists consider that they are detached and independent from what they are researching and regard the phenomena under investigation as objects. Positivists are interested in the interrelationship of the objects they are studying and believe that these objects were present before they took an interest in them. Furthermore, positivists believe that the objects they are studying are unaffected by their research activities and will still be present after the study has been completed. These assumptions are commonly found in research studies in the natural sciences, but they are less convincing in the social sciences, which are concerned with the activities and behaviour of people. Various studies have shown that the process of inquiry can influence both researchers and those participating in the research.
- In contrast, interpretivists consider that researchers have values, even if they have not been made explicit. These values help to determine what are recognized as facts and the interpretations drawn from them. Most interpretivists believe that the researcher is involved with that which is being researched.

3.3.4 Rhetorical assumption

We now move on to the *rhetorical assumption*, which is concerned with the language of research. This is particularly important when you write your research proposal and your final dissertation or thesis. These documents should be complementary to your paradigm, but they must also be written in a style that is acceptable to your supervisors and examiners.

- In a positivist study, it is usual to write in a formal style using the passive voice. For example, instead of writing, 'As part of my research, I observed a group of employees …' in your dissertation or thesis you will write, 'As part of the research, observations were made of a group of employees …' This is because you should try to convey the impression that your research was objective, that rigorous procedures were adopted and any personal opinions and values you possess were not allowed to distort the results. You will use the future tense in your proposal. For example, 'Observations of a group of employees will be made'.
- The position is less clear in an interpretive study. In many disciplines, the preferred style will reflect the immediacy of the research and researcher's involvement. Therefore, you would write in the first person using the future tense in the project proposal and the present tense in your dissertation or thesis. However, we advise that you review the literature in your discipline and find out what is acceptable to your supervisor.

3.3.5 Methodological assumption

The *methodological assumption* is concerned with the process of the research:

- If you are a positivist, you are likely to be concerned with ensuring that any concepts you use can be operationalized; that is, described in such a way that they can be measured. Perhaps you are investigating a topic that includes the concept of intelligence, and you want to find a way of measuring a particular aspect of intelligence. You will probably use a large sample and reduce the phenomena you are examining to their simplest parts. You will focus on what you regard are objective facts and formulate hypotheses. Your analysis will look for association between variables and/or causality (one variable affecting another).
- If you are an interpretivist, you will be examining a small sample, possibly over a period of time. You will use a number of research methods to obtain different perceptions of the phenomena and in your analysis you will be seeking to understand what is happening in a situation and looking for patterns which may be repeated in other similar situations.

3.3.6 A continuum of paradigms

Morgan and Smircich (1980, p. 492) offer 'a rough typology for thinking about the various views that different social scientists hold'. Table 3.3 illustrates two of the core assumptions and the associated research methods for the six categories they identify.

Starting at the extreme positivist end of the continuum (which Morgan and Smircich refer to as the objectivist end), there are those who assume that the social world is the same as the physical world. Their ontological assumption is that reality is an external, concrete structure which affects everyone. As the social world is external and real, the researcher can attempt to measure and analyse it using research methods such as laboratory experiments and surveys.

At the second stage of the continuum, reality is regarded as a concrete process where 'the world is in part what one makes of it' (Morgan and Smircich, 1980, p. 492). The third stage is where reality is derived from the transmission of information which leads to an ever-changing form and activity. At the fourth stage, 'the

Table 3.3 Typology of assumptions on a continuum of paradigms

	Positivism					Interpretivism
Ontological assumption	Reality as a concrete structure	Reality as a concrete process	Reality as a contextual field of information	Reality as a realm of symbolic discourse	Reality as a social construction	Reality as a projection of human imagination
Epistemological stance	To construct a positivist science	To construct systems, process, change	To map contexts	To understand patterns of symbolic discourse	To understand how social reality is created	To obtain phenomeno-logical insight, revelation
Research methods	Experiments, surveys	Historical analysis	Interpretive contextual analysis	Symbolic analysis	Hermeneutics	Exploration of pure subjectivity

Source: Adapted from Morgan and Smircich (1980, p. 492)

social world is a pattern of symbolic relationships and meanings sustained through a process of human action and interaction' (Morgan and Smircich, 1980, p. 494). At the fifth stage individuals through language, actions and routines create the social world. At the sixth, and extreme interpretivist end of the continuum (which Morgan and Smircich refer to as the subjectivist end), reality is seen as a projection of human imagination. Under this assumption, there may be no social world apart from that which is inside the individual's mind.

3.4 Comparing the two main paradigms

The particular paradigm you adopt for your research will be partly determined by your assumptions, but it will be influenced by the dominant paradigm in your research area and the nature of the research problem you are investigating. It is important to remember that one paradigm is not 'right' and the other 'wrong', but you may find that a particular paradigm is more acceptable to your supervisors, examiners or the editors of journals in which you wish to publish your research. It may not be clear as to why they favour a particular paradigm, as in some cases they are merely following a tradition in the discipline.

To help you discuss your decision with your supervisor, Table 3.4 compares the main features of the two paradigms, which we have polarized in order to contrast them.

As we have already suggested, it is helpful to think of the two main paradigms as being at opposite ends of a continuum. Regardless of which paradigm you employ, it is important to pay attention to all its features and ensure there are no contradictions or deficiencies in the way you design your research. The table introduces some new terms and concepts, which we will now discuss.

3.4.1 Sample size

A sample is a subset of a population. In a positivist study, the sample is chosen to be representative of the population from which it is drawn. Therefore, care is taken to ensure that the sample is unbiased in the way it represents the phenomena under study (a random sample, for instance). A population is any precisely defined body

Table 3.4 Features of the two main paradigms

Positivism tends to:	Interpretivism tends to:
Use large samples	Use small samples
Have an artificial location	Have a natural location
Be concerned with hypothesis testing	Be concerned with generating theories
Produce precise, objective, quantitative data	Produce 'rich', subjective, qualitative data
Produce results with high reliability but low validity	Produce findings with low reliability but high validity
Allow results to be generalized from the sample to the population	Allow findings to be generalized from one setting to another similar setting

of people or objects under consideration for statistical purposes. Examples of a set of people in a business research project might be the working population of a particular country; all skilled people in a particular industry; all workers of a certain grade in a particular business, or all trainees in a particular department of that business. A collection of items might be all green saloon cars registered in a particular year in a particular region, or one day's production of medium-sliced wholemeal bread at a particular factory.

Sample size is related to the size of the population under consideration. There is no need to select a sample if it is feasible to study the entire population. In Chapter 10, we describe the methods for selecting a representative sample and the minimum size that allows positivist researchers to generalize the results from the sample to the population. This is not an issue for interpretivists because their goal is to gain rich and detailed insights of the complexity of social phenomena. Therefore, they can conduct their research with a sample of one.

Key definitions

A **population** is a precisely defined body of people or objects under consideration for statistical purposes.

A **sample** is a subset of a population. In a positivist study, the sample is chosen to represent an unbiased subset of the population.

3.4.2 Location

Location refers to the setting in which the research is conducted. For example, a positivist might design an experiment in a laboratory where it is possible to isolate and control the variables being investigated. It would be important to investigate the research problems in an artificial setting if you were investigating the effect of lack of sleep on drivers or the effect of alcohol on drivers or shift workers, as it would not be safe to do it in the workplace. However, most positivist research in the social sciences today is based on secondary data (published data) or in natural locations (for example the workplace). Some researchers refer to this as *field research*, a term that illustrates the longevity of the link with the methods of the natural scientists. An example of field research is a study that evaluates the impact of a new training scheme on the productivity levels in a factory. One of the challenges if you are conducting research in a natural setting is how to control for the influence of other variables, such as noise and temperature levels or the activities of other employees.

Studies designed under an interpretive paradigm are likely to be conducted in a natural setting rather than an artificial location. As the researcher is interested in exploring the complexity of phenomena, he or she will not attempt to control any characteristics of the phenomenon under study.

3.4.3 Theories and hypotheses

The normal process under a positivist paradigm is to study the literature to identify an appropriate *theory* (sometimes referred to as a theoretical model) and then construct a *hypothesis*. A hypothesis is an idea or proposition that is developed from the theory, which you can test using statistics. For example, contingency theory (Fiedler, 1964) contends that that there is no 'best' way to manage an organization because effective management is contingent on the fit between the organization and its environment, and the fit between the organization's subsystems. It is also contingent on the appropriateness of the management style to the nature of the work group and their tasks. Just taking one of these factors, you might decide to test the hypothesis that there is a relationship between effective management (the dependent variable) and the amount of information the manager has about the tasks undertaken by subordinates (the independent variable). You would have to decide how to measure the two variables first and then collect the data and use a statistical test for association.

Under an interpretive paradigm, you may not wish to be restricted by existing theories or there may be no existing theory. Therefore, you may carry out your investigation to describe different patterns that you perceive in the data or to construct a new theory to explain the phenomenon. If the research was an exploratory study, the findings could be used to develop hypotheses that are tested in a subsequent main study.

Key definitions

Empirical evidence is data based on observation or experience.

A **hypothesis** is a proposition that can be tested for association or causality against empirical evidence.

A **theory** is a set of interrelated variables, definitions and propositions that specifies relationships among the variables.

A **variable** is a characteristic of a phenomenon that can be observed or measured.

3.4.4 Quantitative and qualitative data

In contrast to a number of researchers, we prefer to reserve the use of the terms *quantitative* and *qualitative* to describe data rather than paradigms. This because the data collected in a positivist study can be quantitative (that is, data in a numerical form) and/or qualitative (that is, data in a nominal form such as words, images and so on).

In a positivist study, it is likely that the purpose of collecting qualitative data is to ensure that all key variables have been identified or to collect information that will be quantified prior to statistical analysis. This contrasts with a study designed under an interpretive paradigm, where there is no intention of analysing data statistically and therefore no desire to quantify qualitative research data. Some researchers blend the qualitative and quantitative data to such an extent that it is difficult to determine which paradigm is being used. We advise students to be wary of doing this, as it may not be acceptable to your supervisors and examiners.

If you adopt a positivist paradigm, it is essential that your research data are highly specific and precise. Because measurement is an essential element of the research process under this paradigm, you must apply considerable rigour to ensure the accuracy of the measurement. Under an interpretive paradigm, the emphasis is on the quality and depth of the data collected about a phenomenon. Therefore, the qualitative data collected by interpretivists tend to be rich in detail and nuance (that is, levels of meaning).

Bonoma (1985) argues that all researchers desire high levels of *data integrity* and *results currency*. Data integrity describes characteristics of research that affect error and bias in the results, whilst results currency refers to the generalizability of results. Bonoma claims that positivist methods, such as laboratory experiments, are higher in data integrity than the methods used by interpretivists. However, methodologies used by interpretivists, such as case studies, tend to be high in results currency because they have contextual relevance across measures, methods, paradigms, settings and time. In any research project, there is likely to be a trade-off between data integrity and results currency. In other words, data integrity can only be achieved by sacrificing results currency.

Key definitions

Qualitative data are data in a nominal form.
Quantitative data are data in a numerical form.

3.4.5 Reliability

Reliability is concerned with the findings of the research and is one aspect of the credibility of the findings; the other is validity. You need to ask yourself whether the evidence and your conclusions will stand up to close scrutiny (Raimond, 1993, p. 55). For a research result to be reliable, a repeat study should produce the same result. For example, if you found that a group of workers who had attended a training course doubled their previous productivity levels, your result would be reliable if another researcher replicated your study and obtained the same results. Replication is very important in positivist studies.

Whereas reliability tends to be high in positivist studies, under an interpretive paradigm, reliability is often of little importance or may be interpreted in a different way. The qualitative measures do not need to be reliable in the positivist sense. However, importance is placed on whether observations and interpretations made on different occasions and/or by different observers can be explained and understood. As interpretivists believe that the activities of the researcher influence the research, the replication in the positivist sense, would be difficult to achieve. Therefore, the emphasis is on establishing protocols and procedures that establish the authenticity of the findings.

It is often possible to design a research study where reliability is high, but validity, which we discuss in the next section, is low. For example, perhaps you are attempting to establish the criteria on which bank managers decide to grant overdrafts to customers. There are some very rational criteria, such as income levels, security of employment, past evidence of repayment and home ownership, and it is possible that repeated questionnaire surveys of bank managers would demonstrate that these are the important criteria. However, observation or in-depth interviews might establish other criteria that are equally important. These could be apparently less rational criteria, such as the bank manager not liking the look of the applicant or how he or she speaks.

Key definitions

Reliability refers to the absence of differences in the results if the research were repeated.

3.4.6 Validity

Validity is the extent to which the research findings accurately reflect the phenomena under study. 'An effect or test is valid if it demonstrates or measures what the researcher thinks or claims it does' (Coolican, 1992, p. 35). Research errors, such as faulty research procedures, poor samples and inaccurate or misleading measurement, can undermine validity. For example, you may be interested in whether employees in a particular company understand their company's pension scheme. Therefore, you ask them to calculate their pension entitlements. However, you do not know whether their answers reflect their understanding of the scheme, whether they have read the scheme, how good they are at remembering the details of the scheme, or their ability to make calculations.

Because positivism focuses on the precision of measurement and the ability to be able to repeat the experiment reliably, there is always a danger that validity will be very low. In other words, the measure does not reflect the phenomena the researcher claims to be investigating. On the other hand, interpretivism focuses on capturing the essence of the phenomena and extracting data that provide rich, detailed explanations. The interpretivist's aim is to gain full access to the knowledge and meaning of those involved in the phenomenon and consequently validity is high under such a paradigm.

There are a number of different ways in which the validity of research can be assessed. The most common is face validity, which simply involves ensuring that the tests or measures used by the researcher do actually measure or represent what they are supposed to measure or represent. Another form of validity that is important in business research is *construct validity*. This relates to the problem that there are a number of phenomena which are not directly observable, such as motivation, satisfaction, ambition and anxiety. These are known as hypothetical constructs which are assumed to exist as factors that explain observable phenomena. For example, you may be able to observe someone shaking and sweating before an interview. However, you are not actually observing anxiety, but a manifestation of anxiety.

With hypothetical constructs, you must be able to demonstrate that your observations and research findings can be explained by the construct. It would be easy to fall into the trap of claiming that employees achieve high levels of productivity because they love their work, when in fact they are working hard because they are anxious about the security of their jobs during a period of economic recession.

Key definitions

Validity is the extent to which the research findings accurately reflect the phenomena under study.

3.4.7 Generalizability

Generalization is concerned with the application of research results to cases or situations beyond those examined in the study. Generalizability is 'the extent to which you can come to conclusions about one thing (often a population) based on information about another (often a sample)' (Vogt, 1993, p. 99). If you are following a positivist paradigm, you will have selected a sample and you will be interested in determining how confident you are in stating that the characteristics found in the sample will be present in the population from which you have drawn your sample.

However, Gummesson (1991) argues that using statistics to generalize from a sample to a population is just one type of generalization; interpretivists may be able to generalize their findings from one setting to a similar setting. He supports the view of Normann (1970) who contends that it is possible to generalize from a very few cases, or even a single case, if your analysis has captured the interactions and characteristics of the phenomena you are studying. Thus, you will be concerned with whether the patterns, concepts and theories that have been generated in a particular environment can be applied in other environments. To do this, you must have a comprehensive and deep understanding of the activities and behaviour you have been studying.

Key definitions

Generalization is the extent to which the research findings (often based on a sample) can be extended to other cases (often a population) or to other settings.

3.5 Pragmatism

We have emphasized that the two main paradigms represent two extremes of what can be described as a continuum of paradigms and that paradigms are based on mutually exclusive philosophical assumptions about the world and the nature of knowledge. Most students will find their paradigm falls broadly within one of the two main paradigms. This is also true for experienced researchers, who over time may modify their philosophical assumptions and move to a new position on the continuum. Thus, the philosophical assumptions of the researcher's paradigm provide the theoretical framework that underpins the methodology in the majority of research studies in business and management.

In the past few decades, however, some researchers have begun to argue that *pragmatism* should be the key factor in determining the methodology. Rather than be 'constrained' by a single paradigm, pragmatists advocate that researchers should be 'free' to mix methods from different paradigms, choosing them on the basis of usefulness for answering the research question(s). Pragmatists suggest that by ignoring the philosophical debate about reality and the nature of knowledge, the weaknesses of one paradigm can be offset with the strengths of the other. This pluralist approach is an attempt to 'cross the divide between the quantitative and the qualitative and the positivist and the non-positivist' (Curran and Blackburn, 2001, p. 123).

Drawing on his interpretation of other writers, Creswell (2003) sets out seven strictures of pragmatism and compares them with his views of mixed methods research. We discuss three of the knowledge claims he extracts below.

- *Pragmatism is not committed to any one system of philosophy and reality.* This is certainly one of the main claims by pragmatists, but your supervisor and examiners may not be sympathetic to this view if they believe that without a commitment to one paradigm, there is no theoretical framework to support your methodology. Our advice is to consider the views of your supervisor (and your eventual examiners) very carefully before declaring yourself a pragmatist in your proposal. You may find that what you are trying to do is to mix methods from the same

paradigm, rather than abandon your assumptions completely. This is known as triangulation and is discussed in Chapter 5.
- *Individual researchers have freedom of choice.* Although one is always sympathetic to claims of academic freedom, having a choice should not lead to an absence of rationality in your choice of research design and rigour in the application of your methods. If you are seeking a higher qualification or research publications, you will find that those who will evaluate your research may have strong opinions on what is good research. Certainly, you have a choice but you should know why you make a particular choice.
- *Pragmatists believe we need to stop asking questions about reality and the laws of nature.* A quick search of the literature will produce numerous articles that ask questions about reality, but few of them come up with satisfactory answers. Most students will need to demonstrate their understanding of the debate and be able to defend the position that they adopt.

Our advice to students who are thinking of adopting a pragmatic approach is to discuss it with your supervisor as soon as possible. You must be able to justify your stance if you seeking a higher degree or considering publishing an article based on your research in an academic journal. At the undergraduate level, it is unlikely that you will be required to discuss your paradigm, as most supervisors will be focusing on your methodology and your ability to apply your methods and draw conclusions. They may expect you to analyse both qualitative and quantitative data; not because you have adopted any particular paradigm, but because they want to be certain you know how to handle both.

In several parts of this chapter, we have used the terms *method* and *methodology* and this is a good point at which to distinguish between them. A *method* is a technique for collecting and/or analysing data. As a general term, methodology refers to the study of methods (for example, a student on a taught course might study research methodology). However, in the context of a specific study, it refers to the approach to the process of the research, encompassing a body of methods (for example the methodology chapter in a proposal, dissertation or thesis that describes and justifies the overall research strategy and methods). In some cases, a research strategy embodying a particular set of methods has become established through widespread use in particular disciplines (for example grounded theory, which we discuss in Chapter 9.)

Key definitions

A **method** is a technique for collecting and/or analysing data.

A **methodology** is an approach to the process of the research, encompassing a body of methods.

3.6 Conclusions

We have introduced a number of concepts in this chapter that may be new to you. It is essential for you to understand your research paradigm, as this provides a framework for designing your study. The two main paradigms are positivism and what can be loosely referred to as interpretivism. In this chapter, we have examined how the core ontological, epistemological, axiological, rhetorical and methodological assumptions of the two main paradigms differ. Positivism and interpretivism lie at opposite ends of a continuum of paradigms with a range of other paradigms between them. Two key features that characterize research findings are reliability and validity. Reliability refers to being able to obtain the same results if the study were replicated. Reliability is likely to be higher in a positivist study than in a study designed under an interpretive paradigm. Validity refers to the research findings accurately representing what is happening in the situation. Validity is likely to be higher in an interpretivist study than a positivist study.

If you are doing research at Master's or doctoral level, you will need to explain your paradigm and justify your methodology and methods. Methodological triangulation is where the research design includes complementary methods from within the same paradigm. It is essential that triangulation is an integral part of the design and not an attempt to rectify a poorly designed study and you are not advised to mix methods from opposing paradigms.

Once you have identified your paradigm, you can determine which methodology and methods will be appropriate. This will mean you have reached the research design stage and you will be in a position to develop your research proposal. If you are doing research at the undergraduate level, it is likely that you will not have to concern yourself too much with paradigms and will concentrate instead on managing the research process, collecting the data and analysing them. This is covered in subsequent chapters.

Activities

1. You have a set o weighing scales that always register 5 kilos above your actual weight. Your friend has a set of scales that measures his or her weight accurately, but sometimes shows it as 7 kilos above or below her true weight. Explain how these occurrences can be regarded as issues of reliability and/or validity or reliability.

2. You are planning a research study that will investigate the feelings of the devoted fans of a local sports team in situations when it wins and when it loses. Compare the advantages and disadvantages of the two main paradigms for this purpose and decide which approach would give you the best understanding.

3. The marketing director of a company promoting health clubs asks you to assess the effectiveness of a recent advertising campaign they ran in a magazine. Compare the advantages and disadvantages of the two main paradigms for this purpose. Then decide whether the marketing director will expect a qualitative or quantitative analysis and which would be the easiest paradigm for you to adopt.

4. Thousands of years ago a Buddhist monk called Chuang Tzu wrote: 'I dreamt I was a butterfly, flitting around in the sky; then I awoke. Now I wonder, am I a man who dreamt he was a butterfly, or am I a butterfly dreaming I am a man?' Decide which of the five core assumptions associated with the main paradigm this addresses and how you would you answer Chuang Tzu's dilemma.

5. **Paradigm quiz**
   Indicate whether you agree (tick the box) or disagree (put a cross in the box) with the following statements. There are no right or wrong answers and the exercise should not be taken too seriously!

   a) Quantitative data are more scientific than qualitative data. ☐
   b) It is important to state the hypotheses before collecting data. ☐
   c) Surveys are probably the best way to investigate business issues. ☐
   d) Unless a phenomenon can be measured reliably it cannot be investigated. ☐
   e) A good knowledge of statistics is essential for all approaches to business research. ☐
   f) Case studies should only be used for exploratory research. ☐
   g) Using participant observation to collect data is of little value in business research. ☐
   h) Laboratory experiments should be used more widely in business research. ☐
   i) It is impossible to generate theories from research into business issues. ☐
   j) Researchers must remain objective and independent from the phenomena they study. ☐

   Interpretation:
   More ticks than crosses = positivist
   More crosses than ticks = interpretivist
   Equal number of each = undecided

   Once you have finished, critically reflect on why this quiz might not be very effective in diagnosing your paradigm.

PROGRESS TEST

Complete the following sentences:

1. A philosophical framework that guides how scientific research should be conducted is known as a research _____.
2. The two main paradigms can be loosely described as _____ and interpretivism.
3. The extent to which the research findings can be extended to other cases or to other settings is known as _____.
4. A technique for collecting research data is known as a research _____.
5. A technique for analysing research data is known as a research _____.

Are the following statements true or false?

6. Empirical evidence is data collected from an interview or a survey.
7. Only interpretivists conduct exploratory or descriptive studies.

8. Only positivists conduct analytical studies.
9. Only quantitative data are collected in a study based on a positivist paradigm.
10. A study designed to test a hypothesis is based on a positivist paradigm.

Multiple choice questions:

11. The belief that the researcher is independent from that being researched is based on his or her:
    a) ontological assumption
    b) epistemological assumption
    c) axiological assumption
    d) methodological assumption

12. The belief that the process of research is deductive and context-free is based on the researcher's:
    a) ontological assumption
    b) axiological assumption
    c) rhetorical assumption
    d) methodological assumption

13. The belief that research is value-free and biased is based on the researcher's:
    a) ontological assumption
    b) epistemological assumption
    c) axiological assumption
    d) rhetorical assumption

14. The belief that reality is objective, singular and external is based on the researcher's:
    a) ontological assumption
    b) epistemological assumption
    c) rhetorical assumption
    d) methodological assumption

15. The belief that the research should be written in an impersonal, formal style is based on the researcher's:
    a) ontological assumption
    b) axiological assumption
    c) rhetorical assumption
    d) methodological assumption

References

Bonoma, T. V. (1985) 'Case research in marketing: Opportunities, problems, and a process', *Journal of Marketing Research*, XXII, May, pp. 199–208.
Burrell, G. and Morgan, G. (1979) *Sociological Paradigms and Organisational Analysis*, London: Heinemann.
Coolican, H. (1992) *Research Methods and Statistics in Psychology*, London: Hodder & Stoughton.
Creswell, J. W. (1994) *Research Design: Qualitative and Quantitative Approaches*, Thousand Oaks, CA: Sage.

Creswell, J. W. (1998) *Qualitative Inquiry and Research Design: Choosing Among Five Approaches*, Thousand Oaks, CA: Sage.
Creswell, J. W. (2003) *Research Design: Qualitative, Quantitative, and Mixed Methods Approaches*, 2nd edition, Thousand Oaks, CA: Sage.
Curran, J. and Blackburn, R. A. (2001) *Researching the Small Enterprise*, London: Sage.
Fiedler, F. E. (1964) 'A contingency model of leadership effectiveness', *Advances in Experimental Social Psychology*, 1, pp. 149–90.
Gummesson, E. (1991) *Qualitative Methods in Management Research*, Newbury Park: Sage.
Kuhn, T. S. (1962) *The Structure of Scientific Revolutions*, Chicago, IL: University of Chicago Press.
Kuhn, T. (1970) *The Structure of Scientific Revolutions*, Chicago, IL: Chicago University Press.
Mingers, J. (2001) 'Combining IS research methods: Towards a pluralist methodology', *Information Systems Research*, September, 12 (3) p. 240. Available from: http://proquest.umi.com.
Morgan, G. and Smircich, L. (1980) 'The case of qualitative research', *Academy of Management Review*, 5, pp. 491–500.
Normann, R. (1970) *A Personal Quest for Methodology*, Stockholm: Scandinavian Institute for Administrative Research.
Oxford Compact Dictionary & Thesaurus (1997) Oxford: Oxford University Press.
Raimond, P. (1993) *Management Projects: Design, Research and Presentation*, London: Chapman & Hall.
Smith, J. K. (1983) 'Quantitative v qualitative research: An attempt to classify the issue', *Educational Research*, March, pp. 6–13.
Strauss, A. and Corbin, J. (1990) *Basics of Qualitative Research: Grounded Theory Procedures and Techniques*, Newbury Park, CA: Sage.
Van Maanen, J. (1983) *Qualitative Methodology*, London: Sage.
Vogt, W. P. (1993) *Dictionary of Statistics and Methodology*, Newbury Park, CA: Sage.
Walliman, N. (2001) *Your Research Project*, Sage: London.

Glossary

Axiological assumption	A philosophical assumption about the role of values.
Data integrity	Characteristics of the research that affect error and bias in the results.
Empirical evidence	Data based on observation or experience.
Epistemological assumption	A philosophical assumption about what constitutes valid knowledge in the context of the relationship of the researcher to that being researched.
Generalizability	The extent to which the research findings (often based on a sample) can be extended to other cases (often a population) or to other settings.
Interpretivism	A paradigm that emerged in response to criticisms of positivism. It rests on the assumption that social reality is in our minds, and is subjective and multiple. Therefore, social reality is affected by the act of investigating it. The research involves an inductive process with a view to providing interpretive understanding of social phenomena within a particular context.
Location	The setting in which the research is conducted.
Method	A technique for collecting and/or analysing data.
Methodological assumption	A philosophical assumption about the process of research.
Methodology	An approach to the process of the research encompassing a body of methods.
Ontological assumption	A philosophical assumption about the nature of reality.
Phenomenon (plural phenomena)	An observed or apparent object, fact or occurrence, especially one where the cause is uncertain.
Population	A precisely defend body of people or objects under consideration for statistical purposes.

Positivism	A paradigm that originated in the natural sciences. It rests on the assumption that social reality is singular and objective, and is not affected by the act of investigating it. The research involves a deductive process with a view to providing explanatory theories to understand social phenomena.
Qualitative data	Data in a nominal form.
Quantitative data	Data in a numerical form.
Reliability	The absence of differences in the results if the research were repeated.
Replication	Repeating a research study to test the reliability of the results.
Results currency	The generalizability of the research results.
Rhetorical assumption	A philosophical assumption about the language of research.
Sample	A subset of a population. In a positivist study, a random sample is chosen to provide an unbiased subset of the population.
Validity	The extent to which the research findings accurately reflect the phenomena under study.
Variable	A characteristic of a phenomenon that can be observed or measured.

CHAPTER 4
Scientist or ethnographer?
Two models for designing and doing research

KEY QUESTIONS

- How can I answer my research questions?
- What are the scientific and ethnographic approaches to research design?
- What is the 'logic of research' for business and management research?
- What roles do theory and data play in management research?
- What are the assumptions underlying the scientific and ethnographic approaches?

LEARNING OUTCOMES

At the end of this chapter, you should be able to:

- Decide whether to answer your research questions using a scientific, ethnographic or eclectic approach
- Explain the research process and content associated with each approach
- Explain how research philosophy enables us to understand the principles underlying consistent research design

CONTENTS

Introduction
4.1 What are the scientific and ethnographic approaches?
4.2 Why does the research approach really matter?
4.3 How does research approach influence research design?
Summary
Answers to key questions
References
Additional resources
Key terms
Discussion questions
Workshop

Introduction

Part 1 explained how you can define your research topic and the research questions that you will be working on, and plan and schedule how you will carry out your project. In **Part 2**, we consider the next stage of your research process – that of research design. A research design includes the general approach you will take to answering your research questions, as well as the specific techniques you will use to gather, analyse and interpret data.

This chapter introduces two major research design approaches, whilst the remaining chapters in **Part 2** consider how to gather data and the chapters in **Part 3** consider how to analyse data. The approach you select influences your research plan, your role in the research process and how you assess the quality of your research. We characterise the first approach as the scientific approach, exemplified in this book by Frederick W. Taylor and the Hawthorne researchers, and the second approach as the ethnographic approach, exemplified by William Foote White. The scientific approach is influenced by the logic of research in the natural sciences and is associated with research projects that focus on quantitative data. The ethnographic approach is influenced by the logic of research in the social sciences and is associated with research projects that focus on non-quantitative – or qualitative – data.

Before you can decide which approach may best suit your research project, you need to know more about them. In **Section 4.1**, we describe each research approach, and the essence of each approach. This is vital. You should make sure that you understand this before continuing with your research. In **Section 4.2**, we explain how each approach influences the timing and sequence of your research tasks, especially the use of theory and the relationship between theory and data in the research process. In **Section 4.3**, we explore the broader implications of each research approach, which include not only the process of your research project but also its content: each research approach is linked with a different world-view and 'theory' of research, which influences what research questions you can ask, what methods you can use and what data you can collect.

We provide a summary table at the end of each section. We believe understanding your research approach will improve your project. First, understanding these two

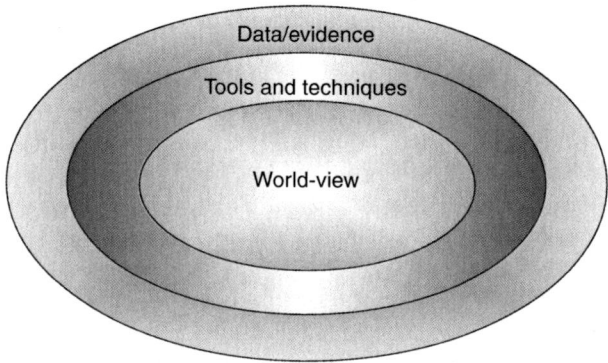

Figure 4.1 The Structure of Chapter 4

approaches will help you to understand why there are so many different ways to do business and management research. It will help you to make good choices about your selection of research methods, make them in a justifiable way and recognise the implications of these choices. If you are using this book to help you to conduct a research project, the approach you choose will affect your research process from this point forward and, as a result, your path through the rest of this book. **Chapters 6, 10 and 11** focus on research methods associated with the scientific approach. **Chapters 7, 8 and 12** each focus on research methods associated with ethnographic research. How you interpret and report your research, discussed in **Chapters 13** and **14**, will depend on which approach you choose. Both approaches have implications for how you work inside an organisation, as we discuss in **Chapter 9**.

Second, understanding your research approach will help you to assess other people's research, particularly the business and management research you find in your literature search. After you have read this chapter, you should understand why research is a better way to answer questions about the world than is journalism or consulting.

4.1 What are the scientific and ethnographic approaches?

Once you have identified your research questions, you need to put together a plan that describes how you will collect and analyse data to answer those research questions. Every research project follows roughly the same process outlined in the plan for this book:

1. Define a research topic and research questions
2. Design your research
3. Do your research – collect and analyse your data
4. Describe your research – interpret and report your findings.

However, this only describes the research process in a very generic way. There is still quite a bit of variety in how you might design, do and describe your research. In an ideal world, you could choose the best combination of research methods – how you will collect and analyse your data – to answer your research questions.

However, as we show in **Figure 4.2**, your research design will be subject to various constraints. In the real world, your choices are limited by the time and resources you have available and the amount of effort you are prepared to invest in your research project. These constraints also include the theory and any prior studies you are looking to emulate or repeat, and any subject preferences. If you are working on a sponsored project or placement, you may be limited to investigating the practical problem and setting of this project. Your personal preferences also need to be taken into account – you may prefer certain kinds of research questions and certain research methods, and you may select the best research topic to suit these questions and methods. We will return to these issues later in this chapter.

A major influence on your research design will be the topic you are studying and the 'rules' for doing research on that topic and in general. These rules deal with the **logic of research**, and describe what research questions you can ask and what methods you can use to answer them.

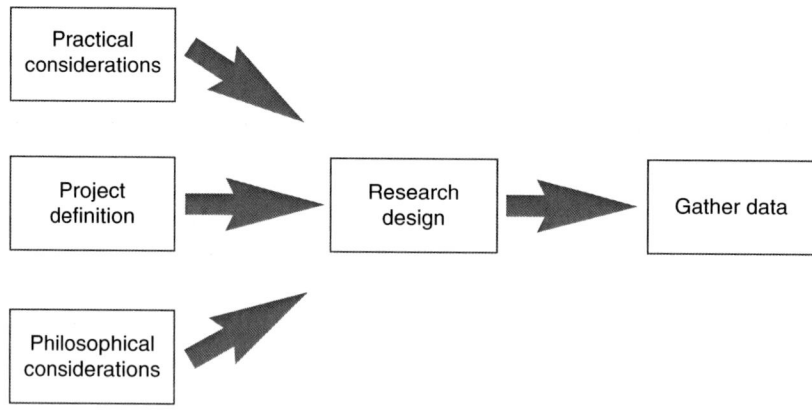

Figure 4.2 Where do you go from here?

As noted above, the two main approaches to research design in business and management can be described as the scientific and the ethnographic. Before we describe these two approaches in detail, **Student research in action 4.1** shows how an awareness of the differences between these two approaches led a student project team to radically redefine their project brief and do an outstanding project. It also demonstrates the choice of research design and the interplay between this and your research questions.

> *Student research in action 4.1*
>
> **A LITTLE DAB'LL DO YA**
>
> A toiletries manufacturer sponsored an undergraduate student project team to find out why sales of their male grooming products had the highest marketing share among 14 to 16-year-olds but only a miniscule share among 18 to 22-year-olds. The company had already commissioned extensive consumer marketing research that gave them specific details about product usage. The company wanted some more in-depth information before they invested in a revised advertising campaign.
>
> The students started by discussing how to find out more about this problem. The company could provide the students with access to point-of-sales data from supermarkets, pharmacies and other retail outlets. The students first considered using a traditional market research approach to find out more about attitudes towards the brand among university students. Whilst they did not have the resources to send out an army of market researchers armed with clipboards or personal computers to ask male university students a barrage of questions, they could use focus groups and questionnaires to find out what grooming products the men used and why they used those particular products. They were certain to be able to get enough students to complete the questionnaires to carry out statistical analysis of the questionnaire results. The focus groups would help them understand what questions to ask on the questionnaires.

This type of research, gathering data by asking questions that you have decided in advance, is consistent with the scientific approach to business and management research. As you will see in **Chapter 6**, questionnaires are a popular method of gathering data that answer specific, well-defined questions, whose answers can be expressed as numbers for statistical analysis. If they chose this research design, the students would need to make sure that they constructed their surveys carefully, selected a representative sample of students, and collected enough data for statistical analysis to be valid. This is consistent with the scientific approach to research, which focuses on quantification. Many researchers prefer the scientific approach, because they understand what the numbers mean and can take action based on them, for example to advise the company how it could reverse the drop among older consumers by targeting its marketing to likely buyers.

> ### *Student research in action 4.1 cont'd*
>
> On reflection, however, the students realised that the interesting question for them was not 'who' purchased (or didn't purchase) the company's products, but 'why' the market share changed so emphatically with age group. They decided to study the role that grooming products played in the life of male students – something that market research and POS figures could not reveal. They used video diaries, collages and other creative research techniques to find out more about what was going on. This focused their attention on the question of 'what influences what products male university students purchase', rather than who purchases them and how much they purchase.
>
> The use of video diaries, collages and other creative techniques resulted in data that were mainly impressions, words and pictures, rather than numbers. To make sense of these data, the students needed to find patterns of common meanings and interpret them as themes, rather than analysing them statistically.

This type of research, gathering data to answer questions that are themselves suggested by the data, is consistent with the ethnographic approach to business and management research. As you will see in **Chapter 7**, direct observation is a popular way of gathering data that answer questions that cannot be specified in advance and are better represented as words than numbers.

> ### *Student research in action 4.1 cont'd*
>
> At the end of the project, the students had made some fascinating and revealing findings about male university students and their relationship to male grooming products, including the significant amount of time most male students spent in front of the mirror getting their look just right, the need to have the 'right labels' in their rooms or bathrooms and the widespread sniffing and even borrowing of products among friends. These findings helped the company to understand that the popularity of their products among 14–16-year-olds actually created the sales gap when men got to university, in particular when their mothers were no longer buying their toiletries and they made their own choices.

By choosing between a scientific approach and an ethnographic approach, the students were choosing between measuring behaviours and finding meanings associated with those behaviours. Because measurement and meaning are different aspects of social behaviour, the scientific approach and the ethnographic approach are associated with different research methods, although this is a matter of 'more often' than 'always'. If the students had chosen the scientific approach, they could have used surveys to gather students' impressions and feelings in the form of words, or they could have counted the occurrence of various motifs or behaviours in the video diary and other qualitative data. The students could even have combined different methods in a single study, which we will consider in **Chapter 8** on case study and multi-method research designs.

4.1.1 Scientific and ethnographic approaches to research and the research process

In this chapter, we will use the terms 'scientific' and 'ethnographic' to contrast the two main research approaches. This does not mean that ethnographic research is *unscientific*, or that scientific research excludes the study of cultures. We have chosen these terms because they reflect the main world-views associated with the two approaches, as well as the main sources of methods, techniques and thinking. The key characteristics of the two approaches are summarised in **Table 4.1**.

In the example above, the students chose between collecting data that were best expressed as numbers – quantitative data – and data that were difficult to reduce to numbers – qualitative data. Because different research methods are often used for the collection or analysis of quantitative and qualitative data, the research methods themselves are often described as quantitative or qualitative. Indeed, the terms 'quantitative' and 'qualitative' are often used to describe the overall research approach. According to O'Leary (2004: 99), however: 'For my money, the two most confusing words in the methods world are quantitative and qualitative.'

Whether you choose a scientific or an ethnographic approach will have a major effect on your research process. These two approaches have 'alternative starting and concluding points, [and] different steps between these points' (Blaikie 2000: 25). In the scientific approach, you develop a complete research plan before you start to collect data. If the students had chosen a scientific approach, they would decide exactly what data they wanted to collect to find what was happening with the brand and its customers. Before they started collecting data, they would specify in precise detail what questions they needed to ask to collect those data, so that they could

Table 4.1 A comparison of the scientific and ethnographic approaches

Characteristic	Scientific approach	Ethnographic approach
Questions that can be answered	What, how much	Why, how
Associated methods	Survey Experiment Databases	Direct observation Interviews Participant observation
Data type	Predominantly numbers	Predominantly words
Finding	Measure	Meaning

develop a standardised questionnaire to give to a large number of male students. This approach often requires a fairly extensive literature review, in order to make sure that you ask the right questions. By deciding on the questions in advance, you can limit the responses to a simple set of responses or even just numbers (for example 'What hair products do you currently buy?', 'How frequently do you buy them?'). These answers can be quickly transcribed onto a spreadsheet and analysed using statistics to identify patterns of behaviour. This is a highly *structured* approach to doing research: the students could identify each stage in advance and each stage could be carried out relatively independently.

In contrast, by choosing the ethnographic approach, the students let the precise nature of the observations of male student behaviour and even some of the questions to emerge as they were doing their research. In this case, the students decided they needed to closely observe how male students actually used grooming products 'in the wild', so that they could build up a picture of these behaviours rather than trying to identify all the questions and data they would need in advance. They needed some starting point to help them to decide where to look and what to look for, but they didn't do a detailed literature review until they started making sense of the materials they had collected. The data themselves – video images, collages and verbal impressions – are different from survey responses. As you can see, this represents a more *unstructured* approach to doing research. Each stage of the study depended on what emerged from the data they had collected – in particular by analysing the themes they saw.

4.1.2 The scientific approach – a brief overview

A brief look at the management literature will show the influence that the scientific approach has had on the development of the body of knowledge. The workshop in **Chapter 1** discussed Frederick W. Taylor and the Hawthorne experiment researchers as examples of the scientific approach to business and management research, along with Stanley Milgram.

A fundamental principle of the scientific approach is: 'If you can measure it, you can understand it' (Michael Faraday). For example, F.W. Taylor was concerned with applying the 'scientific principles' he had used in experimenting with tool steel to managing workers. Here, he analysed what the workers did by measuring their movements – the loads, the distances moved and the time that each movement took. By understanding what they did, he was able to redesign the work they undertook and propose better methods for doing tasks. He also proposed extending this logic to how workers should be supervised and managed. This shows an early emphasis on the scientific approach and on measurement in business and management research.

We will now discuss some other characteristics of the scientific approach, the world-view of scientists and the subjects associated with the approach.

How do scientists view the world?

The scientific approach originated in the natural sciences, including biology, chemistry and physics, which are mainly concerned with natural objects and phenomena. Research from a scientific approach is based on making observations using our senses or through the use of scientific instruments or other measuring devices.

Scientific research focuses on measurement as the way of understanding something of interest. The scientific researcher looks for general patterns, which can be interpreted as theories or 'laws'. Consider Newton's laws of physics, for instance, which predict general properties of matter and motion and are predominantly derived from experimentation and observation. Scientists view the natural world as real and capable of being studied *objectively*, that is, scientists do research 'as if' they can study the world without being influenced by personal opinions or beliefs about what they will find. Whether scientists support a particular political party, religion, or football team should not influence what they discover or what they choose to study.

This approach to doing research on the natural world has been adopted by many researchers for doing research on the social world, including business and management research. Instead of looking for physical laws, scientific researchers may seek to develop general principles about how people, organisations or social systems behave. They focus on what these social units have in common, rather than individual differences. For example, the market research carried out by the consumer products firm identified a general problem – that sales of their products dropped as their target consumers aged. But this only identified what happened, not the reasons underlying the drop. Scientific research by the students might have clarified this, but might not have revealed the deeper meaning of the drop in market share.

Who are the 'scientists' in business and management research?
Business and management researchers who use the scientific approach in their research often come from subjects that look at physical systems or the general behaviour of people, organisations or other social units. For example, finance research often investigates the behaviour of investors in financial markets, with personal information about these investors being irrelevant. Subjects associated with the scientific approach include economics, finance, consumer marketing, operations management, information systems and decision sciences such as operations research and management science. This does not mean that researchers in these areas only take a scientific approach, but it is the 'prevailing approach' in each of these areas.

The role of theory in developing a research design
In the scientific approach, an extensive literature review often takes place as part of developing the research design. The concepts and relationships identified in previous research often form the foundation for the present research project. In some cases, the research project itself focuses on collecting data to test a theory or set of propositions put forward by another researcher. Motivations for doing this kind of research include:

- *Replication* – can we duplicate what the original researchers found out?
- *Extension* – can we find similar results in different contexts?
- *Comparison* – which theory (among competing theories) is the most useful to explain or predict the world?

For instance, one student wanted to test whether the Balanced Scorecard (Kaplan and Norton 1992) could be used to motivate employees. The student formally stated the relationship as the hypothesis: 'The level of employee motivation will be higher where the Balanced Scorecard has been adopted than where it has not been

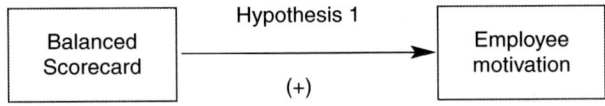

Figure 4.3 A conceptual framework

adopted.' He then developed a research project to collect data to test this hypothesis. In this case, he found that the staff reported being more motivated in the departments where the Balanced Scorecard was being used. Whilst this particular research did not prove that adopting the Balanced Scorecard *caused* motivation to be higher, only that they occurred simultaneously, the data supported this link between the Balanced Scorecard and motivation.

In the scientific approach, researchers often use a literature review to develop a **conceptual framework** that describes both the key issues and concepts they are interested in and the relationships they expect to find between them (Blaikie 2000: 27). A conceptual framework or model is often included as part of an academic article that takes the scientific approach. For instance, the student who was studying the relationship between the Balanced Scorecard and employee motivation had a simple conceptual model, as shown in **Figure 4.3**.

The scientific method

The scientific approach is derived from a particular way of doing research known as the **scientific method**, a generally accepted set of procedures for developing and testing theories. It is an idealised model to arrive at what scientists consider to be truth. The key ideals of this model are objective observation and measurement and careful and accurate analysis of data. In applying the scientific method, scientists try to set aside their preconceptions about how the world works and gather data using 'objective' methods such as laboratory experiments, where they are able to control conditions and repeat experiments over and over again with only slight variations. Such a *closed system* allows them to rule out alternative explanations for their findings and propose that (at least under certain conditions) one thing is linked to another.

We can only use objective methods if we ourselves are objective. The researcher must be separate from what he or she is studying in order to be objective. This distance may come from physical distance (for example sending out a postal survey), social distance (for example the authority of the researcher as a 'social scientist') or procedure (for example separating the planning and execution of research). This distance, as well as external control by peer review (see Chapter 4), makes sure that personal bias is minimised.

When the social sciences started to become recognised areas of study, they were highly influenced by the logic and process of scientific research, so they borrowed the scientific method for the social sciences. The scientific model for research has thus significantly influenced social research, both as 'the way' to do research and as a way not to do research. Although business and management researchers study different topics and use different methods from natural scientists, many researchers believe that the scientific method is the best way to do research, 'as if' we are natural scientists.

The scientific approach – a practical example

As described above, if you take the scientific approach, you may be able to write nearly all your research report before you ever collect any data. Because this approach is highly structured it is often appropriate for a short project since you know how long each stage will take.

Suppose that you were researching customer satisfaction with an online travel retailer and have decided to use an online questionnaire to gather data about customer satisfaction. Before you start collecting data, you could:

- Come up with a series of research questions and hypotheses to test customer satisfaction, for example 'Customers who are highly satisfied with their first online purchase are more likely to repurchase from the same retailer.'
- Specify each aspect of your research plan before you start collecting data (this will be covered in detail in **Chapter 6**).
- Design, pre-test, and pilot your survey before you started collecting your data.
- Set up a spreadsheet for your data, and even run some statistical analysis with dummy data.
- Calculate the number of responses you need to test your hypotheses.
- Design your research report.

As described above and shown in **Figure 4.4**, quantitative research is relatively straightforward once you have decided what research questions you will ask. Although you might have to revisit some issues, once you have decided how you will collect and analyse your data you have made all the major decisions that will affect your research process.

4.1.3 The ethnographic approach – a brief overview

Although the scientific method and the scientific approach unquestionably influenced the early development of business and management studies, the ethnographic approach and the ethnographer as role model are equally important. **Ethnography** is concerned with the study of culture and is an important research approach in areas such as anthropology and sociology. Early ethnographic research focused on exotic, faraway people, such as the American Samoans studied by Margaret Mead in the South Pacific. However, many ethnographers today focus on cultures closer to home, such as high-tech workers, Harley-Davidson owners or even *Star Trek* fans.

An ethnographer is more likely to pick up on differences between cultures if he or she tries to blend in and learn from watching rather than walking around with a clipboard and a list of questions. Ethnographic study is more open-ended – ethnographers start not knowing exactly what they might find or even how they might get there. Much of the learning will emerge along the way and from the journey itself. Ethnography is much better at finding out about meaning rather than measurement, through investigating feelings, attitudes, values, perceptions or motivations, and the state, actions and interactions of people, groups and organisations. In interpreting these, researchers consider their properties – hence the association of ethnography with qualitative research.

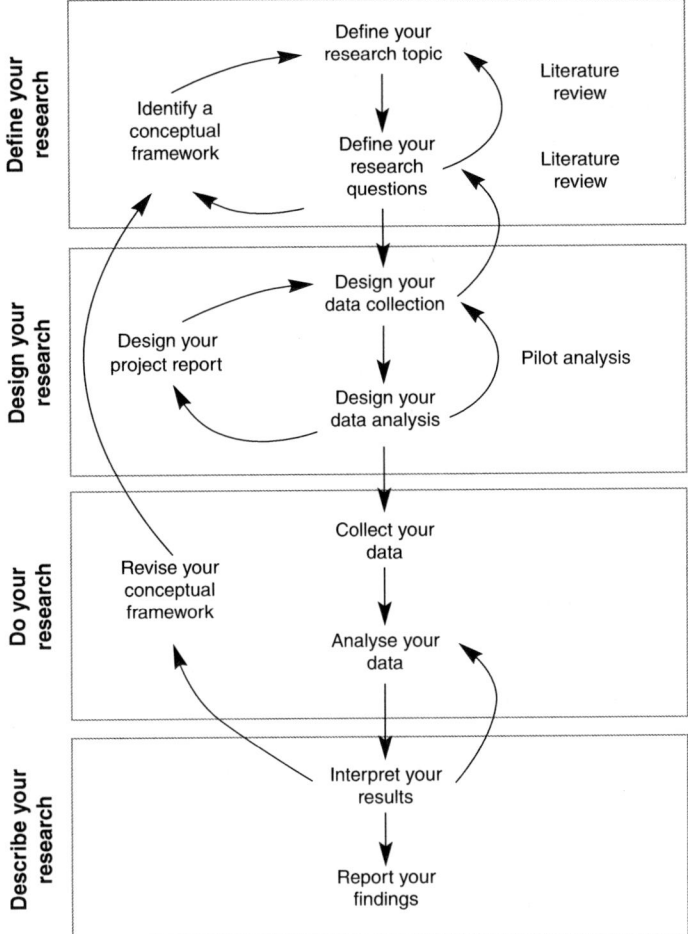

Figure 4.4 The scientific approach to the research process

The study of 'street corner society' by William F. Whyte described briefly in **Chapter 1** is often cited as a classic professional ethnographic study. In a brief student project, it might be impossible to achieve this deep immersion, but many placement or sponsored projects offer students a chance to experience life from the perspective, albeit a temporary one, of a member of or a participant in the organisation or social unit being studied. Even if this isn't possible, many student projects can benefit from using the unstructured tools and techniques associated with ethnography, including observation and interviews, as an alternative to the structured tools and techniques associated with the scientific approach.

How do ethnographers view the world?
Whilst the scientists claimed objectivity about what they were researching, ethnographers emphasise the extent to which the world, especially the social worlds such as business and management, is subjective and shaped by our perceptions. If we perceive what we are studying (for example the complex dynamics in

employer–employee relations) to be a certain way, there is rarely an instrument that will confirm or deny that view. Any view of what is happening is thus *subjective* – it depends on your viewpoint. Ethnographers emphasise the extent to which views differ between individuals, and across cultures, so that the extent to which research is actually based on indisputable social 'facts' is limited. For instance, consider a course of study you have undertaken. It is likely that there will be differing views on the success of the course – some people will have enjoyed it, others may not have done so. In evaluating the course, we could compile quantitative measurements describing how students viewed the course that would provide us with data about the course, focusing, for instance, on the average ratings of the lecturer. Under this approach, the perception of each individual matters less than the average. This would fit with a scientific approach. We could also investigate satisfaction with the course through different students' perceptions. Here, all views would be considered to be relevant, and reveal more about the expectations of individual students, how their views (or perceptions) of the course were formed, and why they viewed the course in different ways. This would be an ethnographic approach. What you learnt about the course would differ significantly between the two different studies.

Who are the 'ethnographers' in business and management research?
Ethnographers often have backgrounds in the subjects mainly concerned with studying people, either individually or collectively, and how they behave. They draw on those disciplines for theory and research methods. In business and management research, these subject areas include human resources management, organisational behaviour and organisational science.

Ethnographic method
In the discussion of the scientific approach, we saw that scientists are concerned predominantly with trying to uncover general laws or patterns, similar to the laws being investigated by natural scientists. Ethnographers try to uncover meaning in a specific situation by studying it intensively. This *depth* is characteristic of ethnographic research.

Wherever possible, ethnographers study issues of interest in their 'natural settings', by involving themselves in the workplace or, in the case of the student project discussed at the start of the chapter, in the lives of the group of people they researched. This emphasises field work – being physically present in the setting being studied. Ethnographic research, thus involves the role of the researcher, the effect of the researcher on what is being studied (you can imagine the impact a loud person may have on the group dynamics of an otherwise quiet group, and the effect this would have on the research if they are concerned with studying group dynamics) and potential sources of bias. Because it takes place in these natural settings, where the researcher cannot control conditions, ethnographic research takes place within an *open system*.

Ethnographers point out that all researchers are human and cannot be completely objective, and therefore will inevitably introduce some sort of bias or subjectivity into the research process. Even experimental research, usually held up as a model of objectivity, can be influenced by researchers, as summarised in **Research in action 4.1**.

> **Research in action 4.1**
>
> **RESEARCHING THE ROLE OF THE RESEARCHER**
>
> Rosenthal and Fode (1963) conducted an experiment to test the effect of experimenter bias, specifically whether experimenters' expectations affected experimental outcomes. Rosenthal and Fode gave student subjects five rats to train to run a maze. Students were told that they had either 'bright' rats, specially bred to run mazes quickly, or 'dull' rats, which were not.
>
> The students found that the 'bright' rats performed significantly better over 50 trials than the 'dull' rats, but the two groups had been actually given rats bred under identical conditions and randomly labelled as either 'bright' or 'dull'.

Just how objective were the experimental results reprinted by the students? Was it not a scientific study carried out in a laboratory environment? Were the conditions not controlled? The students' preconceptions impaired their objectivity in both training and measuring the performance of the rats. This reinforces the ethnographers' belief in subjectivity, and they argue that a challenge in research is recognising your own biases. We will return to this theme later. Natural science researchers argue that objectivity is improved when individual research experiments are designed with controls, such as the 'double-blind' experimental design for conducting medical research, where neither the doctor nor the patient knows whether an active or inactive (placebo) treatment has been administered. They also argue that the scientific community as a whole minimises individual researcher bias through replication. For example, the inability of the scientific community to replicate 'cold fusion' showed that the original study was biased in some way and so disproved its existence.

Practical application of ethnography

Many ethnographers prefer to enter the field (that is, start their data collection in the setting they are investigating) with a completely open mind about what they will find. They will do everything possible to rid themselves of their own biases about the situation into which they are going and prevent other biases developing (for example by reading a critical newspaper article concerning their research setting). They will then let the data (for example what people tell them) dictate the way they proceed with the study and the findings. This is known as 'being led by the data'. They argue that this minimises the likelihood that what they observe and record in the field will be determined by prior beliefs.

In many instances, though, it is not truly possible to do this; all researchers go into the field with some orienting ideas. Thus, many researchers prefer to enter the field with at least some preparation, without developing explicit conceptual frames or instruments such as questionnaires for testing or gathering data, so that the themes (the conceptual framework, as discussed above and in **Chapter 4**) will emerge during the study. This is more typical of student projects and dissertations, where time constraints and other practical considerations (such as people wanting to know what you are going to ask them before they will agree to interviews) are important.

As we have already seen, if you choose an ethnographic approach, you will spend less time planning your research, since you can begin collecting data with a relatively broad topic, and more time actually gathering and analysing data. Ethnography as carried out by Whyte may not be the best approach for a short project – it is fundamentally uncertain and we do not recommend this approach, unless you are being closely supervised by an experienced researcher who has specifically selected the research setting and research method and will work with you on making sense of the data as you go along. However, we do suggest that a form of **bounded ethnography** is entirely appropriate – it combines the practicality of the time-limited project with the ethnographic method. In a bounded situation, you may not reach the level of depth that you would if you were able to explore an issue in unlimited depth. However, you need to finish a project report and provide at least limited answers to your research questions. For this reason, we advocate bounded ethnography as an entirely appropriate approach for student projects.

We can demonstrate this by returning to the earlier example of researching customer satisfaction with an online travel retailer and take an ethnographic approach. Rather than setting up hypotheses, an appropriate research question might be: How do customers judge the quality of travel websites? To answer this question, you could decide to use interviews and observation (for example sitting with customers as they try to make enquiries and bookings online) and, consistent with this, only specify the broad outline of your research process before you start collecting data. Once you have started collecting data, you might:

- Change the data you collect and the methods you use to collect it. For example, if it becomes clear, after the first round of interviews and observations, that speed of response/refresh rates are vital for some people, you could investigate why this is so by conducting further targeted interviews. If you wanted to know if different customers rate speed differently, you could revert to a scientific approach and prepare a questionnaire.
- Decide how to analyse and interpret your data – again emergent, so only planned as far as the analysis of your first set of data.
- Once you have done the first set of data analysis, you will have identified the main themes emerging from your data and can search the literature for conceptual frameworks to support your findings.

As you can see from this example and **Figure 4.5**, if you choose an ethnographic research approach, it will be more recursive than the scientific approach. To put it more formally, it will be an *iterative* (stages looping back to previous stages) rather than a *linear* process (one stage follows another in sequence). Defining, designing, doing and describing overlap significantly. As we have seen, your data collection and data analysis strategies might only emerge once you have started doing research. You may start describing your research, as you will see in **Chapters 7** and **12** before you have finished doing it, and you might identify your conceptual frameworks late in the process.

This messiness is characteristic of ethnographic research. In some ways, it represents the natural way that we solve problems in real life, compared with the linear process of the scientific approach.

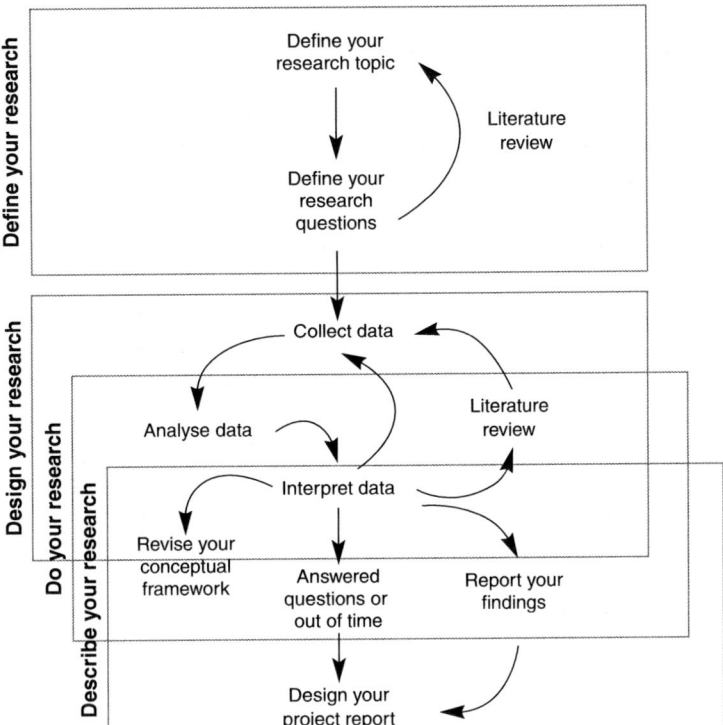

Figure 4.5 A qualitative research process

A final thought on the practicalities of the ethnographic approach to research concerns your own attitudes and preferences. Some researchers are content to live with this messiness and relative lack of structure; others believe that you should do some preliminary research so that you are adequately prepared to observe and record data. If you are the kind of person who might travel alone for the first time by hopping on a plane to the other side of the world, with no hotel reservations, no return ticket and no fixed plans, you might find that a completely 'data-led' approach might suit your personal beliefs and preferences. On the other hand, if you are the kind of person who needs to know what you are doing every day, where you will be staying and when you will be coming home, you might find this an unsettling experience.

As we noted above, most business and management researchers prefer to start collecting data with at least some preparation, although they may not develop an explicit conceptual framework or structured approaches to collecting data (**Chapter 6**). This is more likely to lead to success in a student project, since you do not have the luxury of starting over again if things go wrong and you face many practical constraints such as time.

4.1.4 The logic underlying the two approaches

We have seen that your approach must be consistent with the question you are answering, and your choice will limit the appropriate research methods. If you take the scientific approach, you will need to develop a detailed research plan before you start collecting data. Your first step is to translate your research questions into hypotheses or specific questions, which will determine what data you will collect and how you will collect them. If you take an ethnographic approach, you may only develop a broad research plan before you start collecting data. Your first step is to translate your research questions into a research setting and a preliminary method for collecting data – but not what data you will collect.

But why is this so? Couldn't you collect data and then decide what hypotheses to test, or develop a detailed plan before you start an ethnographic study? Neither of these is impossible, but to do so violates the spirit of each type of study described earlier. The different process for each approach reflects a different logic of research. In scientific research, you will start by developing a specific question based on your research problem, or a hypothesis from a theory or conceptual model that you develop or borrow from the literature.

Your data are then used to answer that specific question or prove or disprove the hypothesis. This is known as **deduction** because the literature will lead to your question or hypothesis. In ethnographic research, your major logical task is to develop concepts and/or a conceptual framework from your data, which is known as **induction** because the data will lead to it.

Deduction – the logic of the scientist

The purpose of deduction is to provide a structured process for testing a general rule or theory using data about a specific instance. Starting with a theory or conceptual framework that may explain a behaviour or a social phenomenon you are interested in studying, you deduce one or more hypotheses from the theory to test, which will guide how and what data you collect. You then analyse your data to see whether they do or do not support the theory. Hypothesis testing in quantitative research usually takes place through the following process:

1. Select a method such as an experiment, survey or secondary data analysis (**Chapter 6**) to collect data
2. Collect data in the form of numbers or transform them into numbers (**Chapter 10**)
3. Use statistical techniques to analyse these quantitative data (**Chapters 10** and **11**)
4. Decide whether to accept or reject the hypothesis based on the statistical analysis
5. Decide whether the results challenge or support the theory or conceptual framework from which the hypotheses were generated (**Chapter 13**)
6. Report the results in numbers, tables and charts (**Chapter 14**).

If you are not testing a specific theory or hypothesis (as in the marketing research project described in **Student research in action 4.1**), omit step 4.

We stated that the methods for scientific research were typically good for collecting quantitative data. However, as we will see in subsequent chapters, you can also test your hypotheses using qualitative data collected using qualitative methods (Blaikie 2000: 10). For now though, we will associate quantitative methods with the scientific approach.

Within the scientific method, going from data back to hypotheses to theory is known as **verification**. You can only show whether your hypothesis is true for the data that you have collected and analysed. If you have done a good job of deducing your hypotheses from your theory, you can make the argument that your theory has been strengthened or weakened by your findings. As you and other researchers test hypotheses in different studies, then theories become stronger or weaker. As theories become weaker, they are replaced by better theories; as theories become stronger, they replace weaker theories. In **Student research in action 4.2**, the student sets out to challenge whether an 'accepted theory' holds in a particular context.

Student research in action 4.2

BIG HAT, SMALL CATTLE

Neil was interested in using his research process to investigate SMEs. He noticed that much of the management literature, in particular the literature on 'best practices', was based on studies conducted on large, often multinational corporations. He wanted to find out how relevant these 'best practices' were to SMEs, and specifically whether his experience that they rarely produced benefits for SMEs – also suggested in the small business literature – was more generally true.

Neil conducted a study to see whether SMEs were adopting 'big business' best practices and whether these practices were associated with performance improvement. His conceptual framework was based on the proposed link between the issues or concepts of 'employing big business best practices' and 'achieving performance improvement'. His hypothesis was 'Employing big business best practices is associated with achieving performance improvement.' This was consistent with the mainstream management literature, but not the small business literature or his own experience, and was what sparked his interest in the project in the first place. He prepared and piloted a questionnaire and then surveyed some small businesses.

Neil discovered that SMEs who had adopted best practices based on big businesses were failing to see any benefits from them. He failed to verify the hypothesis from mainstream management literature and he concluded that these big business ideas were questionable for SMEs. This helped support the small business literature, which argued that a 'one-size-fits-all' approach of using big business ideas in SMEs was inappropriate. Neil's conclusions suggested that researchers should specifically consider the small business context in future research.

The philosopher of science Popper (1959) argued that there is no such thing as objective observation and thus since theories can never be proven to be true, they can only be proven to be false. His classic example concerned swans. If we have never visited the southern hemisphere (or zoo), we might believe that all swans are white. No matter how many white swans we saw, however, we would never be able to prove this unless we could examine every swan in the world. On the other hand, if we set out to disprove the hypothesis that all swans are white, then we could do so by seeing just one nonwhite swan. Popper's argument was that since a single exception such as one single black swan anywhere would disprove a hypothesis, we should only accept a hypothesis as provisionally true (not disproved) rather than proved. As a result, he recommended that a researcher should set up a hypothesis so that it can be disproved (doable) rather than proved (impossible). This approach is known as *falsification*.

Induction – the logic of the ethnographer
As shown above, the logic of induction is that the researcher will generate theory from data. The data can be analysed to identify **patterns**, for instance if there appears to be a pattern that people you meet at the weekend smile more than people you meet during the week, you may conclude that there was something in this. You can generalise these patterns as a conceptual framework or theory, for instance by stating that from your observations, either 'people in general are more happy at the weekend than they are during the week,' or that 'the people you associate with at the weekend are generally more happy than those you associate with during the week'. Such general patterns are what we mean by theory. They are different from the kind of grand theory that you have read about during your literature reviews, but can be classed as a theory, nonetheless.

Researchers often rely on induction when they are researching an area without theory to guide the development of hypotheses (and hence which data to collect). In this case, a researcher will want to collect data about as many aspects as possible of what he or she is studying, and induce the theory from the data, as you will see in **Chapter 12**.

Researchers also use induction when studying an area in which they believe that relying on a conceptual framework or even a high-level theory might bias data collection towards evidence that supports (or in some cases contradicts) that framework. For example, ethologists (researchers who study animal behaviour) may go into the field without having studied primate behaviour intensively, so that they do not try to impose existing research frameworks on what they observe, which might prevent them from observing something important.

4.1.5 The relationship between research approaches and theory

If the scientific approach to research relies on a deductive logic, where you collect data to test theory, and the ethnographic approach relies on an inductive logic, where you collect data to generate theory, clearly the relationship between theory and data differs significantly in the two approaches. Philosophers have debated this relationship between data and theory for many centuries (Easterby-Smith et al. 2002: 27).

The deductive logic is associated with individual projects that emphasise theory *testing*. A stream of quantitative research projects can be used to build theory by testing, revising and then retesting the new theory. However, this does require multiple projects and multiple testing phases, of which a student project could form a small part.

The inductive logic is associated with research projects that emphasise theory *building*. A stream of projects can be used to test theory by comparing the theoretical arguments generated in each, for instance in different contexts.

You will also see researchers alternate between research approaches in a single project. For example, a researcher might use an ethnographic research design for

Table 4.2 Summary of the scientific and ethnographic approaches (1)

Characteristic	Scientific approach	Ethnographic approach
Archetype	Experimenter operating in a laboratory	Researcher present or participating in the field of interest
Questions that can be answered	What, how much	Why, how
Starting point	Structure for data – you know what you need to collect – theory-led	Unstructured – what you need to do emerges – data-led
World-view	Objective – the researcher is independent	Subjective – the researcher is part of what is being researched
Objective	To find general patterns or laws – generality	To understand meaning in one specific situation – depth
Underlying logic	Deduction	Induction
Who uses?	Predominant in economics, finance, operations research, management science, marketing	Predominant in human resource management, organisational behaviour, organisational science
Role of theory	Testing of theory through development of hypotheses, collection of data, verification	Generation of theory through pattern analysis
Process	Predominantly linear, sequential, ordered	Predominantly iterative, overlapping, messy
Associated methods	The scientific method, of which surveys are an example. Modelled on closed-system experiments, minimising bias, but limiting the possibilities of discovery	Video diaries. Recognises social systems are most likely to be open systems, and tries to recognise personal biases and keep an open mind
Data type	Predominantly quantitative, predetermined	Predominantly qualitative, for example a series of statements or impressions
Finding	Measure	Meaning

theory-building research, and then follow it up with a scientific design for theory-testing research.

Table 4.2 provides a summary of **Section 4.1**. It builds on the content of **Table 4.1** and is further expanded on in **Tables 4.4** and **4.6**.

4.2 Why does the research approach really matter?

Up to this point, we provided a general overview of the research approaches. This is important, because you need to identify or select your approach before you go any further in your research process. In this section, we show that the approach you choose will significantly affect your research content as well. Although you might select either approach to study a given research topic, you might not be able to ask the same research questions, because the two approaches make different assumptions about 'How do I understand the world?' and 'How can I study the world?' These are actually two sophisticated questions. They go beyond the logic of research and the relationship between theory and data. Research philosophy provides a way to answer these questions because it allows us to identify and understand the logic of inquiry the 'rules of the game' for a research approach.

If you have the freedom to choose your research design, whether you choose a scientific or an ethnographic research approach will influence:

1. *What research questions can I ask?* – should I focus on 'why', 'how', or 'what'?
2. *What methods or techniques will I use to collect my data* – methods taken from science or social science?
3. *What type of data will I be collecting?* – quantitative or qualitative data?
4. *How will I analyse my data?* – statistical analysis or thematic analysis?

You do not necessarily need to understand research philosophy to answer these questions. Indeed, if you see your research project as a one-off, or if you are working to a narrowly defined project brief, you can plan your research pragmatically. You may not need to address these questions in your research project, but you should understand whether the decisions you make in the rest of the research process are consistent with your research questions. In the bigger picture, the approach you take will affect what you study, how you study it and why you study it. Understanding the two research approaches will also help you to read and understand the business and management literature. This section explores how research philosophy underlies the two approaches.

4.2.1 Research philosophy – where does it fit?

Your choice of research approach reflects deeper issues about research and your own personal beliefs and values. So that we can discuss research philosophy, we will start by defining some terms we need, and later incorporate the elements of **Table 4.2**. Unfortunately, there isn't general agreement in the research literature on where these elements fit into the hierarchy, or even what elements belong in the hierarchy, so the best we can do is try to be consistent in this book. Whilst we can't completely avoid engaging with complex issues, there is an underlying simplicity to research philosophy, which we will describe here as a hierarchy from abstract to concrete, as shown in **Figure 4.6**.

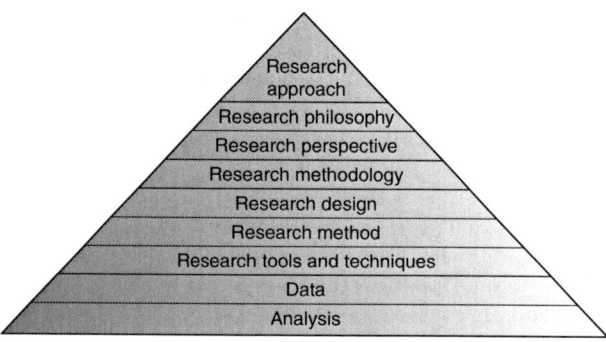

Figure 4.6 The hierarchy

At the highest level of our hierarchy is **research approach**, a strategy or a general logic for answering research questions. We have already identified two main research approaches for business and management as scientific and ethnographic. Knowing or deciding which research approach you will take roughly defines how you will actually do your research and what you will study.

Next comes **research philosophy**, which is the 'rules of the game' or the logic of inquiry governing each approach. You can think of research philosophy as being 'the study of study' – it studies how we study issues. The two branches of research philosophy that concern business and management research are the **philosophy of science**, the high-level rules that set out the ideal way to carry out scientific research on the natural world, and the **philosophy of social science**, the high-level rules that set out the ideal way to carry out research on the social world. We have already examined the philosophy of science through the scientific approach, and the philosophy of social science through the ethnographic approach.

Because of the fundamental assumptions made by the philosophy of science and philosophy of social science (objectivity and subjectivity, for instance) about the world and the best way to study it differ, we can never combine the two in one part of one study – they are incompatible ways of studying the world. They might be used to great effect at different times and for different purposes, for example in sequential studies.

We can further break down the research approach into the **research perspective**, which describes the set of assumptions about the world and the best way to study it, that underlie your research.

Research methodologies, describe how to translate the research perspective into a way of studying the world. If research philosophy concerns the 'study of study', then research methodology concerns the 'study of how to study'.

A research methodology may be implemented through several different **research designs**, the plan for conducting your study, through translating your research methodology into specific **research methods**, the techniques you use to collect and analyse data. In turn, research methods comprise specific techniques and tools, the physical or electronic artefacts associated with particular methods, for example a web survey, a questionnaire or an interview schedule. At the bottom of the hierarchy we have data and analysis. Methodologies, designs, methods, data and analysis are the subject of **Section 4.3**.

4.2.2 Research philosophy – what is it?

Research philosophy describes a 'theory' of research in a particular field and explains the assumptions that underlie the research approaches. These assumptions mainly concern the nature of reality and how we can know reality. Research philosophy describes our **ontological** assumptions about the nature of reality – what is considered to exist and, just as importantly, what does not exist in the environment we are studying.

Wait a minute, how can we study something that doesn't exist? You might reasonably treat social objects, such as organisations, jobs, work roles and so on, as being just as real as physical objects, such as rocks, cars and buildings. However, rocks and work roles are real in different ways. Rocks can be argued to have an objective reality independent of researchers and their understanding, even if you didn't know what a rock was, you would probably recognise it as real if you stubbed your toe on it. Researchers who study physical objects usually find that an **objectivist** ontology suits what they want to research and how they want to research it – they deal with what is physically real and do not consider anything that does not fit in with this 'reality', such as social objects.

On the other hand, although the person with the work role of 'manager' is a real person, the concept of manager isn't a natural concept, and therefore the idea of a manager has been **socially constructed** – it isn't a physical or tangible idea. The role of the manager has evolved over the past couple of centuries and different people have different ideas about what a manager is/does, depending, for example, on their national culture, the point in time they are considering and their experience of people who have borne the title 'manager'. Many social researchers argue, therefore, that even though we treat social concepts such as 'manager' or 'organisations' as real in everyday life, it is inappropriate to treat them as objective in the same way that a geologist would a rock. A **subjectivist** ontology may therefore be more appropriate for studying many business and management phenomena since human behaviour, whether at the level of the individual or the social system, differs significantly from the behaviour of natural objects.

Ontology therefore helps us identify what we accept to be real and therefore what we can study – the objectivist focuses on physical evidence, while the subjectivist accepts that reality can be constructed, by patterns of behaviour for instance.

Another major idea to take away from research philosophy is that your research approach should be consistent with your **epistemology** or epistemological assumptions. Epistemology concerns what is and isn't considered as knowledge in a field. For instance, to an ethnographer, people's opinions provide useful data about a situation – this is acceptable knowledge in this field. To a scientist, however, objective data are preferable, and the use of people's opinions as data may require rigorous scrutiny, for example only in the form of multi-item scales.

The two extreme epistemological positions in business and management research are **positivism**, which is derived from the philosophy of science, and **subjectivism**, which is derived from the philosophy of social science.

We will build the above into our hierarchy at the end of this section. There are, however, some variations in the epistemological approach that a researcher can take between positivism and subjectivism. **Table 4.3** below describes some of these. They may be relevant to your project, or at least help you to make sense of some of the business and management literature you have come across.

In our experience, few business and management undergraduate or taught master's student projects go much further in exploring research philosophy, especially ontology and epistemology, than we have gone this far in this chapter. Indeed, should you wish to go further, we strongly recommend that this is agreed with your supervisor and be part of the requirements of the project.

Table 4.3 demonstrates the variety and complexity of research in the business and management area. It has been studied for over a hundred years, and draws on methods that have been developed over considerably longer than that. If you need to go down one of the above routes, you should consult a specialist source – many examples are contained in the additional resources at the end of this chapter.

Table 4.3 Research approaches

Epistemology	Ontology	Comments
Positivism	Objectivist	Used extensively in the management literature
Realism	Objectivist	Becoming much more popular
Critical realism	Objectivist	Acknowledges that management researchers cannot directly know reality but they can study the world 'as if' they can – the knowledge of reality can be 'good enough'
Interpretivism	Subjectivist	The goal of research is not to explain human behaviour, but to understand it. A fairly mainstream epistemology for business and management researchers
Constructionism	Subjectivist	Focuses on the collective construction of social phenomena
Subjectivism	Subjectivist	Focuses on the 'multiple realities' that exist when social reality is imposed by social actors rather than being constructed or interpreted

The content is therefore the set of beliefs about what we are researching and the world. **Table 4.4** builds on **Table 4.2** and now includes the research philosophy and perspective.

4.3 How does research approach influence research design?

Most students do not usually sit around and debate the nature of reality existence and knowledge. So, what can a knowledge of research philosophy in particular ontology and epistemology, do for you as a researcher? Specifically, how does the research approach influence the research process?

As we have noted above, whether you take a scientific or ethnographic approach to research will affect many, if not all, subsequent decisions you make about your research. This section discusses two implications you should think about before you start making your decisions about research methods:

- The criteria by which the quality of research is assessed
- Auditing your intentions of your research using a research profile.

4.3.1 Quality criteria in research

The goals of scientific research
Researchers who follow the scientific approach generally agree on the standards for judging whether research is good or not good. The goal of such research is *statistically significant* and *generalisable results*. Statistically significant means that the findings are unlikely to have occurred by chance alone (discussed further in **Chapters 11 and 12**).

The goal of many quantitative studies is generalisability – drawing conclusions about a group from a sample. You can only generalise the findings of quantitative research if you can first show that they are valid and reliable.

Table 4.4 Summary of the scientific and ethnographic approaches (2)

Characteristic	Scientific approach	Ethnographic approach
Research philosophy	Philosophy of science	Philosophy of social science
Research perspective	Positivism Realism Empiricism	Interpretivism Constructivism Subjectivism
Archetype	Experimenter operating in a laboratory	Researcher present or participating in the field of interest
Questions that can be answered	What, how much	Why, how
Starting point	Structure for data – you know what you need to collect – theory-led	Unstructured – what you need to do emerges – data-led
World-view	Objective – the researcher is independent	Subjective – the researcher is part of what is being researched
Objective	To find general patterns or laws – generality	To understand meaning in one specific situation – depth
Underlying logic	Deduction	Induction
Who uses?	Predominant in economics, finance, operations research, management science, marketing	Predominant in human resource management, organisational behaviour, organisational science
Role of theory	Testing of theory through development of hypotheses, collection of data, verification	Generation of theory through pattern analysis
Process	Predominantly linear, sequential, ordered	Predominantly iterative, overlapping, messy
Associated methods	The scientific method, of which surveys are an example. Modelled on closed-system experiments, minimising bias, but limiting the possibilities of discovery	Video diaries. Recognises social systems are most likely to be open systems, and tries to recognise personal biases and keep an open mind
Data type	Predominantly quantitative, predetermined	Predominantly qualitative, for example a series of statements or impressions
Finding	Measure	Meaning

Validity refers to how accurately we have conducted our research. For instance, if you were trying to measure customer satisfaction, have the measures you used really measured customer satisfaction or a related concept? Also, did you have enough responses to justify the findings you are claiming? If, as the scientific method proposes, the world is objective and knowable, then the main source of error in our data will be our research method.

Reliability means that you or another researcher would get the same findings if you repeated your study. For example, if you studied the relationship between the location of the till and theft from the till in your high-street bookstore, you should find the same relationship in the bookstore on any high street. Another way of describing reliability is repeatability. Research findings are only reliable if the world itself is uniform.

The goals of ethnographic research

People take one of two positions on the criteria for assessing the quality of ethnographic research, depending on where they start. Some researchers, mainly North American, see the goal of such research to be as rigorous as scientific research. They therefore apply the scientific method to data gathered using ethnographic research designs, or qualitative data gathered using quantitative research designs such as surveys. These researchers usually design their research projects to follow the process that we defined in **Section 4.1** as being closer to the scientific method. This group would be more likely to seek the same qualities in the their findings as scientific researchers – validity and generalisability.

Others do not agree, stating that scientific criteria are incompatible with the ethnographic research approach. Most ethnographers argue that the standards for assessing the quality of qualitative research must differ from those for quantitative research. If the goal of scientific research is statistically significant and generalisable results, then the goal of qualitative research is *valuable*, and idiographic or *transferable* results (O'Leary 2004: 7). Either way, ethnographic researchers need to be as careful as quantitative researchers in reporting how they designed their research and how they collected and interpreted their data.

In understanding the value of the research, the process for analysis of data needs some further discussion. The ethnographic researcher may rely on intuition to guide the analysis and interpretation of findings, rather than rules or procedures. It is in this uniqueness of the situation and the intuitive analysis that the value arrives. It is valuable because it is original.

Most ethnographers disagree that researchers can be objective, and even question whether objectivity is a desirable quality in research. Instead, researchers should recognise that all human beings are subjective, but that subjectivity can be managed in social research. Two ways of managing subjectivity are **neutrality**, developing strategies to avoid unrecognised subjectivity that might bias research findings, and **transparency**, acknowledging subjectivity (O'Leary 2004: 59). Following an agreed procedure for generating theory from data helps to demonstrate neutrality. Explicitly stating your own position helps to demonstrate transparency.

Ethnography requires the researcher to see through other people's eyes and interpret events from their point of view (Bryman 1988). The ethnographer may even need to adopt the viewpoint of the people being researched in order to understand what is going on. This may be illustrated by thinking about how you might research business and management in another culture. If you try to study it from your own (native) perspective, you may not really comprehend what is going on. You might need to think as a person from that culture in order to understand the social reality. This is a major concern in international business research – in part it is about resisting the 'Americanisation' of management, in part about the value of differences between cultures.

If the world is not uniform, dependability may be a more realistic research goal than reliability. **Dependability** refers to the repeatability of the process of inducing theory from data, rather than the repeatability of the findings themselves.

Some researchers question whether uniform criteria can actually be established for ethnography, since every study will differ on essential criteria. They regard the emphasis on universal standards as trying to promote an artificial and unworkable consensus, in the presence of 'multiple realities'.

On the other hand, you will probably need to refer to some standards to assess the quality of your research, if you take an ethnographic approach. You might want to suggest that your work:

- makes a contribution to understanding some aspect of social reality
- is original in some way
- has been conducted in a correct manner, as far as possible, and you have identified any potential source of bias
- is both interesting and true.

4.3.2 Auditing your research using a research profile

You can profile your research design and decide whether your plan is consistent or inconsistent. We show a research profile in **Table 4.5**. This researcher is obviously confused, mixing elements of scientific and ethnographic research approaches inconsistently.

You might want to build a profile of your research and perhaps the key exemplars you have identified in your literature search. Good research tends to be consistent – by consistent we do not mean that every box must be ticked for one or the other approaches, but that there is a logic for any deviation. For example, you could use statistics and inference on data that were collected in qualitative form, but you might want to consider if this is the best method or the best use of your data.

Table 4.5 A research profile

Aspect	Scientific		Ethnographic	
Focus	Measurement	✓	Meaning	
Definition	Collecting and analysing data	✓	Exploring instances and examples	
Objective	Testing general principles		Examining individual differences	✓
Ideal model	Natural sciences	✓	Social sciences	
Research questions	What, how much		How, why	✓
Theory	Theory-testing	✓	Theory-generating	
Reasoning	Deductive	✓	Inductive	
Researcher	Objective and independent		Subjective and involved	✓
Data	Quantitative – numbers and categories		Qualitative – words and symbols	✓
Data collection	Remote or brief	✓	Up close and extended	
Typical methods	Surveys, experiments		Observation, interviews	✓
Data analysis	Statistics	✓	Thematic	
Quality	Validity, reliability, generalisability	✓	Dependability, richness	

Table 4.6 Summary of the scientific and ethnographic approaches (3)

Characteristic	Scientific approach	Ethnographic approach
Research philosophy	Philosophy of science	Philosophy of social science
Research perspective	Positivism Realism Empiricism	Interpretivism Constructivism Subjectivism
Archetype	Experimenter operating in a laboratory	Researcher present or participating in the field of interest
Questions that can be answered	What, how much	Why, how
Starting point	Structure for data – you know what you need to collect – theory-led	Unstructured – what you need to do emerges – data-led
World-view	Objective – the researcher is independent	Subjective – the researcher is part of what is being researched
Objective	To find general patterns or laws – generality, statistically significant results	To understand meaning in one specific situation – depth and valuable, transferable results
Underlying logic	Deduction	Induction
Who uses?	Predominant in economics, finance, operations research, management science, marketing	Predominant in human resource management, organisational behaviour, organisational science
Role of theory	Testing of theory through development of hypotheses, collection of data, verification	Generation of theory through pattern analysis
Process	Predominantly linear, sequential, ordered	Predominantly iterative, overlapping, messy
Associated methods	The scientific method, of which surveys are an example. Modelled on closed-system experiments, minimising bias, but limiting the possibilities of discovery	Video diaries. Recognises social systems are most likely to be open systems, and tries to recognise personal biases and keep an open mind
Data type	Predominantly quantitative, pre-determined	Predominantly qualitative, for example a series of statements or impressions
Finding	Measure	Meaning
Data analysis	Statistical, through rules or procedures	Thematic, through intuition
Quality	Validity, reliability, generalisability	Makes a contribution, good use of recognised method, neutrality or transparency

4.3.3 Scientific versus ethnographic research

Table 4.6 summarises all the elements of each approach, as constructed through this chapter.

Summary

In this chapter, we have presented the two main approaches to business and management research. The scientific approach is based on the logic of scientific inquiry, and uses the scientific method as the model for research endeavour. The ethnographic approach rejects scientific inquiry as inappropriate for studying the social world, and takes the methods of social science, particularly ethnography, as its model.

We began by describing the implications of choosing the scientist or ethnographer as the role model for your research. Quantitative research is relatively linear and predictable once you have decided how you will collect and analyse your data. On the other hand, qualitative research is cyclical and unpredictable – how you will collect and analyse your data emerges as you are actually doing your research.

Besides the process implications, it is important to understand the implications of your research process for what you can study and how you can study it. Some research is associated with research designs that try to replicate the scientific process in social settings. Other research is associated with research designs that try to replicate ethnography. Research philosophy helps us to understand the differences between the two and make sure that a research design is internally consistent.

Answers to key questions

How can I answer my research questions?
- You must select an appropriate research design
- You must collect and analyse data
- You must report your findings

What are the scientific and ethnographic approaches to research design?
- The scientific approach is focused on the collection and analysis of numerical data – a process known as social measurement
- The ethnographic approach is focused on the collection and interpretation of a wide array of data – a process for understanding social meaning

What is the 'logic of research' for business and management research?
- Scientific research follows a deductive logic
- Ethnographic research follows an inductive logic

What roles do theory and data play in management research?
- Theory can be used to develop hypotheses for scientific research, and guide the collection of data
- Data can be used to develop theory in ethnographic research and guide the selection of theory

What are the assumptions underlying the scientific and ethnographic approaches?
- Underlying the scientific research approach are the assumptions that the world is real and knowable, we can be objective and all phenomena can be reduced to a set of numbers

- Underlying the ethnographic research approach is the prime assumption that the world is complex and only knowable through interaction with the social systems that it contains

References

Blaikie, Norman. 2000. *Designing Social Research*. Cambridge: Polity Press.
Bryman, A. 1988. *Quantity and Quality in Social Research*. London: Routledge.
Cooper, D.R. and Schindler, P.S. 2001. *Business Research Methods,* International edition. Singapore: McGraw-Hill Book Company.
Easterby-Smith, Mark, Thorpe, Richard and Lowe, Andy. 2002. *Management Research: An Introduction,* 2nd edn. London: Sage.
Kaplan, R.S. and Norton, D.P. 1992. 'The Balanced Scorecard – Measures That Drive Performance', *Harvard Business Review,* Jan–Feb, pp. 71–9.
O'Leary, Z. 2004. *The Essential Guide to Doing Research*. London: Sage.
Popper, K. 1959. *The Logic of Scientific Discovery,* London: Hutchinson.
Rosenthal, R. and Fode, K. L. 1963. The effect of experimenter bias on the performance of the albino rat, *Behavioural Science,* 8: 183–9.

Additional resources

Crotty, Michel. 1998. *The Foundations of Social Research: Meaning and Perspective in the Research Process*. London: Sage.
Hollis, M. 1994. *The Philosophy of Social Science: An Introduction*. Cambridge: Cambridge University Press.
Kaplan, A. 1964. *The Conduct of Inquiry: Methodology for Behavioural Science*. San Francis-co: Chandler.
Potter, G. 2000. *The Philosophy of Social Science: New Perspectives*. Harlow: Prentice Hall.
Rosnow, R.L. and Rosenthal, R. 1997. *People Studying People: Artifacts and Ethics in Behavioural Research*. New York: W.H. Freeman.
Schutt, R.K. 1996. *Social World: The Process and Practice of Research*. Thousand Oaks, CA: Pine Forge Press.
Searle, C. 1996. *The Quality of Qualitative Research*. London: Allen Lane.
Shermer, M. 1997. *Why People Believe Weird Things: Pseudoscience, Superstition, and Other Confusions of Our Time*. New York: W.H. Freeman.
Weick, K.E. 1979. *The Social Psychology of Organising,* 2nd edn. Reading, MA: Addison-Wesley.

Key terms

bounded ethnography, 80
conceptual framework, 75
deduction, 82
dependability, 91
epistemology, 88
ethnography, 76
induction, 82
logic of research, 69
neutrality, 91
objectivist, 88

patterns, 84
philosophy of science, 87
philosophy of social science, 87
positivism, 88
reliability, 90
research approach, 87
research designs, 87
research methodologies, 87
research methods, 87

research perspective, 87
research philosophy, 87
scientific method, 75
socially constructed, 88
subjectivism, 88
subjectivist, 88
transparency, 91
validity, 90
verification, 82

Discussion questions

1. Why should you consider research philosophy between the research definition stage and the research design stage?
2. Are there any research methods that can only be used in quantitative research and any that can only be used for qualitative research?
3. If the overall goal of research is to find 'truth', why should we judge qualitative research by the standards of quantitative research, or vice versa?
4. Is it acceptable in quantitative research to develop hypotheses from 'interrogating' a large data set with statistical techniques? What principles might this violate?
5. Why do we need to know about research philosophy?
6. What subject areas within business and management are likely to take a quantitative or qualitative approach?
7. Why should we try to disprove a hypothesis rather than to prove it?
8. What is 'truth' in the context of the research that you have come across? How close to 'the truth' do these research projects come?

Workshop

Task

Review the cases discussed in the Chapter 1 workshop.

1. Classify each of these projects as having used either a scientific or an ethnographic approach.
2. Use the research profile of Table 4.5 and profile two of these projects. How consistent is the research design in each case (as far as is possible to tell from the descriptions)?
3. Identify your own 'natural' research approach (the one that fits best with your own world-view), using Table 4.1, 4.2 or 4.3. Identify the strengths and weaknesses of this approach.
4. Find someone with a different 'natural' approach and compare views.

CHAPTER 5
Quantitative research designs
Using scientific methods for social measurement

KEY QUESTIONS

- What methods for collecting data are associated with the scientific approach?
- How can I design a research project to analyse documents or databases, conduct a survey or run an experiment?
- How can I use these methods as part of a qualitative research design strategy?

LEARNING OUTCOMES

At the end of this chapter, you should be able to:
- Design a research study using secondary analysis, a survey or an experiment
- Discuss the strengths and weaknesses of each design
- Identify how we judge the quality of research designs for social measurement

CONTENTS

Introduction
5.1 Designs for secondary analysis
5.2 Designs for surveys
5.3 Designs for experiments
Summary
Answers to key questions
References
Additional resources
Key terms
Discussion questions
Workshop
Postscript to activity 4

Introduction

> 'Don't you know anything about numbers?'
>
> 'Well, I don't think they're very important', snapped Milo, too embarrassed to admit the truth.
>
> 'Not important!' roared the Dodecahedron, turning red with fury. 'Could you have tea for two without the two – or three blind mice without the three? Would there be four corners of the earth if there weren't a four? And how could you sail the seven seas without a seven?'
>
> 'All I meant was –' began Milo, but the Dodecahedron, overcome with emotion and shouting furiously, carried on.
>
> 'If you had high hopes, how would you know how high they were? And did you know that narrow escapes come in all different widths? Would you travel the whole wide world without ever knowing how wide it was? And how could you do anything at long last,' he concluded, waving his arms over his head, 'without knowing how long the last was? Why, numbers are the most beautiful and valuable things in the world.'
>
> (**Juster**, The Phantom Tollbooth, 1954: 174)

After reading **Chapter 5**, you should have an idea whether you will model your research on the scientist or the ethnographer. If your role model is the scientist, you will find this chapter especially useful, because the research methods here are most closely associated with the scientific approach, even though you could also consider using the research methods presented in **Chapter 7**. The methods in this chapter are secondary analysis, surveys and experiments, and are commonly used in business and management research.

This chapter provides a general overview of these research designs, provides some preliminary guidance for designing an informal study and describes their main strengths and weaknesses. They are worth considering if you want your findings to be quantitative, statistically significant and generalisable, and for your research to be as objective, reliable and reproducible as possible.

In **Section 5.1**, we describe how you can collect data to answer your research questions through methods that involve indirect contact only with organisations or people as a data source. This is known as secondary analysis because the sources of data, such as government surveys, proprietary databases, documents or statistical databases, have almost always been created for purposes other than your research project. Secondary analysis can reduce difficulties with gaining access to people or organisations, but it may be difficult to find exactly the data you need to answer your research questions compared with more direct methods. You might select secondary analysis as a main technique if you can answer your research questions using data other people have already collected, or if you can construct your own data set from documents or other materials, but it is often combined with other research methods.

If your research questions can't be answered by analysing existing data, or if you need direct contact with organisations to collect data specifically for your research project, you may want to consider using a survey, described in **Section 5.2**. Survey research is so popular that many people often considered it to be synonymous with business and management research. A survey collects the same information about some or all of a group's members, and includes familiar techniques such as interviews, questionnaires and structured observations. Since you want to draw conclusions about all the group's members without necessarily gathering information from each member of the group, you will need to consider sampling issues carefully. You can use a survey to collect information directly through face-to-face or voice-to-voice interviews, or at a distance through the post, email or web questionnaires. Because surveys are so common, if you choose a survey design you may be able to use an existing survey, build your own survey from existing questions or even develop your own questions.

We also describe experiments as a research design for business and management research in **Section 5.3**. Experiments come closest to the ideal of the scientific model of research because they let researchers test cause-and-effect relationships. However, laboratory experiments are rare in business and management research because little business and management takes place in controlled settings; there is a good deal of use of experiments in natural settings such as field and quasi-experiments like taste tests. No matter what setting, important ethical issues as well as design issues are raised by experiments, because they can affect people's lives, as shown in **Research in action 5.1**.

Research in action 5.1
OUCH!

In June 2004, British newspapers and television news programmes reported on a study presented at the European Society of Human Reproduction and Embryology conference claiming that even just carrying a mobile phone in a pocket reduced men's sperm counts. Based on a survey of 221 men over 13 months concerning their mobile phone usage and their sperm counts, Hungarian researchers proposed that mobile phone usage reduced sperm counts by about one-third.

A report such as this, if accurate, would be alarming in view of the widespread usage of mobile phones in developed countries. Many people were sceptical, however, of the report's conclusions. The survey compared heavy and light/nonusers of mobile phones, but failed to take into account any other factors that might be associated with lower sperm counts among mobile phone users or other studies that found higher sperm counts generally in countries with high mobile phone usage, such as Finland.

After reading this chapter, you should have a better idea why and how you might use one of these designs, choose the most appropriate one for your research, and understand each well enough to get started, although you may need to consult more specialised guides for detailed design. You can read about different statistical techniques in **Chapters 9** and **10**, which cover basic and advanced statistics. Even if you don't plan to use one of these methods in your research project, these designs are commonly used to collect data which can then be cited in journalism and consulting, for example public opinion polls and medical research such as clinical trials. Furthermore, an understanding of these three methods will be helpful if you want to analyse critically how people have collected and analysed data in the articles you have found in your literature search.

5.1 Designs for secondary analysis

In this section, we will describe how you can use **secondary analysis**, analysing previously collected data as your main research design. Secondary analysis is used to describe a research design based around collecting (or acquiring) and analysing secondary data, data that you do not directly collect from organisations or people in their natural settings. In its strictest sense, secondary analysis means analysing data that someone else has already analysed, but it also is used for analysing data that you collect indirectly about people and organisations rather than from them. Your data may have been collected by other people for other purposes, or extracted by you from such sources. This section will describe the main sources of data for secondary analysis and how you can use secondary analysis to analyse data from:

- An existing data set such as a large-scale survey or a commercial database
- A data set that you have created yourself from published or unpublished materials such as company archives, document analysis, or from observing people or organisations without interacting with them (unobtrusive analysis), as shown in **Student research in action 5.1.**

You might choose to use secondary analysis as your research design when:

- Someone else has already collected the data you need, and you can use them to answer your own research questions
- You want to study a social unit that you cannot contact directly because of geographic distance or other access problems
- You want to study the historical activities of social units or social units that no longer exist (historical data), or covering an extended period of time (longitudinal data).

Student research in action 5.1

Frances and Kate were interested in whether high-street banks were responding to pressures for corporate social responsibility (CSR). They decided that one measure of this would be whether the banks had included a statement of their policy regarding diversity on the company website and the content of that policy (if there was one). They collected data from the 25 major banks and building societies in the UK. They also used publicly available information such as reported profits and return on assets to see what influenced these statements. Although this only revealed information about a small part of the banks' CSR activities, it agreed closely with other information about this sector, including market research on customer perceptions and regulatory actions. This secondary analysis gave them some good ideas for doing further research in which they collected information directly from bank customers about their perceptions of their own banks.

Research projects that are based on indirectly collected data are sometimes called **desk/library research** projects, because you do not have direct contact with organisations or people in collecting your data. If you decide to use secondary analysis as your main research method, you should check with your project supervisor and/or business sponsor to see if this meets your project guidelines, because some project guidelines require you to collect primary data. If you are working on a sponsored project, you should check to see if secondary data are acceptable to your project stakeholders, as they may want you to collect primary data to support your findings.

5.1.1 Using existing data sets: surveys, commercial databases, and other sources

Despite the volume of data available in business and management research, few students consider analysing data already collected for other purposes (Saunders et al. 2003: 188). However, it may be worth looking to see if someone has already collected data that may be relevant to your research problem. We have already described library and internet search processes in **Chapter 4** as two ways to find information about your research problem and research setting, an essential part of any research project. You can also use these search processes to identify data to answer your research questions. If you are lucky, someone has already collected the data you need to answer your research questions, and, if you are especially lucky, they have created an electronic database with the kind of information you need in an appropriate format. If you are inordinately lucky, you can gain access to this information and it will be free.

Secondary data are stored in data archives, commercial databases, market reports and company archives. Government departments, trade associations, market research organisations, commercial research organisations, academic research units, newspapers, businesses and other organisations all collect and publish information that may be relevant to answering your research questions. This information may be available in printed form, CD-ROMs, online computer databases or internet sites.

Researchers who use this method usually describe the data differently depending on how it is stored and organised. A **data set** is a set of information collected by academic or professional researchers about one or more social units using a consistent research design or research protocol. A **database** is a structured data set, usually a matrix of data that allocates a row to each social unit (for example organisation, household or person) and a column to each variable or other measure related to that social unit. An **archive** is a collection of documents, images and other data in unprocessed form, which you might process into a data set or a database.

You can use this method to analyse documents and other records you collect from organisations, data that are stored in data repositories such as archives and data collected through unobtrusive measures. You are collecting data specifically for your research project, but your research design still counts as 'secondary analysis' because you are not directly observing, interviewing or surveying the people or organisations you are studying. The documents you are using as sources have already been produced for another purpose rather than being created specifically for your research project, even though your data do not exist until you 'interrogate' the documents (O'Leary 2004: 180).

If you are considering secondary analysis, some questions you might want to explore early on include:

1. *Are the data free, or will you have to pay for them?* In some cases, buying a particular data set will cost hundreds or even thousands of pounds – beyond the reach of most student projects.
2. *Are the data available in computer files, or will you have to enter the data yourself?* Many older data sets are only available in printed tables, or sometimes in obsolete computer formats such as punched cards.
3. *Do the data cover the organisations and the phenomena you are interested in?* It is unlikely that the people who collected the data originally were interested in exactly the same research questions you want to answer in your research, so they may have omitted some data that are relevant to your research and included irrelevant data. Furthermore, data sets tend to focus on large industrial organisations so the sample may be biased.
4. *Are the data accurate?* Research on commercially produced data sets such as Compustat has shown that the data are not always correct, due to either collection or entry errors. You will sometimes need to spend as much time checking your data as if you had originally collected and entered it yourself.

Advantages and disadvantages of secondary analysis

Analysing secondary data may save you time and effort (although not always money). People collect data in many fields of business and management and make those data available. Some companies who conduct market research and publish market reports and consult, such as Mintel and Gartner, specialise in making data available for a fee.

Some areas of management use secondary analysis as a core research design. Secondary data abound in accounting and finance, because companies have to report their financial performance. For example, many financial studies are based on data from financial databases that have been put together by government or for-profit organisations, such as records of stock prices. Studies of technological innovation may use counts of patents derived from patent databases.

Some of the advantages and disadvantages of secondary analysis are listed in **Table 5.1** below. Bryman and Bell (2003: 213) discuss some of these aspects in more depth.

Producers of secondary data

Secondary data can be found everywhere. People and organisations collect information about many aspects of business and management. Governmental and quasi-governmental bodies such as international trade bodies collect and publish statistics about a wide variety of activities, such as trade statistics. Corporations publish annual reports and file information related to stock offerings and other significant activities. Markets such as the New York Stock Exchange are a source of detailed information about transactions such as share prices. Any of these could be used in research. Although it is relatively rare for undergraduate or taught master's research projects compared with postgraduate research projects, sometimes you may be expected to analyse data that have already been collected by your supervisor or your institution.

You may find the terms primary and secondary confusing (just to complicate things even more, you may even see references to tertiary data or sources). **Primary data**

Table 5.1 Secondary analysis in perspective

	Advantages	Disadvantages
Effort	Saving money and time in data collection Allowing more time for data analysis	Need to familiarise yourself with the data Need to manage large and complex data sets May be expensive
Analysis	Access to high-quality data Comparing subgroups or subsets within the data sample Comparing subgroups or subsets in other countries Opportunity to analyse data longitudinally	Lack of control over data quality Limited to data already collected May be biased in unobservable ways May not answer your research questions
Contribution	Reinterpret original findings Fully exploit data set	May not be seen as being as rigorous or relevant as purposefully collected data Does not build as many research skills as direct methods

are data you have collected yourself specifically for your project and **secondary data** are data other people have collected for their own research projects or commercial purposes. Understanding what terms you should use for your data and sources is not as important as understanding why we want to know whether your data are primary, secondary or tertiary.

The main thing to keep in mind is the difference between 'primary' and 'secondary' as the difference between 'new' data and 'reused' data. Your distance from the source of the data will affect the quality of the data and ultimately the quality of your findings or recommendations. The farther away you are from the data source, the more cautious you need to be about its reliability; on the other hand, the closer you are to the data source the more cautious you need to be about the potential bias of the researcher and the researched.

Social surveys as sources of secondary data

A major source of information about organisations, households and people is **survey data**. The internet has revolutionised researchers' ability to identify and access large-scale survey data for secondary analysis. These survey data include data from **censuses**, surveys that collect data from every member of the group being studied, **repeated surveys**, surveys that collect data continuously or at regular intervals, and **ad hoc surveys**, surveys that collect data only once. Since we will discuss survey designs in **Section 5.2**, in this section we will focus on using survey data rather than how to design and administer a survey.

The UK, in particular, is taking a leading role in making survey information available through the web with the Economic and Social Data Service (ESDS), founded jointly in January 2003 by the Economic and Social Research Council (ESRC) and the Joint Information Systems Committee (JISC). The ESDS coordinates storage and access to **data archives**, which are repositories for survey data. Four ESDS research centres currently provide access to key economic and social data for secondary analysis:

- The UK Data Archive (UKDA) at the University of Essex
- The Institute for Social and Economic Research (ISER) at the University of Essex

Table 5.2 Examples of online data sources provided through ESDS

ESDS Government Surveys

Labour Force Surveys/Northern Ireland Labour Force Survey	General Household Survey/Continuous Household Survey (Northern Ireland)
Family Expenditure Survey/Northern Ireland Family Expenditure Survey	National Food Survey/Expenditure and Food Survey (new combined National Food Survey and Family Expenditure Survey)
Family Resources Survey	ONS Omnibus Survey
Survey of English Housing	Health Survey for England/Welsh Health Survey/Scottish Health Survey
British Crime Survey/Scottish Crime Survey	British Social Attitudes/Scottish Social Attitudes/Northern Ireland Life and Times Survey (and the former Northern Ireland Social Attitudes)/Young People's Social Attitudes (periodic offshoot of the BSA)
National Travel Survey	Time Use Survey

ESDS Longitudinal

British Cohort Study (BCS70)	British Household Panel Survey (BHPS)
Millennium Cohort Study (MCS)	National Child Development Survey (NCDS)

ESDS Qualidata

The Peter Townsend collection featuring studies on poverty and the life of older people, *Family Life of Old People* (1955), *The Last Refuge* (1959) and *Poverty in the UK* (1979)	The Paul Thompson collection comprising the major life history interview study of *The Edwardians* (1975)
Stan Cohen's (1967) *Folk Devils and Moral Panics* focusing on the genesis and development of 'moral panic'	Dennis Marsden and Brian Jackson's research papers, including their data for *Education and the Working Class* (1962)
Goldthorpe et al. (1962) *The Affluent Worker* undertaken to test the thesis of working-class embourgeoisement	

ESDS International

OECD Main Economic Indicators	OECD Main Science and Technology Indicators
OECD Quarterly Labour Force Statistics	OECD Social Expenditure Database
OECD Measuring Globalisation	OECD International Development
OECD International Direct Investment Statistics	OECD International Migration Statistics
NS Time Series Data	UNIDO Industrial Statistics
UNIDO Industrial Demand Supply	IMF Direction of Trade Statistics
IMF International Financial Statistics	IMF Balance of Payment Statistics
World Bank World Development Indicators	World Bank Global Development Finance
United Nations Common Database	Eurobarometers
European Social Survey	International Social Survey Programme
World Values Surveys and European Values Surveys	

- The Manchester Information and Associated Services (MIMAS) at the University of Manchester
- The Cathie Marsh Centre for Census and Survey Research (CCSR) at the University of Manchester.

If you are studying in the UK, you may be able to access many different kinds of data through these centres, including large-scale government surveys, qualitative data sets, international data sets and longitudinal data sets, as shown in **Table 5.2**, and illustrated in **Research in action 5.2**.

Research in action 5.2
BRITAIN AT WORK

Many academic researchers have conducted secondary analysis on the Workplace Employee Relations Survey (WERS) data set. The survey is conducted by the Centre for Social Research (formerly SCPR). It started in 1980 as the quadrennial Workplace Industrial Relations Survey (WIRS), surveying British establishments with 25 or more employees, and was renamed WERS in 1998 and extended to workplaces with 10 or more employees. The survey provides 'statistically reliable, nationally representative data on workplace relations and employment practices'.

The research team publishes primary analysis of each survey. Secondary analysis of the data has been conducted by other researchers, who may not have any connection with the project except through the data. These secondary analyses include journal articles, master's dissertations and doctoral dissertations.

See for example:

http://www.data-archive.ac.uk/findingData/werAbstract.asp;

http://www.niesr.ac.uk/niesr/wers98/Bib2004a.pdf

There are many advantages to using archived survey data as a source of data for a research project. The survey data provide you with access to much larger samples than you could hope to ever collect. Surveys such as these are designed and conducted by teams of experts, so that the quality of the research design, instruments, data collection and data processing is very high.

As well as data from a single source such as WERS, you can also combine data from different sources, as shown in **Research in action 5.3**.

Research in action 5.3
COUNTRY MUSIC ... THE MUSIC OF PAIN

To see whether country music and suicide rates were linked, sociologists Steven Stack and Jim Gundlach combined data from the Radio and Records Rating Report, which reported on the size of the country music listening audience in 49 US metropolitan areas, with suicide rates for those areas from the annual Mortality Tapes compiled by the Inter-University Consortium for Social and Political Research at the University of Michigan in the US (Stack and Gundlach 1995). They proposed that the two would be related, because the themes of country music dealt with the same issues that sociologists associate with suicide. This touched off a debate in the journal *Social Forces* over the link, with other sociologists arguing that divorce, gun ownership, living in the south and poverty accounted for both suicide and listening to 'country radio' (also see Stack and Gundlach 1992, 1994).

To use archived survey data, you first need to find out what surveys exist and then gain access to them, which is not always easy. Projects such as ESDS provide comprehensive listings of the survey data they hold, but you may have to use some of the tools and techniques for searching discussed in **Chapter 4** to find other surveys.

Even if you find a survey or other source whose data may help you answer your research questions, you may not always gain access to that data. Whilst many government and academic research centres make summary results and even raw data from their surveys available to researchers, you may only be able to obtain summary results of surveys conducted by commercial research organisations by paying and they may charge more than most student projects could afford. In some cases, however, they may not want to share this information with anyone else.

Commercial databases as sources of secondary data

Proprietary databases are data sets or databases created to be sold. These are often the best source of access to company financial data. You may have access to some proprietary data sets through your department or library, if they subscribe. **Company-specific databases** give company names, sales, profits, geographic profiles, industry profiles and other useful data. Because these databases are compiled and published by commercial organisations, they typically sell the results or charge for access to them. **Chapter 4** discussed some of these databases, but a few of the most popular ones include market research archives such as Mintel, and financial databases such as AMADEUS and FAME.

AMADEUS and **FAME** are two popular company financial databases. These are based on the financial reports and other data provided by companies to governments, securities overseers and investors. You can use these databases to find company accounts data for public and private companies, and can download selected data to create your own custom database.

Marketing information can be essential for projects involving either consumer or industrial products, especially if you are studying a marketing problem or your research setting is consumer-oriented. **Market research reports** are another type of proprietary information that students find useful for research projects. These reports may be published by commercial market or consumer research organisations, or trade associations.

Many business schools subscribe to Mintel market reports. **Mintel** is a consultancy company that:

> publishes over 45 reports each month, covering a wide range of sectors and focusing on topical marketing issues. Divided between UK-specific, European and USA reports, Mintel reports analyse market sizes and trends, market segmentation, and consumer attitudes and purchasing habits, as well as assessing the future of the market. By providing a comprehensive picture of the consumer, Mintel's reports provide thorough analyses of specialist sectors, breaking down often complex issues into easy-to-understand sections.
>
> (http://www.mintel.com/docs/pubs.htm)

For example, if you were studying food consumption, you might want to consult Mintel's June 2004 report extensively exploring the yoghurt market in the US. Other reports listed on the site examine the beer market, book retailing, analgesics and household cleaning products.

Trade associations are another good but often overlooked source of information about the commodity or organisations they represent. For example, the National Hot Dog and Sausage Council's website (http://www.hot-dog.org/) provides extensive information about the sales of 'tube steak' in the US. Information on this site includes:

- General market information (reports on *The Size and Scope of the US Market for Hot Dogs 2003* and *The Size and Scope of the US Market for Sausages 2003*)
- Consumption by geographic area (reports on the *Top Ten Hot Dog Eating Cities* and *Top Ten Sausage Eating Cities*)
- Special reports, such as how many hot dogs are eaten at baseball games in the US (a report on 2004 *Major League Ballpark Consumption*).

5.1.2 Creating your own data sets: archival research and unobtrusive observation

In the previous section, we described surveys and databases as sources of data for secondary analysis where the data had already been collected and processed for you. If you are interested in secondary research but you can't identify a data set or database that contains the information you want to analyse to answer your research questions, you may want to create your own data set from materials that you collect or that have been collected by organisations or other researchers but not processed and analysed. As we noted above, although you might be the first person to collect and analyse this data, it is still generally considered as secondary analysis because you are relying on data you are not collecting directly from organisations or people. Below, we will describe some features of archival research.

Data from documents and archives

In some research projects, you may want or need to gather data without any direct contact with organisations or people. You might choose to analyse documents, whether they are company records, publications or other sources.

Research that takes a historical perspective can often only rely on documents and other records for evidence, since the organisations and people being studied no longer exist to be interviewed or studied. These materials may be held in library or company **archives**, collections of documents or other artefacts that organisations or people create as part of their ongoing activities. Research that uses only secondary data, especially if it focuses on documents, is sometimes called **archival research**, whether the information is actually held in an archive or not, because the same techniques are used for recording and analysing information. Many placement projects involve investigating archival data, as shown in **Research in action 5.4**.

> **Research in action 5.4**
>
> **KATE'S ABC**
>
> As part of a summer job between completing her MBA and starting her PhD, Kate worked on a project for a telecoms manufacturer looking for ways to reduce the costs of materials management. As part of this project, the author and her colleague analysed the purchase orders that had been made over the past year, to identify the items that fell into A*, A, B and C purchase categories. This meant organising and sorting through tens of thousands of purchase orders (historical data), using data downloaded from the division's mainframe into a format viewable in a spreadsheet program. This allowed the organisation to identify the costs associated with purchase orders and thereby assess whether electronic purchasing would be cost-effective.

Secondary data can provide otherwise lost insights into management decisions outside any respondent's living memory, so business history and management history tends to focus largely on archival research. A company's archives can be a rich source of data, since it may contain detailed information that has never been made public and hence never analysed. Company archives may contain catalogues, reports, records of transactions and minutes of meetings, all of which tell us what happened in the past. Researchers may also use other archival materials such as images (photographs, film, video), sounds and other nonwritten materials in doing their research. Archival records can show what people actually (recorded as) thought or did at the time, since organisational members have not reinterpreted archival records through hindsight – as the saying goes, 'Success has many fathers but failure is an orphan.' On the other hand, archives typically only capture a small part of what goes on in an organisation, because they cannot capture informal and verbal interactions.

Some organisational researchers have used archival research to look at how change unfolds over decades, rather than the few months or years that a particular research project would normally take. They may even span centuries, as illustrated in **Research in action 5.5**.

> **Research in action 5.5**
>
> **I'LL DRINK TO THAT!**
>
> Glenn Carroll and Anand Swaminathan (2000) were interested in how the emergence of microbreweries contradicted a long trend towards greater concentration in the beer brewing industry. Carroll and Swaminathan used archival sources to identify the companies that entered and exited the brewing industry in the US over a long period. They used archival sources to construct life histories of 2251 breweries in the country, including microbreweries, brewpubs, contract brewers and mass producers. To identify all the brewers, they relied on industry histories, trade publications and web pages, rather than collecting information directly from existing firms. This is something that would have been, practically, almost impossible to achieve by direct measurement – not just in terms of the logistics of visiting all the firms, but the relative availability of data on firms that no longer existed.

You can also analyse 'texts' that are not words, such as films, television commercials and programmes, magazines advertisements, advertising coupons or bumper stickers. This kind of research can be extremely creative. Even though it is unlikely that you could find a database or a data set of, let's say, how commercials portray people drinking coffee, you could gather these materials and create your own data set to analyse. Consumer researchers, for example, have reported studies in the *Journal of Consumer Research* based on materials as diverse as comic books, romance novels, television commercials and popular television programmes. These are all artefacts created by organisations and used by people.

You might only want to use archival materials as a source of descriptive information, such as names, to create a record of key events in a company's history or as a source of illustrations, but you can also use them in a much more structured way to generate information you can analyse statistically. Various techniques are available for **structured content analysis** to find and count how often concepts, ideas or other 'meaning units' occur within documents or other texts. There are various computer programs you can use to make this task easier.

Major issues in archival research are similar to issues in large-scale survey data archives:

1. *How do you find out what archives exist?* As we noted in **Section 5.1.1**, public organisations such as the government, charities, trade associations and universities may make information available about their archives and even provide public access to those archives, but company archives are usually private, closely controlled, and difficult to find out about and access. Additionally, corporate and other business records may disappear when those businesses disappear through merger, acquisition, bankruptcy or dissolution.
2. *How do you gain access to these archives?* Access to most archives, especially those in private hands, is usually tightly controlled. You may need to use some of the tips for gaining access to people to gain access to archives. We discuss this issue in more detail in **Chapters 8** and **12**.
3. *What data do I need and how should I structure them?* Since you are not working with data in a predefined data set or database as for survey or proprietary databases, you will need to make these decisions yourself. It may take two or more passes through the data to collect all the information you need.
4. *How much time will it take?* Archival research is often time-consuming and open-ended. Archival research is usually slow compared with the other kinds of data gathering described in this chapter and the next, since you will have to go through many documents, and you may not be able to make photocopies or even take notes by hand if there are restrictions because of confidentiality or the condition of the materials. Therefore, extensive archival research may not be appropriate for short-or medium-length research projects, since the time needed to identify, access and collect data may be longer than the time you have available.
5. *Is there another way to get these data?* Can you interrogate any company sources or databases to get the same information? Archival data may be the only records relating to long-ago events or defunct organisations.

Data from unobtrusive measures

You can also use secondary analysis with **unobtrusive measures**, data gathered indirectly from research subjects (Webb et al. 1966) by observing the traces they leave in the physical environment or other natural settings. These data are collected in the natural setting of organisations and people, unlike archival data. There can also be traces such as the forwarding of emails, posts on message boards, and so on.

Such **found data** result from the identification of physical traces, physical changes in the environment due to erosion or accretion. Whilst a variety of unobtrusive data are available to the researcher, researchers need the skills of a forensic scientist, detective or archaeologist to find and interpret these clues. Creative sources of unobtrusive data include:

> wear on the floor tiles surrounding a museum exhibit showing hatching chicks to measure visitor flows; the size of suits of armour as an indicator of changes in human stature over time; and (tongue in cheek) the relationship between psychologists' hair length and their methodological predilections. (Lee 2000: 2)

An unusual but interesting source is described in **Research in action 5.6**

Research in action 5.6

IT'S NOT RUBBISH, IT'S RESEARCH ... HONESTLY!

In studies of household consumption, people often consciously or unconsciously misreport what and how much they consume of various products. To find out what people actually buy, consume and throw away, many researchers have turned to analysing household waste – finding out what's in people's rubbish bins. This can be used to complement survey data ('what people said they did' versus 'what they actually did') or as a stand-alone research design.

In 1973, the Garbage Project at the University of Arizona started to analyse people's household rubbish using the same techniques that archaeologists use for studying ancient populations. A number of studies have used 'household archaeology' or garbage-ology to study business and management problems. For example, Wallendorf and Nelson (1986) studied the contents of nearly 1600 waste bins to determine whether Americans of European and Mexican backgrounds differed in the use of body care products, including 'personal cleansers, household cleansers, oral hygiene products, odour fighters, hair care products, skin care products, cosmetics, feminine protection products, over-the-counter drugs, and aspirin'. In another project, Reilly and Wallendorf (1987) studied differences between the foods consumed by these two groups based on the contents of their rubbish bins.

Unobtrusive measures can complement other data especially if you want to collect data about sensitive issues or do not have direct access to respondents, they are unwilling to answer questions or the act of asking questions might affect the answers (Lee 2000: 1). For example, when people are asked questions directly, they tend to overreport behaviours or attitudes they perceive as positive or **socially desirable**. If recycling household rubbish and giving to charity are considered as positive social behaviours, people will report doing more of these than they actually do.

Not surprisingly, people also tend to underreport undesirable behaviours, such as drinking too much or wasting food.

> **Activity 1**
>
> List three behaviours of interest to business and management researchers that might not be accurately reported.
>
> How could you get accurate information about these behaviours?
>
> Would it be easier or harder than studying attitudes or beliefs?

Is secondary analysis right for you?

Whether you are taking a scientific or ethnographic approach to research, you will probably find yourself doing some secondary analysis, even if it is not the only method you use for collecting data to answer your research questions. If someone else has collected the right data and you can gain access to it, you should make use of it if you can. People and organisations create large amounts of secondary data as part of their everyday activities, and, as we have seen, some proprietary secondary data sources are even deliberately created and maintained as a source of revenues.

Some researchers find the challenge of archival research or unobtrusive measures exciting because it requires 'thinking outside the box'. If you are a fan of Sherlock Holmes, for example, you may recognise some of the detective's methods in unobtrusive research. If you are interested in historical or longitudinal research, this may be the only way to find out about people and companies.

Other business and management researchers, particularly in areas such as finance, accounting and business history, consider secondary analysis to be the only proper way to do research. (This makes writing chapters on methods for data collection in research methods books in these areas fairly simple.) This is often the only way they can accumulate the large number of observations they need to do statistical testing.

You may want to look ahead to **Figure 5.8** if you think you might be interested in secondary analysis, but are not sure. You should also read through **Sections 5.2** and **5.3** before you decide.

5.2 Designs for surveys

Many people think first of survey designs such as questionnaires when they think about business and management research. Interviews and questionnaires are popular ways to gather data about organisations and people (Gray 2004) and find out what people and organisations think, believe or do. They are a fairly natural way of getting information, because we usually ask someone else when we want to find something out. You may want to conduct your own survey to gain information directly from people or organisations, especially when secondary data aren't available.

Surveys can be the quickest and cheapest way of finding out information when you don't have time for intensive research designs such as observation or you are especially interested in studying groups rather than individuals. On the other hand, most people underestimate how difficult and time-consuming it is to design an effective survey that will actually answer their research questions. Questionnaire design and administration can be surprisingly difficult to get right, and the effort involved in getting enough people to agree to be interviewed or return your questionnaire is often underestimated. Unless you do a good job of designing your questions and sample, you may not get the information you need or be able to draw any conclusions. You might even end up discarding all the data you have gathered because the answers are irrelevant, wasting your time and resources and your respondents' time. The worst-case scenario is getting few – or even no – completed questionnaires back.

This section will describe the basics of survey design and administration, including the three main techniques of structured interviews, questionnaires and structured observations. You may want to follow up this information with a specialist book on interviewing or questionnaires from the **Additional resources** at the end of this chapter. Neither, however, will substitute for hands-on experience:

> Questionnaire design cannot be taught from books; every investigation presents new and different problems. A textbook can only hope to prevent some of the worst pitfalls and to give practical, do-it-yourself kind of information that will point the way out of difficulties. (Oppenheimer 1992: 1)

Activity 2

Unsurprisingly, 95 per cent of adults say they wash their hands after using the toilet. However, the American Society of Microbiology reports that only 78 per cent of people actually wash their hands after using the toilet. Of those who wash their hands, only half use soap and only half wash for 15–20 seconds.

What do you think accounts for the difference in the figures above?

How could you collect data to see which figure was more accurate?

Are there any legal or ethical questions that this might raise?

5.2.1 What is a survey?

A **survey** is a way to collect data from a range of respondents by asking them questions. Surveys are especially useful for capturing facts, opinions, behaviours or attitudes. Some familiar tools and techniques are associated with survey designs, including questionnaires, structured interviews and structured observations.

Although survey design can be identified by general principles, a particular survey can take many different forms. **Structured interviews** are conducted face to face, over the telephone or electronically, but they are still based on a standard set of questions (which may be called an instrument or a schedule). **Structured observations** record your observations of people's behaviours over a period of time, for example in work study. **Questionnaires** ask people to record their answers to a series of questions on paper or electronic forms; and are sometimes sent by post. However, you can also hand out questionnaires to respondents in person, and collect them in person, or leave them somewhere for people to collect themselves and return (for example store comment cards). Most surveys are conducted at only a single point in time, but surveys can also be used to collect longitudinal information if conducted continuously or at regular intervals of time.

Is a survey the right design for you?
A survey is not always the best way to answer your research questions. You might want to look ahead to **Figure 5.8** if you are considering a survey.

You should consider a survey if you want to collect data from a large number of respondents and have a limited time for collecting data from each of them or cannot visit them in person, or if you need to collect a large number of responses to analyse statistically. If you want to use a structured interview or questionnaire, your respondents must be able to understand and answer your questions with minimal explanation or without your being physically present. If you want to use structured observation, you may need to do this unobtrusively. You should also consider whether you are asking questions that your respondents might find sensitive or data they might only provide anonymously.

On the other hand, you should rule out a structured survey technique if it is not clear who might have the answers to your questions, you do not know in advance what you want to ask, you need to explain your questions in detail or you need to capture this kind of unstructured information by observation or other means. You should also rule out this approach if your questions or data will change as you do your research. If any of these are true, you might consider the unstructured interview and other techniques presented in **Chapter 7**.

Structured interviews
One of the most common techniques used in all types of business and management research is the **interview** – asking someone questions directly. The structured interview – where you ask the same questions in the same order to every interviewee – is the type of interview mostly closely associated with the scientific approach. (We will discuss other types of interviews in **Chapter 9**.) Taking a structured approach makes sure that the data you collect are consistent across interviews, by minimising the differences between the people you have interviewed and differences between different researchers or different interviews. This fits with the scientific model described in **Chapter 5**.

Ways of conducting structured interviews include:

- *Face-to-face interviews* – typically a one-to-one interview where you and your interviewee are present in the same location. Face-to-face interviews capture the most detail, both verbal and nonverbal, but are the most expensive to conduct because of time, distance and travel. Occasionally, you might conduct the interview as part of a team. You might also interview more than one person at a time, for example all adult members of a household in a consumer marketing study of how the decision to buy a new refrigerator is made.
- *Telephone interviews* – typically a one-to-one interview over the telephone between you and your interviewee. Since neither of you needs to travel, telephone

interviewing is less expensive than face-to-face interviewing, and you may be able to conduct more telephone interviews in a given amount of time. However, the large number of unsolicited telephone interviews for marketing and political research may make people reluctant to participate in them and, if you are trying to interview people in organisations, you may find it difficult to get past the reception switchboard. The growth in web cameras and mobile phones equipped with video capabilities may increase the popularity of telephone interviews for business and management research, and overcome the loss of nonverbal information. You might also interview someone by email or fax, rather than over the phone, but this is more similar to questionnaires, which we explore below.

- *Structured observations* – although in structured observation you are not directly asking any questions, you are interrogating the behaviour of the person being observed and recording the information on a schedule. Mystery shoppers may use such a schedule when they unobtrusively follow people around and record details of what merchandise people look at, touch, try on and purchase, as described by Underhill (2000). Another use of structured observation is the time and motion study, associated with F.W. Taylor.

Issues in interview administration

Although we will go into sampling in more detail in **Section 5.2.3**, you should consider which respondents you are likely to include in or exclude from your survey if you choose one of the three structured interviewing techniques we list above. For example, telephone surveys have been found to undersample people with low or high incomes. In the UK, while most households have a landline, a high percentage of numbers are ex-directory (unlisted), so that you may have trouble developing an accurate sample frame. Furthermore, many people, mostly younger ones, are giving up land lines in favour of mobile phones, which are also ex-directory. Similarly, many people do not have email accounts, so you may be limiting your sample if you send them out this way.

Your 'script', or list of questions, is known as an **interview schedule**. You may standardise not only your questions, but also the range of answers that your respondent can choose from, as we discuss below. Using an interview schedule is convenient because it usually provides space for you to record the answers directly on the form. Standardising your questions, however, doesn't completely limit what you can ask. You may want to probe, ask for further information or explore unexpected answers.

Most professional survey researchers now use **computer-assisted protocols for interviews** (CAPI). Besides making it easier to standardise questions and responses, CAPI allows you to record responses directly on the computer and transfer them to the program you will use to analyse them. You are less likely to create errors than if you are entering them from a paper-based form.

You should try not to influence the answers you get by how you conduct your interviews. **Chapter 7** will discuss how you should behave as an interviewer in more depth. Some issues that apply specifically to structured interviews include:

1. *Consistency.* Make sure that you ask questions in exactly the same way and the same order during each interview. If you need to explain a question to your interviewee, make sure that you are consistent with the instrument and building

standard **prompts** into your interview schedule may help to maintain this consistency. If you interpret or embellish the question with an example or additional information based on what you think, such as 'Well, I think that this means ...', you may influence the answer you get.
2. *Completeness*. Make sure that you have asked every question and not left any out. You may sometimes be tempted ask questions out of order if your interviewee starts talking about a subject you know comes up later in the interview schedule, but besides making it more likely that you will omit questions, this can contribute to a lack of consistency between interviews.
3. *Accuracy*. Make sure that you are recording the replies exactly. If you are only recording answers to closed-ended questions, make sure that you are ticking the right boxes. If you are recording answers to open-ended questions, make sure that you are capturing them exactly.

Even using an interviewing schedule, you may have a hard time maintaining consistency across interviews if several people in your project group are conducting interviews. You should hold a practice session before you start interviewing, so that everyone asks the same questions in the same way. You might try round-robin interviewing until you are satisfied with the consistency across interviewers. You may need to hold a refresher session after a certain number of interviews to make sure that variation hasn't crept in. This is especially important if there are major differences between interviewers. In the *International Service Study*, for example, researcher Chris Voss flew over from the UK to the US to train the American interviewers (Voss et al. 2004). By doing this, he made sure that no significant differences in the way the research was being conducted could creep in.

Because interviewing is so often used for commercial research, including consumer marketing and public opinion research, codes of ethics have been developed that address most of the issues you might encounter if you use a structured interview. Obviously, you need to consider ethical issues and informed consent if you plan to record a telephone interview. We will discuss this issue further in **Chapter 9**.

Self-administered questionnaires
Probably the most familiar survey design is the questionnaire, in which a respondent answers your questions directly, without you present. This difference in who does the asking and recording is significant. Your respondents interact with you only through the structured and standardised list of questions (and often answers), in a **self-administered questionnaire**.

Like interviews, questionnaires vary in how they are delivered to and collected from the respondent. The main methods are:

- *By post* – you send your questionnaire to your respondent by post and the respondent returns the completed questionnaire the same way. This postal questionnaire is popular because of its geographic reach – you can send a questionnaire to anywhere in the world that post is delivered.
- *Deliver and collect* – the questionnaire is handed out or left in a convenient location, and the respondent returns the completed questionnaire to the surveyor or a convenient location such as a clearly labelled box. Comment cards on restaurant tables and in hotel rooms are simple examples.

- *Email surveys* – the questionnaire is sent as an email or attachment to an email for your respondent to complete and return. You will obviously need a list of email addresses to send surveys. It is ethically unacceptable for you to send unsolicited mass emails (**spam**), no matter how well intentioned.
- *Web surveys* – you direct respondents to a web address – or they arrive at it from other links – to fill out a computer-assisted set of questions. This is becoming increasingly popular, not least because the software can record answers for you in a file or database and you do not have to re-enter them manually. You can also post intermediate or final feedback on the results on your website, which may be interesting to your participants. Although, increasingly facilitated by proprietary and general purpose software, there is less control over who answers and how many times they answer.

Issues in questionnaire administration

Your questionnaire design will have to be very clear because you are not interacting with your respondent. If you are considering using a self-administered questionnaire, there is a well-established literature on best practice for questionnaire design and administration (for example Foddy 1993; Oppenheimer 1992). We will present some of the main topics in questionnaire design and administration in this section, but we can cover only a few here. If you decide to use a questionnaire, you should consult some of the sources listed at the end of this chapter in **Additional resources**.

The main advantage of questionnaires over interviews for collecting data from a large number of people becomes obvious when you consider the cost per response. Once you have developed a questionnaire, the cost of administering one additional questionnaire is very low – the cost of photocopying and postage or hosting the website. The costs of scaling up from 100 to 200 questionnaires, or 1000 to 2000 questionnaires, are relatively small. By comparison, each additional interview is as expensive as every other interview. On the other hand, if you are scheduling interviews rather than cold-calling, you are only out the cost of a phone call or letter if your contact decides not to participate; given the low response rate to unsolicited questionnaires, you may be sending out 5–20 questionnaires for each one you get back – this can add up if you want to get a large set of responses to analyse.

The trade-off is the quality of the information you collect in an interview or questionnaire. You can only get the answers to the questions you have asked on your questionnaire, but a structured interview does allow some potential for capturing additional information and insights. Furthermore, you are less likely to have missing data problems with interview data, since you are interacting directly with your respondent. People often skip questions on questionnaires if they do not understand them or are bored. We have seen many questionnaires returned only half-complete. You also can capture more spontaneous feedback from your respondents, especially nonverbal feedback, in an interview, although in a questionnaire you can include a section at the end such as 'Any other comments?'

Since you are not asking the questions in person, your respondent cannot ask for directions, clarifications or prompts, so good questionnaire design becomes essential. If you want people to fill out a questionnaire, it needs to be short and clear, which usually means simple questions with predefined responses (we discuss this below). If you make a major design error, you cannot easily correct or recall a questionnaire once it has been delivered. If you do change your questionnaire or web questionnaire, you may not be able to use the early data. Since you usually interview people one at a time rather than simultaneously, you have more of a chance to mend your interview schedule if you find out that it is flawed.

5.2.2 Survey design and administration

Although many students think that survey design is simple and quick, for example you can design a survey in an afternoon session, survey design and administration is actually an intensive process and you must go through quite a few rounds drafting and redrafting your questions before your first participant is interviewed or fills out a questionnaire.

Developing or adopting a survey instrument

Although we discuss instrument design in detail below, you should consider using an existing survey and/or questions before you design your own. We recommend that you look at some examples of surveys from your literature search. Many articles and books include a copy of key questions – or even the entire survey instrument – or offer to provide them on request. For example, Zeithaml et al.'s *Delivering Quality Service* (1990) includes a copy of their *Service Quality Questionnaire*. Remember to ask permission to use a survey or a questionnaire unless the author has explicitly given permission in the source. (If you can't find any examples of how someone has investigated your research topic using structured interviews or questionnaires, you might question whether survey design is appropriate before trying to develop your own.)

We also recommend that you look at some examples of large-scale social surveys. In the UK, the Economic and Social Research Council (ESRC) supports the Social Survey Question Bank in the Centre for Applied Social Surveys at the University of Surrey, which makes available a large number of the questions asked in economic and social surveys (the data are archived separately, as discussed in **Section 5.1**). Some of these surveys are quite extensive: the National Food Survey has been running since the 1940s.

You may also be able to find a book that provides questions on your research topics. Books that collect together a large number of questions about your topic are known as 'question banks'. These are good sources of questions because experienced researchers will have already tested the questions.

Designing your own survey

If you cannot find a predesigned instrument or questions for your research topic, and you are still interested in designing a survey, we describe some of the major elements of the process below. Because surveys, especially postal questionnaires, are so popular, people have carried out extensive research into survey research and know a lot about what works and what doesn't. We also list some more detailed sources of advice in the **Additional resources** at the end of this chapter. However, you can learn some of the tricks of the trade only by hands-on experience with designing and administering surveys. You may want to consult your project supervisor and/or anyone in your university who is expert in survey design before you launch a full-scale effort.

The survey design process
The work that you put into getting your survey instrument right – whether it is an interview schedule or questionnaire – is critical. Software for designing and analysing questionnaires or online surveys, such as SNAP, makes the technical job of developing an instrument much easier. However, this may result in poorer content, because it focuses more attention on the design and layout of the survey than on the content. We receive many questionnaires that look good, but are poorly conceived and designed, with missing or unclear instructions, poor or confusing questionnaire wording and the entire questionnaire being irrelevant because it has been sent to the wrong person. This agrees with the survey expert Oppenheimer (1992: 5–8), who says that the most common problems with surveys are too little design and planning, not asking the right people and not asking the right questions.

How to design a survey
Figure 5.1 presents a simplified overview of the survey design process. The backwards loops are especially important in survey design, because you won't have a chance to revise your structured interview schedule or your questionnaire once you launch into full-scale research mode.

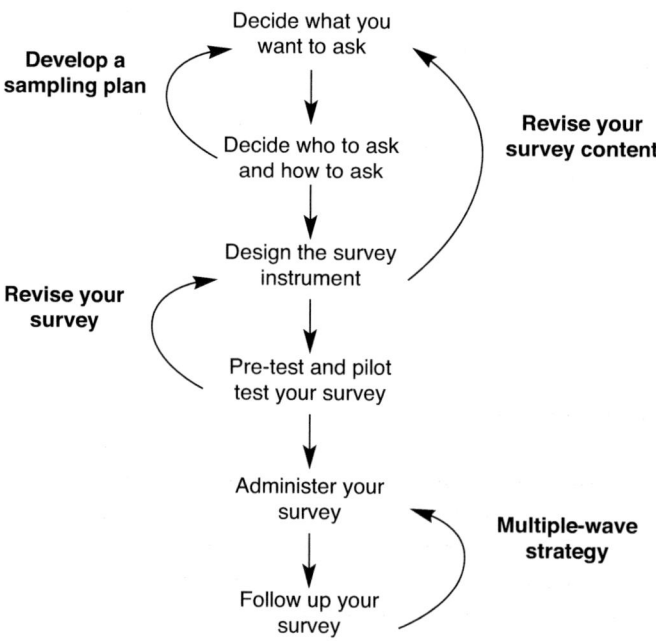

Figure 5.1 An overview of the survey process

Step 1. Decide what you want to ask

Students often decide to use a survey, without knowing whether a survey can actually answer their research questions and so often end up being limited in what they can study by their research design. Starting with your research questions and conceptual framework, you should see how – and whether – you can capture the information you need using a survey. List the major concepts and relationships you need to measure. Will you need additional sources of data? Is there a better way to capture this information?

Step 2. Decide what respondents you want to ask and how you want to ask them

The next step is to identify the people with the information you need. Who can answer the questions you want to ask? Do the people you want to interview or answer your questionnaire have the information to answer your questions, and answer them accurately? The 'good subject' effect (discussed in **Section 5.3**) may lead them to give an answer, even if they have to guess.

Also, will your proposed respondents actually have any interest in being interviewed or answering your questionnaire? CEOs of Fortune 500 companies are extremely unlikely to answer a student's (or even a professor's) unsolicited questionnaire. What incentives, if any, are there for your proposed respondents to participate in your survey – you are asking for a commitment of their time, which they might use better in other ways. Although this is not a unique problem for questionnaires, it is probably most critical for them, since you have to provide some incentive for people both to fill in the form *and* to return it.

You might think that your respondents have a duty to fill out your questionnaire, or they will want to just because you have asked, but this is not necessarily true. One of us saw a form letter sent out by a Japanese company's UK site in response to a request to fill out a questionnaire. The company politely returned the questionnaire and explained that it would have to hire a full-time employee just to fill out questionnaires, it received so many of them! On the other hand, other students on your course or in your halls of residence, members of an organisation or society, people you work with and so on will be much likelier to participate because of a shared interest or connection. We will consider this again in this section when we look at sampling and response rates.

You should also think about how you will administer your survey during this step, whether you will collect data using an interview or a questionnaire. Interviews are good at getting answers to questions, but can be difficult to arrange. You can send a questionnaire anywhere in the world, but they typically have low response rates – even as low as 1 in 100. We know of a student group who sent out several hundred questionnaires, including stamped self-addressed envelopes for the replies. They received two responses. This is unusual, but you should calculate the total costs of your research design, including your time and effort, per response. It doesn't make any sense to use a research design whose strengths are large-scale research and only collect a small set of replies. We do not advocate widescale postal surveys for student projects, unless you have managed to secure external funding and sponsorship from an organisation that will give your project the 'stamp of approval' and perhaps even access to a mailing list, as in **Student Research in action 5.2**.

> **Student research in action 5.2**
> **LIKE THEY DO ON THE DISCOVERY CHANNEL**
>
> Five final-year undergraduate students were working on a project sponsored by an animal welfare group, which we will disguise – for reasons that should become apparent below – as the Hamsters and Gerbils Conservation Society (HGCS). The organisation raised money in the UK to fund refuges for hamsters and gerbils that had been abandoned or abused by their owners, and feral colonies of hamsters and gerbils. It also carried out political campaigning to try to strengthen the laws on hamsters and gerbils in the UK and internationally. Some of this it carried out on its own, some of it with similar groups in other countries and some of it with organisations interested in other rodents.
>
> The organisation wanted the group to survey its members to see how satisfied they were with its strategy. The organisation had a list of its members, to whom it sent publications about its activities and requests for funds. It also distributed a monthly newsletter specifically to junior members (memberships were popular as birthday gifts for children aged 12 and under).
>
> The students developed a survey, which the HGCS enclosed with its next newsletter to junior members. The response rate was high, so the students were able to argue that they had a clear picture of what the organisation's current members thought. They would never have been able to capture this information through interviews or observation. Thus, the students believed that they had captured both information of interest to the society (which they had), and information that could help them to solve an academic (theoretical) problem (which they hadn't, as we discuss below.)

Step 3. Design your survey

Once you get the questions themselves right, you can then think about the order you want to present the questions in, which has a surprising influence on your respondent's willingness to answer and the answers themselves. You should also design the instructions carefully. Once you have the content right, you can work on the look and feel of the questionnaire, including the layout and design on the page, which will make it easier for you to conduct a structured interview or observation, or your respondent to fill out a questionnaire. The final step is to think from your respondent's perspective – have you actually created something that he or she can and will answer? We give some pointers on each of these areas below.

Design your questions. Our advice is that you should try to use an existing survey or existing questions wherever possible, because these have already been extensively tested. If you do want to design your own questions, there are two main types of survey question, closed and open-ended.

You can specify the answers to a **closed-ended question** in advance, so that your respondent chooses the most appropriate response from a list. In a structured interview, you would read your question and then the list of answers or prompts. In a structured observation, you might tick a category that you have already defined. In a web-based questionnaire, your respondent might answer a closed-ended question by indicating their response on a tick box, a radio button or a scrolling list, as shown in **Figure 5.2**.

QUANTITATIVE RESEARCH DESIGNS

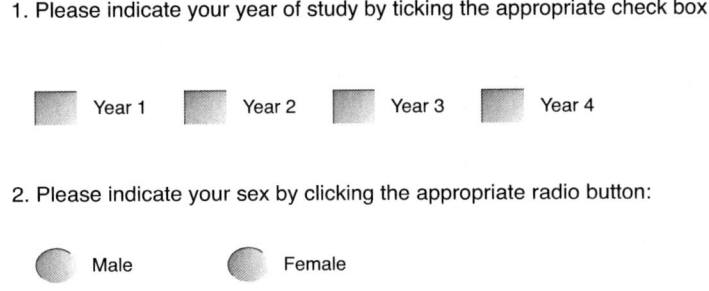

Figure 5.2 Common formats for closed-ended questions

The advantages of closed-ended questions for quantitative research include:

- *Speed* – Interviewers can record the answers and respondents can answer closed-ended questions more quickly.
- *Accuracy* – Interviewers or respondents are less likely to record inappropriate answers.
- *Data entry* – You can enter data from an interview schedule or questionnaire more quickly.

In a closed-ended question, your respondents can only choose from the responses you have already selected. You can also ask an **open-ended question**, where you allow our respondent to give any response. You can ask an open-ended question such as 'Who would you say are your top three competitors?' and record the response directly on your interview schedule or computer, if you are using CAPI. Open-ended questions are often used in structured interviews, since the interviewer is there to provide quality control.

In a web questionnaire, you might ask your respondent to fill in an open-ended answer in a text box. You can make this text box long or short, to give your respondent a clue as to the length of the expected answer. We show some examples in **Figure 5.3**.

You can mix both open-ended and closed-ended questions in a survey. If you are more interested in asking open-ended rather than closed-ended questions, you might consider using a questionnaire, but it might be more appropriate to use an interview (see **Chapter 7**). If you want to ask a large number of questions about a large number of respondents, you should emphasise closed-ended questions. First, since your respondents can only choose from a limited range of answers, you only have to deal with a limited number of different answers per question. Second, you can convert these answers from text into numbers, which makes it easier to record (or 'code') the answers in a computer spreadsheet and analyse them using statistics.

Some common mistakes that students make in designing questions are forgetting about:

1. *Clarity* – if you are using questions whose responses may ask for judgements such as 'seldom' or 'frequently', whenever possible, structure your responses so that it is clear what each response means instead of making your respondent interpret them. How would your respondent know whether 'seldom' means less often

3. Where did you hear about our website?

☐ Another website   ☐ Word-of-mouth

☐ Television advertisement   ☐ Radio advertisement

☐ Other – please indicate below

[   ]

4. What other features would you find helpful on this website?

[   ]

Figure 5.3   Common formats for open-ended and mixed questions

than 'rarely'? Why not specify 'Once a month' and 'Once a year' – unless you are actually investigating how people interpret terms such as seldom and rarely.
2. *Simplicity* – avoid questions that are actually multiple questions or general questions. If you ask a double-barrelled questions such as 'How often do you walk or use the bus and train to get to work?', you are losing any information about the individual activities. Don't use technical terms that may be unfamiliar to your respondent: 'Does your manufacturing plant use JIT/TQM/BPR' might be more intelligible as 'Does your manufacturing plant use just-in-time, total quality management or business process engineering?', although it's still not a good question. Check to make sure that each question is only a single question. Even if it takes up more physical space, you might want to rephrase the last question as 'Please place a tick beside each of the following techniques that your manufacturing plant is using' and list each of the options separately.
3. *Brevity* – avoid long questions, in interviews because it is difficult for your interviewee to remember the entire question and answer it accurately, and in questionnaires because your respondent may lose interest and skip the question.
4. *Neutrality* – avoid asking leading questions, such as 'Are you in favour of raising taxes to waste money on able-bodied people who could work but don't?' You are conducting research to find out information, not confirm your own opinions.

Even if your respondent has the relevant information, you might still get inaccurate answers depending on how you ask the questions. Rather than asking your respondent to estimate a figure in response to 'How many times did you go to the cinema last year', it might be better to ask 'On average, how often do you go to the cinema' and give a range such as weekly, monthly, and so on.

Design your instrument. Once you are happy with your individual questions, you need to check the order you are asking them in and how the whole interview schedule or questionnaire flows together. Some tips for smoother flow are:

- Begin with simple questions and put difficult questions at the end of the questionnaire. This keeps you from putting people off at the beginning.
- Put awkward or potentially embarrassing questions last.
- If your questionnaire is long, or covers different areas, divide the questionnaire into sections. This gives your respondents a break and helps to avoid 'respondent fatigue'.
- Make sure that you have provided clear and explicit instructions on how to answer the questions, and what to do when the questions have been answered – especially important for self-completion questionnaires!

Lay out your questionnaire. Finally, once you are happy with the individual questions and overall structure, you should work carefully on the physical design and appearance of your instrument. Good design can substantially improve your response rate. For informal or small-scale questionnaires, a neatly word-processed and photocopied questionnaire (or a web-based questionnaire you have designed yourself) will usually do. For formal or large-scale questionnaires, or where respondents are of high status, you may need to have them professionally designed and printed.

Using a software package such as Snap may make designing the instrument and entering the data much simpler, but the trade-off is the time involved in learning to use the package and the temptation to focus on design at the expense of content.

Check the questionnaire length. Check to make sure that your interview schedule or questionnaire is not too long and you have not asked too many questions. When people get tired, they may give incorrect answers, may not complete all the questions, or may even not fill it out at all.

To maximise your response rate, your questionnaire should fit entirely on one folded A3 page (that is, no more than four A4 pages), including your instructions. You may have to decide whether to drop some questions, or settle for a lower response rate. Using design tricks such as narrow margins or smaller fonts may actually discourage people from answering it. The same principle applies to online surveys – if you try to disguise a long survey by breaking it into multiple screens, people can still get survey fatigue.

If you absolutely must ask a large number of questions for your research, you might divide the questions into two or more questionnaires for different respondents. An example of a project that did this is the World Class Manufacturing Project, where researchers administered 26 separate questionnaires at each plant site, so that no respondent had to answer more than 100 questions. Each questionnaire could thus be answered in a reasonable amount of time, before the respondent got bored or fatigued. If a single respondent had been asked to give all of this information, he or she would have had to answer more than 1500 questions! You should also consider what information you could collect yourself, for example information that is already published in company annual reports or industry publications.

Pilot your survey

If you test your interview or questionnaire using a pilot test before you start using it to collect data from your sample, you are more likely to pick up serious problems with your questions, instructions or survey design. You should:

1. Make sure that people know who you are, why you are asking for their help and that you have dealt with any reservations about providing you with the data (for example, through a statement on confidentiality).
2. Try out your questions – do people understand what the questions mean? Missing or incorrect responses may indicate that people do not understand what you are asking.
3. Time how long it takes for the interview or your respondents to fill out your questionnaire – too short or too long, and you either miss data or people do not complete the forms.
4. See how they deal with the instructions on the forms, including what to do with the completed form.
5. Enter the data – set up the necessary databases or spreadsheets to feed your data into – how easy is it for you to enter data from the spreadsheets?

Revise your survey

Once you have pilot tested your survey, you should revise anything that you identified as a problem. If you make major changes, you should pilot test your survey again before you administer it. Keep doing this for as long as it takes to get it right, no matter how eager you are to start collecting data. Once everything seems to be OK, check it one more time. You will probably find some errors or ambiguities you have not previously spotted. Fix these and then start interviewing people, making observations or sending out questionnaires.

Administer your survey

If you are using a postal questionnaire, you may want to keep track of the response rate to your questionnaires, so that you can take corrective action if necessary. Some researchers follow a multiple-wave strategy, in which they do not leave their project's success to a single mail shot. This might involve following up nonresponses with a letter or polite phone call after a reasonable period of time to remind people to respond. You may need to send out reminder letters after an appropriate period (two to four weeks), and perhaps even send out more surveys to the same sample or a new sample. As we have mentioned above, a lot of research has been done on this method, so you may want to look to the specialist literature for guidance on more complex survey designs.

5.2.3 Sampling

Except for a census, which is administered to every member of a population (or at least as close as possible), surveys gather data from a subset, or sample, of the population, who represent the entire population you want to study. How you select your **sample** is therefore the second key factor for successful survey research besides instrument design. This will determine your ability to draw conclusions about the social units you are studying.

Sampling allows you to make conclusions about the social units you are studying by selecting units that are representative of your population. To sample you need to understand what population you want to sample and what characteristics you want to measure. 'The first step in understanding and representing a population is to be able to name that population' (O'Leary 2004). Your **population** is the set that contains all members of the social units you want to study. A population might consist of all Chinese restaurants in the UK, all university students or all Honda drivers. Your sample is the subset of those social units you have selected to study for example students at your own university to represent all university students.

Your list of all the units in the population is known as your **sampling frame**, although in many cases it will be difficult to accurately list these units. If you have defined your population as all of O2's mobile phone customers, even if you had access to the company's customer database, this might include customers who no longer have a mobile phone but who haven't cancelled their accounts, or exclude customers who have signed up in the last week.

Your sample must be representative of your population if you want to generalise from your sample to your population (Bryman and Bell 2003: 91); otherwise, your results will be inaccurate because your sample is **biased**. The two main approaches to sampling are probability sampling and nonprobability sampling. In **probability sampling**, the units you study are drawn randomly from your population, whilst in **nonprobability sampling**, you systematically or purposefully select these units.

Activity 3

Nadia and her project group want to collect data for a research project on the environmental effects of low-cost air travel from England to Portugal. They plan to stop students outside the student union and ask them a few questions, which they estimate will take about ten minutes per student. They plan to entice students into answering their question by giving each respondent a chocolate bar.

Do you think that this is a good plan? What issues do you think they should take into account in designing a sampling plan?

Probability sampling

If you want to use statistical tests to measure how likely it is that your findings about your sample are representative of your sample (see **Chapter 10** for more on quantitative analysis), you should use probability sampling. The goal of probability sampling is to make sure that your sample is representative by making sure that each unit in your population has a known and equal probability of being selected. Most probability samples also rely on the units you study being randomly selected. If you want to draw conclusions about household wealth by sampling only footballers' wives, you would be doing journalism or consulting rather than research.

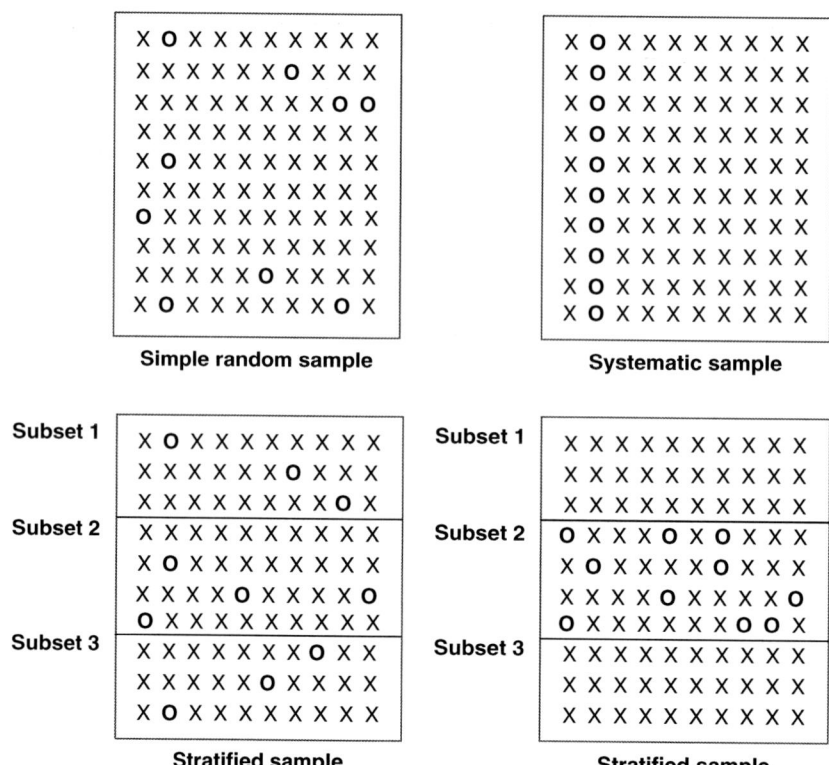

Figure 5.4 Probability sampling illustrated

We describe four techniques that you can use for probability sampling below and illustrate them in **Figure 5.4**:

1. *Simple random sampling* – You are equally likely to select any particular member of the population to study. If you want to sample 10 out of 100 employees, you should have a 10 per cent (10/100) chance of selecting any individual employee for your study. If you have access to a spreadsheet or a table of random numbers, you can use random numbers to select the employees from your sampling frame. If you assigned a random number between 1 and 100 to all 100 employees, you might use a rule that you would select any employee whose random number fell between 41 and 50.
2. *Systematic sampling* – Similar to simple random sampling in that you are equally likely to select any member of the population to study, but instead of using random numbers you take a systematic approach. You might decide to study every tenth employee on the list (2, 22, 32, …). However, if your list is in a nonrandom order, your sample may be biased (for example all women in the first half of the list and all men in the second half).
3. *Stratified random sampling* – If your population is not uniform, you may want to make sure that you select enough members of certain subsets. You may want to make sure that each subset is proportionally represented. If you are trying to

sample students from three years of your degree course, you may want to assign each year its own sampling frame and then use random sampling within the subgroup. This helps you make sure that your sample is representative if simple random sampling might not result in equal representation in your study.

4. *Cluster sampling* – If you have a nonuniform population, you may want to select your entire sample from a particular subset that is representative of the entire population. This is known as a cluster. You might choose a particular police station to be representative of all police stations, or a particular house to represent all first-year student houses. Again, unless your cluster is perfectly representative of your population, you risk building sample error into your sampling plan.

Although this does not describe every possible probability sampling plan, these four techniques illustrate two important aspects of sampling. Probability sampling can be random or systematic. You can draw your sample in a single stage, as in simple random or systematic sampling, or in more than one stage, as in stratified random or cluster sampling. We will discuss other issues related to probability sampling when we describe sample bias and error.

Nonprobability sampling

In nonprobability sampling, you have a greater chance of selecting some units to study than other units. Four techniques that you can use for nonprobability sampling are:

1. *Convenience sampling* – You choose a sample because you have access to it, for example all the students who live in your hall of residence. This may get you enough responses, but you will have trouble convincing anyone else that you can draw any sort of general conclusions from it. The best use of a convenience sample is to pre-test or pilot your instruments, and then just discard the data from your sample.
2. *Volunteer sampling* – You advertise for a sample, for example in a newsgroup or on a bulletin board at school. This pretty much violates all the random sampling rules – researchers have found people who volunteer to be different from the general population. Anyone who watches shows such as *Oprah* or *Tricia*, or reality TV, can vouch for that!
3. *Snowball sampling* – Your sample evolves from a small sample, often a convenience sample, to take in contacts known to or suggested by your original respondents. This is often an effective way to study a social network or otherwise invisibly connected group. Again, you may have problems with drawing conclusions beyond your sample.
4. *Quota sampling* – You choose the characteristics you want your sample to have, and then sample until you have enough representatives of each category. This is not a random or systematic sample, because each unit does not have an equal chance of being selected. However, a quota sample can provide a good approximation to a probability sample. Quota sampling is often used to make sure that you have equal representation of male and female respondents, or respondents by age. If you need, for example, to interview 50 men and 50 women, you

would stop interviewing men after you had reached 50, even if you only had 40 women at that point. Quota sampling is often associated with research that attempts to represent a large population, for example opinion polling for election research.

Each of these techniques lacks one or more characteristic of probability samples that would let us make some general conclusions about the population from the sample. You should be wary of generalising if you use one of these techniques. On the other hand, these can be useful ways to sample when your main goal is not generalisation: you might be sampling for the purposes of qualitative research. Researchers who take a qualitative approach are not interested in how well the sample represents the population, but the lessons learnt from the sample (O'Leary 2004). They describe their samples as theoretical or purposive rather than nonrandom to make this clear.

Sampling error

Using probability sampling allows you to draw conclusions about your population from your sample. The difference between the sample you select and the population you take it from is known as **sampling error**. Sampling error is a threat to generalisability. If you have an accurate sampling frame and you use probability sampling correctly, it is less likely that you will over- or undersample certain members of your population. However, you may still end up with sample error if you cannot contact all the social units you have selected or if some of these refuse to participate. This sampling error is due to **nonresponse**. Selective or systematic nonresponse may skew your sample away from your design, because your findings will be biased towards your respondents and away from your nonrespondents. Even if there is no sampling error, a low response rate can create both practical and theoretical problems for your survey research, as we discuss below.

Response rate

Response rate creates a big headache for students and their supervisors. Students often underestimate how many surveys they will need to administer in order to get a specific number back. (We will describe sample size separately below.) Most surveys are lucky to achieve a 10–15 per cent return rate. Even legally required surveys such as the National Census don't achieve a 100 per cent return rate: you may need to send out 20 or even 100 questionnaires by post in order to get a single survey back. If possible, look at the survey response rates reported in the articles in your literature review. To estimate how many questionnaires you need to send out, divide the number of responses you want by your most likely response rate. So, if you need 100 responses and you estimate your response rate is 10 per cent, you will need to send out 1000 surveys. For interviews, divide the number of interviews you want by the likely conversion rate of contacts to interviews.

As well as reflecting people's dislike of filling out forms or lack of time, a low response rate can suggest problems with your study. This is where good survey design can make a difference. If you plan to use a questionnaire, make sure that it is short and clear, and that you have given people a good reason to fill it out and return it. If there are any serious problems with your survey, then pilot testing, follow-up and multiple-wave survey designs can identify the most serious problems and improve your response rate.

Sample size

'What sample size do I need?' is one question that project supervisors are repeatedly asked. The simple calculations often reported in methods books only apply to some types of surveys such as public opinion polls, where you want to draw relatively simple conclusions about your population, you do not need to investigate differences between subgroups and you only want to know the answer to each question in isolation. You can look up sample sizes on charts or calculate them. The calculation depends only on how confident you want to be that your conclusions accurately represent your sample, and what percentage of the population is likely to give each response to your question. In this case, as Bryman and Bell (2003: 101) point out, the *absolute* size of your sample is more important than the *relative* size. This is due to the statistical properties of sampling – the sample size you need does not increase proportionally with the size of the population you are studying.

In business and management we are seldom interested in questions that are as simple as those posed in opinion or electoral polls, so calculating sample size is rarely straightforward. To estimate the sample size you need, you will need to know not only details of your population and the variables you want to study, but also the precise statistical tests you will use to analyse your data and the confidence level you want to achieve. (We will discuss this further in **Chapters 10** and **11**.) In general, you will need a larger sample size when:

1. you plan to use sophisticated statistical methods
2. you plan to test the relationships between two or more variables
3. your variables can take on more values
4. your data do not follow a normal distribution
5. you are investigating weaker relationships among your variables.

The best advice is to get as large a sample as you can within your time and cost constraints. If calculating sample size is essential to the success of your project, you should probably consult an experienced statistician.

An experienced statistician can also give you useful advice on choosing statistical tests to suit the sample size that you can reasonable obtain. Some statistical analyses cannot be conducted except on very large data sets, whilst some statistical tests can be conducted on very small numbers of responses. As the administrative scientist James March and his colleagues observed, a sample size of one is sufficient, if it's the right one! (March et al. 1991). Sample size is a consideration, as shown in **Student research in action 5.3**.

> **Student research in action 5.3**
>
> **BACK ON THE CHAIN GANG**
>
> Rob and his project group wanted to show that the more hours per week a full-time student worked in paid employment, the less likely they were to get a good degree. They decided to survey past students to see whether the number of hours that students worked in paid employment affected their final degree classification. So, how many questionnaires to send out? First, Rob and his group needed to think about the likely response rate to their survey: some students might have moved, some might not reply.
>
> Second, the way Rob and his group defined student work in their hypothesis was likely to have a big effect on the number of cases they needed to collect:
>
> - Students who worked versus students who didn't work
> - Students who worked more than eight hours per week
> - The number of hours worked
> - The definition and distribution of 'good degrees' in the programme, for example, if only 5 per cent of students received a first, versus 20 per cent received a first. On the other hand, if the group defined a 2.1 or above as a good degree and 95 per cent of the class achieved that level, it would be difficult to show that work accounted for the other 5 per cent.

5.3 Designs for experiments

The final research design that we will discuss in this chapter is the experiment. An **experiment** is a structured process for testing how varying one or more inputs affects one or more outcomes. Many people forget to include the experiment as a research design for business and management research, because it is associated in the popular imagination with the natural and applied sciences. However, you are probably already familiar with experiments from everyday life, even if they go under names such as 'taste test' or 'trial offer'.

5.3.1 Principles of experimental design

An experiment may be your best choice if you want to test hypotheses that concern cause-and-effect relationships. You are interested in such a relationship when a hypothesis states a relationship between two or more concepts, and you propose that at least one concept is an **independent variable** (cause or input) and one concept is a **dependent variable** (effect or outcome). To be able to test this, you must also be able to measure and vary the independent variable, and measure the change in the dependent variable, as well as measuring any other variables that might explain the change in the dependent variable (alternate explanation).

This is one of the major drawbacks of using the experimental design for studying complex business and management situations. In **Chapter 5**, we used the scientist conducting laboratory experiments (perhaps on white mice) as the exemplar of the scientific approach to business and management research. An experiment is often carried out on a limited part of the phenomenon or context that is being studied.

Researchers in natural science and engineering fields are often able to study the systems they are interested in studying in controlled settings such as laboratories, and keep most of the aspects of the system and the environment constant whilst varying only one factor at a time. Researchers may study natural or physical systems by breaking them down into smaller systems or parts that can be studied in isolation from the whole system (reductionism). They can study how a car engine works without having to study the entire automobile, or how an artificial hip joint works, without having to study the entire human body.

On the other hand, people who take the ethnographic approach as their model for doing research often regard the experiment as an inappropriate design for studying complex organisations and human behaviours. They argue that the social units and systems that we research in business and management are difficult to reduce to a simple enough system to study in a laboratory. This doesn't mean that experiments are not used in business and management, just that business and management research (with the exception of some subjects) seldom applies the experimental method in the same way and with the same rigour as the natural sciences.

You should be wary of concluding that the experiment is completely out for business and management research. It *is* possible to carry out an experiment by varying one or more aspects of a situation and observing the effect on some outcome, such as sales or customer satisfaction, as shown in **Student research in action 5.4**. In fact, much of what we know about business and management has been learnt from field experiments, starting with Taylor's scientific management experiments and the Hawthorne experiments. You may even have unwittingly participated in quite a few business and management experiments. Fast-food companies often test out new sandwiches in just a few locations before offering them nationwide – the fast-food company McDonald's even has a mock-up of an entire McDonald's restaurant on the campus of McDonald's University, where new menus and new processes can be tried out before they go public (Bradach 1997). Heinz has tried out different colours of ketchup around the world, to see whether total ketchup sales will increase (BBC News 11 July 2000).

Student research in action 5.4

ONE FROM COLUMN A, ONE FROM COLUMN B

Xin decided that he wanted to test David Maister's eight principles for managing service queues in his MSc dissertation.

Xin decided that his summer job in a Chinese restaurant would be a good place to test these principles with real customers. One of Maister's predictions is that 'unexplained waits seem longer than explained waits' (Maister 1993). In order to test whether this was true, one evening he told some groups of customers who were waiting to be seated why they had to wait and told other groups nothing. At the end of the meal, each group of customers was asked to fill out a questionnaire rating their satisfaction with the meal. Xin expected that if Maister's principle were true, those groups who had been informed would be more satisfied with the meal – everything else being equal of course!

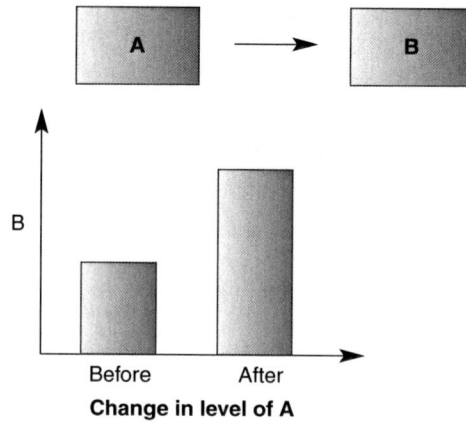

Figure 5.5 A simple experimental framework

It does mean, however, that the conclusions we can draw from an experiment in business and management research are not necessarily as strongly supported as in scientific research.

Cause-and-effect relationships

An experiment is the strongest method for showing a relationship between two or more concepts, especially if you want to show that a change in one causes a change in another – a **cause-and-effect relationship**. Because an experiment allows you to see what effect varying an independent variable has on the dependent variable, holding everything else constant, it is the strongest design for showing a cause-and-effect relationship between concepts.

As noted above, natural scientists are able to study a system in isolation from the environment and hold everything constant except for the one input or condition they are trying to vary. What you can vary is known as your **experimental treatment**. This means that you have more chance of ruling out the observed change in the dependent variable being due to a factor you have not controlled or observed, rather than the change in the independent variable. For example, a company wants to know why the pay-for-performance programme (A) that it implemented didn't result in higher employee performance (B). We might naively conclude that pay-for-performance didn't work, but if we also knew that the company had laid off a significant number of workers during the same period, we might instead decide that we need to include other things that are going on.

In business and management research, you need to rule out the possibility that your observed outcome B isn't due to the other factor (C) that you have not identified. You need to identify any other factor (C) or factors that could affect the outcome, the relationship or offer an alternative explanation. These factors might include any other potential causes of changes in the results, difference in the people or organisations being observed or even our own expectations about what the outcome of the experiment should be.

The most important step in experimental design is the step where you are deducing your hypothesis or hypotheses from your theory. If you do not identify all the

QUANTITATIVE RESEARCH DESIGNS

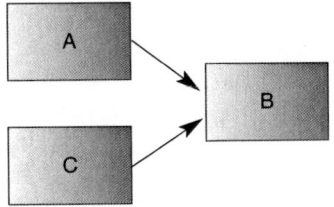

Figure 5.6 Alternate causes

alternate causes and measure or control them, your experiment will be pointless. Being able to identify at least one independent variable and one dependent variable is an important aspect of the experimental design, and one that makes it different from secondary analysis and surveys, where we may only study relationships between variables.

An experiment is the best research design if you want to rule out the possibility that any other factors have affected the relationship between the two (or more) factors that you are looking at. If you can systematically examine the relationship between varying your input factor and changes in the output factor you are observing, and you consistently find changes in the outcome, it is easier to propose that changes in A lead to changes in B.

Ruling out alternate explanations for the relationships between two or more concepts is always difficult, especially when you are doing research with people or organisations rather than natural systems. In scientific research, being able to study a small part of a system in a controlled setting such as a laboratory makes it much easier to do this. In business and management, however, when you start considering what else might be going on in what you are studying, the picture almost always becomes more complex.

If you do find that C (or D and so on) has an effect on B or the relationship between A and B, you may need to revise your model or even your theory. You might need to come up with an alternate hypothesis for the role of C. First, A might not really have any effect on B and a variation in the level of C might be causing the change in B rather than A. Second, although A might have an effect, the effect of C might overwhelm or cancel out the effect of A. Alternatively, A and C might both affect B, but it might be difficult to disentangle their relative effects, especially if A and C always occur together.

It is difficult in many cases to show cause and effect, because for one factor to cause another, the factor that we argue is the cause must precede the result in time, consistently. If you can eliminate as many other factors as possible – which we will discuss in more detail below – you can be even more confident that you have found a cause-and-effect relationship. But this is not the same as proving that A causes B. What if it is impossible to show that the variation in A happens before the variation in B? In real life, this is difficult, so usually we can only make statements about associations, or correlations, which are much weaker than statements about cause and effect.

Experimental treatment and control

Scientists have developed a structured approach to ruling out as many alternate causes or explanations as they can in an experiment. This relies on a design that enables you to hold constant those factors you want to rule out as causing the changes in the output variable so that you can maximise your certainty that the changes are due to varying your input. In experimental language, this is known as **control**. Control is essential for examining cause-and-effect relationships. There are four types of variables that you will need to measure and/or control in an experiment:

1. *Experimental variables* are the inputs you intend to vary to see the effects on outcomes, for example varying the drink (water or Red Bull) as the input to see the effects on test performance
2. *Dependent variables* are the outcomes that you predict will vary in response to changes in the experimental variables
3. *Controlled variables* are any elements of the experiment that you will try to eliminate as potential causes of the variation in outcomes by excluding them from the experiment, holding them constant during the experiment or by randomising some element of the experiment
4. *Uncontrolled variables* are variables you do not know about or are unable to control, which might lead you to make mistakes about concluding there is (or isn't) a cause-and-effect relationship.

Developing your conceptual framework thus becomes crucial for the experimenter because you must be able to identify and specify not only all the variables you want to manipulate and observe, but also any other ones that might affect your experiment.

If you are considering using an experiment, you should already realise that it is difficult to control any systems except simple systems, or any human behaviours except basic or readily observable behaviours. You might also be able to observe the behaviour and interactions of two people (a dyad). Large groups, or complex systems, such as organisations, are extremely difficult to manage in an experiment, although it has been done. This means that true (that is, scientific) experiments are difficult to conduct in business and management, and hence rare. On the other hand, business and management research often draws successfully on experiments done in other areas such as social psychology, in drawing up conceptual frameworks and explaining what is observed in organisations.

Control group

Since we can never be sure that we have eliminated or controlled all other alternate causes besides our independent variable, we need to make sure that the change in our dependent variable wouldn't have happened anyway. The second principle of experimental design is the control group. The term **control group** is often used to describe the group that gets no experimental treatment. If we have two groups – one a control group and one a treatment group – we will be more convinced that our independent variable has created our change in our dependent variable if it only happens to the treatment group and not to the control group.

As you can see in **Figure 5.7**, the control group has stayed the same despite the experimental treatment (change in the independent variable A), whilst the treatment group has changed. Thus, we are more confident that our experimental treatment has caused the change in the dependent variable.

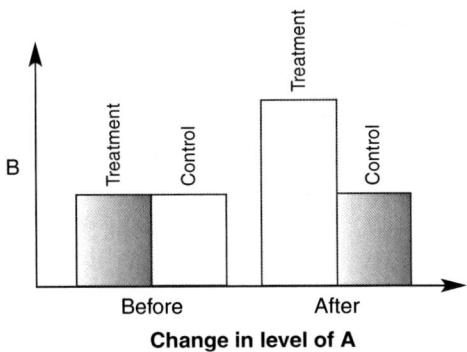

Figure 5.7 Treatment versus control group

Random assignment

Can you really be certain that the experimental treatment has caused the change in the dependent variable, even if you have a control group? Perhaps the two groups would have changed anyway, whether the experimental treatment was applied or not. You need to make sure that there were differences between the treatment and the sample groups that could have caused the change independently of the experimental treatment. This can only be ruled out if you have randomly assigned the experimental participants to the two groups (which you can check by comparing characteristics of the two groups).

Random assignment is the third principle of experimental design, and one that is often violated in business and management experiments. Since people and organisations usually vary significantly one from another, unlike laboratory rats, **random assignment** helps to rule out any variations due to differences between the people or organisations assigned to different levels of your experimental treatment. Random assignment helps you to ensure that differences in your experimental outcomes (dependent variables) aren't due to pre-existing or systemic differences between the people in your groups. We discussed the importance of sampling in **Section 5.2**. Probability sampling is used in the survey design to apply the logic of random assignment.

Statistical analysis

Although it is not a principle of experimental design, you want to make sure that the change you have observed in the dependent variable has actually occurred, and any difference before and after the treatment is not measurement error or natural fluctuations. Ideally, you should design your experiment so that your experimental data provide the strongest empirical evidence (that is, statistical analysis of data) to support (or overturn) this hypothesis. Control, including random assignment, makes the experiments the best method to test an **experimental hypothesis** – what you predicted would happen *before* you conducted the experiment.

You should use statistical tests to make sure that you are not arguing for a cause-and-effect relationship based on a systematic association where this relationship is actually due to change. This is one area where journalism and consulting often fail to measure up to research.

Research shows that people are not very good at actually interpreting results accurately, and without statistical tests they often reach the wrong conclusions. Knowing how to design a statistical test and which statistical test you can use is important to being able to correctly interpret the results of an experiment. However, statistical probability and common sense don't always coincide. This could lead to concluding that there is no relationship when one exists, or that there is a relationship when one doesn't exist. People often overestimate or underestimate the probability that certain events will occur, or the probability that the distribution of events that have occurred differs significantly from randomness, as shown in the activity below.

> **Activity 4**
>
> If you flip a coin 20 times, you expect on average to get 10 heads and 10 tails, if it is a fair coin. If you get 12 heads and 8 tails, you might not be too surprised. If you get 1 head and 19 tails, though, you would probably begin to expect that you might not have an average coin or your flipping technique might be suspect.
>
> Suppose we asked you to mentally flip a penny 10 times and record the number of times it comes up heads and the number of times it comes up tails. How many times would you expect it to come up with no heads or no tails in 10 tosses? 1 or fewer? 2 or fewer? Record your answers in the table below.
>
> | | 0 | 1 | 2 |
> |---|---|---|---|
> | Heads or Tails | | | |
>
> Suppose you did flip the penny ten times and it came up with zero, one or two heads or tails. Would you think that the coin was dodgy? We flipped a simulated penny 10 times, for 100 trials. The exact distribution is shown in the Postscript at the end of this chapter.
>
> If you thought that it was unlikely that a fair penny would come up heads or tails 0 times, then you are right – this might happen by chance once in less than 1000 times, and it never occurred in our simulated 1000 trials. Coming up with one head or tail is also unlikely – this might happen as often as 1 in 100 times. Once we get to two heads or two tails, this might occur 1 in 10 times. This is well above the level of 1 in 20 times that is the accepted level for statistical testing.

What you are investigating in an experiment may be much more subtle than flipping a coin. This means that you need to be careful so that you do not draw the wrong conclusions from an experiment (or indeed any other relationship). **Chapters 10** and **11** will help you identify some useful statistical tests.

5.3.2 Types of experiments

Although you might think of the stereotypical scientist conducting experiments in a laboratory an experiment doesn't necessarily have to take place there. Researchers classify experiments as **true experiments** if all the principles of experimental design – experimental treatment, random assignment, control groups, before-and-after measurement – are met. If one or more of these are lacking, but the general design is experimental, these research studies are known as **quasi-experiments**.

Researchers also classify experiments according to the relationship between the experiment's setting and the natural setting of the system or phenomenon being studied. Experiments can take place in any kind of setting, but the amount of control you will have over variables and random assignment will differ.

Laboratory experiments

In a **laboratory experiment**, you are conducting your experiment in an artificial setting, not the natural setting where participants would normally be found. In natural and behavioural sciences, this setting is usually literally a laboratory, as in Stanley Milgram's experiment on people's obedience to authority, described in **Chapter 1**. However, laboratory settings for business and management research can include settings such as classrooms. Many business and management experiments take place in classrooms, for the convenience of the experimenter and the participants, even though classrooms (and students) are not necessarily identical to organisations (and managers). Other artificial settings for experiments include reality television shows such as *Big Brother* or *Fame Academy* where participants are isolated from the world.

The laboratory experiment gives you the most control over your participants, your experimental treatment and the experimental setting. In areas such as medicine, science, engineering or psychology, this setting might well be a laboratory, but it can be any setting where you have a high degree of control. A formal laboratory setting lets you maximise your control over the experimental setting, the experimental treatment and the assignment of your participants to a particular treatment or control group. An extreme example of a laboratory experiment is a computer simulation, where the experimenter can control all aspects of the experiment, and variation in the outcome results from the application of statistical variations (for example Monte Carlo simulation) and rules for the behaviour of the system that is being simulated.

Even in a laboratory setting, there may be factors that you are not testing but you can't control. These variations might be systemic, recurring in some fashion, or they might be extraneous, nonrecurring. If you conduct an experiment where your outcome variable is participant performance, the room temperature might be higher in the afternoon sessions than in the morning sessions, and the heat might negatively affect your afternoon participants' performance by putting them to sleep. This would be a systemic variation. On the other hand, the noise caused by drilling outside the room might be a one-off and hence extraneous, even though it might still affect the participants.

Laboratory experiments are often criticised as unrepresentative of what actually goes on in organisations. The laboratory setting can be artificial and simplified compared with organisations. The treatment may not closely represent people's actual tasks in organisational settings. The experimental participants themselves are often undergraduates, or business/management students, rather than representing typical organisational populations. All this means that laboratory settings are most appropriate when you are investigating basic aspects of how people behave, independently of the setting, rather than complex social and organisational phenomena.

Field experiments

An experiment that takes place in its natural setting is called a **field experiment**. Xin's Chinese restaurant experiment in **Student research in action 5.4** was a field experiment; so were F.W. Taylor's experiments in work methods. Natural settings for business and management experiments include the workplace (office, shop, factory), the classroom, the household and public spaces such as shopping malls or public streets. Although field experiments minimise the artificiality of the experimental setting on what you are studying, you may have less control over your participants, experimental treatment and other factors than in a laboratory experiment.

Laboratory experiments are high in control, but low in realism. In a field experiment, you trade off some control for a more realistic setting. A field setting might be a classroom, a shopping mall, or even a public space such as public transport – the setting in **Research in action 5.7** is a summer camp. However, you typically can exert only a moderate degree of control over the people, conditions and/or environment.

> ### Research in action 5.7
> #### STOP, THIEF!
>
> Sherif (1956) and Tajfel (1970) both tested whether 'simply being a member of a group was enough to cause people to discriminate against members of another group'. Sherif set up an experiment known as the 'Robber's Cave' in a summer camp, where he allocated boys randomly to different groups and got them to compete on different tasks. Even when the boys in different groups had previously been friends, the rivalries grew so intense that the experiment had to be modified!
>
> Similarly, Tajfel found that when boys were allowed to allocate rewards, they discriminated against members of the other group (the outgroup) in favour of their own group (the ingroup). The ingroup–outgroup hypothesis has been widely used in social psychology and organisational behaviour to explain and predict people's behaviours.

Even if you study people in natural settings, experiments can have surprisingly misleading effects on their behaviours and our interpretation of research findings. Soft drink giant Coca-Cola found this out the hard way in the 1980s when it replaced Coke with New Coke, whose taste customers had preferred in market research blind taste tests. People refused to buy New Coke in the supermarkets, and an embarrassed Coca-Cola was forced to bring back Classic Coke (the original, less-preferred recipe) at enormous expense.

Quasi-experiments

A quasi-experiment is not a true experiment but is a naturally occurring situation that you are taking advantage of as a researcher. You can only observe what is going on directly or indirectly but not manipulate it. You have little control over your participants, the experimental treatment or other experimental conditions. You might be interested in a quasi-experiment because you can analyse the data using the same logic as a true experiment. **Research in action 5.8** illustrates how useful a quasi-experiment can be for a researcher.

> *Research in action 5.8*
> **STRIKE THREE, YER OUT!**
>
> Stanford doctoral student Alan Meyer (1982) developed an ingenious quasi-experiment as part of his dissertation research. In the middle of Meyer's research on hospital management, hospital anaesthesiologists in the San Francisco Bay area went on strike. Although this disrupted his data collection, he realised that the strike created 'before-and-after' conditions – in other words, an experimental treatment – and that he could collect additional data after the strike to complement the data he already had before the strike.

Many natural quasi-experiments let you collect useful data and apply the logic of experimental design. Suppose you are interested in studying the provision of online shopping by supermarkets, you should be able to identify which supermarkets have adopted online shopping, and which haven't, even though you have no influence over which ones do or don't. In this case, you will be observing a quasi-experiment. Your ability to support your hypothesis, though, will be weakened because you can neither randomly assign supermarkets to adopters and nonadopters, nor can you rule out as many systemic or extraneous sources of variation.

ACTIVITY 5

We described Xin's research study in **Student research in action 5.4** as an experiment. Do you think his study was closer to a true experiment or a quasi-experiment? How much control do you think he had over:
- Queuing time – long versus short wait to be seated
- Waiting time – long versus short wait to receive meal
- Number of people in party – couple to group
- Quality of meal.

5.3.3 Experimental design issues and ethical considerations

The principles of experimental design enable researchers to minimise the risk of mistaking a chance result or spurious cause for the cause-and-effect relationship you are interested in. Other issues might still cause your experiment to lose credibility. We discuss some of these below.

Minimising potential sources of bias

Although the principles of experimental design rule out some sources of error, you need to rule out other sources or error or bias when you are designing and conducting your experiment. Your experimental results will be more believable if you can show that you have minimised potential sources of bias. Social psychologists Rosnow and Rosenthal (1997) list the major sources of experimental bias as experimenter effects, and experimenter expectancies, as well as subject effects.

Experimenter effects are intentional or unintentional mistakes in how you collect, record, interpret or report your data and findings; or interactions between you and the experimental treatment, participants and/or setting, especially **experimenter expectancies** – your expectations about the outcomes of the experiment might influence your design of the experiment to increase the likelihood that that outcome actually occurs.

This isn't the same as deliberate fraud (which has been known to occur in scientific and other experiments). It is sometimes known as a 'self-fulfilling prophesy'. Educational experiments have shown that teachers are more encouraging towards students classified as 'bright', and less encouraging towards those designated 'not bright'. These 'bright' students were actually found to outperform the other students at the end of the year, even though there was no difference between the two groups at the beginning. This is similar to the experiment with 'bright' and 'dull' rats by Rosenthal and Fode (1963) described in Chapter 5.

Another source of experimental bias is **subject effects**, also known as demand characteristics. The **good subject effect** occurs when participants change their behaviours to help (or hinder) the experimenter, thus making the experimental results invalid because they do not represent how people usually behave. The **volunteer subject effect** occurs when people who volunteer to participate in studies differ from the general population, and again the experimental results may not represent how people in general (rather than experimental subjects) usually behave.

When other people assess the quality of your research, any experiment will be measured as to the extent you have designed your experiment to minimise – even if you can't rule out – these potential sources of bias. These biases are the major threats to the experimental design.

Ethical issues in experiments: consent

Many ethical issues have been identified for laboratory experiments, and now these experiments nearly always have to be approved by an ethics committee or board before they are allowed to proceed. One element you must absolutely consider in designing an experiment is any potential harm that might come to participants – even inadvertently – because of your experiment. Any experiment with human participants carries some risk of some temporary or permanent effect, so many institutions require approval to minimise the risk of harm. Field experiments pose many of the same issues, so they are often required to undergo the same approval process. Quasi-experiments may need to be approved, even if you are just observing a naturally occurring process, because of the risk that you might pose to confidentiality. If you are considering the use of an experiment of any kind, besides reading this section carefully, you may want to find out about your university's policy, and read Oliver's book *The Student's Guide to Research Ethics* (2003). You may also want to read **Chapter 9** in this book, where ethical issues are covered further.

In laboratory and field experiments, you are always manipulating some experimental treatment that may affect your participants. One way of minimising risk to

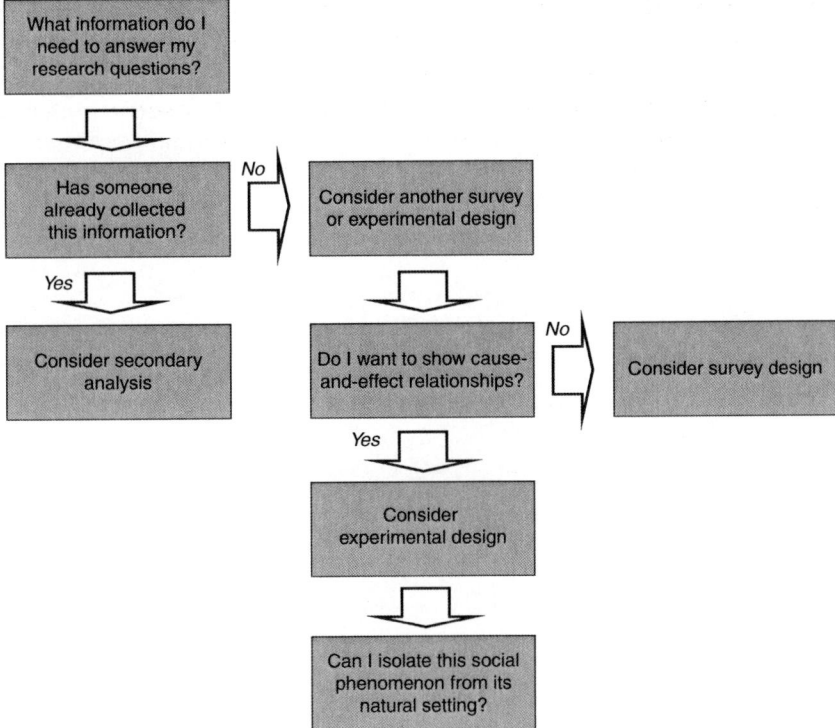

Figure 5.8 A decision tree for this chapter

your participants is by getting their **informed consent**. You will typically need to give your participants information about the experiment before they agree to participate, before you begin the experimental treatment and after the experiment. Especially when you are experimenting on individuals, you will need to give them enough information about the experiment's purpose and content so that they can give fully informed consent to participate. You should also brief your participants at the beginning of the experiment, and give them the opportunity to withdraw from the experiment if they have changed their minds. At the end of the experiment, you should debrief your participants about the experiment – always remember to thank them! – and give them a chance to give you feedback about the experiment.

Summary

In this chapter, we have considered three research designs that are often associated with the scientific approach to business and management research.

Section 5.1 introduced the secondary analysis of data as a research design. Secondary analysis can be used to analyse data that have already been collected, and sometimes analysed, by other people. The sources of this secondary data include archived surveys and proprietary databases. Secondary analysis can also be used to analyse data that you collect yourself from indirect sources, including documents and other artefacts or unobtrusive observation. Although nearly all research projects involve some secondary data, they are underused as a research design when the potential sources of high-quality data are considered.

Section 5.2 discussed a familiar research design, the survey, which includes interviews and questionnaires. Surveys can be used to gather information about a sample that can be generalised to the population from which it comes. Survey design needs care and experience, so you should first see whether there is an existing survey or question bank related to your research topic before you decide to design your own survey and questions. You should also think about the trade-off between the cost of information and the quality of information, especially with postal or online questionnaires.

Section 5.3 explained how you can use experiments to investigate cause-and-effect relationships. Laboratory experiments are seldom used in most areas of business and management, but field experiments and quasi-experiments are common designs. In designing experiments, you should try to minimise experimenter and participant effects, and be mindful of ethical issues that you may need to address before you do your experiment.

Answers to key questions

What methods for collecting data are associated with the scientific approach?

- A secondary analysis, a survey or an experimental research design for social measurement all provide ways to capture quantitative data

How can I design a research project that analyses documents or databases, conducts a survey or runs an experiment?

- By understanding the advantages and disadvantages of the methods presented in this chapter, I can choose between:
- Secondary analysis to analyse data that other researchers have already captured, to analyse data from documents and other artefacts produced for purposes other than research by individuals and organisations, or to capture information about distant or historical activities
- A survey to capture structured information about a sample by asking the same questions of all respondents in a face-to-face or other contact situation, or at a distance from the researcher
- An experiment such as a true experiment or a quasi-experiment in a natural setting – field experiments – or an artificial experiment – laboratory experiments

How can I use these methods as part of a qualitative research design strategy?

- These methods can be adapted to gather qualitative data
- These methods may be useful in case studies or mixed-method research

References

BBC News. 2000. Heinz to launch green ketchup, Tuesday 11 July.
Bradach, Jeffrey L. 1997. Using the plural form in the management of restaurant chains, *Administrative Science Quarterly*, **42**(2): 276–303.

Bryman, Alan and Bell, Emma. 2003. *Business Research Methods*. Oxford: Oxford University Press.

Carroll, Glenn R. and Swaminathan, Anand. 2000. Why the microbrewery movement? Organizational dynamics of resource partitioning in the US brewing industry *American Journal of Sociology*, **106**(3): 715–60.

Foddy William. 1993. *Constructing Questions for Interviews and Questionnaires: Theory and Practice in Social Research*. Cambridge: Cambridge University Press.

Gray David E. 2004. *Doing Research in the Real World*. London: Sage.

Lee, R.M. 2000. *Unobtrusive Methods in Social Research*. Maidenhead: Open University Press.

Maister, David H. 1984. *The Psychology of Waiting in Lines*. Boston: Harvard Business School.

March, James G., Sproull, Lee S. and Tamuz, Michal. 1991. Learning from samples of one or fewer, *Organization Science*, **2**(1): 58–70.

Oppenheimer, A.N. 1992. *Questionnaire Design, Interviewing, and Attitude Measurement*, New edn. London: Continuum.

O'Leary Zina. 2004. *The Essential Guide to Doing Research*. London: Sage.

Reilly Michael D. and Wallendorf, Melanie. 1987. A comparison of group differences in food consumption using household refuse, *Journal of Consumer Research*, **14**(2): 289–94.

Rosenthal, R. and Fode, K.L. 1963. The effect of experimenter bias on the performance of the albino rat, *Behavioural Science*, **8**: 183–9.

Rosnow, R.L. and Rosenthal, R. 1997. *People Studying People: Artifacts and Ethics in Behavioural Research*. New York: W.H. Freeman.

Saunders, Mark, Lewis, Phillip and Thornhill, Adrian. 2003. *Research Methods for Business Students*, 3rd edn. Harlow: Financial Times/Prentice Hall.

Sherif, M. 1956. Experiments in group conflict, *Scientific American*, 195: 54–8.

Stack, Steven and Gundlach, James. 1992. The effect of country music on suicide, *Social Forces*, **70**(5): 211–18.

Stack, Steven and Gundlach, Jim. 1994. Country music and suicide: A reply to Maguire and Snipes, *Social Forces*, **72**(4): 1245–8.

Stack, Steven and Gundlach, James. 1995. Country music and suicide – individual, indirect, and interaction effects: A reply to Snipes and Maguire, *Social Forces*, **74**(1): 331–5.

Tajfel, H. 1970. Experiments in intergroup discrimination, *Scientific American*, **223**: 96–102.

Underhill, Paco. 2000. *Why We Buy: The Science of Shopping*. Texere.

Voss, Christopher A., Roth, Aleda V., Rosenzweig, Eve D., Blackmon, Kate and Chase, Richard B. 2004. A tale of two countries: Conservatism, service quality, and feedback on customer satisfaction, *Journal of Service Research*, **6**(3): 212–40.

Wallendorf, Melanie and Nelson, Daniel. 1986. An archaeological examination of ethnic differences in body care rituals, *Psychology and Marketing*, **3**(4): 273–99.

Webb, E.J., Campbell, D.T., Schwartz, R.D. and Sechrest, L. 1966. *Unobtrusive Measures: Nonreactive Research in the Social Sciences*. Chicago: Rand McNally.

Zeithaml, Valarie A., Parasuraman, A. and Berry, Leonard L. 1990. *Delivering Quality Service: Balancing Customer Perceptions and Expectations*. New York: Free Press.

Additional resources

Aldridge, A. and Levine, K. 2001. *Surveying the Social World: Principles and Practice in Survey Research*. Maidenhead: Open University Press.

Bell, Judith and Opie, Clive. 2002. *Learning from Research: Getting More from Your Data*. Maindenhead: Open University Press.

Blaikie, Norman. 2000. *Designing Social Research*. Cambridge: Polity Press.

Boone, Christopher, Carroll, Glenn R. and van Witteloostuijn, Arjen. 2004. Size, differentiation and the performance of Dutch daily newspapers, *Industrial and Corporate Change*, **13**(1): 117–48.

Dobrev, Stanislav D., Tai-Young Kim and Carroll, Glenn R. 2003. Shifting Gears, Shifting Niches: Organizational Inertia and Change in the Evolution of the US Automobile Industry, 1885–1981, *Organization Science*, **14**(3): 264–82.

Easterby-Smith, Mark, Thorpe, Richard and Lowe, Andy. 2002. *Management Research: An Introduction*, 2nd edn. London: Sage.

Johnson, Roxanne T. 2000. In search of E.I. DuPont de Nemours and Company: the perils of archival research, *Accounting, Business and Financial History*, **10**(2).

Maguire, Edward R. and Snipes, Jeffrey B. 1994. Reassessing the link between country music and suicide, *Social Forces*, **72**(4): 1239–43.

Mauk, Gary W. and Taylor, Matthew J. 1994. Comments on Stack and Gundlach's 'The Effect of Country Music on Suicide: An Achy Breaky Heart' ..., *Social Forces*, **72**(4): 1249–55.

McKendrick, David G. and Carroll, Glenn R. 2001. On the genesis of organizational forms: Evidence from the market for disk arrays, *Organization Science*, **12**(6): 661–82.

Meyer, Alan D. 1982. Adapting to environmental jolts, *Administrative Science Quarterly*, **27**(4): 515–37.

Oliver, Paul. 2003. *The Student's Guide to Research Ethics*. Maidenhead: Open University Press.

Parry, Vivienne. 2004. The panic button, *Guardian*, 29 June, G2: 16.

Snipes, Jeffrey B. and Maguire, Edward R. 1995. Country music, suicide, and spurious-ness, *Social Forces*, **74**(1): 327–9.

Webb, E. and Weick, K.E. 1979. Unobtrusive measures in organisational theory: A reminder. *Administrative Science Quarterly*, **24**(4): 650–9.

Key terms

ad hoc surveys, 103
archival research, 107
archive, 101
archives, 107
biased, 125
cause-and-effect relationship, 132
censuses, 103
closed-ended question, 120
company-specific databases, 106
computer-assisted protocols for interviews, 114
control group, 134
control, 134
data archives, 103
data set, 101
database, 101
dependent variable, 130
desk/library research, 101
experiment, 130
experimental hypothesis, 135
experimental treatment, 132
experimenter effects, 140

experimenter expectancies, 140
field experiment, 138
found data, 110
good subject effect, 140
independent variable, 130
informed consent, 141
interview schedule, 114
interview, 113
laboratory experiment, 137
market research reports, 106
nonprobability sampling, 125
nonresponse, 128
open-ended question, 121
population, 125
primary data, 102
probability sampling, 125
prompts, 115
proprietary databases, 106
quasi-experiments, 137
questionnaires, 112
random assignment, 135
repeated surveys, 103

sample, 124
sampling error, 128
sampling frame, 125
secondary analysis, 100
secondary data, 103
self-administered questionnaire, 115
socially desirable, 110
spam, 116
structured content analysis, 109
structured interviews, 112
structured observations, 112
subject effects, 140
survey, 112
survey data, 103
trade associations, 107
true experiments, 137
unobtrusive measures, 110
volunteer subject effect, 140

Discussion questions

1. What research designs are associated with the quantitative approach?
2. What is secondary analysis?
3. How can I use secondary data to answer my research questions?
4. What are the main advantages and disadvantages of secondary analysis?
5. Does secondary analysis always mean quantitative data and hypothesis-testing?

6. What reliability and validity issues does secondary analysis present?
7. From a research methods point of view, what might be wrong with the statement, 'I haven't decided what to look at yet, but I will be using a questionnaire'?
8. What are good practices in setting up a survey?
9. How do laboratory experiments, field experiments and quasi-experiments differ?
10. Sherif's experiment (**Research in action 5.7**) was set in a summer camp – literally a field experiment. Although he could control the random assignment of boys to groups, and the boys competed on similar tasks in a similar environment, Sherif couldn't control the boys' interactions with other campers, the weather and so on. What do you think would have been different if the experiment had taken place in a laboratory setting (for example, choosing the group from students in a classroom)?

Workshop

This workshop will give students practice in gathering data using a scientific approach.

Background

Capacity is often a problem for frontline service operations because demand tends to be higher in certain parts of the data and lower in others. For example, a coffee shop, cafeteria, restaurant or other food service facility will probably experience peaks and troughs of demand during the day. The operation needs to collect information on these variations in demand so that it can set service levels and decide how many service operatives it needs to deploy at a given time.

Task

Form into teams of no more than three people. Each team should pick a food service facility to observe and set aside several hours to complete the activity.

1. Decide how you would collect data to determine the number of customers arriving at the facility, how long each customer had to wait before being served, and any other information that you think would be relevant.
2. Decide how you would record and analyse these data.
3. Collect these data. (It is a good idea for each team member to collect data independently for at least part of this exercise, so that you can see how accurately people can collect data.)
4. Analyse the data and present the results to your instructor.
5. Hold on to these data for the workshops at the end of **Chapters 11** and **12**.

Postscript to Activity 4

Heads	0	1	2	3	4	5	6	7	8	9	10
	0	9	45	131	187	244	223	97	51	13	0

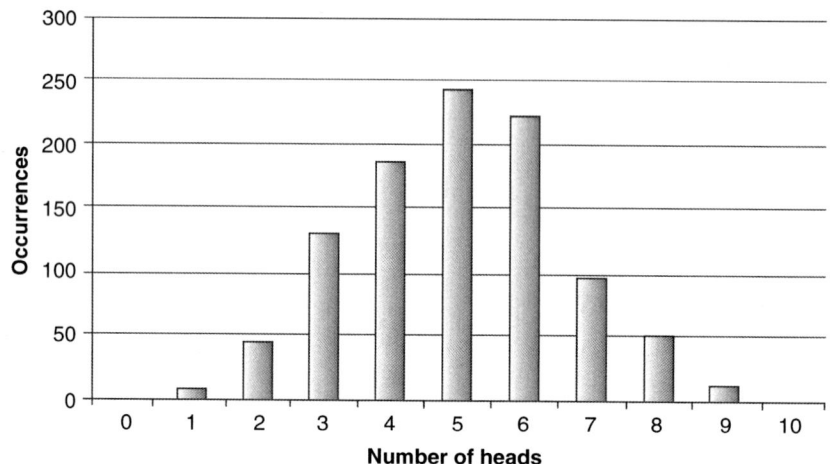

CHAPTER 6
Designing qualitative research
Using ethnographic methods for uncovering social meaning

KEY QUESTIONS

- What research designs can I use to collect data to uncover social meaning?
- How can I use remote data collection, observation, interviews or participant observation?
- How can I use these designs as part of a scientific research approach?

LEARNING OUTCOMES

At the end of this chapter, you should be able to:
- Decide whether an ethnographic approach is appropriate for your research
- Choose between designs for indirect data collection, nonparticipant observation, unstructured interviews and participant observation
- Evaluate the relative practical challenges associated with each method, and how these might affect your study

CONTENTS

Introduction
6.1 Indirect data collection
6.2 Nonparticipant observation
6.3 Unstructured interview/discussion
6.4 Participant observation
Summary
Answers to key questions
References
Additional resources
Key terms
Discussion questions
Workshop

Introduction

> Words are merely utterances: *noises* that stand for feelings, thoughts and experience. They are symbols. Signs. Insignias. They are not Truth. They are not the real thing. Words may help you understand something. Experience allows you to *know*. Yet there are some things that you cannot experience. So I have given you other tools of knowing. And these are called *feelings*. And so too thoughts.
>
> (**Walsch** 1995: 4)

In **Chapter 5**, we introduced the ethnographer as the second role model for business and management researchers. Many interesting research studies in business and management research use qualitative research designs and methods as part of an ethnographic approach to studying people and organisations. Even in areas we usually think of as mostly quantitative, such as consumer marketing, taking this kind of approach can help us ask – and answer – some interesting questions about how and why people behave in certain ways. For example, why do people take up extreme sports such as skydiving? What explains the revival of motorcycling among middle-aged accountants and other professionals – the born-again bikers known as 'bambis'? Why do secretaries gossip? Does the chatting that goes on during surgical operations help to prevent medical errors (such as leaving instruments inside patients) or contribute to them? Is accounting really as objective as we are led to believe? These kinds of questions occur in many business and management settings.

If your research questions ask 'how?' or 'why?' rather than 'what?', you should consider taking an ethnographic approach, which means that you should consider using one of the qualitative research designs presented in this chapter to gather your data. You can choose from many different qualitative methods that people have used effectively, all justified and supported by guidelines practical tips and tricks. Qualitative methods and data require different skills than do the quantitative methods and data discussed in **Chapter 6**.

If you decide to use a qualitative design after reading this chapter, make sure you read **Chapter 12** on analysing qualitative data before you start collecting data. It is vital that you collect your data with how you will analyse it in mind. You should also be aware of some issues that commonly arise in doing qualitative research.

How qualitative designs differ from quantitative designs

Before we look at qualitative methods in detail, we should revisit the root of this approach. In qualitative research, your research questions will focus on increasing your understanding of a particular issue – and will be 'why?' or 'how?' questions. Although you can also use quantitative research designs to answer 'how' and 'why' questions, they are usually different kinds of how and why questions.

Qualitative methods are important because research in business and management deals not only with organisations but also with the people in them. As the opening passage in this chapter indicates, people can ascribe meanings, thoughts and feelings to the situation in which they find themselves. Organisations are both social systems and the setting for social behaviour. Since people construct and maintain social systems, research on them is different from research on the physical objects and systems that are studied in the natural sciences.

This situation is therefore multidimensional. Your research also has the potential to be far more personal. As we shall see, you can bring in your own views of the world, and make a feature of your interpretation. Such interpretation would not be appropriate in quantitative research designs, especially research where the researcher is presumed to be objective and uninvolved (see **Chapter 5**).

One final word. Many students find the tone of discussion in some qualitative methods texts aimed at more advanced researchers daunting. However, although many authors suggest that there is a degree of 'mystique' surrounding qualitative research, which may put off new researchers, don't let 'dictionary overload' put you off. Qualitative research is actually much more straightforward than you might think. Boiled down to its essentials, qualitative data-gathering is built on skills that we already possess: reading, asking questions, talking to people, participating in everyday activities and observing what is going on around us. Remember from **Chapter 5** that qualitative research draws on the skills of the ethnographic researcher.

Designs for qualitative research

Although there many different tools and techniques you can use as part of a qualitative research design, in this chapter we will concentrate on the main ones you might use for your project. As with quantitative research, you can be creative in your research design. You can combine different qualitative methods, and even combine quantitative and qualitative methods. Indeed, this can be highly desirable, since you can investigate your research problem from multiple perspectives this way. In addition to suiting your research problem and questions, the particular technique you choose will also be influenced by the practical issues associated with each method.

Figure 6.1 arranges the main qualitative designs by how involved the researcher is with the subject of the investigation. At the left-hand end of the scale, there is little involvement. Remote data collection, as you will see, is close to the surveys, experiments and secondary research designs that we explored in **Chapter 6**. As your design moves to the right, you become part of whatever situation is being investigated – you will explore the issues through your personal experience. Participant observation, where you actually become part of the organisation or other context that is being explored, is the most different from quantitative designs. Below, we will discuss remote data collection, observation, interviews and discussion, and participation in turn.

6.1 Indirect data collection

In **Chapter 6**, we introduced the ethnographer as the role model for qualitative research designs. Like the ethnographer, in most qualitative research, you will be present to collect data directly from people or organisations. However, you may sometimes want or need to collect data when you can't be present for various reasons. Sometimes organisations will not give you access to the data you need for your project. Other times, you may need to investigate a particular issue through secondary data, especially if they are the only data available.

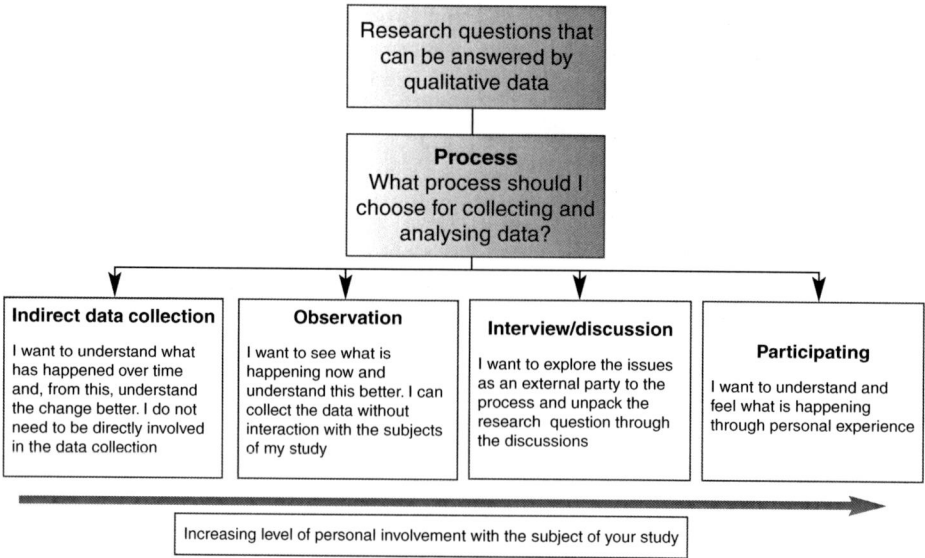

Figure 6.1 Qualitative research designs

To answer your research questions, you may be able to use **indirect data collection**, sometimes called **remote data collection**. Indirect data collection may be your only option if you are studying a historical phenomenon. This was the case for a student who was investigating the spending patterns of people in postwar Europe. He was not able to travel back in time to directly observe people's behaviour, so he had to rely instead on contemporary diary accounts.

This approach has many similarities with secondary analysis, which we presented in **Chapter 6**. However, our focus in that chapter was on data that were already in the form of numbers (for example official statistics or computer databases), whilst in this chapter the focus is on non-numeric data, including words, pictures, sounds and other qualitative data. You can start your data collection by asking the two questions: 'How should I collect the data?' and 'When should I collect the data?'

You can also use the techniques associated with **indirect observation**, discussed in **Chapter 6**, as a way to collect qualitative data. Such indirect data are useful, especially if you combine them with a complementary direct method. As we noted, archaeologists, forensic scientists and garbologists rely mostly on physical clues to our behaviour and may never talk to the people they are researching. They have a well-developed set of tools for compiling these kinds of data. An advantage of indirect observation is that these data are not affected by social pressures for people to give the 'right answers' (the socially desirable responding described in **Chapter 6**).

Finding out what people *really* think creates all sorts of challenges for researchers, as people do not always answer truthfully when questioned. In the UK general election of 1993, the pre-election polls predicted that the Conservative Party would be roundly defeated. They actually won the election by a comfortable margin. The people who had been polled felt under social pressure to say they would vote a particular way, influencing the answers they gave in public, but they actually cast their secret ballots for different candidates. These social pressures affect the responses given by participants in many areas of business and management research.

6.1.1 *How* should you collect the data?

Secondary sources such as publications or web pages can be a good source of qualitative data about individuals and/or organisations. Your challenge here is to identify potential sources of secondary data and gather data from them. You might find the techniques from **Chapter 4** for reviewing the literature, and from **Chapter 6** for secondary data analysis, appropriate for doing this. You might also collect data about individuals and/or organisations directly from their original source in real time, without being directly involved in capturing the data.

For example, suppose you were studying decision-making and in particular the history of a particular kind of decision. Because the decision-making process is usually both confidential and sensitive, you might have difficulty in getting 'real-time' access to observe a decision being made within an organisation. However, an organisation might agree to provide you with access to its archives, for example to see copies of reports and correspondence on past decisions, even if it did not allow you to be present. Company documents such as the minutes of meetings can provide valuable data, especially about the timing of issues and decisions. You could use these documents to track the organisation's decision processes by analysing the minutes from organisational meetings, as they contain the formal records of decisions and notes of the actions that need to be completed prior to the next meeting. (If you are considering doing a project based on this kind of documentary analysis, you should remember that you are relying on the documents providing a faithful record of the discussion, although in practice they may be incomplete as a source. If the minutes of the previous meeting have been confirmed as the first item on the agenda of the subsequent meeting, standard practice for many organisations, at least you have some confidence in their accuracy. Similar concerns apply to other organisational records.)

6.1.2 *When* should you collect the data?

If you are studying a research problem that occurs in 'real time' rather than in the past, ideally you will gather the data directly from organisations or participants immediately as events unfold, with an immediate 'up-link' to your research database. You should try to get your data regularly and quickly. In reality, you may have to keep encouraging (or even nagging) people to provide you with your data, and you may not get it until well after the events they report have happened. Any compromises will undoubtedly affect your data, as people's recollections become far more 'selective' after even a short lapse.

6.2 Nonparticipant observation

In indirect data collection, you will have little or no direct contact with the organisation or people that you are studying, and have only their words and other records to speak for them. In **nonparticipant observation** you will actually collect data directly by watching someone doing something, but you will still have little or no direct interaction with them. You might not even be physically present, as we discuss below. Nonparticipant observation may therefore be as simple as watching and noting how people behave under different circumstances, as in the coffee bar case in **Student research in action 6.1**.

> *Student research in action 6.1*
> **CENTRAL PERK – AND WAIT**
>
> For a coursework assignment, a student project group decided to investigate service quality in a local service operation. The group wanted to see how the varying workload caused by changes in customer demand over time affected a local coffee shop. In particular, they wanted to see how customers responded to the queues that built up at peak times and how staff responded.
>
> The students observed that first thing in the morning customers were able to get a seat easily once they had collected their coffee and cakes. Customers seemed happy to sit for a while in the café and enjoy the experience. As the day progressed, particularly at lunchtime, customers had to queue to get served and then were unable to get a seat. Not only was customer satisfaction dropping off, with customers becoming frustrated by trying to get seated whilst balancing their coffee and shopping bags, but the shop also was losing business to less-crowded neighbours.
>
> On several Saturdays, the students recorded how customers reacted to the different queue lengths during the day, including counting the number of people who walked in, looked around and then walked out again. They used this as a measure of the lost business that the shop could have captured, if only it had had the capacity. The study identified the likely 'tolerance' of potential customers to waiting, its cost and its effect on customer satisfaction. As a result, they were able to recommend how the coffee shop should change its layout and process for serving customers.

As well as observing people's behaviour and actions in person, some researchers are starting to take advantage of electronic technologies such as videotaping. If you have an opportunity to do this, you should think carefully about the ethical implications for your participants. If you have obtained permission to video participants as part of a research project, for example the discussion in a focus group, then it is certainly appropriate to use these recordings as a source of data for that particular research project.

It is usually OK to observe people in public settings such as streets or fast-food restaurants, and take notes, but recording them may raise ethical issues. Town planners and store designers frequently use videos as a research tool, for instance to see how people move (speed, direction or what causes them to change direction). You should always seek such permission from people you are observing if you can, especially if it might affect them, as **Student research in action 6.2** illustrates.

> **Student research in action 6.2**
> **HOW TO WIN FRIENDS AND INFLUENCE PEOPLE (NOT)**
>
> A student was undertaking a placement project at a large car factory. As part of his work, he was asked to investigate the practices associated with the assembly of a car door. Taking the initiative, he took his clipboard, stopwatch and white coat, and headed out to the factory floor. He then started observing the work of the people who were assembling the doors, noting the tasks they were doing and the times that each task took.
>
> When the union convenor saw the student and his stopwatch, he jumped to the conclusion that the student was retiming the jobs that people were doing on behalf of the organisation. This was a perennially sensitive issue, as the timing of a job determined an individual's rate of pay, and any retiming had to be pre-agreed with the unions. Since no such agreement was currently in force, the union ordered all work in the factory to stop. Needless to say, our student was not too popular with the factory management after that.

We recommend that you do *not* use **covert observation** in your project, that is, observing people using surveillance technology or in semi-private or private settings. Even though we are used to being observed – there appears to be CCTV on every street corner in many parts of the world, and there are even television shows that use such footage, which may give the impression that it is acceptable to observe anyone at anytime – this contravenes the ethical guidelines that we recommend for your projects, which we cover more completely in **Chapter 9**. You may need to consider other methods of obtaining such data if you need them for your research.

6.3 Unstructured interview/discussion

In indirect data collection and nonparticipant observation, you have very little direct contact with the people (and organisations) you are studying. A method that involves more contact is unstructured interviews and/or informal discussions. As noted, interviews are one of the most widely used methods in student projects, not least because they draw on familiar skills of finding out things by asking questions. You can use interviews to collect **non-standardised** data as well as the standardised data described in **Chapter 6**. You can make sure that your study maximises its benefits by carefully considering key issues such as:

- Should I interview individuals or groups?
- How should I choose my interview subjects?
- How should I structure the interview/discussion?
- What sort of questions should I use?
- Should the issues be structured or should I be *led by the data*?
- How should I record the interview data?

- How do I make sure that I avoid possible sources of bias in the interviewing process, both from myself and the interviewee(s)?

We will now discuss each of these in turn.

6.3.1 Should I interview people one by one or together?

The question here is whether you should carry out individual or group interviews. Each has a different purpose and will draw on different data collection and analysis techniques. If you are part of a group project, you should also decide whether you should carry out your interviews singly or in pairs. You will not be able to standardise your interviews as much as in the structured interviews discussed in **Chapter 6**, but you can multiply your efforts by splitting interviews between team members. In **Student research in action 6.3**, the five students in one group conducted ten interviews each, giving them fifty interviews in total to analyse. By carefully coordinating the questions they asked and checking the transcripts (see below), they were able to cover a much wider perspective than five researchers working alone. Although one-to-one interviews are fine, working with another interviewer can generate synergies between researchers, as shown in **Student research in action 6.3**.

Student research in action 6.3
BLAME THE PROJECT MANAGER

In a research project with a major airline to investigate a failed IT project, students were considerably younger than most of the people they were interviewing. Working together in pairs gave them extra confidence. An unexpected benefit was that it allowed their different perspectives on the issue to be brought out when they began to discuss their findings. One student thought, for instance, that the project manager was causing the problem they were investigating. The other argued firmly that it had resulted from cultural resistance within the company. By carrying out the interviews together and discussing the results, they were able to overcome their individual opinions and move closer to the truth.

Table 6.1 summarises some of the strengths and weakness of the various combinations of interviewers and interviewees.

6.3.2 How should I choose my interview subjects?

When you are deciding whom you will interview, you should consider the sampling issues discussed in **Chapter 6**. Quantitative research designs emphasised random sampling as a key to being able to generalise results based on statistics. For qualitative research design, instead of random sampling, you should try to select your sample so that it is represents the concepts, rather than the population, that you want to generalise your findings to. You may want to consider either **theoretical or purposive sampling**. Here, instead of choosing people to interview based on how well they represent the group you are studying, you will select them to create the

Table 6.1 A comparison of individual and group interviews

	Interviewee	
Interviewer	One	More than one
One	Most common type of interview, relatively easy to arrange. Susceptible to the biases of both parties. The most appropriate method for confidential or sensitive subjects	Group interview – such as a focus group. Can generate a large volume of data in a short time. Susceptible to biases and group dynamics. Can be difficult where there is a lack of true consensus in the group. Can be difficult for a new researcher to manage alone
More than one	A panel interview. Can be used to remove the biases of one of the interviewers, but can be intimidating for the interviewee if there is a power differential – unlikely with students as interviewers. Good for building the confidence of novice interviewers and to make sure that all relevant points are covered	Group discussions are used to look for some issues. Due to the limitations of the dynamics of both groups, less likely to be useful for in-depth explorations

maximum variety in their responses. However, given the practicalities of arranging interviews, many people use **convenience sampling**, that is, sampling those people to whom you have easy access.

If you can use theoretical/purposive sampling, your interviews will provide a range of views about the issue being researched, rather than define what any particular group thinks. This is not a drawback – remember that the standards by which you will assess the quality of qualitative research are different from quantitative research, which we will discuss further in **Chapters 10** and **12**.

You will need to manage access issues if you decide to gather data using interviews. Gaining physical access to your subjects – agreeing to meet or interview them by some other means – is important. This access needs to be arranged in advance. Ideally, you could decide exactly whom you will see and for how long. In most projects, you are using people's goodwill to gain you the interview, so you are at their mercy. You should tell people in advance what you expect to talk to them about, how long it will take and what they might hope to gain from it. It is often tempting to promise a full report to the organisation of your findings. The rule here is that you should always exceed your promises – a good compromise might be to agree to provide some up-to-date articles on what you are researching.

As well as physical access, getting your interviewees to agree to provide information is important. Having arranged all the logistics of the interviews, you will sometimes find that you will not be given full information. These two factors – physical access and incompleteness – will affect how many people you should plan to interview.

6.3.3 How should I structure the interview/discussion?

In a qualitative interview, you do not go in with an interview schedule with precisely worded questions in a strict order. Despite this unstructured format, this doesn't mean you will be going in without a plan or agenda. You might make use of the 7-I structure introduced below:

1. *Introduce* – state who you are, who you represent, your purpose in seeing that person or people and how long you will be (see note on time below). Reassure them about the confidentiality of the information you hope they will give you. Gain agreement to use any recording equipment you intend to use (see below).
2. *Icebreak* – start to establish rapport with the person or people you are interviewing. Don't forget that they might not have a clear idea why you want to talk to them. It is also worthwhile to start with some easy questions to get the ball rolling. Show an interest in what they are doing. Ensure that you appear relaxed about the discussion – people pick up on anxiety very easily.
3. *Increase the intensity of the questioning* – ask the questions either as prestructured or as the discussion leads (see following section).
4. *Intervene* – when a discussion goes off track, you may need to intervene. If you need to be focused because of time constraints, you should politely but firmly refer the person back to the original question. Some interviewees will have pre-prepared speeches of their own, and will 'play their tape' whether it answers your question or not. You might go with the flow for a short while, but when you absolutely must collect specific information and time is limited, simply letting someone ramble on about their favourite topic may be cathartic for them, but of limited use to you. A more extreme experience – but thankfully rare – is described in **Research in action 6.1**. You should think about how you might handle an awkward interviewee – perhaps to thank them graciously for their time and cut your losses and run.

> ### Research in action 6.1
> #### I'LL NEVER BE YOUR BEAST OF BURDEN
>
> Having arranged an interview with the research director of a large multinational company, I went excited about the good material I hoped the interview would yield for my doctoral work. The discussion started with the interviewee asking me about the research I was doing. That was OK, until he stated that this was, of course, 'missing the point'. He then proceeded to tell me what my research should have been about. His opinion was that whilst what I was asking about was interesting, it was all stuff that had been done ten years previously, and was already well documented. He then patted me on the head as I left and said that he hoped his contribution would be recognised in my thesis. Given that I was already established in this area, with a half-dozen books in print, I found this quite ironic. It could very well happen to you, so please don't feel so bad about it when it does!

5. *In conclusion* – wrap up the session at the end and thank the interviewee for their time. Check details such as how to get out of the building. Attempting an exit through the broom cupboard at this stage is going to blow any credibility you had with the interviewees!
6. *In case* – always request that you can get back to the person you have just spoken with to clarify any points. This is vital for when you start your analysis. You cannot

always cover everything you need to in one session, and there will be some areas that you will have missed altogether. Don't count on being able to follow up any missed material, though.
7. *Interpret your data* soon after the interview – many researchers do this in the car park before they leave or within a few hours of the event. Otherwise, it is easy to forget that critical point that you didn't note down, or be unable to interpret some ambiguous and cryptic notes you have made to yourself.

6.3.4 What sort of questions should I ask?

Chapter 6 provided examples of open-ended and closed-ended questions. You may want to start out with some closed-ended questions, where you provide your interviewee with a limited set of prescribed answers. For instance, you might start out a discussion on motivation by asking:

Q: Would you say that your motivation level was high, moderate, or low?

You could follow this up with an open-ended question to elicit more detail:

Q: Why was your level of motivation low at this point?

Open-ended questions are more exploratory in nature and can lead to many other questions that cannot always be determined in advance. You may also use them to clarify or probe an issue more deeply, such as

Q: Does your work environment determine your level of motivation?
Q: Would you say that there are any other external factors that affect your motivation?

There are some simple rules for asking questions. Start with easier, closed-ended questions – as suggested in Icebreak above. As you develop rapport with the person or people you are interviewing, seek confirmation or further discussion of key points. This should then lead to your most in-depth questions, but only after the people are comfortable with what you are doing. Even when you have interviewed that person before, start gently and allow the flow of information to be established.

A golden rule of interviewing is to respect the time of the people you are interviewing. More than once, after someone has told me repeatedly they are so busy they can only give me ten minutes, I have offered to close the meeting after ten minutes, only to be told that it is fine for me to continue. The important issue here is that if they say ten minutes, it is *your* responsibility to watch the clock. After that time, offer to go. It is rare that an interview that is going somewhere will be terminated, but your courtesy will be respected.

A final note is that the location is important. If the interview is in someone's office, which often happens when you are interviewing managers, any disruption can prove fatal to the process. A ringing telephone or other interruption can cause a break in the flow that makes it difficult to restart the interview afterwards. Where possible, try to arrange the interview in a neutral location where you are less likely to be interrupted.

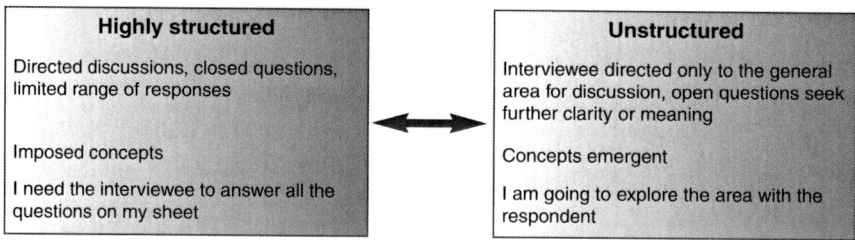

Figure 6.2 Structured versus unstructured interviews

Tip. Something that can totally ruin an interview is when *your* mobile phone goes off. Check before you go into the interview that your phone is turned off.

6.3.5 Should the issues be structured or should you *be led by the data*?

In structuring your interviews, beyond the type of questions you use, consider how you intend it to progress. The extremes of your choices are shown in **Figure 6.2**.

If you are asking exploratory research questions, you will probably find it more natural to use the unstructured approach, although an interview doesn't have to be entirely structured or unstructured. In an unstructured interview, you direct your interviewee to the general area you want to discuss, and then allow the issues to emerge from the conversation.

Getting this to happen is a specialised skill that you have to hone over time. If you reflect on the interview process as you go along by analysing your recordings or transcripts, this will greatly help you to improve. If you are planning to use unstructured interviews, it may be useful to look at Glaser and Strauss's (1967) text on grounded theory. We present a simplified version of grounded research in **Chapter 12**.

You should also consider some other issues in unstructured interviewing:

- *Don't* impose your own preconceptions or ideas by the language you use. In discussing the uncertainty caused by a merger of two large companies, an interviewer was trying to determine its effects on workforce morale. If he were to ask the question 'How angry do you feel about the possibility of being made redundant?', he would clearly be imposing *anger* and *redundancy* into the discussion. If the interviewee has not previously mentioned these two ideas, this might well bias the resulting discussion.
- *Do* use the interviewees' language. If they are talking about something you don't understand, clarify what they mean and then use their language. (The technical term for this is 'native categories'.) In most organisations, people have their own codes, or even TLAs (three-letter abbreviations), for most things.

One respondent answered a question with:

> The first stage of the NPI process is to prepare a PID which includes an MRA. We then gate and get all the LUGs to look over the specs before we move to second-stage EDM.

We could translate this as:

> The first stage of the New Product Introduction Process is to prepare a Project Initiation Document that includes a Manufacturing Readiness Assessment (a document reporting on the ability of the firm and its suppliers to actually produce the product being considered). We then stop and have a review of the process so far (gate) and determine whether we continue, and get the Lead Users Group (a group of customers who are prepared to be involved in the new product process) to look over the specifications (product description and technical data) before we move to the second stage Engineering and Design for Manufacture (the part of the process where the technical specification is turned into actual tangible parts for the product).

You also need to think about precisely how you will elicit information and opinions from your interviewees. On the one hand, imposing your concepts on them through the questions you ask is clearly contrary to the spirit of qualitative research. As Whyte (1978: 111) notes:

> The interview structure is not fixed by predetermined questions, as it is in the questionnaire, but is designed to provide the informant with the freedom to introduce materials that were not anticipated by the interviewer ... a genuinely non-directive interviewing approach simply is not appropriate for research. Far from putting informants at their ease, it actually seems to stir anxieties.

Such a naive approach may be inappropriate in a professional setting, such as when you are interviewing managers – see our comments above about respecting their time.

This suggests that, at least in opening the interview, you will need some structure so that you can develop a rapport with the interviewee and establish mutual credibility. When you start discussing the key issues you are investigating, you should follow the guidelines recommended by Whyte (1978) for interviewing, which we have quoted briefly above. You may need to apply these 'rules' flexibly, however, by varying your degree of directness (guiding the respondent in the type of answer) and restrictiveness (guiding the respondent in the length of answer), depending on the situation.

All this should indicate that **qualitative interviewing** is very different from quantitative interviewing, where your goal is to find answers to the questions on your sheet. It does raise the criticism that unstructured data-gathering is 'unscientific' because the content *emerges* as you progress the interview. However, where your objective is to build your understanding, this continual evolution is to be expected. Eisenhardt (1989: 539) warned researchers that:

> This flexibility is not a licence to be unsystematic. Rather, this flexibility is *controlled opportunism* in which researchers take advantage of the uniqueness of a specific case and the emergence of new themes to improve resultant theory.

That controlled opportunism is part of the skill set that you will develop as you use the methods – it takes practice and reflection to make this happen.

6.3.6 How should I record the interview data?

The best method to ensure that you faithfully capture your qualitative data is to record your interviews, wherever possible, and **transcribe** them word for word later on. This is a painstaking process, but it has significant benefits, as we show in **Student research in action 6.4**.

> *Student research in action 6.4*
>
> **THE BEST MAN FOR THE JOB?**
>
> As mentioned in **Student research in action 3.9**, Anjali was investigating the criteria by which managers were selected for particular jobs. Despite her discussions with both managers and various human resource professionals, she never felt she was making any real progress finding out the criteria or how decisions were made. She had started out looking for a formal, identifiable process, but felt frustrated by the answers she was getting. Going back to the recordings of her interviews, she noticed that when she looked for evidence of a rational selection process, the HR interviewees became more careful and frequently tried to change the subject.
>
> This provided the evidence for one of her findings – there was little to suggest that rational selection processes were taking place in the firms she was investigating, and that whilst they may think this undesirable, it was with the consent of the HR professionals. This was quite a surprise, but one that could not be proved directly in the position she was in – an outsider with the interviews only proceeding out of goodwill. Being seen in that context to be implicitly critical of the interviewees was not going to help her to carry out the project. Instead, she was able to rely on other non-verbal communication signals.

Some dos and don'ts in recording your interviews include:

- *Do* get permission to record the interview.
- *Do* reassure your interviewees about confidentiality.
- *Do* make sure that your recorder is working, including testing in the actual situation to ensure that you can hear what is on the tape. Background noise often makes the conversation inaudible.
- *Do* have a system worked out for keeping tapes – mark those that have been used and those that are available for recording.
- *Don't* use recording equipment that is so intrusive that the interviewees are put off talking openly.

You should never assume that recording takes the place of **taking notes**. During the interview, you should note down any issues that might be worth returning to during the interview, should any topics need probing or the conversation needs more direction.

What should you do if you can't get permission to record your interviews? In a quantitative design where you have a structured interview schedule and mainly closed-ended questions, recording short answers on your interview scripts may be good enough. When you are using mainly open-ended questions, however, to summarise responses you will have to filter the data – decide what is important and what is not. This is definitely something you should avoid: whatever you don't write down, you won't have available to analyse, and you could lose important data because you only realise its significance later on. Furthermore, no matter how fast you can write, you also need to listen to what the person is saying, so that you can seek clarification where necessary or be ready with the next question. Very few people manage both simultaneously. This alone is a good reason to interview in pairs if you are allowed only to take notes.

Transforming verbal data into written form makes it relatively simple to work through and perform the analysis. The usual stage between recording and analysis is **transcription**, where you convert the spoken word into written text, which then becomes your raw data for analysis. Also, transcribed data, if you manage the process carefully, will allow you to trace particular themes or issues back to particular people you have interviewed.

As a rough rule, it will take at least three to four hours of transcription work for each hour of interviews, and may take as much as six to eight hours. Professional typists can work faster, but it does get expensive quickly.

After you have transcribed your interviews, you should check your transcripts, especially of key points, against your recordings to make sure that they have been faithfully reproduced. This will be useful anyway as the first stage of the analysis process – you can use it to refamiliarise yourself with the material you have collected. Try not to summarise or filter your data here. Do not discount any material at this stage, just because it may appear to be out of line with other material. You should wait until the analysis stage to look for the reasons as to why it was different.

6.3.7 How should I avoid bias in the interview process?

So that you can give appropriate attention to the statements made by interviewees during coding and analysis (see **Chapter 12**), you should think about the kind of data and the source in deciding how much to weight the data. If you are collecting **descriptive data**, for example background or general information, you should include in your notes the proximity of the interviewee to the issue being considered (level and nature of involvement) and the likelihood that it was being faithfully reported.

In the case of **evaluative data** (people making judgement statements about an issue or individual), you should consider (Whyte 1978):

1. ulterior motives for sharing insights, experiences and so on
2. the apparent level of desire to please the interviewer
3. idiosyncratic factors, such as mood, feelings guided by dominant events and so on.

Whyte (1978) suggests that you should use the following steps to ensure that your data are as free from such distortion as possible. The first is to check whether a story seems plausible. The second is to consider the reliability of the interviewee. The third is to list and evaluate obvious influence biases (such as political). These should be supplemented by comparing accounts between interviewees and other observations. Where accounts produce conflicting arguments, you should cross-check them using the process above to detect whether this is likely to be a genuine perceptual difference.

You should also recognise that interviewees may hold simultaneously conflicting viewpoints. They may either not be sure themselves, or be prepared to have a different position on an issue depending on who they are talking to. The viewpoint presented to you is influenced by many factors, including those given above. Good listening, asking follow-up questions and just a small dose of cynicism are useful here.

6.4 Participant observation

The last design for qualitative research that we will consider is **participant observation**. Participant observation requires personal involvement with the subject of your investigation, with the objective of deriving knowledge from a total experience of the situation. In the study reported in *Street Corner Society* (summarised in **Chapter 1**), researcher William Foote Whyte (1955) joined a street corner group to explore the lives of its members, even going bowling with the out-of-work men he was studying. Whilst most student research projects are not quite so 'hands-on', this illustrates participative research very well. Indeed, many organisations use some sort of participant observation as part of their normal data-gathering processes, as shown in **Student research in action 6.5**.

> *Student research in action 6.5*
>
> **SOME PEOPLE HAVE ALL THE LUCK**
>
> Mark was working in the IT department of a brewery as part of his course of study. Periodically, office staff members were required to act as mystery customers in the pubs that the brewery also ran. This involved their going to the pub and spending an evening there. The company paid for all their drinks and transport home was even provided at the end of the evening. All the staff had to do was to provide a short report on their experiences of the evening. This helped the firm to understand better the service system that customers required, as well as providing some immediate feedback from a 'customer perspective' of how a particular pub was performing.

Mystery customer studies can be useful for an organisation as a form of short-term participant observation. Indeed, some senior managers have been known to use participant observation to find out what is really going on in their firms. In MBNA Bank, for instance, senior managers regularly spend time answering the phones, as this gets them speaking with customers. The experiences they have are carried back into the decision-making process (this is a key element of the BBC television series *Back to the Floor*, which puts CEOs to work in the front line for a few days).

Participant observation is probably the most classic ethnographic method, which means that it is closest to the 'role model' for qualitative research that we presented in **Chapter 5**. An ethnographic study investigates the culture of a particular organisation or group and tries to make sense of the particular situation. For instance, what are the mechanisms that lead to changes in worker productivity around the times that company bonuses are announced?

The object of using an ethnographic approach is to build the richest possible picture of the *context*, that is, the circumstances surrounding the events and actions you are analysing. This affects both data collection and analysis. The data you collect must provide evidence that the actions you see people taking are connected to the particular events at the time. This is entirely feasible for student projects, and the language, such as that used in the quotation from Rosen (1991: 12) below to describe this kind of research, should not put you off:

> The goal of ethnography in general is to decode, translate and interpret the behaviours and attached meaning systems of those occupying and creating the social system being studied. Ethnography therefore is largely an act of sensemaking, the translation from one context into another of action in relation to meaning and meaning in relation to action.

Participatory action research is participant observation with a twist. An essential aspect of this approach is that you are trying to change the organisation in some way through your involvement as a researcher, not just analysing and reporting the situation. In participatory action research, you are involved in making a change and participating and observing the consequences. For instance, you might use this approach if you were investigating a system for handling customer complaints. Your recommendations for changes are implemented, and you then spend time with the team working in the new system.

In general, action research is associated with research on issues that have a social component, such as equality, fairness or the environment. For example, if you are a participant-observer in a charitable organisation, you might actually try to change the organisation so that it better accomplishes its goals. A real danger here, though, is 'going native' and letting the participation and action aspect overwhelm the research aspect. It also raises some ethical questions, especially if you are participating in an organisation or a context that has legal or moral aspects.

There is much to recommend participant observation as a research method, provided you can manage the risks involved, which we discuss below. This method is often a natural fit with placements or sponsored projects where you are carrying out work for the organisation as well as doing research on it. You can take advantage of this access and the insights gained in doing your research, which would be difficult if not impossible to gain through other types of research. We will cover some other relevant issues such as honesty and confidentiality in **Chapter 9**. You may want to look ahead as they are particularly pertinent here: participation often yields personal insights from the people you are working with.

6.4.1 Risks of participant observation

Whilst you are unlikely to be allowed to do a student project in business and management that poses as much risk to your personal safety as Whyte's *Street Corner*

Society (1995) did to his, you should be aware of several risks posed by participant observation. First, if you are unfamiliar with an organisation, participant observation can take more time than you have available. To gain any real insights, you will need considerable preparation (applying for your project to be supported by an employing organisation, for instance), must collect data over a period usually of months, and then will need time to assimilate and analyse the large amount of data you have amassed. The time requirements mean that participant studies are less often used for student projects than the other qualitative research designs.

Second, you must rely heavily on the organisation you are studying and this creates a significant risk to your project's success. Any organisational changes could mean that your project is no longer supported (it does happen), and you are left exposed, with your data collection only partly completed and not enough time to start again with another organisation.

Finally, in participant observation you must deal with your split role of researcher and participant, and retain some **critical subjectivity** about the situation. You should not become so involved with the situation that you are unable to carry out the reflection necessary for it to be a useful piece of research. When you fail to maintain some separation, you have 'gone native', and your research may only reflect what the organisation thinks and believes, not what is true. This happened to a student project group that spent one day per week for most of a year in their sponsoring organisation (the Hamsters and Gerbils Conservation Foundation mentioned in **Chapter 6**). They lost any critical perspective and, as a result, turned in a poor piece of work from both the supervisor's and the organisation's perspectives, as it was simply market research and a 'puff piece' at that.

6.4.2 Recording observations

When you are doing participant observation, you will usually record your data in a personal **research diary** during the period of the study. You will need considerable discipline to keep a research diary, but you will lose or distort your thoughts and impressions if you do not record them straight away. You will usually need to make time for such recording time away from your research context, otherwise you might compromise your status as a participant.

Summary

This chapter addresses the key question: 'What design should I choose for collecting qualitative data?' You can choose from a large range of methods, depending on your research question and the practicalities of your available time and places to carry out your research. We discussed possible difficulties with access early in the chapter, but this is an issue that is central to all research methods, not just those described here.

We classified qualitative methods according to the level of involvement you would have in each with the subject of your research. You can carry out observation remotely, and collect data collected about what people do. Remote observation is the least involved of the methods and can be either direct or indirect. More involved methods included the direct interview. These are very common and there is much to guide the practices you use to make your study highly effective. You can achieve even higher levels of involvement under the heading of participant observation – there are well-formulated research designs for both ethnographic and action research. Furthermore, you do not have to use any of these methods in isolation, as one method can provide further evidence to support or question the findings of another method.

Answers to key questions

What research designs can I use to collect data to uncover social meaning?
- Remote data collection
- Observation
- Interviews
- Participation

How can I use remote data collection, observation, interviews or participant observation?
- To understand how participants view the social world, rather than have your view imposed upon it
- To collect data directly from participants in their own words and behaviours

How can I use these designs as part of a scientific research approach?
- Transform the qualitative data into numbers and analyse the numbers using statistical techniques

References

Eisenhardt, Kathleen M. 1989. Building theories from case study research, *Academy of Management Review*, **14**(4): 532–50.
Glaser, B. and Strauss, A. 1967. *The Discovery of Grounded Theory: Strategies of Qualitative Research*. London: Wiedenfeld & Nicholson.
Rosen, M. 1991. Coming to terms with the field: Understanding and doing organisational ethnography, *Journal of Management Studies*, **28**(1): 1–24.
Walsch, Neale D. 1995. *Conversations with God:* Book One. London: Hodder & Stoughton.
Whyte, William F. 1955. *Street Corner Society*. Chicago: University of Chicago Press.
Whyte, William F. 1978. 'Interviewing in field research'. In Burgess, R.G. (ed.). *Field Research: A Source-book and Field Manual*. New York: Allen & Unwin, pp. 300–18.

Additional resources

Denzin, Norman K. and Lincoln, Yvonne S. (eds). 2000. *Handbook of Qualitative Research*, 2nd edn. Thousand Oaks, CA: Sage. See particularly Fontana, A. and Frey, J.H. Chapter 22, Interviewing – the art of science, pp. 361–76.
Gummesson, Evert. 2000. *Qualitative Methods in Management Research*, 2nd edn. Thousand Oaks, CA: Sage.
Lee, R.M. 2000. *Unobtrusive Methods In Social Research*. Milton Keynes: Open University Press.
Mintzberg, Henry. 1979. An emerging strategy of 'direct' research, *Administrative Science Quarterly*, **24**: 582–9.

Rathje, William and Murphy, Cullen. 1992. *Rubbish! The Archaeology of Garbage.* New York: HarperCollins.

Reason, Peter and Bradbury, Hilary (eds). 2000. *Handbook of Action Research: Participative Inquiry and Practice.* Thousand Oaks, CA: Sage.

Richardson, S.A., Dohrenwend, B.S. and Klein, D. 1965. *Interviewing: Its Forms and Functions.* New York: Basic Books.

Strauss, A.L. and Corbin, J. 1999. *Basics of Qualitative Research: Grounded Theory Procedures and Techniques,* 2nd edn. Thousand Oaks, CA: Sage.

Symon, Gillian and Cassell, Catherine. (eds) 1998. *Qualitative Methods and Analysis in Organisational Research: A Practical Guide.* Thousand Oaks, CA: Sage.

Van Maanen, John. 1982. 'Fieldwork on the beat'. In Von Maanen, J., Dabbs, J.M. Jr. and Faulkner, R.R. (eds). *Varieties of Qualitative Research.* Thousand Oaks, CA: Sage.

Key terms

- convenience sampling, 155
- covert observation, 153
- critical subjectivity, 164
- descriptive data, 161
- evaluative data, 161
- indirect data collection, 150
- indirect observation, 150
- nonparticipant observation, 152
- non-standardised data, 153
- participant observation, 152
- participatory action research, 163
- qualitative interviewing, 159
- remote data collection, 150
- research diary, 164
- taking notes, 160
- theoretical or purposive 154
- transcribe, 161

Discussion questions

1. What are the main methods associated with a qualitative research design?
2. How can an interview be used in both quantitative and qualitative designs?
3. Think of three examples of data that could be collected by remote observation. What would be the main method of actually gathering the data in each case?
4. Why is it a good idea to tape record unstructured interviews?
5. What is the role of the interview schedule and how does this compare with a questionnaire?
6. How is ethnographic research different from nonparticipant observation?
7. What are the risks involved with participant observation?
8. Why is it a good idea for you to transcribe your own data? What are the drawbacks of this?
9. Are verbal statements really data?
10. What forms of data, other than words, could you collect as part of a qualitative research study?

Workshop

This workshop focuses on how to use unstructured interviews to find out information. At the end of the workshop, you should have a better understanding of what it is like to be both interviewer and interviewee, by playing both roles.

Background

As the **Chapter 2** workshop explained, people have to make significant changes in their lives when they go into higher education. To assist in this process, we need to understand the nature of these changes better.

Task

Conduct interviews in pairs – not necessarily from the same subgroup.

1. Set-up – Two-minute individual preparation (silence) to think about the issues involved.
2. Interview – Spend five minutes with one person interviewing the other on the subject of their experiences of moving into higher education (all aspects of the change – not just educational). The interviewer is responsible for recording the interview – take notes, tape or video record it if possible – it will be used again in the Chapter 12 workshop.
3. Debrief – what types of questions were asked (open/closed, structured/loose) and what was the role of the interviewer (how much did they impose their own views on the interviewee, intervene) and so on?
4. Now change roles – those that were interviewing now become the interviewee – again a five-minute interview and interviewer is responsible for taking a record of the interview.
5. Debrief – what questions were asked this time, how were they put and how did the interviewer ensure that they did not impose their view on the situation? What form did your record of the interview take? What did you write down – everything they said or just what appeared important (to you)?
6. Break into subgroups (four or more usually works well, the key is to have no more than five or six students per group) – collate the information using thematic groupings – combine your interviews with your own experiences in the group (use good processes from the Chapter 4 workshop to ensure that maximum input is achieved). It is suggested that a mind map display may be appropriate here.
7. Debrief the rest of the group – one minute 'show and tell' of what you found about the subject and the process of carrying out unstructured or semi-structured interviews (such as how much of what was said you were able to capture using notes).

CHAPTER 7
Case studies and multi-method design

KEY QUESTIONS

- How can I design and conduct a case study?
- How can I design and conduct research studies that use more than one method or approach?
- How can I combine quantitative and qualitative methods to study social phenomena?
- What are the advantages and disadvantages of integrating quantitative and qualitative methods to study social phenomena?

LEARNING OUTCOMES

By the time that you have completed this chapter, you should be able to:
- Decide whether a case study or other multi-method design is appropriate for your research project
- Design and conduct a case study or other multi-method design
- Incorporate ideas about triangulation into your research design, of any type

CONTENTS

Introduction
7.1 The case study
7.2 Multi-method research and triangulation
Summary
Answers to key questions
References
Additional resources
Key terms
Discussion questions
Workshop

Introduction

Chapters 6 and **7** introduced you to some common quantitative and qualitative research methods that fit with the scientific and the ethnographic approaches to doing business and management research. Not every research design is based on a single research method, however. Before surveys and participant observation became popular in social research, case studies were the main style of social research (Blaikie 2000). Case studies are still widely used in social research, including psychology, sociology, education and economics, as well as in business and management. This chapter will consider the case study, which is often used in business and management research, and other multi-method research designs. The case study is not really a research method, but it is important enough as a research design to deserve a discussion of its own. Multi-method research combines research methods, which makes it worth considering but particularly tricky to get right. We will also consider mixed-method research, which combines both the scientific and the ethnographic approaches.

As you will see in this chapter, a case study is defined by the boundaries of data collection – *what* you collect data about – rather than research methods or techniques – *how* you collect your data. This is particularly useful when you're not sure where the boundaries between the phenomenon you are investigating and its context should be drawn, or exactly what you will find when you begin to explore the phenomenon. If you organise your research around the social unit you are studying, this will make defining the boundaries of your data collection and therefore your research easier. For example, if you are working on a sponsored project, you might collect data about the organisation that is sponsoring you, using as many different methods as you find appropriate, and use all your information to study the company. Case study designs, because they focus on a 'natural' unit of observation, are popular for student research projects.

This inclusion of many different methods and sources of data makes the case study one of the most powerful, yet challenging, research designs because it comes closer than most other methods to the complexity of real organisational settings and phenomena. A case study can be a good way to investigate a phenomenon in its real-life setting, particularly the dynamics that take place in this setting.

Although the 'case' you study in business and management research will often be an organisation or an organisational subunit, you can study an individual, a group, an organisation or even an industry – the range of case study is unlimited. One case study already discussed in this book is William Foote White's (1955) study of street corner life, where he focused on a particular group of people in society. Other significant case studies include Philip Selznick's (1949) study of the Tennessee Valley Authority and Alfred Chandler's (1962) study of the historical development of American industry. In these examples, the focus of the case study can be large organisations and long periods of time, but a case study can be as small as a single person (Sigmund Freud's psychological case studies) or a short period of time (teaching case studies).

Section 7.1 presents the case study. Our discussion of the case study gives us a natural starting point for discussing multi-method research designs, and triangulation in **Section 7.2**.

After you have read this chapter, you should be able to decide whether you want to use a case study approach or a mixed-method approach in your own research project. You might want to go back to **Chapters 6** and **7** to review the tools and techniques we have presented, to see which might be appropriate for your design.

7.1 The case study

Creswell (1994: 61) defines a case study as a single, bounded entity, studied in detail, with a variety of methods, over an extended period. Compared with the research methods presented in **Chapter 6** and **Chapter 7**, the case study method is not a 'pure' research method, because you will normally collect your data from multiple sources and using several methods such as surveying, interviewing, participant observation and archival research. A case study design does not dictate the use of any particular technique for collecting or analysing data, but it does have definite implications for the choice of the unit of analysis to which you will apply one or more techniques.

The social unit being studied defines your **case study**, whether it is a person, a programme, a company, a situation or whatever. For instance, in a study of management coaching you might collect data about each individual person coached as a **case**, in the way that a case is usually used in quantitative research, but you could also define your case study around a team or the organisation. You could write about the performance of a team following coaching (focused on the team as the case), or the performance of all or part of the organisation under the influence of the coaching (the organisation is the case). Although every research design involves the study of cases, only the case study is defined by the case as unit of analysis rather than the techniques for collecting data.

Just as with any other way of doing research, if you choose a case study you need to show that it is the best way to answer your research questions. A case study is as valid as any other research design we have described in the previous two chapters. There are a number of different ways of carrying out a case study, and you need to justify which particular approach you select.

Business and management researchers carry out case studies for both practical and theoretical reasons. A case study is particularly useful if you want to conduct a limited or exploratory study. A case study, like archival research, may be a good approach if you want to study an organisation or phenomenon that you cannot study directly – you can use a case study when you have no control over the events you are interested in studying *and* the phenomenon takes place at least partly during the period you are doing your research. You may want to select a case study approach if you are conducting an individual research project and you have a limited budget and limited time (Blaikie 2000). Group projects can also take a case study approach. However, good case study research, like surveys, takes careful planning and execution (Yin 1989).

As Yin (1994: 3) comments:

> We were once taught to believe that case studies were appropriate for the exploratory phase of an investigation, that surveys and histories were

appropriate for the descriptive phase, and that experiments were the only way of doing explanatory or causal inquiries. [This] view reinforced the idea that case studies were only an exploratory tool and could not be used to describe or test propositions. This ... view, however, is incorrect. Experiments with an exploratory motive have always existed. ... case studies are far from being only an exploratory strategy. Some of the best and most famous case studies have been both descriptive (for example, Whyte's *Street Corner Society* 1943/1955) and explanatory (see Allison's *Essence of Decision: Explaining the Cuban Missile Crisis*, 1971).

If you are not overly limited by practical considerations, you should consider a case study approach if your research questions lend themselves to this approach – specifically if the unit of analysis is right. A case study can answer either exploratory and descriptive or analytic research questions – 'how' and 'why' research questions. A case study can explain, describe, illustrate, explore or evaluate the social phenomenon you are interested in (Yin 1994). You can use a case study approach to test theory as well as to build theory.

Many groups find that the case study approach is a good approach for their research project because of this diversity. If more than one person in your group is doing research (multiple investigators), then each person may pick up aspects of the case that the others have missed. This is especially useful when you can conduct site visits in pairs or teams. Splitting the group, then comparing and contrasting experiences can be an excellent way of gaining insights from multiple perspectives.

If you decide to use a case study, you should note that research case studies are usually more complex than teaching case studies you have encountered in textbooks and in class. These teaching case studies are usually prepared to illustrate part of a situation for specific teaching purposes. Even if they are based on case study research, they have usually been simplified. So, we recommend that you do not use a teaching case study as the model for investigating and/or writing up your research.

7.1.1 Designing and conducting case studies

The key elements of a case study design are:

- defining the case to be studied
- determining what data to collect and how to collect them
- deciding how to analyse and present the data.

We will consider each of these in turn.

7.1.2 Defining the case to be studied

Issues for getting started on your research design include:

- how you will identify the case or cases you plan to study
- where you will draw the empirical boundaries of the case
- whether you will assign cases to pre-existing theoretical categories.

When you identify the case (or cases), you decide what you are going to study, as shown in **Student research in action 7.1**. If you are doing a sponsored or placement project, then the general setting of the case is usually obvious. You will still need to decide what the boundaries of the case will be. Is it your work group, department, business unit, organisation or industry? If you are free to choose the context of your research, then you need to decide what you are going to study, which gives you both more freedom but also less guidance than for a research project linked to a particular business sponsor.

> ### Student research in action 7.1
> **THE BIGGER THEY ARE**
>
> Rebecca wanted to do her MSc dissertation on why English biotech firms survived or failed. Since she only had three months to design, conduct and write up her research and she didn't already have access to any biotech firms, she decided to do a comparative case study of two firms – one which had survived and one which had failed – to see if she could identify factors that contributed to these outcomes. She selected her two cases to create the maximum contrast between firm success in the biotech field; she could thus test various propositions about what factors, for example early venture capitalist involvement, influential people sitting on the corporate board, differed between the two.

Determining the boundaries of the case means deciding what is relevant and what is not to your case. Although this sounds simple, it's a lot more difficult in practice. It is sometimes difficult to separate the case, or social unit, that you are studying from its context. Ragin and Becker (1992: 6) suggest that 'A researcher probably will not know what their cases are until the research, including … writing up the results, is virtually completed'. You may need to describe the department you are working in so that your reader understands the context of your work group. So is the department or the work group the focus of your case?

This also brings in some issues that relate back to **Chapter 5** and the scientist/ethnographer distinction. Quantitative and qualitative researchers may define cases differently. If you take more of a quantitative perspective, you will probably perceive cases as 'out there', existing independently of you as a researcher. Once you have identified a case, then you will assume that its boundaries are set by the case you have defined. For example, if your case is a company, then you will not need to investigate the industry as part of the case, although it may be relevant to the overall research in describing the context and so on. You will probably identify your cases using pre-existing categories based on general or conventional social units such as individuals, teams, families, organisations, cities and nations. You main task is to identify these cases and investigate them.

On the other hand, if you take more of a qualitative perspective, you might be interested in investigating cases that are theoretical constructs created by investigators, which are specific to a piece of research and are developed during the research itself. The boundaries of the case you are studying do not exist until you have defined them – they are not set by the definition of the case (the 'object' you are studying). The 'type A personality' or the 'newly developing country' did not exist before someone defined them. As you accumulate empirical evidence, your cases will emerge. Therefore, your task is not only to identify and investigate cases, but also to bring them into being.

Single versus multiple case studies

Another important issue in designing your research project is whether to study a single case, an in-depth case that includes more than one 'sub-case', or more than one (independent) case. A **single case study** focuses on a single unit of analysis, such as a corporation. A single case study may naturally occur when you are studying something that is unique – such as the Enron scandal. Students often conduct a single case study when they are working in a company and using it as their research setting, or when they are working to a project brief and their sponsor has asked them to focus on a single internal problem. Note that, although you might find that someone doing questionnaires might scoff at you for having only a single case, rather than many, as we have noted above many classic examples in business and management research have been single case studies.

Not every case study is a study of a single case (which is a major difference between a teaching case study and a research case study). You can also study multiple units of analysis, or cases, in a single case study. A **multiple case study approach** is useful if you want to identify which features are unique to a case and which are common across cases. You might decide, for example, to study corporate scandals by doing case studies on both Enron and Parmalat. This replication and contrast provide a significant advantage over the single case study design when you are building and testing theory. You can test or build theory by looking for patterns across cases, use individual cases to support or disconfirm your propositions or develop a more complete theoretical picture. However, you will have less time and effort to spend on each case than if you were doing a single case study.

When you are reading research reports, you may sometimes find it difficult to tell whether a case study is a single case study, a multiple case study conducted within a single setting, or a multiple case study conducted within multiple settings. The multiple case, single-setting design described in example 2 in **Student research in action 7.2** is an **embedded case study**. An embedded case study might involve the study of multiple divisions within a single company, or multiple project teams within new product development. By holding the setting or context constant, you can eliminate external sources of variation and look systematically for patterns of actions, behaviours or practices. You can also use an embedded case study to investigate multiple hierarchical levels within a single study, for example, industry, firm and division level as in example 4.

We are often asked by our students how many cases they should do in a multiple case study design. Whilst there is no way of calculating sample size, as there is for more quantitative methods such as surveys, a good rule of thumb is that you should do between two and eight case studies, given of course that each case study is to an adequate depth. You might also consider doing a single in-depth case study as your main study, and then collect a number of shallower and smaller contrast case studies.

Deciding whether you should study one or several cases in your case study will usually require you to think about whether you are more interested in depth or breadth. **Student research in action 7.2** illustrates student projects that used different forms of case study design.

Student research in action 7.2
EXAMPLES OF CASE STUDIES

Example 1: Strategy implementation

Derkhart was working for a large German bank, and was interested in how the bank implemented its stated corporate strategy. Specifically, his research question concerned how the bank controlled the many activities that were concerned with this strategy implementation. This is an example of a single case approach – he considered many examples of the activities within the one organisation without focusing on any specific activity, group or part of the organisation. He mixed his insights as a manager in this organisation with some survey work of the organisation and interviews with individual senior managers to provide a rich picture of this issue in the organisation.

Example 2: Programme management

Liz was working with a large public sector organisation, looking at how they implemented organisational change projects. The total number of projects carried out at any one time was over 100, so she decided to consider some key cases that would illustrate her research question -'what would constitute "best practice" in such an organisation?' Specifically, she considered a small number of cases that had been successful and some that had failed. The key aspects of the successful projects could then be compared with those aspects of the failed projects, and allow further comparison with the best-practice literature in the area. This is a good example of an embedded case study, because she sampled more than one case from the same organisation.

Example 3: Capacity and capability management at a county council

Ian's project was set in a county council where there had been some problems – notably that it had been audited and labelled as a failing council. A key aspect of this failure concerned its ability to deliver services and make changes. Ian's project was to consider the way the council managed the capacity and capability – literally to find whether it had the workforce or ability to deliver all that it was required to do. He soon found that nobody really knew how much work the organisation was capable of doing. The result was that the organisation regularly took on far more work than it could handle, resulting in chaos. Having spent the majority of his available research time with the council exploring the project in depth and identifying his key findings, he then contacted local organisations from both the public and private sectors to provide contrast cases – and explored each of his key issues at those organisations. In this way, he was able to gain insights into those specific issues of importance. This is an example of a multiple case study, because Ian's other cases came from outside his original case study site (compare with Liz's selection of cases in example 2).

Example 4: Empowerment in construction

Ann's study of empowerment practices in the construction sector investigated the research question, 'what is the policy and reality of empowerment in the construction sector today?' In answering this research question, she looked at the overall patterns of empowerment, as cited in various reports on the sector. She then looked at one firm thought to be 'typical' of the sector. Here she considered the firm's policies on empowerment and how these fitted with the overall managerial philosophy of the firm. She also considered what really happened in the enactment of that policy, by considering examples from a division within the firm – again through management statements such

> as policy statements, and then particular projects – by short site visits conducting interviews of site personnel. This multi-level approach was particularly good at providing a contrast between policy and practice in empowerment – as she did find that there was considerable variation between the views at different levels. This is another example of an embedded case study, where the cases are selected vertically, rather than horizontally as in example 2.

Compare examples 2 and 3 with examples 1 and 4 in **Student research in action 7.2**. If you take a quantitative research approach (as in example 1), identifying common patterns will help you show that your findings are valid and reliable. This does not mean that the quantitative approach to the case was necessarily better than that adopted in the other examples – which were more qualitative – it just answered a different type of research question.

Activity

Fast-food corporations have a choice between franchising new units and opening these units themselves. This decision has obvious financial implications. A less obvious implication is the opportunity to use a company-owned site for getting closer to customers and creating learning, and trying out different policies and procedures, and new products.

Suppose you were interested in how a fast-food corporation changed its advertising and product offerings in response to government initiatives on obesity, and changes in public opinion due to anti-fast-food films and campaigns. How might you develop a case study to investigate this? Try to think about how you would:

- Define the case and its boundaries
- Decide how many cases and what sort of sampling logic to use to select cases.

How would these decisions affect what you find out in your research? Does it make a difference?

The logic of multiple case studies is similar to the logic of qualitative research – you don't need to go on adding cases if you find the same results in all cases, that is, you are not adding any new information. In a multiple case study approach, you should review the contribution each new case is making, rather than wait to the end of your study to note that the findings were the same in all cases.

If you do start to find great consistency in areas where you didn't expect to find it, perhaps it is time to investigate the reasons behind this consistency, rather than simply continue with the same research questions. In this kind of situation, you will find that the case study design is often more evolutionary, and therefore akin to qualitative research.

Logic of sampling

If you decide to investigate more than one case, you will need to think about how you will choose your cases. Whether you take a quantitative or qualitative perspective, you will probably *not* make your case selection based on the principles for probability sampling presented in **Chapter 6**: this is actually the opposite of what you need to do. In most cases, you will want to generalise the findings from your case study to theory, not to a population of similar cases.

There are two ways to think about choosing your research cases. One is to choose either an extreme situation (for example a 'best-practice' or 'worst-practice' company), or a set of cases that varies widely on one or more aspects of either the setting or the main variable you are interested in researching (the 'theoretical variable'). For instance, if your research question was 'what effect does firm size have on the nature of marketing activity carried out?', you may wish to select one small, one medium-sized and one large company as cases, and investigate what 'marketing' constitutes in each case. This theoretical (or purposive) sampling will allow you to select your case or cases so that you can study one or more theoretical propositions. Once you have completed your research, you will be able to draw some conclusions about the effect of size on marketing, rather than what small companies do in marketing, what medium-sized companies do and so on.

The second way to choose your cases is to take a replication approach – choose a set of cases that are similar to each other and look for differences and what causes those differences. For example, you could select a set of small companies to investigate that use similar marketing strategies. You could then try to tease out differences within that similarity about marketing. How robust is the association between marketing and size, for example?

7.1.3 Determining what data to collect and how to collect it

So why haven't we included the case study in either **Chapter 6** on quantitative methods or **Chapter 7** on qualitative methods? In a case study, you may collect quantitative data (numbers), qualitative data (words) or both, using any of the methods discussed in previous chapters (except experiments). Most case studies use more than one technique for collecting data. Nearly all case studies rely on some archival or indirect methods of collecting information. Some stop there, but many go on to use various direct methods, including interviews, questionnaires and non-participant observation.

Although case studies always involve a real-life context, in student projects you would not necessarily be limited to using only the ethnographic and participant observation methods described in **Chapter 7**, even though researchers using these two methods describe what they are studying as cases. If you are an undergraduate or taught master's student, you will probably have too little time to conduct your project using ethnography or participant observation. You will probably combine survey methods such as questionnaires and interviews with participant or nonparticipant observation and archival research. You can use these different methods to collect different information, or you may use them to collect information on the same issues so that you can triangulate your findings, as we describe in **Section 7.2**, rather than using each technique to collect different information.

Table 7.1 Typical quantitative versus qualitative research designs

	Quantitative approach	Qualitative approach
Number of observations	Many	Few or single
Research questions	Who, what, when, where	How, why
Variables	Specified ahead of time, based on theoretical concepts	Emerge from study, based on grounded research
Collection of information	One variable at a time	One case at a time
Analysis	Level of variables and relationships among them; statistical analysis	Finding patterns of events or processes
Goal	Generalisable to observations or contexts beyond sample	Generalisable to theoretical concepts

To see where the case study fits with quantitative and qualitative research methods, you should think about the points discussed earlier in understanding research approaches (**Chapter 5**) and research designs (**Chapters 6** and **7**). These are summarised in **Table 7.1**.

As you saw in **Chapter 5**, quantitative research follows a characteristic pattern where the researcher relies on random sampling, a priori (before data collection starts) definitions of constructs and their measures, specification of research questions, multiple respondents, previous literature, a priori development of research instruments and protocols. The final argument is often structured around producing statistics about the observations. Because of the focus on a single social unit, the case study doesn't fit neatly with quantitative research designs.

On the other hand, qualitative case studies usually begin with loosely defined research objectives and evolve according to the data that are collected. They are often single case designs, involving only a single informant and methods such as ethnography, participant observation or action research. They usually start without any theory in mind and no hypotheses to test: since only the most naive or inexperienced researcher will not have been exposed to some theoretical thinking, this means having a research problem and perhaps some key variables in mind, but not any specific relationships between variables or a theoretical perspective.

The logic of the qualitative case study design is thus closer to a qualitative research design than a quantitative design; however, you may rely on quantitative or qualitative methods for gathering your data. The case study doesn't always fit with qualitative research designs either, because case study researchers may also draw on quantitative approaches, especially in multiple case study research designs. Most case study designs in study projects involve collecting quantitative data using the methods described in **Chapter 6**.

Nevertheless, most case studies will draw heavily on the methods for analysing qualitative data in **Chapter 9** to support their interpretation. **Figure 7.1** illustrates how the case study as a design integrates aspects of both quantitative and qualitative designs.

Whether the case study takes more of a quantitative or qualitative perspective depends on how the researcher designing and conducting the case is guided by the relative methodological perspectives and assumptions and practical considerations.

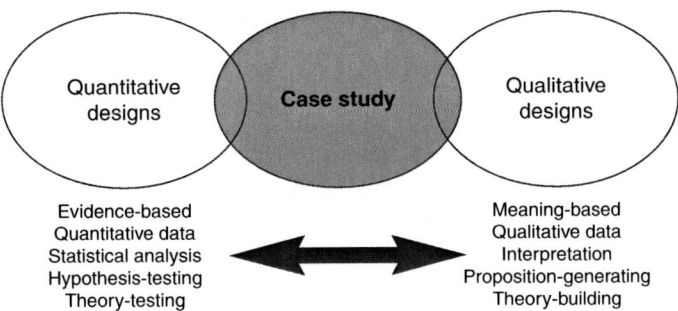

Figure 7.1 Case study as research design

Student research in action 7.3 shows how qualitative data were turned into quantitative data, as a pragmatic approach to dealing with a large data set.

> ### Student research in action 7.3
> Although it was a bigger project than most undergraduate or master's student projects, this is a good example of a case study that relied heavily on quantitative analysis to identify key findings, which then fed into the further analysis. Peter, a Swedish research student, spent several years immersed in a company making office products. He made notes of every conversation or meeting he observed on the days he was present at the company. At the end of his three-year observation period, he had over 6000 observations saved on his computer. Peter used content analysis to identify key themes in his data, then plotted the frequency with which those themes came up over time.

7.1.4 Deciding how to analyse and present the data

Although using multiple methods and multiple data sources improves the quality of case study data and analysis, this can make deciding how to present your case study data tricky. In quantitative research designs such as surveys, reporting your findings is usually straightforward – you can analyse your data statistically and then present them in tables and charts, and structure your discussion around these exhibits. In a case study, you first need to decide how you will analyse and present your results. There are many different ways to do this, depending on whether your research perspective is aligned more with a quantitative or qualitative methodology, which will influence how you develop a coherent analysis and present and organise your data. If your research is more oriented towards the scientific approach, you should try to be consistent with the style and content of a scientific analysis and report; if more ethnographic, with the style and content of an ethnographic analysis and report.

Either way, the first step in most case study research is to develop a coherent narrative that tells the story of your case study. This still leaves the question open of exactly how you will do it, since you can usually identify many possible themes around which you could organise your story, including chronologically, around actors (such as people, groups or organisations) or around processes (such as work activities or technologies). Once you have developed your story, you can use guides to qualitative analysis such as Miles and Huberman (1984) to identify the techniques you can use in analysing your case study data.

How to analyse individual cases

You should write a detailed case study for each case, for example each plant site you have visited. This is usually a descriptive write-up, although you can also provide quantitative information such as graphs and tables to illustrate your case. At the end, your reader should understand the detailed and unique features of each case by itself. Tracy Kidder's *The Soul of a New Machine* (1981), for example, describes how Data General developed the Eclipse computer by telling it as a story in more or less chronological order from the founding of the company through to the introduction of the new computer. This is often the easiest way to organise your narrative, especially if you are telling the story of a company or a person. The most common way that student projects report case study research is to arrange the narrative around a timeline. **Within-case analysis** is the process by which you focus your analysis only on an individual case, without trying to bring in the findings or lessons from any other cases you might have been investigating.

How to analyse multiple cases

When you have conducted multiple cases or have used an embedded case design, you should next search for patterns across cases. This process is to conduct within-case analysis, followed by cross-case analysis if you have multiple cases. When you have conducted within-case analysis on each of your cases, then you should analyse all the cases simultaneously, which is known as **cross-case analysis**, to look for common patterns or significant variations across your cases.

One way of doing this cross-case analysis is to select a number of categories and see how each case fits into that category. Are different cases more similar or more different? Another way to do this is to identify common themes across all the cases, and then see which individual case best illustrates each of those themes. In *Microsoft Secrets*, for example, Michael Cusumano and Richard Selby (1995) organise their story around the key themes they identified in their study of Microsoft:

- organising and managing the company
- managing creative people and technical skills
- competing with products and standards
- defining products and development processes
- developing and shipping products
- building a learning organisation.

They then bring in different aspects of the organisation to illustrate each of them.

You can also analyse multiple cases using a **paired-case analysis**, as illustrated in **Student research in action 7.4**, where you list the similarities and differences between pairs of cases. This can help you to identify new concepts and categories from the data. People who feel more comfortable with the scientific approach may find the paired-case analysis a more natural way to analyse their findings, because it draws more on the scientific reasoning described in **Chapter 5**.

> **Student research in action 7.4**
> **WHY CAN'T WE BE FRIENDS?**
>
> Teh-Yuan's project was concerned with the management of science and scientists in collaborative biotech research projects. He wanted to establish how such projects could be managed well, in particular focusing on the exploitation of the knowledge produced during the research. His work was to take place partly in the UK and partly in his home country – Taiwan. He chose two cases – one in each country.
>
> Initially he noted the difference in productivity between UK and Taiwanese researchers in terms of their key outputs – specifically papers in scientific journals, where UK researchers were at least twice as productive (in terms of papers per researcher) as their Taiwanese counterparts. The difference in terms of patents registered was similar, with the UK researchers being more than twice as productive.
>
> His paired-case analysis would establish some of the differences in the way that scientists worked – by looking at comparable cases from the UK and Taiwan. His work showed that there were many similarities in the motivations of scientists, but that the need to 'publish or perish' was much stronger in the UK. It became clear that the UK researchers were given more time for this activity and when they didn't get it as part of their working hours, they would put in more of their own time to complete the writing tasks.

Grounded case study designs

Many business and management researchers have found the procedure for grounded case study research presented by Kathleen Eisenhardt (1989) helpful. Since in a case study you are often analysing multiple sources of data and multiple methods, you may find that you can best capture the evolving insights and determine your evolving research design using a grounded research approach where data collection and data analysis overlap. Here, grounded refers to a weaving back and forth between theory and data (for example Bryman and Bell 2003), which is different from the deductive (theory determines what data you collect) and the inductive (data determine what theory you develop) that we described in **Chapter 5**.

A grounded approach can be extremely helpful when you haven't started with a particular theory (or conceptual model), and when trying to induce theory from your observations is difficult. In some case studies, you may be examining a phenomenon that no one else has studied before, so it may not be clear before you start your research either what models are relevant or what data you need to collect. For instance, you might be the first person to do research in a particular type of firm, or on a particular practice. In this case, you might not be able to identify what sorts of things you need to be looking for, or even what sorts of things you might expect to find. This grounded approach will help you to capture both theoretical and empirical insights in such situations.

Eisenhardt (1989) presents an extremely useful road map for using a **grounded case study** research approach to build theories from case study research. This road map is appropriate for research that combines both quantitative and qualitative approaches. The steps she suggested are as follows:

1. Getting started – problem definition
2. *Selecting cases* – theoretical sampling

3. *Crafting instruments and protocols* – preparing multiple data collection methods
4. Entering the field – collecting data
5. *Analysing data* – within-case analysis followed by cross-case analysis
6. *Shaping hypotheses* – building evidence and explanation
7. *Enfolding literature* – comparing findings with the literature
8. *Reaching closure* – knowing when to stop.

Steps 1–4 of the grounded case study design are common to all case study research. However, whilst you can use the same methods to collect data for a grounded case study and a case study from the scientific approach, typically you will need much more time to interpret the data and understand what they mean.

Steps 5–8 are worth looking at in more detail. Teh-Yuan's project given in **Student research in action 7.4** illustrates the data analysis – within-case followed by cross-case analysis. First, Teh-Yuan analysed each of his UK cases and Taiwanese cases using a within-case logic. Next, he compared pairs of similar cases using cross-case analysis, based on the case's background (for example size of project, type of technology being worked on (predominantly biotechnology) and stage in the research (basic research or commercial development). Teh-Yuan used this to examine whether how the research process was managed had an impact on its outcome.

Based on this, Teh-Yuan could then use speculations about the differences between cases that he found in his cross-case analysis to develop his propositions. For instance, if he found that a key difference between the projects was the presence of a scientist-manager – someone with the specific remit to manage the project – he could propose that 'the presence of a scientist-manager in such research projects is associated with higher productivity'. He would only need to show that this proposition was reasonable based on the case study data – it need not hold for cases outside the sample. This proposition would then give him something to add to his section on 'areas for future work' in his final research report, and a point for discussion and comparison with the literature.

This is where Step 7, **enfolding the literature**, comes in. Eisenhardt's seventh step is completely in line with the second reason for the existence of the literature review – once a researcher has analysed and speculated from the cases, he or she can now turn to the literature to find vital points of reference and comparison. For example, Teh-Yuan could use the literature to find support for his proposition about the importance of the role of the scientist-manager. If your findings are outside the scope of your previous literature review, you may need to conduct a mini-literature review to find relevant research. Your work can be used to reinforce key findings and provide evidence for the need for research to be carried out to explore the areas of difference further.

Step 8 – **closure** – comes when you are confident that if you stop gathering data you will not miss anything new. This is a powerful reason for closely linking your data collection and your data analysis. You will have reached conceptual saturation when relatively few new concepts are coming out of your cases. At this point, you should be working on the further analysis of the data, through coding and testing out different propositions on the data you have collected. You may need to return to the field later to collect specific data about issues that have emerged from your work, and check that the scope of the work you had envisaged has or has not changed.

Presenting the case study

As we mentioned above, even if you take a quantitative approach to your case study, the design and outputs of a case study are considerably more complex than projects based on research methods such as experiments or surveys and are closer to qualitative research. This can present a challenge when you start writing up and presenting your findings.

There is no 'one best way' to present a case study. During your literature review, look at how case studies are presented in the literature on your research topic, which should provide you with some good examples. For instance, if your evidence is mainly:

1. *questionnaire or other quantitative data* – present the case study evidence as statistical summaries and tables, using the case study detail to illustrate or explain the findings
2. *archival* – present the case study evidence as a narrative, often in chronological order
3. *interview* – present the case study evidence around themes, illustrated with quotes
4. *ethnographic* – present the study as a narrative, often around themes, illustrated with quotes.

Remember that as well as using the literature to support your findings, you can also use the literature to show how your findings have filled a gap in the existing literature or how they challenge existing theoretical explanations.

The following example illustrates how one student chose to present his work at this stage. Sam's project considered the failure of a major new product development project, despite the application of conventional and accepted methods for managing project risks. Sam identified eight key issues that emerged from his analysis – these were concepts that emerged consistently during discussions with people at many levels in the organisation and in his analysis of company documents. Having considered all the options for presentation, Sam used a basic table to present his findings and reintegrate them with the literature. (We will discuss this method of presenting your results in detail in **Chapter 13**.) A summary is given below in **Table 7.2**.

Assessing the quality of a case study

The criteria that may be used to judge your case study include:

1. Have you conducted your research in a systematic way?
2. Does the story that you tell make sense?
3. Does your evidence support your story?
4. Is there any other story that could equally well be told?
5. Have you shown something new?

7.2 Multi-method research and triangulation

The case study is probably the most well-known example of a research design where you employ multiple methods for collecting and analysing your data. However, the case study is not the only example of a multi-method research design. For example, in marketing, studies often employ focus groups, interviews and questionnaires in a single study. Focus groups are used to capture what respondents think are the most important issues or aspects of an issue, usually in a fairly nondirective way. These

Table 7.2 Sam's findings table

Issue	Theory/best practice	Case findings
Use and deployment of risk management systems	If you use a formalised risk management process, it is likely that you will avoid costly problems during the project	Despite the use of formalised risk management systems, problems emerged, particularly during the early stages of the project
Project complexity	Even complex projects can succeed if formal risk management is used	Clear evidence that project managers underestimate risk and complexity so there was no clear view of what the project really entailed
Organisational structure untested	Insufficient organisation will have serious consequences	It did have serious consequences
Senior management interference	Senior management intervention should be minimal once the project has started	Senior management interfered and increased project complexity
Reporting of 'bad news'	Communication channels should be open and used with a no-blame system	People afraid of passing on bad news as management and customers tended to 'shoot the messenger'
Proactive risk management	Formal risk management minimises risk exposure	Risk management seen as secondary and not implemented effectively
Attitudes to risk	Attitudes towards risk should be based on individual experience and training	Attitudes to risk based on overoptimism and wild guesses
Risk deferral	Effective risk management avoids crisis management	Management almost always by crisis, but could have been avoided if addressed early

issues or aspects can then be used to shape a structured interview or questionnaire as the next stage of the research process.

There are three situations where you might want to use multiple methods in a single research project. First, in some projects you won't be able to capture all the information you want to find out using a single method. For example, if you are on a placement project, you might be able to interview managers in your local department about the issues you are investigating. However, if you need to find out information about past decisions, you may need to rely on secondary sources if no one has the relevant knowledge. In this case, you are using different methods to investigate a single issue or a single aspect of that issue. This pluralism in your choice of methods is very much 'horses for courses', so you can usually justify each method you use.

A second reason for using multi-method research occurs when you find out different answers depending on what method you use, and no one method reveals 'the truth' you want to get at. This is why researchers may come up with different findings about the same issue or phenomenon – the answers are method-dependent. For example, in the garbage study described in **Chapter 6**, researchers were interested in whether people could accurately report their use of packaged foods. What people reported they had consumed in their weekly surveys was significantly different from the evidence provided by what they discarded in their rubbish. If the answers you get from different methods converge, even if they are not identical, then you should have more faith in the conclusions you draw from the different methods. For example, even if the amounts discarded in the rubbish varied, if you found that consumers in neighbourhoods with an active recycling programme discarded less waste than those in other neighbourhoods, whatever method you used, you would be more confident in arguing that recycling programmes were effective in promoting desirable behaviours.

Different methods are especially likely to result in different answers when you are asking sensitive questions. People will often give the answers they think are socially appropriate in face-to-face interviews, they are slightly more likely to be honest in telephone interviews, since they can't be seen, and much more likely to be honest in anonymous surveys or computer-based questionnaires. We have already mentioned the differences between people's reports on how often they wash their hands after going to the loo and direct observation. You may be interested or appalled to find out that socially desirable responding makes it difficult for toilet paper manufacturers to find out how people actually use toilet paper – fold or crumple – despite significant consumer research budgets.

You might also consider using different methods when you are asking people to recall or estimate behaviours for which recall may not be accurate. Perhaps the people in the garbology study weren't trying to mislead the researchers, they might actually not have had accurate recall of how much they discarded (how much attention do you actually pay to your rubbish?). Here, the more methods that you can bring to bear, the more chance you have at finding a reliable set of answers.

If you have the time and resources, you may want to experiment with different methods to find out how the information you find out differs according to what method of data collection you use. You can then select the best method – or combine information from the different methods – in answering your research questions. You can capture information about the same issue or aspects of that issue using different methods to see if the information is consistent or inconsistent. The principle of using different methods to collect information on the same thing, rather than on different things, is known as 'triangulation', and is so important for doing research that we will return to it below.

A final reason for using more than one method in your research project is when you want to conduct your research in stages, and different methods are appropriate for each stage of your research. This would actually be a series of linked mini-research projects examining the same research question. For example, you might identify a general topic and conduct a few pilot case studies to identify the important characteristics of the topic. The outcomes of the case study analysis could be used to generate input to interviews, and interviews to surveys. Over time, the research methods could be used to converge progressively on more detailed refinements of your investigation.

At this point, you might be asking yourself whether using multiple methods doesn't conflict with the differences between the scientific and ethnographic approaches. However, these tools and techniques are extremely flexible. You can use a questionnaire to collect unstructured verbal data about why people attend *Star Trek* conventions, if you like. You can use observation to collect detailed measurements on how people navigate through particular websites, if you would rather. At this level, you need to consider the differences between the scientific and ethnographic approach to choose the best set of tools and techniques for what you want to find out, but the 'research methods police' will not hunt you down and arrest you for 'mix-and-match' violations.

Differences between the scientific and ethnographic approach become important when you consider the sequence of activities in the research process. Remember that one of the emphases in the scientific approach is deduction, where you draw on theory to determine what data you collect, whilst the ethnographic approach emphasises the role of data in guiding what theory you choose to explain your observations. It should be obvious that you cannot conduct a research study using the scientific and the ethnographic approach simultaneously, because you cannot let theory determine your observations without selecting a theory, or data determine your theory if you haven't collected data. (The grounded research approach described in **Section 7.1** is a way of 'bootstrapping' your way if you want to choose the middle ground – you are going back and forth between theory and data.)

This also ties into our discussion in **Chapter 5** on the underlying world-views associated with the scientist and the ethnographer. It would be quite a juggling act to believe that we can simultaneously research the social world as real, objective and independent of us, and constructed, subjective and dependent on us. Thus, we argue that it is not possible to conduct mixed-approach research – at least within a single stage of multiple-stage research – even if we can mix tools and techniques. (We will also allow that researchers can mix approaches across stages of multiple-stage research, even if this requires some major flexibility on the researcher's part.) For now, though, you should set this discussion in the context of using multiple tools and techniques.

The contradictions between the process and the world-view associated with each approach may, paradoxically, explain why you can also observe mixed methods across some subjects if you look across researchers, or at the stream of research projects conducted by an individual researcher. This reflects the way that research methods change as a topic moves from being new and not well understood to being established and fairly well understood.

Quite commonly, the methods that people use to investigate a particular topic or phenomenon vary over time across different research projects in predictable fashion. Some researchers even argue that there is a hierarchy, or natural cycle of methods, starting with case studies and ending up with large-scale surveys. However, this has been argued to be a quantitative way of thinking: from a qualitative viewpoint, it may be that any sequence of methods might be valid in investigating a phenomenon.

7.2.1 Triangulation

When you are studying the same phenomenon from several perspectives, for example using more than one method or more than one source of data, this is known as **triangulating** your research. As you might remember from basic maths, the triangle is the strongest and most stable geometry. Some of the different approaches to triangulating your research include:

1. multiple methods
2. multiple sources of data

3. multiple measures
4. multiple viewpoints.

Multiple methods
As mentioned above, you can use multiple methods for collecting your data to strengthen your conclusions. This is especially important when what you find out using one method conflicts with another method, or where you can't capture the information you want using a single method.

Multiple sources of data
Most data are inherently unreliable. If you collect data about the same thing from different sources, you are more likely to spot data that are unreliable. To take a trivial example, imagine reading the same news story in a tabloid, a conservative broadsheet and a liberal broadsheet. How many of the facts and opinions will be consistent? How many of the facts and/or interpretations will differ? You may need to collect some data from only one source, for example the country where the firm's headquarters are located.

Multiple informants
A special case of multiple data sources is asking several people the same question. Many research projects rely on just one person – a single informant – as the source of data about an organisation, work group, household or other group of individuals. Obviously, you need to choose someone who is well informed! Single-informant designs, especially in strategy research, have been widely criticised (for example Van Bruggen et al. 2002). Multiple informants are particularly desirable when you are asking opinion or other subjective questions. For example, if you are studying new product introduction, you could ask the same questions of both marketing and manufacturing managers and see how consistent their answers are.

Multiple informants can be especially useful when you are asking questions for which there is no 'right answer'. You are more likely to reveal a diversity of opinion, if there is one, than if you sample only one person and take their response as representative of the whole. For example, it has been our experience that if you ask a range of people in an organisation what the corporate strategy is, you will get a range of answers – when presumably there is just one corporate strategy being pursued. The marketing manager will see it differently from the manufacturing manager and so on.

If the different responses converge, then you can have more confidence that you have the right answer – at least for that organisation and set of respondents. Opinion polls, especially electoral polls, go to great lengths to get multiple informants so that the answers to the questions they ask are as representative of the whole population as they can possibly be.

Multiple measures
Another way of triangulating is to collect more than one measure for each significant concept (or aspect of an issue) you are investigating. Again, you are trying to get convergence, and divergence between the measures may signal that you need to pay careful attention to some problem.

In attempting to assess, for instance, the level of motivation of a group of employees, you could think of many different measures that can be applied. For instance, you could assess the amount of their own time they were prepared to invest in their work, the level of excitement they felt on a Monday morning going to work and the number of sick days they took off when they weren't really ill.

A word of caution here on developing multiple measures. It is easy to assume that different measures are of the same aspect, but you might well be measuring different aspects that aren't related. For example, absenteeism might reflect employee motivation but lateness to work might reflect extra-work responsibilities that have nothing to do with motivation. If you are taking a scientific approach to measuring intangible aspects such as emotions or beliefs, you may need some expert help in devising multiple measures for the same emotion or belief. You may want to read ahead about measurement scales, which contain a number of different items that (at least in theory) measure the same underlying aspect. We will discuss these in **Chapter 11**.

Multiple viewpoints

A final way to triangulate is to think about what you are researching from as many different angles as you can, and try to include as many possible explanations for what you have found out as you can. If you would arrive at the same conclusions from different perspectives, this should give you more confidence in your results than if a 'scientist' might interpret your research in one way and an 'ethnographer' might interpret it in another.

If you are doing a group project, this sort of triangulation of multiple viewpoints may come naturally. Try to make sure that your group is receptive to these different perspectives, and that 'groupthink' or premature convergence doesn't keep you from being as creative as you can be.

If you are doing a placement or sponsored project, you may find it helpful to have a discussion with your co-workers or your manager to get different perspectives and make sure you haven't missed anything out. Of course, if you get agreement, you need to make sure that you have not gone native – you might try consulting with someone outside the company, within the limits of confidentiality. You should also try to make sure that the received 'company line' does not overwhelm your own findings if they are not what the company wants to hear. You might want to read ahead in **Chapter 10** if this seems to be happening.

If you are doing an individual research project, it may help to discuss your research and findings with someone else, to make sure that it is making sense. If you have kept a research diary along the way, as we recommend, go back and read through your emerging thoughts. Have you left out some promising insights by focusing on the major themes, which you can recapture now? It might also be useful to try to see your research from a different perspective – how would this look to me if I were a scientist/ethnographer? **Figure 7.2** summarises the discussion of triangulation.

7.2.2 Advantages and disadvantages of mixed-method research

If there are so many advantages to doing mixed-method research, why don't all researchers use mixed-method research in every research project? Some of the reasons include:

- you must invest more time and other resources in doing mixed-method research
- you may have difficulty in reconciling the answers from different methods

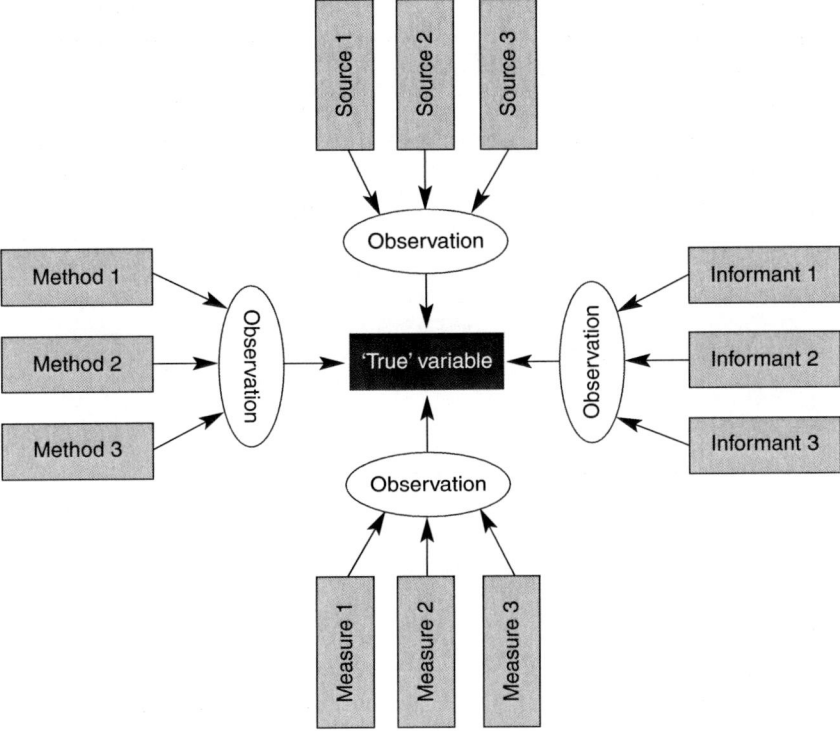

Figure 7.2 Triangulation

- different methods may not give you additional information
- only a single method (or narrow set of methods) may be considered appropriate in your research area or subject
- different methods may reflect different and incompatible research approaches (at the process and world-view levels).

Despite these potential disadvantages, however, we suggest that you consider a mixed-method design if you have the time and resources to carry one out. The advantages that you will gain in terms of confidence in your data, your interpretation and your conclusions may well make a mixed-method approach worth the extra investment in carrying out your research.

Summary

This chapter presents some guidelines on how to design and execute a case study. The case study design combines both quantitative and qualitative research designs, whilst remaining unique. We briefly review the grounded case study approach proposed by Eisenhardt.

The case study is only one type of research design to use multiple methods. The logic of using multiple methods is explained in **Section 7.2**.

Triangulation explains how you can combine quantitative and qualitative data, techniques, methods or approaches with multiple methods and other approaches to strengthen your findings. Triangulation, whether you use multiple informants, researchers, sources of data, techniques, methods or approaches, can increase your insights and the credibility of your research.

Answers to key questions

How can I design and conduct a case study?
- Cases can use predefined issues or take a grounded approach
- Case studies can be single cases, multiple cases, embedded cases and paired cases

How can I design and conduct research studies that use more than one method or approach?
- Similar to the logic of the case study, different methods can be combined to answer different parts of a research question and provide different insights into a research problem

How can I combine quantitative and qualitative methods to study social phenomena?
- Case studies allow the application of multiple methods in the design, collection and analysis of data
- Multiple methods can be used at different times and on different aspects of a case

What are the advantages and disadvantages of integrating quantitative and qualitative methods to study social phenomena?
- Advantages include the generation of a greater insight into the phenomenon being studied
- Disadvantages include more work and the need to reconcile often conflicting data

References

Blaikie, Norman. 2000. *Designing Social Research*. Cambridge: Polity Press.
Bryman, Alan and Bell, Emma. 2003. *Business Research Methods*. Oxford: Oxford University Press.
Chandler, Alfred D. 1962. *Strategy and Structure: Chapters in the History of the American Industrial Enterprise*. Boston: MIT Press.
Creswell, John W. 1994. *Research Design: Qualitative and Quantitative Approaches*. Thousand Oaks, CA: Sage.
Cusumano, Michael A. and Selby, Richard W. 1995. *Microsoft Secrets: How the World's Most Powerful Software Company Creates Technology, Shapes Markets, and Manages People*. London: HarperCollins Business.
Eisenhardt, Kathleen M. 1989. Building theories from case study research, *Academy of Management Review*, **14**(4): 532–50.
Kidder, Tracy. 1981. *The Soul of a New Machine*. New York: Avon Books.
Miles, Matthew B. and Huberman, A. Michael. 1984. *Qualitative Data Analysis*. Beverly Hills, CA: Sage.
Ragin, Charles and Becker, Howard S. (eds). 1992. *What is a Case?* Cambridge: Cambridge University Press.
Selznick, P. 1949. *TVA and the Grass Roots*. Berkeley: University of California Press.
Van Bruggen, Gerrit H., Lilien, Gary L. and Kacker, Manish. 2002. Informants in organizational marketing research: Why use multiple informants and how to aggregate responses, *Journal of Marketing Research*, **39**(4): 469–78.

Whyte, William Foote. 1955. *Street Corner Society*. Chicago: University of Chicago Press.
Yin, Robert K. 1994. *Case Study Research: Design and Methods*, 2nd edn. Thousand Oaks, CA: Sage.

Additional resources

Eisenhardt, Kathleen M. 1991. Better stories and better constructs: The case for rigor and comparative logic, *Academy of Management Review*, 16(3): 620–7.
Glaser, Barney G. and Strauss, Anselm L. 1967. *The Discovery of Grounded Theory: Strategies of Qualitative Research*. London: Weidenfeld & Nicholson.
Gomm, Roger, Hammersley, Martyn and Foster, Peter (eds). 2000. *Case Study Method: Key Issues, Key Texts*. London: Sage.
Jick, Todd. Mixing qualitative and quantitative methods: Triangulation in action, *Administrative Science Quarterly*, **24**: 602–11.
Kanter, R.M. 1983. The Changemasters. New York: Simon & Schuster.
McClintock, C., Brannon, D. and Maynard-Moody, S. 1979. Applying the logic of sample surveys to qualitative case studies: The case cluster method, *Administrative Science Quarterly*, **24**(4): 612–29.
Schroeder, R.G. and Flynn, Barbara B. 2001. *High Performance Manufacturing: Global Perspectives*. New York: John Wiley & Sons.
Stake, Robert E. 1995. *The Art of Case Study Research*. London: Sage.
Strauss, Anselm L. and Corbin, Juliet. 1999. *Basics of Qualitative Research: Techniques and Procedures for Developing Grounded Theory*. London: Sage.
Travers, Max. 2001. *Qualitative Research Through Case Studies*. London: Sage.
Yin, Robert K. 2002. *Applications of Case Study Research*, 2nd edn. London: Sage.
Yin, Robert K. 2003. *Case Study Research: Design and Methods*, 3rd edn. London: Sage.

Key terms

case, 171
case study, 171
closure, 182
cross-case analysis, 180
embedded case study, 174
enfolding the literature, 182
grounded case study, 181
multiple case study approach, 174
paired-case analysis, 180
single case study, 174
triangulation, 186
within-case analysis, 180

Discussion questions

1. What is a case study?
2. Why are case studies so popular among student research projects?
3. What are the different forms of case research?
4. How many cases are enough?
5. Can you use questionnaires and ethnography in the data collection of one case study?
6. What does triangulation mean and how might it be applied in other (non-case) areas of research?
7. Surely cases are just like journalism and consulting?
8. How can having multiple researchers be helpful to the quality of your research?
9. How do you know when to stop collecting data?
10. Can you do a case study on an organisation without visiting it?

Workshop

Task

You have been asked to demonstrate how you would use a case or multi-method research design in the project to find the changes that people experience as they move into higher education. Using the results of the previous workshops on this, or starting afresh, identify:

1. Opportunities for using cases – what questions might cases be good at answering? What types of case analysis could you use here, for example would an embedded multiple case design be appropriate?

2. Opportunities for using triangulation – again, what questions might such an approach be good at answering?

3. Choose a main research question from this work and construct a research design that will enable you to answer this in detail.

PART 3
Literature review and writing your research proposal

CHAPTER 8
Searching and reviewing the literature

LEARNING OBJECTIVES

When you have studied this chapter, you should be able to:
- identify potential sources of secondary data
- search the literature
- record your references
- review the literature, citing your sources
- identify your main research question.

8.1 Introduction

Before you can start the process of searching and reviewing the literature, you need to have identified a *research topic*. Most students have no difficulty in doing this because they have a particular interest in an aspect of one of the subjects they have studied. In some cases, the topic may be allocated. If you are having difficulty in identifying a research topic, try one of the techniques we explained in Chapter 3 to help you generate ideas.

The task of searching and reviewing the literature represents a significant proportion of the total time you will spend on your research and you need to start both activities as soon as possible. In this chapter, we will explain how to conduct a systematic *literature search* and a critical *review* of the literature that is relevant to your study. Many researchers do much of their searching on the internet, using websites that give access to databases containing academic journal articles and other scholarly papers. We recommend that you are selective about the websites you search, to ensure that you only collect information from authoritative sources.

It is essential to keep accurate records so that you can acknowledge the sources of the information that provides the basis of your research. You will need to apply the rules of the bibliographic referencing system that is appropriate to your discipline and acceptable to your supervisor. Once you have collected the literature that is relevant to your study, you will need to write a literature review that evaluates this body of knowledge. In this chapter we will explain what this entails.

8.2 Searching the literature

Your *literature search* can start as soon as you have your first thoughts on a potential topic and it will continue until you submit your dissertation or thesis. In this context, the *literature* refers to the existing body of knowledge. Therefore, a literature search can be defined as a systematic process with a view to identifying the existing body of knowledge on a particular topic. Knowledge is disseminated through various types of publication, which can be in hard copy or digital form, and the data can be qualitative (such as text or illustrations) or quantitative (such as tables or statistics).

The underlying purpose of the literature search is to collect as many relevant items of literature as possible and read them. In the process, you will learn more about the subject and the methodologies used in previous research, which is necessary before you can write a critical review of the literature. This will provide an analysis of what is already known about the phenomena you are going to study and also identify gaps and deficiencies in our knowledge, some aspect of which your study will address.

Key definitions

The **literature** is all sources of published data on a particular topic.

A **literature search** is a systematic process with a view to identifying the existing body of knowledge on a particular topic.

8.2.1 The literature

The *literature* refers to all sources of secondary data that are relevant to your study. Secondary data are data collected from an existing source, such as:

- books on the topic and on methodology
- research reported in books, articles, conference papers and reports
- coverage of business topics in professional journals, newspapers and broadcast media
- government and commercially produced statistics and industry data
- archives
- statutory and voluntary corporate reports
- internal documents and records of organizations
- e-resources, such as on-line databases and the internet.

At undergraduate level, it may be acceptable to refer to textbooks, but at Master's and doctoral level, you must locate original sources of knowledge. By exploring what others have contributed to your area of interest, you will be in a better position to identify a particular research problem or issue to investigate. Your reading should help you understand the main issues within the topic and also the methodologies used in previous studies. If you are a positivist, you will be looking for theories and models so that you can develop a theoretical framework and hypotheses for your study. You can see how your ideas compare with what has gone before, and develop existing ideas or create new ones. Your literature search will continue throughout your study, so that your literature review will reflect the current state of knowledge.

Key definitions

A **theoretical framework** is a collection of theories and models from the literature which underpins a positivist study. Theory can be generated from some interpretivist studies.

8.2.2 Procedure for a systematic literature search

In Chapter 1, we defined research as being systematic and methodical and you can demonstrate this in your methodology chapter when describing how you conducted your literature search. Initially, the subject of your research is likely to be fairly broad, which means your search will be in general terms only. Box 8.1 shows a general procedure for conducting a systematic literature search.

Box 8.1 Procedure for a systematic literature search

- Draw up a list of sources (journal databases, subject-related websites, bibliographic catalogues and other lists your business librarian suggests).
- Define the scope of the research.
- Determine key words you can use for searching, including alternative spellings and synonyms.
- Search each source, keeping a record of your progress (for example: *Journal of Drinking Habits*: Searched 1990–2009 using keywords ...) and full details of relevant publications so that you can read them later and, if relevant, reference them in your work.
- Only collect literature that is relevant to your research in terms of the topic, theory and methodology. In the academic literature, select articles from high-quality journals that review the literature, describe the methods used, discuss the results and draw conclusions.
- Start with the most recent publications and work back in time, using the references at the end of relevant publications to lead you to previous studies.
- When you start to recognize the references cited in other works, you are nearing the end of your first search.
- To keep up to date with the literature, continue searching the literature throughout the project.

8.2.3 Defining the scope

The first step is to define the *scope* and context for your search, which will help limit the material you collect to that which is relevant. Limitations include:

- *Time* – for example, it may not be worth searching more than five years back if the phenomenon you are interested in is some kind of new technology. Find an appropriate cut-off date; it can be adjusted if necessary.
- *Geography* – for example a city, region, country or a comparison of two or more of these.
- *Single or multidisciplinary approach* – for example the development of new software programmes in accountancy.
- *Single discipline, but multi-concept approach* – for example the role of employee appraisals in staff development.

The next step is to decide what sort of information you require. Very recent topics are not likely to be covered by books; journals and newspapers will be the most relevant places to look for information relating to recent events. You may find that some information, for example about a company's corporate strategy or organizational structure, may only be available in internal documents. These may be confidential or difficult to obtain. However, by considering carefully what type of information you expect to find, you can restrict your search to those types only, thus saving yourself valuable time.

You may be able to find much of the information you need from your own institution's library and subscriptions to databases. You need to read abstracts of articles and peruse the information from other sources; if the article or other item of literature is relevant to your research, you will need to print or photocopy a full copy. This may mean visiting another library, or requesting an inter-library loan, for which there may be a charge. You need to allow plenty of time to allow for such delays.

8.2.4 Determining key words

Once you have decided where to start searching, you must identify the key words associated with your research topic that you will use to start off your first search. Although you will later develop some more words from reading the literature you find, you may need some lateral thinking to get you started, such as alternative English spellings and synonyms. For example, if your research is going to focus on the marketing of lager and beer in the UK, you might start your search using key words such as 'marketing' 'advertising', 'lager', 'beer' and 'UK'. As you develop your literature search you may want to widen your search by including 'alcoholic beverages' or narrow it to 'mild', 'bitter', 'real ale' or 'stout'.

When searching, you need to bear in mind that you are seeking authoritative sources. Although you might find it helpful, your supervisors and examiners are not likely to consider sources such as lecture notes (from your institution or another) and open resources such as Wikipedia as authoritative; you will need to seek out the original sources, to which their authors refer. You need to adopt a systematic approach and general surfing of the internet is not advised. We recommend that you take advantage of any tutorials run by your library on how to access and search the e-resources to which your institution subscribes. You can also try academic search engines such as *Google Scholar*, the websites of national and international professional bodies, government departments and other organizations with activities that are relevant to your research topic.

In a simple search, you enter all your key words together in the search box. However, you may be overwhelmed by the thousands of 'hits'. We advise you to investigate the advanced search options that may be available. In many cases, this permits the use of Boolean proximity and adjacency operators to narrow the search or, in the case of too few 'hits', to broaden it. Table 8.1 gives examples of Boolean operators used in ProQuest, an e-resource that contains millions of articles from academic journals and other publications.

The advantages of on-line searching of academic and other databases include:

- ease of access from your computer, wherever you are and have an internet connection
- currency, since printed versions of journals and other documents take longer to reach the library shelves

Table 8.1 Examples of Boolean operators used in ProQuest

Operator	Description
AND	Find <u>all</u> the words. When searching for keywords in "Citation and Document Text," AND finds documents in which the words occur in the same paragraph (within approx. 1000 characters) or the words appear in any citation field. Use W/DOC in place of AND when searching for keywords within "Citation and Document Text," or "Document Text" to retrieve more comprehensive results. *Example:* internet AND education
AND NOT	Find documents which have the first word, but <u>not</u> the second word. *Example:* Internet AND NOT html
OR	Find <u>any</u> of the words. *Example:* Internet OR intranet
W/#	Find documents where these words are <u>within</u> some number of words apart (either before or after). Use when searching for keywords within "Citation and Document Text" or "Document Text." *Example:* computer W/3 careers
W/PARA	Finds documents where these words are <u>within</u> the same <u>paragraph</u> (within approx. 1000 characters). Use when searching for keywords within "Document Text." *Example:* internet W/PARA education
W/DOC	Find documents where all the words appear <u>within</u> the <u>document</u> text. Use W/DOC in place of AND when searching for keywords within "Citation and Document Text" or "Document Text" to retrieve more comprehensive results. *Example:* Internet W/DOC education
NOT W/#	Find documents where these words appear but are <u>not within</u> some number of words apart (either before or after). Use when searching for keywords within "Citation and Document Text" or "Document Text." *Example:* computer NOT W/2 careers
PRE/#	Find documents where the first word appears some number of words <u>before</u> the second word. Use when searching for keywords within "Citation and Document Text" or "Document Text." *Example*: world pre/3 web

Source: ProQuest (2008) Advanced search, Search tips

- cross-disciplinary searching, since journals specializing in different subjects are held in the same publishers' database
- flexibility, as you can carry out a free-text search using any combination of terms and subjects, and you can develop your search strategy as you progress to focus on a particular research problem or issue of interest within the general topic area
- speed, since thousands of sources can be searched in seconds, compared with many hours searching a printed index and the library catalogue and then going to the library shelves to find the publication.

However, you need to bear in mind that searching can still be very time-consuming, particularly if you do not read what you are collecting and therefore do not focus your search at an early stage and adjust your search words accordingly. In addition, you will need to print the documents that are relevant to your research and this may incur some costs. You also need to remember that the results of your search will reflect the quality of the databases and other sources you search. Therefore, we advise you to use a combination of digital and hard copy publications. You will know the end of your search is near when you start to recognize the references in the literature you are reading, but you should continue to search throughout your project to keep your knowledge up to date.

8.2.5 Recording references

Finding relevant information in the first place is hard enough, but finding it again later on can be even harder if you are not careful. It is good practice to make a note of everything you find, even if you eliminate it later because it is not relevant after all. In the long run this will save time by avoiding duplication and helping you with the selection and rejection of material. You will need to set up a filing system on your computer for storing copies of articles, notes, quotations, references (and a parallel system for hard copies you collect). You will soon find that your material can be collated into different categories, which you can place in folders with labels that help identify their contents.

You may have access to bibliographic software, such as *Reference Manager, ProCite, RefWorks* (Write-N-Cite). The main features of most of the bibliographic software are:

- References from most e-resources can be 'dragged' into your personalized database.
- You can also import charts, diagrams and images.
- You can cite publications you have in your database as you write, and the software will generate a list of references at the end of your document when you are ready.
- You can choose from a number of alternative formats for presenting the references, which is useful if you subsequently write articles for submission to journals that have different house styles.

It is by no means essential to use bibliographic software and some researchers find them time-consuming and inconvenient for relatively small studies. The alternative is to keep a list of your references in an ordinary *Word* document (or equivalent) and store it in alphabetical order by author's surname. We suggest you do this in the format that is required for your dissertation or thesis. Whichever method of record keeping you adopt, the main reasons for maintaining accurate records are to:

- identify a particular item accurately so that you can locate it again on-line, in the library or order it through inter-library loan and avoid duplication of effort
- develop links between authors, topics, types of study, main findings and year published by searching your records
- allow you to use a citation in the text of your work to acknowledge the source of information taken from other authors
- allow your supervisor, examiner and other readers to find full bibliographic details of the works of the authors you have cited.

Table 8.2 gives examples of the key data you need to record for a book or journal article.

8.3 Referencing

Whether you are an undergraduate, postgraduate or doctoral student, you must ensure that you follow one of the standard systems for *referencing*. All systems provide rules for making citations and references.

8.3.1 Citations and references

A citation is an acknowledgement in your text of the original source of information or ideas, whether reproduced exactly, paraphrased or summarized. This means the originator of theories, models and arguments, illustrations, diagrams, tables, statistics and any other information that you are using in your work must be acknowledged. Citations are important because they:

- provide evidence of your literature searching and the range of your reading
- help you support your arguments using the authority of the source you have cited
- help the reader to distinguish between your work and the existing body of knowledge, thus avoiding accusations of plagiarism.

References are a list containing the bibliographic details of the sources cited in the text. They are important because they:

- provide full bibliographic details that support the citations
- allow supervisors, examiners and other researchers to locate the source of the works you have cited.

Table 8.2 Key data required for referencing

Books	Journal articles
Name(s) of author(s) or editor(s)	Name(s) of author(s)
Year of publication	Year of publication
Title of book	Title of article
Edition (if not the first)	Title of journal
Place of publication	Volume number and issue
Name of publisher	Page numbers

We distinguish between a *bibliography* and a *list of references* because a bibliography can be a catalogue of publications, not a specific list of those that have been used and, therefore, cited. Some researchers use the terms interchangeably and you should check what the preferred terminology is in your institution.

Key definitions

A **citation** is an acknowledgement in the text of the original source from which information was obtained.

References are a list containing bibliographic details of the sources cited in the text.

There are two main groups of referencing systems: author–date systems, such as the *Harvard system* or the *American Psychological Association (APA) system*, and number-based systems, such as the *Vancouver system*. You will need to find out what is appropriate in your discipline and acceptable to your supervisor before deciding which method to adopt. The important thing to remember is to apply the rules consistently. This means you must first study the rules. Do not be tempted to copy someone else's style, as publishers often use adaptations to create their own house style. Of course, if you are submitting your work for publication, follow the journal's house style. The examples of the Harvard system we show in the next section are based on British Standards, BS 5605:1990.

8.3.2 The Harvard system

The Harvard system is widely used in most business and management research, and other social sciences. It is also used in anthropology and some of the life sciences. The APA system is more commonly used in North America. It is very similar to the Harvard system and both use the author–date system to acknowledge the source of information. Thus, citations in the text are shown as the surname of the author(s) and the date of publication, plus the page number if a quotation is used (or any other exact reproduction of data, such as a table, diagram or illustration). If a printed document or on-line material is not paginated or not dated, use n.p. or n.d. as appropriate.

When citing more than one source, you should place the author–date information in chronological order with the oldest first. If there are two authors, both should be named in all citations. If there are three or more authors, all their names should appear the first time you refer to the publication and thereafter you need only use the name of the first author followed by *et al*. This is the abbreviation of the Latin phrase *et alia*, which means 'and the others' (hence the abbreviation is in italic followed by a full stop). If you are citing more than one author with the same surname, you should include their initials in the text to avoid confusion. Box 8.2 shows a range of examples of how to make citations under the Harvard system.

Under the Harvard system, the bibliographic details of the sources cited in the text are presented in the list of references in alphabetical order by author's name. This list is shown at the end of the document, which means you can still use numbered footnotes or endnotes. The list of references is not included in your word count.

Box 8.2 Citations under the Harvard system

Authors' words are paraphrased

The availability of data is a key factor in determining the successful outcome of a research project (Collis and Hussey, 2003)

or

Collis and Hussey (2003) argue that the availability of data is a key factor in determining the successful outcome of a research project

or authors' words are quoted to emphasize authority of source

'The availability of data is crucial to the successful outcome of your research' (Collis and Hussey, 2003, p. 116).

First citation for three or more authors

Exploratory research by Collis, Dugdale and Jarvis (2001) identified ...

Thereafter

Building on Collis *et al.* (2001), Collis and Jarvis (2002) and Collis, Jarvis and Skerratt (2004) studied ...

More than one source

A number of studies (Carsberg, Page, Sindall and Waring, 1985; Barker and Noonan, 1996; Pratten, 1998) have investigated ...

Author with more than one publication in the same year

Quarterly surveys by Business Monitor (2005a, 2005b, 2005c and 2005d) indicated that ...

Secondary citation

Findings from a case study by Bloomfield (cited in Melrose, 2009) suggest that ...

Distinguishing authors with the same name

R. Hussey (2006) and A. Hussey (2006) examined the effect of ...

Box 8.3 shows examples of references (and their punctuation) under the Harvard system and Box 8.4 illustrates how they are presented in alphabetical order in the list of references at the end of the document. With e-resources, you need to add the URL for the item (the web link) and date you accessed the item. The latter is shown in square brackets. You are advised to copy and paste the URL, as a full stop, comma or slash in the wrong place can lead to problems for you or anyone else wanting to locate the item. We also advise that you test the URL to ensure that it does not need updating, before submitting your work.

8.3.3 The Vancouver system

We will explain the *Vancouver system* because it is used in some business disciplines, such as computer sciences. It is also used in mathematics, biochemistry, physics and

> **Box 8.3 Examples of references**
>
> *Article in an on-line journal*
>
> Collis, J. and Jarvis, R. (2002) 'Financial information and the management of small private companies', *Journal of Small Business and Enterprise Development*, 9 (2), pp. 100–10. http://www.emeraldinsight.com/10.1108/14626000210427357 [Accessed 25 August 2008].
>
> *Article in a printed journal*
>
> Collis, J., Jarvis, R. and Skerratt, L. (2004) 'The demand for the audit in small companies in the UK', *Accounting and Business Research*, 34 (2), pp. 87–100.
>
> *On-line report*
>
> Collis, J. (2003) *Directors' Views on Exemption from Statutory Audit*, URN 03/1342, October, London: DTI. http://www.berr.gov.uk/files/file25971.pdf [Accessed 30 June 2008].
>
> *Book*
>
> Collis, J. and Hussey, R. (2003) *Business Research*, 2nd edition, Basingstoke: Palgrave Macmillan.
>
> *Chapter in a book*
>
> Collis, J., Dugdale, D. and Jarvis, R. (2001) 'Deregulation of Small Company Reporting in the UK', in McLeay, S. and Riccaboni, A. (eds) *Contemporary Issues in Accounting Regulation*, Boston: Kluwer, pp. 167–85.

> **Box 8.4 List of references under the Harvard system**
>
> *References*
>
> Collis, J. (2003) *Directors' Views on Exemption from Statutory Audit*, URN 03/1342, October, London: DTI. http:// www.berr.gov.uk/files/file25971.pdf [Accessed 30 June 2008].
>
> Collis, J., Dugdale, D. and Jarvis, R. (2001) 'Deregulation of Small Company Reporting in the UK', in McLeay, S. and Riccaboni, A. (eds) *Contemporary Issues in Accounting Regulation*, Boston: Kluwer, pp. 167–85.
>
> Collis, J. and Hussey, R. (2003) *Business Research*, 2nd edition, Basingstoke: Palgrave Macmillan.
>
> Collis, J. and Jarvis, R. (2002) 'Financial information and the management of small private companies', *Journal of Small Business and Enterprise Development*, 9 (2), pp. 100–10. http://www.emeraldinsight.com/10. 1108/14626000210427357 [Accessed 25 August 2008].
>
> Collis, J., Jarvis, R. and Skerratt, L. (2004) 'The demand for the audit in small companies in the *UK'*, *Accounting and Business Research*, 34 (2), pp. 87–100.

> **Box 8.5 Citations under the Vancouver system**
>
> *Authors' words are paraphrased*
> The availability of data is a key factor in determining the successful outcome of a research project.[1]
> or
> Collis and Hussey[1] argue that the availability of data is a key factor in determining the successful outcome of a research project.
> *or authors' words are quoted to emphasize authority of source*
> 'The availability of data is crucial to the successful outcome of your research.'[1]
> *First citation for three or more authors*
> Exploratory research by Collis, Dugdale and Jarvis[2] identified …
> *Thereafter*
> Building on Collis et al.,[3] Collis and Jarvis[4] and Collis et al.,[5] examined …
> *More than one source*
> Several studies[6–8] have investigated …

other natural sciences. In the Vancouver system, citations are acknowledged using sequential superscript numbers throughout the text (instead of author–date) and the references are shown as footnotes or as end notes in numerical order (instead of alphabetical order). Numbered footnotes or endnotes are easy to insert in *Word* and other software programs. However, one of the drawbacks of the Vancouver system is that it prevents you from using numbered footnotes or endnotes for other purposes. Box 8.5 shows how the Vancouver system works in the text and Box 8.6 shows the list of references in numerical order.

In this section we have concentrated on the most common needs of students when using citations and references. However, Winkler and McCuen-Metherell (2007) are an excellent source of further information.

8.4 Reviewing the literature

Once you have collected the literature that is relevant to your study, you will need to write a *literature review*. A literature review is a critical evaluation of the existing body of knowledge on a topic, which guides the research and demonstrates that relevant literature has been located and analysed. Therefore, it should provide 'a statement of the state of the art and major questions and issues in the field under consideration' (Gill and Johnson, 1991, p. 21).

At the proposal stage, a preliminary review of the literature helps develop your subject knowledge and provide a context for your research questions. A preliminary review is relatively brief and usually focuses on the seminal studies (the most influential previous research) and the main theories (if appropriate to your paradigm). Most researchers highlight the limitations of their work and suggest avenues for

> **Box 8.6 List of references under the Vancouver system**
>
> References
>
> [1] Collis, J. and Hussey, R. (2003) *Business Research,* 2nd edition, Basingstoke: Palgrave Macmillan.
>
> [2] Collis, J., Dugdale, D. and Jarvis, R. (2001) 'Deregulation of Small Company Reporting in the UK', in McLeay, S. and Riccaboni, A. (eds) *Contemporary Issues in Accounting Regulation,* Boston: Kluwer, pp. 167–85.
>
> [3] ibid. (the Latin abbreviation of *ibidem,* meaning from the same source as previously cited).
>
> [4] Collis, J. and Jarvis, R. (2002) 'Financial information and the management of small private companies', *Journal of Small Business and Enterprise Development* 9 (2), pp. 100–10. http://www.emeraldinsight.com/10.1108/14626000210427357 [Accessed 25 August 2008].
>
> [5] Collis, J., Jarvis, R. and Skerratt, L. (2004) 'The demand for the audit in small companies in the UK', *Accounting and Business Research,* 34 (2), pp. 87–100.
>
> [6] Carsberg, B. V., Page, M. J., Sindall, A. J. and Waring, I. D. (1985) *Small Company Financial Reporting,* London: Prentice Hall.
>
> [7] Barker, P. C. and Noonan, C. (1996) *Small Company Compliance with Accounting Standards,* Dublin: Dublin City University.
>
> [8] Pratten, C. (1998) *The Uses of the Accounts of Small and Medium-sized Companies and the Effects of the Audit Exemption Regime,* London: ICAEW.

future research. This is useful, because you are looking for gaps and deficiencies in the literature that suggest a business problem or issue to investigate.

When you write a full review of literature for your dissertation or thesis, you will also need to demonstrate an appropriate level of intellectual ability and scholarship. At that stage, your literature review will be large enough to occupy at least one chapter (more than one if the literature is large or your study has been designed as an exhaustive review of the literature).

Key definitions

A **literature review** is a critical evaluation of the existing body of knowledge on a topic, which guides the research and demonstrates that the relevant literature has been located and analysed.

8.4.1 Nature and purpose of a literature review

It may be very satisfying to know that you have a fine collection of literature neatly filed away (or piling up impressively in the corner), but you need to start reading and analysing it in order to develop your research proposal and design your study. As you read, you will learn more about the subject and the methodologies used in

> **Box 8.7 Checklist for reading the literature**
>
> - What was the purpose of the study and how does it differ from other studies and my own research?
> - How was the research conducted and how does that differ from other studies and my own research?
> - What were the findings and how do they differ from other studies and my own research?
> - What were the limitations and weaknesses of the study?

Table 8.3 Recording and categorizing previous studies

Author and date	Subject categories	Methodology categories	Sample size	Response rate (if applicable)	Date of study	Location/country

previous research. You may find the questions shown in Box 8.7 useful as a checklist when you first start reading the literature.

8.4.2 General analytical approach

You need to adopt a systematic approach when analysing your collection of articles and other items from the literature. Many researchers adopt a thematic approach, which involves categorizing the themes in the relevant literature. Both subject-related categories and methodology-related categories are likely to be broken down into various subgroups, which will emerge from your reading of the article. Without formally recognizing it, you will begin this process when you generate your key words for searching the literature. Your thematic analysis of the literature can be facilitated if you record key details of the previous studies in a spreadsheet. This allows you to sort the data into different groups to help you structure your literature review (one article is likely to be included in many subgroups). Table 8.3 suggests a basic format, which you can adapt to suit your needs. We have included the standard author–date information to identify the publication, but also the date when the study was conducted, as many articles are not published for a year or more after the research has been completed.

8.4.3 Network analysis of primary citations

Ryan, Scapens and Theobald (2002) offer a structured approach to analysing the literature, using a network diagram to illustrate relationships between primary citations. This approach is based on the assumption that articles in the literature are 'a series of nodes in an interlinked network of theoretical and empirical developments' (Ryan *et al.*, 2002, pp. 186–7). Box 8.8 shows the main steps in constructing a network diagram for this purpose.

> **Box 8.8 Procedure for generating a network of primary citations**
>
> 1. From the literature you have collected, select all the articles that are published in what you consider are the top two or three journals among those represented. From these articles, select those that have been published in the most recent year. These are the ones you will analyse first.
> 2. Examine each article to identify which item from the literature is the most important to the author's study. This is the primary citation for that article. Do the same for the other articles published that year.
> 3. Place all the primary citations for the most recent year as nodes in an oval text box at the bottom of your diagram and use Author (Date) to label them.
> 4. Repeat this process at five-yearly intervals to add new nodes to the diagram that reflect the year of publication. Draw links between nodes to identify the literary antecedents (similar to a family tree). Identify the node that lies at the core of the literature (the one with the most 'descendants') by putting it in a rectangular text box. This allows you to illustrate the theoretical framework that unites the literature.
> 5. The final step is to determine the motivation for each article, and the methodological rationale that links them.
>
> *Source*: Adapted from Ryan et al. (2002)

> **Box 8.9 Guide to writing a literature review**
>
> - Select only material that is relevant to the topic, industry, methodology and so on
> - Identify themes and group the material
> - Define key terms and draw out the important features
> - Compare results and methods of previous studies
> - Be critical and demonstrate relevance to your research
> - Set the context for your study (a deductive approach suggests you will identify a theoretical framework and hypotheses)
> - Identify gaps or deficiencies in the literature that your study will address
> - Conclude with your research question(s)
> - Acknowledge other people's contribution to knowledge using the Harvard system of referencing.

8.4.4 Writing the literature review

Once you have reflected on your analysis, you are ready to start structuring and writing your review of the literature. Box 8.9 provides a general guide to writing a literature review.

You need to ensure that you have included all the major studies that are relevant to your study. You may also consider it diplomatic to refer to any relevant publication by your supervisor(s) and external examiners! A previous study may be relevant because it focuses on the same or a similar research problem or issue to the one you have in mind. Sometimes students become disillusioned because they think there is no literature on the issue they want to investigate. For example, if you are investigating labour turnover in hotels in Poland, perhaps you will not be able to find any other similar studies. However, you may find research has been done on this topic in other countries or there are studies of other HRM issues in Poland that illuminate your research. A second way in which previous research can be relevant is the methodology used. References to studies that have used the research methodology you propose using, or a different research methodology in a similar subject area, are essential. If you decide the item is not relevant, put it in a safe place in case you change your mind later.

A critical analysis of the literature identifies and appraises the contribution to knowledge made by others and comments on any weaknesses. Such comments may focus on such matters as the reliability, validity and generalizability of the findings, which we discussed in Chapter 4. The gaps and deficiencies in the literature are relevant because they suggest the specific areas where further research is needed. Most researchers highlight the limitations of their work and suggest avenues for future research. If you have difficulty in identifying a specific research problem or issue, consider:

- testing a theory in a different setting
- making a new analysis of existing data
- replicating a previous study to provide up-to-date knowledge.

Reviewing the literature involves 'locating, reading and evaluating reports of research as well as reports of casual observation and opinion' (Borg and Gall, 1989, p. 114). Therefore, a literature review is not merely a description of previous studies and other material you collected during your literature search but requires a critical analysis. Unfortunately, some students do not recognize this, as Bruce (1994) found out. She analysed the views of 41 students at an early stage in their studies and identified six ways in which they viewed the literature review. It may be useful to think of these categories as being successive layers in a student's understanding of the nature of and purpose of a literature review, with the deeper level of understanding captured by the last three descriptions:

- a list, with the primary focus on listing what was read, rather than extracting and using the knowledge in the literature
- a search, with the emphasis on finding the existing literature
- a survey, where the researcher is interested in the knowledge in the literature, but does not relate it to his or her own activities
- a vehicle for learning, where the researcher considers he or she is improving his or her personal knowledge on the subject
- a research facilitator, where the researcher improves not only his or her own knowledge, but the literature has an impact on the research project itself
- a report, which is a synthesis of the literature and the earlier experiences the researcher has engaged in.

> **Box 8.10 Avoiding a shopping list approach**
>
> *Shopping list approach*
>
> Davis (2005) found that white rabbits bred more prolifically than those with dark coloured fur.
>
> Smith (2006) argued that Davis had not defined 'dark' fur.
>
> Jones (2007) used five well-defined colours of rabbit in his study and found white rabbits were the most prolific breeders.
>
> *Attempt at synthesis*
>
> The identification of the colour of a rabbit's fur as a predictor of fertility is controversial. Although it has been claimed that white rabbits are more prolific breeders than other colours (Davis, 2005), the reliability of this conclusion has been questioned on the grounds that non-white colours have not been clearly defined (Smith, 2006). Evidence from a recent study by Jones (2007) suggests that white rabbits are indeed more prolific breeders than four other well-defined colours of rabbit.

Box 8.10 shows a simple example of how to avoid summarizing one article after another and turning your review into the equivalent of a shopping list.

8.5 Avoiding plagiarism

Plagiarism is the act of taking someone's words, ideas or other information and passing them off as your own because you fail to acknowledge the original source. It is a form of academic misconduct that is taken very seriously, as it is the equivalent of stealing intellectual property.

Plagiarism is easily avoided if you follow the rules of one of the standard referencing systems, such as the Harvard or Vancouver systems we have described in this chapter. In this chapter, we have emphasized the absolute necessity of applying the rules of the referencing system you are using when writing your literature review, but we would now like to emphasize that this is necessary throughout your work, whether you are writing your research proposal, the final dissertation or thesis, or an academic paper after you have completed your research.

The reason why it is imperative you avoid plagiarism is that your supervisors, examiners and others evaluating your research need to distinguish between the contribution to knowledge made by others and the contribution made by your study. It is your responsibility to ensure that your work is meticulously referenced, that every quotation is enclosed in quotation marks and, whether it is text, a table, a diagram or other item that is reproduced, you show it exactly as it is in the original. This includes the punctuation, any emphasis (such as capital letters, italics or bold) and layout. This does not apply if you are using your own words or developing someone else's table, diagram or other item, where you still acknowledge the source but can present the data as you choose.

SEARCHING AND REVIEWING THE LITERATURE

> **Box 8.11 Checklist for referencing under the Harvard system**
>
> - Have I acknowledged other people's work, ideas and all sources of secondary data?
> - Have I enclosed quotations in quotation marks and cited the author(s), date and page number in the original source?
> - Have I acknowledged the source of all tables, diagrams and other items reproduced, including the number of the page in the original source?
> - Have I applied the rules consistently?
> - Have I included full bibliographic details for every source cited in my list of references?

We now want to explain a different example of plagiarism, which concerns submitting a piece of your own work for assessment if you have already received credits for it on another course. You cannot use the same research report you had assessed as part of a previous course or degree programme as your dissertation or thesis for a subsequent award.

It is not a defence to say you were not aware that you had committed plagiarism. Therefore, you need to familiarize yourself with the regulations (and penalties) that apply in your institution. If you are still in any doubt about what constitutes plagiarism, seek advice from your supervisor. To help you avoid the pitfalls, Box 8.11 provides a checklist for referencing.

8.6 Conclusions

Searching and reviewing the literature is a major part of your research and, although an intensive phase at the start of the project, will continue on a smaller scale until you submit your dissertation or thesis. Therefore, it is essential to start as soon as possible. This will be when you have chosen a general topic that is relevant to your course; it does not matter that you have not yet identified a particular research problem or issue to investigate, because you will identify this from studying the literature and identifying the need for your study. Most students will be required to incorporate a preliminary literature review in their research proposal, and this will be essential if you are applying for funding. All students will need to write a comprehensive critical literature review for their dissertation or thesis.

Searching the literature is time-consuming. It is rarely a problem locating literature but often a matter of not becoming overwhelmed by the number of items found. In this chapter we have given you guidance on how to define the scope of your research and narrow your search so that you focus as closely as possible on the relevant literature. You will then need to become familiar with the literature, which means setting aside plenty of time to read it, select what is relevant to your study and analyse it using a systematic method. You will write about the methods you used to search the literature (and what sources you searched) and how you analysed the material in your methodology chapter in your dissertation or thesis. In

> **Box 8.12 Checklist for the literature review**
>
> - Have you cited the most important experts in your field?
> - Have you referred to major research studies which have made a contribution to our knowledge?
> - Have you referred to articles in the most important academic journals in your area?
> - Have you identified any major government or other institutional study in your research field?
> - Have you identified studies that use the same paradigms and methodologies you propose?
> - Have you identified serious criticisms of any of the studies conducted?
> - Have you avoided plagiarism?

your proposal, you only need to indicate the main sources you will use, such as the journals and databases to which your institution subscribes.

In your literature review, and throughout your research, you must cite your sources correctly and provide full bibliographic details in your list of references. We have explained the principal rules of the Harvard and Vancouver systems, but you must check which system you are expected to use. If your institution uses the APA system, you will find it is very similar to the Harvard system. More information on referencing will be available from your lecturers, supervisors and librarians. It is your responsibility to ensure that you have not committed plagiarism. Many institutions use detection software to check for this and your supervisor will also be alert to this form of cheating. We have warned you about the dangers of plagiarism because it is taken very seriously and the penalties are harsh.

Remember that your literature review is not a shopping list and you must write a critical analysis that provides the context for your research, and concludes by identifying the need for your study and the main research question(s) it addresses. If you are a positivist, an important function of the literature review is to identify your theoretical framework and hypotheses. Box 8.12 shows a checklist for a literature review that draws together some of the key issues.

> ### Activities
>
> 1. Take four different journals from different disciplines in your library and identify which system of referencing each journal uses.
> 2. Using an appropriate bibliographic database, search for information on a well-known company in your own country. Limit your results by date, country or any other variable available on the database. Repeat this with another database and compare the number of 'hits' you get and the features of the search facilities and presentation of the results.

3. Identify a major author in your field of research and conduct a search for all articles he or she has written. If any are co-authored, search for articles published by each author individually.
4. List the main findings of six key articles on your field of research. Then write a synthesis of the findings in no more than two paragraphs.
5. Literature review exercise.

The following reviews have been written by two students who have read the same articles. Which do you think is the better review and why?

Review 1

The popularity of roller-blading in the UK has its roots in the 1990s. Jane Iceslider (1990) describes roller-blading as a means of keeping fit for ice skating during the summer months. In a later article she reinforces this view, as evidenced by her comment, 'All my ice-skating friends use roller-blading as part of their fitness training' (Iceslider, 1992, p. 56).

Greg Sniffer, a reformed drug dealer, argues that roller-blades provide 'quick escape from any nosy cops' (Sniffer, 1998, p. 122).

Social worker, John Goodchild, describes roller-blading as 'a non-contact dance replacement activity for young people' (Goodchild, 1996, p. 29). He cites the growing popularity of children's roller discos in support of his claim. In a later article he notes that 'rollerblading is becoming an environmentally friendly means of transportation in urban locations' (Goodchild, 1999, p. 30).

In his school magazine, Jason Scruff, describes roller-blading as being great fun, adding that all his mates go roller-blading (Scruff, J., 1996). In the same article he mentions how using roller-blades allows him to finish his paper round much faster than when walking. In an accompanying article, Melanie Scruff (Jason's sister), contends that 'roller discos are a great place to meet boys' (Scruff, M., 1996, p. 3) and that she would rather roller-blade into town to meet friends on a Saturday than walk or catch the bus.

Review 2

There is little agreement between authors for the reasons why people roller-blade in the UK. Initially it appears to have been a keep-fit activity (Iceslider, 1990 and 1992), but over time roller-blading appears to have become a fashionable activity (Goodchild, 1996), a social activity (Scruff, M., 1996) and a means of transport for work (Sniffer, 1998; Goodchild, 1999) and leisure (Scruff, M. 1996).

There is some evidence that young people have multiple reasons for roller-blading. For example, one teenager's motivation for roller-blading was in part due to following trends, but also to the speed of transportation compared with walking (Scruff, J., 1996).

Although it is possible that Goodchild (1996 and 1999) has based his conclusions on observation of particular cases of children's behaviour, there appears to have been no formal research into the reasons for the popularity of roller-blading in the

UK. Therefore, there is scope for an exploratory study to identify the main motivations for the popularity of this activity.

References

Goodchild, J. D. (1996) The sociology of rollerblading', Journal of Street Credibility, 1 (1), pp. 29–33.

Goodchild, J. D. (1999) 'Rollerblading to save the planet', Journal of Street Credibility, 3 (3), pp. 8–9.

Iceslider, J. (1990) 'Why I rollerblade', Journal of Fitness, 3 (2), pp. 21–2.

Iceslider, J. (1992) 'Rollerblade your way to fitness', Journal of Fitness, 5 (1), pp. 53–6.

Scruff, J. (1996) 'Roller discos and boys', Kingston School Magazine, Summer term, p. 4.

Scruff, M. (1996) 'Rollerblading is cool', Kingston School Magazine, Summer term, p. 3.

Sniffer, G. (1998) 'How I kicked the habit', Rehabilitation Quarterly, Winter, pp. 122–5.

Adapted from 'A Mock Literature Review' (Anon.)

PROGRESS TEST

Complete the following sentences:

1. In research, the existing body of _____ is known as the literature.
2. A literature search involves collecting secondary _____.
3. Before you can search the literature, you need to identify a number of _____ so that you can search for items that are relevant to your study.
4. The bibliographic list of all the sources of information cited in a document is known as a list of _____.
5. The systematic way in which you search and review the literature is described in your _____ chapter.

Are the following statements true or false?

6. A literature search is not needed if a literature review has already been published on your research topic.
7. A literature review only covers previous research and other sources of relevant published material on the research topic.
8. A literature review is a way of learning about the research topic.
9. A literature review is a systematic survey of relevant publications.
10. A literature review identifies the research questions the researcher will address.

Multiple choice questions:

11. The literature is a source of:
    a) perfect data
    b) primary data
    c) historical data
    d) unpublished data

12. The purpose of a critical literature review is to be:
    a) analytical
    b) complimentary
    c) derogatory
    d) descriptive

13. The result of criticizing constructively or setting out a reasoned argument in steps is known as:
    a) a debate
    b) a devolution
    c) an evaluation
    d) an evolution

14. Using analogy to identify a research topic or methodology involves:
    a) using physical variables to represent numbers
    b) determining the constituent parts of variables
    c) reasoning based on parallel cases
    d) conducting an exploratory study

15. The rationale for using a referencing system is that:
    a) references can be pasted from digital sources
    b) software can be used to organize references
    c) previous studies are identified
    d) the source of existing knowledge is identified

References

Borg, W. R. and Gall, M. D. (1989) *Educational Research: An Introduction*, 5th edition, New York: Longman.

Bruce, C. S. (1994) 'Research students' early experiences of the dissertation literature review', *Studies in Higher Education*, 9 (2), pp. 217–29.

Gill, J. and Johnson, P. (1991) *Research Methods for Managers,* London: Paul Chapman.

Winkler, A. C. and McCuen-Metherell, J. R. (2007) *Writing the Research Paper: A Handbook*, 7th edition, New York: Harcourt Brace Jovanovitch.

Ryan, B., Scapens, R. W. and Theobald, M. (2002) *Research Method and Methodology in Finance and Accounting*, 2nd edition, London: Thomson Learning.

Glossary

Bibliography A list of publications relating to a topic.

Citation An acknowledgement in the text of the original source from which information was obtained.

Literature	All sources of published data on a particular topic.
Literature review	A critical evaluation of the existing body of knowledge on a topic, which guides the research and demonstrates that the relevant literature has been located and analysed.
Literature search	A systematic process with a view to identifying the existing body of knowledge on a particular topic.
Plagiarism	The act of taking someone's words, ideas or other information and passing them off as your own because you fail to acknowledge the original source.
References	A list containing bibliographic details of the sources cited in the text.
Theoretical framework	A collection of theories and models from the literature which underpins a positivist study. Theory can be generated from some interpretivist studies.
Vancouver system	A system of referencing where citations are shown as an in-text number each time the source is cited and the references are listed in numerical order at the end of the document.

CHAPTER 9
What should I study?
Generating and clarifying ideas for your research project

KEY QUESTIONS

- Where do ideas for research topics come from?
- How can I choose between several potential research topics?
- What characterises a good research topic?
- Why should I use research questions to focus my research?
- How can I use a project proposal to define my project scope?

LEARNING OUTCOMES

At the end of this chapter, you should be able to:
- Generate ideas and select an idea for your research project
- Identify your research topic
- Distinguish between satisfactory and unsatisfactory research topics
- Develop researchable research questions
- Develop a research proposal

CONTENTS

Introduction
9.1 Generating ideas for your research project
9.2 Selecting the best idea
9.3 Developing a research proposal
Summary
Answers to key questions
References
Additional resources
Key terms
Frequently asked questions
Discussion questions
Workshop

Introduction

The starting point for your research project is deciding what you will study (Lundberg 1999). 'What am I going to research?' is one of the most important questions you will ask. Your research topic will be developed into your research design, which describes how you are going to research it, covered in **Part 2**. Needless to say, you should choose your research topic carefully, because you will have to live with it, often for a long time.

This chapter presents a systematic process for generating, selecting and refining ideas for research topics. If you have been assigned a research problem by your academic supervisor or business sponsor, you may think that you don't need to generate ideas. This may limit your freedom somewhat, but you still can bring some creativity to generating and selecting ideas and defining your project and developing a research design.

In coming up with good ideas, you may have to deal with many creative and personal issues. Not surprisingly, many students find choosing a topic the most challenging stage of their research project. Sometimes this is because they have no idea of what they want to do or how to come up with ideas; other times, it is because they have too many ideas and no notion of how to choose between them. We will suggest how you might manage either problem. This is an example of where understanding the boundaries between chaos and order can help you to manage your research.

Section 9.1 will explain how to generate ideas from real-world organisations, business and management research, and your own personal and career interests. Combined with brainstorming and other methods such as mind mapping – it is vital for you to generate several ideas here – you can identify ideas that are potentially worth researching.

Although you can easily find good advice about *how* to come up with ideas that you can turn into a feasible and worthwhile research topic, you may find surprisingly little specific guidance about *what* a research topic is. This chapter focuses not only on how to generate and select ideas for research topics and turn them into research problems, but also what a research topic actually is.

At this stage, to make sure that your research topic will satisfy your project guidelines and assessment criteria, read them carefully when you are defining your project – another example of 'beginning with the end in mind'. **Section 9.2** describes how you can select the best idea based on the project requirements and your interests. You can filter your ideas against the characteristics of a good research project. We also describe how to refine your idea from a research topic to research problems and research questions.

When you select an idea to develop, you should make sure not only that you will find your project interesting and worth doing, but also that it is manageable – you can actually get it done in the time and with the skills and other resources you have. In **Section 9.3** we describe how you should define the scope of your project once you have selected a promising research topic and a backup – what you are going to do and, just as importantly, what you are not going to do. A good way to do this is to prepare a project proposal, which will answer the questions that your supervisor or sponsor will typically ask about your project. You can also use a well-developed project proposal to tell other project stakeholders what you will do in your project, which makes it easier for them to provide support and feedback.

After you have finished this chapter, you should be much clearer about what you are going to research, even if you have to revise your research topic once you have done some library research on it, as covered in **Chapter 4**. Otherwise, you may be trying to solve a problem that has already been solved, or one that no one can solve. Such revisiting is not unusual in research projects – they are seldom linear. However, if you approach this systematically, you should waste much less time and effort defining your research project.

9.1 Generating ideas for your research project

Deciding what the project will be about and where and with whom it will be conducted is an important part of your research project (Blaikie 2000: 14). Good ideas for research topics come from all kinds of places: the business and management world, the subjects you have studied in your course and your own personal interests. A systematic approach to generating, selecting and refining these ideas is key to project success (Gill and Johnson 2002).

You may already know what you want or must do, but it's important not to close down the idea-generating process too early. While some projects may not allow you any leeway in defining your topic, nearly every project has enough flexibility that you can – or even be required to – be creative about what you are going to study and how you are going to study it. We suggest that in this stage you identify as many ideas as you can, rather than just one perfect idea. You will learn how to rank and select the best one in **Section 9.2**.

We strongly recommend that you don't decide *what* you will research based on *how* you will research it. That is, don't choose a research topic just because you want to try out a particular way of gathering data – such as a survey – or a particular way of analysing data – such as conjoint analysis (unless your project requirements make this unavoidable). While you should definitely take research methods into account, you should cast your net more widely when you select your topic, otherwise, as the old saying among project supervisors goes, 'if the only tool you have is a hammer, everything starts to look like a nail'.

You should balance order and chaos in generating ideas. Creativity lies on the border between them, where you have generated enough ideas so you can choose the best one, but not so many that you feel overwhelmed and unable to get started, or too few so that you ignore the chance to learn. You should try to identify enough ideas so that you can choose the one that suits you and satisfies your project stakeholders, including your sponsors. You can often incorporate features of the ideas you reject into your research project.

As you can see in **Figure 9.1**, people start from different places in generating ideas. Some people start with many ideas, others with no ideas and a few with one main idea that they will end up researching. Most people start somewhere between the two extremes. If you start with many ideas, you should aim to converge on a few possibilities, and then select one main idea. If you start with no ideas, you should aim to generate several ideas that you can choose among. Even if you start with one

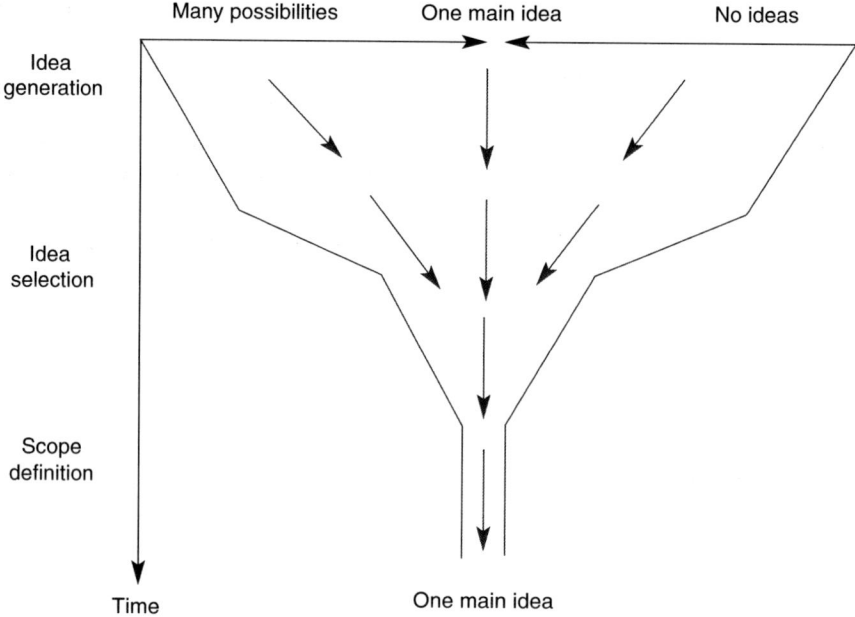

Figure 9.1 Getting to one idea

main idea, you should revisit that idea to see whether it will actually lead to the best project that you can do.

Although this figure may make the process seem simple – generate some ideas and pick the best one – many students find this stressful. Some students have absolutely no idea of what they would like to research for their project, and no clue about how to come up with some ideas. You cannot truly own your project unless you want to find out more about some practical or theoretical problem. You will be just 'going through the motions' (Whedon 2001). We describe how to overcome this in **Section 9.1.1**.

Other students come unstuck the first time they have an unconstrained brief – they can do anything within the entire subject area of business and management – resulting in an overload of possibilities and uncertainty about where to get started. This uncertainty conflicts with the pressing need to get on with the project, which leads to **project paralysis**. If this describes you, don't worry, there are many ways out of it and we will be describing them in **Section 9.2**.

Students who start off with a single fixed idea, an unshakeable view of what they are going to do and how they are going to do it often run into significant problems later on in their research project. This is more risky than not being able to come up with ideas. If you choose your topic without exploring other possibilities, you are unlikely to be successful. You have probably not considered the possibilities adequately and have rushed into making a choice too early. You will miss what you might learn from the early exploration of a subject area, and might have to change your topic significantly anyway. Indeed, absolute certainty at this stage is usually a cover-up for massive ignorance – 'not knowing what you don't know' – as illustrated in **Student research in action 9.10**. The antidote for too much early certainty is to explore your research topic and come up with possibilities to investigate further. Once you start to explore potential ideas, you will find that your certainties are replaced by questions, rather than vice versa.

For instance, suppose you are looking at how to motivate employees in your organisation and have decided that you will take Maslow's 'hierarchy of needs' as the main theoretical basis for your research. Without doing some background research on this model of human behaviour, you may not realise that many studies question the basis of Maslow's model, its applicability and usefulness. If you don't find these articles early on, you risk 'building on sand'. If you only find these studies when you are writing up your research, you may have to go back and make major changes to your project, which you may not have the time for. Even worse, if you don't find them and you turn in recommendations or findings based on at least partially discredited research, you will be embarrassed, at best, when this is pointed out to you. Don't assume that your work will be so compelling that your project examiners will overlook this flaw.

9.1.1 Generating ideas

According to Weick (1992), good research often starts with an issue that catches your attention – something that presents a puzzle or is interesting. Although you may find ideas to explore anywhere, student projects usually come from either real-world business and management settings (practical problems) or from business and management research (theoretical problems). However, you may also find ideas in your own personal interests and experiences, the subjects you have already studied and projects that other students have already carried out, or even from brainstorming.

You can think of an idea as an interest or a general area of inquiry that you want to pursue (Booth et al. 2003: 36). Lundberg (1999) suggests that a **research idea** is general enough to describe anything that you might research:

- a phenomenon
- an issue
- a problem
- a question to study
- a general theme
- an area of behaviour
- a body of theory.

Early on, your ideas may be as broad as 'service management', 'research and development', 'the film industry', or 'humour'. As we noted above, don't worry so much about the quality of your ideas at this point but on quantity: generating enough good ideas so that you can choose the best idea (and possibly a backup if the first idea is risky). *Don't lose your ideas: write them down.* Maintaining a file of your ideas will help you to keep track of potential research topics. You will need to nurture your most promising ideas into research topics, and your best topics into research problems and research questions through further reading and some library research.

These ideas are too general to research, but we describe how you can focus them into research topics and then into research problems and research questions. Your

research topic is a general area of business and management that you can investigate and describes what your project is about. A good research topic will lead to either a practical or a theoretical problem that you can address in your research. As well as a research topic and research problem, you will need to identify a **research setting** where you will conduct your project, and a **sample** of organisations, people or other social units where you will collect your data.

9.1.2 Sources of ideas

Ideas from real-world managers and organisations

Many interesting ideas come from problems that face business and management organisations in the real world, **practical problems** that the organisation needs to solve. If you are sponsored by an organisation or are working in an organisation while you are doing your research, you will probably be expected to focus on a practical problem identified by either you or the organisation. For instance, your organisation or sponsor may want to know how to answer questions such as:

- How can we reduce our purchasing costs through developing a supply strategy (implementing a particular practice)?
- How can we retain customers who are defecting because of bad service (solving a particular organisational problem)?
- How can we get more undergraduate students to apply for our credit card (improving the organisation's performance)?

Your ideas may also be the result of personal experience, as was the case in **Student research in action 9.1**.

Student research in action 9.1

A RESEARCH TOPIC THAT 'STUCK'

Elmar had been an IT consultant before he started as a postgraduate research student. He was shocked and appalled by the number of large IT projects that failed, despite the millions of pounds spent on them. Such failures were often reported in newspapers. When he started his studies, he found that many academic articles also investigated the problem of why IT projects failed. But no one had any definite answers – indeed the literature was littered with prescriptions that did not appear to provide any benefit to managers in managing their projects successfully. Clearly, there was an opportunity for him to do some interesting research. The research project has clear practical implications for managers.

Even if your research is not sponsored by a particular organisation, you may be interested in practical problems faced by organisations or other social units. You might try looking at journals such as the *Harvard Business Review* or *European Management Journal,* magazines such as *Fortune* or *Management Today* or newspapers such as the *Financial Times* or *Wall Street Journal* for those practical problems that are currently 'hot'. Some of the topics recently suggested by such sources include:

- Should charities try to brand themselves (a type of organisation)?
- How do traditional music retailers plan to compete with music downloaded over the web (an industry)?
- How is Nike responding to ethical concerns about the labour practices of its overseas subcontractors (an organisation)?
- Under what conditions should companies buy back their own stock (an organisational problem)?
- Do women managers still face a 'glass ceiling' in investment banks (a group of employees)?
- How do children exercise 'pester power' to get their parents to buy them products advertised on television (a group of consumers)?

If you are required to apply or test a management theory or model as part of your research, you should be aware that not every interesting real-world problem is relevant to academic knowledge. This is important. We have seen research projects fail because the student has not identified a problem for which the research project is a solution. This often happens when a student falls in love with a computer model or other abstract solution and tries to find a business or management problem to apply it to. Remember the hammer analogy. Or, the solution is already well known, and there is nothing new about applying it, but the student hasn't done enough reading to see that this has been discussed already. We will give some tips later on how you can investigate business and management research to find out which ideas you can turn into researchable topics.

Notice that each question above involves a problem that an organisation, its members or society must solve. For example, if downloaded music didn't affect either current or future sales of recorded music, there wouldn't be much to go on. If no problem is involved – you just want to gather information – you might ask yourself whether it is really research.

One useful way to generate a research topic is to take an idea from one context and examine its application in another. **Student research in action 9.2** is an example of this.

Student research in action 9.2

THE CATHERINE WHEEL

As a committed vegetarian and ethical consumer, Catherine was interested in farmers' markets, farm shops, and other places that people could buy organic fruit and vegetables besides the major supermarket chains. In her MSc dissertation, Catherine had surveyed customer attitudes towards online grocery shopping. For her PhD, she decided to combine her ethical interests with her interest in e-business and find out more about what kinds of customers bought organic fruit and vegetables online, and how small organic producers tried to market their products to customers. As she worked on her idea, she realised that it would be interesting to find out whether the models of service quality that she had applied in studying online supermarkets could actually be applied to studying small producers.

Starting with a practical problem will help you to identify the research setting where you will do your research. This will often be centred on the organisation you are sponsored by, are working in or are interested in. You might study a part of the organisation, the entire organisation, its supply network or its industry. On the other hand, you may want to study another research setting to find out information that will be useful to your **focal organisation**. If you want to investigate a practical problem faced by a legal firm, you may want to research how the problem is handled in the medical profession. Research on charities may involve investigating for-profit firms. Part of the solution will be to describe how to implement what you learn in this new context.

Ideas from business and management research
Your other main source of ideas is the research that has been done on business and management. Many interesting ideas for research projects come from **theoretical problems** faced by business and management researchers rather than the practical problems faced by business and management in the real world. If you aren't working for or with an organisation, you might decide to start by identifying theories, models or concepts that other researchers have developed to see whether you can confirm, disprove or extend them. Even though you may be able to apply what you learn in your research to practical problems faced by business and management, your main goal is to increase knowledge by filling in any 'gaps' in what we know about that theory or model.

Theoretical problems are problems of incomplete knowledge that researchers need to solve to understand the world better than when they started. A theoretical problem exists when researchers lack complete knowledge about a theory or model that applies to some aspect of business or management, when they cannot use the existing theory or models to explain what goes on in the real world, or when they do not know which theory or model to apply in a particular situation. They may need more knowledge of the contexts in which to apply this theory or model, or of the concepts to include or exclude from the model. It might also mean that they do not know what concepts belong to that theory or model.

You might look for theoretical problems in various places. You might decide to investigate a particular theory, model or concept mentioned in your studies, such as 'lean production' or 'virtual teams'. You can look for theoretical problems in textbooks (for example Kotler et al.'s *Principles of Marketing* (2004) or Grant's *Contemporary Strategy Analysis* (2004)), academic books (for example *The Machine that Changed the World* (Womack et al., 1995) *Laboratory Life* (Latour and Woolgar, 1986)), or academic journals (for example *Academy of Management Journal* or *European Management Journal*). You might have read about some interesting research findings in a newspaper or a journal. Even looking through the tables of contents of some management journals may give you some ideas about what concepts, models and theories are currently on the research agenda. Your academic supervisor might have some suggestions for you to investigate.

You may have read about a particular theory, model or concept and want to know more about it, or disagree with it and want to challenge it. You might identify an interesting research topic by asking 'what if' you try to apply a theory or model in a new context. For example, you might investigate whether you can apply a model of employee motivation developed for manufacturing employees to lawyers. If you find out that the model does apply, this makes the model more universal or more 'robust'; on the other hand, if it does not apply, this makes the model less universal and more limited.

You can also identify theoretical problems by thinking about generic questions such as the 'practice–performance link' discussed in **Chapter 1**. Is there a theoretical problem that interests you and is relevant to business? Are practices developed in the context of large, multinational companies, for example ISO 9000, applicable in other contexts, for example small and medium-sized enterprises (SMEs) or public services?

You could also start with a concept instead of a problem. Based on what you have learnt about organisational citizenship behaviour (OCB) in your organisational behaviour classes, you could think up questions such as:

- What behaviours should we include in OCB? (concepts)
- Are there differences in OCB between full-time and part-time workers? (context)
- Do Western models of OCB apply in China? (context)
- Does OCB affect customer loyalty? (outcomes)
- Does deviant workplace behaviour affect business unit performance? (outcomes)

If you start with a theoretical problem, as with a practical problem, you will need to identify a research setting where you can investigate your theory, model or concept, and a sample of organisations, people or other units from which you will gather your data. Since you don't have a ready-made research setting, you may need to do some library or internet research to see what research setting might be appropriate.

Projects often benefit from a degree of serendipity. Hence the statement we made in the **Preface** that you will not necessarily end up where you intended with your research. **Student research in action 9.3** illustrates just one of the times that this has happened in the work of the authors of this book.

So which is a better place to start, a practical problem or a theoretical problem? Research that starts with a practical problem often focuses on developing

---

Student research in action 9.3

AN ABSORBING PROJECT

Intrigued by an article on technology cycles by Tushman and Anderson (1986), Kate decided to investigate how major changes in technology affected company survival in high-tech industries. Her supervisor brought an article on a new theoretical concept, absorptive capacity (Cohen and Levinthal 1989, 1990), to her attention as a factor that might affect company survival in turbulent environments. To study whether absorptive capacity affected company survival, Kate needed to find at least one industry or sector where she could gather data. She investigated a number of industries, and narrowed them down to reduced-instruction-set-computing microprocessors, high-definition television, and supercomputers. Even though all three industries were interesting, a chance conversation during a transatlantic air flight with a venture capitalist convinced her to study supercomputers for her thesis.

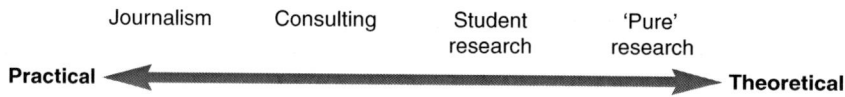

Figure 9.2 The range of approaches to solving interesting problems

recommendations for solving the particular practical problem in that particular context. Remember the discussion in **Chapter 1**, though, so that you can keep your project from being strictly a consulting project (unless that is your remit). You will need to link your research back to larger issues of business and management knowledge. If you are working on a sponsored project, you need to keep in mind that the organisation's main focus is on resolving the practical problem it faces. On the other hand, you need to be clear on how your project will contribute to business and management knowledge.

If you start with a theoretical problem, you will usually emphasise your contribution to knowledge, the findings about the particular theory, model or concept that you have investigated in your particular research setting. Your findings should contribute to knowledge about that theory or model. As we noted, this does not always mean that you have to come up with a new theory or a new model. Your project might simply add to our understanding of which theories and models do or do not apply in this type of organisation (or other context), find out something new that can be used to improve the model or theory, or even, in some cases, discredit it. The organisation will expect you to deliver some useful output, usually in the form of an analysis, recommendations and an implementation plan.

People have strong opinions on whether the main emphasis of business and management research should be to solve practical problems (**mode II research**) or theoretical problems (**mode I research**). This is part of a longstanding debate over whether research should be immediately relevant to solving industry's problems or to increase knowledge without any immediate application. This is illustrated by the differences between basic research, development and commercial research, described in **Chapter 1**.

As shown in **Figure 9.2**, all business and management research has both a practical and a theoretical side, but the balance between the two may vary. Business and management research is more than information-gathering (journalism) or applied problem-solving (consulting) as we argued in **Chapter 1**: research adds to our knowledge about business and management. Your research project will contribute to this knowledge, no matter how small your contribution.

Other sources of ideas

What if you have considered these sources and still don't have any ideas? If you are stuck for ideas and haven't been able to identify any practical or theoretical problems that really 'grab you', you might want to be a bit more creative. Why not brainstorm? **Brainstorming** is a technique for generating and selecting ideas. You should try to come up with as many ideas as you can, without censoring them or subjecting them to critical review. Brainstorming is probably more practical for a group than an individual, but try sitting down somewhere quiet with a blank sheet of paper and free-associating. Include a variety of potential sources of ideas for brainstorming such as your personal interests, your studies or other students' projects. If your idea doesn't interest you, you probably won't be committed enough to do a good project.

Your personal interests
Many students overlook an obvious source of ideas, their own interests. Whilst this is not always necessary or even possible, it is worth considering your interests as you define your project. You may be able to develop one or more of your hobbies, sports and other interests into a topic that reflects your own personality and character. After all, you have to live with the project – sometimes for up to a year – so it may as well be something that inspires you!

Finding something about your project that interests you is especially important if you are working on a project that extends over several months, even if you are working on an assigned project or as part of a research team. You need to 'own' some part of the project, even if it is just part of the process, such as finding out how to design a questionnaire, use a particular statistical technique that you are interested in, or taking responsibility for editing or doing the graphic design of the finished report.

Some examples of projects that students have developed from their own interests are given in **Student research in action 9.4**. Each student developed a research project that allowed him or her to explore a personal interest, and also led to a research problem with both practical and theoretical aspects.

> ### *Student research in action 9.4*
> #### PROJECTS BASED ON STUDENT INTERESTS
>
> - A football fan combined his love of Manchester United with his interest in marketing to develop a study of the impact of sports sponsorship on the sponsoring organisation.
> - A student with a serious interest in 'retail therapy' carried out a study of the e-marketing potential of luxury goods.
> - A highly entrepreneurial student studied the practices and associated success (or otherwise) of local entrepreneurs.
> - A student who did a lot of work with local charities conducted a human resources study of the work performance differences between the voluntary and the private sectors.
> - A student who had served in the military conducted research into commercial project management, and used the project to establish an interest, which subsequently led to a job.

Your studies
You should also consider ideas that come from your studies more generally, such as classes that you have enjoyed or where you have performed your best, since these usually reflect your natural interests and abilities. Your academic performance may

also indicate what you are interested in or good at: it is difficult to do a good project if you don't have the knowledge or skills to carry it through. One of Harvey's students, whose best marks were in finance, initially refused to consider a finance project because he didn't intend to pursue a career in that area. When he thought about his personal and research goals for the project, however, he relented and decided to do a project in financial management, which he carried off with distinction. You should also look at your past coursework assignments to see whether you have already completed a short assignment that you could expand or follow up, given more time, to investigate a topic more deeply.

If you start with a project based on a taught course or coursework assignment, you may find it easier to identify the main topics and relevant research. This will be important when you get started on your literature search and literature review, as we will see in **Chapter 4**. This may also make it easier to identify an academic supervisor who can support your research project.

Other students' projects

A look at projects that other students have completed might spark off some ideas. Many schools keep lists of previous student research projects in the projects office or library or even let you look at previous projects. They may also be listed on your library's web catalogue. If you can look over a list of previous projects, or even at some projects themselves, it may be worth spending some time to see if you can generate some ideas of your own. The following are some examples of recent projects:

- An investigation into knowledge management in the use of rehearsal for natural disaster planning
- Cross-cultural management – the role of individual managers
- Environmental policies – are they worth the recycled paper they are written on?
- A Delphi study on the future of B2B e-commerce platforms
- Virtual teams or virtual chaos? A study of a dispersed workplace
- Information systems strategy and cost justification: visible and invisible benefits
- The impact of ISO 9002 on company performance
- The role of information intermediaries in the distribution of corporate financial reports
- An investigation of the role of regional development agencies in improving business performance
- How much does it cost to gain a customer? A study of the economics of marketing in a law firm
- Will the new requirements for financial reporting prevent another Parmalat or Enron?
- The use of humour in management
- A review of the construction of the facilities for the Athens Olympics

If you still haven't come up with any ideas that seem appealing, you might consider:

1. *Reflecting on your own personal experiences* related to business and management. Frustration is often a great seed for management research ideas. If you have had a bad experience of service quality in a shop, you may want to find out just how widespread bad service is or the causes of such encounters.

2. *Thinking back to lecturers and other speakers you have heard.* Has anyone presented you with an idea that you thought was particularly well thought-out or you could relate to and wanted to find out more about?
3. *Talking to other people to see what they are interested in.* What are the pertinent issues at the moment? For example, you might find out that someone you know has bought or sold something interesting on eBay. This might lead to a question such as 'Can we start to make all our purchases through eBay or other auction sites?'
4. *Reading general articles, journals, books and newspapers.* Good sources for current topics include the *Financial Times, Fortune* magazine, *Harvard Business Review,* and trade publications such as *Computer Weekly* and *The Grocer.* These can help you to identify 'hot topics' that may present good opportunities for both interest and career, and add some relatively unique element to the work.
5. *Surfing the internet using a search engine such as Google.* Do a random search just to see where it leads you.

9.1.3 Which research ideas are worth pursuing?

Once you have developed some potential ideas, before you select one to develop into your research topic you should make sure that none is a 'dead end' in practical or theoretical terms. Just being interesting does not mean that something is worth studying. An idea is only worth exploring if you can develop it into a research topic, a statement of the general area that you plan to research. A research topic 'sets the researcher on a specific path and defines the territory to be explored' (Blaikie 2000: 45). We suggest that you spend a few minutes now to make sure that you could transform any of these ideas into a good research topic. If you can state your research topic as a problem, you are doing well.

In **Section 9.2**, we will describe how to actually narrow down the contenders into one or two ideas that you can take forward. We suggest that you ask the following questions about each of your ideas:

1. Does it meet the project requirements?
2. Is it relevant to at least one practical problem faced by business and management?
3. Is it relevant to at least one theoretical problem faced by business and management researchers?
4. Can I identify a research setting and research sample in which I could gather data?
5. Can I do it with the time and resources available to me?
6. Am I interested in doing it?
7. Is it worth studying?

We suggest that you score each of your ideas using the following system: 0 = No, 1 = Yes, 2 = Outstanding. You should drop any projects that score one or more 0s from further consideration. We will explain in **Section 9.2** how to choose the best idea out of those that are feasible. Use your project requirements to think about what your project needs to do and the criteria it needs to meet.

If you forget to apply the second and third criteria above to potential research topics, this can create significant difficulties later in your research process. Whether you start with a practical or a theoretical problem, your research must apply both to what goes on in the real world – the practical problems faced by businesses and managers – and to business and management theory – our accumulated academic knowledge about organisations and the people in them. Every business and management research project should therefore be relevant for practice – what business and management actually do – and theory – what we know about business and management. We describe how to use the library, internet and other knowledge resources to do this in **Chapter 4**. You may also want to get advice from your supervisor. Don't forget about your coursework.

You may need to do some research to link potential research topics to theoretical problems before you go any further. Even if you start with a practical problem, you will need to identify the business and management knowledge you can apply to define your research topic, design how you will investigate it and describe what you find out. Managers often lack this knowledge and/or the time or skills to find it. This business and management knowledge that you apply may be a theory or model that you have learnt about in your coursework. For example, if you have studied purchasing and supply management, you can identify appropriate models for analysing the organisation's purchasing and supply practices, and other models for improving it. If you can't identify any relevant theories or models from your studies, you will need to search for a theory or model that applies to this specific situation, which we explore in more detail in **Chapter 4**.

There must be something about your research topic that we do not know, but we ought to know, either to solve a practical problem or to add to incomplete information. A potential topic is only worth pursuing if it leads to one or more research problems you can investigate. As we will discuss later in this section, this means you need to be able to link your research topic to one or more areas of business and management studies and to a practical problem faced by business and management.

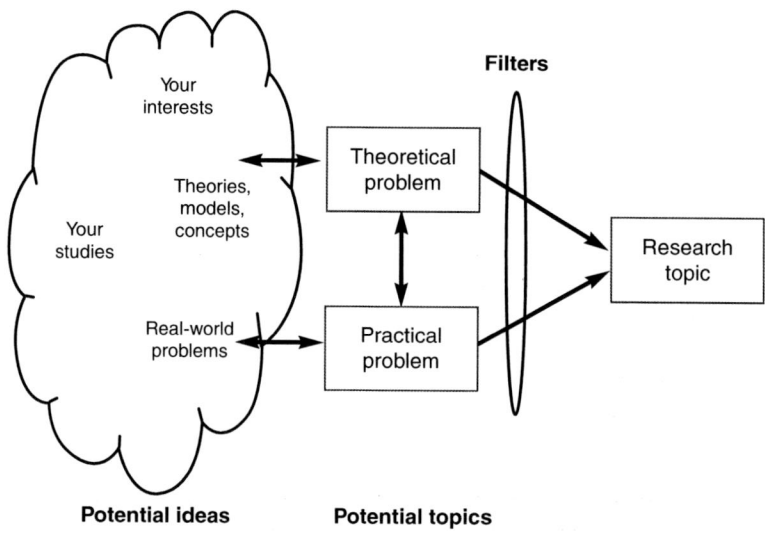

Figure 9.3 Research definition

This investigation can focus on solving a real problem or applying, extending or clarifying a theory or model.

Suppose that you don't have any particular practical or theoretical problem in mind when you are getting started on your research project. How can you bring together a practical problem and a theoretical problem? As we have said previously in this book, you may have to go through several rounds of identifying a practical problem and seeing if you can possibly link it to some area of business and management knowledge, or identifying a theoretical problem and seeing if you can possibly link it to a research setting. No matter whether you start with a practical or a theoretical problem, you must bring both of them together when you define your research problem. So, if you start with a practical problem, you can use theoretical knowledge from your business and management studies to solve that practical problem. If you start with a theoretical problem, you can add to our understanding of that problem by investigating a practical situation. You can see this in **Figure 9.3**.

9.2 Selecting the best idea

Once you have developed a list of potential research topics that meet the basic criteria we described above, your next step is to decide which idea you will actually go forward with. If you are doing an individual project, you may want to pick the idea that interests you the most. If you are not sure which one you should pick, or if you are working in a project team, here is a structured approach from project management you might find useful.

9.2.1 Characteristics of a good research topic

You can use the characteristics of a good research topic that we list below as the baseline for identifying suitable topics and ideas. The most important things to consider are your project requirements, but there are other characteristics of a good research topic that you should consider. They are fairly general, but you can use them to filter research topics as they emerge and revise others. They will also help you decide among different projects you might pursue.

Topic satisfies project guidelines
Any project you take on must satisfy your project requirements and any other expectations of your project supervisor and your examiners. A sponsored or placement project must also satisfy your manager and the organisation's expectations as agreed in the project brief or sponsorship agreement. Balancing the needs and expectations of your academic and business sponsor can be tricky, as we discuss in **Chapter 10**, because they can often come into conflict.

Your project requirements may list specific skills and knowledge you need to demonstrate in your project, such as:

1. Demonstrating your knowledge of the work covered during the course.
2. Identifying and constructively critiquing the work already carried out in the area.
3. Relating theory/best practice to actual practice in organisations.

4. Designing appropriate research questions and selecting appropriate methods to carry them out.
5. Analysing and reporting your findings.
6. Drawing conclusions from the work.

To see how to meet these criteria, you may find it helpful to look at some project reports submitted by former students, as we suggested in **Section 9.1.1**, to see how much work you will need to do and what standard of work you need to achieve. You might also want to talk to your supervisor and/or sponsor to see what effort they expect. For some academic projects, such as a dissertation, you may well be expected to put in as much effort as you would for a full-time job. This would obviously affect your ability to take paid work during this period. For other projects, you might be expected to put in the equivalent of one day per week during the project period.

Topic is feasible

A research problem is not feasible unless you can investigate it with the time and other resources that you have available. This sounds obvious, but students often propose research topics or problems that require more time than they have to spend or access to resources beyond their means. **Chapter 2** explained how to use project management to plan your project, including your project plan, milestones and work breakdown. You should rule out any project that will take more than 80% of the time you have available to work on it.

You should also think about what other resources you will need to investigate this topic. For instance, if you plan to investigate the marketing strategies of blue-chip companies by interviewing top managers, needless to say, you should reconsider your idea unless you already have personal contacts in those firms who already have agreed to take part in such a study. It is unlikely that you will be able to interview even one manager based on 'cold calling', so you will have to rely on publicly available information, which rarely gives any particular insight into the actual strategies being pursued or why and results in unsatisfactory projects. We showed this in **Student research in action 2.4**.

Topic has a manageable scope

A project should have an identifiable beginning, end and boundaries. A good research problem has a well-defined and realistic purpose. It doesn't try to change the world. Many students start out with an overambitious project, for example they aim to 'change the world', or at least significantly 'fix it'. Whilst we applaud this sentiment, you will rarely be able to achieve this – nor is it really appropriate – in a student project. A project with realistic goals, for example understanding a particular area better or applying something you have learnt in your course to solve a particular problem, is much likelier to succeed. Finding out something revolutionary is a bonus, not an objective.

Like other project supervisors, we have given this piece of advice to students more times than we can count. Your idea must be focused enough for you to do a thorough job, but not so small that it is trivial. This chapter will discuss how you can narrow down a research topic. Project scope will come up formally in **Section 9.3.2**.

Topic has symmetrical outcomes

Even if you will not be formally assessed on your research project's outcomes, you will put a lot of time and effort into it. You should therefore make sure that whatever the outcome of your early work, you will still have a project to work on and your outcome will not be irrelevant or trivial. Make sure that your research topic leads to **symmetrical outcomes**, so that no matter what you find out, your findings are both interesting and relevant, or your recommendations are valid and relevant. Not having symmetrical outcomes will be fatal to your research if you are investigating a 'yes or no' question, and the answer is only interesting if you find one. This is especially important if your research is done in sequential stages: one part of your project depends on what you find out in an earlier part. This is often true of exploratory or qualitative projects. The need for symmetry is illustrated in **Student research in action 9.5**.

Student research in action 9.5
BRUCE'S FRUIT MARKET

Bruce was asked to investigate a major supermarket's supply chain for fresh fruit. The project brief stated that he should investigate the supply chain and identify where suppliers were consolidating their products. If, as the supermarket expected, this was in northern France, how might the supermarket influence the supply chain by providing additional facilities, warehousing, and so on?

In the first phase of his study, Bruce found that suppliers mainly consolidated and stored fruit in the UK. This meant that the second part of Bruce's project, which had originally been intended to be the main part of the investigation, was now irrelevant because the supermarket already had enough warehouse facilities in the UK. Thus, he could only complete half of the project, which left him without enough material to flesh out a full research project.

Guess what? Bruce hadn't designed his research so that the first part of the project investigations had symmetrical outcomes. If only he had known about the concept of symmetric outcomes, he could have framed his research questions so that the second half of his project would be worth doing no matter what he found out.

You should think carefully about the questions you are asking in your research in order to spot any asymmetric outcomes. For example, 'Why do lower income households tend to die younger?' assumes a positive answer to the implied question – 'Do people from lower income households (however you decide to define this) actually die younger?' If you can show that people from lower income households do die younger, for example using national statistical records, you can investigate the question, 'Why might this be true?' On the other hand, if you initially found out that people from lower income households didn't actually die younger, the answer to your question is, 'Well, they don't', and your project would not be wildly successful. It might be better to ask 'How does household income affect health and mortality rates?'

Topic is relevant to business and management practice

Your findings and/or recommendations should have more general usefulness, that is, someone else could take your findings and apply them to a similar set of companies or people, or use your project as a starting point for further research or application. A good research project will add to our knowledge about a practical problem and/or theoretical problem, if not both. This continues the theme of building on previous research.

Topic is linked to business and management knowledge

You should have selected a research topic that you can link to at least one area of business and management research (or research in supporting disciplines such as economics or psychology) so that you can develop the theoretical problem. As we will see in **Chapter 4**, you will need to use previous studies when you define your research problem and questions, and when you select your research methods. You will need to develop a literature review (**Chapter 4**) and discuss key findings (**Chapter 12**).

This can be a problem if you are looking at leading-edge technologies or other new areas. For example, when the web was first becoming popular in the 1990s, students researching e-commerce found it difficult to find enough articles to do a good literature review, because the area was so new.

What you find out in your research should contribute to our knowledge of a practical or theoretical problem, that is, it has at least one original aspect. You do not have to provide a new grand theory or make a substantial addition to our existing knowledge, but you should enable us to understand one small aspect of what you have covered a little better than when you started.

Findings/recommendations will satisfy all your project's stakeholders

Students often find that academic and business sponsors have different ideas about what they should do in their project. If you have different project stakeholders who each have conflicting needs and expectations, you may find it difficult to satisfy all of them. You need to think about these competing project stakeholders from the start and make sure that you build in the necessary work to meet the needs of each into your project plan. We cover more of the issues of managing in-company research projects in **Chapter 9**.

Your examiners will probably focus on how your research can help them to understand a theoretical problem – aspects of your topic that they want to know more about. Your academic institution requires an academically sound piece of work that demonstrates knowledge of the subject area and an ability to design and carry out research, present, analyse and draw conclusions from the results.

On the other hand, your business sponsor or collaborator will probably focus on how your research can help them to understand a practical problem – aspects of business and management practice that they need help with. They will worry less about how this was arrived at rather than whether your recommendations can be implemented and whether they will help to solve that particular problem. Sometimes, and this can be very difficult for students to resolve, you may be expected to produce recommendations that support what the manager has already decided, not what the best solution is for the organisation, as illustrated by **Student research in action 9.6**.

> *Student research in action 9.6*
>
> **THAT'S NOT WHAT WE WANTED TO HEAR!**
>
> A team of students spent a year studying the excellent community outreach work being done by a faith-based organisation. Towards the end of their research, the students found out that very few of the underprivileged young people being serviced by the organisation were actually aware of its strong religious beliefs, and those who did know, did not want to be associated with that particular religion. Although this was an interesting finding, with significant implications for their sponsor, the students were told, in no uncertain terms, that they should not mention this finding in their project report.

You may even need to write a different report for each important stakeholder. Few managers will wade through a 20,000-word report to reach your recommendations in your last chapter, even if your report is beautifully bound and laid out! One managing director commented, 'if the blurb on the front doesn't grab me, I don't bother reading it'. This is not what you want to hear if you have worked hard on every page of your project report. We will return to this in **Chapter 14**.

Finally, don't leave yourself out of this equation. You should identify what you want to get out of the project in terms of your research and personal objectives, as discussed in **Chapter 2**. As you start to define what you will do in your research project, you should give some serious thought as to why you are doing the project and what you want to get out of it. A good research project should satisfy your own needs, as well as those of project stakeholders. Even if you have been assigned a research topic or sponsored project that you are not really interested in, you may need to complete your degree requirements or fulfil your project placement requirements. On the other hand, you may be passionate about what you plan to study or see it as a stepping stone to a good job or a promotion. You may be interested in part of the research project, such as learning how to do an action project or analyse questionnaire data.

9.2.2 Selecting the best idea

So, how do you identify the best project? We suggest that you follow the process described in **Student research in action 9.7**. You can construct a similar table by listing your ideas and rating them against the assessment criteria and any other criteria you decide are important. You can make the ranking process more complex by using numerical ratings and/or weighting the factors by their importance. Whether you use a simple or more complex table to rank potential projects, this structured approach allows you or your project team to make a reasonable choice based on your own criteria, and can greatly assist the group in uniting behind a particular decision.

Student research in action 9.7

OOPS! WE DID IT AGAIN

As part of a course at the University of Bath, a group of students must run an event or carry out a particular task to demonstrate their ability to plan, execute and review a group project. They are assessed on the originality of their idea, the quality of the planning process and the content of the report reflecting their experiences during the project.

One group had a meeting and came up with a number of ideas. The group wanted to choose the best project out of the following:

- Producing a yearbook for their class group
- Developing a short video to promote the course they are studying
- Organising a formal ball for the entire department
- Organising a treasure hunt one Sunday
- Organising an 'accident awareness' day for schoolchildren.

The group's next activity was to decide what criteria to judge the proposal against. They first identified three criteria based on how the project would be assessed:

- whether the idea was original
- whether the idea would demonstrate project management skills
- whether it would enable them to produce a good report.

The group then added four more characteristics of their own that they wanted their project to have. These were:

- it should sufficiently stretch the group
- it should not depend too heavily on other people for its success
- it must not require them to undertake any large financial risk
- it must be fun for the group to do.

They then put the projects into a table, and agreed a set of ratings, as shown in **Table 9.1**.

Table 9.1 An example rating table

	Originality	Demonstrates skills	Produces a good report	Stretching	Independent of others	Avoids financial risk	Fun
Yearbook	✗	✓	✓	–	–	✗✗	
Video	✓	✓	✓	✓	✓	✗✓	
Ball	–	✓	✓	✓	✗	✗✗✗	✓
Treasure hunt	✗	–	✗	–	–	✓	–
Accident awareness day	✓	✓	–	✗	✗	✓	–

Given these ratings, they saw that there was one clear choice for them – the video – as it had the most ticks. They also saw that they needed to manage the project's financial risk (cost of hiring editing facilities and production of the finished product) carefully.

Even if one idea is clearly ranked higher than others when you have gone through the ranking process, we recommend that you identify a second project as a backup in case the first one doesn't work out. Having an alternate or 'safety' project available is especially important when your first project is risky, for example if you need to arrange access to an organisation or data set, as such access often falls through.

9.2.3 Refining your research topic

So, now you are down to a single research topic that you have identified or been assigned. What next? For most students, this is narrowing down the research topic to a manageable scope. (Most students start out with a topic so broad it would take a thousand students working for a thousand years to finish their research project.) We suggest that you do this by developing research questions.

Research questions
If your research topic describes the general area you will investigate, your **research questions** define those areas of the topic you will investigate. They will be the main focus of your project, because they will guide what you do in your project. For example, you might develop a research topic of 'service quality' from service management, or 'dual-career ladders' from 'research and development'. These topics could then generate research questions.

Well-constructed research questions will identify the scope of your research project and guide the plan for your project, because they will determine the business and management research that you use to support your project, the data you collect and how you report your research. According to O'Leary (2004: 29), your research questions should:

- Define your research topic – the business or management phenomenon that you will focus on
- Define the nature of your research – whether your main goal is to describe, explore or explain this phenomenon
- Define the issues you will explore – what aspects of the phenomenon you will find out about
- Indicate whether you foresee a relationship between the concepts you are exploring – develop any propositions or hypotheses.

You should try to express any good research problem as a question that is interesting to both managers and academic researchers. **Student research in action 9.8** describes how one student developed some potential research questions.

Student research in action 9.8
UP THE ARSENAL

Alex needed to come up with an idea for her summer research project. She was a passionate fan of the Arsenal football team, which she had followed since she was a child. Putting together the idea of doing research on one or more football teams with the

> topics she had studied in service management, Alex came up with some potential research questions, including:
>
> - Were football stadiums trying to become friendlier to female fans?
> - Were football clubs focusing more on retailing merchandise or entertaining fans?
> - What physical aspects of football stadiums encouraged or discouraged female fans from attending?
>
> Alex also made sure that there was enough support in the academic literature to support her project at a level appropriate for an MSc dissertation. She identified previous studies of female sports fans by Coddington (1997) and Crawford and Gosling (2004) that she could use for her academic framework.

Other research questions that our students have asked include:

- Why do people buy organic produce from small farmers over the internet?
- Do project management techniques reduce IT project failures?
- How can we calculate all the environmental impacts associated with projects such as building a road or bridge?
- Do multinational top management teams work together differently from single nationality ones?

Most students find that they need to cycle between their research topic and research questions several times to end up with a feasible set of research questions and a suitably focused research topic. It is not unusual for students doing a PhD to spend a year clarifying their research questions, even if they have started with a well-defined research topic. Most undergraduate or master's students don't have the luxury of spending so much time! We highlight some of the most common problems below.

No significant contribution. You should avoid, where possible, asking research questions that have already been answered, since you run the risk of doing trivial research. On the other hand, if we only *think* we know the answer, usually because we think the answer is 'common sense', the question might well be worth asking. **Research in action 9.1** demonstrates where a researcher believed that the existing answers to a particular question were inadequate, and went on to make a major contribution to business and management research as a result.

> ### Research in action 9.1
> #### I CAN'T BELIEVE IT'S NOT FAYOL!
>
> Like Henry Mintzberg, you have probably encountered a number of models of 'what managers do' during your studies. At the time Mintzberg started his doctoral thesis, researchers and managers accepted Henri Fayol's description of what managers do, which is to 'plan, organise, control and coordinate'. For his doctoral research, Henry Mintzberg watched five managers for a week each, and recorded what each one did during that week, analysing their incoming and outgoing post, and their conversations. Mintzberg concluded that Fayol and other formal models of managerial

> decision-making did not describe adequately what managers actually did, which he identified as comprising ten different roles (Mintzberg 1971). As well as being a significant triumph of 'fact over folklore', Mintzberg's research led to significant research in managerial decision-making.

Biased or self-answering questions. You should try to avoid choosing or stating research questions so that you have already determined what the answer will be before you start by how you frame the question. Even if you expect to find a certain answer, based on your experience, the theory or model you are using or what your academic supervisor or project sponsor expects, you should frame your research questions so that you remain open to contradictory evidence or unexpected findings. If you don't, you may miss out on the opportunity to discuss what you have found. In **Student research in action 9.9**, the student was open to findings that were not expected and as a result produced a most interesting piece of work.

> *Student research in action 9.9*
>
> **ONE-POTATO, TWO-POTATO ... YOU'RE HIRED!**
>
> Anjali was studying how small and medium-sized companies recruited and selected their employees. She expected to find that they used selected structured methods, as these were widely discussed by both academics and practitioners. However, in the firms who had agreed to give her access to their recruitment methods, it became clear that they selected employees based on interviews only, and that supposedly 'objective' methods (for example personality profiling) were not used. This presented great opportunities for discussion, and then gave rise to further questions, including 'Why didn't these firms use structured techniques for recruitment?'

On the other hand, unexpected findings can become gifts to your research project. In the Hawthorne experiments, researchers failed to find any link between lighting and worker output, but this led them to question what factors actually influenced output in the relay assembly group. Was it the style of supervision? Was it the chance to make more money? Was it the attention from the supervisor? Elton Mayo's explanation that strong social ties created higher performance, even if his interpretation of the data has been challenged by later researchers (see Gillespie 1993), was significantly more interesting for management research than the original question about electric lighting, since it opened up many possibilities for research into the human and social side of managing employees.

Unanswerable questions. Beware of research questions that you cannot answer by gathering and analysing data. Some research questions are simply unanswerable, for example metaphysical questions about good and evil, or right or wrong. This is not the same as the study of business ethics or topics such as corporate social responsibility, though!

Using the literature to support your research topic and questions

Students who have been exposed to natural sciences research often wonder whether they should develop propositions or hypotheses from their research questions. The answer is, 'it depends'. In some research projects, as we will see in **Chapter 5**, you may be expected to further refine your research questions into more specific statements about what you expect to find in your research project at this point. Depending on how specific these statements or predictions are, they may be called research propositions or research hypotheses. You may need to read **Chapter 5** and then come back to this section to see whether this is the case for your own research project.

The work that you do now exploring the area is vital, and will initially expand the possibilities for your work – in line with the model presented in **Figure 9.1**. You may find this easier to do if you use a mind map, a hierarchy of concepts or a Venn diagram, which we describe below.

If you can't find at least one business and management area that your topic fits into, then you may find it difficult to develop and support the theoretical side of your research project. Although this sounds obvious, students often take such a narrow view of a research topic that they conclude that no one else has ever identified it, as shown in **Student research in action 9.10**.

Student research in action 9.10

I AM THE GREATEST

Roy walked into his potential supervisor's office and claimed that the issue of staff pay and rewards in lean manufacturing systems had not been properly studied, but 'the rest of the management world had been too dull to notice'. When the potential supervisor asked him to support this claim, Roy said that he could find little of any relevance on this topic in the operations management literature, and his research project would therefore break new ground.

Roy's proposed research topic was clearly important, relevant and of interest to business. It was also probably true that there was little research in operations management on pay and rewards. So what might be wrong with this picture? Management has been formally studied for over 100 years, and the chances that everyone had ignored such a major research problem are small – not zero, but small, as most topics have been covered in some way, in some form. Relatively little is completely new in management.

Roy's potential project supervisor, therefore, found it hard to believe that no research had been done on the topic and, in fact, he knew that a major study of pay and rewards in lean manufacturing had been published by Delbridge and Lowe (1997). Roy had ignored the fact that pay and reward is a major concern of human resource management (HRM), not of operations management. Not surprisingly, a brief review of the HRM literature revealed that his proposed topic had been extensively studied. Even so, there was scope for him to investigate this topic by building on the existing research on pay and rewards in HRM and lean manufacturing in OM.

If Roy had identified the two different concepts he wanted to study as 'pay and reward' and 'lean production' and realised that they belonged to two different areas, he would

WHAT SHOULD I STUDY?

> have realised that he should be looking at his topic not only as 'how pay and reward affect lean production' but also 'lean production affects pay and reward', which would have led him to both the HRM and the OM literature. Then, rather than trying to invent a new area of study, with the risk that his project findings would merely replicate previous research such as Delbridge and Lowe's study, he could have used this research to focus or frame his study more clearly. For instance, he could have tested the findings of Delbridge and Lowe's study in his own sample of manufacturing firms that had adopted lean production. This would have added to both the HRM and OM literature, since his findings could be used to validate Delbridge and Lowe. Furthermore, he could potentially have used Delbridge and Lowe's research methods to help to design his own research study, which would have saved a lot of time and effort.

As this example suggests someone, somewhere has covered almost any business and management topic you could think of. Don't try to reinvent the wheel unnecessarily. Most research projects that are worth doing build on one or more existing areas of knowledge, and in **Chapter 4** we will discuss some ways you can identify those areas. This also presents a challenge if you can draw on more than one area: you will need not only to select your topic carefully, but also to consider what subject or perspective you will approach that topic from. This will make a big difference in how you define and execute your research topic, and help you to avoid some problems that commonly plague students.

At this stage you should look for two main types of material:

- *General overviews* of your topic, for example textbooks or review articles
- *Model studies* – the type of study you would like to carry out, which yours can add to, provide points of discussion or generally be based around in some way.

> ### Student research in action 9.11
> #### IS ANYBODY LISTENING?
>
> One student found an article by Barclay and Benson (1990), who reported that fewer than 8% of the managers they studied were aware of any recent published studies on the areas in which they were working. He decided to investigate whether the management literature actually affected managers' behaviour. The student decided to see whether his study would find similar low levels of awareness and try to find reasons for the low level of awareness. This would both replicate Barclay and Benson's findings and try to extend them.

Using a mind map to refine your research topic

Figure 9.4 shows a mind map (aka a spider diagram) that Omozo, an MBA student, used to help structure his thoughts on his project on graduate recruitment practices in UK retail banking. He put the main topic in the centre of the map and the main issues related to this around it. The sub-issues are then clustered around each of the main issues.

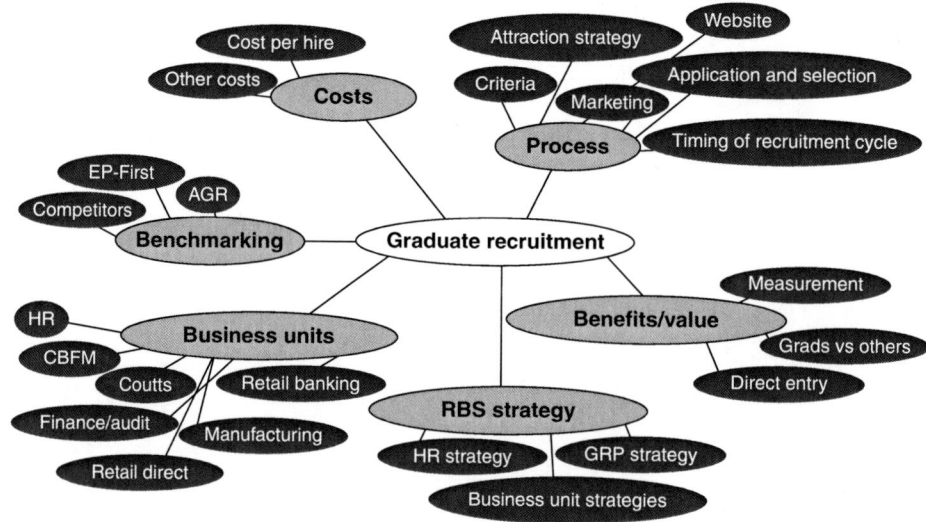

Figure 9.4 Mind map of graduate recruitment project
Source: Courtesy of Omozo Ehigie

Using a hierarchy of concepts to refine your research topic

One way to narrow down what you want to research is to draw a **hierarchy of concepts**, which will help you get specific with your practical and/or theoretical problem. Some students start off with a really broad focus, such as 'Why do organisations fail?' This is a perfectly good starting point, but it would be impossible to investigate in a single research project. Often, students need to go through several iterations on each concept in their research questions to narrow them down into a manageable topic and questions. For example, if your particular interest is marketing, this can be broken down into business-to-business marketing (B2B) and business-to-consumer marketing (B2C). You decide that your interest is in the B2C area. How might this area be broken down? The potential hierarchy of concepts for this project is shown in **Figure 9.5**.

Many concepts easily fall into hierarchies. Thinking about how your research might fit into a conceptual hierarchy can be useful at many points in your project, as you will see in **Chapter 4**. If you go up a level in the hierarchy, you have a more abstract, and therefore broader, concept to deal with; if you go down a level, you have a less abstract, and therefore narrower, concept to deal with.

Using a Venn diagram to refine your research topic

An important aspect of refining your research topic is to see where it fits into the business and management research. If your proposed research project fits into two or more areas of study, you may want to use a mapping technique such as Venn diagrams to show where your topic fits with the subjects that you have studied, because this makes it much easier to see what research people have already done in the area.

Drawing a **Venn diagram** can help you focus your search for previous research (see **Chapter 4**). Some research topics are studied only within one field, for example the ethics of marketing to children is mainly of interest in marketing. Many research topics, however, fit into several areas. For example, total quality management (TQM)

WHAT SHOULD I STUDY?

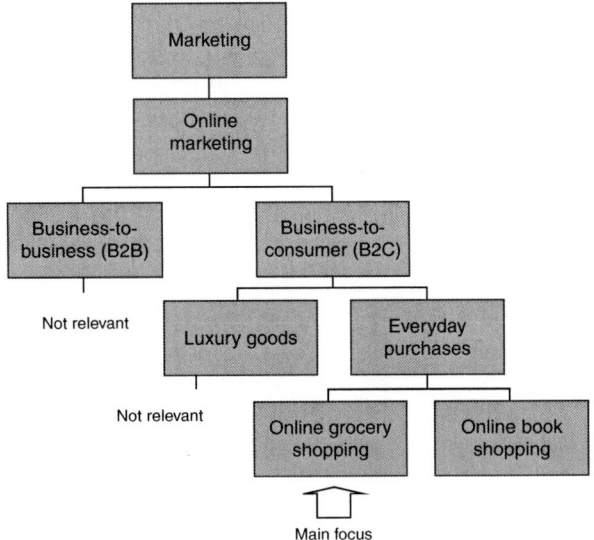

Figure 9.5 A hierarchy of concepts

is a substantial topic in both operations management and human resource management. Some research topics are also studied within business and management's base disciplines, such as economics, sociology or psychology.

As shown in **Figure 9.6**, by looking at the overlap between more than one topic, or more than one field, you can narrow down the scope of your topic considerably. Although each of the areas in **Student research in action 9.12** was well known, the project's originality came from integrating the three. Original work often takes place at the intersection between different areas of study, because you can then draw on relevant aspects of each, but also combine multiple views of your topic.

Student research in action 9.12

TALK TO ME

Amit decided that he would investigate call centres. He started by trying to identify previous research on the specific topic of 'call centre management', but not much had been published under that specific topic heading. After talking to his supervisor, he realised that call centre management was studied in three areas: human resource management (well understood), operations management (well understood) and service management (also well understood). The project therefore existed at the intersection of the three areas, as shown in **Figure 9.6**. His challenge was to bring these three areas together.

Amit could not possibly investigate HRM, OM and services in a single project. His next step was therefore to choose one as his main perspective on the topic. For instance, Amit could choose to take an operations-based approach, if he were mainly interested in the process (what people do), a service-based approach, the way in which the employees interact with the customers, or an HRM-based approach, the human interactions with the system.

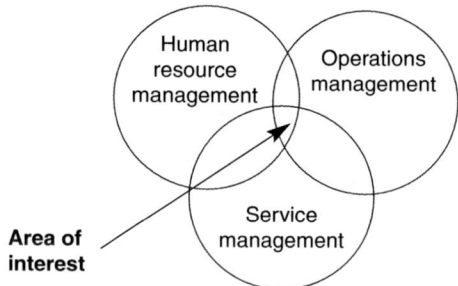

Figure 9.6 A Venn diagram for investigating call centres

9.3 Developing a research proposal

Once you have identified your research problem and research questions, you are ready to start on your research. First, however, you need to communicate it to both yourself and other people. You might try writing down what you want to do as:

- A 'working title' – doesn't have to be snappy, just a few words that say what it is you are doing.
- A picture – some people find it most helpful at this stage to draw a mind map, or represent their project with a picture, photograph, collage or drawing.
- A 'sound bite' or 'elevator pitch' – imagine a friend asking you what you are doing for your project. You have precisely 15 seconds to tell them, before his or her eyes glaze over and he or she rushes off. What will you tell him or her about your work?
- An **abstract** – 100–150 words that summarise what you are thinking of doing.
- A research proposal – a formal document that describes what you plan to do in your project.

9.3.1 Writing a research proposal

Once you've narrowed down your topic area and identified your research problem and research questions, you can now formally state them in a **research proposal** to your academic advisor and/or business sponsor as part of your project. Whether or not you are required to present a formal project proposal, we recommend this as part of your research process. There are many reasons that you should do this, including to:

- Clarify your own ideas
- Document your ideas so that you can discuss your project with other people, including potential supervisors, partners and collaborators
- Provide a formal starting point for the project and a point of reference that you can come back to during the study should things not progress as you plan.

If you have been given a proposal format to follow by your organisation, you should follow it. If you haven't, many students have successfully used the format

Table 9.2 An example of a research proposal

Working title	Don't worry too much about the title at this point, it is generally accepted that it will change during the project – but insert a few words that summarise your ideas.
Main discipline (for example strategy, finance, operations and so on)	What approach will you be taking? Use a Venn diagram to help with this one.
Project discussed with	This should include anyone relevant to your project, and anyone else who could usefully ask pertinent questions on the subject, maybe an academic or tutor, or someone related to the application of the issue you are planning to investigate. We always suggest that you gather as many opinions as possible at the start of the project.
Background to the study	Fill in how the project came about – was it your idea? If not, how did it emerge?
Management issues	What are the people who are working with this problem facing? How is the problem evident? What has been done already about the issue, and how is it manifesting itself today? For instance, it may be the issue of interest is an ongoing problem with industrial relations that results in regular stoppages or industrial disputes. It may recently have come to a head because of new commercial pressures.
Research questions/ propositions/hypotheses	Insert the main and the subsidiary questions/propositions/hypotheses here.
Project objectives	What do you hope to achieve by carrying out this piece of research? What are your personal goals? What do you hope the project will find?
Project scope	What is going to be covered by this project and is there anything you want to specifically exclude? (See further note below.)
Sources of academic information	What are the main review articles, books and your 'hook article', if relevant?
Sources of data	This will be covered later, but for now, have an idea of what you might do to answer your research questions, within the constraints of the available time and resources. In particular, you should consider whether you will be able to answer your research questions by using: • existing information, desk or library research • indirect contact with organisations, for example questionnaires • direct contact with organisations, interviews or in-company research.

in **Table 9.2** for a variety of projects. It is worth putting some effort into completing the proposal at this point. If you can fill in all the boxes, you have at least considered the major issues.

9.3.2 Identifying your project scope

Your **project scope** states 'what's in and what's out'. Identifying your project scope will help you focus your work. It is a good touchstone later on when you are in danger of being distracted or face a choice about what direction your project should take. If you are working as part of a project group, it can help to keep the whole group focused.

The project scope will describe your research topic, research questions and the main perspective you will take on your topic.

This does not stop you from considering other perspectives but, pragmatically, you will have to limit the input from other areas. You will also need to put some boundaries around the subject material you will be considering. For instance, will you consider a single firm, a sector, a type of organisation (for example not for profit, governmental, small to medium-sized enterprise) or a generic view of your topic?

Summary

In this chapter, we have described how to generate ideas for your research project. Some research will start with a practical problem. You may be interested in this practical problem, or you may be assigned a project brief by a business sponsor. Other research starts with a theoretical problem, a problem of incomplete knowledge that you may discover or are assigned by an academic supervisor or lecturer. Either way, business and management research usually involves finding both a practical and a theoretical aspect to your research topic.

This chapter has also provided some guidance on generating research ideas and filtering them to find the best idea. If you start with too few ideas, you may not have enough to select a high-quality idea. On the other hand, if you start with too many ideas, you may not be able to narrow them down. We have discussed a ranking mechanism for selecting the best idea for your research project.

Once you have selected a topic, you should be able to develop a project proposal – a document for communicating to others what you plan to do. You can use a project proposal to gain academic approval and practical support for your project.

Answers to key questions

Where do ideas for research topics come from?
- By creating some initial chaos, reading, discussing a wide range of potential issues, creating a number of possible topics, then focusing your work onto one issue that you will develop
- The process of developing ideas includes reflection on experience, teaching and looking at previous projects, as well as considering why you are doing the project, then choosing the subject perspective you will use to approach the topic

How can I choose between several potential research topics?
- You should choose between topics by defining the criteria your project will be evaluated on and selecting the one that most closely matches the criteria. If there are areas that do not match the criteria, the project should be specified to make sure that key criteria are met

What characterises a good research topic?
- These can be summarised in seven general points – a well-defined purpose, wider implications than the project context, it is feasible, there is a basis in the literature but there is something novel about the study, it is practical, the outcomes are symmetrical and the project satisfies the stakeholders

- It must interest you
- It must fit with the requirements of your institution

Why should I use research questions to focus my research?
- A main overall question will provide a focus for your work
- Breaking the main question down into smaller research questions should provide a comprehensible breakdown of the activities you will need to carry out
- Research questions are a readily understandable means for you to explain 'what is my research project about?'

How can I use a project proposal to define my project scope?
- The proposal will allow you to demonstrate the background and importance of your work, the research questions, hypotheses and propositions, state the intended methods for carrying it out and the basis for it in the literature
- The proposal requires you to start being specific about your ideas – to define what you are going to investigate and, just as importantly, what you are not going to investigate

References

Barclay, I. and Benson, M.H. 1990. The Effective Management of New Product Development, *Leadership and Organisation Development Journal* Special Issue, **11**(6): 1–37.
Blaikie, Norman. 2000. *Designing Social Research*. Cambridge: Polity Press.
Coddington, A. 1997. *One of the Lads: Women who Follow Football*. London: HarperCollins.
Cohen, Wesley M. and Levinthal, Daniel A. 1989. Innovation and learning: The two faces of R&D, *Economic Journal*, **99**(397): 569–96.
Cohen, Wesley M. 1990. Absorptive capacity: A new perspective on learning and innovation, *Administrative Science Quarterly*, **35**(1): 128–52.
Crawford, Garry and Gosling, Victoria K. 2004. The myth of the 'Puck Bunny': Female fans and men's ice hockey, *Sociology*, **38**(3): 477–93.
Delbride, R. and Lowe, J. (1997). Manufacturing control: supervisory systems on the 'new' shop-floor, *Sociology*, **31**(3).
Gill, John and Johnson, Phil. 2002. *Research Methods for Managers*, 3rd edn. London: Sage.
Gillespie, Richard. 1993. *Manufacturing Knowledge: A History of the Hawthorne Experiments*. Cambridge: Cambridge University Press.
Grant, R.M. 2004. *Contemporary Strategy Analysis*. Oxford: Blackwell Publishing.
Kotler, P., Saunders, J. and Armstrong, G. 2004. *Principles of Marketing: European Edition*. Harlow: FT/Prentice Hall.
Lundberg, Craig C. 1999. Finding research agendas: Getting started Weick-like, *The Society for Industrial and Organizational Psychology*, American Psychological Society available on http://www.apa.org.
Mintzberg, Henry. 1971. Managerial work: analysis from observation, *Management Science*, **18**(2): 97–110.
O'Leary, Zina. 2004. *The Essential Guide to Doing Research*. London: Sage.
Tushman, Michael L. and Anderson, Philip. 1986. Technological discontinuities and organisational environments, *Administrative Science Quarterly*, **31**(3): 439–65.
Weick, Karl E. 1992. Agenda setting in organizational behaviour: A theory-focused approach, *Journal of Management Inquiry*, **1**(3): 171–82.
Whedon, Joss. 2002. *Once More with Feeling*. New York: Simon & Schuster.
Womack, J.P., Jones, D.T. and Roos, D. 1995. *The Machine That Changed the World: The Massachusetts Institute of Technology 5-million-dollar, 5-year Report on the Future of the Automobile Industry*, New York: Rawson Associates.

Additional resources

Campbell, John P., Daft, Richard L. and Hulin, Charles L. 1982. *What to Study: Generating and Developing Research Questions*. Beverly Hills, CA: Sage.

Collis, Jill and Hussey, Roger. 2009. *Business Research*, 2nd edn. Basingstoke: Palgrave Macmillan.

Daft, Richard L. 1984. Antecedents of significant and not-so-significant organizational research. In T.S. Bateman and G.R. Ferris (eds). *Method and Analysis in Organizational Research*. Reston, VA: Reston Publishing.

Davis, Murray S. 1971. That's interesting: Toward a phenomenology of sociology and a sociology of phenomenology, *Philosophy of Social Science*, **1**: 309–44.

Easterby-Smith, Mark, Thorpe, Richard and Lowe, Andy. 2002. *Management Research: An Introduction*, 2nd edn. London: Sage.

Jankowicz, A.D. 2000. *Business Research Projects*, 3rd edn. London: Business Press/Thomson Learning.

Kaplan, Abraham. 1964. *The Conduct of Inquiry*. San Francisco: Chandler Press.

Lawrence, Paul R. 1992. The challenge of problem-oriented research, *Journal of Management Inquiry*, **1**(2): 139–42.

Lundberg, Craig C. 1976. Hypothesis generation in organizational behavior research, *Academy of Management Review*, 3(1/2): 5–12.

Maslow, A. H. 1970. *Motivation and Personality*, 2nd edn. New York: Harper & Row.

Partington, David. 2002. *Essential Skills for Management Research*. London: Sage.

Robson, Colin. 2002. *Real World Research*, 2nd edn. Oxford: Blackwell.

Saunders, Mark, Lewis, Phillip and Thornhill, Adrian. 2003. *Research Methods for Business Students*, 3rd edn. Harlow: Financial Times/Prentice Hall.

Sekaran, U. 2000. *Research Methods for Business*, 3rd edn. Chichester: Wiley.

Taylor, Frederick W. 1947. *Scientific Management*. New York: Harper & Row.

Weick, Karl E. 1983. Management thought in the context of action. In S. Srivastva (ed.) *The Executive Mind*. San Francisco: Jossey-Bass.

Weick, Karl E. 1989. Theory construction as disciplined imagination, *Academy of Management Review*, **14**(4): 516–31.

Wren, Daniel A. and Greenwood, Ronald G. 1998. *Management Innovators: The People and Ideas that Have Shaped Modern Business*. Oxford: Oxford University Press.

Zikmund, W.G. 2000. *Business Research Methods*, 6th edn. Orlando, FL: Dryden Press/Harcourt College Publishers.

Key terms

abstract, 244	practical problems, 222	research setting, 222
brainstorming, 226	project paralysis, 220	research topic, 222
focal organisation, 224	project scope, 245	sample, 222
hierarchy of concepts, 242	research idea, 221	symmetrical outcomes, 233
mode I research, 226	research proposal, 244	theoretical problems, 224
mode II research, 226	research questions, 237	Venn diagram, 242

Frequently asked questions

- **Does the project have to be leading edge in management terms: does it have to address a hot topic from the current management literature?**

  No – the project does not have to be fashionable to be good. Many topics have disappeared from the management agenda for no reason other than the field appears

- **How do I know the precise objectives of the project and the balance that is required between theoretical and practical issues?**

  The precise objectives of the project should be set out in course documentation and are always worth referring to – not least because they can clarify the requirements of the project and the balance point between theoretical and practical issues. The discussion of the role of theory/best practice and other practices is in **Chapter 4**.

- **Why do I need to include this theory when what I am looking at is profoundly practical?**

  This is easy to understand, but where does this theory generally come from? It comes from people studying the practical, and theorising from it. As Hebb (1963) famously commented, 'There's nothing so useful as a good theory'. In addition, you will usually need to show that you have covered the existing knowledge on a topic – it is usually a central purpose of the project work. Moreover, the existing knowledge base should help you to make sense of, or at least structure the issues in the area that you are considering.

- **Do I really have to prepare a written scope and proposal?**

  Whilst some institutions require you to present a written proposal, others will accept a discussion of your proposals. We suggest that the few minutes that it takes to prepare the proposal are worthwhile, as it provides a point of reference for the project as it progresses and will help to keep you on track, if you refer back to it regularly.

> ### Discussion questions
>
> 1. If you have access to a set of project requirements for your academic work or business project, use them to answer this question. What are the requirements of projects that you will be carrying out? Investigate the documentation provided by your institution and compare them with the characteristics of a 'good project' included in this chapter.
> 2. 'Previous work is so yesterday. Why not just start it again? After all, it was about time there was some fresh thinking in management.' What do you think of this statement?
> 3. Where do you position yourself in **Figure 9.2**?
> 4. What are the sources of ideas that you could usefully use for your project either to start you off or expand on the ideas that you have?

5. Does every research project have to be linked to a particular business and management area of study? Why or why not?
6. What are the ethical implications of using previous student projects as a source for your own project ideas?
7. How would you express your ideas at different stages in the development of those ideas? How would a mind map be used here?
8. How can filling out a research proposal improve the quality of the research process?
9. How can defining your project scope at this stage of the research process improve the quality of the research project?

Workshop

This workshop comprises two short group exercises, intended to illustrate the different processes that people go through in trying to reach a decision when there are a large number of possibilities for that decision.

10-minute exercise (1)

Your group has been awarded a (fictitious) potential business start-up grant of £100,000. What are you going to do with this? You have 10 minutes to agree on an idea and present it in order to 'win' this money.

Debrief discussion questions (1)

1. What are your ideas (summarise to one idea per group)?
2. How did you choose which of your ideas to run with?
3. What happened in the 10-minute session – was there any structure to the activity? Did all people contribute or was it dominated by one person? How was the information collected?
4. How effective was this process at getting to 'the best idea'?
5. Plot the process that the group went through onto **Figure 9.1**. How did each of you respond to such a wide brief?

10-minute exercise (2)

We now introduce some 'rules' for the process:
1. At the start of the next exercise, the first three minutes are to be conducted in silence to allow everyone to develop their ideas first.
2. Appoint someone as facilitator (not the most dominant person from the first exercise). The role of the facilitator is to clarify ideas and help to ensure that everyone is assisted in making their contribution.
3. No ideas are rejected and nobody is criticised for ideas (some of the wackiest ideas when combined with others can produce superb concepts).

4. Combine but don't eliminate ideas.
5. Use Post-its (or index cards) to write your ideas down (one idea per Post-it or index card) and then compile a mind map of the issues as in **Figure 9.4**.

Task

You have been assigned to a project team to carry out a research project. The general area that you have come up with is the evaluation of critical success factors for small businesses. Your initial evaluation of the area shows it to be large and you will need to focus the topic onto a more limited question that you want to ask.

1. For three minutes, working individually, write down your ideas.
2. For two minutes review each other's ideas, without discussion.
3. For five minutes, arrange the topics into a mind map (as **Figure 9.4**). Which is the most interesting of these that the group would pursue?

Debrief discussion questions (2)

1. What were your main ideas?
2. How did the group work this time round (better or worse)?
3. How did you make decisions?
4. What would you do differently in group situations in future – both to avoid the potential for failure from the issues you have identified, and in terms of the process for making decisions in project groups?

Task

Use the basic idea you have identified to complete a project proposal similar to the one provided in **Table 9.2**.

CHAPTER 10
Writing your research proposal

LEARNING OBJECTIVES

When you have studied this chapter, you should be able to:
- identify a research problem or issue
- determine the purpose of the research
- identify the main research question(s)
- choose the research strategy and methods
- write a research proposal.

10.1 Introduction

Having identified your research paradigm, selected a research topic and begun to investigate the relevant literature, you are now ready to design your study and write your *research proposal* If you are a student, the intellectual sophistication and length of your proposal will depend on the level and requirements of your programme, but once accepted by your supervisor(s), this critical document provides you with a detailed plan for your study. If you are bidding for research funds, your proposal will also play an important role.

This chapter draws together much of the information and guidance given in earlier chapters. For most students, writing their research proposal is the first formal milestone in their studies and paves the way for their dissertation or thesis. If you are studying for a Master's degree or a doctorate, it is likely that your research proposal will need to be more substantial than that required at the undergraduate level. This means you will have to spend some time working on it to obtain the approval of your supervisor(s) and/or research committee.

We start by guiding you through the process of designing your research and then go on to explain how to communicate the main features of your proposed study in your research proposal. It is important to remember that we are only able to give general advice, and you will need to follow the specific requirements of your institution.

10.2 Overview of research design

Before you can write your research proposal, you must spend some time designing your proposed study. *Research design* is the 'science (and art) of planning procedures for conducting studies so as to get the most valid findings' (Vogt, 1993, p. 196). Determining your research design will give you a detailed plan which you will use to guide and focus your research. Whether you are on an undergraduate course or are a postgraduate student, you will be expected to set out your research design in a document known as a 'research proposal'. This is an important step because it is on the basis of your proposal that your research study will be accepted or rejected.

Before you can begin designing your project, you need to have identified your research paradigm and have chosen a research topic. You will remember that your choice of paradigm has important implications for your choice of research strategy and methods for collecting and analysing data. It also influences your choice of research problem and research questions. Figure 10.1 shows the main steps in research design. This simple model suggests the process is linear and moves smoothly from the research problem to the expected outcome. In practice, however, the process is often circular, reiterative and time-consuming, so do not be surprised if you find yourself constantly reviewing previous stages as you progress.

The frst step in designing your research is to identify a *research problem* or issue to investigate. However, you must remember that this does not take place in a vacuum, but in a particular context. Although you may have already determined your research paradigm, you might find that you have selected a research problem where you consider it is necessary to change some of your basic assumptions. Therefore, you may have to review your choice of paradigm and reflect on how appropriate it

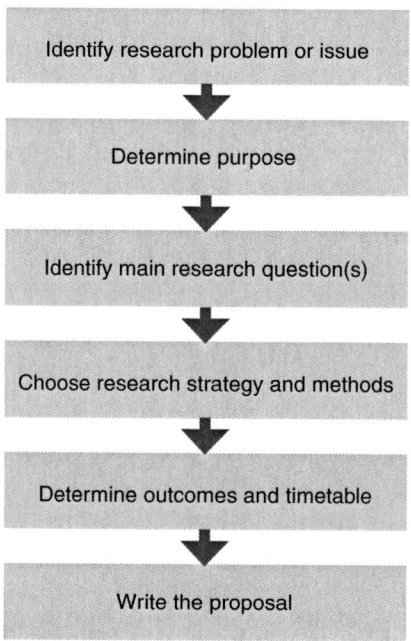

Figure 10.1 Main steps in research design

is to the problem you have identified. Another possibility is that you have picked a problem which is not acceptable to your supervisor or which for practical reasons cannot be investigated.

You will need to refine your research problem by providing a succinct *purpose statement* and developing *research question(s)*. In a positivist study, you will develop a *theoretical framework* which will lead to *hypotheses*. In an interpretivist study, you are more likely to determine the purpose of your research and construct only one or two questions that you will refine and modify, and set within a theoretical context during the course of the research itself. The final stages of your research design will be defining terms, establishing your methodology and giving an indication of the expected outcome. It is important to remember that 'the more sophisticated and rigorous the research design is, the greater the time, costs, and other resources expended on it will be' (Sekaran, 2003, p. 118).

In the following sections we consider each of these activities separately. However, it is important to remember that although we have shown them in a linked sequence, in practice, research is seldom quite so straightforward and orderly. It is highly likely that you will have to retrace your steps and review some of the earlier stages as more information and more problems come to light in the later stages of constructing your research design. We will now examine each of the stages of research design shown in Figure 10.1 in detail.

10.3 The research problem

10.3.1 Identifying a research problem

You will remember from previous chapters that a research project must focus on a specific *problem* or issue. If you are a student, this topic must be relevant to your degree programme and, if you are receiving funding, it must be relevant to your sponsor. Of course, it must also be a topic that is of interest to you!

When you have chosen your research problem, you will find it useful to write a simple statement describing it to help you to remain focused while planning the design of your research. Table 10.1 gives some examples of business research problems other students have identified.

Key definitions

The **research problem** is the specific problem or issue that is the focus of the research.

Identifying a research problem or issue is always an exploratory and reiterative phase in your research. There are a number of ways in which you can develop your ideas within a general topic of interest. These include reading the relevant literature, discussions with your lecturers and other students, and looking at previous students' dissertations and theses. When choosing a research problem, you need to bear in mind that your study must be achievable in terms of the resources available, your skills and the time constraints imposed by the submission date. It must also be sufficiently challenging to meet the academic standards expected at your level of study.

Table 10.1 Examples of research problems

Research topic	Research problem
Accounting regulations	Whether accounting practices should be regulated by the government or by the accounting profession
Corporate governance	How corporate governance can be extended to employee communications
Financial accounting in the NHS	The use of financial accounting by doctors in general practice
Financial reporting	The most effective ways for communicating financial information to stakeholders
Environmental issues in accounting ethics	The criteria by which shareholders measure 'green' companies
Environmental issues in manufacturing	The influence of 'green' factors on supplier selection in the manufacturing sector
Gender issues in employment	The effect of career-break schemes on the recruitment and retention of skilled staff
Public service announcements as a method of communication	The effectiveness of public service announcements for communicating with students

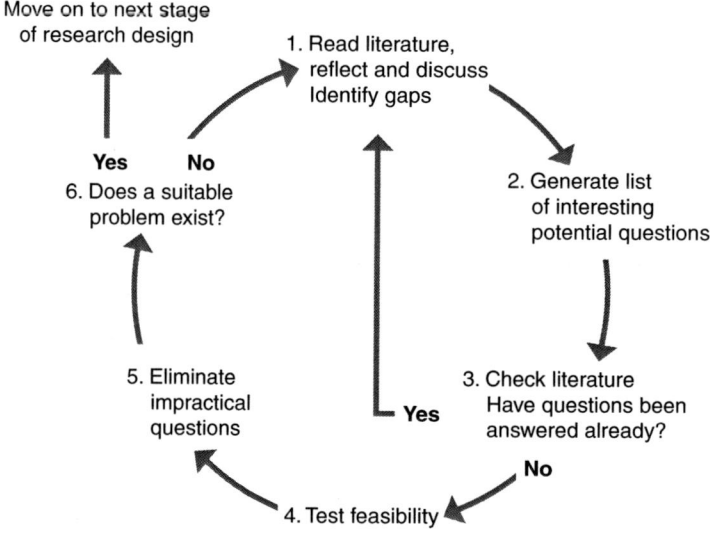

Figure 10.2 Identifying a research problem

The classic way in academic research is to read the literature on the topic of interest to you and identify any gaps and deficiencies in previous studies, since these will indicate opportunities for further research. Figure 10.2 shows a useful procedure for doing this. Identifying a research problem or issue can be a lengthy business since you have to keep revising your initial ideas and referring to the literature until you arrive at a business problem or issue you think will lead to a researchable project. You know that you are arriving at this stage when you can start generating suitable research questions.

Your initial search will probably result in three or four projects within your broad area of interest. You now need to compare them so that you can select one. At this stage it is helpful to eliminate any research problem which you consider is less likely to lead to a successful outcome. Although you may select a topic that is of great interest to you (and your supervisor), at the end of the day you will want to submit a research report which receives a high mark from the examiner or is accepted by the research/doctoral committee. Therefore, you need to examine your list of potential research problems critically and make certain that you select the one which is likely to give you the highest chance of success. We next discuss the specific issues that give some indication of which of the research problems or points you identify are likely to be the most researchable.

10.3.2 Access to data

The availability of data is crucial to the successful outcome of your research. The term data refers to known facts or things used as a basis for inference or analysis. You will need to find out whether you will be able to have access to all the secondary and/or primary data you need for your study. Although you may be able to think of a number of interesting problems, your final choice may be constrained because the necessary data is either not available or is very difficult to collect.

Key definitions

Data are known facts or things used as a basis for inference or reckoning.

Many students fail to appreciate the barriers to collecting data. For example, postal questionnaire response rates are often very low; 20% is typical. Companies will rarely give commercially sensitive information and in many cases may not have suitable records to allow them to give the required data. Therefore, before deciding on your research project, you must be sure that you will be able to get the data and other information you will need to conduct your research. Table 10.2 provides a checklist which you may find useful for assessing the availability of data.

10.3.3 Your skills and resources

When planning your research, you need to consider what you will need to know and do to complete your research. You should be able to gain a reasonable understanding of your subject area by reading the relevant literature search, but you will also need other skills, such as:

- IT skills for searching the literature and analysing data
- creative skills for designing questions and communicating concepts
- verbal communication skills for interviewing
- knowledge of statistics if you are planning a quantitative analysis
- general analytical skills if you are planning to interpret qualitative data
- verbal and written communication skills for presenting your research.

If you know that you have certain weaknesses, you need to assess whether you can overcome them in the time available. Your project is a period of development and you should welcome any opportunity to improve your skills and exploit your existing strengths.

Table 10.2 Assessing the availability of data

Type of data	Source
The literature	Check databases containing academic articles, the library catalogue, and internet resources.
Official statistics	National jurisdictions, the European Commission and international organizations such as the World Bank publish statistics on their websites. Some may be available in your library.
Industry data	You may need background information about a particular industry. Check your library catalogue, databases and the internet.
Company data	Information is available on the company's website and the company's annual report and accounts (which contains extensive narrative information in the case of listed companies). Check your library catalogue for other publications.
Internal data	List the information you will require and get permission/confirmation of access in writing. Do not use unethical methods, such as asking a friend who happens to work in the accounts department!
People	How many will you need to see? Do you know them already? Have you got the necessary communication skills and recording equipment? Do you have sufficient funds and time?
Surveys	Where will you find a list of relevant organizations and contact details? How many interviews or questionnaires will you need for your analysis? What response rate to do you anticipate? Do you have sufficient funds and time?

Box 10.1 Criteria for assessing a research topic

- Is the topic researchable, given time, resources, and availability of data?
- Is there a personal interest in the topic in order to sustain attention?
- Will the results from the study be of interest to others [...]?
- Is the topic likely to be publishable in a scholarly journal (or attractive to a [research] ... committee?
- Does the study (a) fill avoid, (b) replicate, (c) extend, or (d) develop new ideas in the scholarly literature?
- Will the project contribute to career goals?

When considering different research problems, it is useful to look at the implications of your choice. Creswell (1994) offers the criteria shown in Box 10.1 which can be used in assessing a research topic.

10.4 Purpose of the research

10.4.1 Determining the unit of analysis

Once you have chosen a suitable research problem or issue, your next task is to identify the overall *purpose* of the research and determine the *unit of analysis*. The unit of analysis is the phenomenon under study, about which data are collected and

Table 10.3 Units of analysis

Unit of analysis	Example
An individual	A manager, union member, lender, supplier or customer
An event	A merger, strike, relocation, acquisition, change of leadership, decision to diversify or expand
An object	A machine, a product, service, or document
An organization or group of people	A type of business, division, department, committee or level of employee
A relationship	A customer/supplier relationship, manager/subordinate relationship, management/union relationship or head office/branch relationship
An aggregate	A collection of undifferentiated individuals or bodies with no internal structure, such as companies in a certain industry, businesses of a certain size or in a particular location

Source: Adapted from Kervin (1992, pp. 87–9)

analysed, and is closely linked to the research problem and research questions. In business research, a unit of analysis might be a particular organization, division or department within an organization, or a more general group, such as business owners, managers, advisers or regulators. It could also be an inanimate object such as a particular type of event, decision, procedure, contract or communication (Blumberg, Cooper and Schindler, 2005).

Key definitions

The **unit of analysis** is the phenomenon under study, about which data are collected and analysed.

Kervin (1992) suggests that it is generally best to select a unit of analysis at as low a level as possible. This should be at the level where decisions are made. Table 10.3 shows the different units of analysis, starting at the lowest and simplest level.

Once you have determined your unit of analysis, you can state the purpose of your study clearly and succinctly. This can be achieved by writing a *purpose statement*. The purpose statement is usually only two or three sentences long and is normally provided in a separate section in the research proposal (and subsequently in the final research report). The content of the purpose statement depends on whether you are designing your research under a positivist or an interpretivist paradigm.

10.4.2 Purpose statement in a positivist study

In a positivist study, a purpose statement identifies the variables to be studied, the relevant theory and the methods to be employed. It should also refer to the sample and the unit of analysis.

When writing your purpose statement for your proposal, you will use the future tense, but in your research report, dissertation or thesis you will use the past tense because the study will have been completed. Your writing style will reflect your

> **Box 10.2 Simple model of a purpose statement for a positivist study**
>
> The purpose of this _____ (experimental? survey?) study _____ (is? was? will be?) to test the theory of _____ that _____ (compares? relates?) the _____ (independent variable) to _____ (dependent variable) for _____ (subjects? sample?) at _____ (research site). The independent variable(s) _____ will be defined generally as _____ (provide general definition). The dependent variable(s) will be defined generally as _____ (provide general definitions), and the intervening variable(s), _____ (identify the intervening variables) will be statistically controlled in the study.
>
> *Source*: Creswell (1994, p. 64)

rhetorical assumptions. You will write in a formal style using the passive voice, accepted quantitative words and set definitions. For example, instead of writing 'I will hold interviews with ...' or 'I held interviews with ...' you will write 'Interviews will be held with ...' or 'Interviews were held with ...'. You are trying to convey the philosophical assumptions (see Chapter 4) that are appropriate to your paradigm, emphasizing your independence from what you propose to study and your objectivity in measuring reality.

Key definitions

A **purpose statement** is a statement (usually two or three sentences long) that describes the overall purpose of the research study.

Creswell (1994) suggests that scripting can be useful when preparing a purpose statement, which involves filling in blanks in text based on cues in the sentence. Box 10.2 shows a simple model for a positivist study that can be used as the basis for constructing your purpose statement (the alternatives in brackets are the prompts).

10.4.3 Purpose statement in an interpretivist study

There is more variation among purpose statements relating to interpretivist studies. It is normal to emphasize the methodology employed and to imply the inductive nature of the research. The central phenomenon being explored should be described as well as the location for the study. To reflect the rhetorical assumption of this paradigm, you should write in an informal style and use the personal voice, accepted qualitative terms and limited definitions. For example, instead of writing 'Interviews will be held with ...' or 'Interviews were held with ...', you will write 'I will hold interviews with ...' or 'I held interviews with ...'. Throughout the purpose statement, you are trying to convey the philosophical assumptions that are appropriate to your paradigm, emphasizing your interaction with what you propose to study and your subjectivity in interpreting reality.

Box 10.3 illustrates a simple model that can be used as the basis of a purpose statement for an interpretivist study.

> **Box 10.3 Simple model of a purpose statement for an interpretivist study**
>
> The purpose of this study _____ (is? was? will be?) to _____ (understand? describe? develop? discover?) the _____ (central concept being studied) for _____ (the unit of analysis: a person? processes? groups? site?) using a _____ (method of inquiry: ethnographical design? grounded theory design? case study design? phenomenological design?) resulting in a _____ (cultural picture? grounded theory? case study? phenomenological description of themes or patterns?). At this stage in the research the _____ (central concept being studied) will be defined generally as _____ (provide a general definition of the central concept).
>
> *Source*: Creswell (1994, p. 59)

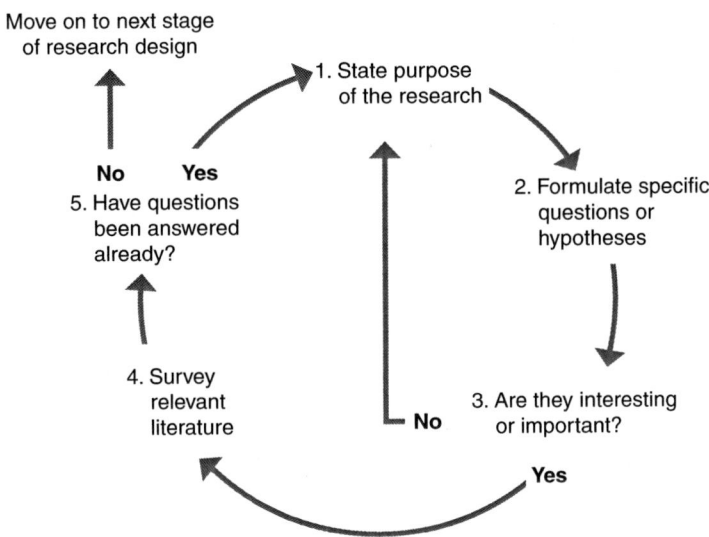

Figure 10.3 Identifying research questions

10.5 The research questions

10.5.1 Identifying research question(s)

Whereas the purpose statement gives details of the general direction of the study, a *research question* states the specific line of enquiry the research will investigate and attempt to answer. Therefore, your research questions provide a focus for your endeavours and are not the actual questions you might use in a questionnaire or interview. Identifying the research question(s) is a crucial stage in your research because it lies at the heart of your research design.

Figure 10.3 shows a simple model of how you can develop research questions. At each stage in the process you need to read, reflect and discuss what you are doing with others. The people you discuss your research with may be fellow students as well as your supervisor. We have already identified research as a process of enquiry, so the outcome of your investigation will be answers. However, you must ensure that the answers will be of interest or importance, otherwise your research will not receive much attention.

Key definitions

A **research question** is a specific question the research is designed to investigate and attempt to answer.

Before launching your investigations, you must search the relevant literature to see if anyone else has already answered your particular questions. If not, you can commence your research. However, if work has already been done in your chosen area, you may have to find ways of amending your proposed research so that it will produce new findings by extending or updating the existing body of knowledge.

10.5.2 Role of theory

A *theoretical framework* is a collection of *theories* and models from the literature. It is a fundamental part of most research studies and underpins the research questions. However, these can also be suggested by empirical evidence (from an exploratory study, for example), from which you subsequently develop a theory and construct propositions to test. A *theory* is 'a set of interrelated constructs (variables), definitions and propositions that presents a systematic view of phenomena by specifying relationships among variables with the purpose of explaining natural phenomena' (Kerlinger, 1979, p. 64). On a more simple level, theories are 'explanations of how things function or why events occur' (Black, 1993, p. 25).

Key definitions

A **theoretical framework** is a collection of theories and models from the literature which underpins a positivist study. Theory can be generated from some interpretivist studies.

A **theory** is a set of interrelated variables, definitions and propositions that specifies relationships among the variables.

A **hypothesis** is a proposition that can be tested for association or causality against empirical evidence.

Although some applied research has no theoretical background, if theory exists, you can develop a testable *hypothesis*. A hypothesis is a proposition that can be tested for association or causality against empirical evidence using statistics. Thus, hypotheses are associated with the positivist paradigm where the logic of the research is deductive and quantitative methods of analysis are used. However, Blaikie (2000, p. 10) argues that in some studies 'the testing is more in terms of a discursive argument from evidence' rather than the results of statistical tests.

According to Merriam (1988), theories can be classified into three types:

- grand theories, which are most often found in the natural sciences
- middle-range theories, which are placed higher than mere working hypotheses, but do not have the status of a grand theory
- substantive theories, which are developed within a certain context.

Laughlin (1995) argues that in the social sciences it is not possible to have a grand theory, only skeletal theory, where 'empirical data will always be of importance to make the skeleton complete in particular contexts' (Laughlin, 1995, p. 81). This does not mean that the theory will be changed or permanently completed, but will remain as a general framework within which a study can be conducted. Glaser and Strauss (1967) emphasize the importance of substantive theories, where theory is derived from the data (which they describe as *grounded theory)*.

Given these differences of opinion, you may find it confusing trying to develop a theoretical framework. However, there are a number of theories, concepts and models from which you can draw, and you will discover them when you study the literature on your chosen topic. They are important in many studies because they provide possible explanations for what is observed.

10.5.3 Research questions in a positivist study

For a study designed under a positivist paradigm, Black (1993) recommends a specific research question, followed by a number *of hypotheses*. Kerlinger (1986)]suggests that good research questions for a positivist study should:

- express a relationship between variables
- be stated in unambiguous terms in question form
- imply the possibility of empirical testing.

Your hypotheses will be based on theory. Each hypothesis is a proposition about the relationship between two variables that can be tested for association or causality against the empirical evidence you collect for your study.

Your hypothesis will identify the independent variable and the dependent variable. The null hypothesis (H_0) states that the two variables are independent of one another and the alternate hypothesis (H_1) states that they are associated with one another. The null hypothesis is always stated first. For example, if you thought that older employees might work more slowly than young employees, your null hypothesis would be:

H_0 There is no relationship between an employee's age and productivity.
H_1 There is a relationship between an employee's age and productivity.

In this example, age is the independent variable and productivity is the dependent variable. The purpose of your research will be to test specific aspects of any theory you may have found in the literature which suggests that there is a relationship between age and productivity level. Using the null hypothesis ensures that you adopt a cautious and critical approach when you are conducting statistical tests on your data.

Sometimes theory suggests that there is a possible direction for the relationship. In this case, you may decide to use a directional hypothesis. For example:

H_0 Productivity does not decrease as an employee increases in age.
H_1 Productivity decreases as an employee increases in age.

As you will have a number of hypotheses, it is important to use a formal, rhetorical style by repeating the same key phrases in the same order. For example:

> There is no relationship between an employee's age and the level of productivity.
> There is no relationship between an employee's age and the level of absenteeism.
> There is no relationship between an employee's age and degree of skill.

10.5.4 Research questions in an interpretivist study

In an interpretivist study, a theoretical framework may be less important or less clear in its structure. Some researchers attempt to approach their analysis with no prior theories, as they consider doing so would constrain and blinker them. Instead, they focus on trying to develop a theoretical framework, which is sometimes referred to as a model or substantive theory. It has been argued that 'even in wanting to escape theory, to be open-minded or wanting to believe that theorizing was unimportant to science, we would be practising a theory' (Slife and Williams, 1995, p. 9).

In some interpretivist studies, the research question takes the form of a grand tour question (Werner and Schoepfle, 1987), which is a single research question posed in its most general form. For example, 'How do employees cope with redundancy in an area of high unemployment?' By doing this, the researcher does not block off any other potential lines of enquiry. This is necessary where an emerging methodology, such as grounded theory, is used and one stage of the research guides the next stage. Nevertheless, the aim of a grand tour question is to focus the study on certain phenomena or a particular direction. It may need to be refined during the course of the research and this may mean you need to change the title of your project to reflect the final research question(s). Creswell (1994) advises one or two grand tour questions, followed by no more than five to seven subsidiary questions.

The criteria for a good research question are less clear in interpretivist studies than in positivist studies. This is due to the importance of the interaction between the researcher and the subject of the study in the former. If you are planning to conduct an interpretivist study, you will find that your research questions often evolve during the process of research and may need to be refined or modified as the study progresses. You will find that there are different customs in different interpretivist methodologies, which will be apparent from the literature you read on your topic. The best advice is to concentrate on the language of the question. It is usual to begin the research questions with 'what' or 'how' and to avoid terms associated with positivism, such as 'cause', 'relationship' or 'association'. Creswell (1994) suggests that you should:

- avoid wording that suggests a relationship between variables, such as 'effect', 'influence', 'impact' or 'determine'
- use open-ended questions without reference to the literature or theory, unless otherwise dictated by the research design
- use a single focus and specify the research site.

Finally, you should not underestimate the influence of your paradigm on your research design. Box 10.4 illustrates this with two examples based on the same research problem and research questions.

> **Box 10.4   Example of the influence of paradigm on research design**
>
> *Topic*: Gender issues in employment
>
> *Research problem*: The effect of the new career-break scheme in Firm A on the recruitment and retention of skilled staff
>
> *Research question*: How has the new career-break scheme contributed to employment in Firm A?
>
> - What is the nature of the scheme? (descriptive)
> - What effect has it had on recruitment of male and female skilled staff? (analytical)
> - What effect has it had on the retention of male and female skilled staff? (analytical)
>
> *Methodology for a positivist study*:
>
> - Research strategy: Case study
> - Methods: Statistical analysis of (a) secondary data from staff employment records and (b) primary data from a self-completion questionnaire survey of staff
>
> *Methodology for an interpretive study*:
>
> - Research strategy: Case study
> - Methods: Thematic analysis of data from semi-structured interviews with staff (primary data)

10.6   Writing the research proposal

10.6.1   Overview

A research proposal is a document that sets out the research design for a proposed study. It explains what is already known about the research topic, the purpose of the research and the main research question(s). It also describes the proposed methodology (including justification for the methods used to select a sample, collect and analyse the research data), the scope of the research and any limitations. It should incorporate a timetable and often concludes with comments on the contribution of the proposed research (the expected outcomes).

Key definitions

A **research proposal** is a document that sets out the research design for a proposed study.

Most institutions have a formal process for submitting a research proposal and instructions concerning the contents and the maximum word count. Your supervisor and/or research committee will be looking at academic issues as well as the feasibility of the proposed study.

The main academic issues being assessed are:

- The proposed study is based on the literature and is academically robust. You do this by demonstrating that you are familiar with the literature and have identified a main research question.
- The methodology clearly states the source(s) from which you will collect the research data, why you are collecting the data, when you are going to collect the data, and how you are going to collect and analyse the data. Be careful not to overlook the importance of explaining your method for selecting a sample or cases and your method(s) of analysis.
- Postgraduate students may need to state how the proposed study will make a contribution to knowledge and doctoral students may have to identify conferences and academic journals where they plan to disseminate their research.

The main practical issues being assessed are:

- You have access to the research data (primary, secondary or both). If your research requires access to confidential data, you must provide documentary evidence from the organization(s) and/or individual(s) confirming that access has been granted.
- You have access to any finance needed to conduct the research and there are no major time constraints that would prevent the completion of the project. Therefore, if you are struggling on a student grant, do not design a study that requires extensive travelling to obtain your data that would be both time-consuming and expensive.
- The outcome is achievable.

Although it is best to use the standard format if your institution provides one, there is still plenty of flexibility to allow you to put your research proposal in its best light. Table 10.4 shows a typical structure of a research proposal, together with some guidance on the proportion of space you should consider devoting to each section.

The detailed content of your proposal will depend on the nature of your research project and how you intend to conduct it, but we are now ready to look at the main items.

10.6.2 Title

The title of your proposed study should be as brief as possible. Creswell (1994) advises that you should not use more than 12 words and that you should consider eliminating most articles and prepositions, and make sure that it includes the focus or topic of the study. Wilkinson (1991) suggests that you eliminate superfluous words, such as 'Approach to …' or 'A study of …'. If you are carrying out research in one particular company or industry, make this clear.

10.6.3 Introduction

The research problem or issue that is the focus of the study should be stated clearly in your introduction. It can usually be expressed in one or two sentences. Resist the temptation to write in sentences that are so long that no one can understand them! Try showing your explanation of the research problem to fellow students, family and friends; if they understand it, it is likely you will impress your supervisor with your clarity.

Table 10.4 Indicative structure of a research proposal

	% of proposal

1. Introduction
  – The research problem or issue and the purpose of the study
  – Background to the study and why it is important or of interest
  – Structure of the remainder of the proposal
	15

2. Preliminary review of the literature
  – Evaluation of key items in the literature
  – Theoretical framework (if applicable)
  – Where your research fats in and the main research question(s)
	40

3. Methodology
  – Identification of paradigm
  – Justification for choice of methodology and methods
  – Scope of the research and the limitations of the research design
	40

4. Outcomes and timetable	5
References *(do not number this section)*	100

You u may find it helpful to follow this with a little background explaining why this issue is important or of interest, and to whom. This would be an appropriate place to define key terms as they arise in your narrative. You could conclude the introduction by explaining the purpose of the proposed study (using one of the model purpose statements we illustrated earlier, if you find this helpful).

You should define key terms (and any common terms you are using in a novel way) on the first occasion that you use them. You should use a definition from an authoritative academic source, such as a specialist dictionary in your discipline. We do not advise you to use Wikipedia or on-line sources from websites that can be posted or edited by the public. Remember that the definition should be in quotation marks and you should cite the name of the author(s), the year of publication and page number(s) in brackets next to the quotation. In a positivist study, this is essential and enhances the precision and rigour of your research.

10.6.4 Preliminary literature review

Your preliminary review of the literature should be a critical analysis of the main studies published that are relevant to your chosen research problem or issue you intend to investigate. Do not fall into the trap of taking a 'shopping list' approach to writing about the previous research you have identified in academic journals, books and other sources and remember that your lecturer's slides are not publications! At this stage, you are not expected to review the entire body of existing knowledge on the topic. Your supervisor will be familiar with the literature, so it is imperative that you cite the key authors and refer to the main theories and models. If you are using grounded theory in an interpretivist study, you will still write a preliminary review of the literature, but you will not need to identify a theoretical framework. If you are adopting a grounded theory methodology, you will need to provide a convincing argument for this choice in your methodology section.

Your preliminary literature review should conclude with an explanation of where your research fits into the gaps in the literature (for example where no knowledge exists about a particular phenomenon in a particular context) or deficiencies in the literature (for example where existing knowledge is out of date). This will include stating your main research question(s) and hypotheses (if applicable). Of course, your research question(s) must relate to the research problem you identified in your introduction, and they must be feasible. It is better to omit a question if you know it will be very difficult to address, rather than include it because it looks impressive.

10.6.5 Methodology

The methodology section in your proposal is where you explain and justify your proposed research strategy and methods for selecting a sample or cases, and for collecting and analysing the data. This section is important because it shows how you intend to investigate your research questions. You should be aware by now that your choice is dictated by your research paradigm. Therefore, it is essential to recognize the paradigm you have adopted, but you do not need to justify it. You u can provide a rationale for your choice of methodology by weighing up the advantages and disadvantages of alternatives.

Whatever the size of your proposed study, you will have to constrain your enquiries in a number of ways. Therefore, you will need to state the *delimitations* that establish the scope of your research. For example, you may confine your interviews to employees in Firm A or you may restrict your postal questionnaire to particular businesses in a particular geographical area. It can be more difficult to define the scope in an interpretivist study because the nature of the research is one of exploration and discovery.

An approach that can be used under either paradigm is to deconstruct your research question or hypothesis. Parker (1994) illustrates this with a hypothesis from a positivist study, which is shown in Figure 10.4. The process enables you to explain every term in considerable detail within the context of your proposed research. Not only does this give you considerable insight into your research, but you are in a better position to communicate it in your proposal (and dissertation, thesis or research report).

Most students will need to discuss issues such as reliability, validity and generalizability, and all students should state the *limitations* of their study. A limitation describes a weakness or deficiency in the research. For example, you may be planning a small exploratory study, from which only tentative conclusions can be drawn. This might be because you are planning a positivist study using a convenience sample rather than a random sample, or you are planning an interpretivist study but do not have the resources to conduct an in-depth case study. Sometimes additional limitations become apparent after the proposal stage and you will need to comment on these when you write your dissertation or thesis.

Students are often reluctant to mention problems with their research. There is no need to emphasize them at the proposal stage, and a comment is usually sufficient. However, you should not ignore them, as they serve two useful purposes:

- to identify potential difficulties, which can be discussed with your supervisor to ascertain whether they need to be resolved or whether they are acceptable in the context of your research design
- to signal at an early stage some of the issues you will need to address during the course of the research and when writing up the research.

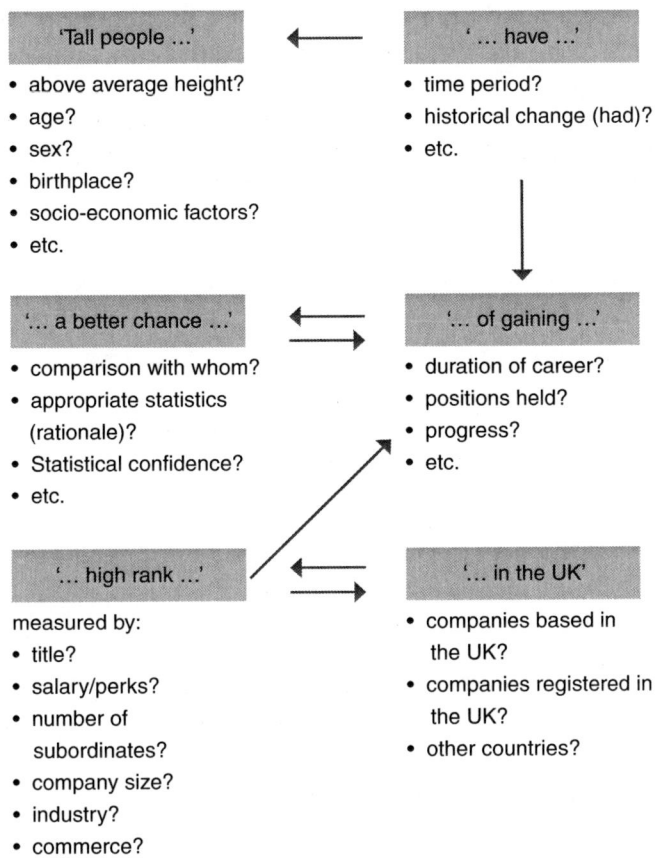

Figure 10.4 Example of deconstruction
'Tall people have a better chance of gaining high rank in the UK'

Source: Adapted from Parker (1994, p. 24)

Key definitions

A **delimitation** establishes the scope of the research.

A **limitation** is a weakness or deficiency in the research.

10.6.6 Outcomes and timetable

At the proposal stage, you cannot describe the outcome of your research in terms of your findings. Therefore, the final section in your proposal is brief and will focus on the expected contribution of the research. One way to express this is to refer to the purpose of the research. For example, if the purpose of your research is to investigate the impact of a new career-break scheme in Firm A, your expected outcomes are a description of the new scheme and an analysis of the impact of the scheme on the recruitment and retention of staff in Firm A. At all levels of research, but particularly at the doctoral level, it is important to emphasize that one outcome of the research is expected to be a contribution to knowledge. In your proposal, this can be stated in terms of the gaps and deficiencies you have identified in the literature.

Your proposed study must take account of the time constraints placed on the project by the submission date. You can use a Gantt chart with horizontal lines showing the timing of each stage to summarize your timetable. We advise you to discuss your draft timetable with your supervisor. Even experienced researchers find that research always takes up more time than you think it will, so do allow a contingency for delays due to exams, job interviews, holidays, illness and so on. Jankowicz (1991) gives estimates of standard times for some project activities. These include one day for preparing a ten-question interview schedule and four weeks for piloting a large questionnaire. You must be realistic about the amount of time you have available and what you can achieve in that time.

10.6.7 Additional information

In some cases, you may need to include a statement of special resources required in your proposal (for example specialist software or access to particular libraries or organizations). If you are applying for funding, you will need to supply a budget for travelling to interviews, printing questionnaires, postage, purchasing reports and papers that are not available on loan and so on. Table 10.5 shows an example of how you might set out your budget (the figures are illustrative and the cost of the researcher's time is not included).

If you are applying for funding, you may also be asked to provide a *statement of research activities and interests* to provide evidence of your suitability to carry out the proposed study. Box 10.5 shows an example of a suitable succinct statement that can be used as the basis for constructing your own.

10.6.8 References

The Harvard system of referencing is the method most commonly used in business and management. It allows you to avoid plagiarism by acknowledging all ideas and sources of information you have used in your work with a *citation* in the text and providing full bibliographic details at the end under the heading of *references*. Do not number the heading of this section and do not number the items listed, but place them in alphabetical order by author's name. This will allow any reader to locate and consult the original source of information; you can support all your assertions with an authoritative published source; and you can also show your supervisor the extent of your reading. Remember that however fettering it may be to your

Table 10.5 Research budget

Nature of expense	Basis of calculation	Cost €	Comment
Travelling expenses	30 interviews at €30 each	900	Car mileage from the university
Research reports	10 reports at €15 each	150	Not available from library
Research assistant	100 hours at €15 per hour	1,500	Data input and analysis
Conference	Fees, travel and hotel	1,020	Dissemination of results
Submission of article	Submission fee	30	*World Journal of Management*
	Total	3,600	

> **Box 10.5 Statement of research activities and interests**
>
> For the past four years I have been very interested in the financial measures used to evaluate the performance of managers. This interest originated with my MBA. My dissertation, which received a distinction, was entitled' The behavioural aspects of a budgetary control system in a small engineering company'. From this I have developed three main areas of interest:
>
> - Managerial performance measures in small manufacturing companies
> - Managerial performance measures in financial services companies
> - Managerial performance measures in charities.
>
> My research into these issues has resulted in five conference papers and two refereed journal articles, as shown in my CV. In the past two years I have spent approximately 70% of my research time conducting studies in XYZ Charity. This is a national charity to which I have full access, as confirmed in the attached letter from their CEO. My proposed research would take my previous research further by ...

lecturers to be cited, their lecture slides are not a publication and you need to refer to the original publications to which they refer.

A citation is made whether the information from your reading of a publication takes the form of a quotation or is summarized in your own words. If you are quoting, or reproducing a table or figure, your citation must include the page number(s) as well as the name(s) of the author(s) and the year of publication. You should bear in mind that your ability to apply the accepted system of referencing is one of the criteria against which your proposal will be assessed.

The more academic articles, reports, books and so on, you have read on your research topic or on research methods, the more citations you will have made and the longer your list of references will be. Therefore, you need to keep careful records of all the hard copy and internet sources you have used. Check that every citation in your proposal has a corresponding entry in your list of references and that you have not listed any items that you did not use and therefore did not cite. It is likely that your supervisor will do this when marking your proposal!

10.6.9 Evaluating your proposal

You will find that a considerable part of research involves reflecting on the work you have done. Designing your research is no exception. The most common reason for students failing at the proposal stage is because they have not been able to convert their general interest in a topic into the design of a study that will allow them to investigate a specific research problem. You must also ensure your design provides a good ft between your paradigm and the proposed research strategy and methods, and that the research process is logical. Your supervisor or sponsor will be looking at your research design from a practical point of view as well as an academic perspective, and will be assessing the feasibility of the design, given the resources available and the time constraints.

As you get involved in selecting a suitable research problem and developing an appropriate research design, it is easy to forget the big picture. Here are some words of general advice:

- Don't be too ambitious. It is much better to submit a modest research proposal which you can achieve than to come to grief on a project which sets out to remedy all the problems of the world
- Don't try to impress. The use of convoluted language and references to obscure articles does not help. Try to write simply and clearly so that any problems with your proposal can be identified and discussed with your supervisor
- Discuss your proposal with friends and family. Although they may not be familiar with the subject matter, they can often ask the awkward question which you have not spotted
- Be prepared to revise your proposal. It may be that you get part way through and realize that it is not possible to achieve all you set out to do. It is much better to correct this at the planning stage than to start the research and fail to complete it
- Remember that your proposal is a plan. You will have done a considerable amount of work preparing it; do not throw it all away. You should use your proposal to guide and manage the research. This does not mean that you cannot adapt your work as the research progresses, but the proposal is a map which should indicate your course and allow you to decide why and when to depart from it
- Try to allow time between completing your research proposal and submitting it so that you can reflect on it and improve it.

Once you have constructed your research proposal, you can use the checklist shown in Box 10.6 to evaluate it before you submit it to your supervisor and/or potential sponsor.

Just in case you are tempted to think that some of the items in the checklist are optional, Robson (1993) offers ten ways to get your proposal rejected. These are shown in Box 10.7.

10.7 Conclusions

In this chapter we have built on your knowledge from studying the preceding chapters to explain how to design a research study and draw up a detailed plan for carrying out the study. We have explored ways in which you can identify a potential research problem by identifying gaps and deficiencies in the literature, and how the purpose of the research can be communicated succinctly through the use of a purpose statement. We have also discussed the role of the main research question(s), and the importance of determining your main research questions and a theoretical framework (the latter is not applicable if you are using a grounded theory methodology). We have looked at the role of hypotheses in a positivist study and the influence of your paradigm on your choice of methodology. Positivist and interpretivist studies will have different research designs. A positivist research design will

Box 10.6 Project proposal checklist

1. Do you have, or can you acquire, the knowledge and skills to do the research?
2. Do you have the resources, such as computer facilities, travelling expenses?
3. Do you have access to the research data you need? If you need the co-operation of certain organizations or people, have you obtained their consent?
4. Does your title aptly describe your study?
5. Have you described the purpose and importance of your research?
6. Have you written a critical preliminary review of the literature and identified your main research question(s)?
7. Have you described and justified your methodology?
8. Is your timetable realistic?
9. Have you avoided plagiarism and checked that your work is correctly referenced?
10. Have you used the spelling and grammar check?

Box 10.7 Ten ways to get your proposal turned down

1. Don't follow the directions or guidelines given for your kind of proposal. Omit information that is asked for. Ignore word limits.
2. Ensure the title has little relationship to the stated objectives; and that neither title nor objectives link to the proposed methods or techniques.
3. Produce woolly, ill-defend objectives.
4. Have the statement of the central problem or research focus vague, or obscure it by other discussion.
5. Leave the design and methodology implicit; let them guess.
6. Have some mundane task, routine consultancy or poorly conceptualized data trawl masquerade as a research project.
7. Be unrealistic in what can be achieved with the time and resources you have available.
8. Be either very brief, or preferably, long-winded and repetitive in your proposal. Rely on weight rather than quality.
9. Make it clear what the findings of your research are going to be, and demonstrate how your ideological stance makes this inevitable.
10. Don't worry about a theoretical or conceptual framework for your research. You want to do a down-to-earth study so you can forget all that fancy stuff.

Source: Robson (1993, p. 468).

incorporate a stronger theoretical basis and it will be necessary to develop hypotheses. There will be an emphasis on the proposed measurement and analysis of the research data. An interpretivist research design may incorporate a theoretical framework and set out various propositions, but the emphasis is more likely to be on the robustness of the methods that will be used to analyse the research data.

We have described how to write a research proposal, looked at a typical structure and suggested additional items that may need to be included, such as a statement of required resources, a budget or a statement of research activities and interests. Once your research proposal has been accepted, you can start collecting your research data. However, the acceptance of your proposal does not necessarily mean that your research project will be successful. A research proposal is merely a plan and the next step is to execute that plan. The following chapters explain how you can do this successfully.

Although every research proposal is unique, it is useful to look at other proposals. If you can obtain examples of successful proposals from your supervisor, these provide the best guide to what is acceptable at your own institution. The following examples are summaries of proposals submitted by MPhil and PhD candidates. For the purpose of this book they have been abbreviated and therefore do not capture the richness of a full proposal. However, they provide illustrations of the style and content of postgraduate and doctoral research proposals.

10.7.1 Examples of business research proposals

ACCOUNTING DECISION MAKING

RESEARCH AREA

Evaluating investment decisions in advanced manufacturing systems: a fuzzy set theory approach

Research problem and literature overview

An important function of management accounting systems is providing managers with models that evaluate all relevant information needed for making investment decisions (*Accola, 1994*). Although Discounted Cash Flow Models (DCFM) have been widely accepted by both academicians and practitioners as a sound approach to investment decisions (*Klammer et al., 1991; Wilner et al., 1992; Cheung, 1993*), many authors have criticized applying them to evaluate the investment in Advanced Manufacturing Systems (AMS) (for example *Mensah and Miranti, 1989; Medearis et al., 1990*) because these models are biased in favour of short-term investments whose benefits are more easily quantified than longer term projects. Consequently, these authors concluded that DCFM should not be applied to evaluate the investments in AMS. The most difficult task associated with applying DCFM in evaluating AMS investments lies in the existence of many variables which can hardly be measured and expressed in terms of cash flows, especially the benefits that the system will provide, such as greater manufacturing flexibility, learning effects, the effects on employee morale and decreased lead time.

Due to these criticisms some researchers (for example *Medearis et al., 1990; O'Brien and Smith, 1993*) argue to ignore the financial analysis and regard the investment as a strategy that should be implemented regardless of the results of DCFM. Also, several authors suggested many approaches to evaluate the investment in AMS as a substitute of DCFM. These approaches are either numerical or non-numerical.

Thus, the main problem in the evaluation of investment decisions in AMS is how to quantify the expected benefits from these systems. In order to make these decisions in an objective manner, there is a need for a device that can properly treat qualitative variables in addition to quantitative variables. This suggests the use of fuzzy set theory (FST), which reduces the need for precise numerical inputs to decision analysis, in evaluating such decisions. FST provides a method of combining qualitative and quantitative variables for decision-making processes.

Research objective

The main objective of this research is introducing a suggested model for evaluating investment decisions in AMS considering qualitative and quantitative variables through the use of FST.

Methodology and work plan

The main aspects of the proposed research are: First, a model using the mathematical logic of FST will be constructed for evaluating the investment decisions of acquiring AMS. This will be carried on through an extensive theoretical study. So as to ensure that this model is applicable in the UK environment, a limited number of interviews with practitioners will be undertaken during the formulation of the model. Second, there will be an empirical study which can be used as a basis for evaluating the benefit and validity of the quantitative model. Input to the theoretical model will demand an in-depth understanding of particular investment decisions and the co-operation of key players in the decision-making process in order to establish 'fuzzy' variables. This data can only be collected in face-to-face interviews of a semi-structured nature.

References

Accola, W. L. (1994) 'Assessing risk and uncertainty in new technology investments', *Accounting Horizons*, Vol. 8 (3) September, pp. 19–35.

Cheung, J. K. (1993)'Management flexibility in capital investment decisions literature', *Journal of Accounting Literature*, 12, pp. 29–66.

Klammer, T, Koch, B. and Wilner, N. (1991) 'Capital budgeting practices: A survey of corporate use', Journal of Management Accounting Research, *American Accounting Association*, 3, Fall, pp. 113–30.

Medearis, H. D., Helms, M. M. and Ettkin, L P. (1990) 'Justifying flexible manufacturing systems (FMS) from a strategic perspective', *Manufacturing Review*, 3 (4) December, pp. 219–23.

Mensah, Y. M. and Miranti, P. J. (1989) 'Capital expenditure analysis and automated manufacturing systems: A review and synthesis', *Journal of Accounting Literature*, 8, pp. 181–207.

O'Brien, C. and Smith, J. E. (1993) 'Design of the decision process for strategic investment in advanced manufacturing *systems*', *International Journal of Production Economics*, 30–31, pp. 309–22.

Wilner, N., Koch, B. and Klammer, T. (1992) 'Justification of high technology capital investment – An empirical study', *The Engineering Economist*, 37 (4) Summer, pp. 341–53.

ACCOUNTING REGULATION

RESEARCH AREA

The regulation of related party transactions

The problem

Related parties are an everyday occurrence in the business world and the transactions that take place between them are a natural process. However, in the UK, these transactions are not disclosed which gives misleading information and enables companies the chance to act fraudulently (*Mason, 1979*). There are a number of cases of fraud using related parties including Pergamon Press (1969), US Financial (1972) and more recently, the death of Robert Maxwell has revealed the syphoning of funds to related parties, effectively stealing people's pensions. For these reasons, it is essential that the disclosure of related party transactions should be regulated. Attempts to regulate these transactions have been made by the ASC with ED 46 (1989) but so far these have been unsuccessful.

Aim of the research

To enable any future standard concerned with the disclosure of related party transactions to be comprehensive and implementable, certain questions must be researched and answered:

1. Why was the earlier attempt at a standard unsuccessful?
2. How should 'related parties' be defned?
3. What information should be disclosed?
4. What should be the threshold of the influence of the resulting standard?
5. How valuable will the information be to the users of the accounts? This research will aim to answer these questions.

Methodology

The research will be conducted as a longitudinal investigation of the interest in related party transactions in the UK. This will include an extensive literature review of background papers (*Brown, 1980*), previous attempts at issuing a standard ED 46 (*ASC, 1989*) and comments made about the exposure draft (*Hinton, 1989; ASC, 1990*). A critique of ED 46 will be published as a major part of the research. The study will be conducted in the context of agency theory (*Jenson and Meckling, 1976*) and the 'market of excuses' thesis by *Watts and Zimmerman (1979)*. A critical appraisal will also be made of the *'Nobes Cycle' (1991)*. The transfer to PhD will enable the research to include international experience, including *IAS 24 (IASC, 1984)* and SAS no. 6 (*AICPA, 1975*), conducted within the framework of international classification (*Mueller, 1967* and *Nobes, 1992*).

References

AICPA (1975) 'Statement on Auditing Standard no. 6', *Journal of Accountancy*, 140, September, pp. 82–5.

ASC (1989) 'Exposure Draft 46 Related Party Transactions', April.
ASC (1990) 'Comments received on ED 46'.
Brown, H. R. (1980) 'Background paper on related party transactions', ICAEW.
Hinton, R. (1989) 'Relating party transactions the UK *my*', *Accountancy,* 103 (1150) June, pp. 26–7.
IASC (1984) 'international Accounting Standard 24 Related Party Disclosures'.
Jenson, M. C. and Meckling, W. H. (1976) 'Theory of the firm: Managerial behaviour, agency costs and ownership structure', *Journal of Financial Economics,* 3, pp. 305–60.
Mason, A. K. (1979) 'Related party transactions: A research study', CICA.
Mueller, G. (1967) *International Accounting,* Part I, New York: Macmillan.
Nobes, C. (1992) *International Classification of Financial Reporting,* 2nd edn, Lava: Routledge.
Watts, R. L. and Zimmerman, J. L. (1979) 'The demand and supply of accounting theories: The market of excuses', *Accounting Review,* 54, April.

AUDITING

RESEARCH AREA

An analytical study of the effect of confirmatory processes on auditors' decision making and hypothesis updating

Research problem

Motivated in part by research findings in psychology, the auditing literature has recently begun to focus on auditors' use of confirmatory processes in evidence search and evaluation. Confirmatory processes mean that the auditor prefers to search for evidence confirming his initial hypotheses and also evaluates this evidence in a way that confirms his hypotheses (*Church, 1990,* p. 81). As the use of confirmatory processes is still a new trend in auditing, some problems are associated with the use of these processes, for example the impact of confirming and disconfirming approaches on auditors' decisions, the role of hypotheses formulation and the use of audit evidence in hypotheses updating.

Literature review and inadequacy of current research

Most of the previous studies (for example *Bedard and Biggs, 1991; McMillan and White, 1993*) on the use of confirmatory processes in auditing focused on auditors' hypotheses formulation. These studies declared that auditors differ in their abilities to formulate correct or plausible hypotheses and these abilities are affected by various factors. Among these factors are expertise, source of hypotheses, hypotheses frame, professional scepticism, motivational factors and cognitive factors. The stated factors still need in-depth investigation, in addition to determining what other factors can trigger the use of confirmatory processes in auditing. A few studies also examined the process of hypotheses updating. *Einhorn and Hogarth (1985)* formulated a model called 'Contrast/Surprise Model' which investigates the effect of confirming and/or disconfirming evidence on hypotheses updating. *Ashton and Ashton (1988)* investigated the validity of the previous model. However, their study is insufficient for investigating the process of hypotheses updating because they concentrated only on evidence order.

Research objective

The main objective of the proposed research is determining the effect of using confirmatory processes on auditor's decision making, and investigating the process of hypotheses updating. The main research questions to be addressed are:

1. What factors trigger the use of confirmatory processes in auditing?
2. What is the process of hypotheses updating?
3. What theoretical models are relevant to the process of hypotheses updating?
4. What are the most appropriate circumstances for using confirmatory/disconfirmatory approaches?

Methodology and work plan

The research will be carried out through a theoretical and an empirical study. The empirical study will involve survey and experimental studies. The survey will be conducted through interviews with a number of auditors in auditing firms. It is intended to carry out 36 interviews in six auditing firms; two large, two medium and two small. Interviews will be held with two highly experienced, two medium experienced and two relatively inexperienced auditors in each firm. These interviews will help in determining factors affecting auditors' use of confirmatory processes. Following the analysis of this data, 18 experimental studies will be carried out to determine the validity of the proposed model. These experimental studies will be conducted in the same auditing firms as the interviews.

References

Ashton, A. H. and Ashton, R. H. (1988) 'Sequential belief revision in auditing', *Accounting Review*, October, pp. 623–41.

Bedard, J. C. and Biggs, S. F. (1991) 'Pattern recognition, hypotheses generation and auditor performance in an analytical *task'*, *Accounting Review*, July, pp. 622–42.

Church, B. K. (1990) 'Auditors' use of confirmatory processes', *Journal of Accounting Literatures*, 9, pp. 81–112.

Einhorn, H. J. and Hogarth, R. M. (1985) *A Contrast/Surprise Model for Updating Beliefs*, Working Paper, University of Chicago, April.

McMillan, J. J. and White, R. A. (1993) 'Auditors' belief revisions and evidence search: The effect of hypothesis frame, confirmation bias and professional skepticism', *Accounting Review*, July, pp. 443–65.

BUYER BEHAVIOUR

RESEARCH AREA

The influence of children behaviour on the family purchase environmentally friendly grocery products in South Wales

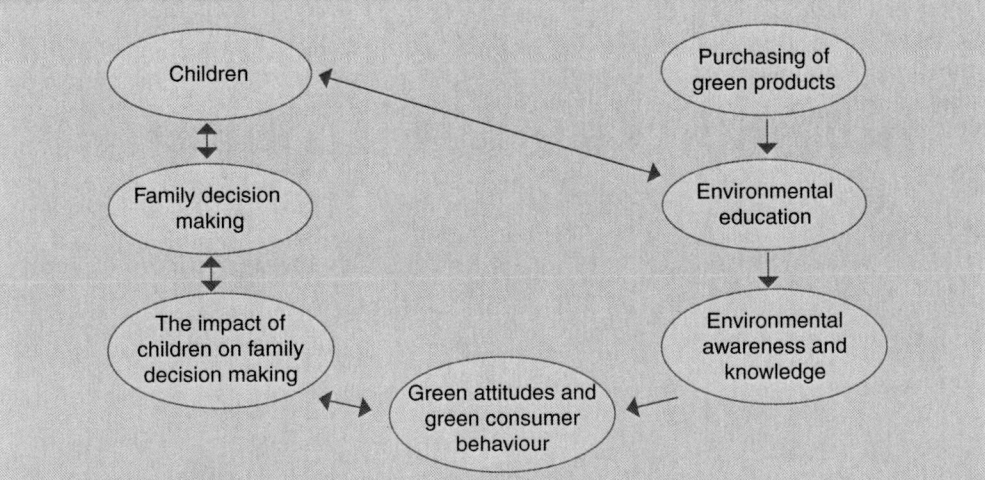

Figure A.1 Diagrammatic conceptual framework

Previous studies of environmental consumerism have addressed the implications of the individual's buyer behaviour (*Ottman 1989; Charter 1992*) and changes in organizational management practices (*Charter 1992; Smith 1993; Welford of and Gouldson 1993*). The majority of studies in the area of green consumerism focus on the greening of the individual's buying behaviour, the development of green consumerism and the reactions of management in a wide sphere of industries. This research will take family buying behaviour models and build in an environmental perspective. The conceptual framework is presented briefly in Figure A.1.

Research by Charter in 1992 revealed that environmental awareness is increasing in schools throughout Europe, with the introduction of environmental topics in range of school syllabuses, together with wide recognition of the importance of environmental issues as a cross-curricular subject. This has resulted in environmental awareness and concern diffusing among children, with the direct result of children acting as important catalysts in raising the environmental awareness of the family group by reporting back what has been learned about the environment at school.

As *Buttle (1993)* discovered, consumer decisions are influenced by systematic relationships of the family which have a variable and determined effect upon the actions of individuals. Most researchers in environmentally responsive buyer behaviour have employed what Buttle (1993) describes as individualistic concepts and constructs. This research intends to take the interactive phenomena of the family and the influence of children on the purchase of environmentally responsible grocery products.

Aims

To investigate the influence of children on the family purchase of environmentally friendly grocery products in South Wales.

The aims of this research centre on an understanding of the influence that children have on family purchase of environmentally friendly grocery products. Grocery products have been selected as the focus of this study because children have a major influence on product choice in this area, and are likely to be involved in product choice selection. The aim of this doctoral study is to determine children's attitudes to and awareness of environmental concerns and the family–child interaction process within the context of environmentally responsive family buying behaviour.

Methodology

The first stage of the research has been a review of the existing literature on green consumerism, environmental education and children, and family buying behaviour. The literature review concentrates on several areas – first, on the diffusion of environmentally responsive buying behaviour; second, on the issues surrounding the development of children's attitudes and awareness of environmental concerns; and third, on the family–child interaction process within the context of family buying behaviour, as Figure A.1. illustrates.

The primary methodology consists of three stages: The exploratory research which is underway, and consists of focus group sessions with primary school children in South Wales. The aims of the exploratory study are to determine the attitudes and behaviour of children towards environmental consumerism and how they believe they influence environmentally responsive family buying behaviour. The legal and ethical aspects of research with children will be adhered to.

Stage two will be an investigation of the family group through focus group sessions in South Wales, with the objective of establishing the actual interactive decision-making process within the sample families. This will be undertaken between September 1995 and March 1996.

The third stage of the research will consist of the development of case studies in order to investigate the holistic characteristics of the real-life situation. The case study sample will be developed from stage two of the research. The in-depth case study analysis will consist of semi-structured interviews and an observational study to be undertaken between March 1996 and March 1997.

Output

This doctoral research will contribute to family buyer behaviour knowledge and the understanding of environmentally responsive consumer behaviour; it will contribute to the understanding of the marketing implications of the influence of children in environmental decision making and the ways in which decision making is undertaken within the family group in the context of environmentally responsive buyer behaviour.

References

Buttle F. (1993) The co-ordinated management of meaning: A case exemplar of a new consumer research paradigm, *European Journal of Marketing*, 28, nos. 8/9.

Charter, M. I. (1992) *Greener Marketing*, Shefield: Greenleaf Publishing.
Ottman, J. (1989) Industries' response to green consumerism', *Journal of Business Strategy*, 13, Part 4.
Smith, D. (1993) 'Purchasing department contributions to company environmental performance', *Purchasing Supply Management*, 20 (1).
Welford, R. and Gouldson, A. (1993) *Environmental Management Business Strategy*, London: Pitman Publishing.

ORGANIZATIONAL CHANGE

RESEARCH AREA

Changing the deal: The role of informal contracts in business transformation and organizational renewal

Introduction and literature review

In the last decade, the belief has grown amongst organizational theorists (Kanter, 1983; Handy, 1989; Pascale, 1990 and others) that in order to be successful in increasingly turbulent markets, organizations need to be able to assimilate – or better, instigate – dramatic shifts in their industries. Change is becoming more discontinuous (Handy, 1989) – or transformational – in nature. The management of discontinuous change demands a more 'holistic approach' (Hinings and Greenwood, 1988) and an ability to recognize – and if appropriate, act on – the limitations of the organization's existing paradigms (Morgan, 1986,1993). It can also require organizations to build more flexibility into their structures and contractual arrangements (Atkinson, 1984). Roles may be restructured; jobs rescoped; new skills demanded; career paths obfuscated: in short, individuals are asked to undertake a radical rethink of their role, both within the organization and in a broader context. Formal contracts and cultures are being developed that aim to meet these challenges, but the informal side of organizational life cannot and should not be ignored.

A pilot project (in an operating company of a leading financial services group) conducted for this proposal, suggested that even when change is accepted at the 'rational' levels it may meet resistance if insufficient attention is paid to its broader implications (Jarvis, 1994). There is a growing need to understand the 'informal contract' between the employer and employee, if both parties' expectations are to be met.

A key output from the research will be a better understanding of the 'informal contract', and if and how it is evolving. At this stage, a working definition is being employed, as follows: 'the expectations – emotional and rational; conscious and unconscious – that employees bring to and take from their work and that are not covered by their job description and formal contract of employment'.

Research aim

The main aim of the MPhil project is to define the informal contract and establish its role in the implementation of major change programmes. PhD research will aim to uncover if and how the informal contract can be 'managed' to support employees through major change.

Research methodology and proposed timetable

Primary research will be qualitative, collaborative inquiry (Reason, 1988) built around 6–8 case studies, each being conducted over a period of 18–24 months. This approach has been selected for its ability to yield data at the unconscious, as well as conscious, level.

Hypotheses will be developed as the case study progresses and each case study will adopt four key research methods: interviews with senior management to provide an organizational context and an understanding of the aims and critical success factors for the change programme; depth interviews, with middle management grades and below, to provide context and a broad understanding of the individual meaning of the informal contract; individual diaries to provide a depth of information – 'felt' and rational – into the meaning of the informal contract to individuals; a series of inquiry groups to develop a shared meaning for the informal contract. Triangulation will be provided through this use of different methods and different sources, while an audit trail will ensure confirmability.

PhD research will test hypotheses for transferability. As well as the opportunities for comparison provided by multiple case studies, it is envisaged that a series of cross-organizational groups, comprising senior managers, will be set up to look at how these hypotheses transfer from theory into practice.

References

Atkinson, J. (1984) *Emerging UK Work Patterns,* IMS Paper No. 145.
Handy, C. (1989) *The Age of Unreason,* Business Books Ltd.
Hinings, C. R. and Greenwood, R. (1988) *The Dynamics of Strategic Change,* Basil Blackwell.
Jarvis, C. (1994) *The Introduction of a Self-Assessment Appraisal System in to FSG OpCo,* unpublished.
Kanter, R. M. (1983) *The Changemasters,* Unwin Hyman.
Morgan, G. (1986) *Images of Organisation,* Sage Publications.
Morgan, G. (1993) *Imaginization,* Penguin.
Pascale, R. (1990) *Managing on the Edge,* Penguin.
Reason, P. (1988) (ed.) *Human Inquiry in Action: Developments in New Paradigm Research,* Saga Publications.

ORGANIZATIONAL CHANGE

RESEARCH AREA

To evaluate input and effectiveness of culture change on individuals and organizations

Background

I have run and co-tutored personal, management and organizational development courses for the last ten years. Co-tutoring has given me the opportunity to observe others' training, receive feedback and reflect on my own practice. The dominant thought area that has emerged from this refection is that the quality of relationship between tutor and learner, and learner and learner, is of critical importance if lasting change and development is to occur.

As a participant in a self-managed learning group at Lancaster University (MAML), I found the experience challenging and, at times, frustrating. I believe this was due to the developmental relationships within the group. While this subject has emerged from reflecting on my own personal experience, I believe it is relevant to tutors, learners and managers. Effective 'engaging' between individuals could be a basis for effective managerial relationships.

The project

The study will explore the nature of 'engaging' (that is, effective developmental relationships) between tutors and learners, and learners and learners. The aim is to define and develop a working model of effective developmental relationships.

Theoretical context

Rowland (1993) has proposed a spectrum of tutoring relationships from 'didactic' to 'exploratory', with the middle ground being occupied by an 'interpretative' model. In his 'exploratory' and 'didactic' models the learning process is seen as being 'a black box, a kind of private psychological process in which the tutor cannot engage' (1993, p. 27). In the 'interpretative' models the tutor deliberately attempts to become part of the learning process. He characterizes the relationship as being one in which there is a free flow of learning and the tutor becomes an important part of the students' learning process. The psycho-therapeutic work of Rogers (1961) clearly defines the characteristics of what he terms a 'helping relationship'. This relationship creates a 'psychological climate' that ultimately releases human potential. Combining the work of Rowland (1993) and Rogers (1961) suggests a definition of 'engaging' as a relationship that creates a developmental psychological climate and a culture of support in which individuals develop shared meanings and collectively become an integral part of each other's reflective processes.

Using Reason's (1988) post-positivist research methodology of co-operative enquiry, I will work with groups to establish how individuals successfully 'engage'.

Reason provides many useful insights into establishing cooperative enquiry groups including creating the 'right' atmosphere for people to examine processes, freely challenge and support one another. He suggests this is not easy and needs to emerge from the group as it matures towards truly authentic collaboration. This is another factor within the process of 'engaging' but between researcher and researched. Thus, the theoretical context of the research methodology parodies the area under study.

Methodology and research process

The proposed study will use a form of co-operative enquiry, which is ontologically based on a belief in a participatory universe and attempts to undertake research with people rather than on them. Cunningham (1988) suggests a broad model of co-operative inquiry which he calls 'interactive holistic research'. This non-linear, or as he puts it 'omni-focussed', model (p. 167) has four elements:

a. Collaborative enquiry – that is with people and either of Type I – in which the group explores its internal processes together or Type II in which the group explores a process which happens outside the group.
b. Action research – research which is concerned with developing practical knowledge or praxis.
c. Experimental research – research which is concerned with how and what I experience.
d. Contextual locating – this represents the backdrop to the whole research study, either intellectually, socially or emotionally.

Within the MPhil phase, I propose to establish a collaborative enquiry group with fellow tutors and learners to explore experiences of 'engaging' (Type II according to Cunningham, 1988). The purpose of this phase is to define and develop a model of 'engaging' between tutors and learners. This will be elaborated in the PhD phase by exploring the nature of developmental relationships within the group (Type I according to Cunningham, 1988) and to look further at this relationship in the context of managing. In this phase the objective is to define 'engaging' between learners and to develop a model of collaborative learning or development. The group will be assembled by invitation and consist of fellow tutors with an interest in exploring developmental relationships. Initial research with learners will be confined to participant observation to enable a working hypothesis to be established and will be undertaken with the many groups that I currently co-tutor. This will be replaced with a more formal collaborative enquiry which attempts to elicit a learner's perspective on 'engaging', initially free of any hypothesis, but later to explore a hypothesis which is either given or developed.

Research with fellow tutors and with learners will take place concurrently. The synthesis of these views will take place through a critical examination of my own practice and experience, through observation and critical subjectivity. Ideas which are developed will then be available for scrutiny and development with the collaborative inquiry group. In each of the groups (that is, learners and tutors) I will be the primary researcher.

References

Cunningham, I. (1988) 'interactive Holistic Research: Researching Self Managed Learning', in Reason, P. (1988) *Human Inquiry in Action – Developments in New Paradigm Research,* London: Sage Publications.

Rogers, C. (1961) *On Becoming a Person,* London: Constable.

Rowland, S. (1993) *The Enquiring Tutor: Exploring the Process of Professional Learning,* London: Falmer Press.

STRATEGIC MANAGEMENT

RESEARCH AREA

Tacit knowledge and sustainable competitive advantage

Introduction and literature review

An enduring problem for strategic management is the sustainability of competitive advantage (Porter, 1985; Barney, 1991; Black and Boal, 1994). The proposed research is concerned with competitive advantage and the link between a heterogeneous firm resource (in this instance tacit knowledge) and the use of relatively homogenous information technology (IT) assets. Much of the literature exploring the link between IT and competitive advantage, holds that innovatory systems are quickly and widely adopted and thus a source of enabling and not critical advantage (Banker and Kauffman, 1988; Ciborra, 1991). Contradictory research shows that this may not be the case as implementation of IT can produce unexpected outcomes (Ciborra, 1991). Other research (for example Cash and McFarlane, 1988; Kremar and Lucas, 1991; Lederer and Sethi, 1991) does not recognize the import of tacit knowledge and sees deviations in performance stemming from a lack of planning. However, recent additions to the literature question this logic, finding that intra-firm structural differences, the source of unexpected outcomes, can be combined with technology as complementary assets to confer a potential source of sustainable competitive advantage (Feeny and Ives, 1990; demons and Row, 1991; Heatley, Argarwal and Tanniru, 1995).

Inadequacy of current research

No empirical research has explored the role of tacit knowledge as a positive intra-firm structural differentiator in the implementation of IT. A priori observation seems to indicate that tacit knowledge is valuable, rare, imperfectly inimitable and non-transferable (Barney, 1991). Evaluating IT strategic successes, Ciborra (1991) identifies serendipity, trial and error, and bricolage as elements of a process of innovation in the use of systems. None of the literature explores the source, nor the effects of this process. Thus, while the literature has speculated as to the role of tacit knowledge in creating sustainable competitive advantage (Spender, 1993), the empirical question, 'Can tacit knowledge provide a source of sustainable competitive advantage?' has not been addressed.

Aims and objectives of research

The research aims to fill this gap in the literature by examining the proposition that tacit knowledge is a source of competitive advantage, and asking, if it is, what the conditions are that are required to support it. The research also aims to answer the question of how tacit knowledge can provide a source of sustainable competitive advantage. This requires an examination of pre-emption, dynamic economies of learning and continuing innovation effects from using IT and tacit knowledge as complementary assets. Thus, the research will test the proposition that combinations of tacit knowledge and IT create core competencies that lead to superior performance, and that these competencies are inimitable in the sense used by *Barney (1991)*. Barriers to imitation can be created by combining tacit knowledge and technology.

Methodology and plan of work

At the highest level of abstraction, it is proposed to use the resource-based view of the firm as a framework to understand asset combinations that can be the source of differences among forms. It is proposed that the research will operationalize measures developed by *Sethi and King (1994)* which were devised to assess the extent to which IT applications provide competitive advantage. In this research competitive advantage is driven by system performance, and this is the dependent variable in this study. The sample will be taken from the population of firms who use SAP business process software. The sample will be stratified for external validity according to Collis and Ghemawat's (1994) resource-based industry typology: along the dimensions of key resources and the nature of the production task. Construct validity will be established using pilot research; in-depth interviews. The focus of the study will centre on deviations from expected performance of a tightly specified and robust business process oriented system which is widely used in a variety of industries. The unit of analysis is at the level of business processes. Deviations in performance between forms having the same IT system constitute differences in the dependent variable and this is a function of knowledge assets, their management and characteristics of the form and system context. A research instrument will be designed which will be administered to collect cardinal and ordinal data on the dimensions of tacit knowledge, group dynamics, form and system characteristics, including data collection on form specific technology trajectories.

References

Banker, R. and Kaufman, R. (1988)'Strategic contributions of IT', Proceedings of 9th Int. Conf. on IS, pp. 141–50.

Barney, J. (1991) 'Firm resources and sustained competitive advantage', *Journal of Management*, 17 (1), pp. 99–120.

Black, J. and Boal, K. (1994) 'Strategic resources: Traits, configuration and paths to sustainable competitive advantage', *Strat. Man. Jnl*, 15, pp. 131–48.

Cash, J. and McFarlane, F. (1988) *Competing Through Information Technology*, Harvard Business School Press.

Ciborra, C. U. (1991) 'The limits of strategic information systems', *International Journal of Information Resource Management*, 2 (3), pp. 11–17.

Clemons, E. K. and Row, M. C. (1991)'Sustaining IT: The role of structural differences', *MIS Quarterly*, September, pp. 275–92.

Collis, D. and Ghemawat, P. (1994) 'Industry Analysis: Understanding Industry Structure and Dynamics', in Fahey, L. and Randall, R. M. (eds) *The Portable MBA*, Wiley, pp. 171–93.

Feeny, D. and Ives, B. (1990) 'In search of sustainability: Reaping long-term advantage from investments in IT', *Jnl Mgmt IS*, 7 (1), pp. 27–45.

Heatley, J, Agarwal, R. and Tanniru, M. (1995)'An evaluation of innovative information technology', *Jnl Strat IS*, 4 (3), pp. 255–77.

Kremar, H. and Lucas, H. (1991) 'Success factors for strategic IS', *Information and Management*, 21, pp. 137–45.

Lederer, A. and Sethi, V. (1991) 'Meeting the challenges of information systems planning', *Long Range Planning*, 25 (2), pp. 69–80.

Porter, M. E. (1985) *Competitive Advantage*, Free Press.

Spender, J. C. (1993) 'Competitive advantage from tacit knowledge? Unpacking the concept and its strategic implications', *Academy of Management*, pp. 37–41.

Sethi, V. and King, W. (1994), 'Development of measures to assess the extent to which IT provides competitive advantage', *Management Science*, 40 (12) pp. 1601–27.

Activities

1. Compare two potential research topics using the following criteria suggested by Creswell (1994).

	Topic 1	Topic 2
a) Is the topic researchable, given time, resources, and availability of data?		
b) Is there a personal interest in the topic in order to sustain attention?		
c) Will the results from the study be of interest to others?		
d) Is the topic likely to be publishable in a scholarly journal or attractive to a research committee?		
e) Does the study fill avoid, replicate, extend, or develop new ideas in the scholarly literature?		
f) Will the project contribute to career goals?		

2. Describe the purpose of your research by writing a positivist purpose statement using the model in the chapter. Then rewrite it as an interpretivist purpose statement.

3. Set down your initial ideas for a proposed study by completing the following form.

Main research question

....

....

a) What is your unit of analysis?
b) What data are you going to collect?
c) Why are you collecting the data?
d) How will you collect the data?
e) When will you collect the data?
f) How will you analyse the data?

4. Now deconstruct your research question as explained in this chapter.
5. Consolidate your answers to the previous questions and construct an outline research proposal. Evaluate the contents of your plan in accordance with the guidance given at the end of this chapter.

PROGRESS TEST

Complete the following sentences:

1. A research _____ is a document that sets out a detailed plan for the proposed study.
2. The phenomenon under study, about which data are collected and analysed, is known as the _____.
3. The term _____ refers to known facts or things used as a basis for inference or reckoning.
4. The specific line of enquiry the research investigates is known as the research _____.
5. The research design is shown in the _____ chapter of the proposal.

Are the following statements true or false?

6. Empirical evidence is data collected about a variable.
7. A variable is a characteristic of a phenomenon under study that is observed or measured.
8. A theory specifies relationships between certain units of analysis.
9. A hypothesis is a proposition that is tested against empirical evidence for association or causality.
10. The purpose of a research proposal is to communicate how the study will be conducted.

Multiple choice questions:

11. The unit of analysis in a research study is:
    a) the research question
    b) the research paradigm
    c) the methods used to collect and analyse the research data
    d) the phenomenon about which data are collected and analysed

12. A theory is:
    a) an exploration of how things function
    b) an exploration of why events occur
    c) an explanation of relationships between variables
    d) an explanation of the research problem

13. A theoretical framework is:
    a) a set of theories and data
    b) a set of theories and empirical data
    c) a set of theories and models
    d) a set of theories and variables

14. A delimitation establishes:
    a) the range and scope of the research
    b) the deficiencies and weaknesses of the research
    c) the outcomes of the research
    d) the timetable for the research

15. A limitation establishes:
    a) the range and scope of the research
    b) the deficiencies and weaknesses of the research
    c) the outcomes of the research
    d) the timetable for the research

References

Black, T. R. (1993) *Evaluating Social Science Research*, London: Sage.
Blaikie, N. (2000) *Designing Social Research*, Cambridge: Polity.
Creswell, J. W. (1994) *Research Design: Qualitative and Quantitative Approaches*, Thousand Oaks, CA: Sage.
Glaser, B. and Strauss, A. (1967) *The Discovery of Grounded Theory*, Chicago, IL: Aldine.
Jankowicz, A. D. (1991) *Business Research Projects for Students*, London: Chapman & Hall.
Kerlinger, F. N. (1979) *Behavioural Research: A Conceptual Approach*, New York: Holt, Rinehart & Winston.
Kerlinger, F. N. (1986) *Foundations of Behavioral Research* (3rd edn), New York: Holt, Rinehart & Winston.
Laughlin, R. (1995) 'Methodological themes – empirical research in accounting: Alternative approaches and a case for "middle-range" thinking', *Accounting, Auditing and Accountability Journal*, 8 (1), pp. 63–87.
Merriam, S. B. (1988) *Case Study Research in Education: A Qualitative Approach*, SanFrancisco, CA: Jossey-Bass.
Parker, D. (1994) *Tackling Coursework*, London: DP Publications.
Robson, C. (1993) *Real World Research: A Resource for Social Scientists and Practitioner Researchers*, Oxford: Blackwell.
Rinehart & Winston. Kervin, J. B. (1992) *Methods for Business Research*, New York: HarperCollins.
Sekaran, U. (2003) *Research Methods for Business*, 4th edition, New York: John Wiley.
Slife, B. D. and Williams, R. N. (1995) *What's Behind the Research: Discovering Hidden Assumptions in the Behavioural Sciences*, Thousand Oaks, CA: Sage.
Vogt, W. P. (1993) *Dictionary of Statistics and Methodology*, Newbury Park, CA: Sage.
Werner, O. and Schoepfle, G. (1987) *Systematic Fieldwork: Foundations of Ethnography and Interviewing*, Newbury Park, CA: Sage.
Wilkinson, A. M. (1991) *The Scientist's Handbook for Writing Papers and Dissertations*, Englewood Cliffs, NJ: Prentice Hall.

Glossary

Delimitation	Establishes the scope of the research.
Harvard system of referencing	A system where citations are shown as author and date (and page number if quoting) in the text and the references are listed in alphabetical order by author at the end of the document.
Limitation	A weaknesses or deficiency in the research.
Purpose statement	A statement (usually two or three sentences long) that describes the overall purpose of the research study.
Research problem	The specific problem or issue that is the focus of the research.
Research proposal	The document which sets out the research design for a study.
Research question	The specific question the research is designed to investigate and attempt to answer.
Theory	A set of interrelated variables, definitions and propositions that specifies relationships among the variables.
Unit of analysis	The phenomenon under study, about which data are collected and analysed.

PART 4
Sampling and data collection

CHAPTER 11
Collecting data: surveys and samples

OBJECTIVES

- To understand the difference between a sampling frame, a sample and a population
- To understand the difference between probabilistic and non-probabilistic sampling
- To know how to select the correct sampling method in different situations
- To understand how to design a questionnaire

Introduction

Many decisions made by business and by the government are the result of information obtained from *sample* data, as it is often too costly or impractical to collect data for the whole population.

Data may already exist or it may need to be collected. When we have to collect our own data, as in the Ipsos MORI survey, we call it *primary data*; when it already exists, as in government statistics, we call it *secondary data*. The collection of data can take many forms, but in this chapter we will concentrate on data that is collected by carrying out surveys. In the Ipsos MORI survey the data was collected using a postal questionnaire. However, there are other ways of collecting the data, such as face-to-face interviews, by telephone interviewing or by online surveys.

Before collecting the data, a representative sample of the target population must be defined. In the Ipsos MORI survey, the sample chosen was representative in terms of business sector, region and size of workforce. These attributes were chosen because it was thought that the responses to the questions were more likely to be influenced by these than by others. The actual choice of method of selecting the sample depends on many factors, including the information available on the target population and the budget. The design of the questionnaire is also important, not only in the type of questions asked but also in their wording. We will be considering all these points in this chapter.

MANAGEMENT RESEARCH CUSTOM PUBLICATION

Quantitative methods in action: Is business confidence in the UK declining?

Each spring and autumn Ipsos MORI carries out a survey for the Regional Development Agencies (RDAs) on issues affecting business in England and Northern Island. The survey published in August 2008 reports on the results collected between April and June 2008. Around 5000 respondents from a broad range of sectors and size of workforce completed the questionnaire.

The Spring 2008 survey concludes that even before the credit crisis of 2008, businesses were pessimistic about the future and 48% of respondents were expecting the business climate to deteriorate in the next 12 months. Businesses were also expecting costs to rise, with energy and transport costs expected to increase most. However there are variations within sectors with construction, hotels and catering likely to suffer the most.

The survey consisted of 27 questions that ranged from factual questions such as size of workforce to subjective questions such as opinion on the business climate. Three sample questions are given in Figure 11.1.

The Ipsos MORI survey is a typical large-scale survey carried out by a commercial organisation. It is a postal survey, although respondents were able to complete it

Q1	Over the next 12 months do you expect the business climate in which your business operates to generally improve, remain stable, or deteriorate?			

Q3	Which of the following costs... (A) have increased for your business over the past 12 months? (B) do you expect to increase over the next 12 months? (C) presents the main upward cost pressure on your business at present?			
		(A) Past 12 months	(B) Next 12 months	(C) Main upward cost pressure at present
Energy costs				
Transport costs				
Staff costs				
Raw materials and bought-in services (other than energy)				
Property costs				
Cost of finance				
Other costs				
None of these				

Q11	To what extent do you agree or disagree with the following statements?					
		Strongly agree	Tend to agree	Neither agree nor disagree	Tend to disagree	Strongly disagree
This location is a good place to invest						
I expect the area in which this business is located to become more attractive to investors in the future						

Q23	How many employees are there at this workplace?					

Figure 11.1 Sample questions in the MORI survey

online. However, the principles of survey and questionnaire design apply to both small-scale and large-scale surveys.

The basics of sampling

I am sure that you have been a *respondent* in a survey at least once in your life. Have you filled in a *questionnaire* or been stopped in the street and asked some questions? You no doubt know that the purpose of a survey is for some organisation or person to obtain *information* about some issue or product. This information could range from what television programme you watched last night to your views on the government of the day.

A survey only collects information about a small subset of the *population*. The word 'population' can and often does refer to all the people in Britain or a town, but for statisticians it is also a general term used to refer to all groups or items being surveyed. For instance, it could refer to the viewing habits of all children in a town or, as you will see in a later chapter, it could refer to the weights of jars of coffee produced by a company during a week. The alternative to a survey is to question every member of the population, and when this is done it is called a *census*. Unfortunately it is expensive and very difficult to carry out a census, and also unnecessary. A survey of a small subset of the population, called a *sample*, can give surprisingly accurate results if carried out properly. Unfortunately, if not carried out correctly, the results can at best be unreliable and at worst misleading. Before you carry out a survey you need answers to several questions, such as:

- What is the purpose of this survey?
- What is my *target* population?
- Do I have a list of the population?
- How can I avoid bias in my sample?
- How accurate do I want my survey to be?
- What resources do I have at my disposal?
- How am I going to collect the required data?

It is crucial to be clear about the purpose of the survey. Not only will this dictate your target population but it will also allow you to formulate your questionnaire correctly. For example, if you are interested in consumers' opinion of a new alcoholic drink it would be pointless targeting people under 18 (and unethical). The target population should contain every person who is likely to buy your product or whose views you are particularly interested in.

Once you have selected your target population, you need to determine whether there is any list that would allow you to identify every member of the population. This list is called a *sampling frame*, and examples include the electoral register, a company's personnel records or even a list of all serial numbers of cars built by one car manufacturer last year. Sometimes a sampling frame is simply not available or is too difficult to obtain, in which case achieving a *representative* sample will be more difficult, but not necessarily impossible.

Activity 11.1

What would be your target population for a survey on motorway tariffs, and would there be a sampling frame available?

If you were only interested in the views of British car drivers then anyone holding a UK driving licence would form your target population. A suitable sampling frame would be records held by the DVLC at Swansea. It would not be 100% accurate as drivers might have changed address and not informed the DVLC, or they might have died.

Once your target population has been chosen and an appropriate sampling frame identified, it is necessary to choose your sample. If the sample is chosen badly your results will be inaccurate due to *bias* in your sample. Bias is caused by choosing a sample that is unrepresentative of the target population. For example, perhaps you wanted to discover people's views on whether a sports field should be sold to a property developer. If your sample contained a large number of people from the local football club, then the sample is likely to be biased in favour of one particular group! To avoid bias you need to ensure that your sample is *representative* of the target population. You will see how this can be achieved later.

The purpose of a survey is to obtain information about a population. All other things being equal, the accuracy of the sample results will depend on the sample size; the larger the sample, the more accurate the results. A large sample will clearly cost more than a small one, although the method that is employed to collect the data will also determine the accuracy and cost of the survey. Methods of data collection range from the use of postal questionnaires to 'face-to-face' interviews. Some methods of data collection are expensive but guarantee a good response rate, while others are cheap to administer but are likely to produce quite a poor response. Table 11.1 compares the main methods of collecting data.

Table 11.1 Methods of data collection

	Postal questionnaire	Telephone interviewing	Face-to-face interviewing	Online
Cost	Low	Moderate	High	Low
Response rate	Low	Moderate	High	Moderate
Speed	Slow	Fast	Fast*	Fast
Quantity of information collected	Limited	Moderate	High	Limited
Quality of information collected	Depends on how well the questionnaire has been designed	Good	High	Depends on how well the questionnaire has been designed

Source: * The speed of collecting the data will be high but travelling time by the interviewers may need to be considered

> **Activity 11.2**
>
> You have been asked to obtain the views of the student population at your institution regarding car parking facilities within the campus. What method of data collection would you use?

The best method would probably be face-to-face interviews, but it is unlikely that you would have the resources for this approach. Telephone interviewing is probably not realistic because of the cost and the fact that students' telephone numbers might be difficult to obtain. This leaves you with either a postal or online questionnaire, both of which should be quite reasonable for this relatively simple type of survey.

There are two types of sampling procedures for obtaining your sample. The first is *probabilistic* sampling, which requires the existence of a sampling frame. The second method is *non-probabilistic* sampling, which does not rely on a sampling frame. Probabilistic sampling is the most important form of sampling as it allows you to use probability theory to calculate the probability that a particular sample could have occurred by chance.

Questionnaire design

Questionnaire design is more of an art than a science and there is no universal design that would be suitable for all situations. The actual design will depend on factors such as:

- the type of respondent (for example, business, consumers, children)
- the method of data collection (postal, telephone, face-to-face or online)
- the resources available.

However, even though no two questionnaires will be identical, it is possible to make a list of some 'dos and don'ts' that should apply to most questionnaires. The most important ones are:

- Do make each question brief and the wording clear and concise with minimal use of jargon. It shouldn't be necessary to explain to the respondent the meaning of a particular question.
- Do keep the length of the questionnaire to a minimum. A maximum of around 20 questions is probably a good guide for most surveys.
- Do make the questions simple to answer.
- Do make the questions as specific as possible. A question such as *'Are you a heavy smoker?'* could be interpreted differently by different respondents. It would be much better to give ranges such as *'Do you smoke less than 10 cigarettes a day?'*, *'Between 10 and 20?'* and *'Over 20?'*
- Do have a logical sequence to the questions.

- Do start with simple questions such as gender, leaving more complicated questions for later in the questionnaire.
- Don't leave the most important question to last. There is a risk that if a respondent becomes bored with answering a questionnaire he or she may not complete the final section.
- Don't use leading questions. For example, *'What are your views on the level of indirect taxation in the UK?'* is better than *'Do you agree that indirect taxation in the UK is too high?'*
- Do try and avoid asking personal questions. Even information on salary is considered by many people to be personal and most respondents prefer to have salary ranges to select. It is often better to ask this type of question later in the questionnaire. If it is necessary to collect really personal information, a face-to-face interview is essential using experienced interviewers.
- Do use a filtering method if not all questions are applicable to all respondents. For example, *'Did you watch The Bill last night?'* may then be followed by questions relating to this episode. To avoid asking non-viewers these questions you will need to have an instruction that allows these non-viewers to jump to the next appropriate question.
- Don't ask two questions in one. A question such as *'Is your job interesting and well paid?'* is unlikely to be answered with a simple yes or no.
- Don't ask questions that rely on memory. Asking respondents if they watched *The Bill* last night is acceptable, but asking if they watched it last week or last month will not necessarily produce very reliable results.
- Don't ask hypothetical questions. Asking someone what he or she would do under a hypothetical situation (such as winning the National Lottery) is unlikely to lead to reliable results. In some surveys this type of question cannot be avoided, but extra care should be taken in its wording.
- It is generally better to use close-ended questions (see later) rather than allow open answers. However, do allow for the fact that your selection of responses might not be complete by having an 'other' category.

  For example, *'What type of property do you live in?'*
  Terraced house   Semi-detached   Detached   Flat
  This question needs an *'Other'* category since you might find someone who lives on a boat or in a windmill!

- Make the questionnaire attractive and easy to complete. Microsoft Word allows you to create forms for use as questionnaires and you can then distribute these forms as an email attachment if this is appropriate for your sample.
- Do conduct a pilot survey on a small but *representative* sample of the target population. This will test out your design and allow you to fine tune it.

Having looked at some of the more important dos and don'ts of questionnaire design we now need to consider the format of the questions and the most effective method of obtaining reliable responses. Questions are of two forms: *close-ended* questions and *open-ended* questions. Close-ended questions give the respondents a choice of answers and are generally considered much easier to answer and to analyse. However, the limited response range can give misleading results. Open-ended questions, such as *'Why did you buy this product?'*, allow respondents more flexibility in the type of response (you may get answers that you hadn't thought of), but of course this type of question is difficult to analyse. Close-ended questions are the most commonly used type and can take many forms, such as:

- *Dichotomous questions* These are questions that have only two answers, such as yes or no.
- *Numeric* Some questions ask for a single number, such as the distance travelled to work each day. Where the question is personal (for example, earnings or age) it is best to give a range, such as:

  Less than £20 000   £20 000 to £30 000   Over £30 000

- *Multiple choice* Respondents select from three or more choices (the question on salary above is an example of a multiple choice question).
- *Likert scale* The question is a statement, such as *'Taxes should be increased to pay for a better health service'*, and respondents indicate their amount of agreement using a scale similar to the one below.

  Strongly agree   Agree   Neither agree   Disagree   Strongly
                             nor disagree   disagree

- *Semantic differential* With this type of question only two ends of the scale are provided and the respondent selects the point between the two ends that represents his views. For example, *'The leisure facilities in my town are'*:

  Excellent _____ Poor

- *Rank order* Respondents are asked to rank each option. This type of question is useful if you want to obtain information on relative preferences, but is more difficult to analyse. The number of choices should be kept to a minimum.

Simple random sampling

With this method every member of the target population has an *equal* chance of being selected. This implies that a sampling frame is required and a method of *randomly* selecting the required sample from this list. The simplest example of this technique is a raffle where the winning ticket is drawn from the 'hat'. For a more formal application a stream of *random numbers* would be used. Random numbers are numbers that show no pattern; each digit is equally likely. A table of random numbers is given in Appendix 1. The method of simple random sampling using random numbers is quite easy to apply, although tedious, as you will see from Example 11.1.

Example 11.1

Table 11.2 is a part of a list of students enrolled on a business studies course at a university.

Say from this 'population' of 25 students you wanted to randomly select a sample of 5 students. How would you do it? You could use the student number (in this case conveniently numbered from 1 to 25) and then try and obtain a match using a stream of two-digit random numbers. For example, suppose you had the following random numbers: 78, 41, 11, 62, 72, 18, 66, 69, 58, 71, 31, 90, 51, 36, 78, 09, 41, 00, 70, 50, 58, 19, 68, 26, 75, 69, and 04. The first two numbers don't exist in our population but 11 does – it is student D. Jeffrey. The next two numbers do not exist but 18 does, and so on. The final sample is numbers 11, 18, 09, 19 and 04, which are students D. Jeffrey, S. Moore, G. Godfrey, F. Muper, and C. Meng.

The majority of random numbers were redundant in this case because the population was so small. In practice the population would be much larger, but the method remains essentially the same. Most sampling frames are held on computer these days so it is much easier to use the computer to select the sample.

Table 11.2 List of students enrolled on a business studies course

Number	Name	Gender
1	N. Adams	Male
2	C. Shah	Male
3	B. Booth	Female
4	C. Meng	Male
5	A. Ho	Male
6	D. Drew	Male
7	K. Fisher	Female
8	P. Frome	Male
9	G. Godfrey	Male
10	J. Bakoulas	Male
11	D. Jeffrey	Female
12	H. Jones	Male
13	M. Li	Male
14	N. King	Female
15	K. Lenow	Male
16	A. Loft	Female
17	T. Georgiou	Female
18	S. Moore	Female
19	F. Muper	Female
20	R. Muster	Female
21	A. Night	Male
22	J. Nott	Male
23	L. Nupper	Male
24	K. Khan	Male
25	O. Patter	Female

COLLECTING DATA: SURVEYS AND SAMPLES

> **Activity 11.3**
>
> Randomly select another sample of 5 students from the list in Table 11.2 using the random numbers: 09, 55, 42, 30, 27, 05, 24, 93, 78, 10, 69, 09, and 11.

You should have noticed that number 09 occurs twice. What did you do in this case? For practical reasons you should have ignored the second 09 and chosen the next number, 11, instead. Your final sample should have been: G. Godfrey, A. Ho, K. Khan, J. Bakoulas and D. Jeffrey.

How representative of the target population are these samples? Since the population is so small it is a simple matter to compare each sample with the population. For instance, there are 15 male and 10 female students, which is a proportion of 60% males to 40% females. In the first sample there were 2 males out of 5, a proportion of 40%, and in the second there were 4 males, a proportion of 80%. From this you can see that the first sample was an underestimate of the true number of males, while the second was an overestimate. Another sample could be different again, and you may even get a sample of all the same sex. This variation is called *sampling error* and occurs in all sampling procedures. In Chapter 9 you will be shown how to quantify this error.

It is possible to reduce the sampling error by a slight modification to the simple random sample method. This is applicable when the target population can be categorised into groups or *strata*.

Stratified sampling

Many populations can be divided into different categories. For example, a population of adults consists of the two sexes, the employed and unemployed, and many other categories. If you think that the responses you will get from your survey are likely to be determined partly by each category, then clearly you want your sample to contain each category in the correct proportions.

> **Activity 11.4**
>
> Using the random numbers 09, 55, 42, 30, 27, 05, 25, 93, 78, 10, 69, 09, 11, 99, 21 and 01, obtain a sample of size 5 that contains the correct proportion of each sex.

You probably realised that your sample should contain 3 males (60% of 5). In order to ensure that you will get exactly 3 males, you should first of all have separated out the two sexes and then obtained two simple random samples, one of size 3 and one of size 2, as shown in Table 11.3.

Table 11.3 Table ordered by gender

Number	Name	Sex
1	N. Adams	Male
2	J. Bakoulas	Male
3	D. Drew	Male
4	P. Frome	Male
5	G. Godfrey	Male
6	A. Ho	Male
7	H. Jones	Male
8	K. Khan	Male
9	K. Lenow	Male
10	M. Li	Male
11	C. Meng	Male
12	A. Night	Male
13	J. Nott	Male
14	L. Nupper	Male
15	C. Shah	Male
1	B. Booth	Female
2	K. Fisher	Female
3	T. Georgiou	Female
4	D. Jeffrey	Female
5	N. King	Female
6	A. Loft	Female
7	S. Moore	Female
8	F. Muper	Female
9	R. Muster	Female
10	O. Patter	Female

The two populations have been re-numbered, although this is not essential. The first sample consists of students 9, 5 and 10, that is K. Lenow, G Godfrey and M. Li, while the second sample consists of students 9 and 1, that is R. Muster and B. Booth.

Stratified sampling is a very reliable method but it does assume that you have a knowledge of the categories of the population. Stratified sampling is often used in conjunction with the next method.

Multi-stage sampling

If the target population covers a wide geographical area then a simple random sample may have selected respondents in quite different parts of the country. If the method employed to collect the data is of the face-to-face interview type, then clearly

COLLECTING DATA: SURVEYS AND SAMPLES

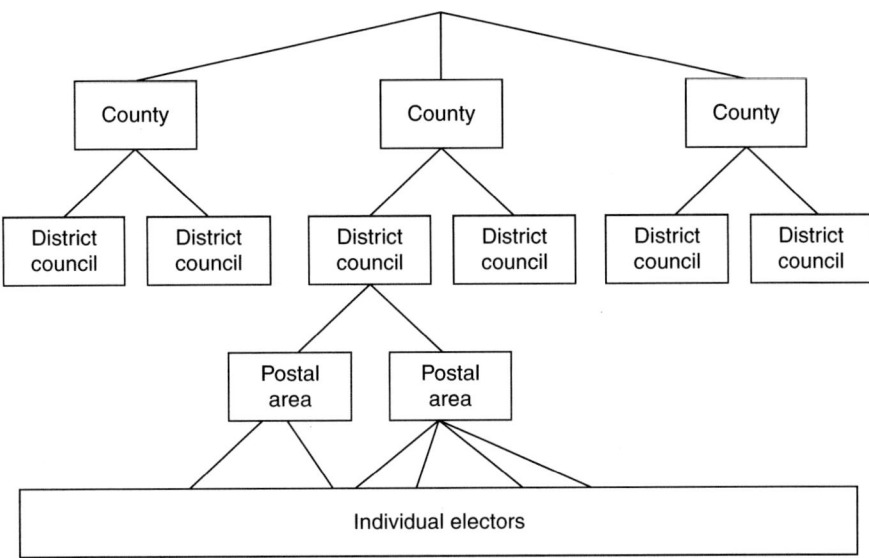

Figure 11.2 Multi-stage sampling

a great deal of travelling could be involved. To overcome this problem the area to be surveyed is divided into smaller areas and a number of these smaller areas randomly selected. If desired, the smaller areas chosen could themselves be divided into smaller districts and a random number of these selected. This procedure is continued until the area is small enough for a simple random sample (or a stratified sample) to be selected. The final sample should consist of respondents concentrated into a small number of areas. It is important that the random sample chosen from each area is the same proportion of the population or bias towards certain areas could result. As it is, bias is likely to occur as a result of similarity of responses from people within the same area, but this is the price you pay for reduced travelling time.

Activity 11.5

You have been asked to obtain a representative sample of television viewers from across Britain using the multi-stage sampling method. How would you select the sample?

The country could be split into counties, or perhaps television regions might be more appropriate in this case. A number of these would be chosen at random, and these areas subdivided into district councils. A random sample of districts within each chosen region could now be selected, and the selected districts divided into postal areas. A random sample of residents within each chosen postal area could then be chosen using the register of electors.

Figure 11.2 illustrates this process in diagrammatic form. At each level you are taking a random sample. Note that it is not until you get to the individual elector that you carry out the actual survey.

Cluster sampling

Cluster sampling is similar to multi-stage sampling and is used when a sampling frame is not available. Again a large geographical area is divided into a number of smaller areas called *clusters*. If necessary these clusters can be further subdivided to obtain clusters which are small enough for *all* members of the cluster to be surveyed. As with multi-stage sampling, a bias will result due to similarities in responses from members of the same cluster. The difference between cluster sampling and multi-stage sampling is that since individual members of a cluster cannot be identified in advance, it is necessary for all members to be surveyed. Random sampling is therefore *not* involved.

> ### Activity 11.6
>
> How would you apply cluster sampling to the population referred to in Activity 11.5?

You would carry out the same procedure to obtain a selected number of postal districts, but these districts could be further subdivided so that individual streets were identified. All households of selected streets would then be surveyed.

Systematic sampling

This method is normally used with a sampling frame but it can also be used where a sampling frame is not available. However, in this case the size of the population must be known. The idea is that every nth member of a population is selected, where the value of n is determined by the size of the population and by the required sample size. For instance, if a 5% sample is to be selected from a population of size 1000, then every 50th person will be selected. The start of the sequence is usually chosen at random. For example, if a 20% sample was to be selected from the student population given in Table 11.2, every 5th person would be selected. If you started with, say, the third student, your sample would consist of B. Booth, P. Frome, M. Li, S. Moore and L. Nupper.

> ### Activity 11.7
>
> You have been asked by a local newspaper to find out what people thought of a particular film that is showing at the local cinema. How would you obtain a sample of 10 people?

Clearly it would be pointless asking people who hadn't seen the film, so your target population would be those people who had recently seen it. The easiest

Table 11.4 Details taken from a register office's records

Name	Date of marriage	Nationality
Mr A. Tan	21/3/93	British
Miss N. Taylor	21/3/93	British
Mr F. Barker	22/3/93	British
Miss F. Addai	22/3/93	Australian
Mr T. Barry	22/3/93	British
Ms K. Larch	22/3/93	Canadian

method would be to wait outside the cinema and select people as they left. If there were 300 people watching the film then you would need to stop every 30th person.

Systematic sampling is a very quick and efficient method of obtaining a sample. The sample should be random, provided there is no pattern in the way people are ordered in the population. For example, if a population consists of married couples then it is possible for the sample to consist of all husbands or all wives. To illustrate this point Table 11.4 refers to records taken from a register office. If you took a systematic sample that selected every second person and you started at F. Barker, all your sample would be males.

Quota sampling

I am sure that you have seen an interviewer in a town centre with a clipboard waiting to pounce on some unsuspecting individual! The interviewer is in fact looking for particular groups of individuals who meet the categories that he or she has been asked to interview. Within each group there will be a number or *quota* of people required and the survey is complete when the quotas have been reached. Quota sampling is a non-probabilistic version of stratified sampling. The quotas within each group should, like stratified sampling, reflect the proportions within the target population.

Activity 11.8

You want to obtain the views of the local population on the creation of an out-of-town shopping complex. You are told that 30% of the population is aged between 12 and 20, 60% is between 20 and 60, and 10% is over 60. You want a sample of 100 individuals. How would you go about choosing your sample?

Your first decision must be the location and time of the survey. An obvious choice would probably be the town centre on a Saturday when many people are out shopping. To reflect the fact that 30% of the population is aged between 12 and 20 you want a quota of 30 individuals in this age range. Similarly, for the other two age bands you would want 60 and 10 individuals respectively.

Quota sampling is a cheap and quick method of obtaining a sample. It is a particularly popular method for market research surveys and opinion polls. Its main disadvantage is that the sample could be heavily biased in favour of one particular group. For instance, in the case of the shopping centre the group of people who do not shop in the town centre will be omitted.

Other sampling methods

There are three other non-probabilistic sampling methods that are sometimes used. These are *judgemental, purposive* and *snowball* sampling. With judgemental sampling the researcher makes a judgement about what constitutes a representative sample. If a government agency was interested in the effects on people's health of car exhaust fumes they would choose areas near cities or motorways to obtain the sample. They would not choose rural areas, except perhaps for a control group.

Purposive sampling is where certain members of the population are purposefully chosen. For example, customers holding store loyalty cards might be asked about planned improvements to the store.

Snowballing is where a sample is chosen using one of the methods mentioned in this chapter and then additional members of the population are generated from this sample. An example could be in the investigation of the mis-selling of pensions that occurred in Britain during the late 1980s. A sample of pensioners could be obtained and any person who was persuaded to leave their occupational pension scheme would be asked to name other people they knew who were also affected. In this way the sample size could be increased.

> ### Activity 11.9
>
> A market research company is interested in consumers' reaction to a new brand of sun cream. What type of sampling method should they adopt?

Although most of the methods mentioned in this chapter would be suitable, judgemental sampling might be the best method to use in this situation. The researcher's judgement together with sales information could be used to select a few holiday resorts where it is likely that the product is being used. Once a resort has been chosen the researcher could use his or her judgement as to which age range should be sampled and at what time of the day the survey should be conducted.

Secondary sources of data

In many cases it is unnecessary to carry out a survey as the relevant data has already been collected and published. Much of the data collected by governments is available in the form of statistical publications and can be found in libraries or on the internet. When data has already been collected we say that it is *secondary* data. Secondary data is obviously easier to collect but its one disadvantage is that the quality of it is unknown. This is less of a problem with official sources, although it is still important to ensure that you know how the data was collected and any particular circumstances that might have made the data inaccurate or distorted in some way. This information is usually given in notes at the end of the publication or in footnotes to the relevant table.

One of the most important sources of official statistics in the UK is the *Monthly Digest of Statistics*, published by the Government Statistical Service. This monthly publication provides information on a wide range of products and services, such as new car registrations, energy usage, road accidents, industrial output and the retail price index, to name a few. Other official sources include *Annual Abstract of Statistics, Economic Trends, Regional Trends* and *Social Trends*. The web page <www.statistics.gov.uk> gives comprehensive details of a large selection of government statistical publications. Within this site you can download statistical data produced by the Office for National Statistics. The site also allows you to download many reports and publications.

Reflection

Sampling is very important in today's complex society. Companies are always keen to find out what consumers think about their products, and governments need to obtain views on all kinds of issues. As we saw at the start of this chapter, the Regional Development Agencies conduct regular surveys of businesses to obtain their views on issues affecting the business community. Ipsos MORI carries out these surveys and for the Spring 2008 survey a sample of over 5000 people was selected. This was a postal survey and follow up letter and emails were sent to ensure that the response rate was adequate for the purpose. However no survey will be 100% reliable. Accuracy is affected by a number of issues. Assuming that a representative sample has been chosen the number of respondents surveyed (the sample size) is the most important factor that determines the *sampling error*. Fortunately, as we shall see in later chapters, it is possible to calculate the sample size required for a given level of accuracy.

One issue with all surveys is whether the respondents have answered the questions truthfully. For example, when there is a question of income some respondents may have income that they do not wish to disclose, particularly if they are on benefits. Face-to-face interviews will usually give more reliable results, provided that the questions are well thought out and experienced interviewers are used.

Another issue with surveys is that they need a great deal of planning and research. It is easy to rush into a survey, only to find later that a vital question has been missed. It is also easy to ask too many questions and either to find that respondents become bored before the end or that the sample size is insufficient to provide meaningful analysis. This latter point is particularly important when you hope to analyse results by several categories and subcategories, such as gender, age and income. Each additional category added can double the number of respondents required.

To resolve many of these challenges it is essential that a pilot study is conducted first. A pilot survey is a small-scale version of the full survey, although it must be large enough that some analysis can be attempted. The pilot survey should also allow the issue of non response to be highlighted. Response rates vary from survey to survey, but 30% is usually considered to be quite good; for some methods, such as postal surveys, the response rate can be in single figures.

Key points

- It is generally impractical to question every member of a target *population*, so a *sample* of this population is selected instead.
- In order to achieve reliable results, a sample should be *representative* of the target population.
- *Probabilistic sampling methods* will give you a representative sample, but these methods require the existence of a sampling frame.
- *Non-probabilistic sampling* is generally quicker to carry out but is not as reliable. Table 11.5 summarises the different methods available.

Table 11.5 A summary of the sampling methods available

	Sampling frame available (probabilistic sampling)	Sampling frame not available (non-probabilistic sampling)
Population resides in one place	Simple random sampling Systematic sampling	Systematic sampling (if the size of the population is known) Judgemental sampling Purposive sampling
Population geographically scattered	Multi-stage sampling	Cluster sampling Judgemental sampling
Population is defined by categories	Stratified sampling	Quota sampling
Population is small and unknown		Snowballing

Further reading

Collis, J. and Hussey, R. (2009) *Business Research. A practical guide for undergraduate and postgraduate students*, 3rd edition, Palgrave Macmillan.

COLLECTING DATA: SURVEYS AND SAMPLES

Exercises

Answers to selected questions can be found in Appendix 3. Answers to the other questions can be found on the companion website for this book.

Practice questions

1. In a Business Studies course at a university there are 320 students in year 1, 250 students in year 2 and 230 students in year 3. There are approximately 60% female students and 40% male students in each year. A survey of 50 students is to be taken to find their views on a course change. How many students of each gender should be selected from each year?

2. A town with historical connections has received a grant of £20m in order to improve its tourist facilities. The town councillors have decided to ask a representative sample of residents how the money should be spent. Given that expenditure for the survey must be kept to a minimum suggest ways in which a representative sample of residents can be chosen.

3. In preparation for the London 2012 Olympics, a survey of the British public is to be undertaken into the form of the opening ceremony. What type of survey should be undertaken and how would the respondents be chosen?

4. Criticise the following questionnaire into people's smoking habits.

Questionnaire on smoking habits	
1. How old are you?	☐
2. What is your marital status?	Single/married/cohabiting
3. Does your partner smoke?	Yes/No
4. How many cigarettes do you smoke a day?	☐
5. Do you understand the health risks of smoking?	Yes/No
6. Would you consider giving up if	
The price increased	☐
A relative died of cancer	☐
There were financial incentives for doing so	☐
7. Did your parents smoke?	Yes/No
8. Which socio-economic class do you belong to?	
A	☐
B	☐
C1	☐
C2	☐
D	☐
E	☐

5. Which of the following are likely to have a sampling frame?
   1. Students at a university
   2. Employees of a company
   3. Concert goers
   4. Shoppers at a shopping mall
   5. Members of a social networking group
6. Table 11.6 represents a target population.
   (a) Using the random numbers 2, 9, 4, 3, 6, 7, select a simple random sample of sample size 3. What is the average age of your sample and what newspapers do they read?
   (b) Stratify your sample by sex and repeat part (a).
   (c) If a systematic sample of size 3 was required and the first person chosen was Steve, who would be the second person chosen?

Table 11.6 Population for Question 6

Name	Sex	Age	Newspaper read
Alan	M	23	Guardian
Steve	M	36	The Times
Jane	F	47	Mirror
Chris	M	36	Mirror
Julie	F	41	Sun
Stuart	M	37	Mirror
Jill	F	37	Telegraph
John	M	38	Express
Kim	M	48	Sun

7. You have been asked to conduct a survey into people's views of the council tax. What would be the target population and what would be a good sampling frame?
8. A football club wants to obtain the views of its supporters on a possible rise in admission charges. It has decided to obtain a simple random sample of members of the supporters' club. Comment on this proposal and suggest alternative target populations and sampling methods.
9. You have been asked to conduct a survey into the attitudes of school leavers to higher education. You intend to carry this out using the face-to-face interview method. How would you obtain your sample?
10. You have been asked to obtain the reaction to the proposal to pedestrianise your local town centre. What survey methods would you use?
11. A clothing company has just been approached by a students' union to supply a range of products suitable for the student market. However, the company wants some evidence that the market would be viable. You have been asked to help design a survey to discover if the students would be prepared to purchase their clothes from this company and what kind of price they would be prepared to pay.
    (a) You are considering using either stratified or quota sampling to obtain your sample. Explain the differences between the two methods and discuss which

method you think would be most suitable. State what categories or 'strata' you might want to consider for this problem, giving reasons why you think that these categories are important.
    (b) Would multi-stage sampling be worth considering for this problem?
    (c) Discuss the types of problems that might arise, both during the design phase and the survey itself. How might you overcome these problems?
12. A company wishes to carry out a survey of its employees to monitor their views on the future of the company. A departmental breakdown of the company's 200 employees is as follows:

Shop-floor/warehouse	80
Service engineers	15
Quality control	20
Marketing and sales	25
Accounts	15
Personnel	10
Administration	25
Catering	10

A survey of 40 employees is to be conducted. A sampling frame is available, listing the employees by surname in alphabetical order, independent of department.
   (a) Explain how the following sampling methods could be carried out to obtain the sample of 40 employees:
   - simple random sampling
   - systematic sampling
   - stratified sampling
   - quota sampling.
   (b) Discuss the benefits and drawbacks of using quota sampling to obtain the sample of 40 employees.
13. A university is considering introducing a third semester so that students can complete their degrees in 2 years by remaining at the university over the summer vacation. To help the university decide whether this would be acceptable to staff and students, it wants to conduct a survey to establish the views of a cross-section of the university community.
   (a) In the context of this problem, describe the terms:
   - target population
   - sampling frame
   - stratified sampling
   - multi-stage sampling.
   (b) Design 5 questions that you might ask the respondents to the survey. Explain how these questions would help you to satisfy the aims of the survey.
   (c) What type of data collection method would you use (postal, telephone or face to face)?

Assignment

Conduct a survey on some aspect of the quality of current television programmes. It is important that you do some research into the relevant issues and then conduct a survey using a questionnaire of your own design.

Information that you collect from your respondents might include:

- Viewing habits (that is, number of hours spent watching television, favourite programmes, and so on).
- Views on the quality of the programmes watched.
- What improvements they would like to see.
- Demographic information such as age, gender, occupation, and so on.

CHAPTER 12
Collecting qualitative data

> **LEARNING OBJECTIVES**
>
> When you have studied this chapter, you should be able to:
> - describe methods based on interviews
> - describe methods based on diaries
> - describe methods based on observation
> - compare the strengths and weaknesses of methods
> - choose a method that reflects your paradigm.

12.1 Introduction

In this chapter we focus on the main methods used to collect *qualitative data*. These methods will be of particular interest if you are designing a study under an interpretive paradigm. Many of the methods used to collect qualitative data have much in common with those used to collect quantitative data, as you will see when you move on to Chapter 10. However, there are important differences, which reflect the assumptions of the two main paradigms. Since positivists often collect some qualitative data that need to be quantified and because *methodological triangulation* may have been incorporated in the research design, this chapter will also be of interest to those designing a study under a positivist paradigm.

Some of the methods we describe in this chapter incorporate the collection and the analysis of the data simultaneously. This makes it hard to identify these elements in the process. Another problem is that some researchers refer to a classification based on 'quantitative methods' or 'qualitative methods'. This can be misleading, as it is the data rather than the means of collecting the data that are in numerical or non-numerical form! However, we agree that 'quantitative methods' is appropriate when referring to statistical methods.

It is essential you set out and justify your method(s) for collecting and analysing your data in your proposal. You would not want to be faced with the problem of having collected a vast amount of material, but not know how to analyse and interpret the data.

12.2 Overview of qualitative data collection

Qualitative data are normally transient, understood only within context and are associated with an interpretive methodology that usually results in findings with a high degree of *validity*. It contrasts with *quantitative data*, which are normally precise, can be captured at various points in time and in different contexts, and are associated with a positivist methodology that usually results in findings with a high degree of *reliability*. The challenge for the researcher using an interpretive paradigm is to apply method(s) that will retain the integrity of the data.

Key definitions

Reliability refers to the absence of differences in the results if the research were repeated.
Validity is the extent to which the research findings accurately reflect the phenomena under study.

Since qualitative data need to be understood within context, you need to collect some background information first. This is known as *contextualization*. Data about the context can relate to aspects such as time and location, or legal, social, political and economic influences. For example, a person working in a declining industry in a remote northern town in Canada, who is confronted with redundancy two weeks before the New Year starts, may have different views of the future than someone working in a booming high-tech industry in California. It is critical to your research that you establish and understand this contextual framework, as this will enhance your sensitivity to the qualitative research data you subsequently collect and aid your interpretation.

Much of the contextualizing data will be found in the literature. Do not ignore statistical data. Information such as the level of unemployment in an area, the economic performance of an industry or employment patterns in a particular company can contribute to setting the framework within which you will be doing your research. Local newspapers are also important, but quite often take a political stance. It is sometimes more revealing to read the readers' letters than the editorials. The former usually express the perceptions and feelings of people who are part of the phenomenon you are studying.

Having established the context, you need to collect data relating to the location of your study and any events taking place before you collect the data. Therefore, equipment such as a camera, video recorder, audio recorder and a notebook will be needed. The notes taken while collecting primary research data are sometimes referred to as *field notes*, a term borrowed from the natural sciences.

We will now examine some of the main methods for collecting data for qualitative analysis. It is important to remember that the methods associated with interpretive paradigms often allow the researcher to collect and analyse the research data in one process. This contrasts with methodologies associated with positivist paradigms, where statistical methods are used to analyse the data. If you are designing a study under an interpretive paradigm, you will need to read this chapter in conjunction with Chapter 9; if you are designing a study under a positivist paradigm, you will need to read this chapter in conjunction with Chapter 10 and the appropriate chapter(s) on statistical analysis.

12.3 Interviews

Interviews are a method for collecting data in which selected participants (the interviewees) are asked questions to find out what they do, think or feel. Prompts and probes may be required. Under an interpretive paradigm, interviews are concerned with exploring 'data on understandings, opinions, what people remember doing, attitudes, feelings and the like, that people have in common' (Arksey and Knight, 1999, p. 2) and will be unstructured. Under a positivist paradigm, interviews are structured, which means the questions are planned in advance (as in a questionnaire). All types of interviews can be conducted with individuals or groups, using face-to-face, telephone, email or video conferencing methods (see Chapter 10).

Key definitions

An **interview** is a method for collecting primary data in which a sample of interviewees are asked questions to find out what they think, do or feel.

12.3.1 Unstructured interviews

An unstructured interview is one where the questions have not been prepared beforehand but evolve during the course of the interview. They are likely to be open-ended, with probes to explore the interviewee's answers in more depth. The most common form of interview is one-to-one, but some researchers find it useful to have two interviewers to help ensure that all the issues are fully explored and notes are kept of nuances, gestures, interruptions and so on. It is helpful to have a record of what occurred during the interview as it can be used to extract a more robust and comprehensive interpretation.

Unstructured interviews are very time-consuming and there may be problems with recording the questions and answers, controlling the range of topics and analysing the data. The questions raised and the matters explored change from one interview to the next as different aspects of the topic are revealed. This process of open discovery is the strength of such interviews, but it is important to recognize that the emphasis and balance of the emerging issues depend on the order in which your participants are interviewed.

Easterby-Smith, Thorpe and Lowe (1991) suggest that unstructured or semi-structured interviews are appropriate when:

- it is necessary to understand the construct that the interviewee uses as a basis for his or her opinions and beliefs about a particular matter or situation
- one aim of the interview is to develop an understanding of the respondent's 'world' so that the researcher might influence it, either independently or collaboratively (as might be the case with action research)

- the step-by-step logic of a situation is not clear
- the subject matter is highly confidential or commercially sensitive
- the interviewee may be reluctant to be truthful about this issue other than confidentially in a one-to-one situation.

Table 12.1 shows examples of different types of interview question and their uses.

To ensure that you gain maximum information, it is essential that you *probe* the interviewee by asking questions that require them to elaborate on their initial statement. There are a number of qualitative characteristics relating to the answers that you must establish and Table 12.2 shows examples of the probes you can use to elicit such data. Probes are questions you asked in response to what the interviewee has said. They are asked so that you can gain greater understanding of the issue under study and are the beginning of the data analysis stage. They are used in an unstructured or semi-structured interview. If you are thinking of asking prepared questions only, you would be using a structured interview, which is a method associated with a positivist paradigm.

You should bear in mind that recent events may affect the interviewee's responses. For example, he or she may have just received news of a promotion, a salary increase, a cut in hours, a reprimand or bad news about a member of the family. If time allows, you will find it useful to arrive at the interview venue 15 minutes beforehand to assimilate the atmosphere and the environment, and spend the first few minutes putting the interviewee at ease. It is difficult to predict or measure bias. Nevertheless, you should be alert to the fact that it can distort your data and hence your findings.

You should always ask the interviewee's permission to *record* the interview using some form of audio recorder and taking notes. After putting your interviewee at ease, you may find it useful to spend a little time establishing a rapport before starting to record. You can offer to switch the recorder off if he or she wants to discuss *confidential* information. You may find that this encourages a higher degree of frankness (see Chapter 3).

Table 12.1 Types of interview question

Type of question	Useful for	Not useful for
Open question (e.g. Tell me what happened when …)	Most openings to explore and gather broad information	Very talkative people
Closed question (e.g. Who did you consult?)	Getting factual information	Getting broad information
Multiple questions (more than one in a sentence)	Never useful	Never useful
Probes (e.g. What happened next?)	Establishing sequence of events or gathering details	Exploring sensitive events
Hypothetical question (e.g. What might happen that could change your opinion?)	Encouraging broader thinking	Situations beyond the interviewee's scope
Comparison question (e.g. Do you prefer weekly or fortnightly team meetings?)	Exploring needs and values	Unrealistic alternatives
Summary question (e.g. So, am I right in thinking that the main issues are …?)	Avoiding ambiguity, validating data and linking answers	Premature or frequent use

Table 12.2 Examples of probes

Characteristic	Probe
Clarity	Can you give me an example of this? What do you mean? Can you explain that again?
Relevance	How do you think that relates to the issue? Can you explain how these factors influence each other?
Depth	Can you explain that in more detail? Can you give me examples?
Dimension	Is it possible to look at this another way? Do you think that is a commonly held opinion?
Significance	How much does this affect you? What do you think is the most important? Would you change your opinion if X was to happen?
Comparison	Can you give me an example where this did not happen? Can you give me an example of a different situation? In what way does your opinion differ from the views of other people?
Bias	Why do you hold this opinion? What might happen that could change your opinion?

Lee (1993) offers the following advice if you are asking questions on *sensitive topics*:

- Use words that are non-threatening and familiar to the respondents. For example, when explaining the purpose of the interview, rather than saying you are conducting research into absenteeism in their workplace, say you are looking at working patterns.
- Lead up to any sensitive question slowly.
- You may find that participants will answer questions about past indiscretions more readily than questions about current behaviour. For example, they may admit to stealing from their employer at some time in the past, but be unwilling to disclose that they have done so recently.

These suggestions raise ethical issues and you must determine your own position on this. If you find your interviewee is showing signs of resisting some topics, the best advice is to drop those questions. However, this will alert you to the likelihood that these may be interesting and important issues and you may wish to find an alternative way of collecting the data, such as *diary methods* or *observation*.

You need to let the interviewee know that the interview is coming to an end. One way of doing so is to say that you have asked all the questions you had in mind and ask whether he or she has any final comments. You should then conclude by thanking them and reassuring them that you will be treating what they have told you as confidential. If you want to improve the validity of your findings, you should arrange to send a summary of your findings to the interviewee for feedback on your interpretation.

After you have left the interview, you should spend as much time as possible immediately afterwards adding to your notes. You will find it helpful if you can share your insights and reflections with your supervisor or fellow students.

12.3.2 Potential problems

Sometimes the interviewee is accompanied by another person (often to ensure that all the questions you ask can be answered). You must be alert to the fact that if there is more than one interviewer or interviewee it will change the dynamics of the interview. Another situation that can arise is that your interviewee may be wearing 'two hats' (in other words, have multiple roles). For example, the finance director of a company you are interviewing may also be on an advisory group that influences EU company law; a factory employee may also be a trade union official. Therefore, when asking questions, you must determine whether he or she is giving a personal opinion or making a policy statement Another problem is that the interviewee may have certain expectations and give what he or she considers is the 'correct' or 'acceptable' answer to the question. Lee (1993) suggests that, to some extent, this can be overcome by increasing the depth of the interview.

When asking questions, you need to be aware of the potential for inadvertent class, race or sex *bias*. For example, a study that examined sex bias more than 40 years ago (Rosenthal, 1966) found that male and female researchers obtained significantly different data from their subjects. The following tendencies were observed:

- Female subjects were treated more attentively and considerately than male subjects were.
- Female researchers smiled more often than male researchers did.
- Male researchers placed themselves closer to male subjects than female researchers did.
- Male researchers showed higher levels of body activity than female researchers did. When the subject was male, both male and female researchers showed higher levels of body activity than they did with female subjects.
- Female subjects rated male researchers as being friendlier than female researchers were, and as having more pleasant and expressive voices than female researchers had.
- Both male and female researchers generally behaved more warmly towards female subjects than they did towards male subjects, with male researchers being the warmer of the two.

12.3.3 Critical incident technique

Unstructured interviews are not merely idle conversations. It is your role to encourage the participant to tell his or her story in his or her own words, while keeping the interviewee to the relevant issues. You are trying to obtain in-depth and authentic knowledge of people's life experiences (Gubrium and Holstein, 2001). One way to do this is to use *critical incident technique*. This method is based on the participant's recollections of key facts and can be used to collect data about a specific activity or event. It was originally developed by Flanagan (1954) as a method to be used under a positivist paradigm, but principles can be modified and adapted according to the circumstances. This makes it very useful for designing interview questions in an interpretive methodology.

> **Box 12.1 Example of how to collect effective critical incidents**
>
> 'Think of the last time you saw one of your subordinates do something that was very helpful to your group in meeting your production schedule.' (Pause until he indicates that he has such an incident in mind.) 'Did his action result in increase in production of as much as one per cent for that day? – or some similar period?'
>
> (If the answer is 'no', say) 'I wonder if you can think of the last time that someone did something that did have this much of an effect in increasing production.' (When he indicates he has such a situation in mind, say) 'What were the general circumstances leading up to this incident?'
> ....
> ....
> 'Tell me exactly what this person did that was so helpful at that time.' ....
> ....
> 'Why was this so helpful in getting your group's job done?'...............................
> ....
> 'When did this incident happen?' ....
> 'What was this person's job?' ....
> 'How long has he been on this job?' ....
> 'How old is he?' ....
>
> *Source*: Flanagan (1954, p. 342)

Flanagan intended the researcher to collect critical incidents using a form, but you can see from the example in Box 12.1 that his questions could form the basis of a semi-structured interview.

Key definitions

Critical incident technique is a method for collecting data about a defined activity or event based on the participant's recollections of key facts.

Critical incident technique helps interviewees to talk about issues in the context of their own experience and discourages them from talking about hypothetical situations or other people's experiences. For example, if you are using interviews with owners of small businesses to investigate a research problem relating to access to finance, the critical incident might focus on their experiences at the start-up stage. You could follow this up by asking them to tell you about the next time they can remember needing capital and what happened, until you have covered all the occasions. If there are a great many of the type of critical incidents you are interested in, it is best to ask about the most recent or to ask the interviewee afterwards why he or she chose that particular event. One of the problems associated with methods based on memory is that the participant may have forgotten important facts. In addition, there is the problem of post-rationalization, where the interviewee recounts the events with a degree of logic and coherence that did not exist at the time.

12.4 Protocol analysis

Protocol analysis is a data collection method used to identify the mental processes in problem solving, and is usually associated with an interpretive methodology. The aim of the method is to find out how people behave and think in a particular situation, particularly in solving a complex problem. Smagorinsky (1989, p. 475) describes protocol analysis as 'an expensive and meticulous research method that has had its share of growing pains'. However, the method offers a tool for the researcher who is interested in how individuals solve business problems.

Key definitions

Protocol analysis is a method for collecting data used to identify a practitioner's mental processes in solving a problem in a particular situation, including the logic and methods used.

The researcher gives some form of written problem to a practitioner who is experienced in that field. As the practitioner addresses the problem, he or she gives verbal explanations of how he or she is doing it and the researcher records the process. Sometimes the practitioner generates further questions, which form the basis of a subsequent stage in the research.

Protocol analysis studies tend to be small, involving fewer than a dozen participants. The process of constructing the problem that is given to the practitioners is diff-cult and is part of the research process. The researcher must seek to contrive a realistic problem and address the fundamental issues, and also define the scope of the study. Furthermore, the researcher must have sufficient knowledge to be able to understand and interpret the logic and methods the practitioner uses to address the problem (it cannot be assumed that a solution is always found).

12.4.1 Generating protocols

There are a number of ways in which the verbal data can be generated. *Retrospective verbalization* takes place when the participant is asked to describe processes after they have occurred. *Concurrent verbalization* takes place when the participant is asked to describe and explain their thoughts as they undertake a task. There are two types of concurrent verbalization: directed reports and think-aloud protocol. The former result when participants are asked to describe only specific behaviours and the latter when they are asked to relay every thought that comes into their heads. Figure 12.1 summarizes the different types of protocol.

Day (1986) identified the following advantages of using protocol analysis:

- It helps to reduce the problem of interviewer bias.
- The possibility of omitting potentially important areas or aspects is reduced.
- The technique is open-ended and provides considerable flexibility.

12.4.2 Potential problems

Bolton (1991) used concurrent verbal protocols to test questionnaires and identify questions associated with information problems. However, he warns that it is 'time consuming and labour intensive' (Bolton, 1991, p. 565). Protocol analysis was used

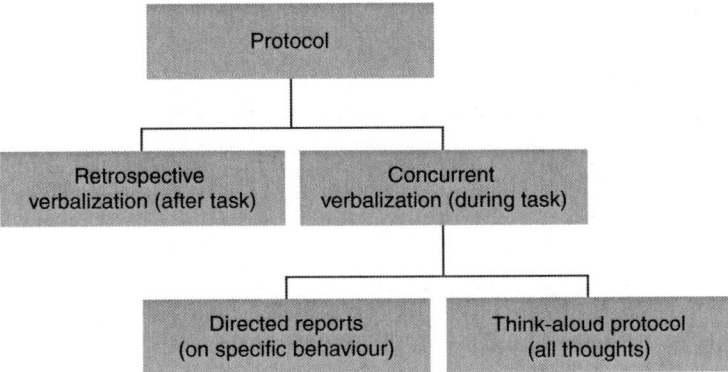

Figure 12.1 Types of protocol

by Smagorinsky (1994) to study writing, and by Clarkson (1962) to examine decisions made by a bank trust investment officer. Day (1986) used it to examine decisions made by investment analysts and points out that a major drawback of using retrospective verbalization is that it does not consider 'a real-time situation, but rather an action replay' (Day, 1986, p. 296). On the other hand, concurrent verbalization requires the researcher to maintain a continuous presence and is usually too time-consuming and disruptive to be considered a feasible choice.

12.5 Repertory grid technique

Based on personal construct theory (Kelly, 1955), *repertory grid technique* is a form of structured interview during which a matrix (the grid) is developed that contains a mathematical representation of the perceptions and constructs a person uses to understand and manage his or her world. The technique 'allows the interviewer to get a mental map of how the interviewee views the world, and to write this map with the minimum of observer bias' (Stewart and Stewart, 1981, p. 5).

Key definitions

Repertory grid technique is a method based on personal construct theory that generates a mathematical representation of a participant's perceptions and constructs.

The underlying theory is that 'people strive to make sense of their world by developing a personal construct system: a network of hypotheses about how the world works' (Hankinson, 2004, p. 146). Our construct system changes as new experiences and knowledge alter the way we look at the world. Our current construct system helps us shape our perceptions about the world and our expectations about future events. It is reality as we know it. Others may share our reality, or part of it, where our construct systems overlap. There are internal inconsistencies in our construct system that may result in our behaviour being at odds with what others perceive as reality. As we all live with these internal inconsistencies, in most cases it causes few problems.

Although it has been used in positivist studies, it is argued that the foundations of personal construct theory lie within the interpretative paradigm (Reason and Rowan, 1981). If you want to use repertory grid technique to collect quantitative data for statistical purposes, you are designing your study under a positivist paradigm. We are going to treat repertory grid technique as being appropriate for a study designed under an interpretive paradigm, but you will need to remember that there is some debate over this when justifying your choice of method in your methodology chapter.

12.5.1 Generating elements and constructs

Repertory grid technique requires the identification of *elements* and *constructs*, and a procedure for enabling participants to relate the constructs to the elements. The elements on the grid are the objects or concepts under discussion, and constructs are the characteristics or attributes of the elements. Following Kelly's original approach, many studies have used people as elements, but other studies have used occupations and work activities (for example Easterby-Smith, 1981; Brook and Brook, 1989; Hunter, 1997) and organizations (for example Barton-Cunningham and Gerrard, 2000; Dackert, Brenner and Johanssen, 2003).

Elements can be generated in several ways:

- by eliciting a topic of interest through discussion with the participants and drawing up a list of elements (usually between 5 and 10, as more could be hard to manage)
- by describing a situation and allowing the participant to identify the elements
- by providing a pool of elements from which the participant selects a certain number of elements
- by providing predetermined elements.

A separate card is used to show the name of each element and these cards are used to elicit the constructs, using *triads* or *dyads*. The classical approach is to use triads, where the interviewer selects three cards at random to show the interviewee. He or she is first asked to decide which two are similar and what differentiates them from the third and then to think of a word or phrase for each similarity or difference between pairs in the triad. The process is repeated until a comprehensive list of personal constructs is obtained. The alternative approach is to use dyads, where pairs of cards are selected at random and the interviewee is asked to provide a word or phrase that describes each similarity or difference. Fransella and Bannister (1977) suggest the researcher adopts whichever method is the most appropriate for exploring the participant's view of the social world they inhabit. The main stages in repertory grid technique are summarized in Box 12.2.

In an *ideographic approach*, the grid is based on the unique elements and personal constructs elicited from the interviewee, and the scores he or she gives that measure relationships between each element and construct. These describe his or her world and the grid may have very little in common with the grids of other interviewees. In a *nomothetic approach*, predetermined elements and/or constructs are used, which facilitate comparison across cases and aggregation of the scores in the grids (Tan and Hunter, 2002). Table 12.3 shows an example of a repertory grid that represents an employee's constructs relating to a set of elements based on organizational systems.

Box 12.2 Procedure for repertory grid technique

1. Determine the focus of the grid.
2. Determine the elements in advance or agree them with each interviewee (approximately 5–10).
3. Write each element on a separate card.
4. Decide whether to use triads or dyads.
5. Select the appropriate number of cards at random.
6. Ask the interviewee to provide a word or phrase that describes each similarity and difference between the pairs of elements.
7. Use these words or phrases as the constructs on the grid.
8. Explain the rating scale to the interviewee (for example 5 = high, 1 = low)
9. Ask the interviewee to indicate the number closest to his or her view and explain the reason.
10. Construct a grid for each interviewee based on his or her responses and scores.

Table 12.3 Example of a repertory grid

Constructs	Elements					
Rating scale 1–7	Inventory management system	Strategic planning system	Office automation	Decision support system	Quality working circle	Collateral organization
Technical quality	6	5	4	2	1	3
Cost	2	1	4	6	5	3
Challenge to status quo	6	1	2	4	5	3
Actionability	1	6	2	4	5	3
Evaluability	6	1	2	5	4	3

Source: Adapted from Dunn and Ginsberg (1986, p. 964)

At a very simple level you can detect emerging patterns. However, it is also possible to take a statistical approach: Dunn and Ginsberg used the data to calculate three indices of cognitive content, thus allowing them to measure differences in the structure and content of reference frames.

12.5.2 Potential problems

At one level a repertory grid 'is nothing more than a labelled set of numbers' (Taylor, 1990, p. 105), but it provides a structured way of assessing an individual's perceptions (Fransella and Bannister, 1977) and 'a framework for the patterning of subjective experiences that has the advantage of being available for statistical analysis' (Taylor, 1990, p. 117). However, the structure approach and a quantitative approach to the analysis is an essential part of the controversy surrounding repertory grid technique. If you are designing your study under an interpretive paradigm, it is essential to seek explanation of the constructs, elements and scores from the interviewee at the time. In all cases, we recommend that you use notes supported by an audio recording. As in any interview, you will need to ask for permission to record.

12.6 Diary methods

Diaries are a method for collecting written data that can be used under both an interpretive and a positivistic methodology. A diary is a record of events or thoughts and is typically used to capture and record what people do, think and feel. Participants are asked to record relevant information in diary forms or booklets over a specified period of time.

Key definitions

A **diary** is a method for collecting data where selected participants are asked to record relevant information in diary forms or booklets over a specified period of time.

12.6.1 Types of diary

Plummer (1983) distinguishes between three types of diary:

- A *log* is a detailed diary in which participants keep a record of the time they spend on their activities. This is a method of collecting quantitative data and is normally used in a positivist study.
- A *diary* is where participants keep descriptive records of their day-to-day lives. These are free-form and present the researcher with several challenges, but also tremendous insights. The diarist should be encouraged to write his or her thoughts as if the diary is secret and to be read by nobody else. This will encourage illuminating revelations but these can be difficult to interpret. It is also challenging to make comparisons if several participants are keeping diaries about the same phenomenon. You may even question whether they are in fact observing the same events, as their perceptions can differ so much.
- A *diary-interview* has the advantage of allowing the researcher to progress to another level of enquiry. The participants are asked to keep a diary in a particular format for a short period. Detailed questions are subsequently developed from the diaries and form the basis of an in-depth interview with the diarist. The extent to which the researcher determines the format is a matter of judgment, but it is one that you must be able to defend. If there is time, we recommend that unstructured interviews are held to agree the format with the participants. Typical formats include those based on time (where the diarist records what they do, think or feel at specific times of the day), events (where the diarist makes the record whenever the activity, thought or feeling occurs) and random (where the diarist makes the choice).

Diary methods offer the advantage of allowing the perspectives of different diarists to be compared. They can be a useful means of gaining sensitive information or an alternative to using direct observation. In contrast to participant observation, where the researcher is involved in the research, in a diary study, data are collected and presented largely within the diarist's frame of reference. Stewart (1965) used diaries as part of a study of managers' jobs and cites the main advantages as:

- Diaries greatly increase the possible coverage of numbers and types of participants, and their geographical and industrial distribution.
- The data can be collected simultaneously, which is less time-consuming than observation.
- The classification of activities is made by the diarist rather than the observer, who may be unfamiliar with the technical aspects of the job.
- The diarist can record all activities, whereas an observer may be excluded from confidential discussions.

12.6.2 Potential problems

Practical problems associated with diary studies include selecting participants who can express themselves well in writing, focusing the diary and providing encouragement over the record-keeping period. You will also find that setting up a diary study involves considerable time and effort. As with many other methods of data collection, there is also the issue of confidentiality. Stewart (1965) points out other disadvantages:

- There are severe limitations if the study is concerned with comparability, although these are reduced if the participants are a homogenous group.
- There may be difficulty in finding a suitable sample and the researcher may have to rely on volunteers.
- There will always be some unreliability in what is recorded.

This last point can be extended to the bias that can easily occur in the individual's recording. For example, the participants may misreport their activities or change their behaviour so that certain activities can be reported to put them in a favourable light. This can also happen when a researcher is using observation to collect data.

12.7 Observation

Observation can take place in a laboratory setting or in a natural setting. A natural setting is a 'research environment that would have existed had researchers never studied it' (Vogt, 1993, p. 150). A natural setting is preferred in a study designed under an interpretive paradigm because of the importance of context and its influence on the phenomenon being studied. This does not necessarily preclude the use of a laboratory setting, if that is an integral part of the research design.

Key definitions

Observation is a method for collecting data used in a laboratory or natural setting to observe and record people's actions and behaviour.

12.7.1 Types of observation

The most common type of observation in business research is *non-participant observation* where the researcher observes and records what people say or do without being involved. The subjects of the research may not be aware that they are being observed, especially if they are being recorded on video or captured in photographs. As in all data collection methods, permission must be sought from the subjects in advance. These forms of data capture mean that if the observer is visible during the observation, he or she is not distracted by having to write notes, which could also influence the subjects' behaviour. If the focus of the research is dialogue, audio recordings can also be made. It is essential that reliable records are made.

Under an interpretive design, the themes relating to the actions and dialogue will emerge during the analysis of the recordings. However, in a study designed under a positivist paradigm, the observer may go on to measure the frequency of occurrence, time of duration or other quantitative data. Alternatively, a positivist observer may have prepared a schedule of phenomena of interest from the literature.

The second type of observation is *participant observation*. In this method, the researcher is fully involved with the participants and the phenomena being researched. The aim is to provide the means of obtaining a detailed understanding of values, motives and practices of those being observed. The main factors to be considered with this method of observation are the:

- purpose of the research
- cost of the research
- extent to which access can be gained
- extent to which the researcher would be comfortable in the role
- amount of time the researcher has available.

12.7.2 Potential problems

There are a number of problems associated with observation techniques. One problem is that you cannot control variables in a natural setting, but by observing the behaviour in two different settings you can draw comparisons. Other problems are concerned with ethics, objectivity, visibility, technology for recording what people say and/or do, boredom, and the impact the researcher has on those observed. Problems of observer bias may arise, such as when one observer interprets an action differently from a colleague. Another problem can be that the observer fails to observe some activities because of distractions. In addition, the grid designed for recording observations may be deficient because it is ambiguous or incomplete.

Observing people in any setting is likely to make them wonder what you are doing. Knowing that they are being observed, may make them change their behaviour by becoming more productive than usual; more docile than usual; take more risks than usual, be less decisive than usual and so on. These are known as *demand characteristics*, because you are making demands on the individual, and this may affect the research. It may be possible to minimize the demand characteristics by not stating the exact purpose of the research. For example, instead of saying you are studying the effect of supervision on the level of productivity, you might say you are investigating the effect of different environments on job satisfaction.

Many years ago such an approach would be acceptable. After the observation you would state the true purpose of the research. However, under the ethical regulations for research now used by many countries and universities it is not acceptable to mislead the participants. It is usually necessary for you to explain beforehand the purpose of the research to the participants and to ensure that they understand it. In some universities it is necessary to obtain the signed consent of the participant. The ethics rules in most countries do not allow you to observe people without their prior permission and without explaining the purpose of your research.

12.8 Focus groups

Focus groups are used to gather data relating to the feelings and opinions of a group of people who are involved in a common situation or discussing the same phenomenon. Focus groups combine interviewing and observation, but allow fresh data to be generated through the interaction of the group. They can be used in an interpretive methodology but are also used by positivists before or after conducting a survey. Focus groups have a long history and were used during the Second World War to examine the effectiveness of propaganda (Merton and Kendall, 1946). In business research, focus groups have long been popular in marketing research, but are increasingly being used in other disciplines.

Focus groups can be useful for a number of purposes, such as to:

- develop knowledge of a new phenomenon
- generate propositions from the issues that emerge
- develop questions for a survey
- obtain feedback on the findings of research in which the focus group members participated.

Key definitions

A **focus group** is a method for collecting data whereby selected participants discuss their reactions and feelings about a product, service, situation or concept, under the guidance of a group leader.

12.8.1 Setting up a focus group

Under the guidance of a group leader, selected participants are encouraged to discuss their opinions, reactions and feelings about a product, service, and type of situation or concept. For example, you might wish to get a group of employees from a company together to discuss what they feel about the profit-sharing scheme in operation, or a group of consumers to discuss their views on a particular brand of cell phone or a television programme. Listening to other group members' views stimulates participants to voice their own opinions. This helps produce 'data and insights that would be less accessible without the interaction found in a group' (Morgan, 1988, p. 12).

If you are planning to hold a focus group, you will need to enlist help. You will probably want to facilitate the meeting yourself, which means you will need someone else to take detailed notes and another person to manage the audio and/or

> **Box 12.3   Procedure for a focus group**
>
> 1. Prepare a list of issues you want to cover.
> 2. Invite a group of people with sufficient experiences in common on the research problem to meet at a neutral location.
> 3. Create a relaxed atmosphere when introducing the group members and explaining the purpose of the focus group and how it will be conducted.
> 4. Start the session with a broad, open question. This can be displayed on an overhead projector or flip chart. If possible, give visual explanations or examples.
> 5. Allow the group to discuss the issue(s) as you introduce them without intervention from you, except to ensure that all members have an opportunity to contribute to the discussion and all the issues are covered.

video recording. Many researchers find it essential to make a video recording of the discussions as the visual cues can be even more revealing than the audio or written records. You will need to prepare a list of issues you want to cover and, if you are the facilitator, you will find it useful to take brief notes of the main points as they emerge. It is very difficult, but not impossible, to run a focus group by yourself and the risk is that data you collect may not have the breadth and depth you are seeking. Box 12.3 shows the main steps involved.

12.8.2   Potential problems

Focus groups are fairly inexpensive to set up. This has resulted in their extensive use to examine industrial, economic and social problems, but the results are sometimes nothing more than the opinions of a small group of people and offer little in the way of deep insights or illumination of the issues under study. To be credible as a data collection technique, focus groups must be properly managed.

One approach is to run a series of groups comprising major categories and compare your findings. For example, you may have separate groups of permanent employees, part-time employees and retired employees discussing their opinion of their employer. Another approach is to have one group containing members from each category. It can be difficult to obtain sufficient volunteers. Too few participants would not generate sufficient data, and too many might mean some do not participate fully; if they do, a large group may be hard to manage. You must remember that you are not trying to obtain a sample from which you can generalize, but to obtain as full a range of perceptions and experiences as possible of the issue or phenomenon of interest to you. Therefore, we advise five to ten participants, but we advise that you try to get acceptances from about 15 to allow for non-attendance on the day.

If the research problem or issue is of interest and relevance to the group, it should not be difficult to generate relevant discussions. In consumer research, participants are invited to try sample goods. This is difficult to replicate when the topic concerns something intangible, such as ethical or equality issues, regulation or corporate governance. It helps if the subject is controversial and often a short documentary will generate discussions. However, sometimes the focus group does not work because one member is highly vociferous and dominates the discussion. Therefore, the researcher needs to explain the purpose of the focus group meeting and how it will be conducted at the onset, and prepare a strategy for encouraging everyone to make a contribution if some remain silent. One approach is to thank the dominant individual for his or her contribution and take the lead for a moment by summarizing the points he or she has made and writing them on a flip chart. Then the rest of the group are invited to give their opinions on these points and add others.

12.9 Grounded theory

Grounded theory is 'a systematic set of procedures to develop an inductively derived grounded theory about a phenomenon. The findings of the research constitute a theoretical formulation of the reality under investigation, rather than consisting of a set of numbers, or a group of loosely related themes' (Strauss and Corbin, 1990, p. 24). We began our discussion of grounded theory in Chapter 5, when we were explaining the main methodologies that are used in business research, and we continue that discussion here.

Key definitions

Grounded theory is a methodology in which a systematic set of procedures is used to develop an inductively derived theory about phenomena.

12.9.1 Procedures

The purpose of grounded theory is to build theory that is faithful to the phenomena under investigation and which illuminates the research problem or issue. The intention is to arrive at prescriptions and policy recommendations with the theory which are 'likely to be intelligible to, and usable by, those in the situation being studied, and ... [which are] often open to comment and correction by them' (Turner, 1981, p. 226).

The theoretical framework is developed by the researcher alternating between inductive and deductive thought. First, the researcher inductively gains information that is apparent in the research data. Next, a deductive approach is used to allow the researcher to turn away from the data, think rationally about the missing information and form logical conclusions. When conclusions have been drawn, the researcher reverts to an inductive approach and tests these tentative hypotheses with existing or new data. By returning to the data, the deducted suggestions can be supported, refuted or modified. Then supported or modified suggestions can be used to form hypotheses and investigated more fully. It is this inductive/deductive approach and the constant reference to the data that helps ground the theory.

'Joint collection, coding and analysis of data is the underlying operation. The generation of theory, coupled with the notion of theory as process, requires that all three operations be done together as much as possible' (Glaser and Strauss, 1967, p. 43).

The relationships between categories and sub-categories discovered during the research should result from the information contained within the data or from deductive reasoning that is verified within the data.

Relationships should not arise from previous assumptions that are not supported by the information in the data. Any views held by the researcher prior to the study may restrict his or her perceptions of the phenomenon under investigation. This might lead to important links and relationships remaining undiscovered or inaccurate deductions about the data, for example. Glaser (1978) suggests that the researcher should enter the research setting with as few predetermined ideas as possible. Of course, no one can completely distance themselves from the beliefs or the structures with which they have grown up or have developed since. However, the researcher needs to be aware of the presence of such prejudices. Once a prejudice has been recognized, its validity can be questioned, and it no longer remains a bias.

Any data collection method associated with an interpretive paradigm can be used in a grounded theory methodology. It is important not to impose boundaries set by prior theory. It is difficult for researchers to rid themselves of the theoretical models and concepts they are familiar with that help them make sense of the world and the way that it works. Imagine you are watching one of the events at the Olympic Games. Try to ignore your existing knowledge about what the competitors, officials and audience are doing by pretending you are from another planet. Now start reflecting and analysing what you observe.

Perhaps the best advice is to approach the research, not with an empty mind, but with an open mind. Therefore, all data can be relevant in illuminating the study. This leads to uncertainty over when you should stop collecting data. The answer is, when you have reached conceptual saturation. In other words, the inclusion of new data does not add to your knowledge of the phenomena under study. We discuss grounded theory again in Chapter 9.

12.9.2 Potential problems

Grounded theory presents a number of problems. These include the difficulty of dealing with the considerable amount of data generated and the question of the generalizability of the findings. Because of the nature of the research process that is time-consuming and set within a particular context, it is usually not possible to generalize from a grounded theory study. Instead of referring to a theory, researchers will refer to the development of a substantive model. This is regarded as a theory that is bounded by, and particular to, the arena in which the study took place. It may be possible to extract themes and patterns that can be observed in similar contexts but one should be hesitant to refer to it as a theory.

However, there is a continuing dissatisfaction with using a priori theories, which do not fully explain business reality. One response has been to encourage the use of grounded theory methodology (Parker and Roffey, 1996). The number of studies doing so includes Barker (1998), Innes (2001), Beattie, Fearnley and Brandt (2004), and Hussey and Ong (2005). However, some researchers are not following the original methods developed by Glaser and Strauss (1967). Instead they have adopted the methods explained by Strauss and Corbin (1994), but have not concerned themselves with the underlying assumptions of the methodology.

12.10 Conclusions

The collection of qualitative data under an interpretative paradigm cannot be separated from the analysis. Although for the purposes of explanation we are discussing collection and analysis in separate chapters, in practice the analytical process starts as soon as you begin collecting qualitative data. If you are collecting qualitative data as part of a positivist study, you will choose quantifying methods in the next stage, followed by statistical analysis. We cover this in the next few chapters. Whichever paradigm you have adopted, it is essential that you do not collect data until you have decided on the method of analysis.

All researchers must consider the ethical issues involved. As a general rule you should inform the participants of the purpose of the research and, where practicable, obtain their written consent to take part. Most of the methods in this chapter are based on the researcher recording the data (interviews, critical incident technique, protocol analysis, repertory grid technique, focus groups and observation) or the participant recording the data (diary methods). We have also mentioned grounded theory methodology again, where any interpretive method(s) can be used. Some of the methods in this chapter are associated with specific analytical methods, which we discuss in the next chapter.

It is also essential that you use rigorous methods for recording research data that also provide evidence of the source. Note-taking allows you to jot down the main points, which is starting off the analysis process. However, it would be difficult to write comprehensive notes and you may miss important information because you are busy writing. Most note-taking involves a degree of instant analysis, which can lead to omissions, distortions, errors and bias as you subjectively filter what data you record. Moreover, even shorthand writers may sometimes find it difficult to decipher their notes afterwards.

Audio or video recording overcomes these problems and leaves you free to concentrate on taking notes of other aspects, such as attitude, behaviour and body language. A specific recording device can be used, or the facilities on your telephone or laptop. The important thing to remember is that you need to obtain the participant's agreement to being recorded. Although the technology has made video easier to use, the cost of the equipment may be a problem. The advantage of video is the relative completeness and complexity of the data thus captured and the permanence of the record it provides. The subsequent analysis can be conducted in any order and at different speeds.

Activities

1. You intend to conduct research to examine the study habits of your fellow students. Select two data collection methods you could use and discuss their advantages and disadvantages.
2. You want to identify the features that employees most like about their workplace. Explain how you would do this.

3. You ask an interviewee the following question: 'How much do you like your job?' The interviewee has replied, 'Not much'. List the probes you would use to improve the quality of his or her answer.
4. Working in small groups (or pairs), one person mimes an action, such as playing a computer game, studying for an examination, carrying out a domestic chore or a work-related task, while the others write down their interpretations and subsequently compare them.
5. In pairs, use repertory grid technique to examine students' study habits. Select roles (researcher or participant) and construct a grid based on the participant's elements and personal constructs. Keep a spare copy of the blank grid. Then complete one copy of the grid for the participant and another for the researcher. Reflect on the similarities and differences. How would you explain them?

PROGRESS TEST

Complete the following sentences:

1. If you are using personal construct theory, you will collect your data using _____ technique.
2. The type of diary where participants are asked to record the time they spend on certain activities is called a _____.
3. The type of interview where the questions are not planned in advance is described as_____.
4. The method where a participant explains verbally how he or she is addressing a specific problem the researcher has constructed is called_____.
5. If you are taking part in the activities of a group you are observing, the method is called _____ observation.

Are the following statements true or false?

6. You must choose separate methods for collecting and analysing your research data.
7. It is acceptable to use participant observation without informing members of the group.
8. Focus groups can be used to collect data under an interpretive paradigm.
9. In grounded theory you stop collecting data when you have conceptual saturation.
10. Probes are used with structured interviews.

Multiple choice questions:

11. Research ethics are important in:
    a) Unstructured interviews
    b) Critical incident technique
    c) Repertory grid technique
    d) All data collection methods

12. Generating personal constructs to collect data is part of:
    a) Unstructured interviews
    b) Critical incident technique
    c) Repertory grid technique
    d) Protocol analysis

13. Using diary methods or observation to collect data:
    a) Is likely to affect the participant's behaviour
    b) Is likely to generate an accurate and reliable record
    c) Can only generate qualitative data
    d) Can only be used as the basis for interviews

14. An effective focus group will:
    a) Have less than five participants
    b) Be dominated by the facilitator
    c) Be dominated by one or two participants
    d) Be recorded by observers using more than one method

15. An effective interviewer will:
    a) Seek permission to record the interview
    b) Do most of the talking
    c) Ask more than one question at a time
    d) Indicate whether the answer was right

References

Arksey, H. and Knight, P. (1999) *Interviewing for Social Scientists,* London: Sage.
Barker, R. G. (1998) 'The market for information: Evidence from finance directors, analysts and fund managers', *Accounting and Business Research,* 29 (1) pp. 3–20.
Barton-Cunningham, J., and Gerrard, P. (2000) 'Characteristics of well-performing organisations in Singapore', *Singapore Management Review,* 22 (1), pp. 35–65.
Bolton, R. N. (1991) 'An exploratory investigation of questionnaire pretesting with verbal protocol analysis', *Advances in Consumer Research,* 18, pp. 558–65.
Brook, J. A. and Brook, J. R. (1989) 'Exploring the meaning of work and non work', *Journal of Organizational Behaviour,* 20, pp. 169–78.
Clarkson, G. P. E. (1962) *Portfolio Selection: A Simulation of Trust Investment,* Englewood Cliffs, NJ: Prentice Hall.
Dackert, I., Jackson P. R., Brenner, S. O. and Johansson, C. R. (2003) 'Eliciting and analyzing employees' expectations of a merger', *Human Relations,* 56 (6), pp. 705–13.
Day, J. (1986) 'The use of annual reports by UK investment analysts', *Accounting & Business Research,* Autumn, pp. 295–307.
Dunn, W. and Ginsberg, A. (1986) 'A sociocognitive network approach to organisational analysis', *Human Relations,* 40 (11), pp. 955–76.
Easterby-Smith, M. (1981) 'The Analysis and Interpretation of Repertory Grids', in M. L. Shaw (ed.) *Recent Advances in Personal Construct Theory,* London: Academic Press, pp. 9–30.
Easterby-Smith, M., Thorpe, R. and Lowe, A. (1991) *Management Research: An Introduction,* London: Sage.
Fearnley, S. and Brandt, R. (2004) 'A grounded theory model of auditor – client negotiations', *International Journal of Auditing* 8 (1), pp. 1–19.
Flanagan, J. C. (1954) 'The critical incident technique', *Psychological Bulletin,* 51 (4), July, pp. 327–58.
Fransella, F. and Bannister, D. (1977) *The Manual for Repertory Grid Technique,* New York: Academic Press.

Glaser, B. and Strauss, A. (1967) *The Discovery of Grounded Theory*, Chicago, IL: Aldine.
Glaser, B. (1978) *Theoretical Sensitivity*, Mill Valley, CA: Sociology Press.
Gubrium, J. and Holstein, J. (eds) (2001) *Handbook of Interview Research*, London, Sage.
Hankinson, G. (2004) 'Repertory grid analysis: An application to the measurement of distant images', *International Journal of Nonprofit and Voluntary Sector Marketing*, 9 (2), pp. 145–54.
Hunter, M. G. (1997) 'The use of RepGrids to gather interview data about information system analysts', *Information Systems Journal*, 7, pp. 67–81.
Innes, J. (2001) 'Social Performance Measures and Management Control: A Grounded Theory Case Study', Discussion Paper, Dundee: University of Dundee.
Kelly, G. A. (1955) *The Psychology of Personal Constructs: A Theory of Personality*, New York: Norton.
Lee, R. M. (1993) *Doing Research on Sensitive Topics*, London: Sage.
Merton, R. K. and Kendall, P. L. (1946) 'The focussed interview', *American Journal of Sociology*, 51, pp. 541–57.
Morgan, D. L. (1988) *Focus Groups as Qualitative Research*, Newbury Park, CA: Sage.
Parker, L. D. and Roffey, B. H. (1996) 'Back to the drawing board: Revisiting grounded theory and the everyday accountant's and manager's reality', *Accounting, Auditing and Accountability Journal*, 10 (2) pp. 212–347.
Plummer, K. (1983) *Documents of Life: An Introduction to the Problems and Literature of a Humanistic Method*, London: Allen & Unwin.
Reason, P. and Rowan, J. (1981) *Human Enquiry: A Sourcebook of New Paradigm Research*, Chichester: John Wiley.
Rosenthal, R. (1966) *Experimenter Effects in Behavioural Research*, New York: Appleton-Century-Crofts.
Smagorinsky, P. (1989) 'The reliability and validity of protocol analysis', *Written Communication*, 6 (4), October, pp. 463–79.
Stewart, R. (1965) 'The use of diaries to study managers' jobs', *Journal of Management Studies*, 2, pp. 228–35.
Stewart, V. and Stewart, A. (1981) *Business Applications of Repertory Grid*, Maidenhead: McGraw-Hill.
Strauss, A. and Corbin, J. (1990) *Basics of Qualitative Research: Grounded Theory Procedures and Techniques*, Newbury Park, CA: Sage.
Strauss, A. and Corbin, J. (1994) 'Grounded Theory Methodology: An Overview', in Denzin, N. K. and Lincoln, Y. S. (eds) *Handbook of Qualitative Research*, Thousand Oaks, CA: Sage.
Tan, F. and Hunter, M. G. (2002) 'The repertory grid technique: A method for the study of cognition in information systems', *MIS Quarterly*, 26 (1), pp. 39–57.
Taylor, D. S. (1990) 'Making the most of your matrices: Hermeneutics, statistics and the repertory grid', *International Journal of Personal Construct Psychology*, 3, pp. 105–19.
Turner, B. A. (1981) 'Some practical aspects of qualitative data analysis: One way of organizing the cognitive processes associated with the generation of grounded theory', *Quality and Quantity*, 15 (3), pp. 225–47.
Vogt, W. P. (1993) *Dictionary of Statistics and Methodology*, Newbury Park, CA: Sage.

Glossary

Critical incident technique	A method for collecting data about a defend activity or event based on the participant's recollections of key facts.
Diary	A method for collecting data where selected participants are asked to record relevant information in diary forms or booklets over a specified period of time.
Focus group	A method for collecting data whereby selected participants discuss their reactions and feelings about a product, service, situation or concept, under the guidance of a group leader.
Interview	A method for collecting primary data in which a sample of interviewees are asked questions to find out what they think, do or feel.
Natural setting	A research environment that would have existed had researchers never studied it.

COLLECTING QUALITATIVE DATA

Non-participant observation	A method of observation in which the observer is not involved in the activities taking place and the phenomena studied.
Observation	A method for collecting data used in the laboratory or in a natural setting to observe and record people's actions and behaviour.
Participant observation	A method of observation in which the observer is involved in the activities taking place and the phenomena studied.
Protocol analysis	A method for collecting data used to identify a practitioner's mental processes in solving a problem in a particular situation, including the logic and methods used.
Quantifying methods	Methods used to analyse qualitative data by converting it into quantitative data.
Repertory grid technique	A method based on personal construct theory that generates a mathematical representation of a participant's perceptions and constructs.
Validity	The extent to which the research findings accurately reflect the phenomena under study.

CHAPTER 13
Collecting data for statistical analysis

LEARNING OBJECTIVES

When you have studied this chapter, you should be able to:
- classify variables according to their level of measurement
- describe the main methods for collecting data for statistical analysis
- discuss the strengths and weaknesses of different methods
- design questions for questionnaire and interview surveys
- select a random sample.

13.1 Introduction

You may be reading this chapter because you are designing a positivist study and you need to identify and discuss your intended method(s) of data collection to finalize your proposal. Alternatively, you may be reading this chapter because your proposal has been accepted, and you are now ready to start collecting original data for statistical analysis. In either case, this chapter will help guide you.

You will remember from Chapter 5 that the two main methodologies associated with positivism are experimental studies and surveys (which may be designed as cross-sectional or longitudinal studies). Since experimental studies are not widely used in business research for practical and ethical reasons, this chapter focuses on the methods used to collect original data when a survey methodology is adopted. The two main methods we discuss are self-completion questionnaires and interviews. We also describe critical incident technique, which can be incorporated in either method. This knowledge should build on what you have learned from studying Chapter 9 because methods are not necessarily identified as positivist or interpretivist by their labels, but by the type of data collected and how the data are analysed. Moreover, studies incorporating *triangulation* may use more than one method for collecting data.

The close relationship between collecting and analysing the research data means it is important to think ahead to the type of statistical analysis you will use when designing questions for self-completion questionnaires and interviews. Therefore, we examine the issues relating to designing questions separately. The final aspect of data collection we examine is concerned with finding a sampling frame and selecting a sample.

13.2 Overview of data collection in a positivist study

Researchers are interested in collecting data about the phenomena they are studying. You will remember that in Chapter 1 we defined data as known facts or things used as a basis for inference or reckoning. Some authors distinguish between data and information, by defining information as the knowledge created by organizing data into a useful form. This obviously depends on how items of data are perceived and how they are used. For example, if you are a positivist, you may have collected data relating to the variables under study via a questionnaire survey, which you subsequently analysed using statistics. You probably consider that this process allowed you to turn data into information that makes a small contribution to knowledge. On the other hand, your respondents may consider that what they gave was information in the first place.

Data can be *quantitative* (in numerical form) or *qualitative* (in non-numerical form, such as text or images). Data can also be classified by source. Your literature review is an analysis of *secondary data* (data collected from an existing source), but your research data may be *primary data* (data you have generated by collecting it from an original source, such as an experiment or survey). Typical sources of secondary data include commercial databases, published books, articles, reports and statistics, or an organization's internal records and documents. Such data can be published in hard copy or in digital form, such as on the internet.

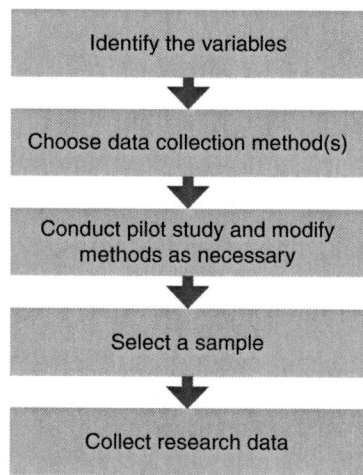

Figure 13.1 Overview of the data collection process

Figure 13.1 shows an overview of the data collection process. However, it is important to realize that this is purely illustrative and the process is not as linear as the diagram suggests. Moreover, research data can be generated or collected from different sources and more than one method can be used.

Key definitions

Data are known facts or things used as a basis for inference or reckoning.

Information is the knowledge created by organizing data into a useful form.

Primary data are generated from an original source, such as your own experiments, surveys, interviews or focus groups.

Secondary data are collected from an existing source, such as publications, databases and internal records.

13.3 Variables

Under positivism, research is deductive. Therefore, one of the purposes of the literature review is to identify a *theory* (or set of theories) to provide a theoretical framework for your study. A theory is a set of interrelated *variables*, definitions and propositions that specifies relationships among the variables. A variable is a characteristic of a phenomenon that can be observed or measured. Researchers collect data relating to each variable, which provide empirical evidence. Your theoretical framework forms the basis for constructing a *hypothesis* (plural *hypotheses*), which is an idea or proposition that can be tested for association or causality against the empirical evidence you collect.

Before you can collect any research data, you need to understand the properties of the variables relating to the phenomena you are studying. A *variable* is an attribute or characteristic of the phenomenon under study that can be observed and measured. You can see from this definition that variables are usually taken to be numerical and this is because any non-numerical observations can be quantified by allocating a numerical code (Upton and Cook, 2006). For example, the responses to open questions in a survey can be examined to identify the main themes and then a number given to each theme or category.

Key definitions

Empirical evidence is data based on observation or experience.

A **hypothesis** is a proposition that can be tested for association or causality against empirical evidence.

A **theory** is a set of interrelated variables, definitions and propositions that specifies relationships among the variables.

A **variable** is a characteristic of a phenomenon that can be observed or measured.

13.3.1 Measurement levels

The level at which a variable is measured has important implications for your subsequent choice of statistical methods. 'A level of measurement is the scale that represents a hierarchy of precision on which a variable might be assessed'

(Salkind, 2006, p. 100). There are four levels of measurement, which we will examine in decreasing order of precision:

- A *ratio* variable is a quantitative variable measured on a mathematical scale with equal intervals between points and a fixed zero point. The fixed zero point permits the highest level of precision in the measurement and allows us to say how much of the variable exists (it could be none) and compare one value with another. For example, using sea level as the fixed zero point, we can measure altitude in feet or metres. This means we can say that one aeroplane is flying at an altitude measured in metres that is twice as high as another aeroplane. If we use kilometres as the measurement scale, we can measure the distance by train from London to Brussels. If we use time as the measurement scale, we would designate the time of departure from London as the fixed zero point and compare the average time of the journey by high speed train with the time by air. This allows us to say that, the mean (average) train journey is only 10% longer than by air.
- An *interval* variable is a grouped quantitative variable measured on a mathematical scale that has equal intervals between points and an arbitrary zero point. This means you can place each data item precisely on the scale and compare the values. For example, the interval between an IQ score of 100 and 115 is the same as the interval between 110 and 125, but it is not possible to say that someone with an IQ of 120 is twice as intelligent as someone with an IQ of 60. Temperature is another example: If the temperature was 1° centigrade yesterday and 2° centigrade today, we know that today is warmer by an interval of 1°, but we cannot say that today is twice as warm as yesterday because 0° centigrade does not mean there is no temperature! With only an arbitrary zero point, we cannot say that the difference between two points on the scale is a precise representation of the variable under study.
- An *ordinal* variable is measured using numerical codes to identify order (ranks). This allows you to see whether one observation is ranked more highly than another observation; for example, degree classifications of a candidate applying for a job (1, 2.1, 2.2 or 3) or their country of location preferences (1st, 2nd or 3rd). Ordinal variables fall between quantitative and categorical measures.
- A *nominal* variable is measured using numerical codes to identify named categories. For this reason, it is described as a 'categorical' variable. Each observation is placed in one of the categories. For example, you may have a variable for the gender of an applicant for a job (two categories), ethnicity (several categories) qualifications (several categories). If it is not possible to anticipate all the categories you can include a category named 'Other'. This is also used if you subsequently find some categories contain very few observations.

One of the reasons why it is important to identify the level of measurement of variables is that it has implications for your statistical analysis. If you have collected data from ratio or interval variables, and the data meet certain distributional assumptions, you can use *parametric* statistic tests, which are based on the mean. On the other hand, if your data come from ordinal or nominal variables you will need to use the less powerful non-parametric methods. We examine this further in the next two chapters.

Key definitions

An **interval variable** is measured on a mathematical scale with equal intervals and an arbitrary zero point.

A **nominal variable** is measured using numerical codes to identify named categories.

An **ordinal variable** is measured using numerical codes to identify order or rank.

A **ratio variable** is measured on a mathematical scale with equal intervals and a fixed zero point.

13.3.2 Discrete and continuous quantitative variables

Quantitative variables measured on a ratio or interval scale can be *discrete* or *continuous*. A discrete variable can take only one value on the scale. For example, the number of sales assistants in a baker's shop on different days of the week might range from 1 to 5 and the variable can only take the values 0, 1, 2, 3, 4 or 5. Therefore, a value of 1.3 or 4.6 sales assistants is not possible.

On the other hand, a continuous variable can take any value between the start and end of a scale. For example, the amount of fruit and vegetables wasted in a hotel kitchen each day might vary from 0 kg to 10 kg and the variable can take any value between the start and end of the scale. Therefore, the data for Monday could be 3 kg exactly, but on Tuesday it could be 3.5 kg and on Wednesday 2.75 kg. In practice, there is considerable blurring of these definitions. For example, it can be argued that income is a discrete ratio variable, because income is a specific value within a range of values. However, because there are so many different possibilities when incomes are taken down to the last penny or cent, income is generally considered to be a continuous variable. Weight is certainly a continuous variable, but if the weighing scales are only accurate to the nearest tenth of a kilogram, the results will be from the distinct range of values, 0.1, 0.2, 0.3, 0.4 and so on.

Key definitions

A **continuous variable** is a ratio or interval variable measured on a scale where the data can take any value within a given range, such as time or length.

A **discrete variable** is a ratio or interval variable measured on a scale that can take only one of a range of distinct values, such as number of employees.

13.3.3 Dichotomous and dummy variables

A *dichotomous* variable is a variable that has only two possible categories, each with an assigned value. 'Gender' is an example of a natural dichotomous variable where the two groups are male and female and can be described as a categorical variable. Sometimes a variable that is not a natural dichotomy can be recoded into a new *dummy* variable. Perhaps you have collected data relating to the variable 'age', which measures the number of years since the business was started in five year periods (<5 years, 6–10 years, 11–15 years, 16–20 years and so on). You could collapse this variable into a new variable called Maturity with two groups coded as 1 = Mature (≥5 years old) and 0 = Otherwise. If you do this, keep the original variable with its precise information in case you need it, because one of the disadvantages of recoding it into a dichotomous variable is that all this detail is lost.

Kervin (1992) suggests a number of arguments to support how you can treat a dichotomous variable in terms of the level of measurement. Using the above example of 'maturity', you might say that since the values represent a named category, it is a nominal variable with two groups named 'young' and 'mature'. Alternatively, you could argue that since the mature group has more of the original variable than the young group, it is an ordinal variable. Since there are only two values, you might decide to ignore the question of equal intervals and treat it as an interval variable. Finally, you might conclude that the 0 represents a natural zero point indicating that the business is not a mature business; in other words, the variable is a dummy variable where 0 = the characteristic of maturity is absent and 1 = the characteristic is present. Therefore, you treat it as a ratio variable. However, you are only likely to find support for the first of these arguments and we advise that you discuss the others with your supervisor before using them to justify your choice of statistical methods in your proposal.

Key definitions

A **dichotomous variable** is a variable that has two categories, such as gender.

A **dummy variable** is a dichotomous quantitative variable coded 1 if the characteristic is present and 0 if the characteristic is absent.

13.3.4 Hypothetical constructs

Finding a measurement scale for variables such as the age of the businesses in your study or financial variables is not difficult, as there are widely accepted measures (the number of years since the business was started and monetary measures respectively). However, if your variables were abstract ideas such as intelligence or honesty, you will need to search the literature to find a suitable measurement scale or develop your own *hypothetical construct*. A *construct* is a set of concepts or general notions and ideas a person has in his or her mind about certain things. Because a construct is a mental image or abstract idea, it is difficult to observe and measure. Consequently, positivists develop a category or numerical scales to measure opinion and other abstract ideas. For example, intelligence has been measured by psychologists as a numerical hypothetical construct called intelligence quotient (IQ). This is a score that is derived from an individual taking a carefully designed test.

Apart from saving you time, the main advantages of finding an existing hypothetical construct, rather than developing your own, are that the validity of the measure is likely to have been tested (Kervin, 1992) and you can compare your results with others based on the same construct. Examples include social stratification categories, frequency categories, ranking and rating scales (see section 13.5.4).

Key definitions

A **hypothetical construct** is a rating scale used to measure opinion and other abstract ideas.

13.3.5 Dependent and independent variables

In many statistical tests it is necessary to identify the *dependent variable* (*DV*) and the *independent variable* (*IV*). A dependent variable is a variable whose values are influenced by one or more independent variables. Conversely, an independent variable is a variable that influences the values of a dependent variable. For example, in an experimental study, the intensity of lighting (IV) in the workplace might be manipulated to observe the effect on the productivity levels (DV), or a stressful situation might be created by generating random loud noises (IV) outside the workplace window to observe the effect on the completion of complex tasks (DV).

An *extraneous variable* is any variable other than the independent variable that might have an effect on the dependent variable. For example, if your study involves an investigation of the relationship between productivity and motivation, you may find it difficult to exclude the effect of other factors, such as a heatwave, a work-to-rule, a takeover or anxiety caused by personal problems. A *confounding variable* is one that obscures the effect of another variable. For example, employees' behaviour may be affected by the novelty of being the centre of the researcher's attention or by working in an unfamiliar place for the purposes of a controlled experiment.

Key definitions

A **dependent variable** (DV) is a variable whose values are influenced by one or more independent variables.

An **independent variable** (IV) is a variable that influences the values of a dependent variable.

13.4 Data collection methods

The two main data collection methods we discuss in this section are self-completion questionnaires and interviews. We also describe critical incident technique, which can be incorporated in either method. These are widely used methods in positivist studies, but you should also explore other methods that you come across when studying previous research on your chosen topic.

13.4.1 Questionnaires

A *questionnaire* is a list of carefully structured questions, which have been chosen after considerable testing with a view to eliciting reliable responses from a particular group of people. The aim is to find out what they think, do or feel because this will help you address your research questions. Of course, this raises the issue of *confidentiality*, which we examined in Chapter 3. When a questionnaire is used in an interview, many researchers call it an 'interview schedule'. You may also come across the term *research instrument*, which is a questionnaire or interview schedule that has been used and tested in a number of different studies. In a face-to-face or telephone interview, the answers to the questions are recorded by the interviewer. However, in a postal or on-line survey, the questionnaire is completed by the respondent. This is cheaper and less time-consuming, but there are a number of other factors that you should be aware of if you are conducting an interview survey and we discuss these in the next section.

Questionnaires or interview schedules are used in a *Delphi study*, where the aim is to gather opinions from a carefully selected group of experts. Once the responses have been summarized, the results are returned to the participants so that they can

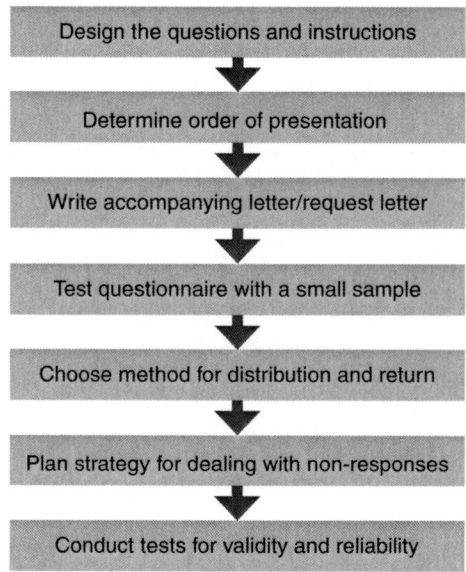

Figure 13.2 Designing a questionnaire or interview schedule

re-evaluate their original answers once they have seen the responses of the group. This process is repeated a number of times until there is consensus. Unlike a focus group, the experts do not meet or know the identities of the other group members.

Before you start designing your questionnaire or interview schedule, you need to have identified the variables about which you need data so that you can address your research questions. You also need to have found a list from which to choose a sample. In a large questionnaire or interview survey, many respondents or interviewees will be needed and you will need to decide on a method for selecting a suitable sample. We look at this important decision in section 13.7. The main steps involved in designing a questionnaire or interview schedule are summarized in Figure 13.2.

Key definitions

A **questionnaire** is a method for collecting primary data in which a sample of respondents are asked a list of carefully structured questions chosen after considerable testing, with a view to eliciting reliable responses.

Question design is concerned with the type of questions, their wording, the order in which they are presented and the reliability and validity of the responses. We discuss this in detail in Section 13.5. You will need to explain the purpose of the study, since the respondents need to know the context in which the questions are being posed. This can be achieved by starting the questionnaire with an explanatory paragraph or attaching a covering letter.

It is essential that you *pilot* or test your questionnaire as fully as possible before distributing it. At the undergraduate level, you could ask your supervisor, friends and family to play the role of respondents. Even if they know little about the subject, they can still be very helpful in spotting a range of potential problems.

However, the best advice is to try your questionnaire out on people who are similar to those in your sample. If you are a Master's or doctoral student, you may find it takes several drafts, with tests at every stage, until you are satisfied, so allow plenty of time for this important part of the process.

There are a number of *distribution* methods, each with different strengths and weaknesses. Cost is often an important factor and the best method for a particular study often depends on the size and location of the sample.

- *By post* – This is a commonly used method of distribution that is fairly easy to administer. The questionnaire and covering letter are posted to the population or the sample, usually with a prepaid envelope for returning the completed questionnaire. If you are conducting an internal survey in a particular company, it may be possible to use the internal mail. If it is a large survey, you will need to consider the cost of printing, postage and stationery. You should also leave plenty of time for getting the questionnaire printed, folding and inserting the contents, sealing the envelopes and franking or stamping them. However, one of the drawbacks is that response rates of 10% or less are not uncommon and this introduces the problem of sample bias because those who respond may not be representative of the population. Response rates can be increased by keeping the questionnaire as short as possible (for example two sides of A4) and using closed questions of a simple and non-sensitive nature.
- *By telephone* – This is also a widely used method to employ as it reduces the costs associated with face-to-face interviews, but still allows some aspect of personal contact. A relatively long questionnaire can be used and it can be helpful with sensitive and complex questions. However, achieving the desired number of responses may require a very large sampling frame and there is the cost of many calls to consider. Moreover, your results may be biased towards people who are available and willing to answer questions in this way.
- *On-line* – Web-based tools, such as Survey Monkey, allow you to create your own survey for a fee and email it to potential respondents. You can view the preliminary results as they come in and the data file can be exported to *Excel*, SPSS and other software packages for analysis. Like the last two methods of distribution, on-line surveys are now so widely used that obtaining sufficient responses may take some time and the results may be biased.
- *Face-to-face* – The questionnaire can be presented to respondents in the street, at their homes, in the workplace or any convenient place. It is time-consuming and can be expensive if you have to travel to a particular location to meet an interviewee. However, this method offers the advantage that response rates can be fairly high and comprehensive data can be collected. It is often very useful if sensitive or complex questions need to be asked. Where the interview is conducted in the interviewee's home, it is possible to use a lengthy questionnaire. It is important that you take precautions to ensure your personal safety when using the face-to-face method (see Chapter 3). We look at interviews in more detail in the next section.
- *Group distribution* – This method is only appropriate where the survey is being conducted in a small number of locations or a single location. You may be able to agree that the sample or sub-groups are assembled in the same room at the same

time, such as the canteen during a quiet period in the afternoon. You can then explain the purpose of the survey and how to complete the questionnaire, while being available to answer any queries. This is a convenient, low-cost method for administering questionnaires and the number of usable questionnaires is likely to be high.

- *Individual distribution* – This is a variation of group distribution. If the sample is situated in one location, it may be possible to distribute, and collect, the questionnaires individually. As well as a place of work, this approach can be used in theatres, restaurants and even on trains and buses. It is normally necessary to supply pens or pencils for the completion of the questionnaires. You may encounter problems with sample bias if you use this method; for example, you may only capture patrons who visit a theatre on a Monday, or travel at a particular time. However, if properly designed, this method can be very precise in targeting the most appropriate sample.

There are two major problems associated with using questionnaires in a survey. The first is *questionnaire fatigue*. This refers to the reluctance of many people to respond to questionnaire surveys because they are inundated with unsolicited requests by post, email, telephone and in the street. The second problem is what to do about *non-response bias*, which can be present if some questionnaires are not returned. Non-response bias is crucial in a survey because your research design will be based on the fact that you are going to generalize from the sample to the population. If you have not collected responses from all the members of your sample, the data may not be representative of the population. Later on in this chapter, we will look at item non-response (non-response to particular questions) and the implications for the reliability and validity of the results.

Wallace and Mellor (1988) suggest three methods for testing for questionnaire non-response:

1. Compare responses by date of reply. One method of doing this is to send a follow-up request to non-respondents. If you intend to do this, you will need to keep a record of those who reply and when. In a postal questionnaire survey, you are advised to send a fresh copy of the questionnaire (perhaps printed on different coloured paper or with an identifying symbol in addition to the unique reference number). The questionnaires that result from the follow-up (late respondents) are then compared with those from the first request (early respondents).
2. Compare the characteristics of respondents with those of the population, assuming you know them.
3. Compare the characteristics of respondents with those of non-respondents in the sample, assuming you know them.

13.4.2 Interviews

Interviews are a method for collecting data in which selected participants (the interviewees) are asked questions to find out what they do, think or feel. Verbal or visual prompts may be required. Interviews can be conducted with individuals or groups using face-to-face, telephone or video conferencing methods (although video conferencing is not likely to be feasible for a large scale survey). A positivist approach suggests a *structured interview* based on a *questionnaire* or interview schedule.

Key definitions

An *interview* is a method for collecting primary data in which a sample of interviewees are asked questions to find out what they think, do or feel.

In a *structured interview*, these questions are likely to be *closed questions*, each of which has a set of predetermined answers. There may be some *open questions*, which allow the respondent to answer in his or her own words. In a large structured or semi-structured face-to-face or telephone interview, a questionnaire is prepared in advance and is completed by the interviewer from the responses given by the interviewee (for example interviews used in market research surveys). In a *semi-structured interview*, some of the questions are pre-prepared, but the interviewer is able to add additional questions in order to obtain more detailed information about a particular answer or to explore new (but relevant) issues that arise from a particular answer. *Unstructured interviews* are associated with an interpretive paradigm.

In a large interview survey, many interviewees are needed and this gives rise to the problem of obtaining access to an appropriate sample. You will need to explain the purpose of the study, since the interviewees need to know the subject of the interview and the context in which you will ask your questions. Obtaining a sample and conducting the interviews can be very time-consuming and there may be travel and hospitality costs to consider. In some studies, a self-completion questionnaire may be more appropriate.

Structured interviews make it easy to compare answers because each interviewee is asked the same questions. However, in a semi-structured (or unstructured interview) the issues discussed, the questions raised and the matters explored change from one interview to the next as different aspects of the topic are revealed. This process of discovery is the strength of such interviews, but it is important to recognize that emphasis and balance of the emerging issues may depend on the order in which you interview the participants. In unstructured and semi-structured interviews, it may be difficult to keep a note of the questions and answers, controlling the range of topics and, later, analysing the data.

In all types of interview, you are advised to ask the interviewee's permission to record the interview using an audio recorder. After putting your interviewee at ease, you may find it useful to spend a little time establishing a rapport before starting to record. You can offer to switch the recorder off if your interviewee wants to discuss confidential or sensitive information; seek permission to continue to take notes. You may find that this encourages a higher degree of frankness. We discussed the issue of *confidentiality* in Chapter 3. Lee (1993) offers the following advice if you are asking questions on sensitive topics:

- Use words that are non-threatening and familiar to the respondents. For example, when explaining the purpose of the questionnaire, rather than saying you are conducting research into absenteeism in their workplace, say you are looking at working patterns.
- Lead up to any sensitive question slowly.

- You may find that participants will answer questions about past indiscretions more readily than questions about current behaviour. For example, they may admit to stealing from their employer at some time in the past, but be unwilling to disclose that they have done so recently.

These suggestions raise ethical issues and you must determine your own position on this. If you find your interviewee is showing signs of resisting some topics, the best advice is to drop those questions. However, this will alert you to the likelihood that these may be interesting and important issues and you may wish to find an alternative way of collecting the data, such as *diary methods or observation* (see Chapter 8).

In a positivist study, you will need to ensure that all the interviews are conducted in the same way to avoid *interviewer bias*. This means that not only should the same questions be asked, but also that they should be posed in the same way. Furthermore, you must ensure that each respondent will understand the question in the same way. This is known as *stimulus equivalence* and demands considerable thought and skill in question design. A checklist for keeping interviewer bias to the minimum is shown in Box 13.1.

There is also potential for inadvertent class, race or sex bias. Another problem is that the interviewee may have certain expectations about the interview and give what he or she considers is the 'correct' or 'acceptable' answer to the question. Lee (1993) suggests that, to some extent, this can be overcome by increasing the depth of the interview. You should bear in mind that recent events may also affect the interviewee's responses. For example, he or she may have just received news of a promotion, a salary increase, a cut in hours, a reprimand or bad news about a member of the family. If time allows, you will find it useful to arrive at the interview venue 15 minutes beforehand to assimilate the atmosphere and the environment, and spend the first few minutes putting the interviewee at ease. It is difficult to predict or measure bias. Nevertheless, you should be alert to the fact that it can distort your data and hence your findings.

Box 13.1 Checklist for reducing interviewer bias

- Read each question exactly as worded in the questionnaire.
- Read each question slowly, using the same intonation and emphasis.
- Ask the questions in the same order.
- Ask every question that applies.
- Use the same response cards (if required as part of the design).
- Record exactly what the respondent says.
- Do not answer the question for the respondent.
- Show interest by paying attention when the respondent is answering, but do not show approval or disapproval.
- Make sure you have understood each answer and that the answer is adequate.

Source: Adapted from Brenner (1985)

The most common form of interview is one-to-one, but some researchers find it useful to have two interviewers to help ensure that all the issues are fully explored and notes are kept of nuances and relevant non-verbal factors. Sometimes the interviewee is accompanied by another person (often to ensure that all the questions you ask can be answered). You must be alert to the fact that more than one interviewer or interviewee will change the dynamics of the interview. Another problem is that an interviewee may be 'wearing two hats'. For example, the finance director of a company may also be a director of other companies or involved in other organizations; an employee may also be a trade unionist or a shareholder. When you are asking questions, you must determine which 'hat' the interviewee is wearing, and whether he or she is giving a personal opinion or making a policy statement.

As well as deciding on the structure and recording of an interview, you must also be able to bring it to a satisfactory conclusion and let the interviewee know that it is ending. One device is to say that you have asked all the questions you had in mind and ask whether the interviewee has any final comments. You should then conclude by thanking them and reassuring them that you will be treating what they have told you as confidential. After you have left the interview, it is beneficial to add further notes.

Despite some disadvantages, interviews permit the researcher to ask complex questions and ask follow-up questions, which is not possible in a self-completion questionnaire. Thus, further information can be obtained. An interview may permit a higher degree of confidence in the replies than responses to a self-completion questionnaire and can take account of non-verbal communications such as the attitude and behaviour of the interviewee. It is important to take precautions to ensure your personal safety when conducting face-to-face interviews.

13.4.3 Critical incident technique

Critical incident technique is a method for collecting data about a defined activity or event based on the participant's recollections of key facts. Developed by Flanagan (1954), it allows important facts to be gathered about behaviour in defined situations 'in a rather objective fashion with only a minimum of inferences and interpretation of a more subjective nature' (Flanagan, 1954, p. 335). Although it is called a technique, it is not a set of rigid rules, but a flexible set of principles that can be modified and adapted according to the circumstances. In Chapter 8, we explained how it can be used as the basis for a semi-structured interview under an interpretive paradigm and we will now look at its use in interviews or surveys under a positivist paradigm.

Key definitions

Critical incident technique is a method for collecting data about a defined activity or event based on the participant's recollections of key facts.

Flanagan recommended that only simple types of judgements should be required of observers, who should be qualified. All observations should be evaluated by the observer in terms of an agreed statement of the purpose of the activity. The procedure for establishing the general aims of an activity, the training of the interviewers and the manner in which observations should be made are all predetermined. What is of

> **Box 13.2 Critical incident technique in a survey**
>
> *These questions are open-ended and I have kept them to a few vital areas of interest. All will require you to reflect back on decisions and reasons for decisions you have made.*
>
> 1. Please think about an occasion when you improved your home. What improvements did you make?
> 2. On that occasion what made you do it?
> 3. Did you receive any help? If 'yes', please explain what help you received.
> 4. Have you wanted to improve your home in any other way but could not?
> 5. What improvements did you wish to make?
> 6. What stopped you from doing it?
>
> *Source*: MacKinlay (1986), cited in Easterby-Smith, Thorpe and Lowe (1991, p. 84)

prime interest to researchers is the way in which Flanagan concentrates on an observable activity (the incident), where the intended purpose seems to be clear and the effect appears to be logical; hence, the incident is critical.

We showed Flanagan's example of a form for collected effective critical incidents in Chapter 8. In this chapter we will look at an example taken from a questionnaire survey of householders (MacKinlay, 1986), which contained six open-ended questions. The questionnaire allowed a third of an A4 page per question for the reply, but some respondents added additional sheets. The questions were preceded by an explanation, as shown in Box 13.2.

It is likely that many researchers use this approach without realizing it. One of the benefits is that it allows the researcher to collect data about events chosen by the respondent because they are memorable, rather than general impressions of events or vicarious knowledge of events. In interviews, it can be of considerable value in generating data where there is a lack of focus or the interviewee has difficulty in expressing an opinion.

One of the problems associated with methods based on memory is that the participant may have forgotten important facts. In addition, there is the problem of post-rationalization, where the interviewee recounts the events with a degree of logic and coherence that did not exist at the time.

13.5 Designing questions

Many data collection methods rely on *questions* as the vehicle for gathering primary research data. In this section, we focus on designing questions for a positivist study, where the research data thus generated will be analysed using statistical methods. Before you can decide what the most appropriate questions will be, you must gain a considerable amount of knowledge about your subject to allow you to develop a theoretical or conceptual framework and formulate the hypotheses you will test. Your subject knowledge will come from your taught and/or independent studies;

your theoretical framework (sometimes referred to as a conceptual framework) that underpins the hypotheses you will test will be drawn from your literature review. The statistical methods you will use will be described in your methodology chapter.

Questions should be presented in a logical order and it is often beneficial to move from general to specific topics. This is known as funnelling. In complex questionnaires, it may be necessary to use filter questions, where respondents who have given a certain answer are directed to skip a question or batch of questions. For example, 'Do you normally do the household shopping? *If YES, go to next question; if NO, go to Question 17.*'

In addition to designing the questions themselves, in a self-completion questionnaire you also give precise *instructions* (for example whether to tick one or more boxes, or whether a number or word should be circled to indicate the response). The clarity of the instructions and the ordering and presentation of the questions can do much to encourage and help respondents. These factors also make the subsequent analysis of the data easier.

Classification questions collect data about the characteristics of the unit of analysis, such as the respondent's job title, age or education; or the geographical region, industry, size or age of the business. If you wish to make comparisons with previous studies, government statistics or other publications, it is essential to use the same categories. Classification questions collect data that will enable you to describe your sample and examine relationships between subsets of your sample. Remember, you should only collect data about variables you will use in your analysis.

There is some debate over the best location for classification questions. Some authors believe that they are best placed at the beginning, so that respondents gain confidence in answering easy questions; others prefer to place them at the end, so that the respondent starts with the more interesting questions. If your questions are of a sensitive nature, it may be best to start with the non-threatening classification questions. If you have a large number of classification questions, it could be better to put them at the end, so that the respondent is not deterred at the start. Remember to allocate a unique reference number to each questionnaire. This will enable you to maintain control of the project and, if appropriate, you will be able to identify which respondents have replied and send follow-up letters to those who have not. If you are using *triangulation*, you will also be able to match data about the unit of analysis from different sources.

13.5.1 General rules

It is essential to bear your target audience in mind when designing your questions. If your sample is composed of intelligent people, who are likely to be knowledgeable about the topic, you can aim for a fairly high level of complexity, but the general rule is to keep it simple. Box 13.3 summarizes the general rules for designing questions.

These fundamental aspects of question design are important, because once you have asked the questions there is often little you can do to enhance the quality of the answers. It can be helpful to the respondent if you qualify your questions in some way, perhaps by referring to a specific time period, rather than requiring the respondent to search their memory for an answer. For example, instead of asking, 'Have you ever bought Fair Trade coffee?' you might ask, 'Have you bought Fair

> **Box 13.3 General rules for designing questions**
>
> - Provide a context by briefly explaining the purpose of the research
> - Only ask questions that are needed for the analysis
> - Keep each question as short and as simple as possible
> - Only ask one question at a time
> - Include questions that serve as cross-checks on answers to other questions
> - Avoid jargon, ambiguity and negative questions
> - Avoid leading questions and value-laden questions that suggest a 'correct' answer
> - Avoid calculations and memory tests
> - Avoid questions that could cause offence or embarrassment

Trade coffee in the past three weeks?' A question can also be qualified by referring to a particular place. For example, 'What are your views on the choice of Fair Trade coffee in your local supermarket?'

If the issue addressed in the question is complex or rigid, we might wish to add some generality to it. For example, 'Do you travel to work in your own car?' might be taken to mean every day. This can be generalized by inserting the word 'normally' or 'usually', thus: 'Do you normally travel to work in your own car?' A question can also be made more general by inserting the word 'overall' or the term 'in general'. For example, 'In general, are you satisfied with the level of service you obtain from the company?' However, in some questions precision may be important and desirable.

Coolican (1992) identifies the following pitfalls to avoid when deciding on the order in which questions should be asked:

- To address the tendency for participants to agree rather than disagree (known as response acquiescence), you should mix positive and negative questions to keep them thinking of their answers.
- The participant may try to interpret the aim of the question or questionnaire, or set up emotional blocks to some questions. Therefore, it is advisable to ensure that both positive and negative items appear and that less extreme statements are presented first.
- Some responses may be considered as socially desirable. For example, if you want to ask 'How often do you take a bath/shower each week?' respondents who do not wash very often may not give a valid answer, but one that fits the image they wish to present. You can try to resolve this problem by putting in some statements that only those respondents who are answering to impress would choose (for example more than twice a day), but if your pilot test produces too many of these responses, you should discard your questionnaire or interview schedule.

In the remainder of this section, we examine the different types of questions you can ask and the importance of incorporating features that will enhance your results and assist in the later analysis of the responses you receive.

13.5.2 Open and closed questions

A positivist approach suggests *closed questions*, which allow the respondent to choose from predetermined answers. For example, questions seeking facts, such as the respondent's age (where the predetermined answers are given in age bands) or job title (where the respondent chooses from a list). Other closed questions may seek opinions (for example a question where the predetermined answers are given in the form of statements with which the respondent can agree or disagree).

Key definitions

A closed question is one where respondents select the answer from a number of predetermined alternatives.

An open question is one where respondents can give the answer in their own words.

However, there may be some *open questions*, which allow the respondents to answer in their own words. Subsequently, each response is examined carefully to identify the key words, phrases or themes across the answers and placed in a category with a numerical code, which represents a nominal variable. For example, in a survey of the directors of small companies, question 3 asked whether they would have the accounts audited even if the company were not legally required to do so, and were given a 'yes' or 'no' choice. Box 13.4 shows this closed question and the open question that followed, which asked them to give their reasons and provided space for the answer. An initial analysis identified nine categories across the responses and the following values allocated to each, with no order implied: 1 = cost savings, 2 = no benefit, 3 = check, 4 = good practice/governance, 5 = assurance for shareholders, 6 = assurance for customers/suppliers, 7 = assurance for bank/lenders, 8 = exit plans, 9 = other.

Closed questions are very convenient and are usually easy to analyse, since the range of potential answers is limited and can be coded in advance. On the other hand, open questions offer the advantage that the respondents are able to give their opinions as precisely as possible in their own words. For undergraduates and Master's students, who often have to work within a tight time frame, it is advisable to keep the number of open-ended questions to the minimum in a large survey.

Box 13.4 Open and closed questions

3. Would you have the accounts audited if not legally required to do so?
   (*Tick one box only*)

Yes, the accounts are already audited voluntarily	☐	(1)
Yes, the accounts would be audited voluntarily	☐	(2)
No	☐	(0)

   Please give reasons for either answer
   ....
   ....

   Source: Adapted from Collis (2003)

Moreover, all researchers need to be aware that a large number of open questions may deter busy respondents from replying.

13.5.3 Multiple choice questions

Multiple choice questions are those where the participant is asked a closed question and selects his or her answer from a list of predetermined responses or categories. It may be difficult to provide sufficient, unambiguous categories to allow the respondent to give an unequivocal answer. An example of this is a question that seeks to ascertain respondents' occupations. Even in a fairly small organization there may be quite a wide range of occupations; you cannot provide a full list because it would take up too much room. As a general guide approximately six predetermined responses or categories are usually sufficient. In interviews, you will find it helpful to have a printed copy of the choice of answers to show the interviewee. This means he or she can study the list rather than have to memorize all the alternatives. The interviewee then simply tells you his or her choice.

When deciding on categories, you must take care to use terms that mean something to the participants, so that you can have confidence in their replies. For example, you may use the term 'Accountant' as one of your job title categories, meaning a person who has passed the necessary exams to become a member of one of the accountancy bodies. However, some respondents may attribute a wider meaning to this term and you may find that a bookkeeper or credit controller sees himself or herself as a belonging to this category.

In a single organization, it is usually possible to construct categories for factual questions that people will understand. If you are taking a random sample of the population, it becomes much harder. If you are uncertain that you have covered all possibilities, you should add an 'Other' category that allows the respondent to provide their own category and a 'Don't know' category if this is likely to apply.

Box 13.5 shows two examples of multiple choice questions and their associated answers. Whereas question 1 expects only one response, question 5 asks respondents to tick as many boxes as apply. It is important to give clear instructions.

Sometimes a question is phrased so that the respondent is presented with a range of opinions and has to select the one that most closely resembles their own. The drawback with this type of question is that it takes up considerable space and does not capture the respondents' opinions in their own words. As a result, you cannot be certain about how closely it matches their opinions. However, it can sometimes be useful for dealing with sensitive issues, since it identifies different responses. It can also be useful as a means of cross-checking other questions by presenting the situation in a different way. Box 13.6 shows an example of a question that could be used to evaluate how well students worked together on a group assignment.

13.5.4 Ranking and rating scales

Another approach is to ask respondents to rank a list of items and Box 13.7 shows an example. Unfortunately, the responses to such questions can be disappointing. Often respondents will not have gone through this type of exercise before and may be unwilling to spare the time to think about it. You may find that after ranking the

Box 13.5 Multiple choice (fact)

1. Is the company a family-owned business? (*Tick one box only*)

   Wholly family-owned (or only 1 owner) ☐ (1)
   Partly family-owned ☐ (2)
   None of the shareholders are related ☐ (0)

5. Apart from Companies House, who normally receives a copy of the company's statutory accounts? (*Tick as many boxes as apply*)
   (a) Shareholders ☐
   (b) Bank and other providers of finance ☐
   (c) Directors/managers who are *not* shareholders ☐
   (d) Employees who are *not* shareholders ☐
   (e) Major suppliers and trade creditors ☐
   (f) Major customers ☐
   (g) Tax authorities ☐
   (h) Other (Please state) .... ☐

Source: Adapted from Collis (2003)

Box 13.6 Multiple choice (opinion)

(i) Thinking about your relationship with others in your assignment group, indicate which of the following statements is closest to your view.
(*Tick one box only*)

We are a very happy and friendly group	☐	(1)
We get on reasonably well and better than many others	☐	(2)
We have our ups and downs the same as any other group	☐	(3)
We tend to be quite argumentative and less friendly than other groups	☐	(4)
We do not work well as a group and there are unresolved conflicts	☐	(5)

Box 13.7 Ranking

(ii) Rank the following learning resources on this module on a scale of 1 to 5, where 1 = most useful and 5 = least useful.

The activities during the lectures ☐
The activities during the tutorials ☐
The lecture notes on *BlackBoard* ☐
The recommended textbook ☐
Feedback from the progress tests ☐

> **Box 13.8 Semantic differential rating scale**
>
> (c) Rate the clarity of the assessment criteria for your group assignment on the following scale where 1 = low and 7 = high. (*Circle the number closest to your view*)
>
> 1   2   3   4   5   6   7

first three, they leave the others blank because they have been unwilling or unable to decide a rank for the remaining items. If you would like to include a ranking question, keep the number of items as low as possible (preferably no more than six).

The most straightforward way to collect opinions is to set a simple question requiring a 'Yes' or 'No' response. This elicits a clear response, but does not offer any flexibility and may force respondents into giving an opinion when they do not hold one. Because opinion and other abstract ideas are difficult to observe and measure, you may decide to use a *hypothetical construct* in the form of a numeric rating scale, to measure opinion and other abstract ideas. This allows respondents to give a more discriminating response than a simple 'yes' or 'no'. One such scale is known as a *semantic differential rating scale*. Two words or phrases are selected to represent two ends of the scale and the respondents are asked to indicate their opinion using a seven point scale. Box 13.8 shows an example.

A second type of rating scale measures intensity of opinion. This also allows respondents to give a more discriminating response and indicate if they feel neutral. Box 13.9 shows an example where respondents are asked to indicate their level of agreement with a set of statements using a rating scale of 1 to 5. If there had been more room, each number might have had a label (for example 5 = Strongly agree, 4 = Agree,

> **Box 13.9 Intensity rating scale**
>
> **4. What are your views on the following statements regarding the audit?**
> (*Circle number closest to your view*)
>
> | | Agree | | | | Disagree |
> |---|---|---|---|---|---|
> | (a) Provides a check on accounting records and systems | 5 | 4 | 3 | 2 | 1 |
> | (b) Improves the quality of the financial information | 5 | 4 | 3 | 2 | 1 |
> | (c) Improves the credibility of the financial information | 5 | 4 | 3 | 2 | 1 |
> | (d) Has a positive effect on company's credit rating score | 5 | 4 | 3 | 2 | 1 |
>
> *Source*: Adapted from Collis (2003)

3 = Neutral, 2 = Disagree, 1 = Strongly disagree). Unlike ranking, where 1 represents the top of the scale, you will find it useful to follow the convention of allocating 1 to the lowest level of agreement, importance, usefulness, or whatever it is your rating scale is measuring. This will make it easier to interpret the results of your statistical analysis.

An advantage of using ranking and rating scales is that a number of different statements can be provided in a list, which makes economical use of the space and is easy for the respondent to complete. Moreover, these ordinal variables are measured at a higher level than a nominal variable requiring a simple 'Yes' or 'No' answer, which has implications for the type of statistic tests that can be used in your analysis. Box 13.10 gives examples of commonly used scales.

13.5.5 Reliability and validity

If you decide to use rating scales or attitude scales in the questions you ask, you will want to be sure that they will measure the respondents' views consistently. The *reliability* of the responses you receive to all your questions is an important issue

---

Box 13.10 Examples of intensity, frequency and evaluation rating scales

General adjectives (unipolar)
5 Very/Extremely/Strongly satisfied, important, agree, etc.
4 Fairly/Quite/Moderately
3 Slightly/Weakly
2 Not very/Hardly
1 Not at all

Directional general adjectives (bipolar)
5 Very/Extremely/Strongly satisfied, important, agree, etc.
4 Moderately/Fairly/Mostly
3 Neutral/Undecided/Unsure
2 Moderately/Fairly/Mostly
1 Very/Extremely/Strongly dissatisfied, unimportant, disagree, etc.

Directional comparisons (bipolar)
5 Much better
4 Better
3 About the same
2 Worse
1 Much worse

Frequency (unipolar)
5 All the time
4 Most of the time
3 Sometimes
2 Seldom/Rarely
1 Never/Not at all

> *Evaluation (unipolar)*
> 5 Excellent
> 4 Very good
> 3 Average
> 2 Poor
> 1 Very poor
>
> *Source*: Adapted from Kervin (1992, p. 319)

in a positivist study. Reliability is concerned with the findings of the research. The findings can be said to be reliable if you or someone else repeats the research and obtains the same results. *Validity* is also important and this is concerned with the extent to which the research findings accurately represent what is happening in the situation; in other words, whether the data collected represent a true picture of what is being studied.

The reason why there may be doubt lies in the problem that our questions may contain errors (perhaps they are worded ambiguously), the respondent may become bored or there may be antagonism between the researcher and the participants leading to *item non-response*. Typical examples include failing to answer questions that apply or not following instructions by ticking more than one box when only one choice was allowed. There are a number of ways of dealing with such problems, ranging from making an educated guess based on the respondent's other answers to statistical methods. If you have a large number of non-responses to a particular question across the sample, it usually means the question design was at fault and the data from that question should not be used in your analysis. If a respondent returns an incomplete questionnaire or one where questions that are crucial to your analysis are not answered, you will have to discard it.

There are three common ways of estimating the reliability of the responses to questions in questionnaires or interviews:

- *Test re-test method* – The questions are asked of the same people, but on two separate occasions. Responses for the two occasions are correlated and the *correlation co-efficient* of the two sets of data computed (see Chapter 12), thus providing an index of reliability. However, this method suffers from the considerable disadvantage that it is often difficult to persuade respondents to answer questions a second time and, if they do, they may think more deeply about the questions on the second occasion and give different answers.
- *Split-halves method* – The questionnaires or interview record sheets are divided into two equal halves, perhaps by putting the responses to the odd numbered questions in one pile and the responses to the even numbered questions in another. Alternatively, the responses to the first half of the questions are put in a separate pile from the answers to the remainder. The two piles are then correlated and the *correlation co-efficient* of the two sets of data computed as above.
- *Internal consistency method* – Every item is correlated with every other item across the sample and the average inter-item correlation is taken as the index of

> **Box 13.11 Checklist for eliminating questions**
>
> 1. Does the question measure some aspect of one of the research questions?
> 2. Does the question provide information needed in conjunction with some other variable?
>   (If NO to both 1 and 2, drop the question; if YES to one or both, retain)
> 3. Will most respondents understand the question and in the same way?
>   (If NO, revise or drop; if YES, retain)
> 4. Will most respondents have the information to answer it?
>   (If NO, drop; if YES, retain)
> 5. Will most respondents be willing to answer it?
>   (If NO, drop; if YES, retain)
> 6. Is other information needed to analyse this question?
>   (If NO, retain; if YES, retain only if the other information is available or can be obtained)
> 7. Should this question be asked of all respondents or only a subset?
>   (If ALL, retain; if ONLY A SUBSET, retain only if the subset is identifiable beforehand or through questions in the interview)
>
> *Source*: Adapted from Czaja and Blair (1996, p. 61)

reliability. Although this is a popular method of computing the reliability of the results where questions have been used as the basis of the data collection method, it requires substantial computing facilities and software that uses a special formula called *Kuder-Richardson (KR20)*.

The responses to your questions may turn out to be highly reliable, but the results will be worthless if your questions do not measure what you intended them to measure; in other words *validity* is low. Therefore, it is important that the questions you ask correspond with the explanation you give respondents regarding the purpose of your study; otherwise, they may lose interest in answering the questions, as these will appear to be irrelevant.

13.5.6 Eliminating questions

Having decided on the questions you wish to ask, it is common to find that you have far too many. Use the checklist given in Box 13.11 to determine which questions you should retain and which you should drop when designing questions for interviews or questionnaires.

You must be alert to the possibility that some of the issues you wish to investigate may be offensive or embarrassing to the respondents. We do not recommend you ask any *sensitive questions* in a self-completion questionnaire. Not only is it likely to deter respondents from answering the sensitive question, but it may discourage them from participating at all.

13.6 Coding questions

Although *coding* is more closely related to data analysis than to data collection, it is important to consider at this stage how you will analyse your research data and what software is available to help you with this task (for example *Excel, Minitab* and *SPSS for Windows*).* *SPSS* is widely used in business research because it can process large amounts of data and we will be introducing the principles of data entry and analysis using SPSS in the next chapter.

13.6.1 Coding closed questions

Pre-coding questions for statistical analysis as part of the questionnaire design makes the subsequent data entry easier and less prone to error. Where this is not possible, it is important to remember to keep a record of the codes used for each question and what they signify. This is essential should you decide to use a third party to input your data, and also for when you start to interpret the analysed data.

It is usual to reserve certain code numbers for particular purposes. For nominal variables where only one can be selected, allocate a different code to each so that the answer can be identified. For nominal variables where more than one answer may apply, each variable is treated independently: use 1 to indicate the box has been ticked (the characteristic is present) and leave blank if it has not been ticked. This will be interpreted by SPSS as a 'missing' data, which means a non-response. Depending on your planned analysis, you may wish to use 0 if the box has not been ticked (the characteristic is not present). Similarly, it is usual to code the answer 'yes' as 1 and the answer 'no' as 0. There is no need to pre-code ordinal variables because they use a numerical rating scale.

You may have noticed that the examples of questions we used in this chapter were pre-coded. Box 13.12 shows an example of a pre-coded questionnaire. Look carefully at the way in which the potential answers have been coded. Each code is discretely shown in brackets next to the relevant box. There are no hard and fast rules about where to place the codes and you may find that it makes more sense to put the codes at the top of a column of boxes for some sets of variables. You simply need to adopt a location that improves the accuracy and efficiency of processing the data, while not confusing the respondent. In this example, a smaller, lighter font has been used to reduce the likelihood of the respondent becoming distracted by codes.

Earlier in this chapter, we suggested that you should pilot your questions before commencing your data collection in earnest. We also recommend that once you have your test data, you also pilot your coding. Amending coding errors now will save you valuable time and effort later when errors can only be painstakingly corrected by hand on every record sheet or questionnaire.

13.6.2 Coding open questions

Statistical analysis can only be conducted on quantitative data. *Open questions* where the answer takes a numerical value do not need to be coded (for example dates or

---

*SPSS is an abbreviation for Statistical Product and Service Solutions (formerly Statistical Package for the Social Sciences).

Box 13.12 A pre-coded questionnaire

URN 42

1. Is the company a family-owned business? (*Tick one box only*)

    Wholly family-owned (or only 1 owner) ☐ (1)
    Partly family-owned ☐ (2)
    None of the shareholders are related ☐ (0)

2. How many shareholders (owners) does the company have?

    (a) Total number of shareholders ☐
    Breakdown:
    (b) Number of shareholders with access to internal financial information ☐
    (c) Number of shareholders *without* access to internal financial information ☐

3. Would you have the accounts audited if not legally required to do so? (*Tick one box only*)

    Yes, the accounts are already audited voluntarily ☐ (1)
    Yes, the accounts would be audited voluntarily ☐ (2)
    No ☐ (0)

    Please give reasons for either answer
    ....
    ....

4. What are your views on the following statements regarding the audit? (*Circle number closest to your view*)

	Agree				Disagree
(a) Provides a check on accounting records and systems	5	4	3	2	1
(b) Improves the quality of the financial information	5	4	3	2	1
(c) Improves the credibility of the financial information	5	4	3	2	1
(d) Has a positive effect on company's credit rating score	5	4	3	2	1

5. Apart from Companies House, who normally receives a copy of the company's statutory accounts? (*Tick as many boxes as apply*)

    (a) Shareholders ☐
    (b) Bank and other providers of finance ☐
    (c) Employees who are *not* shareholders ☐
    (d) Major suppliers and trade creditors ☐
    (e) Major customers ☐
    (f) Tax authorities ☐
    (g) Other (*Please state*)...☐

> **6. Do you have any of the following qualifications/training?**
> (*Tick as many boxes as apply*)
> (a) Undergraduate or postgraduate degree ☐
> (b) Professional/vocational qualification ☐
> (c) Study/training in business/management subjects ☐
>
> *Source*: Adapted from Collis (2003)

financial data). However, open questions where you are unable to anticipate the response (including those where you provide an 'Other' category) will result in qualitative data that cannot be coded until all the replies have been received. The task of recording and counting frequencies accurately and methodically can be helped by using *tallies*. A tally is just a simple stroke used to count the frequency of occurrence of a value or category in a variable. You jot down one upright stroke for each occurrence until you have four; the fifth is drawn horizontally across the group, like a five bar gate. You can then count in fives until you get to the single tallies. Box 13.13 shows tallies being used to help record the frequencies for the second part of question 3, which was designed as an open question to capture the respondents' reasons for a particular action.

13.7 Sampling methods

13.7.1 Sampling frames

A *sampling frame* is a record of the population from which a sample can be drawn. A sample is an unbiased subset that represents the population and a *population* is a body of people or collection of items under consideration for statistical purposes. If

> **Box 13.13   Using tallies to count frequencies**
>
> **3. Would you have the accounts audited if not legally required to do so?**
> (*Tick one box only*)
>
> Yes, the accounts are already audited voluntarily ☐ (1)
> Yes, the accounts would be audited voluntarily ☐ (2)
> No ☐ (0)
>
> *Please give reasons for either answer*
> **Voluntary audit**
> Assurance for third party ℐℐℐℐ ℐℐℐℐ ℐℐℐℐ ℐℐℐℐ ℐℐℐℐ ℐℐℐℐ ℐℐℐℐ   35
> Good practice ℐℐℐℐ ℐℐℐℐ ℐℐℐℐ   14
> **No audit**
> No benefit/no need ℐℐℐℐ ℐℐℐℐ ℐℐℐℐ ℐℐℐℐ ℐℐℐℐ ℐℐℐℐ ℐℐℐℐ I   36
> Cost savings ℐℐℐℐ ℐℐℐℐ ℐℐℐℐ ℐℐℐℐ ℐℐℐℐ ℐℐℐℐ II   32

the population is relatively small, you can select the whole population; otherwise, you will need to select a random sample. 'In a positivist study, it is vital to obtain a random sample to get some idea of variation ... To build general conclusions on ... limited data is a bit like a lazy evolutionist biologist finding a few mutant finches ... in a population on day one of a field outing, then returning home to claim that all finches of this species display the same properties' (Alexander, 2006, p. 20).

A random sample is one where every member of the population has a chance of being chosen. Therefore, the sample is an unbiased subset of the population, which allows the results obtained for the sample to be taken to be true for the whole population; in other words, the results from the sample are generalizable to the population.

Key definitions

A **population** is a body of people or collection of items under consideration for statistical purposes.

A **sample** is a subset of a population. In a positivist study, a random sample is chosen to provide an unbiased subset that represents the population.

A **sampling frame** is a record of the population from which a sample can be drawn.

To find out how many items there are in the population, you need to find a suitable sampling frame. For example, if you were conducting research where employees are the unit of analysis, the Human Resources department of the business may be willing to supply a staff list. However, if businesses are your unit of analysis, you will need to look for a suitable database, such as FAME, Dun & Bradstreet or DataStream. For example, perhaps your research focuses on the financial structure of small companies in the paper recycling industry in the London postal area. Your *unit of analysis* is a small company, which you decide to define as a private limited company with up to 50 employees. You decide to use the FAME database to identify companies that fit your criteria and your investigations show that there are 32 such companies. Obviously, your research findings will relate only to paper recycling companies in London of this size and you will not be able to generalize the results of your study to other companies.

On the other hand, perhaps you are investigating the performance of all small companies in all industries throughout the UK. In this case, your unit of analysis is still a small company and you can still use the FAME database as the sampling frame, but this time you find that there are thousands of companies that fit your criteria. To save the expense and inconvenience of investigating all these companies, it is acceptable to reduce the number to a manageable size by selecting a random sample. Figure 13.3 shows the main steps in selecting a random sample.

13.7.2 Sample size

For a Bachelor's or taught Master's dissertation or thesis, it is common to accept a degree of uncertainty in the conclusions you draw, so selecting a sufficiently large random sample to allow your results to be generalized to the population may not be vital to your study. Nevertheless, you still need a large enough sample to address your research questions because if your sample is too small, it may preclude some important statistical tests among the subsets in the sample (for example looking for

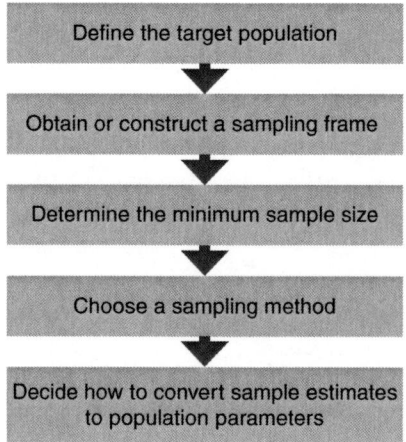

Figure 13.3 Main steps in selecting a random sample

differences between industry sectors). Therefore, the greater the expected variation within the sample, the larger the sample required.

The larger the sample, the better it will represent the population. Therefore, if you want to generalize from your results, you must also determine the minimum sample size to reflect the size of the population. In a questionnaire survey, you will also need to take account of your expected *response rate*, which may be 10% or less. Recent surveys in your field or your own pilot survey will give you a guide.

The minimum sample size to allow results from a random sample to be generalized to the population is much higher for a small population than it is for a large population. 'As the population increases, the sample size increases at a diminishing rate and remains relatively constant at slightly more than 380 cases' (Krejcie and Morgan, 1970, p. 610). This is illustrated in Table 13.1.

Clegg (1990) suggests the three main considerations are:

- the statistical analysis planned
- the expected variability within subsets in the sample
- the tradition in your research area regarding what constitutes an appropriate sample size.

The factors that must be considered when determining the appropriate number of subjects to include in a sample are discussed in detail by Czaja and Blair (1996); essentially, it is a question of deciding how accurate you want your results to be and how confident you want to be in that answer.

13.7.3 Methods for selecting a random sample

One way to select a random sample is to allocate a number to every member of the population and select a sample based on the numbers given in a random number table (see Appendix at the end of this chapter) or random numbers created by a computer. This is the equivalent of a lottery, where every number has a chance of being drawn. An unbiased sample is one that represents every section of a population in the same proportion as the population. However, the sample will be biased

Table 13.1 Determining sample size from a given population

Population	Sample size
10	10
100	80
200	132
300	169
400	196
500	217
700	248
1,000	278
2,000	322
3,000	341
4,000	351
5,000	357
7,000	364
10,000	370
20,000	377
50,000	381
75,000	382
≥1,000,000	384

Source: Adapted from Krejcie and Morgan (1970, p. 608)

if the researcher chooses members of the population, asks for volunteers or offers financial inducements to attract participants. Such methods are likely to produce a biased sample because the volunteers may possess certain characteristics that others in the population do not possess.

In *systematic sampling*, the population is divided by the required sample size (n) and the sample chosen by taking every 'nth' subject, as illustrated in Box 13.14.

Stratified sampling overcomes the problem that a simple random sample might result in some members of the population being significantly under- or over-represented.

Box 13.14 Systematic sampling

Example
Population: 10,000
Sample size: 370

Divide the population by the required sample size:

$$\frac{10,000}{370} = 27$$

Select a randomly chosen number between 1 and the required sample size of 27 (we have chosen 3); then choose every 27th number thereafter until 370 numbers have been selected:

30, 57, 84, 111, 138, 165 and so on

> **Box 13.15 Stratified sampling Example**
>
> **Example**
> Population: 500 (1% senior managers, 5% supervisors, 94% clerical staff)
> Sample size: 217
>
> 217 × 1% =   2 senior managers
> 217 × 5% =   11 supervisors
> 217 × 94% = 207 clerical staff
>   Total = 217

It does this by taking account of each identifiable strata of the population. For example, if your sampling frame consists of all the employees in an insurance company, you may identify the following strata: senior managers, supervisors and clerical staff. You would then need to find out how many there were in each category and work out what percentage of the whole this represents, so that you can ensure that the same proportions are reflected in the sample. Box 13.15 shows an example.

Other types of sampling include:

- *Quota sampling* involves giving interviewers quotas of different types of people to question, for example 25 men under the age of 21; 30 women over 50 and so on. It is widely used in marketing research.
- *Cluster sampling* involves making a random selection from a sampling frame listing groups of units rather than individual units. Every individual belonging to the selected groups is then interviewed or examined. This can be a useful approach, particularly for face-to-face interviews, where for time or economy reasons it is necessary to reduce the physical areas covered. For example, a certain number of project teams within a company might be selected and every member of the selected teams interviewed.
- *Multi-stage sampling* is used where the groups selected in a cluster sample are so large that a sub-sample must be selected from each group. For example, first select a sample of companies. From each company, select a sample of departments and from each department select a sample of managers to survey.

13.7.4 Methods for selecting a non-random sample

If generalization is not your aim or you are conducting a study under an interpretive paradigm, there are a number of methods you can consider to select a non-random sample:

- *Snowball sampling or networking* is associated with interpretivist studies where it is essential to include people with experience of the phenomenon being studied in the sample. For example, supposing you are interested in how people cope with redundancy. Perhaps you are able to find some people who have experienced being made redundant who are willing to take part in your survey. One of the

questions you would ask them would be whether they know of anyone else who has also been through the same experience with whom they could put you in touch. In this way you can extend your sample of participants.
- *Judgemental sampling* is similar to snowball sampling as the participants are selected by the researcher on the strength of their experience of the phenomenon under study. However, in judgmental sampling the researcher makes the decision prior to the commencement of the survey and does not pursue other contacts that may arise during the course of the study.
- *Natural sampling* is fairly common in business research and occurs when the researcher has little influence on the composition of the sample. For example, only particular employees are involved in the phenomenon being investigated or only certain employees are available at the time of the study. It is important to try to avoid the situation where the employer selects the sample on criteria, which are not divulged to you, since it is possible that such a sample will be biased.

It can sometimes be difficult to obtain a sample, particularly if you are dealing with sensitive issues. In addition to the sampling methods we have already identified, Lee (1993) suggests a number of other approaches that can be useful:

- *Advertising* can be used in local or national newspapers, or you can visit locations where members of your population are likely to congregate. Lee calls this outcropping. For example, if you wish to find out how people cope with unemployment, you are likely to find a suitable sample of individuals with experience of this by visiting a Job Centre or employment bureau.
- You may find that you already have access to a suitable sample if you have a full or part-time job. For example, Fineman (1983) used his position as a counsellor on a government-sponsored career review programme to study white-collar unemployment. Another approach is to join a club or society that caters for the phenomenon you want to investigate. For example, you might try joining a fitness club in order to meet people who use exercise as a means of controlling stress at work, or an angling club to find a sample of fishermen in order to investigate their views on licensing regulations.
- *Piggybacking* is where you extract your sample from an existing survey or use another survey to obtain your population simultaneously.
- Finally, you can use screening to select a sample. For example, if you were interested in why people purchase a particular product, you would interview a large number of people and screen out for your sample all those who buy the product.

The methods in this section will produce biased samples, for the main reason that a sampling frame cannot be unambiguously identified in advance and therefore a random sample cannot be selected. In a positivist study, you must recognize that this is an important limitation and in all studies you will need to justify your sample selection method in your methodology chapter. There are some ethical dilemmas concerned with some sampling methods we have described in this section that you need to recognize, in addition to issues concerning your personal safety (see Chapter 3).

13.8 Conclusions

In this chapter, we have investigated the ways in which you can collect original data to supplement the secondary data you have collected, and will continue to collect, from searching the literature. We have examined how you can classify your variables according to their level of measurement and how to identify them according to their role in your analysis. We have examined the main methods of collecting data for statistical analysis and you should now be in a position to make an informed choice. It is important to remember that you can use more than one method, and some methods associated with a particular paradigm can be adapted for use under either paradigm.

In Chapter 8, we drew attention to the importance of using rigorous methods for recording research data that also provide evidence of the source. If the participant is not providing written responses, you will need to jot down the main points in a notebook. This necessarily means leaving out items and all the details, which can lead to distortions, errors and bias. Even shorthand writers sometimes have a problem in deciphering their notes afterwards an you need to be aware that relying on your notes will be inadequate. Audio and/or video recording overcomes these problems and leaves you free to concentrate on taking notes of other aspects, such as attitude, behaviour and body language, if these are relevant to your understanding of the phenomena under study. A specific recording device can be used or the facilities on your telephone or laptop. The important thing o remember is that you need to obtain the participant's agreement to being recorded

The overall design of questionnaires and how they can be distributed offers a number of choices. This is a so true of the way in which questions can be designed under a positivist paradigm, including the use of hypothetical constructs to measure abstract ideas. We have discussed these matters and explained how questions in questionnaires and other data record sheets can be pre-coded for subsequent statistical analysis. The final topic covered in this chapter is the important matter of selecting a sample. Under a positivist paradigm, this can be the whole population or a random sample of sufficient size to represent the population and allow you to address your research questions.

Activities

1. You are interested in environmental issues. Discuss the advantages and disadvantages of collecting secondary data, such as the newspaper or television news coverage, compared with primary data.
2. General lecture questionnaire

    Think about the last lecture you attended and complete the General Lecture Questionnaire on the next page. This is just an exercise and you won't be asked to identify the lecture or the lecturer or reveal your ratings. When you've finished, jot down your thoughts on what you like or dislike about the questionnaire from your perspective as a 'respondent'.

3. Now put on your researcher's hat and redesign the general lecture questionnaire and pilot it with two fellow students. Stay with them while they complete it so you can ask them about how useful they found the instructions and how easy they found it to answer the questions. Ask them what they liked and did not like about it.

GENERAL LECTURE QUESTIONNAIRE

The purpose of this questionnaire is to obtain your views and opinions about the lectures you have been given during the course from this lecturer to help him evaluate his teaching.

Please ring the response that you think is the most appropriate to each statement. If you wish to make any comments in addition to those ratings please do so on the back page.

The lecturer	Strongly agree	Agree	Neither agree nor disagree	Disagree	Strongly disagree
1. Encourages student participation in lectures	5	4	3	2	1
2. Allows opportunities for asking questions	5	4	3	2	1
3. Has a good lecture delivery	5	4	3	2	1
4. Has good rapport with students	5	4	3	2	1
5. Is approachable and friendly with students	5	4	3	2	1
6. Is respectful towards students	5	4	3	2	1
7. Is able to reach student level	5	4	3	2	1
8. Enables easy note taking	5	4	3	2	1
9. Provides useful printed notes*	5	4	3	2	1
10. Would help students by providing printed notes	5	4	3	2	1
11. Has a good knowledge of his subject	5	4	3	2	1
12. Maintains student interest during lectures	5	4	3	2	1
13. Gives varied, lively lectures	5	4	3	2	1
14. Is clear and comprehensible in lectures	5	4	3	2	1
15. Gives lectures which are too fast to take in	5	4	3	2	1
16. Gives audible lectures	5	4	3	2	1
17. Gives structured, organized lectures	5	4	3	2	1
18. Appears to be enthusiastic for his subject	5	4	3	2	1

*Please answer if applicable
Source: Anon.

---

4. Design a one-page, self-completion questionnaire to find out what brand of toothpaste people normally buy and their reasons. If you did this activity in Chapter 5, you may want to make some improvements with the new knowledge you have gained from studying this chapter. It is likely that your first question will list various brands of toothpaste and ask the respondent to indicate the one he or she normally uses. Base your subsequent questions on the information you can extract from the following interview transcript.

INTERVIEWER: Why did you buy the brand of toothpaste you are using at present?

RESPONDENT: Well, my wife and I usually get the one that's on special offer. It's not that money is tight – that's what she chooses to do. So we tend to get the one where there's money off, 25% extra free, two for the price of one, and so on. But last week the brand on special offer was a new one – we hadn't seen it before. It's really good because it has a strong minty taste. I don't like the ones with fancy fruit flavours. This new one's good – I like it a lot. [Pause] What's it called, now? I can't remember the name of it at the moment. [Pause] That's funny because I clean my teeth at least twice a day, so I see the tube often enough! Anyway, my wife likes it too and I think we'll buy it again, even if it's not discounted when we need to buy the next tube. When you get to my age it is important to look after your teeth, you know!

- Number each question and pre-code your variables (apart from any open questions).
- Make a note of whether the level of measurement of each variable is nominal, ordinal, interval or ratio.
- Identify your dependent variable and independent variables.

5. Pilot your toothpaste questionnaire with two fellow students as your respondents. Stay with them while they complete it, so you can ask them about how useful they found the instructions and how easy they found it to answer the questions. Ask them what they liked and did not like about it

PROGRESS TEST

Complete the following sentences:

1. A_____variable is measured on a mathematical scale with equal intervals and a fixed zero point.
2. An_____variable is measured on a mathematical scale with equal intervals and an arbitrary zero point.
3. An_____variable is measured using numerical codes to identify order or rank.
4. A_____variable is measured using numerical codes to identify named categories.
5. A method for collecting data based on the participant's recollections of key facts about an activity or event is known as_____.

Are the following statements true or false?

6. A standard set of predetermined questions is used in a structured interview.
7. Interviewer bias occurs when the participant does not know the answer to a question.
8. A random sample includes every member of a population.

9. A low response rate may lead to a biased sample.
10. Validity is concerned with whether another researcher can obtain the same results.

Multiple choice questions:

11. A closed question is one where:
    a) the respondent chooses from a list of answers prepared in advance
    b) the researcher has piloted the questions in advance
    c) the question only applies to some of the respondents in the sample
    d) more than one question is asked at a time

12. A quantitative variable is measured on:
    a) a continuous scale
    b) an interval scale
    c) a ratio scale
    d) any of the above

13. A categorical variable is measured on:
    a) a continuous scale
    b) a discrete scale
    c) a nominal scale
    d) a ratio scale

14. A dummy variable is measured on:
    a) a categorical scale
    b) a discrete scale
    c) a nominal scale
    d) any of the above

15. A hypothetical construct is measured on:
    a) an interval scale
    b) an ordinal scale
    c) a nominal scale
    d) a ratio scale

References

Alexander, D. (2006) 'The devil with Dawkins', *Times Higher Education*, London: TSL Education, 3 February, p. 20.

Brenner, M. (1985) 'Survey Interviewing' in Brenner, M., Brown, J. and Canter, D. (eds) *The Research Interview: Uses and Approaches*, New York: Academic Press, pp. 9–36.

Clegg, F. G. (1990) *Simple Statistics*, Cambridge: Cambridge University Press. Collis, J. (2003) *Directors' Views on Exemption from the Statutory Audit*, URN 03/1342, London: DTI, October. Available from http://www.berr.gov.uk/files/file25971.pdf.

Coolican, H. (1992) *Research Methods and Statistics in Psychology*, London: Hodder & Stoughton.

Collis, J. (2003) *Directors' Views on Exemption from the Statutory Audit*, URN 03/1342, London: DTI, October. Available from http://www.berr.gov.uk/files/file25971.pdf.

Czaja, R. and Blair, J. (1996) *Designing Surveys: A Guide to Decisions and Procedures*, Thousand Oaks, CA: Pine Forge Press.

Easterby-Smith, M., Thorpe, R. and Lowe, A. (1991) *Management Research: An Introduction*, London: Sage.

Fineman, S. (1983) *White Collar Unemployment: Impact and Stress*, Chichester: Wiley.

Flanagan, J. C. (1954) 'The critical incident technique', *Psychological Bulletin*, 51 (4), July, pp. 327–58.

MacKinlay, T. (1986) *The Development of a Personal Strategy of Management*, M.Sc. thesis, Manchester Polytechnic, Department of Management.

Kervin, J. B. (1992) *Methods for Business Research*, New York: HarperCollins.

Krejcie, R. V. and Morgan, D. W. (1970) 'Determining sample size for research activities', *Educational and Psychological Measurement*, 30, pp. 607–10.

Lee, R. M. (1993) *Doing Research on Sensitive Topics*, London: Sage.

Salkind, N. J. (2006) *Exploring Research*, Upper Saddle River, NJ: Pearson International.

Upton, G. and Cook, I. (2006) *Oxford Dictionary of Statistics*, 2nd edition, Oxford: Oxford University Press.

Wallace, R. S. O. and Mellor, C. J. (1988) 'Non-response bias in mail accounting surveys: A pedagogical note', *British Accounting Review*, 20, pp. 131–9.

Glossary

Categorical variable	A nominal variable measured using numerical codes to identify categories.
Closed question	A question where respondents select the answer from a number of predetermined alternatives.
Confounding variable	A variable that obscures the effects of another.
Continuous variable	A ratio or interval variable measured on a scale where the data can take any value within a given range, such as time or length.
Critical incident technique	A method for collecting data about a defend activity or event based on the participant's recollections of key facts.
Dependent variable (DV)	A variable whose values are influenced by one or more independent variables.
Discrete variable	A ratio or interval variable measured on a scale that can take only one of a range of distinct values, such as number of employees.
Dummy variable	A dichotomous quantitative variable coded 1 if the characteristic is present and 0 if the characteristic is absent.
Hypothetical construct	A rating scale used to measure opinion and other abstract ideas.
Independent variable (IV)	A variable that influences the values of a dependent variable.
Information	The knowledge created by organizing data into a useful form.
Interval variable	A variable measured on a mathematical scale with equal intervals and an arbitrary zero point.
Nominal variable	A variable measured using numerical codes to identify named categories.
Open question	A question where respondents can give a response in their own words.
Ordinal variable	A variable measured using numerical codes to identify order or rank.
Quantitative variable	A ratio, interval or dummy variable.
Questionnaire	A method for collecting primary data in which a sample of respondents are asked a list of carefully structured questionschosen after considerable testing, with a view to eliciting reliable responses.
Random sample	A sample that is representative of the population because every member had an equal chance of being selected.
Rating scale	A hypothetical construct for obtaining ordinal data, such as the Likert scale.
Ratio variable	A variable measured on a mathematical scale with equal intervals and a fixed zero point.

COLLECTING DATA FOR STATISTICAL ANALYSIS

Sampling frame A record of the population from which a sample can be drawn.

Secondary data Data collected from an existing source, such as publications, databases and internal records.

Stratified sample A random sample chosen by selecting an appropriate proportion from each strata of the population.

Systematic sample A random sample chosen by dividing the population by the required sample size (n) and selecting every nth subject.

Tally A simple stroke used to count the frequency of occurrence of a value or category in a variable.

Variable A characteristic of a phenomenon that can be observed or measured.

Appendix: Random number tables

03 47 43 73 86	36 96 47 36 61	46 98 63 71 62	33 26 16 80 45	60 11 14 10 95
97 74 24 67 62	42 81 14 57 20	42 53 32 37 32	27 07 36 07 51	24 51 79 89 73
16 76 62 27 66	56 50 26 17 07	32 90 79 78 53	13 55 38 58 59	88 97 54 14 10
12 56 85 99 26	96 96 68 27 31	05 03 72 93 15	57 12 10 14 21	88 26 49 81 76
55 59 56 35 64	38 54 82 46 22	31 62 43 09 90	06 18 44 32 53	23 83 01 30 30
16 22 77 94 39	49 54 43 54 82	17 37 93 23 78	87 35 20 96 43	84 26 34 91 64
84 42 17 53 31	57 24 55 06 88	77 04 74 47 67	21 76 33 50 25	83 92 12 06 76
63 01 63 78 59	16 95 55 67 19	98 10 50 71 75	12 86 73 58 07	44 39 52 38 79
33 21 12 34 29	78 64 56 07 82	52 42 07 44 38	15 51 00 13 42	99 66 02 79 54
57 60 86 32 44	09 47 27 96 54	49 17 46 09 62	90 52 84 77 27	08 02 73 43 28
18 18 07 92 46	44 17 16 58 09	79 83 86 16 62	06 76 50 03 10	55 23 64 05 05
26 62 38 97 75	84 16 07 44 99	83 11 46 32 24	20 14 85 88 45	10 93 72 88 71
23 42 40 64 74	82 97 77 77 81	07 45 32 14 08	32 98 94 07 72	93 85 79 10 75
52 36 28 19 95	50 92 26 11 97	00 56 76 31 38	80 22 02 53 53	86 60 42 04 53
37 85 94 35 12	83 39 50 08 30	42 34 07 96 88	54 42 06 87 98	35 85 29 48 38
70 29 17 12 13	40 33 20 38 26	13 89 51 03 74	17 76 37 13 04	07 74 21 19 30
56 62 18 37 35	96 83 50 87 75	97 12 25 93 47	70 33 24 03 54	97 77 46 44 80
99 49 57 22 77	88 42 95 45 72	16 64 36 16 00	04 43 18 66 79	94 77 24 21 90
16 08 15 04 72	33 27 14 34 90	45 59 34 68 49	12 72 07 34 45	99 27 72 95 14
31 16 93 32 43	50 27 89 87 19	20 15 37 00 49	52 85 66 60 44	38 68 88 11 80
68 34 30 13 70	55 74 30 77 40	44 22 78 84 26	04 33 46 09 52	68 07 97 06 57
74 57 25 65 76	59 29 97 68 60	71 91 38 67 54	13 58 18 24 76	15 54 55 95 52
27 42 37 86 53	48 55 90 65 72	96 57 69 36 10	96 46 92 42 45	97 60 49 04 91
00 39 68 29 61	66 37 32 20 30	77 84 57 03 29	10 45 65 04 26	11 04 96 67 24
29 94 98 94 24	68 49 69 10 82	53 75 91 93 30	34 25 20 57 27	40 48 73 51 92
16 90 82 66 59	83 62 64 11 12	67 19 00 71 74	60 47 21 29 68	02 02 37 03 31
11 27 94 75 06	06 09 19 74 66	02 94 37 34 02	76 70 90 30 86	38 45 94 30 38
35 24 10 16 20	33 32 51 26 38	79 78 45 04 91	16 92 53 56 16	02 75 50 95 98
38 23 16 86 38	42 38 97 01 50	87 75 66 81 41	40 01 74 91 62	48 51 84 08 32
31 96 25 91 47	96 44 33 49 13	34 86 82 53 91	00 52 43 48 85	27 55 26 89 62
66 67 40 67 14	64 05 71 95 86	11 05 65 09 68	76 83 20 37 90	57 16 00 11 66
14 90 84 45 11	75 73 88 05 90	52 27 41 14 86	22 98 12 22 08	07 52 74 95 80
68 05 51 18 00	33 96 02 75 19	07 60 62 93 55	59 33 82 43 90	49 37 38 44 59
20 46 78 73 90	97 51 40 14 02	04 02 33 31 08	39 54 16 49 36	47 95 93 13 30
64 19 58 97 79	15 06 15 93 20	01 90 10 75 06	40 78 78 89 62	02 67 74 17 33
05 26 93 70 60	22 35 85 15 13	92 03 51 59 77	59 56 78 06 83	52 91 05 70 74
07 97 10 88 23	09 98 42 99 64	61 71 62 99 15	06 51 29 16 93	58 05 77 09 51
68 71 86 85 85	54 87 66 47 54	73 32 08 11 12	44 95 92 63 16	29 56 24 29 48
26 99 61 65 53	58 37 78 80 70	42 10 50 67 42	32 17 55 85 74	94 44 67 16 94
14 65 52 68 75	87 59 36 22 41	26 78 63 06 55	13 08 27 01 50	15 29 39 39 43

Abridged from R. A. Fisher and F. Yate (1953), *Statistical Tables for Biological, Agricultural and Medical Research*, Edinburgh: Oliver and Boyd by permission of the authors and publishers (Longman Group UK Ltd).

PART 5
Data analysis

CHAPTER 14
Analysing qualitative data
Interpreting interview and observational data

KEY QUESTIONS

- How should I prepare my qualitative data for analysis?
- What are the main strategies for analysing qualitative data?
- How can I identify concepts and conceptual frameworks in my data?
- What qualities should I aim for in my analysis?

LEARNING OUTCOMES

At the end of this chapter, you should be able to:
- Decide whether to analyse your qualitative data in a structured or unstructured way
- See if your data analysis is consistent with your research design
- Assess the quality of your data and analysis

CONTENTS

Introduction
14.1 Managing your qualitative data
14.2 Analysing your qualitative data
14.3 Assessing your analysis
Summary
Answers to key questions
References
Additional resources
Key terms
Discussion questions
Workshop

Introduction

> Just as painters need both techniques and vision to bring their novel images to life on canvas, [qualitative] analysts need techniques to help them see beyond the ordinary and to arrive at new understandings of social life. (**Strauss and Corbin**, 1996: 8)

If you have collected all your qualitative data and are sitting in front of a significant pile of transcripts, notes and other documents from your interviews or observations, you are probably wondering: 'What do I do with all of this? Where do I start?' Our advice is actually 'Don't start here!' To analyse qualitative data, you need to analyse your data as you go along, not wait until the end.

Once you start collecting data using a qualitative research design, you will see the major difference between the deductive approach taken in quantitative research and the inductive approach taken in qualitative research. In a qualitative research design, you continually refine your data collection and analysis as you investigate your research problem, opening up new areas and closing off other ones. Your qualitative research design will evolve throughout the research process; a quantitative research design is 'frozen' once your data collection has started.

Because of this evolution and flexibility, you need to approach qualitative research as a creative process that requires your intuition and insight. This is one of the key skills associated with the ethnographer rather than the scientist as a role model. The scientist's creativity comes before and after the data analysis (for which there are strict rules), whilst the ethnographer's creativity is especially important in analysing and interpreting the evidence. This might be new to you, particularly if you come from a technical background where research follows the deductive logic. Although you may find this much less structured than statistical analysis, the procedures you can use for identifying themes in qualitative data are as rigorous, well developed and credible as statistical methods for analysing quantitative data.

This chapter presents the two main approaches to analysing qualitative data, one structured and the other unstructured. Which one you choose will depend on how you collected your data. The four qualitative research designs introduced in **Chapter 7** varied by how involved the researcher was in the research setting and with the research participants. For more detailed guidance, refer to the **Additional resources** at the end of this chapter.

In **Section 14.1**, we deal with some issues you must address before you even start analysing your qualitative data. You must organise your data, decide the general approach you will take – structured or unstructured – and whether you will analyse your data by hand or use specialised computer software.

In **Section 14.2**, we discuss key principles of qualitative analysis. We introduce methods for unstructured data analysis. We begin with Kolb's cycle, which is a general approach to analysing qualitative data. We then discuss principles of coding, concept extraction and framework-building. In **Section 14.3**, we describe the criteria by which you should assess the quality of your analysis.

After you have read this chapter, you should be able to plan how you will analyse your qualitative data. This makes it easier to collect data in a systematic way and analyse them. Since a major advantage of qualitative research design is that it enables you to look for unexpected or counterintuitive patterns in your data, you should make sure you capture as many of these insights as you can. Taking a systematic approach is especially important for an open-ended process such as qualitative analysis.

14.1 Managing your qualitative data

Whether you used one of the quantitative research methods presented in **Chapter 6**, the qualitative research methods presented in **Chapter 7**, or the case study/multi-method designs presented in **Chapter 8** to collect qualitative data, you will end up with data that are quite different from quantitative data. Ultimately you can transform all quantitative data into numbers, which can then be treated the same, no matter what they represent. However, qualitative data have no such common ground.

14.1.1 Managing qualitative data

As we saw in **Chapter 10**, you can easily record quantitative data in a data matrix by hand, in a spreadsheet or a statistical program. You can keep track of and analyse them relatively easily. Managing qualitative data presents more of a challenge because qualitative data:

- *Are not processed or transformed.* You must start your analysis with data in their raw form rather than in processed form. This is a major difference from quantitative research, where you might analyse secondary data from a database where someone has already transformed the raw data into numbers.
- *Take many forms.* Qualitative data include interviews, personal statements, opinions, impressions and recollections, along with documents and other artefacts.
- *Are not standardised.* Each piece of qualitative data will be presented in its own way.
- *Are voluminous.* Because they haven't been transformed or processed, qualitative data cannot be expressed as concisely as quantitative data. It is not unusual for qualitative analysis, for example of the results of a participant observation study, to start with hundreds or even thousands of pages of notes and transcripts.

Before you start analysing your qualitative data, you will need to put them in a form that you can work with. This will be much easier if you have taken a systematic approach to collecting, handling and storing these data.

We start with some simple tips for managing your qualitative data. In working with qualitative data, you must make sure that your data are:

- **Traceable**. You must be able to demonstrate where a particular piece of data came from. Who said (or wrote) it? Which organisation or field setting did it come from? When was it collected? Who collected it? See **Student research in action 14.1** for an example.
- **Reliable**. Your transcripts or other records must faithfully record your discussions or observations. Always write up your notes and impressions within

24 hours – we recommend immediately, if you can. This might even be before you leave the interview site – some researchers have even done this in the toilets for privacy.
- **Complete.** You should keep all your field notes, tapes and transcripts. **Student research in action 14.1** shows how a student did this for a project where she collected data in several different ways and from several different sources.

> ## Student research in action 14.1
> ### HANNAH AND HER CISTERNS
>
> As part of a wine-marketing course, Hannah was investigating how market information gets up the supply chain from the sellers to the wine producers and finally the growers. She arranged to interview people at different stages in the supply process.
>
> Following her interviews, Hannah logged her data sources as shown in Table 14.1. Hannah identified each different data element she collected using a simple system. She used a four-digit code to classify each interview or document according to its source and type. Each code contained information about the category of the organisation, the organisation, the individual who was interviewed and the type of data that were collected. She also kept careful track of the dates of the interviews.
>
> These simple codes helped Hannah keep track of interviews and documents. By organising her data systematically, Hannah made sure that she could trace all her data back to their source. She could easily include the table in her research methods chapter in her project report, so that she could refer to them systematically. Also, since Hannah disguised the firms and individuals before she reported her findings, this table helped her keep track of the disguises she used for her firms.
>
> Finally, during her analysis and reporting, she used these codes to compare the views of participants located in different parts of the supply network.

Table 14.1 Hannah's list of contacts and documents

Place in supply chain	Company	Person interviewed	Date(s) of interview	Code(s)
Retail outlet	A	Store manager	7/12/2001	1-A-1 T (transcript)
		Beverage manager	7/12/2001	1-A-2 N (notes only – recording declined)
	B	Regional manager	14/12/2001	1-B-1 T 1-B-1-D (documents)
Distributor	C	Marketing manager	22/11/2001	2-C-1-T
	D	Category manager	18/12/2001	2-D-1-T
Producer	D	Marketing manager	19/12/2001	3-D-2-T
	E	Brand manager	7/11/2001	3-E-1-T 3-E-1-D
Grower	F	Vineyard owner	12/1/2002	4-F-1-T
		Vineyard manager	12/1/2002	4-F-2-T
	G	Planning manager	25/11/2001	4-G-1-T

Table 14.2 The advantages and disadvantages of using qualitative analysis software

Pros	Cons
Ease of document management – particularly for very large amounts of data	Doesn't do anything that cannot be done by other means
Traceability of concepts ensured	Can result in loss of contextual information
Does allow you to demonstrate your methods and obtain high-quality output	Significant learning curve – takes time to get to be proficient with the software
	Doesn't do the analysis for you
	May deter you from using more effective graphical means
	Requires all data to be entered in the same format – can be highly time-consuming where you have nonstandard data

14.1.2 Software for qualitative analysis

As part of your research design, you should decide early on whether you will analyse your qualitative data by hand, using a word-processing program or a specialised computer program. This will affect not only your analysis, but also how you collect and record your data. If you make this decision early in the research process, you will avoid having to convert your data to a new format before you can analyse it or, more disastrously, having to type it all in at the last minute.

We recommend that you collect and analyse your qualitative data using a simple word-processing program such as Microsoft Word, unless you are collecting a lot of data, working in a team or doing a complex analysis. Even though qualitative research designs usually collect data from a small sample compared with quantitative research designs such as surveys, they result in as much or even more data. As we noted above, you may record or transcribe thousands of words, especially in a long or group project: a doctoral student who takes this approach may often transcribe more than a thousand pages of interviews or observations.

Just as you can use statistical software to manage the complexity of statistical analysis, you can use ethnographic software to manage the complexity of qualitative analysis. You may hear this software generically referred to as **computer-assisted qualitative data analysis software** (CAQDAS). Specialised software such as Ethno-graph, QSR NVivo, and winMAX are all available for the qualitative researcher (see www.scolari.com). Although experienced qualitative researchers have differing opinions about CAQDAS software (Bryman and Bell 2003: 446), you may find it useful if you have the time to spend learning to use it. Professional researchers use this software for the routine mechanical work of coding data and finding all the instances of a particular code so they can concentrate on interpreting the data. As O'Leary (2004: 203) points out, the researcher still needs to 'strategically creatively, and intuitively analyse the data'. Table 14.2 summarises the arguments for and against using CAQDAS software.

14.2 Analysing your qualitative data

compared with quantitative data analysis, where only your interpretation cannot be predicted in your research design, the analysis of qualitative data can be complex and open-ended, so new researchers sometimes find this frustrating. In **Chapter 5**, we characterised the logic underlying quantitative research as deductive and qualitative research as inductive. As we have noted, quantitative research (at least in the abstract) is a more or less linear process. Qualitative research, however, is usually much messier. Research design, data collection and data analysis may overlap; you may even cycle back and forth between them repeatedly. As a result, you may not be able to tell how you will analyse your data until you have collected them. You may not even know what data you will end up collecting.

This has a significant impact on this stage of the research process, because you do not know how much time and energy you will spend analysing your data. This stage may be very time-consuming, but skimping on it will mean that you don't find out anything worthwhile. Worse, if you rush your analysis, even if you do find out something interesting, you may not be able to support your findings.

A fundamental strength of qualitative data analysis is its ability to evolve during the study. We will describe a simple technique – based on Kolb's learning cycle – and a more complicated technique – concept extraction – for this.

14.2.1 Using Kolb's learning cycle for qualitative data analysis

A good model which many researchers use to analyse qualitative data is based on **Kolb's learning cycle** (Kolb, 1985), and is shown in **Figure 14.1**. Kolb's cycle starts with what he terms **concrete experience**. Your concrete experience may be very personal, such as a series of feelings or memories, or research-based, such as transcripts of interviews. Your analysis is based on this concrete experience.

The second stage of **reflective observation** involves three separate activities. The first activity is **familiarisation**, becoming intimately familiar with your data. This is particularly important for group projects or where you are analysing your data after a time lapse. Many researchers believe (re)familiarisation to be key to high-quality qualitative analysis.

The second activity is **spending time with the issues and the data**. You are not specifically looking for anything, but unhurriedly reflecting on what is happening. The final activity is **reordering**, or summarising the data to reflect the patterns you see in the data.

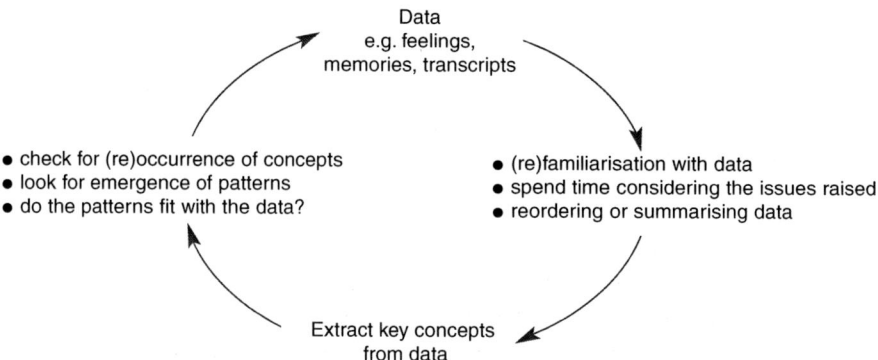

Figure 14.1 Kolb's learning cycle applied to qualitative data analysis

Once you have reordered your data, you should spend some time in **abstract conceptualisation**. This sounds horrendous, but it is actually very simple. You extract concepts (or the key themes) from your data. A **concept** is 'a descriptor for an issue, movement, thought or pattern of words that would be recognisable particularly to the researcher'. A simple example of the identification of what became a very important concept in a piece of research is described in **Student research in action 14.2**.

> *Student research in action 14.2*
>
> **FLUFFY THE VAMPIRE SLAYER**
>
> A student group was interviewing people in a firm about benchmarking. They noticed that they would start talking about benchmarking but become very vague once they had got beyond a simple statement of the word. The students identified this vagueness as 'going fluffy'.
>
> Once they had identified 'going fluffy' as a concept, the students marked the occasions in their transcripts where they thought respondents had 'gone fluffy'. They were then able to relate where this occurred to people's experiences with the benchmarking initiative, and later to its relative success.
>
> By identifying episodes of 'going fluffy' in the transcripts, the students saw that vagueness was associated with low levels of application, and even lower levels of benefits being achieved. They concluded that there were significant pockets within the organisation where knowledge levels were low ('being fluffy') and that if the firm wanted to gain greater success from its initiative, these knowledge deficiencies would have to be addressed.

The final stage of Kolb's learning cycle is **active experimentation** with your data to see where a concept or group of concepts occurs. In this stage, you can see whether any patterns are emerging from your data, or whether your data are starting to fit with theories, models or concepts suggested in the literature. A concept can include actions, so you can analyse actions using Kolb's learning cycle, as illustrated in **Student research in action 14.3**. You will then need to see if these patterns fit with the reality of your data – do they really fit your concrete experience? We will discuss how you can do this in **Section 14.2**.

> *Student research, in action 14.3*
>
> **PLEASE DON'T SQUEEZE THE KIWIS**
>
> A team of students were investigating whether people would purchase fresh vegetables over the internet and what kinds of customers were likely to use internet shopping. They decided to investigate buyer behaviour and spent a considerable amount of time lurking round the vegetable counters of a major supermarket observing and recording the behaviour of different customers. As this was a nonparticipant observation study, they had to unobtrusively record their observations of the movements and actions of shoppers to avoid alerting customers to the fact that they were being watched.

> The students started their data collection by observing how people selected fresh produce. These differences included how the person looked for items (browsers versus list shoppers) and how they then selected the actual produce to buy. They noted the process of produce selection by using a series of symbols (as described in **Chapter 6**) for structured observation. They modified a standard set of symbols to include special activities that emerged from their analysis – specifically 'squeeze', 'sniff or 'tap and listen'.
>
> For each observation they carefully noted the shopper's characteristics. This included whether the shopper was a man or a woman, whether they had a basket or trolley (small or large shopping expedition), their apparent age and their appearance. This provided background information for later analysis.
>
> Once they had observed a sufficient number of shoppers, they examined the sequence of actions by each customer and compared these sequences across the range of shoppers. As part of the abstract conceptualisation stage, they classified shoppers into the following three behaviours:
>
> - *Pickers* – Pick the first thing that they see
> - *Lookers* – Have a perfunctory look to check that it is OK before confirming their selection
> - *Squeezers* – Do a thorough analysis, including one or more of the special activities listed above.
>
> They then tried to see whether each behaviour could be associated with a particular category of customer. Some of the propositions they identified were:
>
> - Older people are more likely be squeezers
> - Younger people are more likely to be pickers.
>
> They tested these propositions by going back to their original data set. They then hypothesized that the main group of prospective purchasers via the internet would be pickers, shoppers who were less discriminating about their vegetables. These would most likely be younger shoppers (under 40). Older people, who checked out their vegetables more thoroughly, were less likely to spend their 'grey pound' via the internet, at least on vegetables, since they would not be able to do a thorough analysis.
>
> By examining how people select fresh produce, the students could understand some general principles of shopping behaviours after observing a small sample of buyers in one store. Since the students hadn't started with any particular hypotheses to test, such as 'Older shoppers are less likely to buy vegetables via the internet', they were free to let the findings emerge from the data they collected rather than imposing an interpretation on it (and making it less likely that they would recognize any unexpected or counterintuitive evidence). They might have missed these different behaviours if they had administered a survey and statistically analysed the data. However, they could argue that their findings were equally as generalisable as survey data, since there was nothing special about the store, its location or the customers). As part of their 'areas for further investigation', they suggested that the findings could be further tested through a survey of a wider population.

14.2.2 Unstructured versus structured analysis

As described above, Kolb's cycle is an unstructured approach to finding out the meaning of your qualitative data. In an **unstructured analysis**, you let meanings and themes emerge from your data, rather than you imposing them on the data. You can then look for conceptual frameworks that help you to understand and explain these themes.

Unstructured approach to qualitative analysis

Although an unstructured approach is excellent for maximising the creativity you can bring to interpreting your data and the chances that you may develop some new and unique insights from your evidence, it can create real challenges for student researchers. An unstructured approach takes no account of deadlines – it is done when it is done and not any sooner. This means that it is open-ended, and that you may take weeks, or even months, to do a thorough job of your data analysis and interpretation.

At this point, you can really start to see the differences between a scientific approach, where considerable project time needs to be spent in planning your research before you start collecting data, down to the statistical tests and tables, and the ethnographic approach, where you can start collecting data almost immediately, but the milestones for analysing and interpreting your data are much fuzzier. This is not to say that we recommend a scientific approach, only that you need to take this difference into account when you are planning and doing your research.

Structured analysis of qualitative data

If you are collecting qualitative data, but you have to meet a project deadline, you might want to consider taking a more structured approach to analysing your qualitative data. Instead of trying to induce everything, up to and including your conceptual framework, from your data, you can use concepts and/or conceptual frameworks from the literature to structure your data analysis and interpretation.

In a **structured analysis** of qualitative data, you compare your findings to a conceptual framework you have developed or found in the literature. This will help to guide your analysis and interpretation, but still allow you to identify those aspects of your evidence that differ from what other researchers have previously found.

Some researchers use pre-existing concepts and frameworks to apply even more structure than the comparative method we have just described. That is, they analyse their qualitative data through the lens of a conceptual framework they have already selected. This process is similar to the 'classical' scientific approach, but substitutes thematic analysis for statistical analysis. If you take this approach, you should realise that this is a quantitative approach, but you are using qualitative rather than quantitative data. The steps in the process are similar to the statistical techniques for analysing quantitative data described in **Chapters 6, 10** and **11**.

Since the structured approach is so similar to the analysis of quantitative data, we will not focus on it in this chapter. Instead, the following considers how quantitative techniques can be applied to qualitative data.

Statistical analysis of qualitative data

You should realise that if you are more aligned with a scientific approach there is nothing to prevent you from statistically analysing data you have gathered using a qualitative research method such as participant observation or unstructured interviews. Indeed, quantitative research is often based on quantitative data that started out as qualitative data. We often reduce the complexity of qualitative data, such as attitudes, opinions or behaviours, to numbers by quantification so that we can analyse them more conveniently using the statistical methods described in **Chapters 10** and **11**. You are likely to be familiar with these shortcuts. For example, many questionnaires ask you to quantify an opinion on a scale of 'completely disagree' to 'completely agree', or a behaviour on a scale of 'rarely or never' to 'frequently or always' by circling a number.

You can analyse any qualitative data set – for example the thousand-page interview transcript or notes based on participant observation – in a quantitative way. If you want to analyse your qualitative data statistically, you will need to make sure that you meet the other requirements for quantitative analysis. Qualitative research designs often involve in-depth investigation of a small number of cases. You will have to make sure that you have a large enough sample to analyse statistically. Small sample sizes and other factors may make it difficult for you to use the inferential statistics described in **Chapters 10** and **11**. Since many qualitative research designs do not meet minimum sample sizes, continuous measurements or normal distributions, you may need to use special techniques, known as nonparametric methods.

However, the main objection to analysing qualitative data statistically is not small sample size. The complexity of the conceptual frameworks (theories and models) that people investigate in qualitative research designs means that multivariate thinking (if not statistical techniques) may be useful in developing and evaluating your findings. If you reduce qualitative data to categorical data, you risk losing much of the data's richness and any unique insights. For example, if you classified people as only 'satisfied' or 'dissatisfied', you might miss out on insights from your data that reveal why they were dissatisfied or whether all dissatisfied customers are alike – are there different kinds of dissatisfaction?

Which approach should you take?
Figure 14.2 shows how the unstructured and structured approaches to analysing qualitative data fit with the different research designs discussed in **Chapter 7**, where we classified quantitative research designs by how close the researcher was to the subject of the research. Your approach should match the data you have collected. Where you position your data analysis depends on your research problem and questions, and on the data you have collected. Research questions that ask 'why?' and look for underlying meaning in situations suggest unstructured techniques, whilst research questions such as 'what?' suggest more structured techniques.

In an unstructured approach to analysing your qualitative data, you will not have a predetermined structure, as in structured qualitative or quantitative analysis. As you analyse your data and collect more data, you will change the methods and perhaps even the questions you are asking. You still need to take a systematic approach to managing the analytic process, no matter what technique you decide to use.

14.2.3 Extracting concepts from your data

A more complex technique for identifying concepts and developing or testing conceptual frameworks is **concept extraction**. Concept extraction is often used in analysing structured and unstructured interviews and participant observation. In concept extraction, your concepts emerge from your data, rather than from your literature review. This can be used in either the structured or unstructured approaches described above.

Concept identification
The first step in concept extraction is to identify the key issues, ideas or other meaning units in your data. Many people find this easiest to do manually, by going

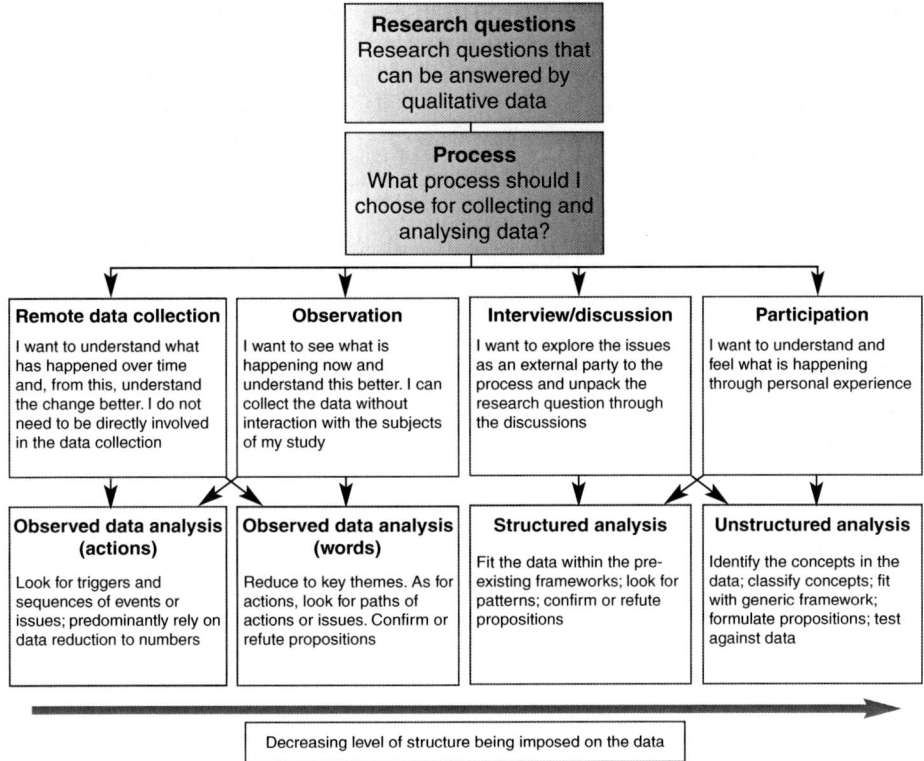

Figure 14.2 Methods for collecting and analysing qualitative data

through a transcript line by line and marking each occurrence of a potential concept. (You can also do this on the computer or using specialised software.) You should try to summarise each concept in a word or a short phrase. You may want to play around with different ways of expressing a concept.

If you have found the concept expressed in different words by different interviewees or sources of data, you may want to call the concepts by slightly different names. This might be easier to see in an example where two interviewees were discussing change in their organisations. They frequently mentioned the measures being applied to the individuals and teams during the interviews, but they focused on different aspects such as those measures that had an impact on pay systems. The researchers identified measures as a concept, but showed the different measures as 'Measures1' and 'Measures2'. You should also note the context in which these issues are being discussed, and any other issues associated with (discussed before or after) them.

Open coding

A systematic process for identifying concepts is **open coding**. Open coding starts with codes that emerge when the researcher highlights the key ideas.

Table 14.3 presents a detailed example of how you can change your raw data – words – into concepts, based on a transcript of an actual interview. The study addressed the research question 'Where do new ideas for changes to new product development

Table 14.3 Transcribed interview

Interviewer's question	Manager's answer	Code/concept
I was just wondering how you find out about other things that are going on in the company?	We used to find out about these things **through colleagues**, and curiously enough it often comes from one particular area of the firm - that of silicon chip design. These chips are at the heart of all our products and are highly complex. The guys working down there tend to generate very quick processes for what they do, and they are then taken up by other parts of the design process, so **they tend to lead the way**.	Internal sources Perceived excellence
So they've got something different going on there? Do they have different pressures on the process that means they have to innovate more quickly?	I think that what is different there is that we do our bit first. They are then under pretty **severe schedule pressure**. It is also a fairly deterministic part of the product in that if you get it right, it stays right.	Time-driven
Is that because it's too expensive to change it?	No, it's because of the nature of the design – it's digital design. Once you've come up with the digital design, you can make a million of them. From the point of view of the rest of the product, there's a lot more to do after you've come up with the design. For some reason, it does generate an immense amount of schedule pressure on those guys up front and as a result of that there is a strong recognition that it is necessary to get the chips right first time, and that's **fundamental to the health of the overall development programme**. So they tend to **invest more in novel techniques** to make it happen right and quickly. They do all sorts of things like they'll think nothing of buying some sort of simulator package that we use that costs say a quarter of a million pounds, to save three weeks on a project. They'll probably only use it for a few weeks, but the **payback is in time, so it's worth it**. To kind of complete that, what happens is that those guys tend to **find out new techniques**, then it kind of **seeps out** if you like. **They start talking about it, you go along, you review it. You think this looks good – I can apply it some way; then you do it yourself**. What does not happen and perhaps ought to happen is we don't get ideas coming from the corporate HQ. They have teams of people studying the product development processes. They then come round and say, '**we've got a great new technique for you**,' and **you don't go to the seminar** because we've discovered in the past that what they've really got is something that invariably you were doing a lot of years ago, because they're actually going round polling all of us and getting the best practices from us; **it doesn't help**.	Critical Investment Time-driven Pull of ideas – chance External push – rejection Evaluation – ineffective
Is there any other help from the corporation?	No – they are just playing at it really. We just have to do it as well as we possibly can.	
Are there any other sources that you use to find new ideas?	Often from **best practice within the corporation** rather than corporate HQ telling you. This is a good way of doing it. Often at the beginning of a programme, you might find yourself, you get this **breathing space when you are planning**, you use this time to go and visit other parts of the corporation that you know are being successful. So you've got the Laser Printer people who have gone and	Pull of ideas – Opportunity available

	seen what the disk people are doing, what techniques they are using and seeing if there is anything here we can use?	
That would be an informal process then?	Yes, it would be up to the **initiative** of the people involved in the new programme. They'd want to go and find out that stuff. For instance, we wouldn't use universities or educational establishments. I can't remember any times when we do.	Individual initiative
Just as a matter of interest, is there any particular reason for that?	**We don't tend to look outside these walls**. Specifically, why we don't go to academia I couldn't tell you, other than whenever something like that happens, often they're not well engaged; you get the impression they've read every book there is but they haven't actually done any of this stuff. There's an element of having to **win your spurs** here.	Internal sources Credibility

processes come from, and how are they implemented?' After some structured questions, the interviewer asked the respondents more open-ended questions about how new ideas came into the department to find out how innovation was being applied to NPD. The table shows how the researcher has highlighted those concepts in the transcript associated with where new product ideas come from.

The researcher has identified the exact words used by the manager with **codes** in the right-hand column that represent concepts. (The term 'coding' is used differently in qualitative analysis, where it is your first step in building theory, whereas in quantitative analysis, it is purely data-recording.) 'Coding' the data this way makes it easier to compare data from interviews from different managers, and starts to create the raw material for the next stage of classification.

Coding starts to translate your respondent's language (here the manager's words) into your own language of concepts. As you can see, people don't speak in concepts, particularly if they are formulating ideas as they speak. In this case, the manager describes what goes on inside his organisation; the researcher translates his words into more abstract codes for concepts that describe the flow of ideas. For example, one code refers to the pull of ideas. Pull is where you go looking for that something; push is where someone from outside your area is telling you to do something. You can identify two examples of the pull of ideas in the transcript in **Table 14.3**.

You will also find that your own questioning may have made perfect sense at the time, but when you read it on the page, it may not be what you intended, or certainly nowhere near as clear – this is a skill that comes with time and reflection on the transcripts. The transcript therefore is a substantially different data source than a report, for instance. You may have some challenges decoding what respondents were talking about before you can do the analysis. Beware here that you don't impose an interpretation – if there is ambiguity, either go back to them to seek clarification or treat this with care.

Bryman and Bell (2003: 435–6) suggest that you:

- Code as soon as possible, preferably as you are going along, to make sense of your data and avoid being swamped at the end

Table 14.4 Organising concepts by themes

Category	Property	Dimension
Source of ideas	Location Mechanism Perception of source	Internal/external Push/pull Excellence/ineffective Credible/not credible
Drivers for ideas	Criticality of process	Time-driven High/low
Idea-searching process	Involvement in searching Type of searching process Instigation	Active/passive Planned/chance Individual/corporate initiative
Implementation	Opportunity	Available/not available

- Read through all your materials before you start coding or interpreting them
- Read through once and generate your basic codes
- Review your codes to see whether you can group codes into common categories
- Start to look for more general theoretical ideas
- Don't worry about generating too many codes, finding a single interpretation of your data or analysing your data.

Classification

Once you have coded your data, you can start to group together the concepts you have identified. Numbering or otherwise identifying your concepts (as in **Table 14.1**) will let you track where your data came from. You may want to write down each code or concept on an index card or Post-it note and group them physically or list them on the computer and start rearranging them. You may see hierarchical patterns in the concepts (concept, subconcept, sub-subconcept and so on).

Table 14.4 shows one possible arrangement of the concepts from **Table 14.3**. As you can see, each significant group of concepts, such as source of ideas, drivers for ideas, search process and so on, defines a **category** representing a real-world phenomenon (Bryman and Bell 2003: 430). A category has **properties**, which are aspects or attributes. Each property has one or more **dimensions**, representing the range of values it can take on, which are derived from your original concepts. For instance, in the transcript, ideas were noted to come from either inside the firm (internal) or outside (external). So, internal and external become the two dimensions of the property 'location'.

Conceptual framework

Once you have developed categories, you can start to develop a conceptual framework and develop propositions about the relationships between concepts, or compare your findings with a pre-existing framework, for example a conceptual framework you have identified in the literature. This provides the input into the next stage of qualitative analysis. **Student research in action 14.4** illustrates how such a framework can emerge as you explore the relationships between concepts.

ANALYSING QUALITATIVE DATA

> *Student research in action 14.4*
>
> **BUDDY, MY BUDDY**
>
> Suzie was considering the role of networks between individuals in knowledge transfer within and between organisations. She focused on the social aspects of knowledge management – she proposed that the more socially active a member of staff was, the more likely he or she was to share knowledge with others. Suzie developed a conceptual framework to show the concepts and relations that she wanted to develop, as shown in **Figure 14.3**.
>
> At the start of her study, Suzie did not know how she would identify socially active employees or measure their behaviour. As she collected and analysed data, she started to see patterns emerge. A concept that consistently emerged during the interviews and observations was the number and duration of non-work-related discussions that took place, either directly or by phone or email. These were often wrapped around discussions of work-related issues. Suzie's analysis suggested that there was a link between nonwork discussions and work-related discussions that was worth investigating further.

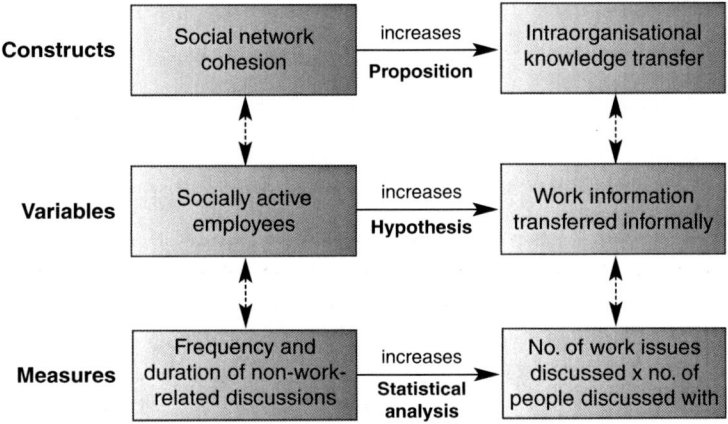

Figure 14.3 A framework for studying individual networks

Axial coding

Strauss and Corbin (1999) present a method for putting the codes back together in a new way once you have completed your open coding, They explain how you can experiment with your codes and categories, so you can test out different scenarios to explain what you think is happening. This approach is helpful if your goal is to build a conceptual model based on your qualitative data.

This process of building up a conceptual model from your open codes and categories is called **axial coding**. Axial coding lets you elaborate each of your data categories in terms of the relationships that may exist between properties and their dimensions. You can use axial coding to figure out what is going in each of these conceptual categories: what it is, when it happens, when it doesn't happen, what are its consequences. Strauss and Corbin suggest that you link your categories to the causal conditions, contexts,

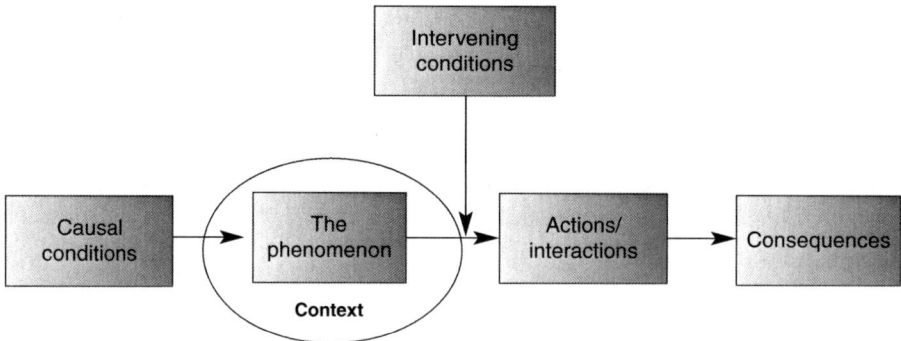

Figure 14.4 Strauss and Corbin's model for axial coding

intervening conditions, actions/interactions and consequences of the phenomenon you are investigating, as shown in **Figure 14.4**.

For example, you might be interested in whether there is any relationship between playing video games frequently and failure in exams. You could use the process of axial coding to examine the conceptual category of video game-playing. The **phenomenon** is the behaviour you are actually studying, whether it is solitary game-playing or group game-playing. You might want to distinguish between high and low levels of game-playing. Is four hours a day a high, moderate or low amount? Does this vary depending on whether it is a school day or a holiday? Finally, you would want to see what consequences game-playing has for study, social activities and so on.

14.2.4 Mapping concepts

Some qualitative researchers find it easier to explore qualitative data using graphical techniques rather than verbal ones such as the axial coding process described above. You could experiment with mind maps, influence diagrams and logic diagrams as ways of identifying patterns in your qualitative data. Mind maps have already been shown in **Chapters 3** and **4** and you might find them useful for graphically displaying and linking the concepts that have emerged from your study.

Influence diagrams

An **influence diagram** not only shows the concepts and whether there are relationships between them, it also shows the proposed cause-and-effect relationships. You can use an influence diagram to show where different forces may be acting in a particular situation (see Coyle 2001). An example influence diagram is shown in **Figure 14.5**.

Logic diagrams

Logic diagrams show the logic or preconditions for an event or set of circumstances to occur. Logic diagrams (see also Schragenheim 1998) provide the ability either to structure the logic of the current situation, or to indicate the necessary conditions for that situation to arise. The example shown in **Figure 14.6** enabled the researcher to determine the root causes of particular phenomena. The basis for the figure is the logic that IF the first condition arises, THEN it will logically lead to those that are indicated by the arrows.

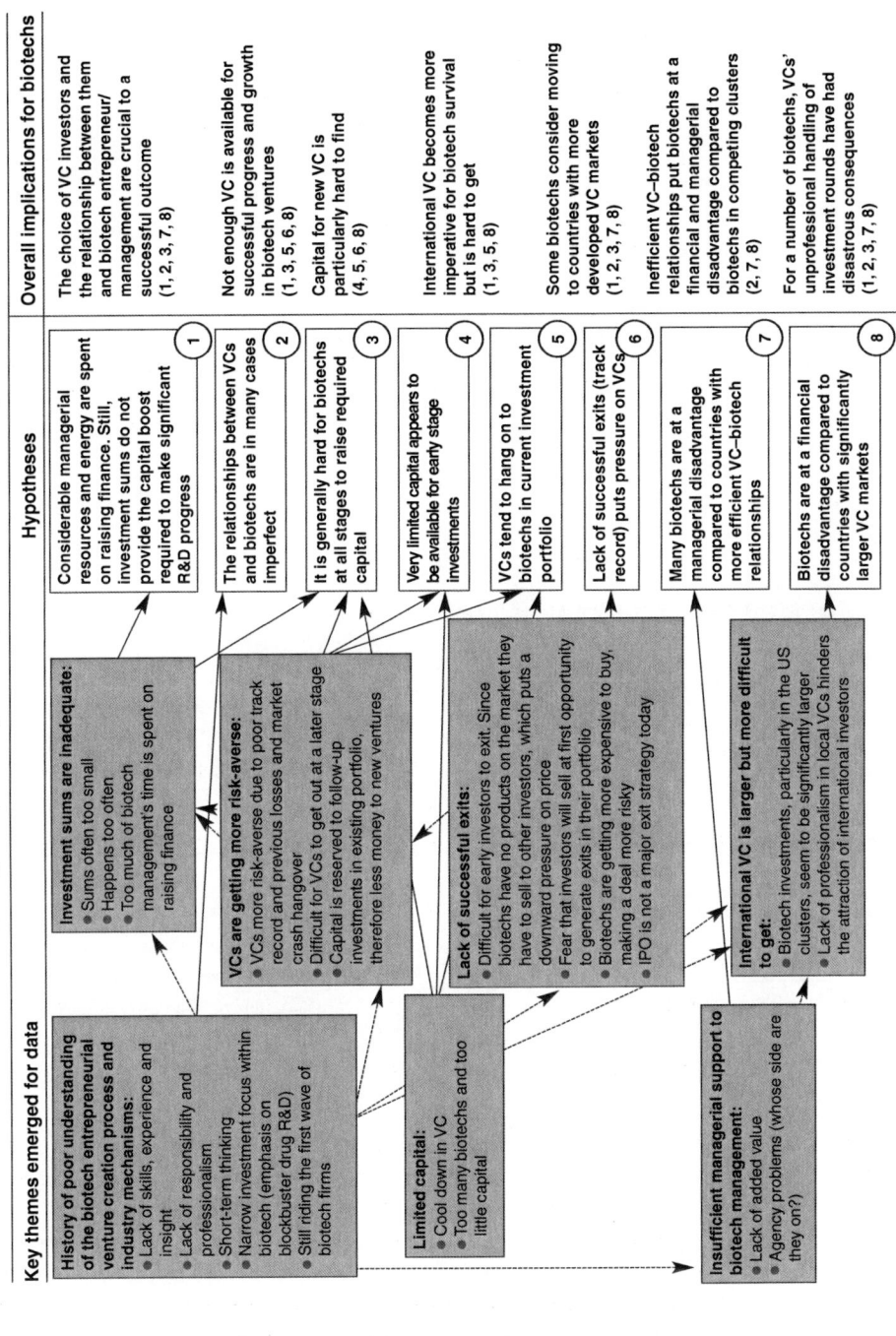

Figure 14.5 An example of an influence diagram

Source: Courtesy of Jes Batting

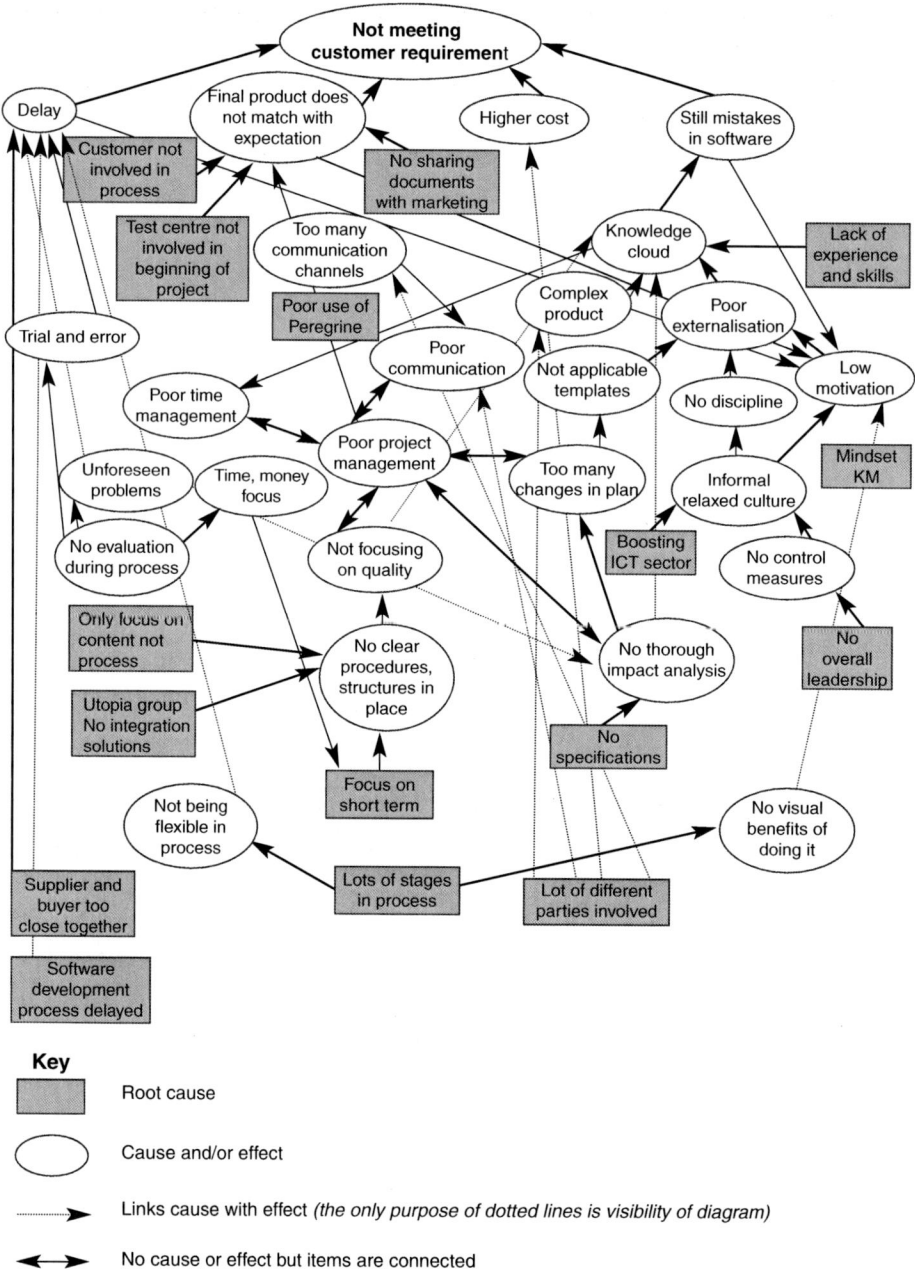

Figure 14.6 An example of a logic diagram

14.2.5 Finishing your analysis

Students frequently ask how they will know when their analysis is complete. Unlike quantitative research designs, where you can determine the sample size required for your statistical data analysis before you start collecting data, in qualitative research designs, it may be difficult to tell when you can stop collecting data and when your analysis is complete. In qualitative research, the term that is often used is **theoretical saturation**. You have reached theoretical saturation when additional data no longer add extra information to your concepts, when you are no longer getting any new insights from coding your data or reviewing your concepts or categories.

You have done enough when you have achieved your goal, which might include:

- *Description.* A better description of a particular phenomenon, the elements that constitute it and its dynamics, for instance how a situation changes over time.
- *Categorisation.* A classification of elements of an issue of interest, for example how people behave or perform particular tasks.
- *Inter-relation.* Establishing relationships between concepts, for instance as described in **Table 14.4**.
- *Explanation.* Explaining a particular action or behaviour by describing what caused it or the circumstances in which it occurred.
- *Prediction.* A better prediction of the circumstances under which some action may work, for example the produce-buying case in **Student research in action 14.3**.

14.3 Assessing your analysis

14.3.1 Assessing the quality of your findings

Figure 14.7 shows the key elements of this assessment and the questions you should ask of your work before, during and after you have analysed your qualitative data. Each element is now discussed in turn.

Is your research **reliable**? Whilst the detailed specification of the conceptual framework and methods of quantitative studies are assumed to lead to higher levels of reliability, qualitative studies – particularly those that are unstructured – would be difficult to repeat exactly. If you were to do a short period of participant observation, it would be unlikely that someone else could go and join the same group

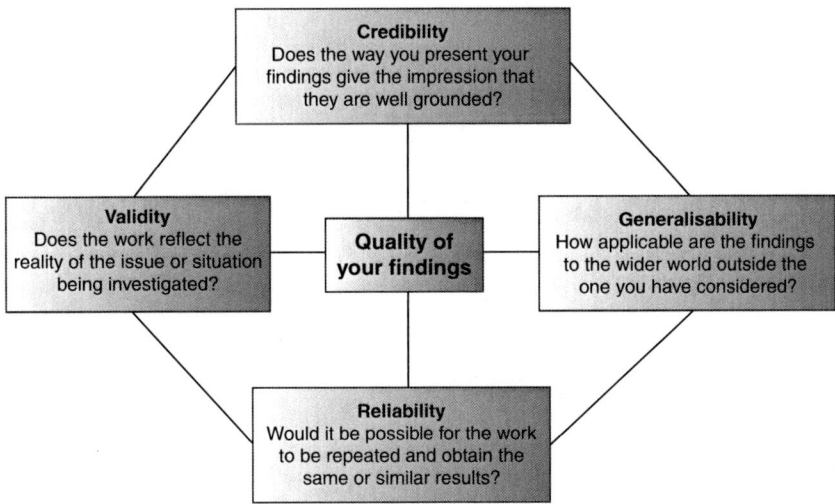

Figure 14.7 A framework for assessing the quality of qualitative research

and achieve exactly the same findings. Situations, people and dynamics change over time, resulting in this being more of a theoretical question – 'if I went back and did this study again, would I get the same results, and if it had been done by someone else, would they have got the same results?' In a qualitative study, it is unlikely that the results would be the same in either case, but the main points and conclusions should be fairly robust rather than fragile. Both of these questions force reflection on your own interaction and influence with the system you are researching.

Is your research **valid**? Validity refers to the extent to which you have captured the underlying truth of the situation and not been misled by particular influences. Student projects can be biased by the views of key individuals – maybe someone who has been closely associated with the project and who may have his/her own agenda to press. Furthermore, there is always the issue of whether you have been *rigorous* in your analysis, or succumbed to a shallow *impressionistic* analysis of your data. Whilst there is ample space in the scope of methods used here to allow you to form impressions from your data, you should be able to demonstrate how you got from there to your findings. Documenting and explaining how you got from your data to your conclusions, using strategies such as those described in this chapter (which are explored in more depth in **Chapter 13**), is one way to show this.

Is your research **generalisable**? This is very difficult to get right. Many projects overstate their findings (this is what we found in this organisation/place and therefore it is true for all organisations/places/the entire world) or understate them (these findings are only true in the situation we investigated and have no relevance anywhere else). In qualitative research, particularly in single case studies, you might think that you have a sample of only one, which makes issues unrepresentative. It is possible to learn from a sample of one (or even fewer) by thinking about areas where the findings of a similar piece of work may be similar, and where its particular circumstances would make it different (for example different competitive/legislative/geographical environment).

Is your research **credible**? This was included by Shipman (1982) and is a vital factor – how you present your findings and your research. It is important that you present evidence to support any contentions made, including key quotations and evidence from numerous sources (see the discussion of triangulation in **Chapter 8**). In analysing your qualitative data, you should identify suitable key pieces of data that can be presented in your report. This is discussed further in **Chapter 13**.

14.3.2 Where to look for more information

In this section, we have only looked at structured and unstructured techniques for analysing qualitative data. However, you will find many different approaches to qualitative data analysis discussed in the research methods literature, including those highlighted by O'Leary (2004: 199–200) and Bryman and Bell (2003):

- *Analytic induction*, a rigorous approach to testing hypotheses from qualitative data
- *Content analysis*, which can be used to identify themes in texts or other materials. Researchers use both qualitative content analysis, where the emphasis is on searching out underlying themes, and quantitative content analysis, where the emphasis is on counting instances of these themes for quantitative analysis

- *Discourse analysis*, which can be used to interpret language in its social and historical context
- *Narrative analysis*, which can be used to interpret the stories told by individuals, which focuses on the patterns people find in their lives over time
- *Conversation analysis*, which can be used to understand the structure of conversations
- *Semiotics*, which can be used to interpret the meaning behind signs and symbols, to show how messages are communicated as systems of cultural meaning
- *Hermeneutics*, which can be used to interpret texts, originally sacred texts such as the Bible, but today applied to both documents and social actions
- *Grounded theory*, which can be used to generate theory directly from data (which we briefly discussed in **Chapter 8** in the context of grounded case studies).

You may want to look at the **Additional resources** at the end of this chapter if any sound interesting. You can find many articles and even entire books written on these approaches.

Summary

This chapter introduces methods for analysing qualitative data. These methods range from highly structured, which are close to quantitative analysis, to highly unstructured, which are not. Which method you should choose depends on how involved you are with the data source, whether you have started with a theoretical framework or expect one to emerge from your analysis, and your research questions.

Many studies start with a conceptual framework, but it is also possible to let the structure emerge, using a grounded theory approach such as that of Strauss and Corbin (1999). You can use various graphical techniques to experiment with your concepts as suggested by Kolb, including mind maps, influence diagrams and logic diagrams, which help you to formulate propositions that can be compared with the data you have collected.

The data analysis process will pass the findings to the discussion and reporting stage of the project in a range of forms. The quality of this outcome is evaluated in terms of reliability, validity, generalisability and credibility. The use of IT support in your process may provide benefits but, for short projects where the volume of data is limited, may take more time to learn how to use than will provide benefit to the project.

Answers to key questions

How should I prepare my qualitative data for analysis?
- Verbal data should be transcribed and put in order, with a reference for eachpiece of data

What are the main strategies for analysing qualitative data?
- Use structured analysis to fit your data into a predetermined framework
- Use unstructured analysis to let your framework emerge

How can I identify concepts and conceptual frameworks in my data?
- Start by coding
- Look for categories
- Elaborate your categories and look for relationships between them

What qualities should I aim for in my analysis?
- Reliability
- Validity
- Generalisability
- Credibility

References

Bryman, Alan and Bell, Emma. 2003. *Business Research Methods.* Oxford: Oxford University Press.
Coyle, R.G. 2001. *Systems Dynamics Modelling: A Practical Approach.* London: Chapman & Hall/CRC.
Kolb, David A. 1985. *Experiential Learning.* Englewood Cliffs, NJ: Pearson.
O'Leary, Zina. 2004. *The Essential Guide to Doing Research.* London: Sage.
Schragenheim, E. 1998. *Management Dilemmas.* Boca Raton, FL: St Lucie Press.
Shipman, M. 1982. *The Limitations of Social Research,* London: Longman.
Strauss, Anselm L. and Corbin, Juliet. 1999. *Basics of Qualitative Research: Grounded Theory Procedures & Techniques,* 2nd edn. Thousand Oaks, CA: Sage.

Additional resources

Bryman, Alan and Burgess, R.G. (eds) 1994. *Analysing Qualitative Data.* London: Routledge.
Buzan, A. 2000. *The Mind Map Book.* London: BBC Books.
Cameron, S. 2001. *The MBA Handbook.* Harlow: Financial Times/Prentice Hall.
Denzin, Norman. 1970. *The Research Act: A Theoretical Introduction to Sociological Methods.* Chicago: Aldine.
Denzin, Norman and Lincoln, Y. 1994. *Handbook of Qualitative Research.* Thousand Oaks, CA: Sage.
Dubin, Robert. 1978. *Theory Building: A Practical Guide to the Construction and Testing of Theoretical Models,* 2nd edn. New York: Free Press.
Gahan, Celia and Hannibal, Mike. 1998. *Doing Qualitative Research Using QSR Nud*IST.* London: Sage (Nud*IST is now renamed QSR NVivo).
Gibbs, Graham R. 2002. *Qualitative Data Analysis: Explorations with NVivo.* Maidenhead: Open University Press.
Glaser, Barney G. and Strauss, Anselm L. 1967. *The Discovery of Grounded Theory: Strategies of Qualitative Research.* London: Wiedenfeld & Nicholson.
Guba, E. 1985. The context of emergent paradigm research. In Lincoln, Y. (ed.) *Organizational Theory and Inquiry: The Paradigm Revolution.* Thousand Oaks, CA: Sage.
Gummesson, Evert. 2000. *Qualitative Methods in Management Research,* 2nd edn. Thousand Oaks, CA: Sage.
Kolb, D.A., Rubin, I.M. and MacIntyre, J.M. 1984. *Organisational Psychology.* Harlow: Prentice Hall.
Reason, Peter and Bradbury, Hilary. (eds) 2000. *Handbook of Action Research.* London: Sage.
Symon, Gillian and Cassell, Catherine. (eds) 1998. *Qualitative Methods and Analysis in Organisational Research.* London: Sage.

Web resources

QSR International: http://www.qsr-software.com/

Scolari: Sage Publications Software. Resources for qualitative analysis software: (http://www.scolari.co.uk/).

Key terms

abstract conceptualisation, 383
active experimentation, 383
axial coding, 391
category, 390
codes, 389
complete, 380
computer-assisted qualitative data analysis software, 381
concept, 383
concept extraction, 386
concrete experience, 382
credible, 396
dimensions, 390
familiarisation, 382
generalisable, 396
influence diagram, 392
Kolb's learning cycle, 382
logic diagrams, 392
open coding, 387
phenomenon, 392
properties, 390
reflective observation, 382
reliable, 379
reordering, 382
spending time with the issues and the data, 382
structured analysis, 385
theoretical saturation, 395
traceable, 379
unstructured analysis, 384
valid, 396

Discussion questions

1. How is qualitative analysis different from quantitative analysis?
2. What techniques for analysis are usually associated with which research methods?
3. Why should you try to capture data as close to the source as possible, for instance by recording all notes within a short time of an interview?
4. What is the role of a learning cycle approach in analysing data?
5. What is coding?
6. What research philosophy might be associated with structured data analysis?
7. Do codes exist in the data or should you impose them?
8. What is the difference between a construct, a variable and a measure?
9. What is the end point of qualitative analysis?
10. How would you assess the quality of the research you have carried out and that reported (for example in journals) by others?

Workshop

Background

In previous workshops you have conducted interviews on the subject of the changes that people go through when they move into higher education.

Task

1. If you did not record the interviews in Workshop 7, in pairs, conduct an interview on the subject of the changes that each other has experienced in their move into higher education. Each interview should last no more than 10 minutes. Use this time to explore any particular issues that the interviewees found challenging and what it was that made the issue challenging or important to them. Record the interviews, if at all

possible (computers, some mobile phones, i-Pods and other devices can be used for recording purposes, if you do not have a tape recorder handy).

2. Relisten to the interview and transcribe the most important two minutes (this is not a general practice, but is used here for pragmatic purposes).

3. Use the coding procedures shown in Table 14.3 to identify the key concepts that emerged from the interviews.

4. How would further data (interviews) help here?

5. If you had many more interviews (say 100), how would you handle the data? Describe a process for storing, retrieving and analysing such a large volume of data.

CHAPTER 15
Analysing data using descriptive statistics

> **LEARNING OBJECTIVES**
>
> When you have studied this chapter, you should be able to:
> - differentiate between descriptive statistics and inferential statistics
> - enter data into *SPSS*, recode variables and create new variables
> - generate frequency tables, charts and other diagrams
> - generate measures of central tendency and dispersion
> - generate measures of normality.

15.1 Introduction

If you have adopted a *positivist paradigm,* you will have collected quantitative data and you will need to quantify any qualitative research data. If your knowledge of statistics is somewhat rusty, you should find this chapter useful as it contains key formulae for some of the basic techniques, together with step-by-step instructions and worked examples. However, you may prefer to enter your data into a software program, such as *Excel, Minitab* or *SPSS.* In this chapter, we introduce you to *SPSS for Windows,*[1] which is widely used in business research because it can process large amounts of data.

SPSS provides a data file where data can be stored, which is similar to a spreadsheet. Once the data have been entered or imported into *SPSS*, frequency tables, charts, cross-tabulations and a range of statistical tests can be performed quickly and accurately. The resulting output can then be pasted into your dissertation or thesis. Whether you decide to calculate the statistics yourself or use software, you will need to determine which statistics are appropriate for the data you have collected and how to interpret the results. This chapter and the next will give you guidance.

[1] *SPSS* is an abbreviation for Statistical Product and Service Solutions (formerly Statistical Package for the Social Sciences).

15.2 Statistics

The term *statistics* refers to the body of methods and theory that is applied to quantitative data. 'A statistic is a number that describes a sample' (Moore, McCabe, Duckworth and Alwan, 2009, p. 210).[2] For example, you could calculate the mean number of employees in a sample of companies to describe the average size of the sample. A statistic can be used to estimate an unknown *parameter*, which is a number that describes a population. Thus, if you had a random sample that was a representative of the population, you could use the sample mean to estimate the average number of employees in the population of companies. A random sample is representative subset of the population where observations are made and a population includes the totality of observations that might be made (as in a census). A statistic 'enables us to recognize and evaluate the errors involved in quantifying our experience, especially when generalizing from what is known of some small group (a sample) to some wider group (the population)' (Rowntree, 1991, p. 186).

Key definitions

A **parameter** is a number that describes a population.
A **statistic** is a number that describes a sample.
Statistics is a body of methods and theory that is applied to quantitative data.

Research data can be *secondary data* (for example a survey of a sample of annual reports using content analysis), *primary data* (for example a survey of a sample of companies using questionnaires) or both. In addition to quantitative data, you may have collected some qualitative data (for example themes you have identified in the narrative sections of the annual reports or categories you have identified from responses to open questions in the questionnaire survey). You can see from the definition of statistics that statistical methods can only be applied to quantitative data, so you will need to quantify any qualitative data beforehand. You can do this by identifying each nominal variable and recording the frequency of occurrence of each category it contains. You will remember that we recommended using *tallies* to aid the counting of frequencies.

Key definitions

Descriptive statistics are a group of statistical methods used to summarize, describe or display quantitative data.

Statisticians commonly draw a distinction between *descriptive statistics* and *inferential statistics*. Descriptive statistics are used to summarize the data in a more compact form and can be presented in tables, charts and other graphical forms. This allows patterns to be discerned that are not apparent in the raw data and 'positively aids subsequent hypothesis detection/confirmation' (Lovie, 1986, p. 165). Inferential statistics are 'statistical tests that lead to conclusions about a target population based on a random sample and the concept of sampling distribution' (Kervin, 1992, p. 727).

[2] The term *statistic* was introduced by Sir Ronald Fisher in 1922 (Upton and Cook, 2006).

In an undergraduate dissertation, the research may be designed as a small, descriptive study. Therefore, the use of descriptive statistics to explore the data from individual variables (hence the term *univariate analysis*) may be sufficient to address the research questions. However, at postgraduate level, you are likely to design an analytical study. Therefore, you are more likely to use descriptive statistics at the exploratory stage and then go on to use inferential statistics (or other techniques) in a bivariate and/or multivariate analysis. We will examine the statistics used in *bivariate analysis* (two variables) and *multivariate analysis* (more than two variables) in the next chapter.

Key definitions

Inferential statistics are a group of statistical methods and models used to draw conclusions about a population from quantitative data relating to a random sample.

15.3 Getting started with *SPSS*

15.3.1 The research data

We are going to use real business data collected for a postal questionnaire survey of the directors of small private companies. You have already seen some of the questions asked, as they were used as examples in the previous chapter. The companies were selected on the basis that they were likely to qualify for exemption from the statutory requirement to have their accounts audited. Do not worry if you know nothing about this topic, as no prior knowledge is required. The Collis Report (2003) was commissioned by the government as part of the consultation on raising the turnover threshold for audit exemption in UK company law from £1 million to £4.8 million, which would extend this regulatory relaxation to a greater number of small companies. The literature showed that although some of the companies that already qualified for audit exemption made use of it, others apparently chose to continue having their accounts audited. This led to the following research question: What are the factors that have a significant influence on the directors' decision to have a voluntary audit?

Very briefly, the theoretical framework for the study was that the emphasis on turnover in company law at that time implied a relationship between size and whether the cost of audit exceeded the benefits. Agency theory (Jenson and Meckling, 1976) suggests that audit would be required where there was information asymmetry between 'agent' and 'principal' (for example the directors managing the company and external owners, or between the directors and the company's lenders and creditors).

Based on this framework, a number of *hypotheses* were formulated. Each hypothesis is a statement about a relationship between two variables and starts with the Latin phrase *ceteris paribus,* which means 'all things being equal'. The *null hypothesis* (H_0) states that the two variables are independent of one another (there is no relationship) and the *alternative hypothesis* (H_1) states that the two variables are associated with one another (there is a relationship). Using inferential statistics, the hypotheses are tested against the empirical data and the alternative hypothesis is accepted if there is statistically significant evidence to reject the null hypothesis (in other words, the null hypothesis is the default). Here is the first hypothesis in the null and the alternative form:

- H_0 *Ceteris paribus,* the likelihood of the directors choosing a voluntary audit does not increase with company size, as measured by turnover.
- H_1 *Ceteris paribus,* the likelihood of the directors choosing a voluntary audit increases with company size as measured by turnover.

Box 15.1 lists the nine hypotheses tested in the null form. You should check with your supervisor which form is acceptable.

The sampling frame used was FAME. This is a database containing data from the annual report and accounts of 2.8 million companies in the UK and Ireland. At any one moment in time, some of these companies are dormant, some are in the process of liquidation, some have not yet registered their accounts for the latest year and some do not qualify for audit exemption on the grounds of the public interest (for example listed companies and those in the financial services sector). A search of the

---

Box 15.1   Hypotheses to be tested

H1 *Ceteris paribus,* the likelihood of the directors choosing a voluntary audit does not increase with company size, as measured by turnover.

H2 *Ceteris paribus,* the likelihood of the directors choosing a voluntary audit does not increase with perceptions that the audit provides a check on accounting records and systems.

H3 *Ceteris paribus,* the likelihood of the directors choosing a voluntary audit does not increase with perceptions that the audit improves the quality of the financial information.

H4 *Ceteris paribus,* the likelihood of the directors choosing a voluntary audit does not increase with perceptions that the audit improves the credibility of the financial information.

H5 *Ceteris paribus,* the likelihood of the directors choosing a voluntary audit does not increase with perceptions that the audit has a positive effect on the company's credit score.

H6 *Ceteris paribus,* the likelihood of the directors choosing a voluntary audit does not increase if the company is not family owned.

H7 *Ceteris paribus,* the likelihood of the directors choosing a voluntary audit does not increase if there are shareholders without access to internal financial information.

H8 *Ceteris paribus,* the likelihood of the directors choosing a voluntary audit does not increase if the statutory accounts are given to the bank and other providers of finance.

H9 *Ceteris paribus,* the likelihood of the directors choosing a voluntary audit does not increase if they have a degree, a professional/vocational qualification or have studied/trained in business or management subjects.

database identified a population of 2,633 active companies within the scope of the study (likely to qualify for audit exemption if the turnover threshold were raised), and which had registered their accounts for 2002. The questionnaire was sent to the principal director of each company with an accompanying letter explaining the purpose of the research and that it had been commissioned by the Department for Trade and Industry which was subsequently restructured as the Department for Business, Enterprise and Regulatory Reform. After one reminder, 790 completed questionnaires were received, giving a response rate of 30%. This unexpectedly high rate was undoubtedly due to the use of the government logo on the questionnaire, since response rates from small businesses are usually considerably lower.

We are going to use this survey data to illustrate some of the key features of *SPSS*. The identity of the respondents will not be revealed as they were assured anonymity. This was achieved through the use of a unique reference number (URN) known only to the researcher. Box 15.2 shows the responses given by respondent 42.

15.3.2 Labelling variables and entering the data

Our illustrations are based on *SPSS 16.0*. You run the program in the same way as any other software. For example, *start* ⇒ **All Programs** ⇒ **SPSS16** (or whatever version is available to you). If your programs are on a local area network, *SPSS* may be located within a folder for mathematical and statistics packages. The program usually opens with a screen inviting you to choose what you would like to do. Select **Type in data** and *SPSS* Data Editor will then open a new data file in **Data View** (see Figure 15.1), in which each row of cells represents a different case (for example a respondent to a questionnaire survey) and each column represents a different variable. If you are using secondary research data that you have exported to an *Excel* spreadsheet, you can simply copy and paste it into *SPSS* Data Editor.

Now switch from **Data View** to **Variable View** by clicking on the tab at the bottom left of the screen and you can start naming and labelling your variables:

- Under **Name**, type a short word to identify the variable. In this survey, each respondent was given a unique reference number (URN) so that primary data from the questionnaire survey could be matched to secondary data from FAME. Therefore, you might decide to type URN as the name for the first variable. The second variable relates to the first question, so you might want to name it Q1. You will find that *SPSS* prevents you from using a number as the first character or any spaces. Initially you will find this a quick and easy way to name your variables.
- Under **Decimals**, amend the default to reflect the number of decimal places in the data for that variable. For example, for Q1 you will select 0 decimal places, whereas for turnover you will need to select 3 decimal places.
- Under **Labels**, type a word or two that adds information to the name of the variable. For example, **Family ownership** for **Q1**; **Total owners** for **Q2a**; **With internal info** for **Q2b**; **Without internal info** for **Q2c**. For **Q4**, you might decide to use a key word, such as **Check** for **Q4a**; **Quality** for **Q4b**; **Credibility** for **Q4c**; **Credit score** for **Q4d**.
- Under **Values**, enter the codes and what they signify. For example, in **Q4**, 1 = **Disagree** and 5 = **Agree** (once you have entered this information, you can copy

Box 15.2 Questionnaire completed by respondent 42

URN 42

1. Is the company a family-owned business? (*Tick one box only*)
- Wholly family-owned (or only 1 owner) ☒ (1)
- Partly family-owned ☐ (2)
- None of the shareholders are related ☐ (0)

2. How many shareholders (owners) does the company have?
- (a) Total number of shareholders [2]
  Breakdown:
- (b) Number of shareholders with access to internal financial information [2]
- (c) Number of shareholders <u>without</u> access to internal financial information [0]

3. Would you have the accounts audited if not legally required to do so? (*Tick one box only*)
- Yes, the accounts are already audited voluntarily ☐ (1)
- Yes, the accounts would be audited voluntarily ☐ (2)
- No ☒ (0)

Please give reasons for either answer

....
....

4. What are your views on the following statements regarding the audit? (*Circle number closest to your view*)

	Agree				Disagree
(a) Provides a check on accounting records and systems	5	4	③	2	1
(b) Improves the quality of the financial information	5	4	3	②	①
(c) Improves the credibility of the financial information	5	4	3	②	1
(d) Has a positive effect on company's credit rating score	5	4	3	②	1

5. Apart from Companies House, who normally receives a copy of the company's statutory accounts? (*Tick as many boxes as apply*)
- (a) Shareholders ☒
- (b) Bank and other providers of finance ☐

(*Other variables omitted in this example*)

6. Do you have any of the following qualifications/training? (*Tick as many boxes as apply*)
- (a) Undergraduate or postgraduate degree ☐
- (b) Professional/vocational qualification ☐
- (c) Study/training in business/management subjects ☐

Turnover data taken from 2002 accounts on FAME: £74,411k

Source: Adapted from Collis (2003).

ANALYSING DATA USING DESCRIPTIVE STATISTICS

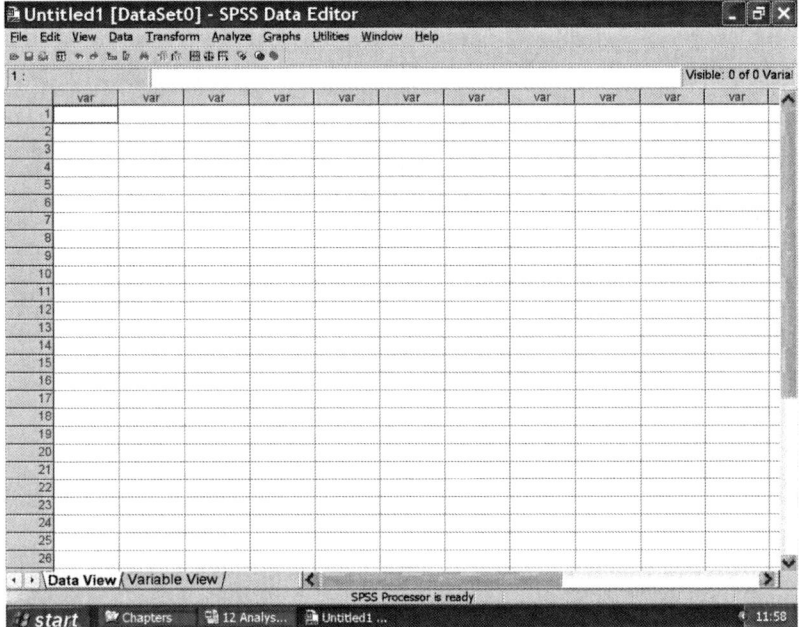

Figure 15.1 *SPSS* Data Editor

and paste it to other variables using the same codes); for **Q6, 1 = Yes** and **0 = Otherwise**. Turnover does not need any codes entered because it is a ratio variable.

- *SPSS* provides a default measure for missing data (or no response), so unless you have a particular reason to enter a code for a non-response, move on to **Measurement**. *SPSS* gives you a choice of **Scale** (use for *ratio* or *interval* variables) **Ordinal** or **Nominal**. If you need to jog your memory to make these decisions, refer to Chapter 10, section 10.3.1).

At this point, save the file (**File, Save As**) and name it **Data for URN 42.sav** (Figure 15.2 shows the screen at this stage in the process).

Next return to **Data View** and enter the data values (the observations) for respondent 42, including the data for turnover, which for the convenience of this exercise is shown as a note at the end of the questionnaire. If you place your cursor over the name of a variable, *SPSS* will reveal the label you added in **Variable View**. For example, Figure 15.3 shows that by placing the cursor on the variable **Q4a**, the label **Check** is displayed, which was used to remind us that this variable relates to the role of the audit as a check on accounting records and systems. This is a very useful feature that helps ensure you enter the data in the appropriate column.

15.3.3 Recoding variables

In the previous chapter, we mentioned situations where you might have collected data in a particular form for one purpose, but want to recode it into a different variable in a new, simpler form called a *dummy variable*. This is a dichotomous variable containing only two categories, where 1 = the characteristic is present and 0 = the

	Name	Type	Width	Decimals	Label	Values	Missing	Columns	Align	Measure
1	URN	Numeric	4	0		None	None	5	Right	Nominal
2	Q1	Numeric	6	0	Family owners	{0, Not related	None	5	Right	Nominal
3	Q2a	Numeric	6	0	Total owners	None	None	5	Right	Scale
4	Q2b	Numeric	6	0	With internal in	None	None	5	Right	Scale
5	Q2c	Numeric	6	0	Without intern	None	None	5	Right	Scale
6	Family	Numeric	5	0	Q1	{0, Otherwise}	None	8	Right	Nominal
7	Q3	Numeric	6	0	Future decisio	{0, No}...	None	5	Right	Nominal
8	Q4a	Numeric	6	0	Check	{1, Disagree}...	None	5	Right	Ordinal
9	Q4b	Numeric	6	0	Quality	{1, Disagree}...	None	5	Right	Ordinal
10	Q4c	Numeric	6	0	Credibility	{1, Disagree}...	None	5	Right	Ordinal
11	Q4d	Numeric	6	0	Credit score	{1, Not import	None	5	Right	Ordinal
12	Q5a	Numeric	6	0	Shareholders	{0, Otherwise}	None	5	Right	Nominal
13	Q5b	Numeric	6	0	Bank	{0, Otherwise}	None	5	Right	Nominal
14	Q6a	Numeric	6	0	Degree	{0, Otherwise}	None	5	Right	Nominal
15	Q6b	Numeric	6	0	Prof/voc qualif	{0, Otherwise}	None	5	Right	Nominal
16	Q6c	Numeric	6	0	Studied bus/m	{0, Otherwise}	None	5	Right	Nominal
17	Turnover	Numeric	11	3	£k	None	None	8	Right	Scale

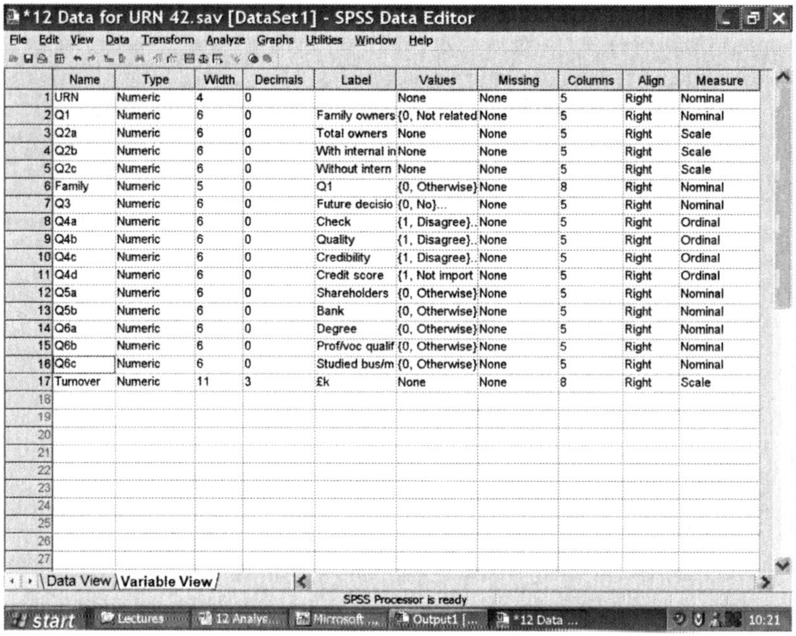

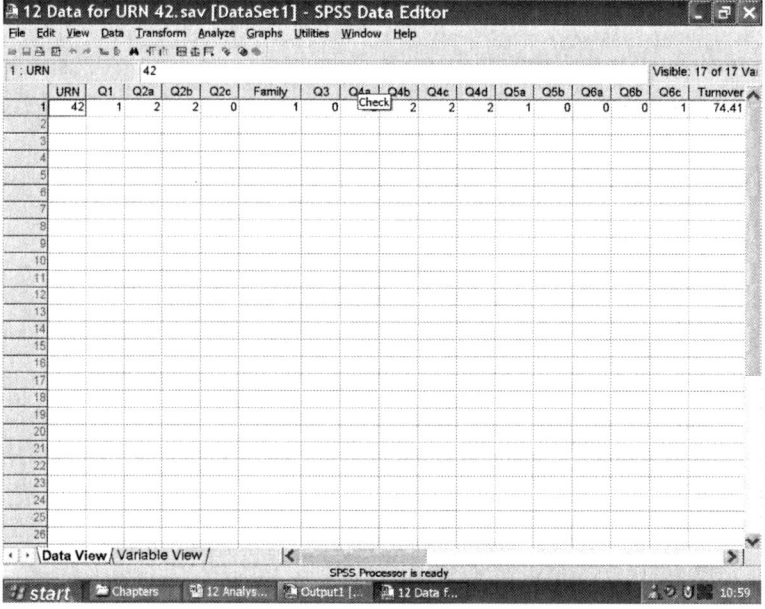

Figure 15.2 Variable view of data for URN 42.sav

	URN	Q1	Q2a	Q2b	Q2c	Family	Q3	Q4a	Q4b	Q4c	Q4d	Q5a	Q5b	Q6a	Q6b	Q6c	Turnover
1	42	1	2	2	0	1	0		2	2	2	1	0	0	0	1	74.41

Figure 15.3 Data view of data for URN 42.sav

characteristic is absent. It is important to keep the original variable in case you need the more detailed and precise information for another purpose. We will illustrate how to recode a variable with Q1, which collected data about the extent to which the company is family-owned. We are going to recode it into a new variable called

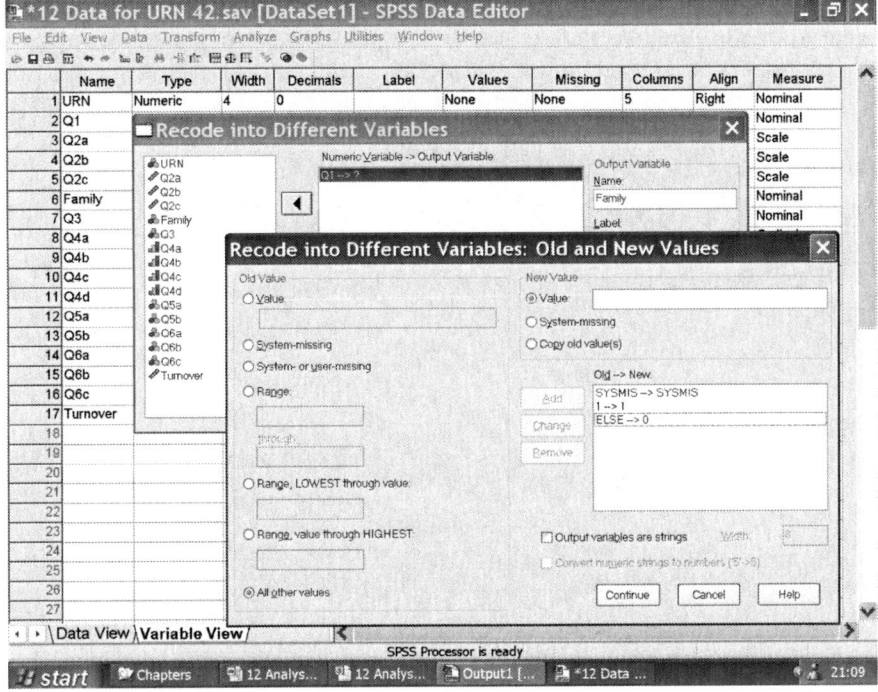

Figure 15.4 Recoding into a different variable

Family, which will have two groups: companies that are wholly-family owned (or have only one owner) and those that are not.

In **Variable View** select the whole of row 6 to position the new variable above it:

- From the menu, select **Edit** ⇒ **Insert Variable**.
- Name the new variable **Family** and label it as **Q1**.
- Under **Values**, enter the details for the two groups: **1 = Wholly family-owned, 0 = Otherwise**.
- Change the measurement level to nominal.

From the menu, select **Transform** ⇒ **Recode into Different Variable**:

- From the list of variables on the left, select **Q1** and use the arrow button to move it into the **Input Variable –> Output Variable** box.
- Type **Family** in the **Output Variable Name** box and click **Old and New Values**.
- Under **Old value**, click **System-missing** and under **New value** click **System-missing** and then click **Add**.
- Under **Old value**, type 1 and under **New value**, type **1** and click **Add**.
- Under **Old value**, click **All other values** and under **New value**, type **0** and click **Add** ⇒ **Continue** ⇒ **Change** and **OK**. Figure 15.4 illustrates this process.

When you have finished, return to **Data View** and carry out a visual check that the value 1 in the new dummy variable coincides with the value 1 in the original variable. This is just an exercise, but when you enter your own research data, you will not start recoding any variables until you have finished entering all the observations for your sample. Remember that it is essential to verify the accuracy of your recoding instructions by checking the outcome. With a large number of cases, it is not practical to use a visual check and we suggest you compare the total frequencies for each category in the old and new variables instead. We will show you how to generate frequency tables in the next section. If you find you have made a mistake, simply go through the steps for recoding the variable again.

You can reinforce and extend your knowledge of recoding by creating three more dummy variables:

- Recode **Q2c into Exowners**, where **1 = External owners, 0 = Otherwise**. Do this by recoding **SYSMIS –> SYSMIS, 0 –> 0, ELSE –> 1**.
- Recode **Q3** into **Volaudit**, where **1 = Yes, 0 = No**. Do this by recoding **SYSMIS –> SYSMIS, 0 –> 0, ELSE –> 1**.
- Recode **Q6a, Q6b** and **Q6c** into **Education**, where **1 = Degree, qualifications or training, 0 = Otherwise**. This is a bit more complicated. As each variable will make a contribution to the new variable, recode 1 –> 1 for each variable in turn. Then check **Data View** to see the new variable accurately reflects your instructions. If so, from the menu select **Transform** ⇒ **Recode** ⇒ **Into same variable** and after selecting **Education**, recode **1 –> 1, ELSE –> 0**. Then in **Data View** carry out a last visual check on the accuracy of the outcome. As already mentioned, this is essential when working with your own data, as you will not do any recoding until you have finished entering the data for your entire sample.

At this point, you may have begun to think that it would be more convenient if the names we used for the four variables in **Q4** were more informative, like the names of the new variables you have created. Renaming them is easy. Go into **Variable View** and under **Name**, type **Check** instead of **Q4a** and under **Label**, type **Q4a** instead of **Check**. Carry out a similar reversal for **Q4b, Q4c** and **Q4d**. Although using the question numbers was useful at the data entry stage, this small change will aid the next stage, which involves analysing the variables and interpreting the results. When you have finished, save the file and exit. Table 15.1 now summarizes the variables in the analysis, where for some tests we will be describing Volaudit as the dependent variable (DV) and the others as the independent variables (IVs).

Key definitions

A **dichotomous variable** is a variable that has two categories, such as gender.

A **dummy variable** is a dichotomous quantitative variable coded 1 if the characteristic is present and 0 if the characteristic is absent.

We are now ready to examine some of the *descriptive statistics* used to explore data in a *univariate analysis*. The methods we are going to use are simple statistical models, which not only help us describe the data, but also help determine whether parametric or non-parametric methods will be appropriate in any bivariate or multivariate analysis. Box 15.3 summarizes the statistics we are going to generate.

Table 15.1 Variables in the analysis

Hypothesis	Variable	Description
	Volaudit	Whether company would have a voluntary audit (1, 0)
H1	Turnover	Turnover in 2002 accounts (£k)
H2	Check	Audit provides a check on accounting records and systems (5 = Agree, 1 = Disagree)
H3	Quality	Audit improves the quality of the financial information (5 = Agree, 1 = Disagree)
H4	Credibility	Audit improves the credibility of the financial information (5 = Agree, 1 = Disagree)
H5	Creditscore	Audit has a positive effect on the credit rating score (5 = Agree, 1 = Disagree)
H6	Family	Whether company is wholly family-owned (1, 0)
H7	Exowners	Whether company has external shareholders (1, 0)
H8	Bank	Whether statutory accounts are given to the bank/lenders (1, 0)
H9	Education	Whether respondent has degree/qualifications/training (1, 0)

Box 15.3 Univariate analysis

Descriptive statistics
Frequency distribution
    Percentage frequency
Measures of central tendency
    Mean
    Median
    Mode
Measures of dispersion
    Range
    Standard deviation
Measures of normality
    Skewness
    Kurtosis

15.4 Frequency distributions

In statistics, the term *frequency* refers to the number of observations for a particular data value in a variable (the frequency of occurrence of a quantity in a ratio or interval variable and a category in an ordinal or nominal variable). A *frequency distribution* is an array that summarizes the frequencies for all the data values in a particular variable (Upton and Cook, 2006). For example, the data values in the survey for the variable **Turnover** were the figures reported in the companies' 2006 annual accounts. If no company had precisely the same figure for turnover as another, the number of observations for each data value would be 1. If the variable is measured on an ordinal scale (for example, **Check**, which is coded 1–5) or a nominal scale (for example, **Family**, which is coded 1 or 0), the data values are the codes and the number of observations are the number of companies in each category.

A frequency distribution can be presented for one variable *(univariate* analysis) or two variables *(bivariate* analysis) in a table, chart or other type of diagram. Even with a very small data set (say, 20 data values or less), an examination of how the values are distributed will aid your interpretation of the data.

15.4.1 Percentage frequencies

A *percentage frequency* is a familiar statistical model, which summarizes frequencies as a proportion of 100. It is calculated by dividing the frequency by the sum of the frequencies and then multiplying the answer by 100. This can be expressed as a formula:

$$\text{Percentage frequency} = \frac{f}{\Sigma f} \times 100$$

where
  f = the frequency
  Σ = the sum of

Example

The survey found that 633 companies out of 790 in the sample had a turnover of less than £1 million. Putting these figures into the formula:

$$\frac{633}{790} \times 100 = 80\%$$

The formula we have used is not difficult to understand, but if you are not a statistician, you may find the mathematical notation somewhat mysterious. However, it is merely a kind of shorthand that speeds up the process of writing the formulae and, once you know what the symbols represent, you can decipher the message. As we are going to show you how to use *SPSS* to generate the statistics you require, we will not examine the mathematical side.

15.4.2 Creating interval variables

In a large sample, you may find it useful to recode ratio variables into non-overlapping groups and create a new variable measured on an equal-interval scale. This allows the overall pattern in the frequencies and percentage frequencies to be discerned. However, much of the detail is lost in the process, so it is important to recode into a different variable (rather than the same variable) and keep the original precise information in case you need it for another purpose later on.

Key definitions

A **frequency** is the number of observations for a particular data value in a variable.

A **frequency distribution** is an array that summarizes the frequencies for all the data values in a particular variable.

A **percentage frequency** is a descriptive statistic that summarizes a frequency as a proportion of 100.

When deciding how many groups to create, you need to bear in mind that too few might obscure essential features while too many could emphasize minor or random features. A rule of thumb might be 5 to 10, depending on the range of values in the data. You need to take care that you can allocate each item of data to the appropriate group without ambiguity. For example, the original variable **Turnover** was recoded into a different variable named **Turnovercat** with five groups containing equal intervals of £1m. However, we should not use intervals of £0–£1m, £1m–£2m, £2m–£3m and so on, because a value of £1m could be placed in either the first or the second group and a value of £2m could be placed in the second or the third group. The correct intervals would be £0–£0.99m, £1m–1.99m, £2m–£2.99m and so on.

15.4.3 Generating frequency tables

Although *a frequency table* can be generated for a ratio variable, it is more usually associated with variables that contain groups or categories, such as interval, ordinal or nominal variables. To generate a frequency table in *SPSS*, start the program in the usual way and open the file named **Data for 790 cos.sav**.

- From the menu, select **A**nalyze ⇒ **D**escriptive Statistics ⇒ **F**requencies …
- From the list of variables on the left, select Turnovercat and use the arrow button ▶ to move it into the **V**ariable(s) box on the right (see Figure 15.5). If you also wanted to generate frequency tables for other variables, you would simply move them into the box on the right at this point.
- The default is to display the frequency tables, so click **OK** to see the output (see Table 15.2).

To copy a table from the *SPSS* output file into a *Word* document, left click with your mouse on the table to select it, and from the menu at the top of the screen, select **E**dit then **C**opy and you will then be able to paste the table into your document. You need to remember that every table should be accompanied by one or more paragraphs of explanation.

Table 15.2 shows the presentation of *univariate* data for a variable containing grouped data, but if you want to analyse data from two such variables, you need to generate a *cross-tabulation*. We will demonstrate this with the grouped data from the interval variable **Turnovercat** and the categorical data from the dummy variable

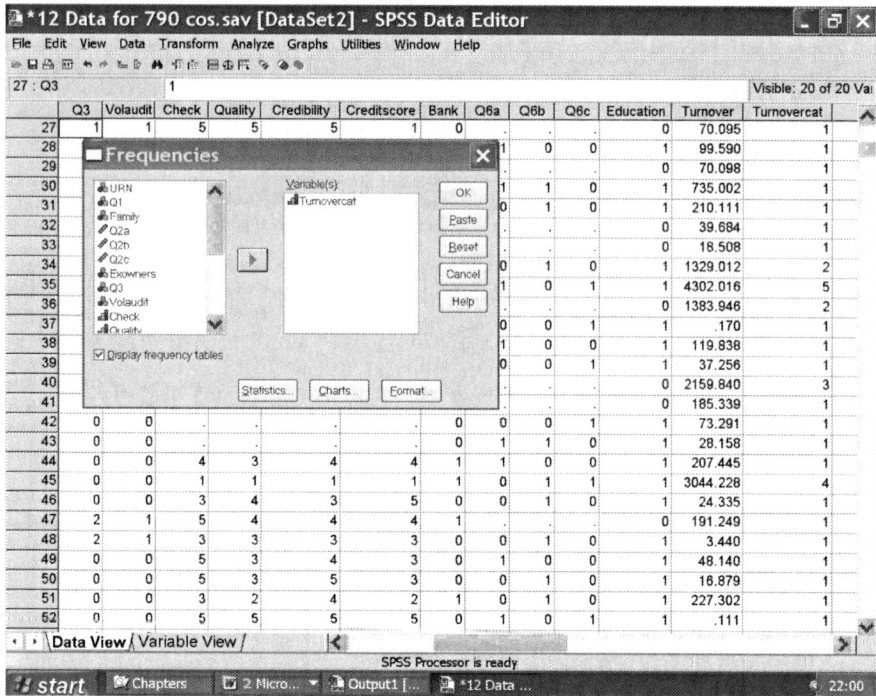

Figure 15.5 Generating a frequency table

Table 15.2 Frequency table for Turnovercat

Statistics

Turnovercat		
N	Valid	790
	Missing	0

Turnovercat

		Frequency	Percent	Valid Percent	Cumulative Percent
Valid	1 Under £1m	633	80.1	80.1	80.1
	2 £1m–£1.99m	55	7.0	7.0	87.1
	3 £2m–£2.99m	37	4.7	4.7	91.8
	4 £3m–£3.99m	40	5.1	5.1	96.8
	5 £4m–£4.9m	25	3.2	3.2	100.0
	Total	790	100.0	100.0	

Volaudit. You can generate a cross-tabulation in *SPSS* using these two variables using the following procedure:

- From the menu at the top, select **Analyze** ⇒ **Descriptive Statistics** ... ⇒ **Crosstabs** and use the arrow button to move **Volaudit** into **Column(s)** and **Turnovercat** into **Row(s)**.

ANALYSING DATA USING DESCRIPTIVE STATISTICS

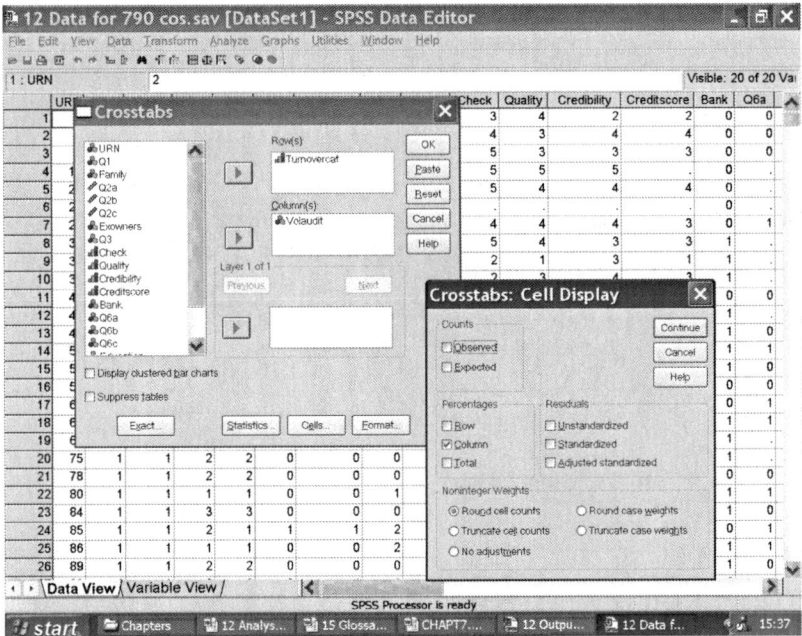

Figure 15.6 Generating a cross-tabulation

- The default is to show the count of the observations, but it is often more useful to show the percentages. Be wary of showing too much data in a table (generally no more than 20 items of data) as this can detract from the main message. As we have put the dependent variable in the column(s), it makes sense to show the column percentages rather than the row percentages. To do this, select **Cells** and under **Percentages** select **Column** (see Figure 15.6).
- Then click **Continue** and **OK** to see the output (see Table 15.3).

Once copied into a *Word* document, a table can be edited in the usual way. In this example, both groups in the dependent variable **Volaudit** follow more or less the same size order. If your data do not conveniently coincide in this way, base the order on the group that contains the larger frequencies and let the other group follow that order.

15.4.4 Generating charts

Charts (and other graphical forms) can also be used to present frequency information. Some people prefer to read summarized information in a chart and detailed information in a table. In both cases, there must also be a written explanation. You need to consider the level at which the variable is measured when choosing the type of chart. If you have entered your data into a spreadsheet or into a specialist statistical program, you will find it easy to produce a variety of different charts. Table 15.4 shows how your choice is constrained by the measurement level of the research data.

Table 15.3 Cross-tabulation for Volaudit and Turnovercat

Case Processing Summary

	Cases					
	Valid		Missing		Total	
	N	Percent	N	Percent	N	Percent
Turnovercat * Volaudit	772	97.7%	18	2.3%	790	100.0%

Turnovercat * Volaudit Crosstabulation

			Volaudit		Total
			0 Otherwise	1 Yes	
Turnovercat	1 Under £1m	Count	406	214	620
		% within Volaudit	92.7%	64.1%	80.3%
	2 £1m–£1.99m	Count	12	42	54
		% within Volaudit	2.7%	12.6%	7.0%
	3 £2m–£2.99m	Count	10	26	36
		% within Volaudit	2.3%	7.8%	4.7%
	4 £3m–£3.99m	Count	5	33	38
		% within Volaudit	1.1%	9.9%	4.9%
	5 £4m–£4.9m	Count	5	19	24
		% within Volaudit	1.1%	5.7%	3.1%
Total		Count	438	334	772
		% within Volaudit	100.0%	100.0%	

Table 15.4 Charts for different types of data

Measurement level	Bar chart	Pie chart	Histogram
Nominal	✓	✓	
Ordinal	✓		
Interval			✓
Ratio			✓

The advantages of using a chart are:

- it is a good way to communicate general points
- it is attractive to look at
- it appeals to a more general audience
- it makes it easier to compare data sets
- relationships can be seen more clearly.

The disadvantages of using a chart are:

- it is not a good way to communicate specific details
- it can be misinterpreted

ANALYSING DATA USING DESCRIPTIVE STATISTICS

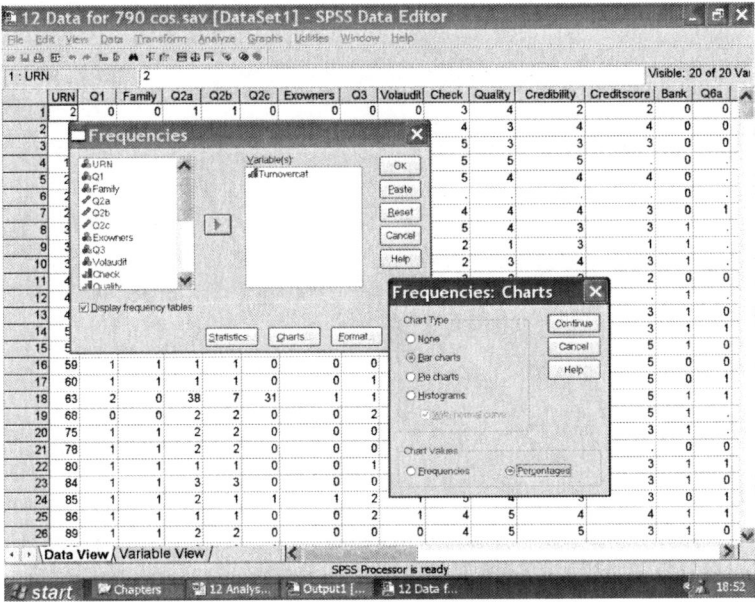

Figure 15.7 Generating a chart

- the design may detract from the message
- designing a non-standard chart can be time-consuming
- it can be designed to be deliberately misleading.

You can create a chart in *SPSS* at the same time as generating a frequency table.

- From the menu, select **Analyze** ⇒ **Descriptive Statistics...** ⇒ **Frequencies**.
- From the list of variables on the left, move **Turnovercat** into the **Variable(s)** box on the right and click **Charts**.
- Under **Chart Type**, select **Bar charts**, and under **Chart Values**, select **Percentages** and click **Continue** (see Figure 15.7).
- **Click OK** to see the output (see Figure 15.8).

Go through the same procedure again, to select a pie chart or a histogram (not surprisingly, *SPSS* does not anticipate that you might want all three, so you can only select one at a time).

In a *bar chart*, the frequency or percentage frequency for each ordinal or nominal category is displayed in a separate vertical (or horizontal) bar. The frequencies are indicated by the height (or length) of the bars, which permits a visual comparison. In a *component bar chart*, the bars are divided into segments. However, these are not recommended, as the segments lack a common axis or base line, which makes them difficult to interpret visually. The alternative is a *multiple bar chart* in which the segments are adjoined and each starts at the base line. This allows the reader to compare several component parts, but the comparison of the total is lost.

In a *pie chart*, the percentage frequency for each value or category is displayed as a segment of a circular diagram. Each segment represents an area that is proportional

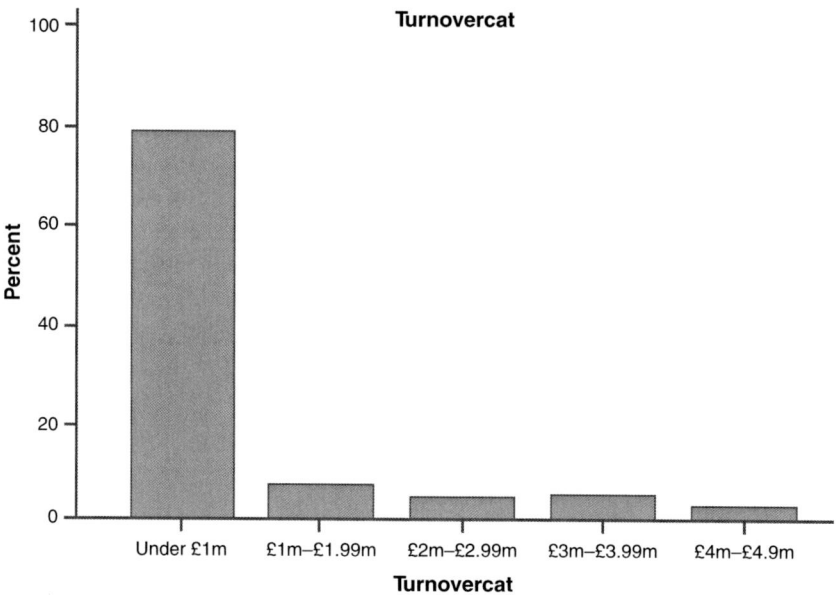

Figure 15.8 Bar chart for Turnovercat

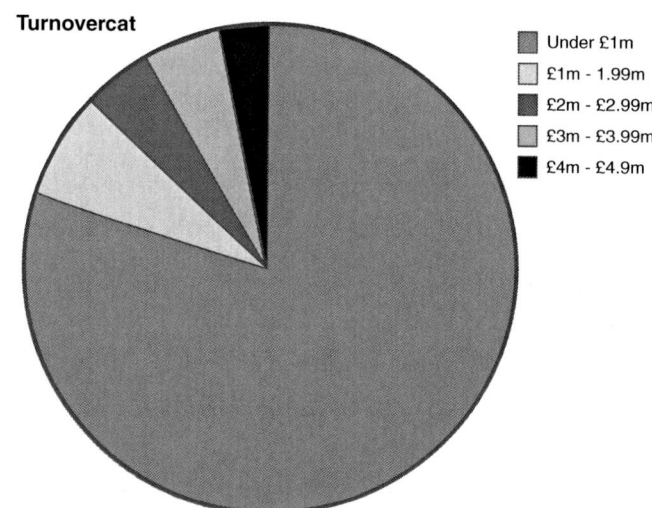

Figure 15.9 Pie chart for Turnovercat

to the whole 'pie'. Figure 15.9 shows a pie chart representing the percentage frequencies for each category in **Turnovercat**.

A *histogram* is a refinement of a bar chart, but the adjoining bars touch, indicating that the variable is measured on an interval or ratio scale. If you have data measured on an interval scale based on equal intervals, the width of the bars will be constant and the height of each bar will represent the frequency because Area = Width × Height. Thus, a histogram shows the approximate shape of the distribution. We will illustrate this with the original variable **Turnover**, which is measured on a ratio scale and the chart is shown in Figure 15.10.

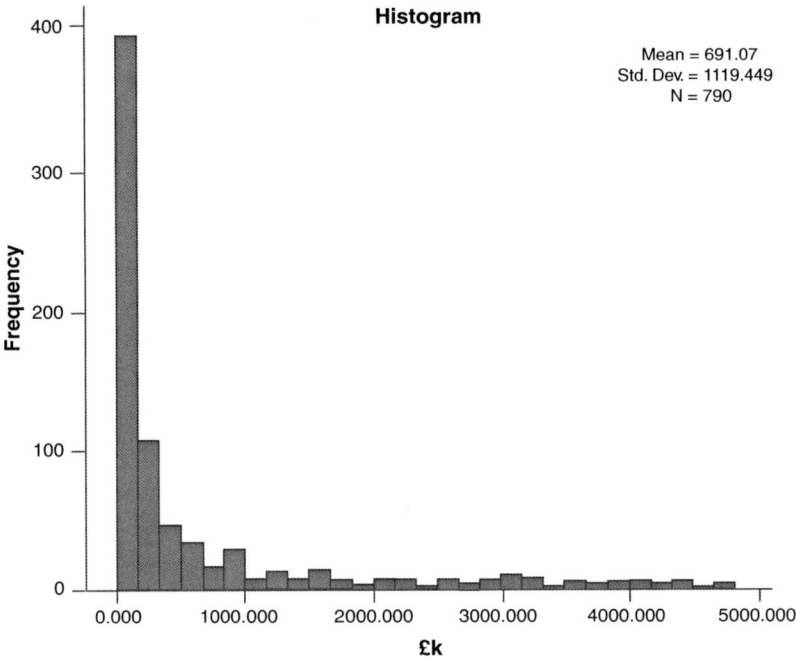

Figure 15.10 Histogram for Turnover

We suggest you run the tutorial on creating and editing charts. To amend the appearance of the chart, double click on the chart to open the **Chart Editor**. For example, in the bar chart and pie chart we have illustrated, it would be useful to add value labels to the segments, but specify 0 decimal places to reduce unwanted 'noise' in the communication. In the histogram for **Turnover**, you might want to use a scaling factor of 1,000, which would allow you to label the values in millions as shown in the bar and pie charts for **Turnovercat**. For future reference, note that the histogram can also show the distribution curve and the default is to show some descriptive statistics that summarize the data. We will examine these in the next section.

To copy a chart from the *SPSS* output file into a *Word* document, left click with your mouse on the chart to select it, and from the menu at the top of the screen, select **Edit** then **Copy** and you will then be able to paste the table into your document. You need to remember that every chart should be accompanied by one or more paragraphs of explanation.

The **Chart Editor** allows you to generate a *line graph* to present continuous data (such as **Turnover**) across a number of categories. It is not appropriate to use a line graph to represent discrete data, such as number of employees. This is because you can represent turnover as a line by dividing it into fractional denominations (such as £1.01, £1.02, £1.03 and so on) but you cannot have 1.1, 1.2 or 1.3 employees. Line graphs are often used to present data collected at different points in time. For example, if you have turnover data for the past five years, you could use a line chart to illustrate any volatility, stability or trend over the period and compare companies with external shareholders with those that are owner-managed. The frequencies are always shown on the vertical axis (the Y axis) and data values for the categories on the horizontal axis (the X axis). In this example, **Turnover** would be shown on the Y axis (in £k or £m) and the years would be shown along the X axis. You might want to use **Exowners** as the variable to define the lines by. If you did this, the two groups in **Exowners** would be described as 'External owners' and 'Otherwise' in the legend.

You can see from this brief description that one advantage of line graphs over other charts is that, providing they share the same scale and unit of measurement, a number of variables can be represented on the same graph (a multiple line graph). This greatly facilitates visual comparison of the data.

15.4.5 Generating a stem-and-leaf plot

A *stem-and-leaf plot* is a diagram that uses the data values (observations) in a frequency distribution to create a display. Thus, it 'retains all the information in the data, while also giving an idea of the underlying distribution' (Upton and Cook, 2006, p. 409). The data are arranged in size order and each observation is divided into a leading digit to represent the stem and trailing digits, which represent the leaf.

The diagram presents the data in a more compact and useable form, which highlights any gaps and *outliers*. An outlier is an extreme value that does not conform to the general pattern. In a small sample, outliers are important because they can distort the results of the statistical analysis. We will demonstrate how to generate a stem-and-leaf plot in *SPSS* using the data for **Turnover**.

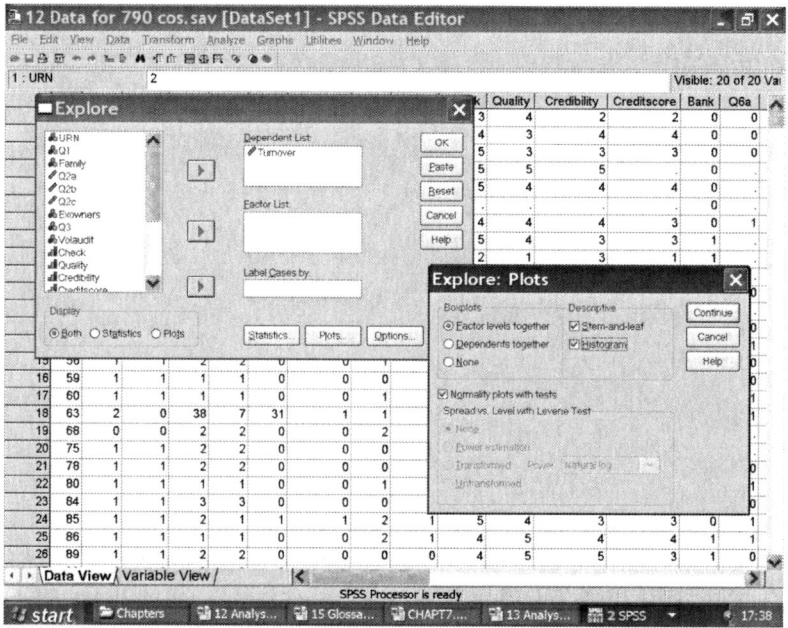

Figure 15.11 Generating a stem-and-leaf plot

ANALYSING DATA USING DESCRIPTIVE STATISTICS

Box 15.4 Stem-and-leaf plot for Turnover

```
Turnover £k
Frequency               Stem & Leaf
 321.00                  0 . 0000011111222223334444555566677788899 9
 104.00                  1 . 0111223456788&
  65.00                  2 . 0123469&
  39.00                  3 . 0123&&
  25.00                  4 . &&&
  18.00                  5 . &&
  18.00                  6 . &&
   6.00                  7 . &
  18.00                  8 . &&
  19.00                  9 . &&
   5.00                 10 . &
   5.00                 11 . &
   8.00                 12 . &
   9.00                 13 . &
   2.00                 14 . &
   6.00                 15 . &
  11.00                 16 . 1&
   3.00                 17 . &
 108.00                 Extremes  >=1795)

Stem width: 100.00
Each leaf: 8 case (s)
& denotes fractional leaves
```

- Select **Analyze** ⇒ **D**escriptive **Statistics**... ⇒ **E**xplore and move **Turnover** into the **V**ariable(s) box on the right.
- From the buttons on the right-hand side, select **Plo**t**s**. Under **Descriptive**, the default is **Stem-and-leaf**, so click Continue (see Figure 15.11).
- Then click **OK** for the results (see Box 15.4).

Box 15.4 illustrates the stem-and-leaf plot for the **Turnover**.

15.5 Measuring central tendency

We are now going to look at a group of statistical models that are concerned with measuring the *central tendency* of a frequency distribution. Measures of central tendency provide a convenient way of summarizing a large frequency distribution by describing it with a single statistic. The three measures are the mean, the median and the mode.

15.5.1 The mean

The *mean* ($\bar{x}$) is the arithmetic average of a set of data in a sample and can only be calculated for ratio or interval variables. It is found by dividing the sum of the observations by the number of observations, as shown in the following formula:

$$\text{Mean} = \frac{\sum x}{n}$$

where

  x = each observation
  n = the total number of observations
  $\sum$ = the sum of

Example

A student's exam marks were as follows:

Module 1	Module 2	Module 3	Module 4	Module 5	Module 6
82%	78%	80%	64%	70%	64%

Inserting the data into the formula:

$$\frac{82+78+80+64+70+64}{6} = \frac{438}{6} = 73\%$$

The advantages of the mean are:

- it can be calculated exactly
- it takes account of all the data
- it can be used as the basis of other statistical models.

The disadvantages of the mean are:

- it is greatly affected by outliers (extreme values that are very high or very low)
- it is a hypothetical value and may not be one of the actual values
- it can give an impossible figure for discrete data (for example the average number of owners in the sample of small companies was 5.8)
- it cannot be calculated for ordinal or nominal data.

15.5.2 The median

The *median* (M) is the mid-value of a set of data that has been arranged in size order (in other words, it has been ranked). It can be calculated for variables measured on a ratio, interval or ordinal scale and is found by adding 1 to the number of observations and dividing by 2. The formula is:

$$\text{Median} = \frac{n+1}{2}$$

where

  n = number of observations

This is very straightforward if you have an even number of observations because the formula will take you directly to the observation at the mid-point. The following example shows what you need to do if you have an uneven number of observations.

Example

The student's exam marks in chronological order were:

Module 1	Module 2	Module 3	Module 4	Module 5	Module 6
82%	78%	80%	64%	70%	64%

The marks arranged in size order are:

| 64% | 64% | 70% | 78% | 80% | 82% |

Inserting the data into the formula:

$$\frac{6+1}{2} = 3.5$$

Therefore, the median is half-way between the third and the fourth of the ranked marks. A simple calculation will tell us the exact value:

$$\frac{70+78}{2} = 74\%$$

The advantages of the median are:

- it is not affected by outliers or open-ended values at the extremities
- it is not affected by unequal class intervals
- it can represent an actual value in the data.

The disadvantages of the median are:

- it cannot be measured precisely for distributions reflecting grouped data
- it cannot be used as the basis for other statistical models
- it may not be useful if the data set does not have normal distribution (we will be looking at this in section 15.7)
- it cannot be calculated for nominal data.

15.5.3 The mode

The *mode* (m) is the most frequently occurring value in a data set and can be used for all variables, irrespective of the measurement scale.

Example

The student's exam marks were:

Module 1	Module 2	Module 3	Module 4	Module 5	Module 6
82%	78%	80%	64%	70%	64%

The mode of 64%

The advantages of the mode are:

- it is not affected by outliers
- it is easy to identify in a small data set
- it can be calculated for any variable, irrespective of the measurement scale.

The disadvantages of the mode are:

- it is a dynamic measure that can change as other values are added
- it cannot be measured precisely for distributions reflecting grouped data
- there may be multiple modes
- it cannot be used as the basis for other statistical models.

One of the things you will have noticed from the analysis in this section is that the mean, the median and the mode each use a different definition of central tendency. Our analysis of the student's marks has produced a different result under each method. The reason for this will become apparent when we look at the importance of examining the spread of data values in section 15.6.

Key definitions

The **mean** ($\bar{x}$) is a measure of central tendency based on the arithmetic average of a set of data values.

The **median (M)** is a measure of central tendency based on the mid-value of a set of data values arranged in size order.

The **mode (m)** is a measure of central tendency based on the most frequently occurring value in set of data (there may be multiple modes).

15.5.4 Generating measures of central tendency

With a large data set, you will need some help in calculating measures of central tendency, but *SPSS* allows you to do this at the same time as generating frequency distributions in tables and/or charts. The procedure is as follows:

- From the menu, select **Analyze** ⇒ **Descriptive Statistics...** ⇒ **Frequencies**.
- We will use the original ratio variable to measure turnover, so use the arrow button to return **Turnovercat** to the list on the left and move **Turnover** into the **Variable(s)** box on the right. If you also wanted to generate frequency tables for other variables, you would simply move them into the box on the right at this point.
- Now click on **Statistics** and under **Central Tendency**, select **Mean, Median** and **Mode** and click Continue (see Figure 15.12).
- Then click **OK** to see the results table (see Table 15.5).

Interpreting the results, you can see that despite being called measures of central tendency, the 'centre' differs for each statistic. The reasons for this will become apparent in the next section. For the time being, we can simply say that the different results arise from the different definitions we used for each measure.

Before moving on to the next subject, we are going to demonstrate the importance of retaining the detailed data in the original variable **Turnover** by comparing

ANALYSING DATA USING DESCRIPTIVE STATISTICS

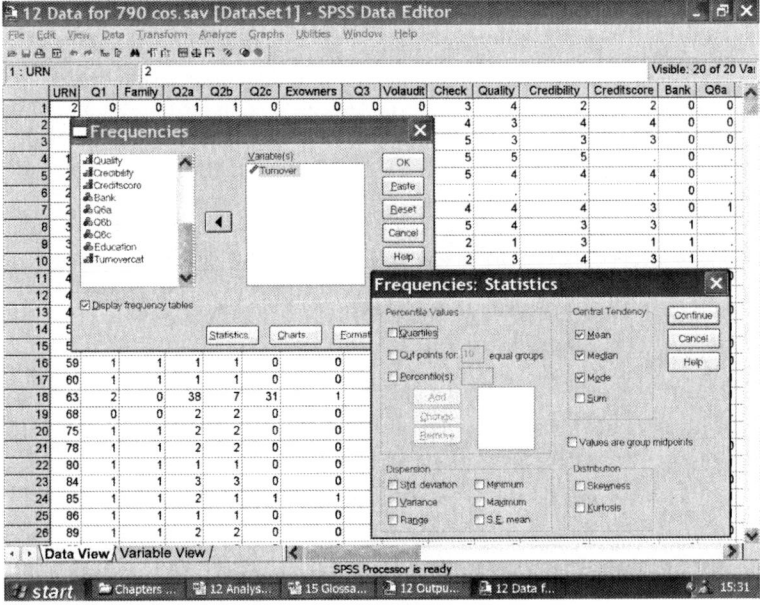

Figure 15.12 Generating measures of central tendency

Table 15.5 Measures of central tendency for Turnover

	Turnover £k	
N	Valid	790
	Missing	0
Mean		691.07062
Median		158.06450
Mode		8.000

the precise mean we have obtained for that variable with the mean we can calculate for the five classes of grouped data in **Turnovercat**. To determine the mean for grouped data, we need to take the mid-points of each class and multiply by the frequency, as shown in the following formula:

$$\text{Mean for grouped data} = \frac{\sum fx}{\sum f}$$

where

    f = the frequency
    x = each observation
    Σ = the sum of

The calculations are as follows:

Turnover	Frequency (f)	Mid-point (x)	(fx)
Under £1m	633	0.5	316.5
£1m–£1.99m	55	1.5	82.5
£2m–£2.99m	37	2.5	92.5
£3m–£3.99m	40	3.5	140.0
£4m–£4.9m	25	4.5	112.5
Total	790		744.0

We can now substitute the figures we have calculated in the formula:

$$\frac{744}{790} = 0.94$$

The results show that the mean for the grouped data in the interval variable **Turnovercat** is £0.94m compared to the mean of £0.69m that we calculated earlier using the precise data contained in the ratio variable **Turnover**. The grouped data can only give an approximation of this important statistic. Moreover, this approximation is larger than the actual mean because it is based on the median in each category rather than every data value (observation). This helps demonstrate the superiority of ratio data over interval or ordinal data when it comes to measuring the mean, which lies at the heart of the most powerful statistical models used in inferential statistics. We will discuss this further in Chapter 12.

15.6 Measuring dispersion

Measures of central tendency are useful for providing statistics that summarize the location of the 'middle' of the data, but they do not tell us anything about the spread of the data values. Therefore, we are now going to look at *measures of dispersion*, which should only be calculated for variables measured on a ratio or interval scale. The two measures are the range and the standard deviation.

Key definitions

The **interquartile range** is a measure of dispersion that represents the difference between the upper quartile and the lower quartile (the middle 50%) of a frequency distribution arranged in size order.

The **range** is a measure of dispersion that represents the difference between the maximum value and the minimum value in a frequency distribution arranged in size order.

15.6.1 Range

The range is a simple measure of dispersion that describes the difference between the maximum value (the upper extreme or E_U) and the minimum value (the lower extreme

ANALYSING DATA USING DESCRIPTIVE STATISTICS

or E_L) in a frequency distribution arranged in size order. You will remember from the previous section that the median is the mid-point, but in a large set of data (say, 30 observations or more) it can be useful to divide the frequency distribution into quartiles, each containing 25% of the data values. This allows us to measure the interquartile range, which is the difference between the upper quartile (Q_3) and the lower quartile (Q_1), and the spread of the middle 50% of the data values. When comparing two distributions, the interquartile range is often preferred to the range, because the latter is more easily affected by outliers (extreme values). The formulae are:

$$\text{Range} = E_U - E_L$$
$$\text{Interquartile range} = Q_3 - Q_1$$

Example

Inserting the data for Turnover (£k) into the formulae:

Range = 4,738.271 − 0.054 = 4,738.217
Interquartile range = 742.76625 − 52.74525 = 690.021

Unfortunately, the drawback of using the range is that it only takes account of two items of data and the drawback of the interquartile range is that it only takes account of half the values. What we really want is a measure of dispersion that will take account of all the values and we discuss such an alternative next.

15.6.2 Standard deviation

The *standard deviation* (sd) should only be calculated for ratio or interval variables, but it overcomes the deficiencies of the range and the interquartile range discussed in the previous section by using all the data. The standard deviation is related to the normal distribution and the term was introduced by Karl Pearson in 1893 (Upton and Cook, 2006). It is based on the *error* and the *variance,* which are two statistical models used to measure how well the *mean* represents the data (Field, 2000).

In this context, the error is the difference between the mean and the data value (the observation). It is called an error because it measures the deviation of the observation from the mean (which is a hypothetical value that summarizes the data). We then add up the errors and make some adjustments. These are necessary because the difference between the mean and each value below the mean produces a negative figure while the difference between the mean and each value above the mean produces a positive figure. Unfortunately, when these are added together, the answer is zero. To resolve this problem, the errors are squared (in mathematics, squaring a positive or a negative number always produces a positive figure).

This allows us to calculate the variance, which is the mean of the squared errors. However, this is very difficult to interpret because it is measured in squared units (for example our turnover data would be in square £). To de-square the units, we calculate the square root of the variance. This gives us the standard deviation, which we can now define as the square root of the variance. A small standard deviation relative to the mean suggests the mean represents the data well; conversely, a large standard deviation relative to the mean, suggests the mean does not represent the data well because the data values are widely dispersed.

Key definitions

The **error** is the difference between the mean and the data value (observation).

The **standard deviation (sd)** is the square root of the variance. A large standard deviation relative to the mean suggests the mean does not represent the data well.

The **standard error (se)** is the standard deviation between the means of different samples. A large standard error relative to the overall sample mean suggests the sample might not be representative of the population.

The **variance** is the mean of the squared errors.

In case you only have a small data set and want to calculate the standard deviation unaided, the formula for individual data is:

$$sd = \sqrt{\frac{\sum(x - \bar{x})^2}{n}}$$

where

x = an observation
$\bar{x}$ = the mean
n = the total number of observations
$\sqrt{}$ = the square root
$\sum$ = the sum of

The formula for grouped data is:

$$sd = \sqrt{\frac{\sum x^2 f}{\sum f} - \frac{(\sum xf)^2}{\sum f}}$$

where
x = the mid-point of each data class
f = the frequency of each class
$\sqrt{}$ = the square root
$\sum$ = the sum of

The advantages of the standard deviation are:

- it uses every value
- it is in the same units as the original data
- it is easy to interpret.

The disadvantages are:

- the calculations are complex without the aid of suitable software
- it can only be used for variables measured on a ratio or interval scale.

The final term we are going to introduce is the *standard error* (se), which is calculated by 'taking the difference between each sample mean and the overall mean, squaring the differences, adding them up and dividing by the number of samples'

ANALYSING DATA USING DESCRIPTIVE STATISTICS

(Field, 2000, p. 9). A small standard error relative to the overall sample mean suggests the sample is representative of the population, whereas a large standard error relative to the overall sample mean suggests the sample might not be representative of the population.

15.6.3 Generating measures of dispersion

By now you will have realized that *SPSS* allows you to generate frequency tables, measures of central tendency and measures of dispersion for one or more variables in one set of instructions under the **Analyze** ⇒ **Descriptive Statistics** menu. We will now show you how to add the measures of dispersion we have been discussing:

- From the menu, select Analyze ⇒ **Descriptive Statistics…** ⇒ **Frequencies** and move **Turnover** into the **Variable(s)** box on the right. If you also wanted to generate frequency tables for other variables, you would simply move them into the box on the right at this point.
- Deselect the default to display frequency tables, as you already have them.
- Now click on **Statistics** and deselect any options under **Central Tendency**, as you have them already. Under **Percentile Values**, select **Quartiles** and under **Dispersion** click all the options and then click Continue (see Figure 15.13).
- Click **OK** to see the output (see Table 15.6).

15.7 Normal distribution

We mentioned in the previous section that the standard deviation is related to the *normal distribution*. This term was introduced in the late 19th century by Sir Francis

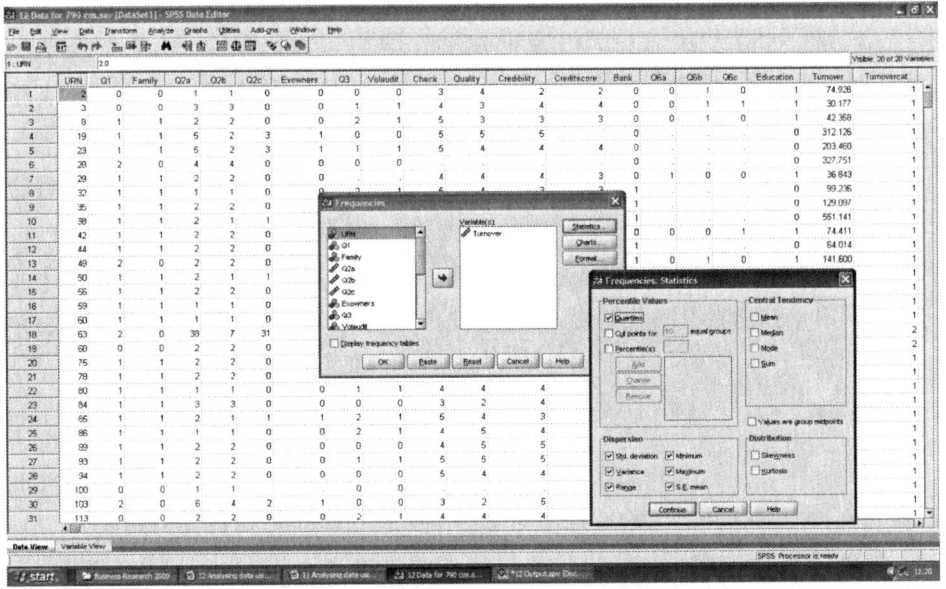

Figure 15.13 Generating measures of dispersion

Table 15.6 Measures of dispersion for Turnover

Turnover

		Statistics
N	Valid	790
	Missing	0
Std. Error of Mean		39.828205
Std. Deviation		1119.448910
Variance		1253165.862
Range		4738.217
Minimum		.054
Maximum		4738.271
Percentiles	25	52.74525
	50	158.06450
	75	742.76625

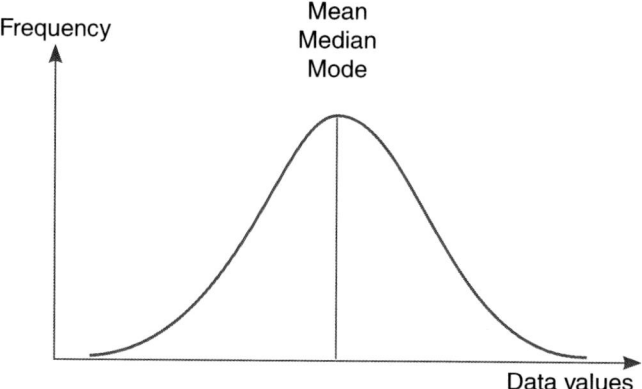

Figure 15.14 A normal frequency distribution

Galton, cousin of Charles Darwin who published *The Origin of Species* in 1859 (Upton and Cook, 2006), and refers to a theoretical frequency distribution that is bell-shaped and symmetrical, with tails extending indefinitely either side of the centre. In a normal distribution, the *mean*, the *median* and the *mode* coincide at the centre (see Figure 15.14). It is described as a theoretical frequency distribution because it is a mathematical model representing perfect symmetry, against which empirical data can be compared.

15.7.1 Skewness and kurtosis

When the frequency distribution does not have a symmetrical distribution, it is described as skewed. Thus, *skewness* is a measure of the extent to which a frequency

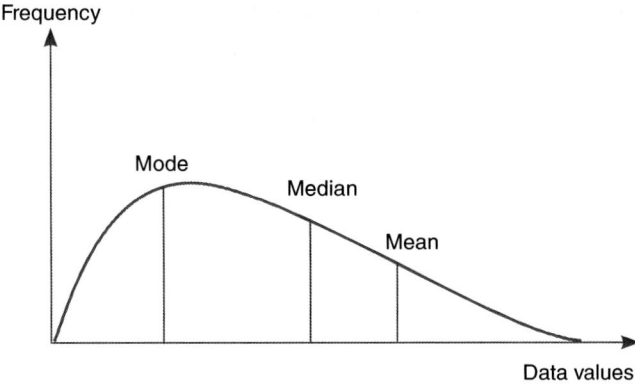

Figure 15.15 A positively skewed frequency distribution

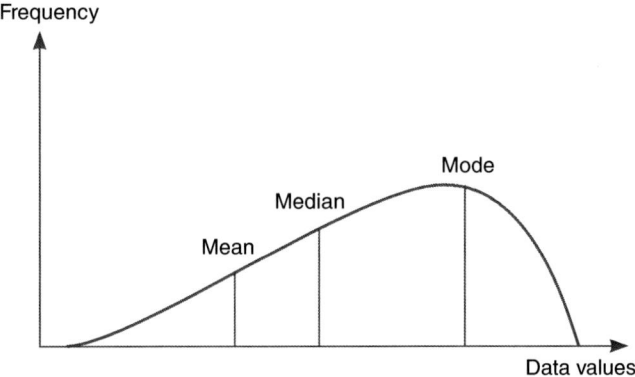

Figure 15.16 A negatively skewed frequency distribution

distribution is asymmetric. In a skewed distribution, the mean, the median and the mode have different values. Indeed, we found that the mean turnover for the sample companies was £691,071, the median was £158,065 and the mode was £8,000. The skewness of a normal distribution is 0 (the distribution is symmetrical). When a distribution has a positive skewness value, the tail is on the right (the positive side of the centre) and most of the observations are at the lower end of the range (see Figure 15.15). When the distribution has a negative skewness value, the tail is on the left (the negative side of the centre) and most of the observations are at the upper end of the range (see Figure 15.16). A skewness value that is more than twice the standard error of the skewness suggests the distribution is not symmetrical.

Key definitions

Skewness is a measure of the extent to which a frequency distribution is asymmetric (a normal distribution has a skewness of 0).

A second important measure is *kurtosis*, which measures the extent to which a frequency distribution is fatter or more peaked than a normal distribution (Upton and

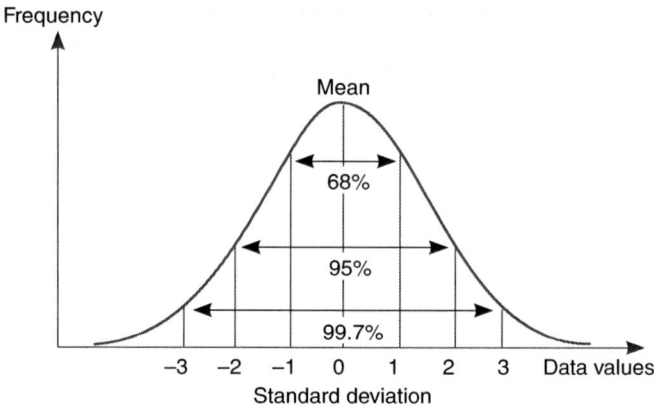

Figure 15.17 Proportion of a normal distribution under 1 standard deviation

Cook, 2006). The kurtosis value of a normal distribution is 0, which indicates the bell-shaped distribution with most of the observations clustered in the centre. A distribution with positive kurtosis is more peaked than a normal distribution because it has more observations in the centre and longer tails on either side. A distribution with negative kurtosis is fatter than a normal distribution because there are fewer observations in the centre and the tails on either side are shorter.

Both the mean and the standard deviation are related to the normal distribution. While the mean represents the centre of the frequency distribution, the standard deviation measures the spread or dispersion of the data values around the mean. If the data set has a normal distribution, 68% of the data values will be within 1 standard deviation of the mean, 95% will fall within 2 standard deviations of the mean and 99.7% will fall within 3 standard deviations of the mean. This is illustrated in Figure 15.17.

Key definitions

Kurtosis is a measure of the extent to which a frequency distribution is fatter or more peaked than a normal distribution (a normal distribution has a kurtosis of 0).

A **normal distribution** is a theoretical frequency distribution that is bell-shaped and symmetrical, with tails extending indefinitely either side of the centre. The mean, median and mode coincide at the centre.

15.7.2 Testing for normality

Although you can obtain measures of skewness and kurtosis under the **Frequencies** menu we have been using so far, if you want to run normality tests at the same time, you need to use the **Explore** menu. The procedure is as follows:

- Select **Analyze** ⇒ **Descriptive Statistics...** ⇒ **Explore** and move **Turnover** into the **Variable(s)** box on the right.
- The default is for both statistics and plots. Under **Statistics**, accept the default of **Descriptives**. However, under **Plots**, select **Normality** plots with **tests** and click **Continue** (see Figure 15.18).
- Click **OK** for the output (see Table 15.7).

ANALYSING DATA USING DESCRIPTIVE STATISTICS

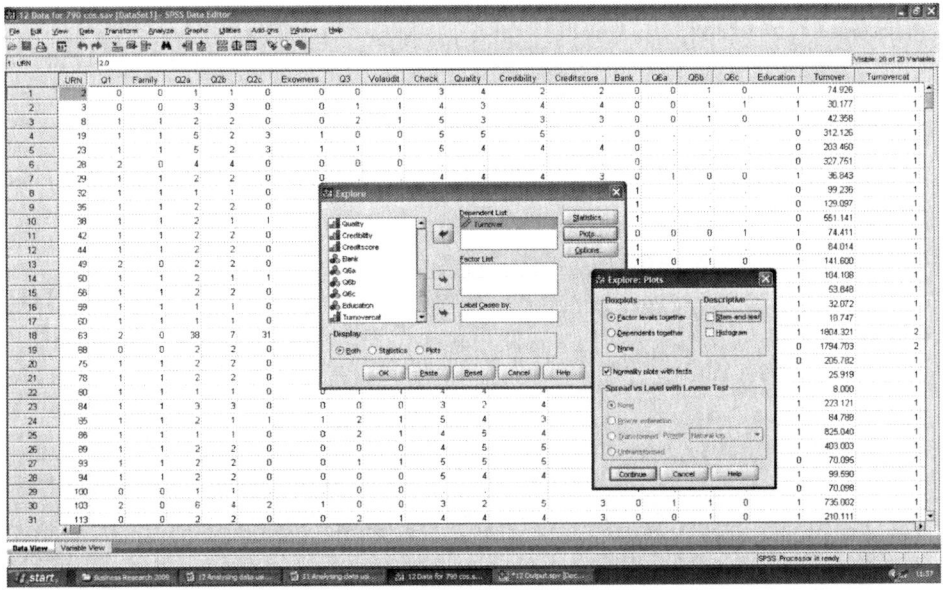

Figure 15.18 Generating descriptive statistics and testing for normality

Table 15.7 Descriptive statistics and normality tests for Turnover

Case Processing Summary

	Cases					
	Valid		Missing		Total	
	N	Percent	N	Percent	N	Percent
Turnover	790	100.0%	0	.0%	790	100.0%

Descriptives

			Statistic	Std. Error
Turnover	Mean		691.07062	39.828205
	95% Confidence Interval for Mean	Lower Bound	612.88884	
		Upper Bound	769.25240	
	5% Trimmed Mean		537.33076	
	Median		158.06450	
	Variance		1253165.862	
	Std. Deviation		1119.448910	
	Minimum		.054	
	Maximum		4738.271	
	Range		4738.217	
	Interquartile Range		690.021	
	Skewness		2.042	.087
	Kurtosis		3.170	.174

Table 15.7 (Continued)

Tests of Normality

Turnover	Kolmogorov-Smirnov[a]			Shapiro-Wilk		
	Statistic	df	Sig.	Statistic	df	Sig.
	.276	790	.000	.643	790	.000

[a.] Lilliefors Significance Correction

These results confirm what we could see from the general shape of the data in the histogram and from the measures of central tendency: **Turnover** does not have a normal distribution. The positive value for skewness confirms the spread of the data is skewed with more observations on the right of the mean; the positive value for kurtosis indicates a more peaked distribution than expected in a normal distribution with a higher degree of clustering of observations around the mean and longer tail(s).

The tests of normality compare the frequency distribution of the sample with a normal distribution with the same mean and standard deviation (Field, 2000). The test statistic is a function of the observations in our random sample. If the actual value is too far from the expected value, the test result is significant and this evidence leads us to reject the null hypothesis. Conversely, if the actual value is close to the expected value, the test result is not significant, and we do not reject the null hypothesis. There are two cases when a test result leads to a correct result (Upton and Cook, 2006):

- H_0 is true and the test leads to its acceptance
- H_1 is true and the test leads to the rejection of H_0.

However, there are also two cases when a test leads to an incorrect result (an error):

- H_0 is true, but the test leads to its rejection (referred to as a *Type 1 error*)
- H_1 is true, but the test leads to the acceptance of H0 (referred to as a *Type II error*).

We need to specify the size of the critical region that determines whether the test result is significant by setting the *significance level*. If you are conducting research into issues relating to health or safety you would want this critical region to be less than 1%, but in most business and management research, a 5% probability of a Type I or II error is usually acceptable. This is reflected in the default on *SPSS*, where the significance level is set at 0.05, which is 5%. Therefore, you will interpret the result of any test as being significant if the probability statistic (which we refer to as *p*) is significant at 5% or less (in other words, $p \leq 0.05$).

Looking at the tests of normality in the second part of Table 15.7, you can see the results are significant (the value under Sig. is ≤ 0.05). This means we can reject the null hypothesis and we accept that the frequency distribution for **Turnover** differs significantly from a normal distribution. If a result showed $p > 0.05$, it would indicate that the size of the deviation from normality in the sample was not large enough to be significant. In this case, a significant result is not surprising, since small and medium-sized businesses account for 99.9% of all enterprises in the UK

(BERR, 2008, p. 1), thus size is positively skewed in the population. When you have finished, save your files and exit from *SPSS*.

Key definitions

The **significance level** is the level of confidence that the results of a statistical analysis are not due to chance. It is usually expressed as the probability that the results of the statistical analysis are due to chance (usually 5% or less).

A **type I error** occurs when H_0 is true, but the test leads to its rejection.

A **type II error** occurs when H_1 is true, but the test leads to the acceptance of H_0.

15.8 Conclusions

In this chapter, we have demonstrated how to conduct a typical exploratory analysis of research data and how to generate tables, charts and other graphical forms, and how to summarize data using descriptive statistics. All students designing a study that includes the analysis of quantitative data need this knowledge. However, it does not matter whether you use *SPSS* or another software program to which you have access. If you have a relatively small data set, you could enter it into an *Excel* spreadsheet, which also has facilities for generating statistics and charts. Although it is possible to calculate percentage frequencies, measures of central tendency and dispersion using a calculator, when time and accuracy are at a premium you will find it invaluable to learn how to use the statistical package at your disposal. These are transferable skills that will enhance your employability.

Table 15.8 summarizes the descriptive statistics we have examined in this chapter and helps you select those that are appropriate for the measurement level of your variables.

In addition to time constraints and your skills, your choice of statistics will depend on research questions, which may require the use of inferential statistics in

Table 15.8 Choosing appropriate descriptive statistics

Exploratory analysis	Measurement level
Frequency distribution	
Percentage frequency	Ratio, interval, ordinal, nominal
Measures of central tendency	
Mean	Ratio, interval
Median	Ratio, interval, ordinal
Mode	Ratio, interval, ordinal, nominal
Measures of dispersion	
Range	Ratio, interval
Standard deviation	Ratio, interval
Measures of normality	
Skewness	Ratio, interval
Kurtosis	Ratio, interval

> **Box 15.5 Checklist for conducting quantitative data analysis**
>
> 1. Are you confident that your research design was sound?
> 2. Have you been systematic and rigorous in the collection of your data?
> 3. Is your identification of variables adequate?
> 4. Are your measurements of the variables reliable?
> 5. Is the analysis suitable for the measurement scale (nominal, ordinal, interval or ratio)?

addition to the descriptive statistics we have explained in this chapter. We discuss inferential statistics in the next chapter, but if these are not required for your study, you may find the checklist in Box 15.5 helps ensure the successful completion of your analysis.

Activities

This chapter is entirely activity-based. If you have access to *SPSS*, start at the beginning of the chapter and work your way through. If *SPSS* is not available, do the same activities using an alternative software package following the on-screen tutorials and help facilities.

PROGRESS TEST

Complete the following sentences:

1. A _____ is the number of observations for a particular data value in a variable.
2. A descriptive statistic that summarizes a frequency as a proportion of 100 is called a _____.
3. A _____ is a display that summarizes the frequencies for all the data values in a particular variable.
4. The analysis of two variables together is known as _____ analysis.
5. A variable that is coded 1 if the characteristic is present and 0 otherwise is known as a _____ variable.

Are the following statements true or false?

6. The alternative hypothesis is written as H_0.
7. A pie chart is suitable for summarizing frequency distributions from nominal or ordinal variables.
8. A histogram is suitable for summarizing frequency distributions from ratio or interval variables.

9. The mean should only be calculated for nominal or ordinal variables.
10. The standard deviation should only be calculated for ratio or interval variables.

Multiple choice questions:

11. A number that describes a sample is called:
    a) a code
    b) a data value
    c) a parameter
    d) a statistic

12. A number that describes a population is called:
    a) a code
    b) a data value
    c) a parameter
    d) a statistic

13. The mid-value of a set of data arranged in size order is:
    a) the mean
    b) the median
    c) the mode
    d) the rank

14. The measure used to describe the asymmetry of a frequency distribution is:
    a) deviation
    b) kurtosis
    c) normality
    d) skewness

15. A Type I error is where:
    a) the null hypothesis is true, but the test leads to its rejection
    b) the null hypothesis is true and the test leads to its acceptance
    c) the alternative hypothesis is true, but the test leads to the acceptance of the null hypothesis
    d) the significance level is set too high

References

BERR (Department for Business, Enterprise & Regulatory Reform) (2008) *Small and Medium-Sized Enterprise (SME) Statistics for the UK and Regions 2007*, URN 08/92. [Accessed 22 August 2008]. Available from http://stats.berr.gov.uk/ed/sme.

Collis, J. (2003) *Directors' Views on Exemption from the Statutory Audit*, URN 03/1342, London: DTI, October. Available from http://www.berr.gov.uk/files/file25971.pdf.

Duckworth, W. M. and Alwan, L. C. (2009) *The Practice of Business Statistics*, 2nd edition, New York: W.H. Freeman and Company.

Field, A. (2000) *Discovering Statistics Using SPSS for Windows*, London: Sage.

Jensen, M. C. and Meckling, W. H. (1976) 'Theory of the firm: Managerial behavior, agency costs and the ownership structure', *Journal of Financial Economics*, 3, pp. 305–60.

Kervin, J. B. (1992) *Methods for Business Research*, New York: HarperCollins.

Lovie, P. (1986) 'Identifying Outliers' in Lovie, A. D. (ed.) *New Developments in Statistics for Psychology and the Social Sciences* 1, London: Methuen.

Moore, D., McCabe, G. P., Duckworth, W. M. and Alwan, L. C. (2009) *The Practice of Business Statistics*, 2nd edition, New York: W.H. Freeman and Company.

Rowntree, D. (1991) *Statistics Without Tears: A Primer for Non-mathematicians*, Harmondsworth: Penguin.

Upton, G. and Cook, I. (2006) *Oxford Dictionary of Statistics*, 2nd edition, Oxford: Oxford University Press.

Glossary

Bar chart	A graphical presentation of a frequency distribution of an ordinal or nominal variable in which the data are represented by a series of separate vertical or horizontal bars. The frequencies are indicated by the height (or length) of the bars.
Confidence interval	A parametric technique for estimating a range of values of a sample statistic that is likely to contain an unknown population parameter at a given level of probability; the wider the confidence interval, the higher the confidence level.
Descriptive statistics	A group of statistical methods used to summarize, describe or display quantitative data.
Dichotomous variable	A variable that has two categories, such as gender.
Error	The difference between the mean and the data value (observation).
Frequency	The number of observations for a particular data value in a variable.
Frequency distribution	An array that summarizes the frequencies for all the data values in a particular variable
Histogram	A refinement of a bar chart where adjoining bars touch, indicating continuous interval or ratio data. Frequency is represented by area, with the width of each bar indicating the class interval and the height indicating the frequency of the class.
Inferential statistics	A group of statistical methods and models used to draw conclusions about a population from quantitative data relating to a random sample.
Interquartile range	A measure of dispersion that represents the difference between the upper quartile and the lower quartile (the middle 50%) of a frequency distribution arranged in size order.
Kurtosis	A measure of the extent to which a frequency distribution is fatter or more peaked than a normal distribution (a normal distribution has a kurtosis of 0).
Line graph	A graphical presentation of a frequency distribution in which the data are represented by a series of points joined by a line; only suitable for continuous data.
Mean (x)	A measure of central tendency based on the arithmetic average of a set of data values.
Median (M)	A measure of central tendency based on the mid-value of a set of data arranged in size order.
Mode (m)	A measure of central tendency based on the most frequently occurring value in set of data (there may be multiple modes).
Normal distribution	A theoretical frequency distribution that is bell-shaped and symmetrical with tails extending indefinitely either side of the centre. The mean, median and mode coincide at the centre.
Parameter	A number that describes a population.
Percentage frequency	A descriptive statistic that summarizes a frequency as a proportion of 100.

Pie chart	A circular diagram showing the percentage frequency distribution of a nominal variable in which the data are represented by a series of segments. Each segment represents an area that is proportional to the whole 'pie'.
Range	A measure of dispersion that represents the difference between the maximum value and the minimum value in a frequency distribution arranged in size order.
Significance level	Level of confidence that the results of a statistical analysis are not due to chance. It is usually expressed as the probability that the results of the statistical analysis are due to chance (usually 5% or less).
Skewness	A measure of the extent to which a frequency distribution is asymmetric (a normal distribution has a skewness of 0).
Standard deviation (sd)	A measure of dispersion that is the square root of the variance. A large standard deviation relative to the mean suggests the mean does not represent the data well.
Standard error (se)	The standard deviation between the means of different samples. A large standard error relative to the overall sample mean suggests the sample might not be representative of the population.
Statistic	A number that describes a sample.
Statistics	A body of methods and theory that is applied to quantitative data.
Stem-and-leaf plot	A diagram that uses the data values in a frequency distribution to create a display. The data values are arranged in size order and each is divided into the leading digit (the stem) and trailing digits (the leaves).
Type I error	An error that occurs when H_0 is true, but the test leads to its rejection.
Type II error	An error that occurs when H_1 is true, but the test leads to the acceptance of H_0.
Variance	The mean of the squared errors.

CHAPTER 16
Analysing data using inferential statistics

LEARNING OBJECTIVES

When you have studied this chapter, you should be able to:
- determine whether parametric or non-parametric methods are appropriate
- conduct tests of difference for independent or dependent samples
- conduct tests of association between variables
- predict an outcome from one or more variables
- use time series analysis to examine trends.

16.1 Introduction

The *descriptive statistics* covered in the previous chapter lie at the heart of a univariate analysis of research data and allow you to examine frequency distributions and measure the central tendency and dispersion of the data. At the postgraduate or doctoral level, this will merely form the exploratory stage of your research and you will need to go on to conduct a further analysis based on *inferential statistics*. Before you start, you need to consider the underlying characteristics of the research data and decide whether *parametric* or *non-parametric* statistical tests are appropriate.

In this chapter, we will explain how to generate inferential statistics based on some of the main bivariate and multivariate methods of analysis. As in the last chapter, we will provide step-by-step instructions using *SPSS for Windows* and use the data from the Collis Report (2003) as our main example. As some studies incorporate the analysis of longitudinal data, we devote a section to preparing data for a *time series analysis*, which is used for forecasting trends.

Our intention is to provide a practical guide and provide sufficient theoretical content to help you gain a basic understanding of the most widely used methods. It is important to remember that we are only looking at a selection of the analytical techniques available and you may find it helpful to discuss other possibilities and further reading with your supervisors. You are strongly advised to do this 'at the design stage of the project, not after you have collected the data' (Robson, 1993, p. 307).

16.2 Planning the analysis

When planning your analysis, you will be guided by your hypotheses and the nature of your data. This will help you determine the appropriate tests and techniques to use. The starting point is to examine your hypotheses and identify the variables to be included in the analysis. You can then determine whether parametric or non-parametric tests are appropriate for your data and decide whether *bivariate* analysis and/or *multivariate* analysis is needed to address your research questions.

16.2.1 Hypotheses and variables in the analysis

You will remember from previous chapters that a *hypothesis* is a proposition that can be tested for association or causality against *empirical evidence* (data based on observation or experience). It is important to remember that the methods used by positivists conducting business research have their roots in the experimental designs used by the natural scientists. This is reflected in the language associated with some tests, when the dependent variable (DV) in the hypothesis is identified, whose values are influenced by one or more independent variables (IVs). In the previous chapter, we gave the example of a study where the intensity of the lighting (the IV) in an office was manipulated to observe the effect on the productivity levels (the DV). You might want to predict that there will be an effect in a specific direction, such as better lighting is associated with higher productivity levels. This is known as a *one-tailed hypothesis*. A *two-tailed hypothesis* is where you predict the IV has an effect on the DV, but you cannot predict the direction.

Key definitions

Bivariate analysis is the analysis of data from two variables.
Multivariate analysis is the analysis of data from more than two variables.
Univariate analysis is the analysis of data from one variable.

The analysis we are going to explain in this part of the chapter is based on the Collis Report (2003). As you can see from Box 16.1, the nine hypotheses tested in that study were one-tailed because in each hypothesis the direction of the effect was predicted.

Table 16.1 summarizes the variables in the analysis, where **Volaudit** is the DV (more accurately described as the *outcome variable* in regression analysis) and the other variables are the IVs (more accurately described as the *predictor variables* in a regression model). The table also shows how the variables are coded, some of which you created in the last chapter.

Box 16.1 Hypotheses to be tested

H1 *Ceteris paribus*, the likelihood of the directors choosing a voluntary audit does not increase with company size, as measured by turnover.

H2 *Ceteris paribus*, the likelihood of the directors choosing a voluntary audit does not increase with perceptions that the audit provides a check on accounting records and systems.

H3 *Ceteris paribus*, the likelihood of the directors choosing a voluntary audit does not increase with perceptions that the audit improves the quality of the financial information.

H4 *Ceteris paribus*, the likelihood of the directors choosing a voluntary audit does not increase with perceptions that the audit improves the credibility of the financial information.

H5 *Ceteris paribus*, the likelihood of the directors choosing a voluntary audit does not increase with perceptions that the audit has a positive effect on the company's credit score.

H6 *Ceteris paribus*, the likelihood of the directors choosing a voluntary audit does not increase if the company is not family owned.

H7 *Ceteris paribus*, the likelihood of the directors choosing a voluntary audit does not increase if there are shareholders without access to internal financial information.

H8 *Ceteris paribus*, the likelihood of the directors choosing a voluntary audit does not increase if the statutory accounts are given to the bank and other providers of finance.

H9 *Ceteris paribus*, the likelihood of the directors choosing a voluntary audit does not increase if they have a degree, a professional/vocational qualification or have studied/trained in business or management subjects.

Table 16.1 Variables in the analysis

Hypothesis	Variable	Description
	Volaudit	Whether company would have a voluntary audit (1, 0)
H1	Turnover	Turnover in 2002 accounts (£k)
H2	Check	Audit provides a check on accounting records and systems (5 = Agree, 1 = Disagree)
H3	Quality	Audit improves the quality of the financial information (5 = Agree, 1 = Disagree)
H4	Credibility	Audit improves the credibility of the financial information (5 = Agree, 1 = Disagree)
H5	Creditscore	Audit has a positive effect on the credit rating score (5 = Agree, 1 = Disagree)
H6	Family	Whether company is wholly family-owned (1, 0)
H7	Exowners	Whether company has external shareholders (1, 0)
H8	Bank	Whether statutory accounts are given to the bank/lenders (1, 0)
H9	Education	Whether respondent has degree/qualifications/training (1, 0)

16.2.2 Parametric or non-parametric tests

The term *inferential statistics* stems from the fact that data are collected about a *random sample* with a view to making inferences about the *population*. You will remember that a population is a body of people or any collection of items under consideration, and a random sample is a representative subset of the population. Your reason for obtaining a random sample is to obtain estimates of theoretical *population parameters*. For example, you may want to use the – sample mean ($\bar{x}$) and the sample standard deviation (s) to make inferences about the population mean (μ pronounced 'mu') and the population standard deviation (s pronounced 'sigma'). Traditionally, sample statistics are represented by Roman letters and population parameters are represented by Greek letters.

Key definitions

Inferential statistics are a group of statistical methods and models used to draw conclusions about a population from quantitative data relating to a random sample

Inferential statistics include *parametric* tests and *non-parametric* tests. Parametric tests make certain assumptions about the distributional characteristics of the population under investigation. To determine whether parametric tests are appropriate, you need to establish whether your research data meet the following four basic assumptions. Drawing on Field (2000), these can be summarized as follows:

- The variable is measured on a ratio or interval scale (therefore, you cannot use a parametric test for ordinal or nominal data).
- The data are from a population with a normal distribution (therefore, you cannot use a parametric test for ratio or interval data with a skewed distribution).
- There is *homogeneity of variance*, which means the variances are stable in a test across groups of subjects, or the variance of one variable is stable at all levels in a test against another variable.
- The data values in the variable are independent (in other words, they come from different cases or the behaviour of one subject does not influence the behaviour of another).

The reason why these assumptions are so important is that the calculations that underpin parametric tests are based on the mean of the data values. However, non-parametric tests do not rely on the data meeting these assumptions because in a non-parametric test, the frequencies are first arranged in size order and the calculations performed on the ranks rather than the data values. You need to bear in mind that since the ranks are proxies for the information contained in the original data, there is a greater chance the test will lead to the type of incorrect result known as a *Type II error*. This refers to the situation where H_1 is true, but the test leads to the acceptance of H_0 (see Chapter 11). Therefore, in a non-parametric test, you might not be able to detect a significant effect in the ranked data, but one exists in the original data (Field, 2000). This explains why non-parametric tests are less powerful and the results less reliable than for parametric tests (Oakshott, 1994).

If you look at the variables we are going to analyse in Table 16.1, you will see that **Turnover** is the only one that is measured on a ratio or interval scale. Therefore,

Table 16.2 Bivariate and multivariate analysis

Purpose	For parametric data	For non-parametric data
Tests of difference for independent or dependent samples	*t*-test	Mann-Whitney test
Tests of association between two nominal variables	Not applicable	Chi-square test
Tests of association between two quantitative variables	Pearson's correlation	Spearman's correlation
Predicting an outcome from one or more variables	Linear regression	Logistic regression

the first assumption is met for this variable. However, the results of the normality tests we conducted as part of our exploratory analysis (see Chapter 11) showed that Turnover does not have a normal distribution (it was positively skewed with the majority of companies having a turnover at the smaller end of the scale). Since all the other variables in the analysis are measured on an ordinal or nominal scale, it is clear that the next stage of the analysis must be based on non-parametric tests.

Key definitions

A **normal distribution** is a theoretical frequency distribution that is bell-shaped and symmetrical, with tails extending indefinitely either side of the centre. The mean, median and mode coincide at the centre.

A **Type 1 error** occurs when H_0 is true, but the test leads to its rejection.

A **Type II error** occurs when H_1 is true, but the test leads to the acceptance of H_0.

The tests you choose for your study will depend on your hypotheses and your research questions. A typical analysis might start with bivariate analysis to explore differences between independent or related samples and to test for relationships between variables and measure the strength of those relationships. This might lead to multivariate analysis where a regression model is developed from one or more predictor variables. Table 16.2 summarizes the parametric and non-parametric methods we are going to examine. We will demonstrate the non-parametric methods using the data from the Collis Report (2003) first and then explain the equivalent parametric method. If you have longitudinal data, you will also need to refer to the final sections of the chapter where we discuss indexation methods and time series analysis.

16.3 Tests of difference

16.3.1 Mann-whitney test

If you have non-parametric data for an IV measured on a quantitative scale (a non-normal ratio or interval scale, or an ordinal scale) and a DV containing two independent samples, you can use the *Mann-Whitney test* to establish whether there is a difference between the two samples. In the Collis Report, **Volaudit** is the DV. This is a dummy variable relating to whether the company would have a voluntary audit, and is coded 1 = Yes, 0 = No. This gives us our two independent samples or groups of subjects. We are going to use the Mann-Whitney test for each of the following IVs: **Turnover**, which is measured on a non-parametric ratio scale; **Check, Quality, Credibility** and **Creditscore**, which are measured on an ordinal scale where 1 = Disagree and 5 = Agree. The null hypothesis (H_0) is that there is no difference between the two groups.

Start *SPSS* in the usual way and open the file named **Data for 790 cos.sav**. Although we are going to run five tests, we can instruct *SPSS* to do this in one procedure as follows:

- From the menu, select **Analyze** ⇒ **Nonparametric tests** ⇒ **2 Independent samples**.
- Move **Turnover, Check, Quality, Credibility** and **Creditscore** to **Test Variable List**. The order does not matter, but our principle is to list them in the order of the hypotheses shown in Table 16.1 (which coincides with the level of measurement).
- Move **Volaudit** to **Grouping Variable** and click **Define groups**.
- The two groups in **Volaudit** are labelled 1 and 0, so in **Group 1** type 1 and in **Group 2** type 0 (see Figure 16.1).
- We want the default test, **Mann-Whitney U**, so click **OK** to see the output (see Table 16.3).

Table 16.3 presents the results of each of the five tests in two tables. The first table summarizes the data after it has been ranked (you will remember that in a non-parametric test, the frequencies are arranged in size order and the calculations performed on the ranks rather than the original data values. Therefore, it tells us which of the two groups in the DV had higher mean rank. The second table shows the test statistic (**Mann-Whitney U**) and the final line shows the probability value (**Asymp. Sig. (2-tailed)**). Since our hypotheses were one-tailed (they predicted the

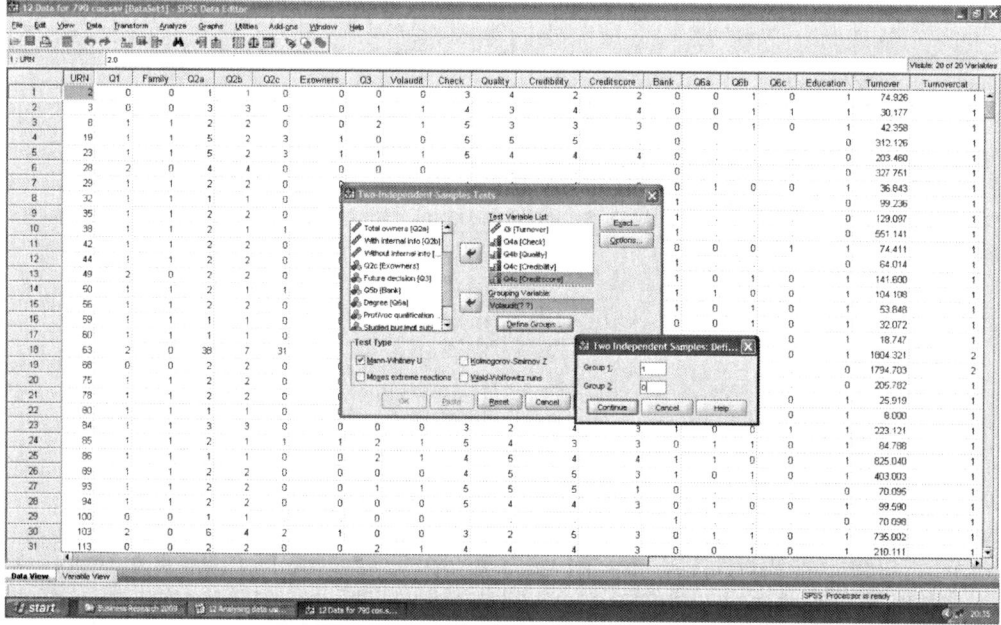

Figure 16.1 Running a Mann-Whitney test

Table 16.3 Mann-Whitney test for Turnover, Check, Quality, Credibility and Creditscore

Ranks

	Volaudit	N	Mean Rank	Sum of Ranks
Turnover	0 No	438	311.29	136344.50
	1 Yes	334	485.13	162033.50
	Total	772		
Check	0 No	362	285.45	103332.00
	1 Yes	320	404.91	129571.00
	Total	682		
Quality	0 No	356	268.62	95629.00
	1 Yes	316	412.97	130499.00
	Total	672		
Credibility	0 No	358	278.17	99584.00
	1 Yes	315	403.86	127217.00
	Total	673		
Creditscore	0 No	355	273.52	97100.00
	1 Yes	312	402.81	125678.00
	Total	667		

Test Statistics[a]

	Turnover	Check	Quality	Credibility	Creditscore
Mann-Whitney U	40203.500	37629.000	32083.000	35323.000	33910.000
Wilcoxon W	136344.500	103332.000	95629.000	99584.000	97100.000
Z	−10.731	−8.519	−9.864	−8.851	−8.928
Asymp. Sig. (2-tailed)	.000	.000	.000	.000	.000

a. Grouping Variable: Volaudit

direction of the relationship), we need to divide the probability values shown in the table for a two-tailed hypothesis by 2. The outcome is unchanged with a very high level of significance $(p < 0.01)$ and we have evidence to reject the null hypothesis for this test in respect of **Turnover, Check, Quality, Credibility** and **Creditscore**.

You may have noticed that the results also show a test statistic labelled **Wilcoxon W** and its associated z score. This is used when there are two sets of scores from the same subjects. For example, in a longitudinal study where you have data from the same subjects that relate to the same variable collected on a previous occasion.

16.3.2 T-Test

If you have parametric data for an IV measured on a ratio or interval scale and a DV containing two independent samples, you can use the *independent t-test* to establish whether there is a difference between the two samples or groups of subjects. The null hypothesis is that there is no difference between the two groups.

In a research design where independent samples are used, you might take groups to participate in difference phases of an experiment. Perhaps you are interested in the fuel consumption of vehicles where some drivers have been on a safe driving course and others have not. The first group is the experimental group and the second group is the control group. One problem with this is that because the two groups are independent, any difference could be due to other factors; for example, some drivers may be more experienced or more cautious than others.

One way round this problem is to adopt a paired-samples design. In this case, you would match a driver in the experimental group with a driver in the control group, who has similar characteristics that might affect his or her driving performance (for example driving experience, accident rate and age). You will also need to use the *paired-sample t-test* for dependent samples if you have two sets of data for a single group of subjects.

The *t*-test was not used in the Collis Report, but if you want to find it on *SPSS*, the procedure is as follows:

- From the menu, select **Analyze** ⇒ **Compare Means** ⇒ **Independent-Samples T Test** ... (or **Paired-Samples T Test** ...).
- Move the appropriate variables into the **Test variable** and **Grouping variable** boxes and then click the **Define groups** to identify the two groups.

The *SPSS* output for an independent *t*-test provides a table with descriptive statistics, which is followed by a second table, which requires a little explanation because you need to decide which of the two rows of results are relevant. You need to look first at the results of the **Levene's Test for Equality of Variances**. If the probability statistic (**Sig**.) is not significant $(p < 0.05)$, you should refer to the *t*-test results in the row labelled **Equal variances assumed**. Conversely, if the probability statistic (**Sig**.) for the Levene's test is significant $(p \leq 0.05)$, you should refer to the *t*-test results in the row labelled **Equal variances not assumed** (Field, 2000).

As discussed in the previous section, if you have predicted the direction of the relationship in your hypothesis, you will need to divide the probability value for the *t*-test by 2. If the result is significant $(p \leq 0.05)$, you have evidence to reject the null hypothesis that there is no difference between the two groups.

16.4 Tests of association

16.4.1 Chi-square test

If you have non-parametric data for two variables measured on a nominal scale, you will remember from the previous chapter that you can use a cross-tabulation as part of your bivariate analysis. If the two variables each contain two categories, a cross-tabulation produces a 2 × 2 table containing 2 columns and 2 rows, with 4 cells altogether. We are going to take this a step further by conducting a *chi-square* (χ^2) *test* to find out whether there is a statistically significant association between the column and row categories. For a 2 × 2 table, the test is based on the assumption that the expected counts in each cell will be 5 or more (Moore, McCabe, Duckworth and Alwan, 2009) and compares the observed frequencies (actual counts) with the expected frequencies (theoretical counts).

We are going to measure the association between the two groups in our **DV** (**Volaudit**) and the dummy variables that represent the remaining IVs in the analysis: **Family, Exowners, Bank** and **Education**. The null hypothesis (H_0) we are testing is that there is no association between the two categories in each variable. Although

ANALYSING DATA USING INFERENTIAL STATISTICS

we are going to run four tests, we can instruct *SPSS* to do this in one procedure as follows:

- From the menu at the top, select **Analyze** ⇒ **Descriptive Statistics**… ⇒ **Crosstabs**.
- Move **Family, Exowners, Bank** and **Education** into **Row(s)**.
- Move **Volaudit** into **Column(s)**.
- Select **Statistics** and click **Chi-square** and **Continue**.
- Select **Cells**. Under **Counts**, you will see that **Observed** is the default, but also click **Expected**. Under **Percentages**, click **Column** and **Continue** (see Figure 16.2).
- Then click **OK** to see the output (see Table 16.4).

Do not be alarmed by the quantity of tables produced! It is simply that after reporting on the number of cases in each test, *SPSS* has generated a cross-tabulation and a table showing the results of the chi-square tests for each pair of variables tested. We will start by looking at the latter.

The chi-square statistic we are interested in is shown in the first row and bears the name of Karl Pearson, who proposed the chi-square test in 1900, following the publication of his work on correlation in 1895–8 (Upton and Cook, 2006; Moore *et al*, 2009). Any deviation from the null hypothesis makes the chi-square value larger. We also need to look at the probability statistic for Pearson's chi-square, which is shown in the third column of the first row under **Asymp. Sig.** (**2-sided**). Since our hypotheses are all one-sided, we need to divide the probability statistic by 2. Apart from **Education**, the significance levels for the variables tested are very high ($p < 0.01$). However, we must check the notes beneath each table to confirm that none of the cells have an expected count of less than 5, which can be a problem with a small sample. However, the notes confirm that this assumption of the test is met.

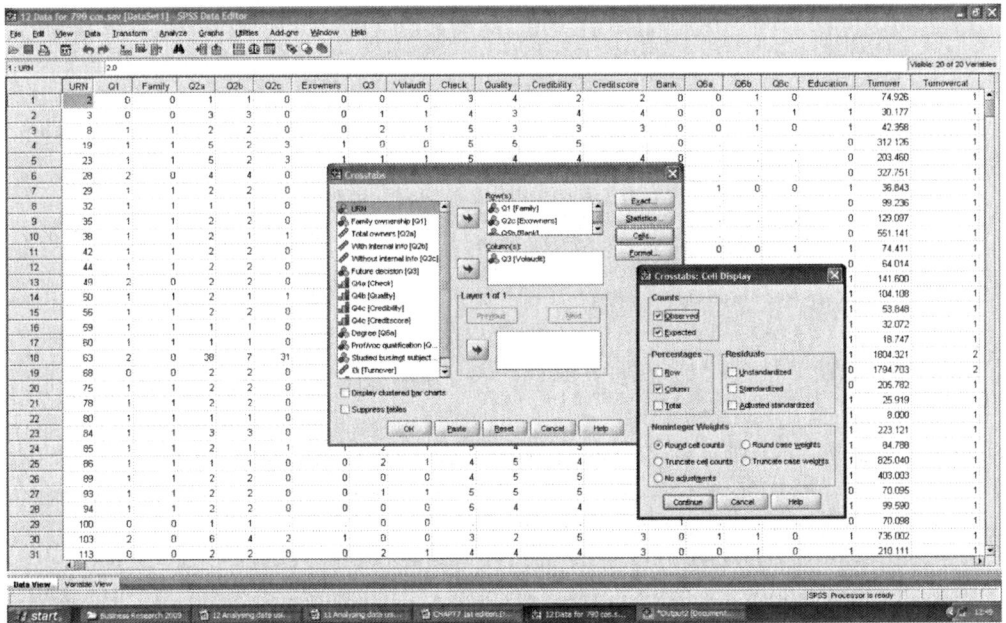

Figure 16.2 Running a Chi-square test

Table 16.4 Chi-square tests for Volaudit against Family, Exowners, Bank and Education

Case Processing Summary

	Cases					
	Valid		Missing		Total	
	N	Percent	N	Percent	N	Percent
Family * Volaudit	767	97.1%	23	2.9%	790	100.0%
Exowners * Volaudit	690	87.3%	100	12.7%	790	100.0%
Bank * Volaudit	772	97.7%	18	2.3%	790	100.0%
Education * Volaudit	772	97.7%	18	2.3%	790	100.0%

Family * Volaudit

Crosstab

			Volaudit		Total
			0 Otherwise	1 Yes	
Family	0 Otherwise	Count	102	144	246
		Expected Count	138.9	107.1	246.0
		% within Volaudit	23.6%	43.1%	32.1%
	1 Wholly family-owned	Count	331	190	521
		Expected Count	294.1	226.9	521.0
		% within Volaudit	76.4%	56.9%	67.9%
Total		Count	433	334	767
		Expected Count	433.0	334.0	767.0
		% within Volaudit	100.0%	100.0%	100.0%

Chi-Square Tests

	Value	Df	Asymp. Sig. (2-sided)	Exact Sig. (2-sided)	Exact Sig. (1-sided)
Pearson Chi-Square	33.103[a]	1	.000		
Continuity Correction[b]	32.212	1	.000		
Likelihood Ratio	33.031	1	.000		
Fisher's Exact Test				.000	.000
Linear-by-Linear Association	33.060	1	.000		
N of Valid Cases	767				

a. 0 cells (.0%) have expected count less than 5. The minimum expected count is 107.12
b. Computed only for a 2 × 2 table

Exowners * Volaudit

Crosstab

			Volaudit		Total
			0 Otherwise	1 Yes	
Exowners	0 Otherwise	Count	338	232	570
		Expected Count	318.0	252.0	570.0
		% within Volaudit	87.8%	76.1%	82.6%
	1 External owners	Count	47	73	120
		Expected Count	67.0	53.0	120.0
		% within Volaudit	12.2%	23.9%	17.4%
Total		Count	385	305	690
		Expected Count	385.0	305.0	690.0
		% within Volaudit	100.0%	100.0%	100.0%

Chi-Square Tests

	Value	Df	Asymp. Sig. (2-sided)	Exact Sig. (2-sided)	Exact Sig. (1-sided)
Pearson Chi-Square	16.289[a]	1	.000		
Continuity Correction[b]	15.483	1	.000		
Likelihood Ratio	16.210	1	.000		
Fisher's Exact Test				.000	.000
Linear-by-Linear Association	16.266	1	.000		
N of Valid Cases	690				

a. 0 cells (.0%) have expected count less than 5. The minimum expected count is 53.04
b. Computed only for a 2x2 table

Bank * Volaudit

Crosstab

			Volaudit		Total
			0 Otherwise	1 Yes	
Bank	0 Otherwise	Count	264	116	380
		Expected Count	215.6	164.4	380.0
		% within Volaudit	60.3%	34.7%	49.2%
	1 Yes	Count	174	218	392
		Expected Count	222.4	169.6	392.0
		% within Volaudit	39.7%	65.3%	50.8%
Total		Count	438	334	772
		Expected Count	438.0	334.0	772.0
		% within Volaudit	100.0%	100.0%	100.0%

Chi-Square Tests

	Value	Df	Asymp. Sig. (2-sided)	Exact Sig. (2-sided)	Exact Sig. (1-sided)
Pearson Chi-Square	49.468[a]	1	.000		
Continuity Correction[b]	48.452	1	.000		
Likelihood Ratio	50.092	1	.000		
Fisher's Exact Test				.000	.000
Linear-by-Linear Association	49.404	1	.000		
N of Valid Cases	772				

a. 0 cells (.0%) have expected count less than 5. The minimum expected count is 164.40
b. Computed only for a 2 × 2 table

Education * Volaudit

Crosstab

			Volaudit		Total
			0 Otherwise	1 Yes	
Education	0 Otherwise	Count	124	105	229
		Expected Count	129.9	99.1	229.0
		% within Volaudit	28.3%	31.4%	29.7%
	1 Yes	Count	314	229	543
		Expected Count	308.1	234.9	543.0
		% within Volaudit	71.7%	68.6%	70.3%
Total		Count	438	334	772
		Expected Count	438.0	334.0	772.0
		% within Volaudit	100.0%	100.0%	100.0%

Chi-Square Tests

	Value	Df	Asymp. Sig. (2-sided)	Exact Sig. (2-sided)	Exact Sig. (1-sided)
Pearson Chi-Square	.888a	1	.346		
Continuity Correctionb	.744	1	.388		
Likelihood Ratio	.886	1	.347		
Fisher's Exact Test				.382	.194
Linear-by-Linear Association	.887	1	.346		
N of Valid Cases	772				

a. 0 cells (.0%) have expected count less than 5. The minimum expected count is 99.08
b. Computed only for a 2 × 2 table

Therefore, we have evidence to reject the null hypothesis of no association in respect of **Family**, **Exowners** and **Bank**.

We need to look at the percentages in the cells of the cross-tabulations to interpret the association. These tell us that demand for voluntary audit is associated with companies that are not wholly family owned, have external owners or give their accounts to the bank/lenders but not with the characteristics of the respondent capture by Education. This means we must accept the null hypothesis represented by H9 in Box 16.1.

16.5 Correlation

Correlation is synonymous with its originator, Karl Pearson, who we mentioned in the previous section. Correlation offers additional information about an association between two quantitative variables (thus excluding those measured on a nominal scale) because it measures the direction and strength of any linear relationship between them. 'Most of the statistics used in the social sciences are based on linear models, which means that we try to fit straight-line models to the data collected' (Field, 2000, p. 11). In statistics, a *correlation coefficient is* 'a measure of the linear dependence of one numerical random variable on another' (Upton and Cook, 2006, p. 101). The two variables are not referred to as the DV and the IV because 'they are measured simultaneously and so no cause-and-effect relationship can be established' (Field, 2000, p. 78).

Key definitions

Correlation is a measure of the direction and strength of association between two quantitative variables. Correlation may be linear or non-linear, positive or negative.

The correlation coefficient is measured within the range −1 to +1. The direction of the correlation is positive if both variables increase together, but it is negative if one variable increases as the other decreases. The strength of the correlation is measured by the size of the correlation coefficient:

   1 represents a perfect positive linear association
   0 represents no linear association
   −1 represents a perfect negative linear association

ANALYSING DATA USING INFERENTIAL STATISTICS

Therefore, values in between can be graded roughly as:

0.90 to 0.99 (very high positive correlation)
0.70 to 0.89 (high positive correlation)
0.40 to 0.69 (medium positive correlation)
0 to 0.39 (low positive correlation)
0 to –0.39 (low negative correlation)
–0.40 to –0.69 (medium negative correlation)
–0.70 to –0.89 (high negative correlation)
–0.90 to –0.99 (very high negative correlation)

You need to take care when interpreting correlation coefficients, since correlation between two variables does not prove the existence of a causal link between them; two causally unrelated variables can be correlated because they both relate to a third variable. For example, the sales of ice-cream and suntan lotion may be correlated because they both relate to higher temperatures.

16.5.1 Bivariate scatterplot

If you have parametric data, a preliminary step is to generate a display of the relationship between the two quantitative variables using a simple *scatterplot*. One variable is plotted against the other on a graph as a pattern of points, which indicates the direction and strength of any linear correlation. The more the points cluster around a straight line, the stronger the correlation.

- If the points tend to cluster around a line that runs from the lower left to the upper right of the graph, the correlation is *positive*, as shown in Figure 16.3. Positive correlation occurs when an increase in the value of one variable is associated with an increase in the value of the other. For example, an increase in the volume of orders from customers may be associated with increased calls to customers by the sales representatives.
- If points tend to cluster around a line that runs from the upper left to the lower right of the graph, the correlation is *negative*, as shown in Figure 16.4. Negative correlation occurs when an increase in the value of one variable is associated with a decrease in the value of the other. For example, higher interest rates for borrowing may be associated with lower house sales.

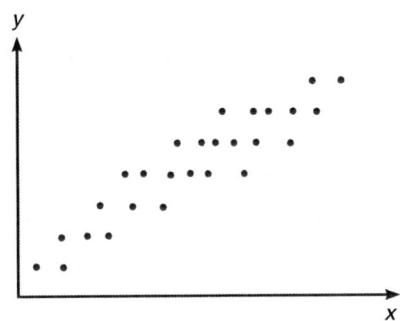

Figure 16.3 Scatterplot showing positive linear correlation

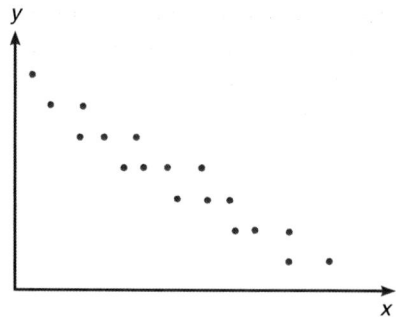

Figure 16.4 Scatterplot showing negative linear correlation

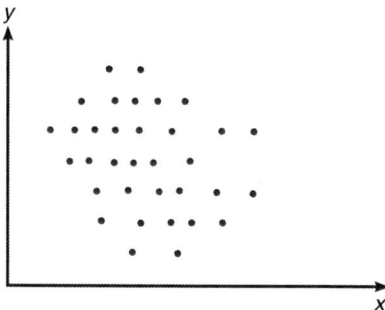

Figure 16.5 Scatterplot showing no correlation

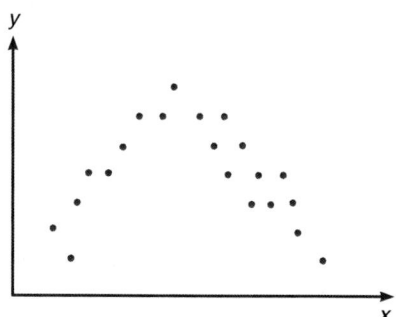

Figure 16.6 Scatterplot showing non-linear correlation

- If the points are scattered randomly throughout the graph, there is no correlation between the two variables as shown in Figure 16.5. Alternatively, the pattern may show non-linear correlation as illustrated in Figure 16.6.

Using *SPSS*, the general procedure is as follows:

- From the menu at the top, select **Graphs** ⇒ **Legacy Dialogs** ⇒ **Scatter/Dot**.
- The default is a Simple Scatterplot, but you will see that you have other choices.
- Move one variable into the **Y Axis** box and the other into the **X Axis** box.
- If you want different symbols or different coloured dots for different groups in the sample, move a third variable into the **Set Markers** by box. For example, if

you used **Bank**, companies giving their accounts to the bank could be shown with a currency symbol and the default dot could be retained for the others.
- With a small data set, you can move a variable into the **Label Cases by** box to use the value labels to label the points on the plot. For example, if you used ID, the points would be labelled with the case numbers; alternatively, you could use the case numbers to label any outliers.
- Move one or more variables that contain groups into the **Panel by** boxes to generate a matrix of charts for each group. For example, if you used **Family**, you could generate one chart for the companies that are wholly family-owned and another for the remainder.

16.5.2 Spearman's correlation

If you have non-parametric data for two variables measured on a ratio, interval or ordinal scale, you can use a correlation coefficient called *Spearman's rho* (or r_s) to measure the linear association between the variables. This overcomes the problem that the data are non-parametric by placing the data values in order of size and then examining differences in the rankings of one variable compared to the other.

We are going to use Spearman's *rho* to measure the correlation between **Check, Quality, Credibility, Creditscore** and **Turnover**. The null hypothesis (H_0) we are testing is that there is no correlation between any two variables and we can instruct *SPSS* to do this in one procedure as follows:

- From the menu at the top, select **Analyze** ⇒ **Correlate** ⇒ **Bivariate**...
- Move **Turnover, Check, Quality, Credibility** and **Creditscore** into **Variables**.
- Under **Correlation Coefficients**, deselect **Pearson** and then select **Spearman**.
- Under **Test of Significance**, click **One-tailed** and accept the default to **Flag significant correlations**.
- Under **Options**, you will see that the default for missing values is to **Exclude cases pairwise**, which we will accept, so you can now click **Continue** (see Figure 16.7).
- Then click **OK** to see the output (see Table 16.5).

The results in Table 16.5 are somewhat confusing because the statistics are shown for every possible pairing and this means some information is repeated. For convenience, we have added a shaded background to the duplicated information you can ignore. We will now examine the results in the cells without shading. A correlation coefficient of 1 (shown as 1.000) indicates perfect positive correlation. You can see this in the results where a variable is paired with itself. In all the other bivariate tests, you can see that the probability statistic (**Sig. 1-tailed**) tells us that the results are significant at the 1% level ($p = \leq 0.01$). Therefore, we can conclude that there is evidence to reject the null hypothesis of no correlation, but you need to remember that this does not mean we have established causality because there may be several explanatory variables.

One of the reasons for conducting this analysis is to check for potential *multicollinearity*. This occurs when the correlation between independent (predictor) variables in a multiple regression model is very high (≥ 0.90), which can give rise to unreliable estimates of the standard errors (Kervin, 1992, p. 608). Multicollinearity can make it

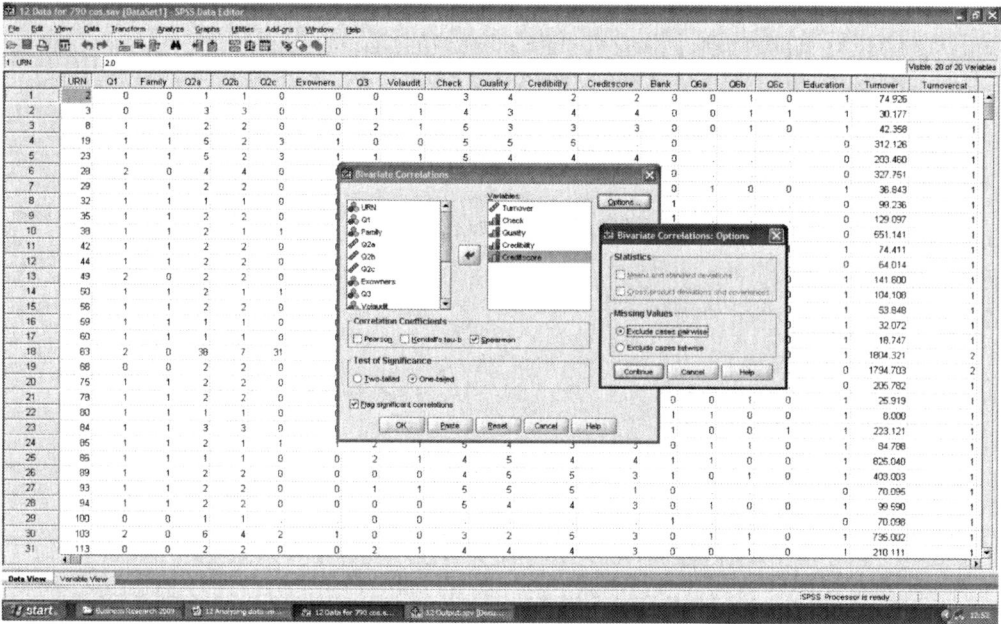

Figure 16.7   Running Spearman's correlation

Table 16.5   Spearman's rho for Turnover, Check, Quality, Credibility and Creditscore

			Correlation				
			Turnover	*Check*	*Quality*	*Credibility*	*Creditscore*
Spearman's rho	Turnover	Correlation Coefficient	1.000	.106**	.112**	.180**	.179**
		Sig. (1-tailed)	.	.003	.002	.000	.000
		N	790	697	687	688	681
	Check	Correlation Coefficient	.106**	1.000	.606**	.609**	.467**
		Sig. (1-tailed)	.003	.	.000	.000	.000
		N	697	697	681	682	674
	Quality	Correlation Coefficient	.112**	.606**	1.000	.651**	.529**
		Sig. (1-tailed)	.002	.000	.	.000	.000
		N	687	681	687	681	671
	Credibility	Correlation Coefficient	.180**	.609**	.651**	1.000	.532**
		Sig. (1-tailed)	.000	.000	.000	.	.000
		N	688	682	681	688	670
	Creditscore	Correlation Coefficient	.179**	.467**	.529**	.532**	1.000
		Sig. (1-tailed)	.000	.000	.000	.000	.
		N	681	674	671	670	681

**. Correlation is significant at the 0.01 level (1-tailed)

hard to identify the separate effects of the independent variables (Judge, Griffiths, Hill, Lutkepol and Lee, 1985, p. 896) and therefore it is essential to establish that there is no major 'overlap' in the predictive power of the variables. Kervin (1992) advises that if two predictor variables are highly related, the one with less theoretical importance to the research should be excluded from the analysis.

If you look at the correlation coefficients in our results, none of them are higher than 0.7, which means that the strength of the correlation is not likely to be a problem at the next stage of our analysis where we will be using multiple regression.

16.5.3 Pearson's correlation

If you have parametric data for two continuous variables, you can use *Pearson's product-moment correlation coefficient* (or *r*) to measure the linear association between the variables. You will remember that a continuous variable is a ratio or interval variable measured on a scale where the data can take any value within a given range (for example turnover or assets but not number of employees). The null hypothesis (H_0) is that there is no correlation between the two variables and the procedure in *SPSS* is as follows:

- From the menu at the top, select **Analyze** ⇒ **Correlate** ⇒ **Bivariate**...
- Move the appropriate variables into the **Variables** box.
- Under **Correlation Coefficients**, accept the default, which is **Pearson**.
- Under **Test of Significance**, select **One-tailed** if your hypotheses specify the direction of the correlation and accept the default to **Flag significant correlations**.
- Under **Options**, accept the default for missing values, which is to **Exclude cases pairwise**, so you can click **Continue** and **OK**.

16.6 Linear regression

We commented earlier that correlation offers additional information about an association between two variables because it measures the direction and strength of any linear relationship between them. *Linear regression* goes further by giving an indication of the ability of an independent variable to predict an outcome in a dependent variable where there is a linear relationship between them. The term *regression* was introduced in the late 19th century by Sir Francis Galton and refers to statistical models where 'the expected value of one variable Y is presumed to be dependent on one or more other variables (x_1, x_2, ...)' (Upton and Cook, 2006, p. 364). Linear regression is based on an algebraic equation that allows a straight line to be drawn on a graph from information about the slope (the gradient of the line in relation to the horizontal axis of the graph) and the intercept (the point at which the line crosses the vertical axis of a graph) (Field, 2000). The equation states the relationship between a dependent (outcome) variable Y and an independent (predictor) variable x (Upton and Cook, 2006, p. 243):

$$Y = \alpha + \beta x + \varepsilon$$

where

α (alpha) = the parameter corresponding to the intercept
β (beta) = the parameter corresponding to the slope
ε (epsilon) = a random error

In a linear regression model, an *error* (ε) is the difference between the observed (actual) values and the expected (theoretical) values in the model and therefore can be described as a *residual*. Drawing on Field (2000), the assumptions underpinning the linear equation can be summarized as follows:

- The dependent (outcome) variable is a continuous quantitative variable (measured on a ratio or interval scale), but an independent (predictor) variable can be continuous or a dummy variable (categorical variables can be used if they are first recoded as dummy variables).
- There is some variation in the data values of the independent variable(s) (in other words, none have a variance of 0).
- There is no perfect multicollinearity between the independent variables.
- None of the independent variables correlates with another variable that is not included in the analysis.
- The errors are uncorrelated and have a normal distribution with a mean of 0 and constant variance.
- The data values in the dependent variable are independent (in other words, they come from different cases).
- The relationship between the dependent variable and each independent variable is linear.

16.6.1 Simple or multiple linear regression

In a *simple regression* model, the outcome in the dependent variable is predicted by a single independent variable, while in a *multiple regression* model it is predicted by more than one independent variable. If your data meet the assumptions of the linear equation we have just described, you can use the following procedure in *SPSS*:

- From the menu at the top, select **Analyze** ⇒ **Regression** ⇒ **Linear**...
- Move your dependent (outcome) variable into **Dependent** and your independent (predictor) variable(s) into **Independent**.
- If you have theoretical reasons for choosing the predictor variables (in other words, your hypothesis is based on theory), accept the default method, **Enter**, which means the variables will be entered simultaneously as one block.
- Click on the **Options** button and under **Statistics and Plots** select any additional statistics you want to help you assess the fit of the model to the data and click **Continue**.
- Then click **OK** for the results.

It is useful at this point to summarize the results of the bivariate analysis for the data from the Collis Report (2003) in which we have tested the variables suggested by the theoretical framework that would influence the demand for the audit. This was represented by the dummy variable, **Volaudit**. The bivariate analysis found a significant difference between the two groups in **Volaudit** and **Turnover, Check, Quality, Credibility** and **Creditscore** and significant association between **Volaudit** when paired with **Family, Exowners** and **Bank**. The association with **Education** was not significant and we have accepted the null hypothesis represented by H9 in Box 16.1.

The next step is to run a multiple regression analysis with **Volaudit** as the dependent (outcome) variable and the remaining eight variables as the independent (predictor) variables. However, if the dependent variable is a dummy variable, the relationship with an independent variable is non-linear, which means the assumptions of the linear equation are not met. To overcome this problem, the dependent variable can be transformed into a logit, which allows a non-linear relationship to be expressed in a linear form (Field, 2000). If the dependent variable is a dummy variable and one or more of the independent variables are continuous quantitative variables, a *logistic regression* model can be used. If none of the independent variables is a continuous quantitative variable, a *logit* model is appropriate (Upton and Cook, 2006).

Key definitions

Linear regression is a measure of the ability of an independent variable to predict an outcome in a dependent variable where there is a linear relationship between them.

Since our dependent variable (**Volaudit**) is a dummy variable and one of our independent variables (**Turnover**) is a continuous quantitative variable, we should choose a logistic regression model.

16.6.2 Logistic regression

As explained above, *logistic regression* is a form of multiple regression that is used where the dependent variable is a dummy variable and one or more of the independent variables are continuous quantitative variables. Any other independent variables can be ordinal or dummy variables. Nominal variables can be used if they are first recoded as dummy variables, as described in Chapter 11. There is also an opportunity to do this automatically under the logistic regression options in *SPSS*. The procedure for logistic regression is as follows:

- From the menu at the top, select **Analyze** ⇒ **Regression** ⇒ **Binary logistic**...
- Move Volaudit into **Dependent**.
- **Move Turnover, Check, Quality, Credibility, Creditscore, Family, Exowners** and **Bank** into **Covariates** (the term used by *SPSS* for the independent variable). As we have mentioned before, the order does not matter, but it seems logical to list them in the order of the hypotheses shown in Table 16.1.
- We have theoretical reasons for choosing the independent variables, so accept the default method, **Enter**, which means they will be entered simultaneously as one block.
- If you have any nominal predictor variables that are not dummy variables, you can click on the **Categorical** button and move them into the **Categorical Covariates** box. You would highlight each variable in turn and under **Change Contrast** select **First** or **Last** to indicate which of these categories represents the characteristic is present and click **Change**. For example, if you did this for Family, the variable would then be shown as **Family(Indicator(first))**, as illustrated in Figure 16.8. Click **Cancel** to leave that dialogue box.
- Now click on the **Options** button and under **Statistics and Plots** select **Hosmer-Lemeshow goodness-of-fit** to help you assess the fit of the model to the data and click **Continue**.
- Then click **OK** for the results (see Table 16.6).

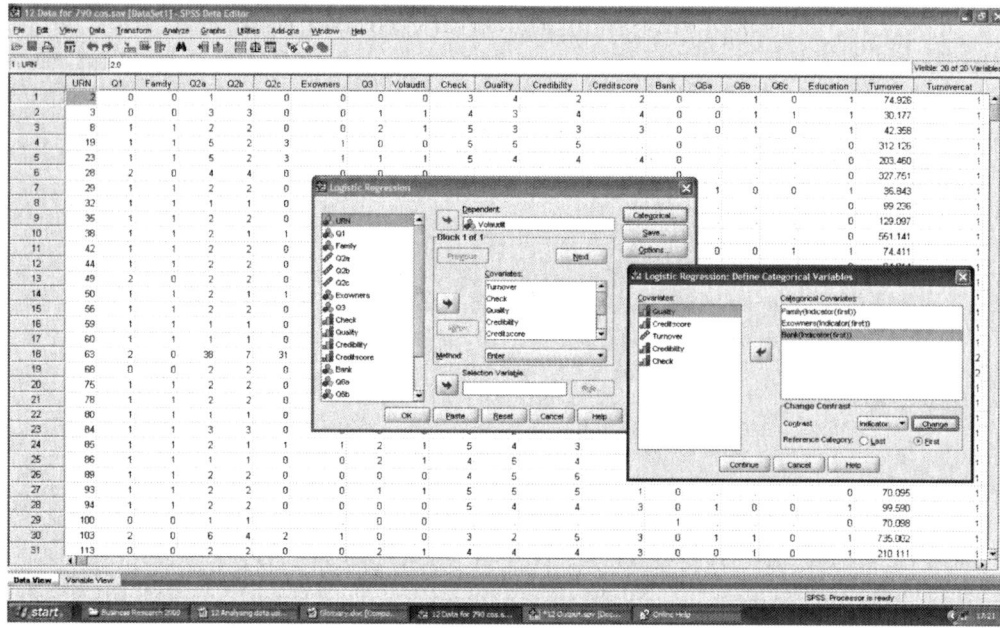

Figure 16.8 Running a logistic regression

TABLE 16.6 Logistic regression for Volaudit

Case Processing Summary

Unweighted Cases[a]		N	Percent
Selected Cases	Included in Analysis	588	74.4
	Missing Cases	202	25.6
	Total	790	100.0
Unselected Cases		0	.0
Total		790	100.0

a. If weight is in effect, see classification table for the total number of cases

Dependent Variable Encoding

Original Value	Internal Value
0 No	0
1 Yes	1

Block 0: Beginning Block

Classification Table[a,b]

			Predicted		
				Q3	
Observed			0 No	1 Yes	Percentage Correct
Step 0	Q3	0 No	306	0	100.0
		1 Yes	282	0	.0
		Overall Percentage			52.0

a. Constant is included in the model
b. The cut value is .500

Variables in the Equation

		B	S.E.	Wald	Df	Sig.	Exp(B)
Step 0	Constant	−.082	.083	.979	1	.322	.922

Variables not in the Equation

			Score	Df	Sig.
Step 0	Variables	Turnover	67.579	1	.000
		Check	58.876	1	.000
		Quality	82.641	1	.000
		Credibility	73.669	1	.000
		Creditscore	65.224	1	.000
		Family	25.419	1	.000
		Exowners	14.612	1	.000
		Bank	39.666	1	.000
		Overall Statistics	173.140	8	.000

Block 1: Method = Enter

Omnibus Tests of Model Coefficients

		Chi-square	df	Sig.
Step 1	Step	205.031	8	.000
	Block	205.031	8	.000
	Model	205.031	8	.000

Model Summary

Step	−2 Log likelihood	Cox & Snell R Square	Nagelkerke R Square
1	609.130[a]	.294	.393

a. Estimation terminated at iteration number 5 because parameter estimates changed by less than .001

Hosmer and Lemeshow Test

Step	Chi-square	Df	Sig.
1	8.306	8	.404

Contingency Table for Hosmer and Lemeshow Test

		Volaudit = 0 No		Volaudit = 1 Yes		
		Observed	Expected	Observed	Expected	Total
Step 1	1	55	55.356	4	3.644	59
	2	50	49.934	9	9.066	59
	3	43	45.181	16	13.819	59
	4	46	40.020	13	18.980	59
	5	31	33.309	28	25.691	59
	6	27	27.177	32	31.823	59
	7	21	23.189	38	35.811	59
	8	14	17.345	45	41.655	59
	9	16	10.681	43	48.319	59
	10	3	3.809	54	53.191	57

Classification Table[a]

		Observed	Predicted		
			\ Q3		
			0 No	1 Yes	Percentage Correct
Step 1	Q3	0 No	225	81	73.5
		1 Yes	71	211	74.8
		Overall Percentage			74.1

a. The cut value is .500

Variables in the Equation

		B	S.E.	Wald	df	Sig.	Exp(B)
Step 1	Turnover	.001	.000	21.810	1	.000	1.001
	Check	.246	.124	3.932	1	.047	1.278
	Quality	.403	.104	15.086	1	.000	1.496
	Credibility	.124	.128	.939	1	.333	1.132
	Creditscore	.256	.097	7.026	1	.008	1.292
	Family	−.794	.214	13.767	1	.000	.452
	Exowners	.644	.268	5.796	1	.016	1.905
	Bank	.448	.218	4.212	1	.040	1.565
	Constant	−4.116	.551	55.779	1	.000	.016

This is another situation where there is no need to be alarmed by the volume of output. The first table to check is the **Case Processing Summary** at the beginning, which shows that 588 cases in the sample of 790 were included in the analysis. In multivariate analysis, a case is omitted if there is missing data for any one of the variables and this can be a problem with small samples. However, it is not a matter of concern here.

We can skip the tables in Block 0 where no variables have been entered in the model and concentrate on Block 1, starting with the **Model Summary**. In this table, the **Nagelkerke R Square** indicates that the model including our predictor variables explains .393 or 39% of the variance in the two groups in the outcome variable (whether the directors would have a voluntary audit). The hypothesis for the Hosmer and Lemeshow test is that the observed frequencies (actual counts) are not associated with the expected frequencies (theoretical counts). The probability statistic (**Sig.**) is .404), which is not significant. This means we can reject the null hypothesis and conclude that there is a good fit between the actual data and the model. The Hosmer and Lemeshow test is 'more robust than the traditional goodness-of-fit statistic used in logistic regression, particularly for models with continuous covariates and studies with small sample sizes ... [This is achieved by] grouping cases into deciles of risk and comparing the observed probability with the expected probability within each decile' (*SPSS*, version 16).

The final table shows the results for the **Variables in the Equation** which we entered in one block:

- The probability statistics (**Sig.**) show that the results for all the predictor variables are significant ($p = \leq 0.05$), apart from **Credibility**.

- The factor coefficient (**B**) for **Family** indicates the expected negative relationship with **Volaudit** (demand for voluntary audit comes from companies that are <u>not</u> wholly family-owned).
- The higher values of the **Wald** statistic and the lower values of the probability statistics for **Turnover, Quality, Creditscore, Family** and **Exowners** indicate that these are the most influential factors.

We now have evidence to reject the null hypotheses for **Turnover, Check, Quality, Family, Exowners** and **Bank** (H1–H3 and H5–H8), but not for **Credibility** (H4). This concludes our interpretation of the statistics, but in a dissertation or thesis would lead on to a narrative discussion with links to previous studies, limitations and theoretical and practical implications arising from the results. You will find further guidance in Chapter 13.

16.7 Time series analysis

If you have collected *longitudinal data* for a random variable, you can use *time series analysis* to forecast future values. A *time series* is a sequence of measurements of a variable taken at regular intervals over time. The purpose of a time series analysis is to examine the *trend* and any *seasonal variation*. Both can be further analysed using linear regression (Moore *et al.*, 2009). However, before the analysis can commence, it is usually necessary to remove the effects of inflation or seasonal fluctuations. You can do this in *Excel* or *SPSS*. We will explain the methods in sufficient detail to allow you to calculate the statistics in *Excel*.

Key definitions

Seasonal variation is where a pattern in the movements of time series data repeats itself at regular intervals.

A **time series** is a sequence of measurements of a variable taken at regular intervals over time.

Time series analysis is a statistical technique for forecasting future events from time series data.

A **trend** is a consistently upward or downward movement in time series data.

16.7.1 Indexation

An *index number* is a statistical measure which shows the percentage change in a variable, such as costs or prices, from some fixed point in the past. The base period of an index is the period against which all other periods are compared. A simple index shows each item in a series relative to some chosen base period value. For example, you may have collected data about a variable whose value changes over time, such as property prices, the cost of a certain component used in manufacturing, the average pay of employees in a particular industry, or consumers' annual expenditure on durable goods.

For a clearer indication of the pattern of movement of the value of such a variable over time, it is customary to choose an appropriate point in time as a base; for example a particular year for a variable that is observed annually.

The base time-point should be chosen to reflect a time when values of the variable are relatively stable. The value of the variable at other points in time can then be expressed as a percentage of the value at the base time-point. The general formula is:

$$\text{Index number} = \frac{\text{Current value}}{\text{Value at base time-point}} \times 100$$

Key definitions

An **index number** is a statistical measure that shows the percentage change in a variable from a fixed point in the past.

The resulting figure (known as the *relative*) is the simplest form of index number. The value of the index number at the base time-point is always 100. The following example shows how to construct a simple index.

Example

You have obtained the following historical data relating to the average price of a house in the UK over six years in the 1970s. You will use the first year in the series as the base year (thus, 1971 = 100) and then apply the following formula:

$$\text{Index} = \frac{\text{Current year price}}{\text{Base year price}} \times 100$$

This generates the index shown in the final column of Table 16.7.

Index figures are very useful for transforming multiple sets of data so that they can be compared in a table or a graph. The following example illustrates how to do this.

Table 16.7 House price index 1971–6

Year	Price	Formula	Index (1971 = 100)
1971	£5,632	$\frac{£5,632}{£5,632} \times 100$	100.0
1972	£7,374	$\frac{£7,374}{£5,632} \times 100$	130.9
1973	£9,942	$\frac{£9,942}{£5,632} \times 100$	176.5
1974	£11,073	$\frac{£11,073}{£5,632} \times 100$	196.6
1975	£12,144	$\frac{£12,144}{£5,632} \times 100$	215.6
1976	£13,006	$\frac{£13,006}{£5,632} \times 100$	230.9

ANALYSING DATA USING INFERENTIAL STATISTICS

Example

You want to analyse the following production data from a factory in your study.

Year	Production units (m)	Number of employees	Units per employee shift
2003	184	602	1.40
2004	180	571	1.45
2005	188	551	1.56
2006	188	524	1.65
2007	185	498	1.72
2008	179	466	1.80

You start by constructing a simple index for each variable, as previously demonstrated, where 2003 = 100. The results are shown in Table 16.8. When these are plotted on a multiple line graph (see Figure 16.9), you can see that the overall production has remained stable despite a steady reduction in the number of employees. This is because the number of units produced per employee shift has increased.

Table 16.8 Production indices 2003–8

Year	Production units index	Number of employees index	Units per employee shift index
2003	100.0	100.0	100.0
2004	97.8	94.9	103.6
2005	102.2	91.5	111.4
2006	102.2	87.0	117.9
2007	100.5	82.7	122.9
2008	97.3	77.4	128.6

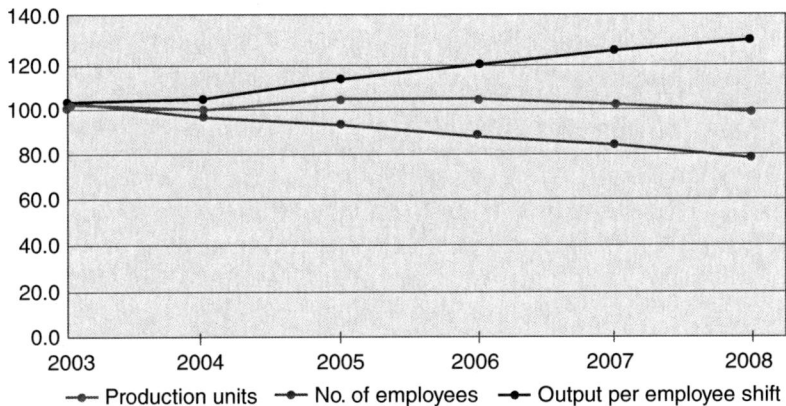

Figure 16.9 Production indices 2003–8

16.7.2 Deflating data

If you have collected financial data over a period when there has been inflation in the economy, this will obscure the underlying trend in the data. However, you can use indexation to *deflate* the data and thus remove the effect of inflation. The resulting data will then reflect the value of money as it was in the base year of the index you use. It is convenient to use an index such as the Retail Price Index (RPI) as it is known in the UK or the Consumer Price Index (CPI) in the USA and some other countries. A price index is the weighted mean of the prices paid by consumers for a set of standard household goods and services. The following example illustrates how to deflate your research data using such a price index.

Example

You have obtained the following historical data relating to a company's profit over a five-year period in the 1980s and the RPI for each year. You find out that the base year for the RPI at that time was 1974 (thus, 1974 = 100). You then apply the following formula:

$$\text{Deflated profit} = \frac{\text{Base year RPI}}{\text{Current year RPI}} \times \text{Profit}$$

This generates the deflated profit figures shown in the last column of Table 16.9.

Table 16.9 Deflated profit 1982–6

Year	Profit	RPI (1974 = 100)	Formula	Deflated profit
1982	£12.0m	320.4	$\frac{100}{320.4} \times 12.0$	£3.7m
1983	£13.5m	335.1	$\frac{100}{335.1} \times 13.5$	£4.0m
1984	£15.1m	351.8	$\frac{100}{351.8} \times 15.1$	£4.2m
1985	£17.0m	373.2	$\frac{100}{373.2} \times 17.0$	£4.6m
1986	£19.0m	385.9	$\frac{100}{385.9} \times 19.0$	£4.9m

The deflated profit figures are now based on the value they would have had in 1974. They can also be plotted on a line graph, as shown in Figure 16.10, which illustrates the distorting effects of inflation very clearly. Far from the dramatic increase shown in the original data, the deflated profit figures show only a modest increase over the period, which puts a different complexion on the financial performance of the company and demonstrates the impact of inflation during the 1980s.

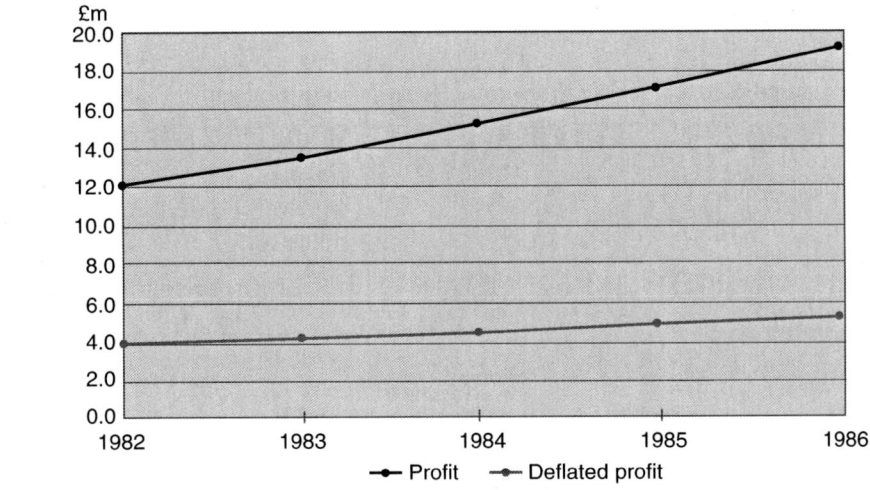

Figure 16.10 Deflated profit 1982–6

16.7.3 Weighted index numbers

A *weighted index number* is constructed by calculating a weighted average of some set of values, where the weights show the relative importance of each item in the data set. This is the basis of a consumer price index, which we have already mentioned. Here, the prices are weighted to reflect the prices paid by consumers for different retail goods and services. The Financial Times Stock Exchange 100 Share Index (FTSE 100 or Footsie) represents the share prices of the largest 100 companies listed on the London Stock Exchange in any quarter and is calculated minute by minute. Unlike other indices, it has a base of 1,000 and this relates to prices on 3 January 1984 (*Oxford Dictionary of Accounting*, 2005).

When calculating weighted index numbers, you should remember that the weights are held constant at their values for the base time-point. Since the weighting may change dramatically over a long period of time, it is only realistic to use weighted index numbers with fixed weights over short periods. An index can be calculated which is the average of a series of price relatives. To be realistic, it should take into account the amount of each commodity used and this is what a weighted index reflects.

Key definitions

A **weighted index number** is an index number constructed by calculating a weighted average of some set of values, where the weights show the relative importance of each item in the data set.

A *Laspeyres index* is a base period weighted index, where the weights used relate to some chosen base period. The formula is:

$$\text{Laspeyres index} = \frac{\Sigma PcQb}{\Sigma PbQb} \times 100$$

where

    Pc = Current price
    Pb = Base price
    Qb = Base quantity

The advantages of a Laspeyres index are:

- The index is easy to calculate for a series of years as it uses the same set of weights each time.
- It allows a comparison of any one year with any other as all use the same weights.
- It requires little data in terms of weights.

The disadvantages of a Laspeyres index are:

- The weights used will gradually become out of date and will no longer represent the contemporary situation.
- It tends to overestimate price increase because it uses out-of-date weights.

A *Paasche index* is a current period weighted average where the weights used rebase to the current period. The formula is:

$$\frac{\Sigma PcQc}{\Sigma PbQc} \times 100$$

where

    Pc = Current price
    Pb = Base price
    Qc = Current quantity

The advantage of a Paasche index is:

- The index always uses the current weights and thus reflects today's situation.

The disadvantages of a Paasche index are:

- The index involves more calculation for a series of years as the weights used are constantly changing.
- It can only be compared against the base year as the weights for each year change.
- It tends to underestimate price increases.
- It requires new weights each period which can be both costly and time-consuming to collect.

16.7.4 Calculating the de-seasonalized trend

We have already mentioned that the main use of time series analysis is to predict *trends*. A trend is a consistently upward or downward movement in the data values over the time period. A *seasonal variation* is where a pattern in the movements repeats itself at regular intervals. The two main statistical models for analysing time series data are the *additive model* and the *multiplicative model*. The formulae are as follows:

$$Y = T + S + C + I \text{ (additive model)}$$
$$Y = T \times S \times C \times I \text{ (multiplicative model)}$$

where

Y = the observation
T = trend
S = seasonal variation
C = cyclical component
I = irregular component

Although the additive model is simpler to analyse, the multiplicative model is generally considered to be more realistic. The adequacy of the multiplicative model may be tested by analysing the irregular component. If this is not random, the suitability of the model must be questioned. Any component may be absent from a particular time series (for example annual data cannot include the seasonal variation component).

Example

Perhaps you have collected quarterly data relating to the number of ice-creams sold (the sales volume) by a particular business over a five-year period.

- First calculate the 4 quarter moving total by adding the sales volume in groups of four.
- Then calculate the 8 quarter moving total by adding the 4 quarter moving totals in groups of two.
- Next, divide the 8 quarter moving totals by 8 to obtain the trend.
- Before you can eliminate any seasonal variations, you will need to calculate the de-trended series by dividing your original quarterly data (Y) by the trend (T).

These calculations are quickly computed on an *Excel* work sheet and Table 16.10 illustrates this stage of the analysis. If you use a calculator, discrepancies may occur due to rounding.

You are now ready to calculate the seasonal variation (S) which you do by averaging the de-trended series you calculated in Table 16.10. These data have been transferred to Table 16.11 to demonstrate how the seasonal index is calculated. The averages should add up to 4 for quarterly data and 12 for monthly data.

The mean for each quarter represents the seasonal variation (S), which we need in order to calculate the de-seasonalized data (Y ÷ S). Table 16.12 illustrates this and summarizes the key statistics we have calculated.

Table 16.10 De-trended series for ice-cream sales (m) 2004–8

Year	Quarter	Sales (m) (Y)	4 quarter moving total	8 quarter moving total	Trend (T)	De-trended series (Y ÷ T)
2004	Q1	106	–	–	–	–
	Q2	192				
			726			
	Q3	278		1,463	183	1.52
			737			
	Q4	150		1,481	185	0.81
			744			
2005	Q1	117		1,488	186	0.63
			744			
	Q2	199		1,492	187	1.07
			748			
	Q3	278		1,518	190	1.47
			770			
	Q4	154		1,541	193	0.80
			771			
2006	Q1	139		1,575	197	0.71
			804			
	Q2	200		1,631	204	0.98
			827			
	Q3	311		1,652	207	1.51
			825			
	Q4	177		1,670	209	0.85
			845			
2007	Q1	137		1,692	212	0.65
			847			
	Q2	220		1,694	212	1.04
			847			
	Q3	313		1,701	213	1.47
			854			
	Q4	177		1,672	209	0.85
			818			
2008	Q1	144		1,591	199	0.72
			773			
	Q2	184		1,551	194	0.95
			778			
	Q3	268		1,412	177	1.52
			634			
	Q4	182		–	–	–

Table 16.11 Seasonal index for ice-cream sales (m) 2004–8

	De-trended series			
Year	Q1	Q2	Q3	Q4
2004	–	–	1.52	0.81
2005	0.63	1.07	1.47	0.8
2006	0.71	0.98	1.51	0.85
2007	0.65	1.04	1.47	0.85
2008	0.72	0.95	–	–
Total	2.71	4.04	5.97	3.31
Mean (seasonal variation)	0.68	1.01	1.48	0.83
Seasonal index	68	101	148	83

Table 16.12 De-seasonalized data for ice-cream sales (m) 2004–8

Year	Quarter	Sales (m) (Y)	Trend (T)	De-trended series (Y ÷ T)	Seasonal variation (S)	De-seasonalized data (Y ÷ S)
2004	Q1	106	–	–	0.68	156
	Q2	192	–	–	1.01	190
	Q3	278	183	1.52	1.48	187
	Q4	150	185	0.81	0.83	180
2005	Q1	117	186	0.63	0.68	173
	Q2	199	187	1.07	1.01	197
	Q3	278	190	1.47	1.48	187
	Q4	154	193	0.80	0.83	185
2006	Q1	139	197	0.71	0.68	205
	Q2	200	204	0.98	1.01	198
	Q3	311	207	1.51	1.48	210
	Q4	177	209	0.85	0.83	212
2007	Q1	137	212	0.65	0.68	202
	Q2	220	212	1.04	1.01	218
	Q3	313	213	1.47	1.48	211
	Q4	177	209	0.85	0.83	212
2008	Q1	144	199	0.72	0.68	213
	Q2	184	194	0.95	1.01	182
	Q3	268	177	1.52	1.48	181
	Q4	182	–	–	0.83	218

If you have tried this for yourself on a spreadsheet, you can now plot the trend for ice-cream sales over the period on a graph and use the seasonal index to forecast the data for the next year in the series.

16.7.5 Evaluating the cyclical and irregular variation

In order to evaluate the cyclical variation (C) you need to obtain the de-trended, de-seasonalized series:

$$\frac{Y}{T \times S} = C \times I$$

Next, smooth out the irregular component (I) by means of a moving average performed on the $\frac{Y}{T \times S}$ series.

Since the aim is to smooth and not to remove the cycle, a three-point moving average could be used. The irregular component (I) is obtained from:

$$\frac{Y}{T \times S \times C}$$

This should be random in nature; otherwise the adequacy of the proposed model must be questioned. Therefore, evaluation of the irregular component yields a measure of method suitability. For multiplicative models, the irregular component should be random about unity (± 1). If the irregular component is evaluated and shown to be random, it can be removed from the series, producing an error-free series:

$$\frac{Y}{I} = T \times S \times C$$

In order to be reasonably certain that components exist in a time series, there should be sufficient data to establish the reality of these components or complementary information to suggest their presence. In a short span of data, random phenomena can appear to be systematic and, conversely, systematic effects can be masked by random variation.

16.8 Conclusions

Apart from the important matter of whether your data meet the four basic assumptions that determine whether you can use parametric tests, you need to consider time constraints and your skills. The data used to illustrate the inferential statistics in this chapter relate to a study that was designed to address a set of hypotheses underpinned by theory. Although the research data was non-parametric, we have also explained the equivalent parametric models.

In the previous sections we have showed how comparison of longitudinal data can be aided through indexation and time series analysis can be used to examine the trend and any seasonal variation. If the latter is present, the de-seasonalized trend can be calculated and any cyclical and irregular variation evaluated. The trend and the seasonal variation can be analysed using linear regression.

Your choice of analysis will depend on whether your research data is parametric or non-parametric and whether you want to:

- summarize and/or display the data (descriptive statistics)
- test for significant differences between independent or related samples (inferential statistics)
- test for significant association between variables (inferential statistics)
- predict an outcome from one or more independent variables (inferential statistics)
- forecast trends from longitudinal data (time series analysis).

It is important to remember that you need to know how you are going to analyse your data before you collect it. We provided a checklist at the end of the previous chapter and Box 16.2 extends this by summarizing the main steps in analysing quantitative data.

Activities

This chapter is entirely activity-based. If you have access to *SPSS*, start at the beginning of the chapter and work your way through. If *SPSS* is not available, do the same activities using an alternative software package following the on-screen tutorials and help facilities.

Box 16.2 Main steps in analysing quantitative data

1. Quantify answers to open questions.
2. Identify each case and enter the data into your software program.
3. Name the variables and the coding labels, and identify the level of measurement.
4. If recoding is required, recode into a different variable, thus keeping the original intact.
5. For most business research, accept the *SPSS* default significance level of 0.05.
6. Decide whether your hypotheses are one-tailed or two-tailed.
7. Identify the dependent variable and the independent variable(s) (not applicable when testing for correlation).
8. Determine whether parametric or non-parametric tests are appropriate.
9. Decide whether you have independent or dependent samples.
10. Explore, describe and analyse the data using appropriate statistical methods to address your research questions.

PROGRESS TEST

Complete the following sentences:
1. A random sample is a representative subset drawn from the _____.
2. A number that describes a _____ is called a statistic.
3. A number that describes a _____ is called a parameter.
4. Parametric tests are underpinned by four assumptions about the characteristics of the distribution of the _____.
5. The analysis of more than two variables together is known as _____ analysis.

Are the following statements true or false?
6. A normality test compares the distribution of the research data with that of a theoretical sample.
7. A test of difference can only be carried out with parametric data.
8. A chi-square test can only be carried out between nominal variables.
9. Regression analysis can only be carried out if the correlation between the dependent and the independent variables is linear.
10. Regression analysis can only be carried out if there is no perfect multicollinearity between the independent variables.

Multiple choice questions:

11. A *t*-test is a parametric test of difference for:
    a) ratio or interval variables
    b) ordinal or nominal variables
    c) dependent or independent variables
    d) dependent or independent samples

12. A Mann-Whitney test is a non-parametric test of:
    a) association
    b) difference
    c) multicollinearity
    d) normality

13. A chi-square test is a non-parametric test of:
    a) association
    b) difference
    c) multicollinearity
    d) normality

14. Measures of correlation are needed to evaluate potential problems with:
    a) kurtosis
    b) multicollinearity
    c) normality
    d) skewness

15. Logistic regression is used where:
    a) the dependent variable is a dummy variable
    b) the independent variable is a dummy variable
    c) there is only one predictor variable
    d) there is more than one predictor variable

References

Collis, J. (2003) *Directors' Views on Exemption from the Statutory Audit*, URN 03/1342, London: DTI, October. Available from http://www.berr.gov.uk/files/file25971.pdf.

Field, A. (2000) *Discovering Statistics Using SPSS for Windows*, London: Sage.

Judge, G. G., Griffiths, W. E., Hill, R. C., Lutkepol, H. and Lee, T. C. (1985) *The Theory and Practice of Econometrics*. Chichester: John Wiley & Sons.

Kervin, J. B. (1992) *Methods for Business Research*, New York: HarperCollins.

Moore, D., McCabe, G. P., Duckworth, W. M. and Alwan, L. C. (2009) *The Practice of Business Statistics*, 2nd edition, New York: W.H. Freeman and Company.

Oakshott, L. (1994) *Essential Elements of Business Statistics*, London: DP Publications.

Oxford Dictionary of Accounting (2005), Oxford: Oxford University Press.

Robson, C. (1993) *Real World Research: A Resource for Social Scientists and Practitioner Researchers*, Oxford: Blackwell.

Upton, G. and Cook, I. (2006) *Oxford Dictionary of Statistics*, 2nd edition, Oxford: Oxford University Press.

Glossary

Bivariate analysis	Analysis of data from two variables.
Chi squared (χ^2) test	A non-parametric test of association for two variables measured on a nominal scale.
Correlation	A measure of the direction and strength of association between two quantitative variables. Correlation may be linear or nonlinear, positive or negative.
Cross-tabulation	A bivariate analysis of frequency distributions (usually relating to ordinal or nominal variables) in the form of a table.
Index number	A statistical measure that shows the percentage change in a variable from a fixed point in the past.
Linear regression	A measure of the ability of an independent variable to predict an outcome in a dependent variable where there is a linear relationship between them.
Logistic regression	A form of multiple regression that is used where the dependent variable is a dummy variable and one or more of the independent variables are continuous quantitative variables. Any other independent variables can be ordinal or dummy variables.
Mann-Whitney test	A non-parametric test of difference for two independent or dependent samples for ratio, interval or ordinal variables.
Multivariate analysis	Analysis of data more than two variables.
Pearson's correlation coefficient (r)	A parametric test that measures linear association between two continuous variables measured on a ratio or interval scale.
Ranked data	Quantitative data arranged in size order so that statistical tests can be performed on the ranks.
Scatter plot	A diagram for presenting data where one variable is plotted against another on a graph as a pattern of points, which indicates the direction and strength of any linear correlation. The more the points cluster around a straight line, the stronger the correlation.
Seasonal variation	Where a pattern in the movements of time series data repeats itself at regular intervals.
Spearman's correlation coefficient (rho)	A non-parametric test that measures linear association between two variables measured on a ratio, interval or ordinal scale.
Time series	A sequence of measurements of a variable taken at regular intervals over time.
Time series analysis	A statistical technique for forecasting future events from time series data.
Trend	A consistently upward or downward movement in time series data.
t-test	A parametric test of difference for two independent or dependent samples for ratio or interval variables.
Univariate analysis	Analysis of data from one variable.
Weighted index number	An index number constructed by calculating a weighted average of some set of values, where the weights show the relative importance of each item in the data set.

PART 6
Describing your research

CHAPTER 17
Answering your research questions
Interpreting your findings and making recommendations

KEY QUESTIONS

- How can I turn my analysis into answers to my research questions?
- How can I present my analysis?
- How do I use the literature to support my findings and discussion?
- How do I discuss my findings?

LEARNING OUTCOMES

At the end of this chapter, you should be able to:

- Interpret your data and analysis with respect to your conceptual framework and theory
- Develop interim findings and recommendations from your research
- Use your data and analysis to support your findings, discussion and conclusions

CONTENTS

Introduction
17.1   Interpreting your quantitative results
17.2   Interpreting your qualitative results
17.3   Developing findings and recommendations
Summary
Answers to key questions
References
Additional resources
Key terms
Discussion questions
Workshop

Introduction

After you have collected and analysed your data, you need to relate your data and analysis back to your research questions to see whether you have answered them. If you have taken the scientific approach as your model, this usually means comparing what you have found out with the conceptual model you started with and then your research questions; if you have taken the ethnographic approach as your model, this usually means comparing the conceptual model you have developed with your research questions. You will also need to compare the answers to your research questions with the theory in your topic area, and consider alternate explanations and unexpected findings from your research.

In many cases, you will need to do this before you write up your final research report. You may need to present interim results to your academic supervisor and/or business sponsor. You may need to understand what you have found out in one stage of your research before you proceed to the next, especially if you have taken a multi-method or multi-stage approach. Most students find interpreting their data and the results of their data analysis a challenging task, especially closing the loop back to their conceptual framework, research questions and theory, with respect to the theoretical problem, and in developing recommendations, with respect to the practical problem. It is difficult to find specific guidance on how to do this. It is tempting to just forge blindly ahead.

In this chapter, we present a systematic process for interpreting your data and your analysis with regard to your conceptual framework and your research questions. If you follow this process, you should be able to identify your findings, discussion and conclusions for your academic report, and identify an implementation plan and recommendations for your report, if you are writing one, to your sponsor. One of your key tasks is to make sure that you have answered your research questions. It may seem farfetched to you that someone might present research that does not do this, but people often get sidetracked during their project and end up doing research that is unrelated to their research questions. In fact, we have read many project reports and reviewed many articles for conferences and journals, some by experienced authors, where the research questions are mentioned in the introduction and never heard of again.

Section 17.1 explains how to interpret the data and statistical tests associated with a quantitative analysis to see whether you have answered your research questions. We describe some useful ways to present your data and your statistical analysis to help you with this interpretation. We also point out some common mistakes you should try to avoid. If you have interpreted what you have found out, you will find it easier to turn your numbers back into words – or at least describe them in words – when you present your research. In interpreting what you have found out, you should also keep in mind the criteria by which the quality of quantitative research is judged.

Section 17.2 examines how to interpret the data and the themes associated with a qualitative analysis to see whether you have answered your research questions. Since qualitative research does not necessarily start with a conceptual framework, and one may emerge from the unstructured or structured analysis, this may be more complex than in quantitative research. However, you still need to relate what you have found out back to your research questions, so that you can see whether you have answered them. We point out some useful strategies and common mistakes associated with this stage of doing your research. The experimenting that you do in this stage can help you see how to present your research in your project report, which is often tricky for qualitative research. As with quantitative analysis, you should compare your findings with the criteria for qualitative analysis.

Section 17.3 describes how you can develop what you have found out into your recommendations and implementation plan if you are conducting in-company research. You should consider alternate solutions to your practical problem in this stage of your research, and be able to explain why your solution is the most appropriate one.

This chapter will also help you to develop the core elements of your project report – your findings, discussion and conclusions – which we discuss in more detail in **Chapter 14**. Many student projects fail to achieve high marks because the students see presenting their data and analysis as the end point of their research, and fail to develop a link back to the theoretical and practical problems they set out to investigate. Your data do not have any value until they have been interpreted and measured against the quality standards for the kind of research you are doing. When you understand what you have found out, you will also be in a much better position to present it to your readers, including your academic examiners and project sponsors.

17.1 Interpreting your quantitative results

The reader of a research report is usually at least as concerned with how you arrived at your findings (your process) as with what your findings are (your content). Academic readers are interested in how you have translated your research questions into a research design, and how your evidence answers those research questions. In other words, their focus is on the generalisability of your report, which requires validity. Practitioners, on the other hand, will be interested in how you propose that your answers might solve a practical problem. In other words, their focus is on the relevance of your recommendations, which requires rigour. As you will see in **Chapter 14**, this may lead you to write two separate reports, one for each audience, although you may be able to include common material in both. Before you start the writing-up process, however, you need to interpret what you have found out. It is not enough to present your raw (or summarised) data and hope that your reader can (or will) make sense of it for him or herself.

Once you have collected and analysed your data, you have three key tasks:

1. *Interpret your data* – Understand what the data mean, with respect to your hypotheses
2. *Interpret your analysis* – Understand what the analysis means with respect to your conceptual framework
3. *Interpret your empirical research* – Understand what your findings mean for your theoretical and practical problem.

If you are doing your research from a quantitative perspective, once you have completed your statistical analysis you should ask yourself some tough questions about what you have found out (for example O'Leary 2004: 186–7). These questions include:

1. Do my data adequately capture the concepts and relationships I want to investigate?
2. Have I adequately measured these concepts and relationships with my statistical tests?
3. Do my data and statistical tests support or not support my hypotheses?
4. How does this analysis fit with my conceptual model?
5. Have I answered my research questions?
6. Do I need to go back to the literature to explain my findings from another perspective? Are there other ways I can interpret my findings? What did I not find out that I expected to find out? What did I find out that I didn't expect to find out?
7. Do I need to do further research to answer my research questions?
8. What have I learnt about my research setting, research methods, research questions or theory? What can this contribute to future research?

Along with your data and your analysis, the answers to these questions will provide the basis for your findings, discussion and conclusions when you present or write up your research.

17.1.1 Interpreting your data

Your first key task is to relate your data to the research questions you set out to investigate – making sure that the data you have collected are relevant to your research questions; as mentioned in the introduction, this is not always the case in research. **Chapters 10** and **11** presented a number of statistical techniques you can use to interrogate your data, ranging from simple descriptive statistics to advanced multivariate techniques. Applying these techniques rigorously, however, is no guarantee that your data have construct validity – they measure the concepts and/or relationships you set out to investigate – or face validity – they measure what you think they measure. This is a matter of judgement and hence research skill, rather than number-crunching.

You will also need to think about how you will identify the most important and relevant data to support your arguments. This can be a problem in both quantitative and qualitative research, because you will have usually gathered a lot more data than you can make sense of. If you have used a quantitative approach such as secondary analysis, survey or experiment, you are likely to begin your interpretation swamped by numbers – many numbers, raw data, tables, statistical formulae, statistical outputs. This may be too many numbers for you to be able to see the forest for the trees, when you are writing up your research report or presenting your findings. Your reader will have no chance.

No matter how interesting you think each piece of data is, do not become a train spotter. The data are nothing – your interpretation is everything. Try to focus first on those data that will help you to answer your research questions. A good way to get started on this is to reduce your data so you can identify the most *important* patterns in your data, not every possible pattern. One of Kate's former colleagues called this 'holding down the data and torturing it until it surrenders'!

Since most of us find visual data easier to interpret than numbers, you might try converting your raw data into charts, graph, figures and tables. You can present many data more clearly in the form of charts or graphs, tables and figures. Most computer software, whether specialised statistical software, spreadsheet software or word-processing software, lets you create illustrations from your data. These should relate back to your conceptual framework and hence back to each of your research questions. You should generally present your data in the same order as your research questions (**Chapter 3**), which will determine the structure of your literature review, conceptual framework and so on.

The main dangers of this for students are that they waste too much time trying to get things to look 'just right', for example three-dimensional charts when two-dimensional would do, and they try to create a graph or chart for every possible aspect of the data, so inducing 'graph fatigue'. Try to create just the right amount of graphics to identify the story your data are telling. These are like the illustrations in a book – try to make 'your book' relatively grown-up rather than a children's picture book.

Tables

A **table** presents data in rows and columns of numbers and/or words. It is the most basic form of exhibit. 'Tables communicate precise numerical information to readers' (Dunleavy 2003: 165). You should organise the layout of any table systematically, with the columns and rows in some logical order such as largest to smallest or most important to least important.

You can usually find many uses for tables in your project report. Tables seldom show raw data; they usually show data that have been processed in some way, for example to summarise or describe data or findings in compact form. Tables of raw data are rarely helpful in interpreting your data with respect to your research questions. If you look at academic research reported in high-quality academic journals such as the *Academy of Management Journal* or the *Administrative Science Quarterly*, you will see that the first table in most of these articles presents an overview of the key concepts and the relationships between them. This is a good idea for you when you are interpreting your data, before you start looking at the results of any statistical tests. The three things commonly reported in such a table are:

1. A measure of central tendency, such as the mean
2. A measure of dispersion, such as the standard deviation
3. A measure of bivariate relationships, such as Pearson's product moment correlation.

Such a table is invaluable to an experienced researcher, since he or she can often predict the significant findings and potential problems with the data based on this table alone, even before you present the results of any statistical tests. **Table 17.1**, from a project investigating the link between communication and group conflict, shows the means, standard deviations and correlations.

In fact, when you look at **Table 17.1**, the data suggest that face-to-face communication and telephone communication are associated with lower group conflict, but email communication is a bit more ambiguous. Perhaps this is because in the group studied, people who talk to each other face to face tend to talk to each other on the phone as well, but people who email do not communicate in other ways.

Table 17.1 A descriptive table for your variables

| | Variable | Mean | SD | Pearson's product moment correlation | | | | | |
				1	2	3	4	5	6
1	Face-to-face contact	13.4	3.1	1.00					
2	Telephone contact	10.2	5.1	.56	1.00				
3	Email contact	18.1	3.5	−.21	−.31	1.00			
4	Liking	4.5	1.01	.47	.20	−.36	1.00		
5	Preference	3.2	.87	.36	.33	.21	.39	1.00	
6	Attachment	3.5	.98	.09	.15	.22	.56	.37	1.00

Charts and graphs

Charts and graphs present numeric data effectively, especially if you want to look for patterns that tell a story. A **chart** is the term typically used for a figure that presents relationships among two or more independent variables. A **graph** is the term typically used for one that presents relationships among one or more sets of independent and dependent variables, especially where data follow a linear pattern. Microsoft Excel and other statistical programs make it easy to explore a range of charts. You should avoid 'dumbing down the data' too much (for example endless pie charts) and making it look like the front page of *USA Today*. Dunleavy (2003: 173) lists eight types of charts and graphs commonly used in research, which are shown in **Table 17.2**.

Table 17.2 Some common charts and graphs

Type	Use to present	Example
Scatterplot (X–Y) chart	The relationship between an independent and one or more dependent variables	Ice cream sales versus average monthly temperature
Line graph	The relationship between time and one or more dependent variables	Sales of Maylor's *Project Management* by month
Vertical bar chart	Discontinuous time-series data	Monthly sales of male deodrants
Horizontal bar chart	Non-time-series categorical data	Amount of time taken to complete activities
Grouped bar chart	Several discontinuous time-series data	Sales of the top three management books by month
Stacked bar chart	Relative shares of multiple categories	Share of grocery spending by different food categories by year for ten years
Pie chart	Shares of a single overall category	Companies by number of employees in your sample
Layer chart	Several continuous time-series (or other continuous) data	Aggregate sales in three industrial sectors over the past 100 years

When you create your graphics, you should follow good practice (for example Dunleavey 2003: 163–4):

1. Label each exhibit with a heading or caption that clearly describes what is being shown.
2. Number each exhibit uniquely and systematically, preferably with a chapter number and unique figure number, for example **Figure 4.1**, **Table 17.2**.
3. Label the elements of the exhibit clearly, for example table columns, chart legends and the units of measurement. Make sure that each exhibit is self-explanatory.
4. Give brief details of where the data come from.

This systematic approach will make your life a lot easier when you present your graphics or incorporate them into your final project report. You must also make sure that you refer to each exhibit and explain it in words in your main text.

17.1.2 Interpreting your analysis

Your second task is to interpret the results of your statistical analysis. The goal of interpretation is not just to present your data and statistical test results, but to tell the story of how these data and tests relate to your research question. The structure of this story is determined by your research questions.

If you have analysed your data using statistical techniques, you need to interpret the results of your statistical analysis and turn this interpretation into your findings. This means not only reporting key data and key aspects of your statistical analysis, but also explaining them with respect to your hypothesis (or whatever statement is driving your research).

For each statistical test, you should always make sure that you describe:

1. *Your data* – What data you are analysing, where they come from and any data reduction or other transformation that you have applied to the data.
2. *Your tests* – What statistical test you have used to analyse your data, any important assumptions and what software package you have used in the analysis. If you are using a statistical test that is unlikely to be familiar to your reader, you may need to include details in an appendix.
3. *Your results* – In enough detail so that your reader can interpret them for him or herself, but not so much detail that it is overwhelming. Include the key details, not every number reported in the analytical results. (If you don't know what those details are, you probably shouldn't be using that test.) You may need to include details of equations or outputs in an appendix if your reader might need to consult them in more or full detail.

As we mentioned above, this is where students often lose all sense of proportion. The purpose of gathering data is to answer your research questions, not to gather as much data as you can. Elegance is better than overkill. Similarly, the purpose of using statistical tests is not to test data in as many ways as possible, nor is it to apply as many different statistical tests as you can. One point in **Chapter 5** about the scientific approach was that ideally you would be able to specify the data and tests in advance of collecting data, to the point that you could mostly write up your project report before you ever started collecting data. Gathering a lot of data and testing it to death is an inductive strategy; data-mining has its place, but usually as the prelude to organised research rather than as part of it (it is sometimes referred to as 'data-gouging' for this reason).

What statistics should I be looking at?

A key part of interpreting your statistical tests will be to figure out what the most important and relevant statistical tests are, what they mean and how to present them. The statistics and statistical tests you are most interested in are those that help you to decide whether you have answered your research questions. If you have been following our advice for a systematic research process, you have translated your research questions into your research design by means of a conceptual diagram.

How you actually report your data and the story you tell will depend on your research project. If your research is mainly descriptive, you will present descriptive statistics, often in reduced form, and explain what they mean. If your research is more analytical, you need to present details of your analysis and relate it to your hypotheses. If your research is explanatory, you need to link it to the literature as well.

Figures

A good way to present your statistical tests (especially if you have more than one) is to integrate them with your conceptual model. Drawing your conceptual model and then showing which concepts and/or relationships you have tested and what the results are is a good way to do this. It is definitely a helpful way to begin visualising the story emerging from your research project.

Figure 17.1 illustrates a simple conceptual model with a single independent and a single dependent concept. Suppose you were investigating the link between communication and group conflict. You want to see whether the frequency with which people communicate with others in the same group, by face-to-face contact, telephone contact and email, affects intragroup contact. Your participants have kept a diary recording the number of contacts with other group members per week. You want to see whether the type and frequency of communication affect how much people like each other, who they prefer to work with on projects and how attached they feel to the group. For this study, you might present the conceptual model in a

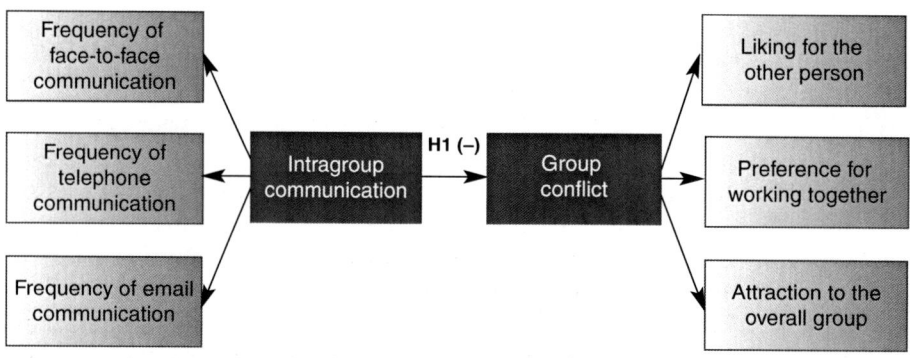

Figure 17.1 A conceptual model

figure and indicate the results of the hypothesised relationships and the direction of those relationships.

Figure 17.1 shows that your main hypothesis is that the more frequently members of a group communicate with each other, the lower the amount of group conflict. An experienced reader will also be able to tell from your figure what kind of data you have collected and what kind of statistical analysis you are likely to have used. Figures such as this are especially useful in showing relationships, which become essential when you have a complex conceptual model that your readers might find difficult to follow if you present it only in words. You can think of a good figure as being a road map for your audience.

Statistical significance

A word to the wise. The ways in which students interpret statistical significance (p) is a source of endless hilarity to examiners and gnashing of teeth by quantitative methods teachers. Do make sure that you understand what a test of statistical significance means and how to interpret the level of statistical significance. The 'golden rule' in business and management research for determining whether a result is statistically significant is $p < .05$, or a 1 in 20 chance that we are falsely accepting a relationship when one does not exist. Any test where the result is $p < .05$ is significant; any test where the result is $p > .05$ is not significant. There is no such thing as almost or nearly significant.

You should also make sure that you are following the conventions for highlighting statistical significance in tables, which we show below:

* $p <= .05$
** $p <= .01$
*** $p <= .001$

17.1.3 Interpreting your empirical research

Once you have interpreted your data and your statistical tests, you have started to create the most important elements of your findings. Your findings are a central element of your research project and hence of any presentation or report. Your third task is to 'close the loop' between these findings and your research questions, to see how well you have done your job as a researcher. This will lead to a discussion of what your empirical research means in light of your research questions, and, usually, the theory that informs and supports those research questions. Remember that your data illustrate those questions and that theory in a particular research setting and sample.

One important aspect of interpreting your findings is to see how well you have done against the criteria on which the quality of your research will be assessed. It is not enough for research to be provocative or interesting; it needs to be done in an appropriate way. One criterion is whether you are able to express your results in the context of the existing knowledge in your area of interest. Your combination of your results with this knowledge makes your research interesting – as demonstrated in **Chapter 8**. It also links with earlier parts of the study – the literature review in particular. You should also demonstrate how you have systematically addressed your research questions.

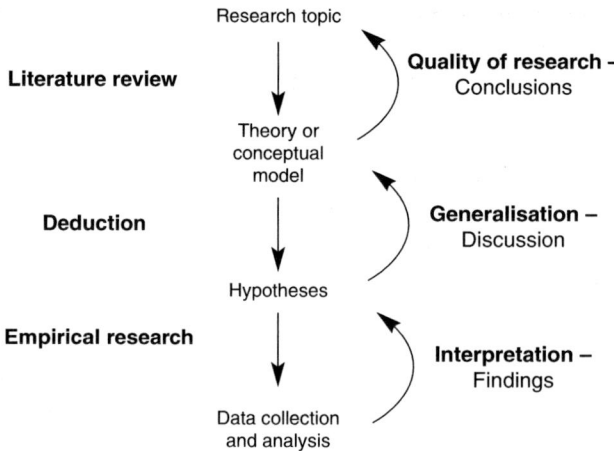

Figure 17.2 The link back to the literature

Although you will show most of the links to your literature in your discussion chapter, in the findings chapter you may need to briefly summarise relevant items to remind your readers what your hypotheses are and why you are predicting a relationship and its direction. In a quantitative research project, you will have started with a theory or conceptual framework that applies to your research topic and develop one or more hypotheses to test. Since you must find your theory somewhere, you have a link back from data to hypotheses to theory to your research problem. **Figure 17.2** is a simplified description of this process.

In order to close this loop, you need to see how the findings from your secondary analysis, survey or experiment fit with your literature. We described how to interpret the results of your statistical analysis above, to see whether your hypotheses are supported or not supported by your data. Since your hypotheses were deduced from your theory or conceptual framework, then you need to link this back to your research questions and the relevant theory (literature). This can help you to show that your data and analysis support your original framework, and whether you should explore any alternate frameworks to explore what you actually found out. You may need to conduct additional research – or at least identify the need to conduct additional research – as a result of this.

17.1.4 Quality in quantitative analysis

The final task in interpreting your evidence is to think about the quality of your research, primarily in terms of what you set out to do, but also with reference to the standards by which research is judged. The two lenses through which you might view your research are:

- *Scientific* – has it increased the reader's knowledge about/of the research problem and/or the method?
- *Advice* – what can the reader do/what is the reader empowered to do now that he/she has read the report?

Compared with qualitative researchers, quantitative researchers have a good deal of consensus on the scientific, or technical, criteria for judging quantitative research. In **Chapter 12**, we described the four criteria by which quantitative research is judged as:

1. *Validity* – are your results accurate?
2. *Reliability* – are your results repeatable?
3. *Generalisability* – do your results have meaning beyond your data set?
4. *Credibility* – does the 'story' that your results tell appear plausible?

You should also highlight any actual or potential problems with the research you actually did, versus the research you planned to do (especially deviations from your research design). These deviations, which might include problems with missing data, sample size, violation of statistical assumptions or your instrument, might affect what you found out. You should also reveal anything that might influence your interpretation of your findings. Perhaps you should have used a different statistical test or added (or taken away) variables to (from) your model. These sorts of issues become important in drawing conclusions from your research.

17.2 Interpreting your qualitative results

In **Chapter 12**, we described a process for thematically analysing qualitative research. In qualitative analysis, you are inevitably interpreting your findings as you are analysing your data, because you need to build codes and categories from the raw data. This means that the interpretation aspect of this stage of your research process differs from this stage of a quantitative research project, where you can separate analysing and interpreting. As with quantitative research, the main issue you need to address is linking what you have done with your research questions.

17.2.1 Interpreting patterns

In interpreting qualitative research, you will need to link your data with a theory you have identified because of doing your research. This means that you will find it difficult, if not impossible, to adopt the same structured approach to interpreting your research as you did for quantitative research. In qualitative research, your main goal is to weave together a convincing narrative from what you have done. A major task in interpreting is to identify the data that support this story, so that it is grounded in your empirical data as well as in your thematic analysis (for example your use of Kolb's cycle or concept extraction, as described in **Chapter 12**).

As the qualitative research process is usually iterative, cycling back and forth between processes of conceptualisation, data collection and data analysis, you will need to combine these in your interpretation of what you have found out. In qualitative research, you end up creating a conceptual framework, rather than starting with one. Your conceptual framework will emerge from your data, rather than being 'borrowed' from the literature. This means that interpreting your qualitative research report can be difficult because you can identify many different ways to

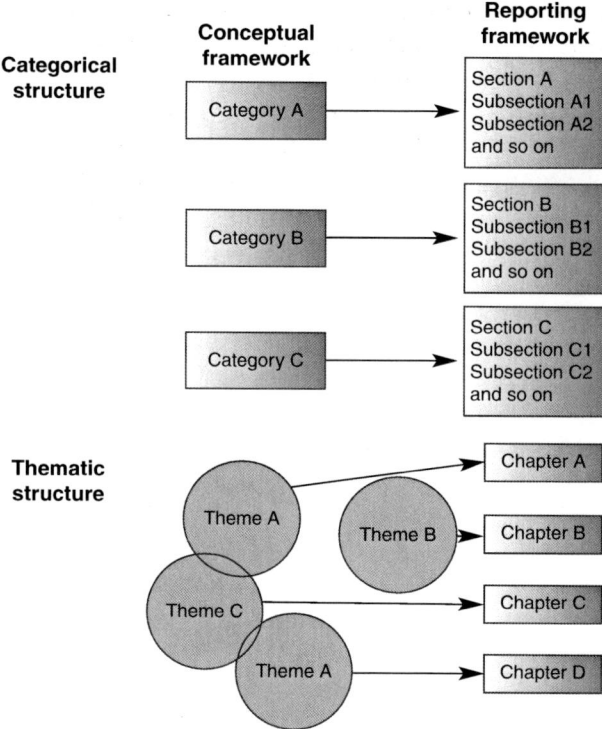

Figure 17.3 Categorical and thematic organisation

make sense of it. Two different ways for organising emerging ideas and themes are (Figure 17.3):

- *categorical* – reporting your categories and progressively focusing in or out. These categories can be predetermined or emerge from your data analysis
- *thematic* – presenting your overall conceptual framework, then reporting each theme.

Many students find it useful to refer to examples of qualitative research to see how other researchers have induced themes and conceptual frameworks from their rich, qualitative data. It is even more important to understand the 'story' emerging from your research, even if it is not the only story that could emerge. You are depending mainly on the story you tell, or the narrative you create, to communicate the essence of the research you have done, and tables and figures are not as much a part of that story.

Students usually find Miles and Huberman's *Qualitative Data Analysis* (1984) useful, because it presents many different ways to organise the interpretation of qualitative data. You should be able to find a good model for your own research among the many examples they present. You might also go back to an article or book you have consulted in your research project, and map how it structured its discussion.

Instead of basing your interpretation on data summarised in the form of tables and charts, as in quantitative research, you will usually need to work with the critical incidents, concepts or themes that emerge from your data. Many students have found it useful to use physical methods of working with keywords or phrases. For example, market researchers have developed sophisticated ways of sorting ideas written on index cards, using either R-sort or Q-sort procedures. (The main differences in sorting approaches tend to be whether you start with every idea in the same structure and split them progressively into smaller and smaller groups, or whether you start with individual ideas and combine them progressively into larger groups.) Other qualitative researchers have found it useful to use whiteboards or Post-it notes at this stage.

Kate Fox's *Watching the English: The Hidden Rules of English Behaviour* (2003), an ethnographic study of the 'everyday' behaviour of English people, provides a good full-length example of organising around themes. Fox identifies two main themes from her investigation, which she describes as 'conversation codes' and 'behaviour codes'. These are then used to organise all subsequent subthemes, for example conversation codes start with 'the weather' and end with 'pub talk', while behaviour codes start with rules that apply at home and take in sex, food and work along the way. Conversation codes and behaviour codes represent 'meta-themes'.

Either way, it may be useful to refer back and forth to 'verbatim quoting' from your transcripts and observation notes, comparing them with your argument, and interpreting and commenting on that evidence as you go along. (You need to have carefully catalogued your data, as recommended in **Chapter 12**, to be able to trace your quotes back to the interview or observation they came from.)

17.2.2 Interpreting qualitative data

Qualitative research is also challenging for students who are using this approach for the first time, especially if this is their first major research project. The outcome of interpreting the qualitative research you have done is another story! If the role model for the quantitative researcher is objective, independent scientist, then the role model for the qualitative research as ethnographer has clear implications for how you interpret qualitative research. Your major task is to develop this story, or narrative, and figure out the best way to tell it.

Reading an account of qualitative research is much closer to reading a work of fiction, such as a novel, than reading a scientific report. You would probably be surprised to read the following in a quantitative report:

> As a single, 30 year old woman, I could uninhibitedly ask other women to go to lunch; however, asking the men, most of whom were also older than me, was not as comfortable and seemed to require more of a justification. (**Schultze** 2000)

Although all qualitative reports have more in common with each other than they do with quantitative reports, there are three important models of how to interpret and present your qualitative evidence:

- as a narrative
- as thick description
- as a personal journey.

Narrative

The narrative form is probably the closest that qualitative research comes to the quantitative approach, and may be a good choice if your research is more structured than unstructured. If you have used a relatively noninvolved qualitative design for your research such as indirect observation or secondary source data, your story may be a chronological story, which relates events – both in what you have studied and your research process – as they happened over time. If you develop your interpretation as a narrative, you may focus mostly on the factual details of what you observed and what it meant.

Thick description

If you have been more involved in your research setting, for example as a participant observer, you may want to include more of your own experience in interpreting your research. The style that is often associated with the more participative types of qualitative research is **thick description**, which incorporates how it felt for you to be doing research as well as what you observed. Thick description comes from the tradition of ethnographic research in anthropology (Geertz 1973), where researchers were describing people and contexts, such as the Pacific Islanders studied by Malinowski and Mead, with whom their readers were unfamiliar. Business and management researchers who are influenced by this tradition use thick description to describe less exotic situations, such as police patrols (Van Maanen 1982), scientific laboratories (Latour and Woolgar 1986), artificial intelligence research (Forsythe 2001) or even retirement homes (Ehrenreich 2002). Even though they are observing cultures much closer to home (for example Po Branson's *Nudist on the Late Shift*), they interpret the setting and events for their readers in much the same way.

The goal of thick description is to make your reader feel as though he or she is actually present in the research setting, and perhaps even as if he or she is doing the research. John van Maanen's *Tales of the Field* gives a number of vivid examples from his own experience as an ethnographer. You may describe the physical situation in detail, for example how it looked, felt, smelt and so on. For example, Diane Forsythe (2001: 170) was a participant observer in a computer lab where several incidents had occurred that made the atmosphere a bit tense for the women in the lab. In her discussion of how the women in the lab reacted to the installation of sexist screensavers, Forsythe describes how she herself reacted to the screensavers, eventually bringing the matter up with the head of the lab. She discusses the feelings and reactions not only of the people she was observing, but also her own reactions, and what these might mean in a wider context.

The reader might also note that Forsythe's work is vividly descriptive. When you read it, you can place yourself in the scene it describes: this style of writing could just as easily come from a novel or short story, and is completely different from the factual description found in a quantitative research report. Another difference is that Forsythe puts herself into the story as a major character and takes part in the action. This is a major break with quantitative research, where the researcher writes as an omniscient, neutral 'we', if at all. Especially in direct observation and participant observation, the researcher becomes an active character in the story being told in the research and, to some extent, your reader does too.

Personal journey

As noted above, some forms of qualitative research include the researcher as a major actor, rather than as an observer who mainly observes and reacts. In some forms of qualitative research, for example participative action research or cooperative inquiry, the researcher becomes as much an object of the study as the people in the organisation or context being studied. In this case, your interpretation of what you have done may focus on reflections on how you felt or changed during the research, as well as what you learnt/observed from the field study.

As in the study quoted above, Ulricke Schultze (2000) incorporated her experiences as a researcher into her description of what she saw. Like Forsythe, Schultze's report is vividly descriptive. She presents her reflections on what is going on (how can I interpret this, how does it make me feel) and her reflections on this reflection – a kind of hyperreflexivity that she describes as 'ex-pressing'. To give her reader a feel for reflexive research as a process rather than an outcome, she presents excerpts from her research diary in her report so that the reader gets a sense of the progress (or lack of progress) she was making at various points in the project. Again, this is very different from the mostly retrospective sense-making imposed on research done from a scientific perspective. (This is not to say that scientists never write in an ethnographic style. James Watson, for example, describes the discovery of the structure of DNA in very much this way. But scientists do this outside reporting research, usually in biographies written for popular audiences.)

You may want to talk to your project supervisor, and look at some previous project reports, before you decide how much of your own experience and reflections you need to incorporate when you are interpreting what you have done. Some academic supervisors will expect and/or encourage it, but some may find it inappropriate.

If you are using this as the basis for a report to your business sponsor, you should tread carefully! Your business sponsor may be completely uninterested in this aspect of your placement or sponsored project (although it is not completely unknown), and it can be politically risky for both yourself and the people in the organisation to reveal detailed information. The major exception would be, obviously, situations in which you were explicitly engaged to do action research or other similar research.

17.2.3 Linking your results to the literature

Because you are not basing your research plan on a deep exploration of the literature, in interpreting your qualitative research it is especially important to link what you have found to the literature. One criticism of qualitative research as currently practised is that too little of this linking is done, so there is very little accumulation of knowledge and much repetition. On the other hand, since you are inducing a conceptual model from your data whilst doing your research, as a qualitative researcher you should be in an excellent position to do a wide sweep for relevant literature, since you will have 'already found out what you are going to find out'.

Your interpretation may point towards particular themes or strands in the literature that might explain your findings or your findings might help to explain. You are moving in the opposite direction of the relationship between theory and data found in quantitative research. Again, it may be helpful to look at some examples of qualitative research on your topic for guidance in this area. There is no reason that a qualitative research project cannot be theoretically rich and use this richness to make sure that it is robust.

17.2.4 Quality in qualitative analysis

The last task in interpreting qualitative data is to assess your research against the standards you have set for your research project and the standards for qualitative research. There is much debate over whether qualitative research should be judged by the standards for qualitative research or those for quantitative research. The description in **Chapter 12** may be useful here.

One aspect of the scientific approach is that there is very little room for innovation or improvisation in the way you interpret and present your research. How you present your data and statistical analysis needs in some ways to stand by itself. On the other hand, the actual style of the writing – the aesthetic effect – matters little as long as you get the job done. Whilst there are wide variations in writing ability among quantitative researchers, this has little effect on the credibility of what they say (although it may affect the willingness of other people to read it in the first place). The scientific style intentionally effaces the researcher – rather than highlights his or her role in the research – the findings are what counts.

In qualitative research, especially in thick description or research as personal journey, the aesthetics of the writing style and presentation play an important role in how the quality of your research is assessed. If you are writing a report using qualitative research, you usually mean your reader to take it seriously as a narrative and as a text. You are also being assessed on the additional criterion – how well is this project report written? This includes the quality of your writing, as well as its effect on your reader. Some of the criteria applied to assessing qualitative research, as well as validity and reliability, may be:

- *Aesthetic* – what reactions does it arouse in the reader?
- *Moral* – does the research raise or clarify any moral issues relating to the research problem and/or the reader him/herself?
- *Activist* – what can the reader do/what is the reader empowered to do now that he/she has read the report?

17.3 Developing findings and recommendations

We advocate that you articulate what you have found in your research so that you have a firmer basis for your findings and recommendations. Here we present a structured way of doing this which will be useful for presenting interim findings and writing up your research.

17.3.1 Summarising what you have found

A good way to make sense of what you have found out, both at the level of your practical problem and the higher level of your theoretical problem, is to summarise what you have found out through your research. We first need to differentiate

Table 17.3 Outcomes of your project

	Quantitative study	Qualitative study
Expectations	Over 60% of people will be aware of the regulations concerning the labelling of GM foods	People will be keen to know about what their food contains and will actively seek out information about it
Findings	32.5% of people were aware of the regulations concerning the labelling of GM foods	The behaviour of the people we interviewed differed from their stated intentions, in that they did not actively seek out information, yet claimed to do so
Discussion	Considerably less people than expected were aware of the regulations concerning labelling. The reasons could be ...	Despite the apparent importance to people of GM issues, they do not reflect this in practice. The reasons could be ...
Conclusions	Awareness campaigns on food labelling have been less successful than claimed	The effort needed to gain information is more than the perceived benefits. Information needs to be more readily available

between the different elements of the process – expectations, findings, discussions and conclusions. An example is given in **Table 17.3**.

Your **expectations** come from the objectives you have defined for your research project. These are formed primarily from theory, literature or, in many business cases, documented best practice. These provide the basis or first point of reference against which you are going to be making comparisons. The literature may include similar studies that you are replicating, or inference from theory. For instance, studies have shown that in the absence of major inertia effects (such as with personal bank accounts), retail customers will change their buying habits if they are dissatisfied. Grounding your work on this is a good starting point. You will then conduct your study to determine whether, in the particular circumstance you are considering, this is true.

Your *findings* focus on your data and analysis. For example, in a quantitative study, your findings chapter will present your data and show whether they support or do not support your hypothesis. You should make sure that you have interpreted your findings with little editorial (that is, personal opinion rather than supported comment) – they should not require elaboration at this point. When you write up these findings in your project report or present them to an audience, you will need to use signposting and other assistance to help your reader through them.

Part of your task is to speculate on why you found what you did or offer an alternate explanation. This is the job of your *discussion*, not your findings. Your discussion places your findings in the context of your expectations, highlighting similarities and differences. That is, where your findings support your initial expectations or existing theory, they should be noted as such. Where there are differences, these should also be noted and, where possible (as shown in **Table 17.3**), an attempt at some explanation provided.

The discussion needs to be well structured, and you should focus on:

- Areas of weakness and opportunities for improvement in the situation you have studied, for instance if your study indicates that a firm has not identified

Table 17.4 A summary table

Issue	Theoretical view/best practice/expectations	Empirical view/reality/findings
1		
2	List the main issues that have arisen from your work	For each issue provide a very brief summary of what you expected to find, based on the literature	For each issue provide a very brief summary of what you found
3		
4		
5		

particular market sectors of interest, your comments, based on the literature, could show how its processes could be improved to make sure that these opportunities are not missed in future.

- Areas where the theory or best practice does not appear to work, for instance one student project commented that the application of ISO 9000 in a small firm led to a massive increase in bureaucracy that was in danger of putting the firm out of business. The literature appeared almost universally to suggest that ISO 9000 was a good thing, with very few authors identifying the major downsides or how these could be avoided. The student was able to provide a critique of the literature on this basis – that the 'theory' was deficient in some way.

These plus the main issues that can be claimed directly from your results are then fed into the conclusions of your work. Your *conclusion* then takes these discussions on a stage further, with the implications of your findings being stated.

17.3.2 Preparing a summary table

Many students find having to summarise their discussion in the form of a table most helpful, as it is easy to drown in the apparent complexity of the issues being dealt with. **Table 17.4** shows the format for the summary table – as used to reintegrate the findings of the case with the literature in **Chapter 8**. The process is summarised in **Figure 17.4**.

17.3.3 Problems with interpretation

Students who have an easy time collecting and analysing data often have a hard time with making sense of it relative to their conceptual framework and research questions, and vice versa. This may be because some people are more comfortable with fact and others with speculation. You should strive, however, for a balance of the two in your research.

The main problems that examiners find in project reports usually happen when students fail to assess the business and management research on the topic, fail to take a critical perspective on this work or fail to take a critical perspective on their own work. We summarise these problems below:

- *'Told you so'* – examiners find little more annoying than someone starting off with a (usually overgeneralised) hypothesis, and then attempting to prove this is correct,

ANSWERING YOUR RESEARCH QUESTIONS

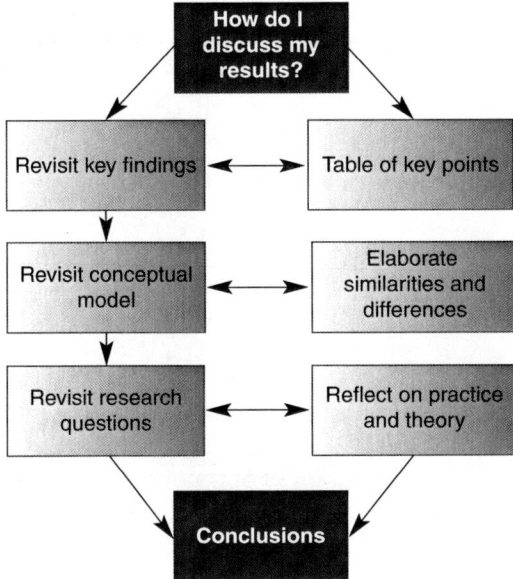

Figure 17.4 Tasks and outputs for your discussion chapter

without any critical analysis of either the idea or the alternatives. This is a solution in search of a problem and rarely makes for good research. It usually happens because a student has fallen in love with a concept, idea, method, model or practice and then looked for a situation in which to apply it. It is much better if you investigate the practical or theoretical problem, identify a number of solutions, evaluate these solutions, and then recommend a particular solution based on your work, even if you do have a particular solution in mind when you start.

- *'Everybody else is stupid'* – where a very limited literature review has been carried out, it is easy for critical analysis to consist of personal opinion. This can occur when commenting on the behaviour of individuals, for example, and then relating this to the expectations you had of their actions. Similarly, for literature, it is always worth considering the context of published work, the associated methods and using these as points for comparison, to gain more insight into the findings.
- *'I'm confused'* – where an author does recognise his/her own confusion over an issue, and presents two sides of an issue, whilst appearing to support both. Where there is no clear preference, this is of interest in itself, provided you recognise it and state why this is so.
- *'Therefore, the world is flat'* – the danger of overgeneralising findings has already been discussed in **Chapter 9**, but is bad for the student, as it shows a lack of understanding of the limitations of whatever method set they are using.
- *'We found nothing of interest'* – often after spending a long time with a project, some of the more interesting findings are lost, as individuals cease to treat them as novel any more. This can result in your work not representing the true value of your findings. Go back to the data, if necessary with the help of someone who is not familiar with the study, and re-evaluate the findings.

- *'It's so obvious'* – well if it is, then you need to look further. If the answer is obvious, was your research question worth asking? Whilst some findings are wonderfully simple in nature, expressing them in terms such as 'all change initiatives need top management support to succeed' has become a truism. It is at times like this when you need to look beyond these basics and be more specific. Who in top management? What does support in this context really mean? What are the cases where change has been successful despite this or not successful even though it was in place?

Summary

In this chapter, we have described how to finish 'doing' your research project by going from your data back through to your research questions. This is the opposite journey you took to get to your data and it is important to close this loop before you start writing your research report. After you have finished this chapter, you should be ready to go on to the final phase of your research, writing your research report.

We discussed the model for interpreting quantitative research in **Section 17.1**. We recommend that you start by interpreting your data with respect to your research questions. Charts, graphs and tables are all useful devices for doing this. You should then move on to interpreting your statistical analysis, perhaps by mapping your results against your conceptual model to see what parts of it your empirical research supports and which parts it doesn't. You should then compare your research with the theory that surrounds your research questions. What did you find that you didn't expect, what did you expect to find that you didn't? You should conclude this stage by considering the quality of your research project. What is good about it? What could be improved?

In a qualitative research report, on the other hand, your focus will be on organising and structuring your words, so that your reader can follow your analysis and to demonstrate the dependability of your research process. You need to decide how to organise your report, identify any schematic presentations of your analysis and tie your findings to your research topic. You will also need to decide how you will communicate your research, whether you present your research as a relatively straightforward narrative, thick description or a personal journey.

Finally, we described the chapter in your project report in which you make sense of your findings, which is your discussion chapter in quantitative research but may be integrated into the description of your research in a qualitative report. We suggest some areas you might want to cover and present some strategies for presenting your discussion chapter.

Answers to key questions

How can I turn my analysis into answers to my research questions?
- Turn data into findings by comparison with prior expectations (quantitative research) or other scenarios (qualitative research)
- Interpret your findings in your discussion

How do I present my analysis?

- For quantitative data and analysis, use graphs, charts, figures and tables
- For qualitative data and analysis, use stories and pictures

How do I use the literature to support my findings and discussion?

- Link key themes back to your literature review to provide points of contrast and similarity
- Link forward to new questions raised by your study that have not been answered by the existing literature

How do I discuss my findings?

- By provision of points of similarity and difference between the findings and the expectations

References

Dunleavy, Patrick. 2003. *Authoring a PhD: How to Plan, Draft, Write and Finish a Doctoral Thesis or Dissertation*. Basingstoke: Palgrave Macmillan.

Ehrenreich, Barbara. 2002. *Nickel and Dimed: Undercover in Low-wage America*. London: Granta Books.

Forsythe, Diana E. 2001. *Studying Those Who Study Us: An Anthropologist in the World of Artificial Intelligence*. Palo Alto, CA: Stanford University Press.

Fox, Kate. 2003. *Watching the English: The Hidden Rules of English Behaviour*. London: Hodder & Stoughton.

Geertz, Clifford. 1973. *Interpretation of Cultures*. New York: Basic Books.

Latour, Bruno and Woolgar, Steve. 1986. *Laboratory Life: The Construction of Scientific Facts*. Princeton: Princeton University Press.

Miles, Matthew B. and Huberman, A. Michael. 1984. *Qualitative Data Analysis*. Beverly Hills, CA: Sage.

O'Leary, Zina. 2004. *The Essential Guide to Doing Research*. London: Sage.

Schultze, Ulrike, 2000. A confessional account of an ethnography about knowledge work, *MIS Quarterly*, 24(1): 213–42.

Van Maanen, J. 1982. 'Fieldwork on the beat'. In Von Maanen, J., Dabbs, J.M. Jr. and Faulkner, R.R. (eds) *Varieties of Qualitative Research*. Thousand Oaks, CA: Sage.

Additional resources

Bell, Judith and Opie, Clive. 2002. *Learning from Research: Getting More From Your Data*. Maidenhead: Open University Press.

Bryman, Alan and Burgess, R.G. (eds) 1994. *Analysing Qualitative Data*. London: Rout-ledge.

Denscombe, Martyn. 2003. *The Good Research Guide for Small-Scale Social Research Projects*, 2nd edn. Maidenhead: Open University Press.

Denzin, Norman and Lincoln, Y. (eds) 1994. *Handbook of Qualitative Research*. Thousand Oaks, CA: Sage.

Eisenhardt, Kathleen M. 1991. Better stories and better constructs: The case for rigor and comparative logic, *Academy of Management Review*, 16(3): 620–7.

Locke, Karen D. 2000. *Grounded Theory in Management Research*. London: Sage.

Key terms

chart, 484	table, 483
graph, 484	thick description, 492

Discussion questions

1. Why shouldn't you assume that your data will 'speak for themselves'?
2. Is it a good idea to present quantitative research in a nonstandard format?
3. Are all numbers forbidden in a qualitative research report? Even page numbers?
4. How should you present case study or mixed-method research?
5. Why should you separate the findings, discussion and conclusions in a quantitative report? Can you separate them in a qualitative report?
6. What should you talk about in your discussion chapter?

Workshop

Task

Choose one of the core articles from your literature review. Read through the article. Now read through it again and:

1. draw a square around key terms
2. underline key themes
3. circle key transition words

which relate to the analysis of data.

Copy these onto Post-it notes and stick them onto the wall.

- Can you identify the structure?
- Can you rearrange them into another, better structure?

CHAPTER 18
Describing your research
Writing up your project report

KEY QUESTIONS

- How should I report my research?
- What are the differences between a report on quantitative research and one on qualitative research?
- What are the differences between an academic and a business report?
- How can I manage the writing process effectively?
- How do I write and edit the project report?
- How do I prepare for an oral presentation or viva?

LEARNING OUTCOMES

At the end of this chapter, you should be able to:

- Prepare your project report, and deliver a written report, oral presentation or viva
- Understand how to vary the project structure and style to suit a particular audience
- Develop a detailed writing plan

CONTENTS

Introduction
18.1 Delivering your project report
18.2 Managing the writing process
18.3 Getting it right
Summary
Answers to key questions
References
Additional resources

Key terms
Frequently asked questions
Discussion questions
Workshop

Introduction

Once you have collected and analysed your data, you may feel as though your project is practically complete, but – don't relax just yet! Writing up your research project is equally as important as actually doing the research. Leaving enough time to write up your research is critical to satisfying your stakeholders and getting a good mark. No research project is really finished until other people know what you have found out; they won't know until you tell them. 'Research is judged not by what you did, but by your ability to report on what you did' (O'Leary 2004: 205).

Your supervisor and business sponsor can only assess your project report. A poorly presented report on even the most brilliant research will underwhelm your examiners. On the other hand, a well-presented report may not totally make up for an imperfect project, but it may tip the scales between passing and failing. How well you define, design and do your project report is a critical aspect of your research. Moreover, anything worth doing is worth doing well: a good project report is something you can be proud of, and writing well is a valuable skill.

To prepare a good report, you need to visualise your finished product – is it a written research report, an oral presentation, a viva, or a combination of these? Your report's structure and content should reflect the characteristics of a good project report, but they will also depend on your project requirements and assessment criteria.

Section 14.1 presents the structure and content of a generic project report, which you can vary to reflect your research approach or customise for a business report. An academic audience will be interested mainly in your findings and theoretical contribution, but a business audience will be interested in your recommendations and practical contribution. If you must present your research to both academic and business audiences, you may need to consider how they differ and what they have in common.

Section 14.2 describes how to manage the writing process better. This is especially important if you are writing a long or technically complex report, or if you are writing with other people. If you have been writing all along, then well done you. You should have enough time to write, edit and polish up your report into a brilliant piece of work without staying up all night consuming massive amounts of caffeine and chocolate or panicking. If you haven't, you should find some practical tips and strategies for rescuing your project or keeping it on track.

Section 14.3 focuses on the technical skills you need to write for either an academic or a business audience. You can use ideas about rhetoric, voice and style to create a high-quality project report, rather than one that just gets the job done.

After you have read this chapter, you should be able to visualise your finished report and work towards achieving it. You should be able to develop a writing plan, develop a detailed outline of your presentation and identify the most appropriate content, structure and style for your audience.

18.1 Delivering your project report

Writing is essential to each stage of the research process (O'Leary 2004: 206), not just the end stage. This is critical to 'beginning with the end in mind'– this is the end you should have been keeping in mind. Earlier we recommended that you visualise your finished project report early on in your project and work backwards to see what you must do to get there. Now you should treat your final write-up as a mini-research project. There are three issues you should think about now:

- *Defining your report* – How are you going to present your research? Why are you writing your report? Who will read it? What should go in and what should you leave out?
- *Designing your report* – What are the major themes of your report? How should you structure your report? What is the main evidence you need to include in your report? What other evidence do you need to support this?
- *Doing your report* – How can you put together a rough draft? How can you turn this rough draft into a first draft? How can you edit this into a finished report?

Most students find the first hurdle not how to write (style), but what to write (content and structure). Although you may need to learn new technical skills to write your project report, you can use a reference book such as *The Oxford Style Manual* (Ritter 2002) to find the answers to specific questions about formal writing such as referencing, page numbering, tables of contents and so on. You are unlikely to find a technical manual that tells you specifically how to write a report for your own unique project. There may be more than one way to do things, depending on what you are writing about and who you are writing it for.

We begin by identifying generic contents and structure for a typical project report. We then explain how you can vary this generic report for an academic or business audience, or to report quantitative or qualitative research.

18.1.1 Visualising your finished product

In our experience, visualising your finished project report *before* you start writing it -ideally even before you start researching it – makes it much easier to manage your writing process and produce a high-quality report. As you learnt in the defining stage of the overall research project – if you do a good job defining your project report, it will be easier to write it; if you drift into it without a plan, you will end up wasting your time and effort.

Beginning with the end in mind is especially important if you are preparing a formal or lengthy written report or presentation. Your project report may be the longest and/or most complex piece of writing you have done, or indeed may ever do if you are writing up a final-year project or dissertation. It is usually impossible to keep everything in your head at once when you are writing a long or complex project report.

The more you can apply a structured process for visualising, outlining and writing your project report or presentation, the easier it will be to see whether you have accomplished it. Similarly, if you are writing with other people, it is easier to work to a clear vision, and you can only achieve this if you can articulate it. If you are a type 2 student (see **Chapter 2**), you may have been able to muddle along in writing essays, coursework or short project reports where you can keep everything in your head and complete the process in one or two writing sessions. However, you may have to abandon your type 2 ways to do a good job on your project report, to avoid the usual 'beginning, muddle, end'.

The key questions to ask yourself here are:

- How will you present your research?
- Who will read this report?
- Why are they reading it?
- What do they expect to get out of it?

How will you present your research?

The first step in visualising your research project is to think about how you will present it. What form will it take – a written project report, an oral presentation, a viva, or more than one of these? Some of the most common formats for research reports are:

- Short project report – 20 pages
- Long project report – 100 pages
- Brief oral presentation – 15 minutes
- Long oral presentation – 1 hour
- Viva.

This will affect not only how you physically present your research, but also how much depth you can go into and what you need to include. Your project requirements should tell you how you will present your research and how it will be assessed. You should also have agreed with your business sponsor, if you have one, what they expect as far as any additional reports or presentations in your project brief.

Who will read your project report?

Besides the physical format, O'Leary (2004: 206) suggests that you should visualise your research as a conversation with your audience. It is important to identify this audience before you start writing or preparing your project report. Who is your ideal or actual **reader**? You need to target not only the contents and structure of your report, but also its style to your audience.

Most project reports are written for an examiner and/or business sponsor, as we discuss in **Chapter 15**. However, your project report may be read by your project supervisor, your academic advisors, your business sponsors, the people who have supported or participated in your research and the wider community of business and management researchers and managers. These different readers may not all bring the same knowledge, assumptions or expectations to your report.

Why are they reading it?

Your academic readers will be more interested in the conceptual, rather than the practical, side of your research problem. They may be less intrigued by the specific details of your answers than the theoretical aspects; the empirical context of your research may be no more than 'local colour'. In presenting your research to an academic audience, therefore, you should focus on showing how you have translated your research topic into research questions, and designed your research to answer those questions. Your report will focus on developing and evaluating your knowledge claim and presenting evidence to support or disprove it.

On the other hand, your business readers will be more interested in the practical, rather than the conceptual, side of your research. Your empirical analysis and recommendations will be more intriguing to them than the most elegant theory or model. Therefore, in presenting your research to business readers, you should focus especially on the practical problem: your analysis, potential solutions and recommendations.

What do you want your reader to get out of it?

Academic readers and business readers will actually read a project report or listen to a project presentation very differently. Your academic readers will expect you to be comprehensive and thorough – within the project guidelines of course. They may even turn to your references first, before they read anything else. On the other hand, the more senior the manager you are presenting your research to, the less time he or she will actually spend reading it. Most senior managers, in fact, will probably only read your report's executive summary or sit through a brief presentation, rather than go into the details.

Given these differences, you may wonder if you can get by with writing just one report if you are presenting your research to both academic and business audiences. Although you may be able to identify common themes and elements across both audiences, it is probably best to think at this stage of your target being two different reports, with some differences but as much in common as possible. We will talk about differences in content, structure and style between academic and business reports in **Section 18.1.3**.

18.1.2 A generic report structure

Once you have visualised your project report and your audience, you can define the basic parameters of your project report – the structure and content. This will help you to answer the following questions:

- How should you structure your report?
- What are the major themes of your report?
- What is the main evidence you need to include in your report?
- What other evidence do you need to support this?

Students often find getting started difficult because they do not know what the project report should contain or how it should be structured. A short informal report and a long formal report will differ substantially in details, but the structure and content will be similar. Your reader expects to read a project report in a familiar structure that presents information in a logical order (Denscombe 2003: 291). We describe this below as a generic project report, which we will show you how to vary depending on how you did your research and your audience.

We start off with the model that would be most appropriate for research that takes the scientific approach, since scientists have developed a standard report. The model that an ethnographer would take is an improvisation on this standard report to reflect the unique characteristics of the research.

Based on these elements, which we will describe below, you should try to develop an outline for your project report before you start writing. Even if you need to revise it later, the process of outlining will help you to clarify your thinking and visualise the finished project report. As you prepare your outline, think not only about what you want to say, but what evidence you want to include, in the form of charts, tables and figures, and how you will include these in your project report. This is also a good time to think about what material you need to include in the body of your report, and what should be put in appendices, especially if you have a limit on the number of words and/or pages in your report.

If you are writing up a report that takes the scientific approach, all you have left to do is write and edit it; if you are writing up a report from the ethnographic perspective, you need to think about how to make these elements part of your story or narrative. Many of the elements will be exactly the same for both kinds of reports, for example the prelims and endmatter should be identical – the main variation will be in the core chapters of the report.

Main text

The **main text** of your report includes everything between the first word of your introduction and the last word of your conclusions. Your main text should be divided into sections (short report) or chapters (long report) that are signalled by headings. You may want to check whether your project requirements for word or page length refer to just this main text or the entire project report.

In a generic project report, your main text would include these sections or chapters in this order:

- *Abstract* – A brief overview of the research problem, argument, themes
- *Introduction* – The problem this research addresses and why it was worth doing
- *Literature review* – What other people found out about this problem
- *Research methods* – How I/we investigated this problem
- *Findings* – What I/we found out about the problem and what it means
- *Discussion* – What our findings say about the more general research problem that I/we investigated
- *Conclusions* – What I/we now know about this problem as a result of this research project.

Introduction

Your **introduction** is an overview of your entire project report. It tells your reader what you did in your project, why it was important, and what you found out.

The introduction should, at a minimum, tell the reader the background, aims, definitions and overview of your report:

- What your research is about
- Why your research is important and interesting
- What your research questions are
- How you answered those questions
- What your main findings were
- A preview of the rest of the paper.

It is usually easier to write your introduction last, even though it comes first in the main text. Word for word, your readers will probably pay more attention to your introduction than any other part of your project, and it pays to put in a lot of effort here to get things just right. Imagine that you have just this chapter to tell someone what your research is about.

Some students believe that if you tell your readers what you found out in your introduction, the reader will not want to read any farther. A research report is not a detective novel: you need to report your findings early on, rather than leaving them to the last chapters.

Literature review

In the introduction, or immediately following it, you should include a **literature review** that provides a critical analysis of the business and management research on your research topic. We discussed doing a literature search and writing a literature review in depth in **Chapter 4**, and mentioned Chris Hart's two excellent books, *Doing a Literature Review* (1998) and *Doing a Literature Search* (2001).

Your literature review should show a critical perspective on business and management research on your research topic, establish any conceptual framework you plan to use (theories, models, concepts, relationships between concepts) and provide the basis for your research questions. If your readers are unfamiliar with your research topic, after they have read your literature review they should know (O'Leary 2004:78–9):

1. The developments in the field
2. If the researcher is credible
3. If the topic is worth studying.

The structure of your literature review may follow a deductive logic, which Dunleavy (2003) describes as a **focus-down strategy**. This structure starts with a broad overview of the topic and progressively narrows it down. This is in line with the hierarchy of concepts model introduced in **Chapter 3** and is based on how scientists report their research, in keeping with the scientific ideal. However, you are not required to follow this model. Your literature review may be more convincing if you compare and contrast themes in the literature you are reviewing. The literature review is a conceptual exploration of your research problem and research questions: once you have finished this chapter, your reader should be able to anticipate your findings, even though you have not yet described how you gathered and analysed your data or what your findings were.

If you wait to start your literature review until you are writing up, you may find that analysing and synthesising the relevant academic literature is just as difficult and time-consuming as analysing your data. You may find it difficult to do a good job on both at once. It is much easier if you have been constantly revisiting the literature as you gather data, analyse it and interpret your findings. Mistakes that students commonly make in writing literature reviews in their final report include:

- Being uncritical or hypercritical
- Lacking focus or having too many focuses
- Not linking the literature review to their research questions
- Not leaving enough time to search and review the literature
- Using the wrong sources.

Research methods

Once you have established your research questions in your literature, you are ready to describe how you will answer them in your **research methods** chapter. You should describe your research design (*how*) and your sources of data (*who* and *where*). You need to tell your reader how the research problem was investigated and why this was the best way to investigate it.

Your research methods chapter should explain how you investigated your research problem and why you used the particular methods and techniques that you did (Bell 1999). Say what you did, but don't feel compelled to report in detail everything you did. You may also be expected to address issues such as validity and reliability in this section. Key aspects of your research you should address include:

- Why you collected the data you did
- What data you collected, where you collected them, when they were collected and how they were collected
- How you analysed the data
- Why you choose these methods
- Strengths and weaknesses of your choices, perhaps with reference to alternative approaches that you might have taken, but didn't.

You may also need to include references for your specific research techniques, for example if you are using a case study, Stake (1995) or Yin (2003), or for action research, Stringer (1996). If you have chosen a well-established set of techniques and procedures for investigating your particular research topic, this may be a fairly short chapter. If there is controversy over the best method, or you have used a nontraditional method, you may need to delve deeper into your research approach.

Some students use their research methods chapter for an extended discussion of research philosophy (**Chapter 5**). The scientific versus ethnographic approach discussion in **Chapter 5** may be relevant here, if you are taking a nonstandard approach and need to justify it. Otherwise, unless you have been instructed by your project guidelines or academic supervisor to discuss research philosophy as part of this chapter (or you are a postgraduate research student), it is usually a good idea to leave it out. It is extremely difficult to get the discussion right, and even experts haven't managed to agree on the core issues.

You may want to use your research methods chapter to describe the research setting and sample, although you may have done this in the introduction for a project that started with a practical problem or qualitative research. This may include a description of the company or industry you studied, how you identified and selected your sample, details of your sample, including population, sampling frame, sample, sample size, and related issues such as response rates and nonrespondent bias.

Findings

Your **findings** chapter will introduce your reader to your data (Denscombe 2003: 294). This chapter tells what you found out in your research and what it means. You need to make sense of the data you have collected in your study, and relate them to both the theoretical literature and the overall research question or problem. Dunleavy (2003) suggests that if you think of this chapter as the answer to 'what does the reader need to know?', then you will focus on reducing the data and communicating them clearly. If your project is data-driven, you may need to summarise your analysis in the main text, in the form of charts and tables, and provide the full analysis and data in an appendix. As we covered this in **Chapter 13**, you should look at this chapter again if you get stuck. Here, to understand what you need to include in your findings, you might spend some time thinking about:

- What is the main evidence you need to include in your report?
- What other evidence do you need to support this?
- What are the major themes of your report?

Discussion

You should also provide a **discussion** of your findings, whether in your findings chapter or as a separate chapter. You need to present your findings before you analyse them and interpret them in light of your research questions (Denscombe 2003). As well as presenting the details of what you found out, you will also need to discuss what they mean within the broader context of the research project, including the theoretical literature and/or the frameworks presented in the literature review. This chapter should describe whether your research answered your research questions, or how it addressed the research problem. Your discussion will focus on your findings with respect to the conceptual models and the literature. It will also look beyond the current research project:

- Your main/most important findings
- How your results relate to the literature
- Any weaknesses/limitations of your findings
- The contribution to knowledge.

The structure of your results section may follow a deductive structure, the structure of your research questions or hypotheses or the main themes of your analysis.

Conclusions and recommendations

In this final chapter you should draw some general **conclusions** and suggest a way forward. Some issues you might address in your conclusions are:

- The main lessons learnt from the study
- The problems you faced and how you overcome them

- What you would do differently if starting the work now
- Any future research that should be conducted
- The implications for stakeholders – academics, managers or policy makers.

You should make sure that you have written a really good conclusions chapter. As we have noted, examiners often read selectively – they skim the middle of your project report and start reading closely again when they reach the conclusions and recommendations. Grab their interest again and help them to make sense of your research.

Preliminary matter (prelims)
All but very informal project reports include some additional material before the main text. You will include more **prelims** for formal or long reports. The prelims help your reader to navigate through your project report, so it is essential for long or complex projects and optional for short and simple projects. Unless otherwise noted, you should number these pages with lower-case Roman numbers (i, ii, iii, …), although the page number is not usually shown on the front pages. The table of contents lists those pages following the contents, with the page numbers visible. You will restart your page numbers with your introduction and use Arabic numerals.

The first page of any report is the **title page**. Your project requirements will usually specify the content and format of this page, which may include the title of your project, the name of the author(s) (unless you are being marked anonymously), the date and the unit or degree for which you are submitting this report.

Make sure that your title expresses your research topic clearly and concisely. Your main research questions may be the best source of your title. Avoid obscure or clever titles – you are supposed to communicate your research to your reader, not show off.

In an academic report, an **abstract** usually follows the title page. Your abstract summarises your research topic, the main themes of your research and your main findings. An abstract may be as brief as 75 words or as detailed as 250 words. Students often make the mistake of writing their abstract as though it is the first part of the introduction – it is separate. Think of the abstract as a mini-report that may be circulated separately from your report, like a commercial for your research.

In a business report, an **executive summary** usually follows the title page instead of an abstract. The executive summary is a brief summary of the practical problem (normally about one page), your analysis of the practical problem, the alternative solutions, your recommendations and any implementation issues. You should write your executive summary so that a busy executive who only reads the executive summary (and not the rest of your report) can make a decision. As with the abstract, you should never write your executive summary as though it is the first part of your introduction – it is separate. In fact, it may well be circulated separately.

What other prelims you include depend on your project requirements and the complexity of your report. A long project (20 pages or more) may include: a **table of contents**, which lists the major elements of the report and their page numbers; a **list of figures**; a **list of tables**; a **list of illustrations**; and a **glossary** and/or a **list of abbreviations** that define unfamiliar terms in one location.

You may want to thank anyone who has helped you with your research. You should put these **acknowledgements** on a separate page in your project report.

Only thank people who have contributed to your research. It's not really appropriate to thank your current girlfriend/boyfriend/best mate unless they have provided you with project resources or data. (Plus, be careful who you thank, as we have noted before in another context, you will have to live with it for a long time!) You may want to thank your academic supervisor or project sponsor, although try not to be too smarmy, especially if he or she will be marking your work.

Endmatter

While the prelims help your reader to navigate through your report, you may also need to include **endmatter** to help your reader to understand what you have presented and amplify their understanding.

The most important endmatter is your **list of sources** or references. This may list either all the resources you consulted for the research project, or only those sources you have actually cited in the main text. You should consult your project guidelines and/or project supervisor to see which one is appropriate.

Make sure that your references are complete, you have included every source you have cited in your main text and have not included irrelevant sources just to pad out your list. This will be much easier if you have been keeping good records of your sources during your project. Many examiners will turn first to your references, as we noted in **Chapter 4**, and interpret the quality of your citations and references as an overall guide to the quality of your research. If your project requirements do not specify a format, you should use the Harvard author–date system.

You should put anything that might be useful to understanding the report, but is not important enough to go in the main text, in an **appendix**. If you have included any appendices, these will follow your list of sources. This might include:

- Copies of your research instruments, such as a blank questionnaire or an interview schedule
- Full details of your research setting and sample, which you have summarised in the main text
- Full details of your analysis, which you have summarised in the main body.

Don't include all completed questionnaires or interview transcripts unless you have been instructed to do so by your supervisor or project requirements. One

Table 18.1 Prelims and endmatter

	Academic report		Business report	
	Short/informal	Long/formal	Short/informal	Long/formal
Title page	✓	✓	✓	✓
Abstract	✓	✓		
Executive summary			✓	✓
Table of contents		✓		✓
Acknowledgements		(✓)		
References	✓	✓	(✓)	(✓)
Appendices	(✓)	✓	✓	✓

example of a questionnaire or transcript will usually do. You should make sure not to hide any of your key points in your appendices (many examiners do not bother to read them), but you should make sure that you don't waste space in your main text with material that doesn't belong there.

18.1.3 Variations on the generic structure

This generic report is commonly used for quantitative research, where researchers fill in the blanks of the generic structure with details of the particular research project. This generic project report structure is based on the scientific reporting style central to quantitative research, but ethnographers also need to report their work. While the generic report suits the deductive approach of quantitative research well, it may not be the best way to report qualitative research. Although you could use the generic structure and the chapter contents described above for any sort of project report, the structure of your report should reflect your research approach.

From this book you will know that qualitative research follows a different research process, and is analysed and interpreted differently. Researchers often report qualitative research using structures (and sometimes content) that reflect the difference between these two approaches. Instead of following the prescribed, highly structured format of quantitative research, qualitative research reports are usually written in a more fluid way, reflecting their emergent nature.

Qualitative research

If you have taken a qualitative approach to your research design, your project report or presentation may reflect this approach in its structure, which is usually more flexible than a quantitative report. Although you still need an introduction and conclusions, you may want to describe your research methods immediately following the introduction.

In **Chapter 13**, we described how to interpret qualitative research. Since in qualitative research you will often identify several themes rather than converge on a single theme through deduction, as in quantitative research, you will probably want to structure the core of your report around these themes. This means that you will probably integrate your literature review and your findings around your theme or themes. You may want to follow the advice given by Miles and Huberman (1984), who suggested structuring qualitative research reports around themes, rather than a focus-down structure. You might want to integrate your literature review with the findings and discussion, especially if you are following a grounded theory approach.

The main body of a typical qualitative research report or presentation might look like this:

- *Introduction* – The problem this research addresses and why it was worth doing
- *Research methods* – How I/we investigated this problem
- *Theme 1* – The first thing I/we found out about this problem and what it means
- *Theme 2* – and so on
- *Theme 3* – and so on
- *Conclusions* – What I/we now know about this problem as a result of this research.

Business report structure

You may want to write a separate report for a business sponsor if you are required to hand in both an academic report for marking and a business report to your business sponsor. In some circumstances, your business sponsor may be satisfied with a copy of your project report, but expect you to make an oral presentation.

Easterby-Smith et al. (2002: 154) argue that the distance between academic and business audiences is decreasing as more managers study business and management. However, we argue that you should consider them as two different audiences because managers and academics will want to know different things and the constraints on their time and attention differ so much.

A business audience will mainly be interested in your recommendations on the particular practical problem they face, and only in anything else such as what you did and how you did it insofar as it supports these recommendations. A top manager has only a few minutes to spend on your project report and will typically only read through a few pages of your report, and at best skim read the rest. Even a manager who reads your report closely, however, may not have any interest in the theoretical aspects of your research project. This means that the sections that are most interesting to your academic reader, including the literature review, research methods, findings and discussion, are completely wasted on the manager.

You should focus on the things that will most interest your project sponsor in the main body of your report or presentation:

1. Your analysis of the practical problem
2. Potential solutions to this practical problem
3. Your recommendation of a particular solution
4. Your implementation, including time, cost, feasibility.

Therefore, we recommend a structure that looks like this:

- *Introduction* – The problem this research addresses
- *Analysis* – Why this problem exists
- *Potential solutions* – How we could solve this problem
- *Recommendation* – How we should solve this problem
- *Implementation* – How we can put this recommendation into practice.

If you are not writing a separate report but do need to provide your business sponsor with a report, you might condense or append your literature review, methods and discussion chapters. However, you should still include the academic literature where it relates to your analysis, options and recommendations, and where you need to give credit to other people's words and ideas. Keep details of any important theory or models and your sample in the main body of the text. You still need to demonstrate to your sponsor or manager that your analysis and recommendations are credible and valid, and backing them up with the weight of the literature will help you do this.

18.1.4 Oral presentations and vivas

Many research projects involve a formal or informal presentation, such as an oral presentation or a viva. Oral presentations include informal presentations to fellow students, and formal presentations to examiners and sponsors, which may be assessed individually or collectively.

Oral presentation

You should prepare an **oral presentation** as carefully as a written report. If you plan to do otherwise, you will not succeed. Planning and rehearsal are essential to successful oral presentations.

Issues you should think about during the planning stage include:

- What should the presentation include?
- Who should present it?
- How sophisticated does it need to be?

If the people attending your presentation haven't read your report in advance, your emphasis should be on summarising the key points and conveying the research story. A typical structure will be:

1. Title slide – project title, researcher name(s), sponsor (if any)
2. Aims and objectives
3. Background and context of the research
4. How you did the research
5. Your key findings
6. Your analysis and discussion
7. Your conclusions and recommendations.

If your audience has thoroughly read your written report in advance, you should try to avoid simply repeating the main points in your report, and instead try to add value through your presentation. Don't forget that your main goal should be communicating your research to your audience, but try to bring something new to the material you are presenting or present some aspects of your research that perhaps you could not include in the written report.

Most students nowadays can use presentation software such as Microsoft PowerPoint to create a professional-looking set of slides. The danger, of course, is that the content is often not as carefully thought out as the presentation. Before you get too wrapped up in selecting colours, music, special effects and so on, you need to plan the content of your presentation. Many of the tips for structuring a written report apply to formal presentations.

Try to avoid slides that are too busy or too dense. These will distract your audience from your content. Try not to overload slides with text – on the other hand, don't put up an overhead with just a few words. A good rule of thumb is to prepare one slide for every five minutes if your presentation is over an hour; one slide for every three minutes if under an hour.

You should rehearse your presentation enough times so that you can deliver your presentation smoothly and in the right amount of time. Rehearsing with technical aids is essential. If you haven't used an overhead projector, slide projector, whiteboard, flip chart, video/DVD, visualiser or other aid before, you should practise with it until you are comfortable. You should also work carefully on timing – presentations that are much longer or shorter come across as ill-prepared.

You might want to consider whether all group members will take turns presenting, or only the strongest and most confident. If you are presenting to examiners, you should probably make every effort to include every team member in the presentation, unless there is a genuine reason why someone cannot actively participate. It is usually better for everyone to play at least some role, even if only to introduce the people who will do the substantive speaking. If you are presenting to a business audience, you may want to let the more confident members dominate, but everyone should still participate.

If you are being assessed on your oral presentation, you should review your project requirements to see if any criteria apply specifically to your presentation or if they differ from the written project criteria. The main things examiners look for are:

- How confidently you present your report
- How well you bring your material to life
- How well you have prepared your materials and visual aids
- How well you can answer questions and, if necessary, depart from the script.

Although many students feel nervous or self-conscious about oral presentations, these help you to build career skills and self-confidence. They can also enhance your written project report by building enthusiasm and support for the project, allowing you to explore project angles you missed in the written report and expand the discussion of interesting areas of the project.

You will sound much better and feel less nervous if you take a deep breath before you speak your first word. If you are not normally a confident speaker, you should practise alone or with friends until you feel comfortable speaking. Practise in front of a mirror to see whether you are using your body language and gestures effectively. Get a friend to give you feedback if possible. If you are really nervous, you might try some sort of humour as an icebreaker – Dilbert cartoons are currently popular – but remember that humour can fall flat. You should also think about any questions that are likely to come up and how you might answer them. Once you get started, your audience will focus on what you are presenting, unless you distract them. As long as you don't fall down, giggle uncontrollably, pass out or run off stage – all things we have seen presenters do – the audience will stick with you.

Even experienced speakers expect to have some butterflies before they start speaking – in fact, many believe that if you don't, your delivery will be flat. Tony Blair, the UK prime minister and an experienced public speaker, has been known to finish presentations with a wringing wet shirt, but he still gets his message across.

Vivas

You may also be expected to answer questions about your research in an oral examination known as a **viva**. This may be relatively informal, such as a question-and-answer session, or a formal examination by one or more examiners.

Murray (2003: 17) suggests that the main concerns of the examiner will be:

- Did you do the work yourself?
- Do you understand the business and management research?
- Do you have a good knowledge of the research project?

- Are you a competent researcher?
- Did you learn anything?

You can look up past projects to see what they are like, but you cannot usually observe a viva to see what one is like, which makes some students nervous. On the brighter side, rarely will you get one or more intelligent examiners to listen so intently to you talking about your research project! If you are facing a viva, you might talk to students who have undergone the same examination to see what it is like – but beware horror stories. Everyone likes to tell stories about awful examinations, as they do about driving tests. You might also look at Rowena Murray's book *How to Survive Your Viva* (2003), although it is primarily aimed at doctoral students.

18.2 Managing the writing process

Once you have identified the structure and content of your project report, writing it should be straightforward, shouldn't it? Well no, in fact the report-writing phase of your research will be cyclical, like the rest of your project. As noted earlier, your project report may often be the biggest written project you have done to date. Word lengths of 10,000–40,000 words (80–150 pages) are not uncommon. They are written differently from short projects of 20 pages or so. Because the project is so much longer and more complex, you will need to help your readers by explicitly guiding them through the main body of the text, for example by linking sections together and signposting what is coming up.

If you are working on a large piece of research such as a dissertation, you might be able to complete much of your written report early on in the research process. About half of a quantitative research project will have been completed before you begin your field research. You will have identified your research problem, research questions and any propositions or hypotheses you are putting forward in your research proposal; defined your methodology, including methods for gathering and analysing data, early on as well; and selected your analysis. This means that you should be able to write your first few sections or chapters whilst you are collecting and analysing your data.

In qualitative research, you will typically be collecting and analysing data and reviewing the literature at the same time, so you won't be able to do as much finished writing early in the project. However, you should be taking field and reflective notes during the process, and therefore you should have much of the text to hand by the time you finish your field work. The challenge is then to work out the structure for presenting your research.

Writing will be much easier if you set yourself a schedule and stick to it. A good description of productive writing habits can be found in Bell (1999: 199), who suggests that writing effectively will be much easier if you create a rhythm of work and get support from others.

If you have been working in a group, this may be the first time you have written anything substantial with other people. The skills that have got you this far in your studies may no longer be adequate. The main challenge will be to manage the group process, as discussed in **Chapter 2**. You will need to manage yourself and/or your group so that you not only finish on time, but also leave yourself plenty of time to get your project report right in the process. This is so important that we discuss this in detail.

18.2.1 Drafting and editing your project report

As soon possible, you should start writing your project report. The main milestones of your project will be a rough draft, a first draft and a finished report. However, some parts of your project may be finished before you start collecting your data, while others may only come together at the last minute.

Your rough draft

We suggest you start by putting together a **rough draft** of your core chapters only – the literature review, methods, findings and discussion – and hold back on the introduction, conclusions, prelims and endmatter until later. Otherwise, you will waste time editing them to reflect a constantly changing report. Your rough draft of these core chapters is critical, because this is the first time you will write down your complete argument in a more or less coherent form. You should aim for a rough draft that is about 60 per cent of your total word length, since you have quite a bit to add to this.

Writing your rough draft will be considerably easier if you have been writing all along, for example early drafts of quantitative research or theoretical memos for grounded research. You shouldn't worry about getting the detailed writing exactly right, but instead try to cover all the points and get the argument right. You can turn this rough draft into a first draft, and then polish up this first draft into your final project report.

Once you have written this rough draft, you can:

1. Add to it – new material, ideas, or thinking
2. Subtract from it
3. Change the structure around
4. Make it communicate better to your readers.

You should try to complete a chapter at a time, rather than lots of unconnected bits. Keep going back to your outline if you need to. You may want to write deductively – 'sculpting in marble' – write an initial draft of complete or longer length, then edit and revise it until it fits the requirements; or inductively – 'sculpting in clay' – start with an outline and fill in each of the points in greater detail until the report is written.

Your first draft

You can revise and edit this rough draft into your **first draft**, your first complete version of your report. The quality of your final report is determined by the quality of this first draft – at least for projects with deadlines – so make sure that you start and finish your first draft on time. Many project reports are marked down because they are essentially edited rough drafts, rather than polished first drafts. After you have written a first draft, you should read through your text and see if you have achieved the following:

- Presented the information in a logical sequence
- Made sure each section has a central message
- Made sure each item leads to the next
- Identified any unnecessary material that could go into an appendix.

You should go back to the outline and see how well the overall structure of your report is working, especially if you have taken a qualitative approach and there is more than one way to present your research.

At this point, don't worry too much about polishing your written text. Booth et al. (2003: 201) suggest that: 'Since readers read each sentence in light of how they see it contributing to the whole, it makes sense to diagnose first the largest elements, then focus on the clarity of your sentences, and only last on matters of correctness, spelling and punctuation.' You may end up editing out or rewriting large sections of your rough draft, so it doesn't really matter how well written those sections were.

The major change between the rough draft and the first draft is in the perspective. Whereas you can write your rough draft from your own perspective, make sure that you write your first draft from your reader's perspective. Constantly remind your reader of the structure of your report and where they are in the report. Write what your reader wants to know, rather than what you want to say.

Most of your editing should focus on making your work communicate to your readers. In particular, you will need to include quite a lot of text that is not about the content of your research but helps your reader to navigate through the document and highlights the important or interesting things you have done. Murray (2003: 195–200) suggests four key things you should do for your reader:

1. *Repetition* – repeating concepts, arguments and other key points for linking and emphasis
2. *Forecasting* – letting readers know in advance what you will and will not be doing in your project report
3. *Signalling* – highlighting links and other key aspects of the text
4. *Signposting* – constantly reminding your readers where they are in the thesis, using headings, topic sentences and other devices.

Students sometimes say to us that they don't need to use repetition, forecasting, signalling and signposting because what they have written is so obvious and straightforward – at least when they read it! However, these writing devices can be key to communicating with your reader.

Editing

Make sure that you have allowed enough time to edit your project report. No matter how bad your rough draft, your skill in editing it into a first draft and a final draft can 'turn a pig's ear into a silk purse'. This kind of editing is not spell-checking and other proofreading but revising how you have organised your paper to make sure that your argument is clear, and revising how you have written it so that it is understandable to your readers.

The length of your first draft is a good guide to whether your report is within the word limit specified in your project requirements. If you haven't formatted your report, a good estimate is 250 words per page (in double-spaced, standard margin, 12-point Times Roman font).

Although some people write concisely and economically even in their first draft, most of us can reduce the number of words by 25–50 per cent without losing any content. Look for wordy phrases you can replace such as 'in the way that' with 'how' or 'in order to' with 'to'. Use charts, figures and tables wherever they make sense. A picture can often replace 1000 words, as tables, diagrams, charts and other forms of illustration are often much clearer than written descriptions. However, make sure that you link these back to the text and interpret them – or highlight their implications – in the text rather than just inserting them anywhere and expecting them to be self-explanatory.

When you are satisfied with your first draft, then, and only then, you should include any additional elements required of your project as a piece of formal writing. These elements may include the title page, table of contents, table of figures, acknowledgements, abstract, executive summary, glossary, index, reference list or bibliography, index and/or appendices. You should check that your page numbering, headers, footers and so on are right and in the correct format. If you start including these too early in the writing process, you will waste a lot of time playing with them. We will describe special issues associated with final editing in **Section 18.3**.

As you edit your project report, you may need to consult a number of specialised sources. You can find dozens of good reference books in your library or book shop on the technical aspects of formal and academic writing. Every writer needs a basic set of reference books, including a dictionary, usage manual and thesaurus.

You may also want to consult a professional style and usage guide such as *The Oxford Style Manual* (Ritter 2002) or *The Chicago Manual of Style,* which are good for answering practical questions such as preparing a table of contents, page numbering, referencing and so on. They are especially useful when you start the final editing, since this will bring up many specific questions. Some standard academic reference books are listed at the end of the chapter.

If you are working on a long report and it contains many tables or figures or several different people are working together and combining electronic documents, you may find it worthwhile investing in a specialist guide to whatever word-processing program you are using. In preparing complicated documents (such as the various drafts of this book), being able to automatically update various fiddly bits of your document such as cross-references or figure numbers and page numbers can save you time and frustration.

If you have time to learn them, you may want to take advantage of the advanced technical capabilities built into modern word-processing software programs such as Microsoft Word. These programs now have many of the same features as professional page-setting programs. You can use these features if you are writing a long document. It can be useful to keep your text broken up into smaller units such as chapters, especially if different people are writing different bits of the text, and then use your word-processing software to edit and print them as a single virtual text.

18.2.2 Managing yourself

Students often turn in poor quality project reports, even if they have done a good job on designing and doing their research project, if they have allowed too little time to write and edit. You will have to manage yourself (and your project group if you have one) as well as your writing process.

Creating a good working environment

One key to writing up is to work consistently and without wasting your writing time. Make sure that you aren't trying to work somewhere that actively destroys your concentration. You don't need to go into monastic solitude – many people write better with some background noise such as the radio, television or music, but choose it carefully so that it isn't distracting.

For many of us, writing is bound up with elaborate rituals and habits. You should be aware of **comfort habits**, those habits and rituals that many of us engage in when getting down to a major piece of writing, for example clearing the desk, cleaning the oven, using a particular kind of writing pad/writing instrument. One PhD student, for example, could not start writing until he had made a cup of tea and allowed it to cool down completely. As Becker (1986) points out, we are often aware of our own habits but ashamed to admit to them, because we assume we are the only ones to have such rituals. Nearly everyone has a different comfort habit, but all are equally embarrassing. You should be mindful of your own habits if they are keeping you from writing well or even writing at all, or take advantage of them if they can help you to start or keep going. A trick that works for Kate when she is desperate is to line up the contents of a bag of Skittles and reward herself with a Skittle each time she completes a set amount of writing. One bag of Skittles later, the entire job is done. Healthier-minded students may promise themselves a run or a session in the gym after they've done a set quota of writing.

Even if you are working alone, finding someone to be a moral support can be an effective way to overcome procrastination. For example, you can talk about your writing with someone else or ask someone else to be your conscience.

Avoiding or overcoming procrastination

Many good research projects are not translated into good project reports because of **procrastination** (Blaxter et al. 1996: 209), the art of putting off until tomorrow what we should be doing today. We are all experts at avoiding things we don't really want to do. Although many students use deadlines to motivate themselves, waiting until the last possible minute does not result in significantly better project reports, but does increase the possibility that something will go wrong.

Procrastination stimulates students (and academics) to new heights of creativity in **displacement activities**, substituting an activity that is indeed worthwhile but not essential to your writing, for example cleaning the cooker, tidying your room/desk or walking the dog. These displacement activities are really just excuses for not sitting down to writing.

From a long list of ways to overcome procrastination provided by Blaxter et al. (1996: 210), four of the most useful are:

1. Make notes on your reading, the results of your research or your discussion with your supervisor or manager.
2. Write one of the easier sections of your report, such as the table of contents, references or bibliography.
3. Prepare the outline of one of the sections or chapters and start adding quotations, points and so on.
4. Set yourself a target for writing a set number of words or a set amount of time; don't do anything else until you have done it and give yourself a treat once you have finished it.

Recognising when you have done enough

Some type 1 students finish early and then keep working because they don't know when to stop. This is unlikely for most of us because we have procrastinated. Most students stop writing only when they absolutely have to stop in order to turn their project report in on time. However, if you have finished early and have met your objectives for the report, hand it in. No project report is ever completely finished, just abandoned.

18.2.3 Strategies for group writing

Many students may find writing the project report challenging, because they must write it as part of a team. Writing collaboratively involves not only technical challenges but also significant interpersonal challenges.

If you are working on a group project, you should discuss as a group how you will organise writing up the research report. Some groups prefer to assign roles, with a single person – or a pair – responsible for editing, and others writing the text. Other groups divide up responsibility equally for writing and editing.

You may find that you will have to solve interpersonal challenges as well as technical challenges in writing as a group. Some may be due to different writing habits, so it might be useful for your team to go through the issues mentioned above before you start writing the full project report draft.

As a project team, you may want to stick with the same strategy you have used in defining, designing and doing your research project, or you may want to try a new pattern. The two basic strategies for dividing up the writing responsibilities are writing individually and writing collaboratively.

If you have taken a quantitative approach, you may find that it is easy to split up the project report chapters or even sections so that individual team members can write independently. One person could take responsibility for the research methods chapter, one the literature review and so on. This may be difficult if you have taken a qualitative approach, since it is much more difficult to split up the different elements.

Although you may find that splitting up the writing task between individuals (or small teams) reduces interpersonal conflicts, if you cut and paste the resulting text together, as in **Figure 18.1a**, you can create a number of problems for your team. First, not everyone on the team may be equally good at writing, so that your overall

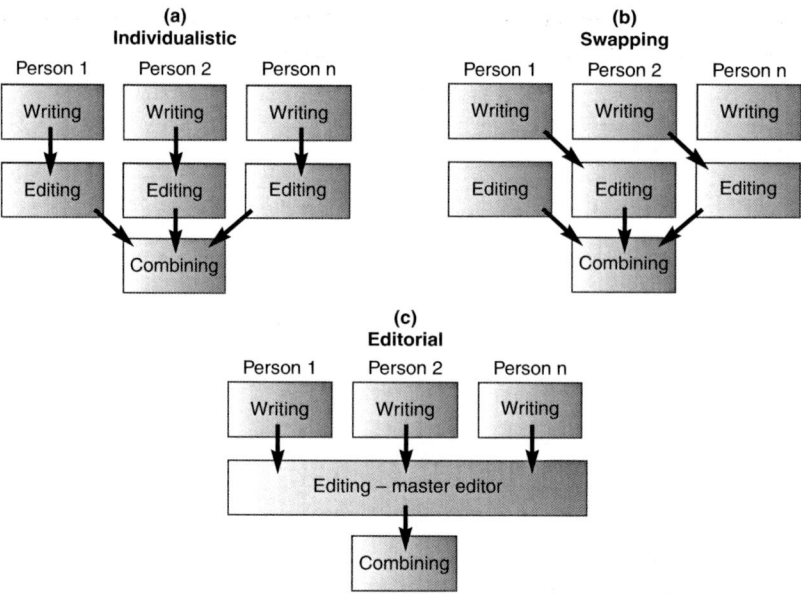

Figure 18.1 Strategies for writing and editing

report will be only as good as your weakest writer. Second, individual writers may go 'off message', so that your report contradicts itself, confusing your readers. Third, since team members will have different styles, it may be difficult to keep a consistent voice and style across the chapters. Thus, you will need to put a lot more effort into editing your report.

Your project report may be more consistent if you switch writing and editing responsibilities, as shown in **Figure 18.1b**. Since different people are responsible for writing and editing, the differences can be homogenised across the different individuals or teams. In addition, if different people are writing and editing, you have more chances to catch any mistakes or misstatements that may creep in. Achieving consistency is more of a challenge than you would think in a group working to deadlines. Some student project reports we have read fail even to agree on a consistent research topic – each section starting with a slightly different interpretation of the main topic! Needless to say, this didn't really impress the examiner, who would have preferred some consensus on whether the topic was corporate social responsibility, corporate ethics or corporate governance.

Your report may also be more consistent if you appoint a **master editor**, as shown in **Figure 18.1c**, to be responsible for editing all the chapters and making sure they are consistent. If you have a group member who is particularly talented at editing, this is a good way of using his or her talent, but it can also be easy to burn that person out if the editing task is too big and there is too little time left to do it well.

If you are writing up quantitative research, shared responsibility for writing and editing may work well, since there are generally accepted conventions for structure and style that most people understand and can imitate. If you are writing up qualitative research, on the other hand, it may work better to have a single editor, especially if different people are writing different sections. It is often difficult to maintain a consistent style across writers, but the use of a master editor can help you attain a seamless style. However, it can be more difficult to identify discrete sections which you can assign to different writers, since you are weaving together your data, conceptual framework and findings as you present them, rather than having them in separate sections.

18.3 Getting it right

Thus far in the research project, you have had to learn and use various sets of skills. Writing the project report is no different. Every project report will be unique, but the process of writing any project report will call on the same set of generic technical skills, which are writing persuasively, correctly and stylishly.

A quick checklist for the technical details is to see whether your report or presentation does each of the following:

- Achieves a good standard of spelling and grammar
- Develops logical links from one section to another
- Uses headings and subheadings to divide the text into clear sections
- Is consistent in the use of the referencing style
- Uses care with the page layout
- Presents tables and figures properly.

18.3.1 Writing correctly

To write correctly you need to master the basic mechanics of writing: spelling, grammar and punctuation. Some students may believe that writing correctly is old-fashioned: we think that you should do it anyway. You may not know who is marking your project report, it might be someone who cares deeply about language. Even if your reader isn't so punctilious, if you make more than a few errors, a reader will mentally downgrade his/her opinion of the quality of your research report and, by extension, your research. At the very least, errors cause the reader's attention to slip, and he/she may notice problems with your logic or other core aspects of your research that might otherwise have gone unnoticed. Finally, if you have put time and effort into your research, why not try to do a good job on the writing? Would you patronise a five-star restaurant where the chef is famous, the ingredients are top-notch, the cooking is superb, but the ingredients are slopped onto a paper plate and slapped down in front of you?

Many students have problems producing error-free prose. You may have dyslexia or another learning impairment. You may not have been taught how to write correctly, but your readers will consciously or unconsciously judge your research as being of poor quality if you make spelling, grammar and punctuation errors in your project report, presentation handouts and overheads, covering letters and any other documents you produce.

Although many students whose native language is not English write English tolerably or even exceptionally well, others find it a challenge. Many universities offer assistance to international students, including pre-sessional English courses, continuing English training and even personal coaching. You should investigate which of these are available to you. You may want to ask your supervisor or project coordinator whether you are allowed to use a proofreader (it is not ethical to hire someone to actually write the report for you).

Spell check

Most readers will assume that, if you misspell more than a few words in your project report, you have spent too little time to do a good job or you are satisfied with shoddy work. Most word-processing programs nowadays include spell-checking routines that highlight misspelt words. Some even query correctly spelt words that are commonly misused – 'it's' for 'its' or 'they're', 'their', 'there'. However, if you substitute a correctly spelt word for the word you meant to write, for example if you mean to write 'from' and type 'form' instead, even the most sophisticated computer spellchecker will not catch your mistake.

You will catch more misspellings if you:

- Use a dictionary when you write
- Leave time between your final editing and printing out your report, so that you can read through with a fresh eye
- Get someone else to read through your report
- Read through your report backwards – from back to front, bottom to top and left to right.

Don't forget to check you have correctly spelt the names of any people or organisations you mention in your report. Misspelling the name of a major researcher in your literature review – which happens more frequently than you would think – makes your command of the literature look shaky. Similarly, if you get the name of a major organisation wrong (Wal-Mart, not Walmart or WalMart), how likely is it that your reader will assume that your data and analysis are right?

You should also refer to your dictionary to make sure that you use words correctly. Students often misuse words when they want to appear more sophisticated than they actually are. This is not usually a good idea and you will come across like Mrs Mala-prop, a character in one of Sheridan's plays who constantly misused words to try to impress her listeners.

A good dictionary will also help you avoid clichés and other hackneyed expressions in your writing. Some of the 'usual suspects' listed by O'Connor (1996) are acid test, bite the bullet, bottom line, can of worms, foregone conclusion, foreseeable future, tip of the iceberg and viable alternative.

Grammar check

As well as checking your spelling in your final draft, you should also check to make sure that you are grammatically correct. Grammar refers to the technical rules governing the parts of speech (nouns, verbs, adjectives, adverbs and pronouns), and how we employ them (agreement, phrases and clauses). A report that is filled with grammatical mistakes gives your reader the impression that you don't really care enough about your research to do a good job in presenting it.

Grammar poses a number of fiendish traps for writers of all types. 'Grammar is a sine qua non of language, placing its demons in the light of sense, sentencing them to the plight of prose' (Gordon 1993a: xv). Cook (1985: viii) suggests that the errors that most commonly cause readers problems in reading and understanding are:

- *Needless words* – A good editor can spot needless words and eliminate them. This is essential for editing your writing to the word limit, if your first draft is lengthy. It will also help with the clarity of what you are writing.
- *Words in the wrong order* – Words are in the wrong order for one of two reasons. First, word-processing makes it easy to shift sentence elements around and leave orphans or dangling bits. It is the editor's responsibility to hunt down and eradicate these. A more subtle problem occurs when words are not in the wrong logical order, but are not in the order that a native English speaker would put them. This takes a more practised ear to find, because it is usually difficult to articulate why 'the red big house', for example, sounds awkward, whereas the 'big red house' doesn't.
- *Equivalent but unbalanced sentence elements* – Writing your entire report in simple sentences would start to sound monotonous after a while. (It worked for Hemingway though!) Whenever we combine simple sentences into complex ones, we run the risk of creating inconsistencies between the joined-up phrases. A simple example would be 'Harvey designed the survey chapters, the data were analysed by Kate, and writing all the report was the job of Helen.' Three different kinds of sentences are joined up here. It would be more consistent to write 'Harvey designed the survey, Kate analysed the data and Helen wrote the report.' Any time you use 'and' or 'or' to join up sentences (or sentence elements, which are incomplete sentences), you should check to make sure they are parallel, that is, written the same way. This may perhaps seem a subtle point but it can definitely distract your reader if you get it wrong.
- *Imprecise relations between subjects and verbs and between pronouns and antecedents* – This is perhaps a fancy way of saying that this is a tricky area of grammar. Make sure that your subjects agree with their verbs. This sounds easy, but it gets difficult when you have a compound subject (Bob and John ... are ... is?), when your subject and verb are separated by other elements of your sentence (the experiment that was carried out by the students under controlled conditions in a laboratory setting ... are ... is?), or when you have a tricky subject such as 'per cent' or 'none'. The same goes for pronoun agreement. Most of us wouldn't say 'John ... she' but things can get tricky (the company ... its or their?), especially when you are trying to avoid sexist terms (the examiner awarded his ... her ... their? mark).
- *Inappropriate punctuation* – the subject of our discussion below.

If you know you have problems with grammar, consult a good usage guide and/or a friend or professional with a good ear for language and a good understanding of the rules. There are many good guides to grammar for beginners and advanced students – see **Additional resources** at the end of this chapter.

Punctuation
Checking punctuation is the final task of the editor. Punctuation is essential to style and communicating with your reader. Punctuation clarifies the structure of a sentence and prevents you from misreading it (Cook 1985: 108).

If you know that you have trouble with punctuation, you can find a wide range of reference manuals in your library or book shop. We can enthusiastically recommend the following two books (full details in the **References**):

- Patricia T. O'Connor's *Woe is I: The Grammarphobe's Guide to Better English in Plain English* (1996: x), which the author describes as a 'survival guide for intelligent people', which provides 'commonsense tips on how to avoid stumbling into ... the worst pitfalls of everyday language'
- Karen Elizabeth Gordon's *The New Well-tempered Sentence: A Punctuation Handbook for the Innocent, the Eager, and the Doomed* (1993b: vii), in which 'the punctuation marks themselves [are] stirring up trouble and inviting raffish comrades in for drinks', not to mention 'taking off their clothes, throwing masked balls, [and] sending insinuating letters to cellists, divas, and Eurobankers'.

Punctuation is also one of the key aspects of style. 'Prose writers are interested mostly in life and commas', argues Ursula Le Guin (1998: 35), a bestselling science fiction writer and expert on creative writing. You can use punctuation to decorate your writing, says Cook (1985). Lynne Truss's book on punctuation, *Eats, Shoots & Leaves* (2003), was a recent bestseller on both sides of the Atlantic.

Punctuating badly is like weaving all over the road when you are driving – you are likely to be pulled over and given a stern warning. It would be nice to think that people only have problems with sophisticated punctuation marks such as the colon, but even the poor full stop is abused in student writing. If you're not confident with your punctuation, stick to simple, short sentences. Your report may sound a bit choppy, or you may come across as the next Ernest Hemingway, but this may help you to write correctly, if not beautifully.

18.3.2 Writing with style

As we have noted above, your examiners will mark your project report based not only on the quality of your research, but also how well you report it. This includes not only the structure of your report, but also how well you describe what you have done – its style. Style also includes the sound of the language you use, punctuation, syntax, sentences and paragraphs.

Style distinguishes a good report from a great report, if they both have the same content. A great chef not only knows how to prepare a good meal, she/he also knows how to arrange it on the plate for maximum impact.

Your audience will not read your project report for its writing style only, unlike readers of poetry or fiction, but how you write does affect their ability to make sense of what you have written and interpret your meaning. Your readers may expect you to write a project report on quantitative research in a scientific style, using the third person, past tense and many passive sentences (Denscombe 2003: 289). On the other hand, for a project report on qualitative research, they may expect an ethnographic style, using the first person, present tense and many active sentences.

Beyond choosing an appropriate style for your research approach, remember that your readers will focus not so much on the aesthetics of your writing, as on your ability to construct sentences and paragraphs, and generate and order ideas (Williams 1990: xiv). O'Leary (2004: 209) suggests that you approach writing as a craft, which includes selecting the style and finding a voice. Another craft element is constructing your report: finding a story and making convincing arguments.

Many books deal with the finer points of style. Strunk and White's short (less than 100 pages) book *The Elements of Style* (1999) has withstood the test of time for generations of American students. Two invaluable handbooks for more advanced skills are Joseph M. Williams' *Style: Toward Clarity and Grace* (1990) and Jacques Barzun's *Simple and Direct* (1985). Both books focus on improving not only the style but also the structure of professional writing. Instead of prescribing rules such as 'avoid passive sentences', these books will help you to understand how to communicate complicated ideas in a simple manner.

Activity

If you are having problems writing clearly, here are some things that you should focus on:

1. *Narrative* – Remember that a research report is a type of story, and try to put yourself in the shoes of the person who is hearing the story for the first time and trying to make sense of it.

2. *Agency* – Name the subjects of your sentences. This is why you are told to 'avoid passive sentences' – passive sentences evade responsibility – 'the staff were laid off' versus 'the division managers laid off the staff. These subjects can be people, organisations, collectivities or figurative ('studies').

3. *Action* – Use active verbs wherever possible. Avoid weak verbs – is, are, were – if you can replace them with stronger verbs that describe physical movements, mental processes, feelings or relationships. If you combine active verbs with agency, you can't help but improve your writing.

4. *Cohesion* – Link your sentences.

Take a representative page from somewhere in your first draft and do one or more of the following activities:

- Circle the subjects of your sentences and underline the verbs. How many sentences have explicit subjects? How many have active verbs? Passive, indirect sentences are like a long stretch of the motorway – they can lull you to sleep.

- Count the number of words in the sentences on the page. Most people average about 20 words per sentence. Make some sentences shorter, and some longer, to vary the pace of your writing.

- If you are using word-processing software such as Microsoft Word, then check out the readability statistics for your work. If you are writing at too high a level (pseudo-academic), look at ways of simplifying your writing. If you are writing at too low a level (elementary), bring up the level.

- Circle the last sentence of each paragraph and first sentence of the next paragraph on the page and see how they relate to each other. If you are having continuity problems, this is a good way to see why this happens.

As well as the technical points we have covered, you will also need to edit for style, so that you end up with a well-written, as well as accurate, account of your research. This is especially important for qualitative research, where your style will help you to paint a picture of the real-life context where you have observed people and organisations. It is also important for quantitative research, because it helps you to establish and maintain the credibility of what you have done, by writing authoritatively.

Style is probably one of the hardest things for beginners to get right. New writers often try to imitate academic writing, and end up with an impenetrable mess. Joseph Williams (1990) suggests three reasons why good writing is difficult:

1. We don't actually intend to write well: we try to impress other people with pretentious writing or academic writing when we think our ideas won't be good enough, like trying to cover up a bad steak with a fancy sauce.
2. We never learnt how to write well: we think that technically correct writing (no spelling or grammatical errors) is enough, without writing clearly as well.
3. We can't write this particular report well: we don't have enough experience in doing this kind of writing or we don't really know for whom we're writing.

The following are some hints for editing by ear from Howard S. Becker (1986: 127), who probably writes better than any other sociologist (or even any social scientist) around:

1. Substitute active verbs for passive verbs when you can. Put crucial actions into verbs and make some important character in the story you are telling the subject of the verb.
2. Use fewer words. Avoid 'throat-clearing' phrases. 'An unnecessary word does no work.'
3. Avoid repeating phrases.
4. How you structure your writing (syntax) should reflect its content. Put important ideas first in the sentence.
5. Use concrete rather than abstract words wherever possible. Use concrete details to give body to abstractions.
6. Avoid overworked metaphors and clichés.

Writing clearly

A logical and clear report is likely to receive higher marks than a report that is muddled and hard to follow, even if both report the same research and same content. For your project report to document and communicate your research, an important part of your job is to write clearly: 'Whatever else a well-educated person can do, that person should be able to write clearly and to understand what it means to do that' (Williams 1990: 2).

As in the old joke about modern art, we may not be able to define clear writing, but we do know it when we see it. Williams (1990) suggests that writing clearly begins with writing clear sentences. These sentences then need to be joined up into coherent paragraphs, which maintain the flow of meaning between sentences.

Paragraphs are joined up into sections. Sections are combined in a chapter. Each chapter needs to flow into the next.

Writing concisely

Good writing is not only clear but also concise. You should use as few words as possible. We can often cut 20 per cent or more words out of our writing without losing any meaning. Most first drafts are full of excess words – the equivalent of verbal throat-clearings such as 'erm' and 'you know' when we speak. The *Journal of Consumer Research*, in fact, suggests that authors cut 20 per cent of the length of their final draft before sending in a paper to the journal.

For example, the sentence 'Williams (1990) suggests that writing clearly begins with writing clear sentences' above started as 'Williams (1990) suggests that the process of writing clearly begins with the ability to write clear sentences.' The new sentence is 50 per cent shorter.

Voice

Good writing also has a distinct voice as well as style. *Voice* refers to the tone that is taken in the relationship between reader and writer, how you express yourself (Blaxter et al. 1996: 221), whilst *style* describes how you write up your research. In choosing a voice, it is important to think about your audience. In quantitative research, you are addressing an academic audience, usually your academic supervisor and/or examiner(s). Choosing a voice in qualitative research can be tricky. Who is your audience? Is it the same audience as for a quantitative report, or is it different? Miles and Huberman (1994) suggest that you should consider your reader as a co-analyst, looking at and interpreting the evidence in your qualitative report. If you are part of a group project, is the paper being written by the group, or by a collective 'we' persona?

Another way of thinking about voice is that it represents the *point of view*. Is the person writing the report omniscient, a perspective typically taken in quantitative research, or is the author's viewpoint limited to what he/she observed, as in much qualitative research?

A final word

Many students do their research project a great disservice by not taking care with how they present it. We would never argue that how you present your research is more important than what you present. However, in our experience, how you present can either detract from or enhance what you have done significantly. If you get the presentation right, your reader should not actually pay any attention to the voice, style or grammar in your report, and your research will be free to speak for itself. If you get the presentation wrong, your reader will be distracted from the content and focus on the presentation and quibble with the research.

Summary

In **Section 14.1**, we describe the process for planning your project report, writing your rough draft, revising your rough draft into a first draft, and editing your project report into a finished draft. **Section 14.2** briefly discusses some of the technical aspects of project report writing: developing an argument, writing correctly and writing with style. **Section 14.3** concludes with some tips for writing alone or as part of a project group.

Answers to key questions

How should I report my research?
- This depends on the requirements of your project – it may be a report and/or a presentation
- The formats for each of these are well defined
- You should follow one of the recommended formats

What are the differences between a report on quantitative research and one on qualitative research?
- The formats for quantitative reports are based on a generic format with little variation
- The formats for qualitative research may vary depending on the narrative or story being told

What are the differences between an academic and a business report?
- Length, audience, purpose and format are all different between these two forms

How can I manage the writing process effectively?
- Plan before you start
- Start early and write often
- Get regular feedback on the process
- Manage your group and yourself

How do I write and edit the project report?
- You should pay attention to style, voice and the technical content of your work

How do I prepare for an oral presentation or viva?
- Prepare your formal presentation
- Check the audience – their interest and purpose for attending
- Practise what you will say
- Anticipate questions

References

Barzun, Jacques. 1985. *Simple and Direct: A Rhetoric for Writers,* rev. edn. Chicago: University of Chicago Press.
Becker, Howard S. 1986. *Writing for Social Scientists.* Chicago: University of Chicago Press.
Bell, Judith. 1999. *Doing Your Research Project: A Guide for First-Time Researchers in Education and Social Science,* 3rd edn. Maidenhead: Open University Press.
Blaxter, Lorraine, Hughes, Christine and Tight, Malcolm. 1996. *How to Research.* Buckingham: Open University.
Cook, Claire Kehrwald. 1985. *Line by Line: How to Edit Your Own Writing.* Boston, MA: Houghton Mifflin.
Denscombe, Martyn. 2003. *The Good Research Guide for Small-Scale Social Research Projects,* 2nd edn. Maidenhead: Open University Press.
Dunleavy, Patrick. 2003. *Authoring a PhD: How to Plan, Draft, Write and Finish a Doctoral Thesis or Dissertation.* Basingstoke: Palgrave Macmillan.
Gordon, Karen E. 1993a. *The Deluxe Transitive Vampire: The Ultimate Handbook for the Innocent, the Eager, and the Doomed.* New York: Pantheon Books.
Gordon, Karen E. 1993b. *The New Well-Tempered Sentence: A Punctuation Handbook for the Innocent, the Eager, and the Doomed,* Boston, MA: Houghton Mifflin.
Hart, Chris. 1998. *Doing a Literature Review: Releasing the Social Science Research Imagination.* London: Sage.
Hart, Chris. 2001. *Doing a Literature Search: A Comprehensive Guide for the Social Sciences.* London: Sage.
Le Guin, Ursula K. 1998. *Steering the Craft: Exercises and Discussions on Story Writing for the Lone Navigator or the Mutinous Crew.* Portland, OR: Eighth Mountain Press.
Miles, Matthew B. and Huberman, A. Michael. 1994. *Qualitative Data Analysis,* 2nd edn. Beverly Hills, CA: Sage.
Murray, Rowena. 2003. *How To Survive Your Viva: Defending a Thesis in an Oral Examination.* Maidenhead: Open University Press.
O'Connor, Patricia T. 1996. *Woe Is I: The Grammarphone's Guide to Better English in Plain English.* New York: Riverhead Books.
O'Leary, Zina. 2004. *The Essential Guide to Doing Research.* London: Sage. Ritter, Robert M. 2002. *The Oxford Style Manual.* Oxford University Press.
Stake, Robert E. 1995. *The Art of Case Study Research.* London: Sage.
Stringer, Ernest T. 1996. *Action Research: A Handbook for Practitioners.* London: Sage.
Strunk, William I. and White, E.B. 1999. *The Elements of Style.* New York: Allyn & Bacon.
The Chicago Manual of Style: For Authors, Editors and Copywriters, 2003 15th edn. Chicago: University of Chicago Press.
Truss, Lynne. 2003. *Eats, Shoots & Leaves: The Zero Tolerance Approach to Punctuation.* London: Profile Books.
Williams, Joseph M. 1990. Style: *Toward Clarity and Grace.* Chicago: University of Chicago Press.
Yin, Robert K. 2003. *Case Study Research: Design and Methods,* 3rd edn. London: Sage.

Additional resources

Booth, Wayne C, Columb, Gregory G. and William, Joseph M. 2003. *The Craft of Research,* 2nd edn. Chicago: University of Chicago Press.
Easterby-Smith, Mark, Thorpe, Richard and Lowe, Andy. 2002. *Management Research: An Introduction,* 2nd edn. London: Sage.
Locke, Lawrence F., Silverman, S.J. and Spirduso, W.W. 2004. *Reading and Understanding Research,* 2nd edn. London: Sage.
Van Maanen, J. 1982. 'Fieldwork on the beat'. In Von Maanen, J., Dabbs, J.M. Jr and Faulkner, R.R., (eds). *Varieties of Qualitative Research.* Thousand Oaks, CA: Sage.

Key terms

abstract, 510	focus-down strategy, 507	oral presentation, 514
acknowledgements, 510	glossary, 510	prelims, 510
appendix, 511	introduction, 506	procrastination, 520
comfort habits, 520	list of abbreviations, 510	reader, 504
conclusions, 509	list of figures, 510	research methods, 508
discussion, 509	list of illustrations, 510	rough draft, 517
displacement activities, 520	list of sources, 511	table of contents, 510
endmatter, 511	list of tables, 510	title page, 510
executive summary, 510	literature review, 507	viva, 515
findings, 509	main text, 506	
first draft, 517	master editor, 522	

Frequently asked questions

How long will writing the report take?

Experience suggests that any piece of written work will take 110 per cent of the time you have available to do it in. However, you can plan for preparing, writing and editing early on.

If you know the length of your project, either total number of words or pages, you can estimate how long it will take based on how quickly you normally work. An average page formatted with double-spacing, 12-point Times Roman font will be about 250 words. The most you can reasonably expect to write in a single day is 6000 words, working at a frenetic pace. A more reasonable target is 2000 words working at a steady pace, or 1000 words if you are a slow writer.

This would require you to work the following amounts of time, just on writing (not researching or reading):

- 1–5 days for a coursework project of 1500–5000 words (6–20 pages)
- 5–20 days for a dissertation of 20,000 words.

You will also need to include time for collecting your materials and planning your report structure, and editing your first draft. Thus, you should allow about three times as long for the entire writing process as for the writing itself. Obviously, if you write as you go along, you will be able to streamline this stage of the research process; if you leave it all to the last minute, forget about it and just go into panic mode, work all night and drink lots of caffeinated beverages.

What should the report look like?

If you have been given specifications for the format of the written report, you should follow these – exactly. In this case, you can use this section to help understand what to do and how to get there. You will probably find it useful to consult student reports from previous years, if you have access to them, so that you can see how other students have presented their research.

DESCRIBING YOUR RESEARCH

If you are not working to a specified format, Section 18.2 will help you visualise your format and decide how to get there.

Who will read this report?

Unlike most things that you have read during your course and research, research reports are typically written for a minute audience. Your main 'customers' will be your supervisor, your examiners (if different), your sponsor (if you have one) and perhaps the participants in your study. Sometimes research reports from student projects will reach a wider audience, but this isn't usual or even desirable.

Discussion questions

1. Why is it important to approach your project report as a special kind of writing rather than just 'business as usual'?
2. Is there a special format that all project reports must follow?
3. Why is it important to understand who will be reading your report before you start writing?
4. Should you write your report in the same order as the chapters?
5. Where can you go to get help with writing if English is not your first language?
6. What challenges occur when you are writing as part of a group that are not relevant when you are writing alone?
7. Why is procrastination an enemy of good reports rather than just a different way of working?
8. Do you have any habits or rituals that you associate with writing? Are these productive or counterproductive?
9. How can good writing help your reader to understand your research project? How can it help you?
10. Why might quantitative and qualitative research reports differ? Academic and business reports? Individual and group reports?

Workshop

Go back to three of the core readings in your literature review (if a quantitative study) or theory (if a qualitative study such as a grounded theory project).

1. Analyse the overall structure of each piece.
2. Is this structure 'standard' or 'customised'?
3. Identify the major uses of literature.
4. How does the contributions and conclusions section build on the findings?

Name index

Agnew, N. M., 15
Alexander, D., 363
Alwan, L. C., 402, 448
Anderson, P., 225
Arksey, H., 315

Bannister, D., 322, 323
Barclay, I., 241
Barker, R. G., 330
Barton-Cunningham, J., 322
Barzun, J., 527
Beattie, V., 330
Becker, H. S., 173, 520, 528
Bell, E., 102, 125, 129, 181, 381, 389, 390, 396
Bell, J., 508, 516
Benson, M. H., 241
BERR, 251, 435
Black, T. R., 262, 263, 285
Blackburn, R. A., 60
Blaikie, N., 72, 75, 82, 170, 171, 219, 229, 262
Blair, J., 359, 364
Blaxter, L., 520, 521, 529
Blumberg, B., 259
Bolton, R. N., 320
Bonoma, T. V., 58
Booth, W. C., 221, 518
Borg, W. R., 209
Bradach, J. L., 131
Brandt, R., 330
Brenner, S. O., 322
Brenner, M., 348
Brook, J. A., 322
Brook, J. R., 322
Bruce, C. S., 209
Bryman, A., 91, 102, 125, 129, 181, 381, 389, 390, 396
Burrell, G., 50

Carroll, G. R., 108
Chandler, A. D., 170
Clarkson, G. P. E., 321
Clegg, F. G., 364
Coddington, A., 238
Cohen, W. M., 225
Collis, J., 203, 286, 353, 355, 356, 362, 406, 441, 442, 445, 448, 458
Cook, I., 339, 402, 412, 420, 427, 430, 432, 434, 449, 452, 457, 459
Cooke, C. K., 525, 526
Coolican, H., 59, 352
Corbin, J., 50, 329, 330, 378, 391, 392, 397
Covey, S., 33
Coyle, R. G., 392
Crawford, G., 238
Creswell, J. W., 49, 50, 51, 54, 60, 171, 258, 260, 261, 264, 266, 287
Curran, J., 60
Cusumano, M. A., 180
Czaja, R., 359, 364

Dackert, I. R., 322
Davis, G. B., 36
Day, J., 321
Delbridge, R., 240, 241
Denscombe, M., 506, 509, 526
Dickson, W. J., 43
Duckworth, W. M., 402, 448
Dunleavy, P., 483, 484, 507, 509
Dunn, W., 323

Easterby-Smith, M., 84, 315, 322, 350, 513
Ehrenreich, B., 492
Eisenhardt, K. M., 159, 181, 182, 189

Faraday, M., 73
Fearnley, S., 330
Fiedler, F. E., 57

NAME INDEX

Field, A., 427, 429, 434, 444, 448, 452, 457, 458, 459
Fineman, S., 367
Flanagan, J. C., 318, 319, 349, 350
Foddy, W., 116
Fode, K. L., 79, 140
Forsythe, D. E., 492, 493
Fox, K., 491
Fransella, F., 322, 323

Gall, M. D., 209
Geertz, C., 492
Gerrard, P., 322
Gill, J., 205, 219
Gillespie, R., 239
Ginsberg, A., 323
Glaser, B., 158, 263, 329, 330
Gordon, K. E., 525
Gosling, V. K., 238
Gray, D. E., 111
Greenwood, R. G., 281
Griffiths, W. E., 456
Gubrium, J., 318
Gummesson, E., 60
Gundlach, J., 105

Hankinson, G., 321
Holstein, J., 318
Huberman, A. M., 180, 512, 529
Hunter, M. G. 322
Hussey, R., 203

Innes, J., 330

Jankowicz, A. D., 270
Johnson, P., 205, 219
Jones, D. T., 210
Judge, G. G., 210
Juster, N., 98

Kanter, R. M., 281
Kaplan, R. S., 74
Kelly, G. A., 321
Kendall, P. L., 327
Kerlinger, F. N., 262, 263
Kervin, J. B., 259, 342, 358, 402, 455, 456
Kipling, R., 31
Knight, P., 315
Kolb, D. A., 382
Kotler, P., 224
Krejcie, R. V., 364, 365
Kuhn, T., 50
Kuhn, T. S., 48

Latour, B., 224, 492
Laughlin, R., 263

Le Guin, U. K., 526
Lee, R. M., 110, 317, 318, 347, 367
Lee, T. C., 456
Levinthal, D. A., 225
Lovie, P., 402
Lowe, A., 315, 350
Lowe, J., 240, 241
Lundberg, C. C., 218, 221
Lutkepol, H., 456

MacKinlay, T., 350
Maister, D. H., 131
March, J. G., 129
Maslow, A. H., 221
McCabe, G. P., 402, 448
McClintock, C., 402, 448
McCuen-Metherell, J. R., 205
Meckling, W. H., 276, 403
Mellor, C. J., 346
Merriam, S. B., 262
Merton, R. K., 327
Meyer, A. D., 139
Miles, M. B., 180, 490, 512, 529
Milgram, S., 41, 73
Mingers, J., 50
Mintzberg, H., 238, 239
Moore, D., 402, 448, 449, 463
Morgan, D. L., 327
Morgan, D. W., 364, 365
Morgan, G., 50, 51, 54, 55, 281
Murray, R., 515, 516, 518

Nelson, D., 110
Normann, R., 60
Norton, D. P., 74

O'Connor, P. T., 524, 526
O'Leary, Z., 72, 91, 101, 125, 128, 237, 381, 396, 482, 502, 503, 504, 507, 526
Oakshott, L., 444
Oliver, P., 140
Ong, A., 330
Oppenheimer, A. N., 112, 116, 118
Oxford Compact Dictionary & Thesaurus, 48
Oxford Dictionary of Accounting, 467

Parker, C. A., 36
Parker, D., 268, 269
Parker, L. D., 330
Plummer, K., 324
Popper, K., 83
Pyke, S. W., 15

Ragin, C., 173
Raimond, P., 58
Reason, P., 282, 283, 284, 322

NAME INDEX

Reilly, M. D., 110
Ritter, R. M., 503, 519
Robson, C., 272, 273, 442
Roethlisberger, F. J., 43
Roffey, B. H., 330
Rosen, M., 163
Rosenthal, R., 79, 140, 318
Rosnow, R. L., 140
Rowan, J., 322
Rowntree, D., 402
Ryan, B., 207, 208

Sagan, C., 33
Salkind, N. J., 340
Saunders, M., 25, 101
Scapens, R. W., 207
Schindler, P. S., 259
Schoepfle, G., 264
Schragenheim, E., 392
Schultze, U., 491, 493
Sekaran, U., 255
Selby, R. W., 180
Sherif, M., 138, 145
Shipman, M., 396
Slife, B. D., 264
Smagorinsky, P., 320, 321
Smircich, L., 50, 54, 55
Smith, J. K., 48, 50, 52
Stack, S., 105
Stake, R. E., 508
Stewart, A., 325
Stewart, R., 321
Stewart, V., 321
Strauss, A., 50, 263, 329, 330, 378, 391, 392, 397
Stringer, E. T., 508
Strunk, W. I., 527
Swaminathan, A., 108

Tajfel, H., 138
Tan, F., 322
Taylor, D. S., 323
Taylor, F. W., 42, 68, 73, 114
Theobald, M., 207
Thorpe, R., 315, 350
Turner, B. A., 329
Tushman, M. L., 225

Underhill, P., 114
Upton, G., 339, 402, 412, 420, 427, 430, 431, 434, 449, 452, 457, 459

Van Bruggen, G. H., 187
Van Maanen, J., 50, 492
Vogt, W. P., 59, 254, 325
Voss, C. A., 115

Wallace, R. S. O., 346
Wallendorf, M., 110
Walliman, N., 49
Walsch, N. D., 148
Webb, E. J., 110
Weick, K. E., 221
Werner, O., 264
Whedon, J., 220
Whyte, W. F., 42, 77, 80, 159, 161, 162
Wilkinson, A. M., 266
Williams, J. M., 526, 527, 528, 529
Williams, R. N., 264
Winkler, A. C., 205
Womack, J. P., 224
Woolgar, S., 224, 492

Yin, R. K., 171, 172, 508

Zeithaml, V. A., 117
Zikmund, W. G., 39

Subject index

abstract
  conceptualisation, 383
  journal articles, 198
  in project report, 510
  of research topic, 244
access, negotiating
  unstructured interviewing, 155
access to data, 257
acknowledgements, in project report, 510
action research, as research method, 163
active experimentation, 383
ad-hoc surveys *see* survey
additive model in time series analysis, 469
AMADEUS database, 106
analysing data
  quantitative data, 401–474
analysis, interpreting, 485–488
analytical procedures
  for reviewing the literature, 207
analytical research, 7
appendix, in project report, 511
applied research, 9, 10
archival research, 107–111
  see also secondary analysis
archive, 107
articles
  searching for, 196
association measures
  chi-square test, 448–452
assumptions
  linear regression models, 458
  parametric tests, 444
audience, 504–505, 513, 514
audio-visual aids, 515
average *see* mean
axial coding, 391–392
axiological assumption, 53

Bachelor's level research, 4, 16
bar charts, 416, 417, 418
basic research, 9
BBC News, 131
beginning with the end in mind, 33, 503
bias
  minimising and avoiding, 139–140
  in sampling, 296
bibliographic software, 200
bivariate analysis, 403, 412, 442, 445, 448
body language *see* oral presentation
Boolean operators, 199
bounded ethnography, 80
brainstorming, as source of ideas, 226–227

case study, 169–191
  analysing data, 179–183
  boundaries, 173
  conducting, 172
  cross-case analysis, 180
  defined, 171–172
  defining, 172–173
  designing, 172
  different from teaching case study, 172
  embedded, 174
  examples, 175–176
  grounded, 181–182
  motives for conducting, 170–172
  not pure research design, 172
  paired-case analysis, 180
  presenting, 178, 179–183
  qualitative versus quantitative, 177–178
  quality criteria, 183
  replication sampling, 177
  sampling, 177
  single versus multiple, 174
  theoretical sampling, 177
  unit of observation, 170
  within-case analysis, 180
category, in qualitative analysis, 390
cause-and-effect relationship, 132–133
census, 103, 295

central tendency measures, 421–426
chart, as means of presenting data, 484–485
   grouped bar chart, 484
   horizontal bar chart, 484
   layer chart, 484
   line graph, 484
   pie chart, 484
   scatterplot, 484
   stacked bar chart, 484
   vertical bar chart, 484
charts and graphs, 415, 416, 417
chi squared (χ^2) test, 448–452
citations and references, 201, 270–271
   Harvard system, 201–203
   Vancouver system, 203–205
classifying research, 5–10
closed-ended question, 120
closed questions, 347, 353
closure, reaching, 182
cluster sampling, 304, 366
coding
   in qualitative analysis, 387–390
   questionnaires, 360–362
collaborative writing *see* group writing and editing
collecting data *see* methods
collection of data, 296
comfort habits, 520
   see also displacement activities
completeness, as attribute of qualitative analysis, 380
composite index number *see* weighted index number
computer-assisted protocols for interviews, 114
computer-assisted qualitative data analysis software (CAQDAS), 381
concept
   axial coding, 391–392
   classification, 390
   defined, 383
   extraction, 386–392
   framework, 75, 390
   identification, 386–387
   mapping, 392–394
conclusions, in project report, 509–510
concrete experience, 382
concurrent verbalization, 320
conference papers
   searching for, 196
confidentiality, 343, 347
construct, 320
   hypothetical, 342
   validity, 342
consulting, 28–29
content analysis, 396

continuous quantitative variable, 341
control group, 134
convenience sampling, 154–155
conversation analysis, 397
correlation measures, 452
   Pearson's correlation (*r*), 457
   Spearman's correlation coefficient (*rho* or r_s), 455–456
covert observation, 153
credibility, as attribute of qualitative research, 396
critical incident technique, 318–319, 349–350
critical subjectivity, as attribute of ethnographic approach, 164
cross-case analysis, 180
cross tabulations, 413
cyclical variation in a trend, 471

data, 257
   access, 257
   collection of, 296
   discrete and continuous, 341
   interpreting, 481–489
   primary, 293
   quantitative, 338
   secondary, 293
data analysis *see* methods
data archive, 103
data collection *see* methods
data integrity, 58
data set, 101–102
database, 101–102
   company-specific, 106
deconstruction, 269
deduction, 82
deductive research, 9–10, 339
deflating data, 466–467
delimitations, 269
Delphi study, 343–344
dependability, as attribute of research, 91
dependent variable, 130, 342–343
descriptive data, 161
descriptive research, 6–7
descriptive statistics, 401–440
de-seasonalized trend, 468–469
designing
   questions, 344–345, 350–359, 354, 360
   research, 254
desk research, 101
diagrams
   scatterplot, 453
   stem-and-leaf plot, 420–421
diary methods, 324–325, 348
dichotomous variable, 342
difference measures
   t-test, 447–448

SUBJECT INDEX

Dilbert, cartoon character, 515
dimensions, 390
discourse, 4
   discourse analysis, 397
discrete quantitative variable, 341
discussion, in project report, 509
dispersion measures, 426–429
displacement activities, 520
   see also procrastination
dissertation, 4, 10, 11, 14, 15
distribution methods for questionnaires, 345
distribution of frequency data, 411–412
doctoral level research, 6
drafting, 517–519
dummy variable, 407–408

Economic and Social Data Service (ESDS), 103–105
editing, 518–519
embedded case study, 174
empirical evidence, 6, 7, 57
end matter, 511–512
enfolding the literature, 182
epistemological assumption, 52–53
epistemology, 88
error
   in linear regression, 458
   standard error of the mean, 428
   type I or II in hypothesis testing, 434, 435
ethnographer, as role model, 76–77, 76–81
   see also scientist, as role model
ethnography, 76
evaluating
   your proposal, 271–272
evaluative data, 161
executive summary, in project report, 510
experiment, as research method, 130–141
   cause-and effect relationships, 132–133
   consent by participants, 140–141
   control, 134
   control group, 134
   control variables, 134
   dependent variable, 130, 134
   ethical aspects, 140–141
   examples of, 132
   experimental hypothesis, 135–136
   experimental treatment, 133–134
   experimental variables, 134
   experimenter effects, 140
   experimenter expectancies, 140
   field experiment, 138
   good subject effect, 140
   independent variable, 130, 132, 133, 134
   issues in, 139–141
   laboratory experiment, 137
   principles of, 130–136
   quasi-experiment, 137, 138–139
   random assignment, 135
   subject effects, 140
   true experiment, 136–137
   volunteer subject effect, 140
explanatory research see analytical research
exploratory research, 5–8

FAME database, 106
familiarisation, as part of qualitative research, 382
field experiment, as type of experiment, 138
figures, in project report, 486–487
findings
   interpreting, 479–499
   in project report, 509
first draft, of project report, 517–518
focal organisation, 224
focus-down strategy, in report writing, 507
focus groups, 327–329
found data, 110
   see also unobtrusive measures
frame, sampling, 295
frequency distributions, 411–412

general analytical procedure
   analyzing the literature, 207
generalizability, 59–60
   as attribute of research, 89–90, 396
glossary, in project report, 510
good subject effect, 140
grammar, importance of, 524–525
graph, 484
   see also chart
graphs and charts, 415, 416, 417
grounded case study, 181–182
   closure, 182
   enfolding the literature, 182
   see also case study
grounded theory, 329–330, 397
group writing and editing, 521–523
grouped quantitative variable, 340

Harvard system of referencing, 201–203
Hawthorne studies, 43, 73
hermeneutics, 397
hierarchy of concepts, 242
histograms, 417, 418, 419
hypothesis, 6, 57, 262, 339, 442
hypothetical construct, 342

ideas see project ideas
independent samples, 445–446
independent variable, 130, 342–343
index numbers, 463–464
   weighted, 467–468

indirect data collection
    as research method, 149–151
    techniques for, 151
indirect observation, 150
induction, 82
inductive research, 10
inferential statistics, 402, 441–474
influence diagram, 392, 393
informed consent, 140–141
intensity rating scale, 356
internal consistency method, 358–359
interpretation, problems with, 496–498
interpretivism, 48, 49–50
interquartile range, 426
interval variable, 340
interview, as research method, 112–115
interview schedule, 114
    see also questionnaires and interview
interviewer bias, 348, 362
interviews, 315, 346–349
    unstructured, as research method, 153–162
introduction, in project report, 506–507
irregular variation in a trend, 471–472

journal articles
    searching for, 195
journalism, compared with research, 27–29
judgemental sampling, 306, 367

key words in literature searching, 198
Kipling's six questions, 31–33
Kolb's learning cycle, 382–383
kurtosis, 431

laboratory experiment, 137
laboratory or natural research
    location, 56
Laspeyres index, 467
limitations, 268
line graph, 419
linear regressions, 457
list of abbreviations, in project report, 510
list of illustrations, in project report, 510
list of sources, in project report, 511
list of tables, in project report, 510
literature, 12, 196
literature review, 201–215, 339
    flaws in, 507
    in a proposal, 268
    in research report, 507–508
    methods of analysis, 207
    plagiarism, 210
    referencing systems, 202
literature search, 195–215
    bibliographic software, 200
logic diagram, 392, 394

logic of research, 82
logistic regression, 459

main text, in project report, 506
Mann-Whitney test, 445
market research reports, 106
master editor, 522
Master's level research, 4, 11
matched-pairs sample, 448
matrix
    repertory grid, 321
mean, 422
measurement level of variables, 339–340
measuring association
    chi-square test, 448–452
measuring central tendency, 421
measuring correlation
    Pearson's correlation coefficient (r), 457
    Spearman's correlation coefficient (r_s), 455
measuring difference
    Mann-Whitney test, 445
    t-test, 447
measuring dispersion, 426
median, 422
methodological assumption, 54
methodological rigour, 17
methodologies, 13, 61
    pragmatism, 60
methodology chapter
    in a proposal, 268
methods, 61
    analysing quantitative data, 401–474
    collecting qualitative data, 313–333
    collecting quantitative data, 337–371
    selecting a sample, 362–367
Mintel, 106–107
mode, 423
mode I research, 226
mode II research, 226
multicollinearity, 455
multi-method research, 183–189
    advantages and disadvantages, 188–189
    motivations for doing, 187–188
    sequential, 183–185
    triangulation, 186–188
    versus single-method research, 183–184
    see also case study; triangulation
multiple case study, 174
multiple-choice questions, 354
multiple regression, 458
multiplicative model in time series analysis, 469
multi-stage sampling, 302–303, 366
multivariate analysis, 403, 445, 458

narrative, for presenting qualitative research, 492
narrative analysis, 397

SUBJECT INDEX

natural sampling, 367
network
    analysis of primary citations, 207
neutrality, 91
nominal variable, 340
non-parametric tests, 444
non-participant observation, 326
nonparticipant observation, as research
    ethics of, 152–153
    in person, 152
    method, 151–153
    recording, 152–153
non-probability sampling, 127–128, 297
    convenience sampling, 127
    quota sampling, 127
    snowball sampling, 127
    volunteer sampling, 127
non-response, as source of error, 128
non-response bias in questionnaires, 346
non-standardised data, 153
normal distribution, 429
normality tests, 432
notes, taking, in qualitative research, 160–161, 164
null hypothesis, 403

objectivism, 88
observation methods, 325, 348
one-tailed hypothesis, 442
ontological assumption, 52
open coding, 387–390
open-ended question, 121
open questions, 353
oral presentation, 514–515
    see also viva voce examination
ordinal variable, 340
originality, 29–30
outcome variable, 442
outliers, 422, 423

Paasche index, 468
paired sample, 448
paired-case analysis, 180
paradigms, 13, 47–64
    link with methodology, 60
    main paradigms, 48, 55
    philosophical assumptions, 51
parameter, 402
parametric tests, 444
participant observation, 326
participant observation, as research method, 162–164
    critical subjectivity, 164
    ethnography, 162–163
    mystery shopping, 162
    participatory action research, 163

    recording, 164
    risks, 163–164
patterns, 84
Pearson's correlation (r), 457
personal construct theory, 321
personal journey, for presenting qualitative research, 493
phenomenon, 48, 338, 390
philosophy, 47
    of science, 87
    of social science, 87
pie charts, 416, 417
piggyback sampling, 367
plagiarism, 210
planning and administration, 268
population, 55, 125, 362
positivism, 48–61, 88
postal questionnaire, 117
postgraduate level research, 4, 11
practical problem, 222
pragmatism, 60
predictive research, 7
predictor variable, 442
preliminary literature review, 267
prelims, 510–511
primary data, 102–103, 293, 402
probability sampling, 125, 297
    cluster sampling, 127
    simple random sampling, 126
    stratified random sampling, 126–127
    systematic sampling, 126
probes, 316
procrastination, 520
    see also displacement activities
project ideas, 226–229
    generating, 219–220
    refining, 237–243
    selecting, 229–231
project ideas, sources of, 226–228
    other students' projects, 228–229
    personal interests, 227
    your studies, 227–228
project outcome, 495
project paralysis, 220
project planning, 501–529
project report, 503–516
    abstract, in project report, 510
    acknowledgements, in project report, 510
    appendix, in project report, 511
    clarity, 528–529
    comfort habits, 520
    concision, 529
    conclusions, in project report, 509–510
    discussion, in project report, 509
    displacement activities, 520
    editing by ear, 529

project report – *continued*
   editing for style, 526–529
   end matter, 511–512
   executive summary, in project report, 510
   findings, in project report, 509
   first draft, of project report, 517–518
   focus-down strategy, in report writing, 507
   generic structure, 505–511
   glossary, in project report, 510
   grammar, importance of, 524–525
   introduction, in project report, 506–507
   list of abbreviations, in project report, 510
   list of illustrations, in project report, 510
   list of sources, in project report, 511
   list of tables, in project report, 510
   main text, in project report, 506
   master editor, 522
   oral presentation, 514–515
   prelims, 510–511
   procrastination, 520
   reader, writing for, 504
   research methods, in project report, 508–509
   rough draft, 517
   table of contents, in project report, 510
   title page, in project report, 510
   viva voce examination, 513–516
   voice, 529
   writing, discussion of, 523–529
project report, preparing, 517–519
   comfort habits, 520
   displacement activities, 520
   first draft, of project report, 517–518
   focus-down strategy, in report writing, 507
   master editor, 522
   oral presentation, 514
   procrastination, 520
   rough draft, 517
project report, structure, 505–512
   abstract, 510
   acknowledgements, 510
   appendix, 511
   business report, 513
   conclusions, 509–510
   discussion, 509
   end matter, 511–512
   executive summary, 510
   findings, 509
   generic, 505–512
   glossary, 510
   introduction, 506–507
   list of abbreviations, 510
   list of illustrations, 510
   list of sources, 511
   list of tables, 510
   main text, 506
   prelims, 510–511
   qualitative, 512
   research methods, 508–509
   table of contents, 510
   title page, 510
project report, visualising, 503–505
   reader, writing for, 504
   writing, discussion of, 523–529
project scope, 245–246
project sponsors
   reporting to, 513
project stakeholders, 34
   see also project sponsors
project supervisor, 35
prompts, in interviewing, 115
properties, as part of qualitative research, 390
proposal, writing, 253–289
   examples, 274
proprietary databases, 106
protocol analysis, 320
punctuation, as essential writing skill, 525–526
pure research *see* basic research
purpose of the research, 3, 4, 258
purpose statement, 259
purposive sampling, 306

qualitative data, 57
   collection, 313–333
qualitative data, analysing, 377–397
   abstract conceptualisation, 383
   active experimentation, 383
   axial coding, 391–392
   category, 390
   coding, 387–390
   complete, 380
   computer-assisted qualitative data analysis software (CAQDAS), 381
   concept extraction, 386
   concrete experience, 382
   content analysis, 396
   conversation analysis, 397
   credibility, 396
   dimensions, 390
   discourse analysis, 397
   familiarisation, 382
   grounded theory, 397
   hermeneutics, 397
   influence diagram, 392, 393
   Kolb's learning cycle, 382–383
   logic diagram, 392, 394
   narrative analysis, 397
   open coding, 387–390
   phenomenon, 390
   properties, 390
   reflective observation, 382

SUBJECT INDEX

re-ordering, 382–383
semiotics, 397
statistical analysis, 385–386
structured analysis, 384–386
theoretical saturation, 395
traceable, as attribute of qualitative data, 379
qualitative data, interpreting, 489–494
   qualitative data, managing, 379–380
   qualitative data, presenting, 489–505
   unstructured analysis, 384–385
   unstructured approach, 384–385
qualitative interviewing, 159
qualitative research, 5, 8, 147–164
   compared with quantitative designs, 148–149
   credibility, 396
   designs, 149
   generalisability, 396
   indirect data collection, 149–151
   nonparticipant observation, 151–153
   participant observation, 162–164
   quality of, 395–494
   reliability, 395
   unstructured interviewing, 153–162
   validity, 396
quantitative data, 57
   analysis, 401–474
   collection, 337–371
   interpreting, 481–488
   presenting, 481–489
quantitative research, 5, 8, 97–141
   experiments, 130–141
   quality of, 488–489
   questionnaires, 111–117
   secondary analysis, 100–111
   surveys, 111–130
quantitative variable, 340
quasi-experiments, 137
questionnaire design, 297–299
questionnaires, 113
   emailed, 116
   issues in, 116–117
   postal, 115
   self-administered, 115–116
   web-based, 116
questionnaires and interview
   designing and coding questions, 344, 351, 359, 360
   distribution methods, 345
   eliminating questions, 359
   non-response bias, 346
   schedules, 343
quota sampling, 305–306, 366

random assignment, 135
random number tables, 374
random numbers, 300
random sampling, 363, 364
range, 426
ranking and rating scales, 340, 354
ratio variable, 340
raw data, 482–483
reader, writing for, 504
recommendations, making, 479–499
referencing, 201, 270
   Harvard system, 202
   Vancouver system, 202
reflective observation, 382
regression, 457
   linear, 457, 458
   logistic, 459
related sample *see* paired sample
reliability, 58, 358
   as attribute for research, 89–92, 379–380
re-ordering, 382–383
repeated surveys, 103
repertory grid technique, 321
replication, 58
research, 3, 23
   applied and basic, 9
   characteristics of good projects, 17
   deductive and inductive, 9
   exploratory, descriptive, analytical and predictive, 5
   planning and timetable, 269
   process, 11, 255
   purpose, 3, 4, 258
   qualitative and quantitative, 8
research approach, 84–86, 89
research contribution, 238
research defined, 24–29
research designs, 13, 87, 89, 254
research diary, 164
research idea, 221
research instrument, 343
research methodology *see* research approach
research methods
   general overview, 87
   in project report, 508–509
   see also methods
research paradigms *see* paradigms
research perspective *see* research approach
research philosophy, 86–87
research problem, 4, 12, 16, 30, 261
research process, 24–25
research profiling, 92
research projects
   contribution, 238
   types of, 31
research proposal
   writing, 244–245
   see also proposal, writing

research question, 3, 13, 16, 30, 237, 261
research report, dissertation or thesis
    citations and references, 201
research setting, 222
research strategy, 15
research topic, 4, 16
    characteristics of, 231–235
    conceptual framework, 75
    database, 101
    generalisability, as attribute of research, 89–92, 396
    refining, 237
    scientist, as role model, 97–141
residuals in linear regression, 458
results currency, 58
retrospective verbalization, 320
rhetorical assumption, 53
rough draft, 517

sample, 55, 362
    bias, 345, 362
    size, 55, 296, 363
sampling, 124–129, 295–308
    bias, 125
    in quantitative research, 124–130
    nonprobability sampling, 127–128
    population, 125
    probability sampling, 125, 125–127
    response rate, 128–129
    sample, 124, 222
    sampling error, 128, 301
    sampling frame, 125, 295, 362
sampling bias, 296
sampling methods, 362
    cluster, 304
    judgemental, 306
    multi-stage, 302–303
    non-probabilistic, 297
    probabilistic, 97
    purposive, 306
    quota, 305–306
    simple random, 299–301
    snowball, 306
    stratified, 301–302
    systematic, 304–305
scatter plot, 453
scientific method, 75
scientist, as role model, 67, 73–75, 94, 97–141
    see also ethnographer, as role model
seasonal variation, 463
secondary analysis, as research method, 100
    advantages and disadvantages, 102
    motivations for, 100–101
    sources of data, 100, 101–107
secondary data, 102–107, 293, 402
    archival, 107–109

constraints on, 102
existing data sets, 101–107
primary, 101–102
producers, 102–103
proprietary, 106
social surveys, 103–106
trade associations, 107
secondary sources of data, 293
self-administered questionnaire, 115–116
semantic differential rating scale, 356
semiotics, 397
sensitive questions, 367
significance level, 434
simple index numbers, 463
simple random sampling, 299–301
simple regression, 458
single-case study, 174
single informant see triangulation
skewness of a frequency distribution, 431
skills and personal qualities, 257
snowball sampling, 306, 366
social construction, 88
socially desirable responding, 110
software
    quantitative data analysis, 401
    referencing, 200
spam, 116
Spearman's correlation coefficient (rho or r_s), 455
spelling, 524
split-halves method, 358
spread see dispersion measures
SPSS
    creating interval variables, 413
    getting started, 403
    labelling variables and entering data, 405
    measuring central tendency, 421
    measuring dispersion, 426
    normal distribution, 429
    recoding variables, 234
stakeholders see project stakeholders
standard deviation, 427
statistical significance, 487
statistical tests
    association, 448
    difference, 445
    normality, 432
    reporting, 487
statistics, 401
stem-and-leaf plot, 420
stimulus equivalence, 348
stratified sample, 265
stratified sampling, 301–302
structured analysis, 384–386
structured content analysis, 109
structured interviews, 113–114

SUBJECT INDEX

avoiding bias in, 114–115
computer-assisted protocols, 114
criteria for assessing, 114–115
face-to-face, 113
interview schedule, 114
issues in, 114–115
structured observation, 114
telephone, 113–114
structured observations, 113–114
student profiles, Type 1 versus Type 2, 521
student *t*-test *see t*-test
subject effects, as source of experimental error, 140
subjectivism, 88
summary table, 496
survey, as research method, 111–130
defined, 123, 124
designing and administering, 117–124
motivations for, 112–113
piloting, 124
questionnaire, 123
questions, 120–122
response rate, 128–129
sample size, 129
sampling issues, 119, 124–130
self-designed versus standard, 117–118
structured interviews, 113–114
structured observation, 112
survey instrument, 117
survey data, 103
symmetric outcomes, 233
systematic approach, 24–25, 481
systematic sample, 365
systematic sampling, 304–305

t-test, 447–448
table of contents, in project report, 510
tables, 413–415
tables, in findings, 483–485
descriptive, 485
taking notes, good practice in, 160
tallies, 362
tests for
association, 448–452
correlation, 452–463
difference, 445–448
multicollinearity, 455
normality, 432–435
theoretical framework, 197, 262, 339
theoretical or purposive sampling, 154, 177
theoretical problem, 224
theoretical saturation, 395
theory, 56–57, 262, 339
thesis, 4, 11, 14
thick description, 492
time series analysis, 463–472

timetable
for proposed research, 269–270
title page, in project report, 510
traceability, as attribute of qualitative data, 379
trade associations, 107
transcribing, 160, 161
transparency, 91
trend, 463
cyclical and irregular variation, 471–472
deflated, 466
de-seasonalized, 468–469
triangulation, 186–188, 337
multiple informants, 187
multiple methods, 187
multiple sources of data, 187
true experiments, 137
two-tailed hypothesis, 442
Type I and Type II errors, 434–435

undergraduate level research, 5, 10–11
unit of analysis, 258–259
univariate analysis, 403, 410, 442
frequency distributions, 412
measuring central tendency, 421
measuring dispersion, 426
unobtrusive measures, 110–111
unstructured analysis, 384–385
unstructured approach, 384–385
unstructured interviewing, 153–162
avoiding bias, 161–162
choosing subjects, 154–155
data-led, 158–159
difference from structured interviewing, 159
motivation for, 153
permission to record, 160
questions, 157
recording data, 160–161
single interviews, 154
structuring, 155–157
taking notes during, 160

validity, 59, 358
validity, as aspect of research, 89–92, 396
Vancouver system of referencing, 203–205
variables, 7, 57, 339–343
creating and recoding in *SPSS*, 412–413, 420–421
labelling in *SPSS*, 405–407
level of measurement, 339–341
variance, in standard deviation, 427
Venn diagram, 242–243
verification, 82
viva voce examination, 513–516
see also oral presentation
voice, in qualitative research, 529
volunteer subject effect, 140

SUBJECT INDEX

weighted index numbers, 467–468
within-case analysis, 180
word processing, 519
working environment, 520
Workplace Employee Relations Survey (WERS), 105
writing, getting started, 520
writing and editing, strategies for, 517–519, 522
writing correctly, 523–529
  see also editing, grammar, punctuation, spelling